DATE DUE	
7-5-18	
GAYLORD	PRINTED IN U.S.A.

ROSA LUXEMBURG

ROSA LUXEMBURG

J. P. NETTL

ABRIDGED EDITION

SCHOCKEN BOOKS · NEW YORK

All rights reserved under International and Pan-American Copyright Conventions. Published in the United States by Schocken Books Inc., New York. Distributed by Pantheon Books, a division of Random House, Inc., New York. Unabridged edition originally published by the Oxford University Press in 1966. Abridged edition first published as an Oxford University Press paperback in 1969.

Grateful acknowledgment is made to Harcourt Brace Jovanovich, Inc., for permission to reprint 'Rosa Luxemburg' from *Man in Dark Times* by Hannah Arendt. Copyright © 1966 by Hannah Arendt. Reprinted by permission of Harcourt Brace Jovanovich, Inc.

Library of Congress Cataloging-in-Publication Data

Nettl, J. P.
Rosa Luxemburg.

Bibliography: p.
Includes index.
1. Luxemburg, Rosa, 1871–1919. 2. Women communists—Biography. 3. Communism—Germany—History—20th century. I. Title.
HX274.7.L89N48   1989   335.43′092′4 [B]   88-43233
ISBN 0-8052-0890-9

Display type by Stephanie Bart-Horvath

Manufactured in the United States of America
First Schocken Paperback Edition

CONTENTS

INTRODUCTION

by Hannah Arendt

I

The definitive biography, English-style, is among the most admirable genres of historiography. Lengthy, thoroughly documented, heavily annotated, and generously splashed with quotations, it usually comes in two large volumes and tells more, and more vividly, about the historical period in question than all but the most outstanding history books. For unlike other biographies, history is here not treated as the inevitable background of a famous person's life span; it is rather as though the colorless light of historical time were forced through and refracted by the prism of a great character so that in the resulting spectrum a complete unity of life and world is achieved. This may be why it has become the classical genre for the lives of great statesmen but has remained rather unsuitable for those in which the main interest lies in the life story, or for the lives of artists, writers, and, generally, men or women whose genius forced them to keep the world at a certain distance and whose significance lies chiefly in their works, the artifacts they added to the world, not in the role they played in it.[1]

[1] Another limitation has become more obvious in recent years when Hitler and Stalin, because of their importance for contemporary history, were treated to the undeserved honor of definitive biographies. No matter how scrupulously Alan Bullock in his book on Hitler and Isaac Deutscher in his biography of Stalin followed the methodological technicalities prescribed by the genre, to see history in the light of these non-persons could only result in their falsifying promotion to respectability and in a more subtle distortion of the events. When we want to see both events and persons

It was a stroke of genius on the part of J. P. Nettl to choose the life of Rosa Luxemburg, the most unlikely candidate, as a proper subject for a genre that seems suitable only for the lives of great statesmen and other persons of the world. She certainly was nothing of the kind. Even in her own world of the European socialist movement she was a rather marginal figure, with relatively brief moments of splendor and great brilliance, whose influence in deed and written word can hardly be compared to that of her contemporaries—to Plekhanov, Trotsky, and Lenin, to Bebel and Kautsky, to Jaurès and Millerand. If success in the world is a prerequisite for success in the genre, how could Mr. Nettl succeed with this woman who when very young had been swept into the German Social Democratic Party from her native Poland; who continued to play a key role in the little-known and neglected history of Polish socialism; and who then for about two decades, although never officially recognized, became the most controversial and least understood figure in the German Left movement? For it was precisely success—success even in her own world of revolutionaries—which was withheld from Rosa Luxemburg in life, death, and after death. Can it be that the failure of all her efforts as far as official recognition is concerned is somehow connected with the dismal failure of revolution in our century? Will history look different if seen through the prism of her life and work?

However that may be, I know no book that sheds more light on the crucial period of European socialism from the last decades of the nineteenth century to the fateful day in January 1919 when Rosa Luxemburg and Karl Liebknecht, the two leaders of the *Spartakusbund*, the precursor of the German Communist Party, were murdered in Berlin—under the eyes and probably with the connivance of the Socialist regime then in power. The murderers

in right proportion we still have to go to the much less well documented and factually incomplete biographies of Hitler and Stalin by Konrad Heiden and Boris Souvarine respectively.

were members of the ultra-nationalist and officially illegal *Freikorps*, a paramilitary organization from which Hitler's storm troopers were soon to recruit their most promising killers. That the government at the time was practically in the hands of the *Freikorps* because they enjoyed 'the full support of Noske', the Socialists' expert on national defense, then in charge of military affairs, was confirmed only recently by Captain Pabst, the last surviving participant in the assassination. The Bonn government—in this as in other respects only too eager to revive the more sinister traits of the Weimar Republic—let it be known that it was thanks to the *Freikorps* that Moscow had failed to incorporate all of Germany into a red Empire after the First World War and that the murder of Liebknecht and Luxemburg was entirely legal, 'an execution in accordance with martial law'.[2] This was considerably more than even the Weimar Republic had ever pretended, for it had never admitted publicly that the *Freikorps* actually were an arm of the government and it had 'punished' the murderers by meting out a sentence of two years and two weeks to the soldier Runge for '*attempted* manslaughter' (he had hit Rosa Luxemburg over the head in the corridors of the Hotel Eden), and four months to Lieutenant Vogel (he was the officer in charge when she was shot in the head inside a car and thrown into the Landwehr Canal) for 'failing to report a corpse and illegally disposing of it'. During the trial, a photograph showing Runge and his comrades celebrating the assassination in the same hotel on the following day was introduced as evidence, which caused the defendant great merriment. 'Accused Runge, you must behave properly. This is no laughing matter,' said the presiding judge. Forty-five years later, during the Auschwitz trial in Frankfurt, a similar scene took place; the same words were spoken.

With the murder of Rosa Luxemburg and Liebknecht, the split of the European Left into Socialist and Communist parties became irrevocable; 'the abyss which the Communists had pictured

---

[2] See the *Bulletin des Presse- und Informationsamtes der Bundesregierung*, of February 8, 1962, p. 224.

in theory had become . . . the abyss of the grave'. And since this early crime had been aided and abetted by the government, it initiated the death dance in postwar Germany: The assassins of the extreme Right started by liquidating prominent leaders of the extreme Left—Hugo Haase and Gustav Landauer, Leo Jogiches and Eugene Leviné—and quickly moved to the center and the right-of-center—to Walther Rathenau and Matthias Erzberger, both members of the government at the time of their murder. Thus Rosa Luxemburg's death became the watershed between two eras in Germany; and it became the point of no return for the German Left. All those who had drifted to the Communists out of bitter disappointment with the Socialist Party were even more disappointed with the swift moral decline and political disintegration of the Communist Party, and yet they felt that to return to the ranks of the Socialists would mean to condone the murder of Rosa. Such personal reactions, which are seldom publicly admitted, are among the small, mosaic-like pieces that fall into place in the large riddle of history. In the case of Rosa Luxemburg they are part of the legend which soon surrounded her name. Legends have a truth of their own, but Mr. Nettl is entirely right to have paid almost no attention to the Rosa myth. It was his task, difficult enough, to restore her to historical life.

Shortly after her death, when all persuasions of the Left had already decided that she had always been 'mistaken' (a 'really hopeless case', as George Lichtheim, the last in this long line, put it in *Encounter*), a curious shift in her reputation took place. Two small volumes of her letters were published, and these, entirely personal and of a simple, touchingly humane, and often poetic beauty, were enough to destroy the propaganda image of blood-thirsty 'Red Rosa', at least in all but the most obstinately anti-Semitic and reactionary circles. However, what then grew up was another legend—the sentimentalized image of the bird watcher and lover of flowers, a woman whose guards said good-by to her with tears in their eyes when she left prison—as if they couldn't go on living without being entertained by this strange prisoner

who had insisted on treating them as human beings. Nettl does
not mention this story, faithfully handed down to me when I was
a child and later confirmed by Kurt Rosenfeld, her friend and
lawyer, who claimed to have witnessed the scene. It is probably
true enough, and its slightly embarrassing features are somehow
offset by the survival of another anecdote, this one mentioned by
Nettl. In 1907, she and her friend Clara Zetkin (later the 'grand
old woman' of German Communism) had gone for a walk, lost
count of time, and arrived late for an appointment with August
Bebel, who had feared they were lost. Rosa then proposed their
epitaph: 'Here lie the last two men of German Social Democracy.'
Seven years later, in February 1914, she had occasion to prove the
truth of this cruel joke in a splendid address to the judges of the
Criminal Court which had indicted her for 'inciting' the masses
to civil disobedience in case of war. (Not bad, incidentally, for the
woman who 'was always wrong' to stand trial on this charge five
months before the outbreak of the First World War, which few
'serious' people had thought possible.) Mr. Nettl with good sense
has reprinted the address in its entirety; its 'manliness' is unparal-
leled in the history of German socialism.

It took a few more years and a few more catastrophes for the
legend to turn into a symbol of nostalgia for the good old times
of the movement, when hopes were green, the revolution around
the corner, and, most important, the faith in the capacities of the
masses and in the moral integrity of the Socialist or Communist
leadership was still intact. It speaks not only for the person of Rosa
Luxemburg, but also for the qualities of this older generation of
the Left, that the legend—vague, confused, inaccurate in nearly
all details—could spread throughout the world and come to life
whenever a 'New Left' sprang into being. But side by side with
this glamorized image, there survived also the old clichés of the
'quarrelsome female', a 'romantic' who was neither 'realistic' nor
scientific (it is true that she was always out of step), and whose
works, especially her great book on imperialism (*The Accumulation of Capital*, 1913), were shrugged off. Every New Left move-

ment, when its moment came to change into the Old Left—
usually when its members reached the age of forty—promptly
buried its early enthusiasm for Rosa Luxemburg together with the
dreams of youth; and since they had usually not bothered to read,
let alone to understand, what she had to say they found it easy to
dismiss her with all the patronizing philistinism of their newly
acquired status. 'Luxemburgism', invented posthumously by
Party hacks for polemical reasons, has never even achieved the
honor of being denounced as 'treason'; it was treated as a harmless,
infantile disease. Nothing Rosa Luxemburg wrote or said survived except her surprisingly accurate criticism of Bolshevik politics during the early stages of the Russian Revolution, and this
only because those whom a 'god had failed' could use it as a
convenient though wholly inadequate weapon against Stalin.
('There is something indecent in the use of Rosa's name and
writings as a cold war missile,' as the reviewer of Nettl's book
pointed out in the Times Literary Supplement.) Her new admirers
had no more in common with her than her detractors. Her highly
developed sense for theoretical differences and her infallible judg-
ment of people, her personal likes and dislikes, would have prevented her lumping Lenin and Stalin together under all
circumstances, quite apart from the fact that she had never been
a 'believer', had never used politics as a substitute for religion, and
had been careful, as Mr. Nettl notes, not to attack religion when
she opposed the church. In short, while 'revolution was as close
and real to her as to Lenin', it was no more an article of faith with
her than Marxism. Lenin was primarily a man of action and
would have gone into politics in any event, but she, who in her
half-serious self-estimate was born 'to mind the geese', might just
as well have buried herself in botany and zoology or history and
economics or mathematics, had not the circumstances of the
world offended her sense of justice and freedom.

This is of course to admit that she was not an orthodox Marxist,
so little orthodox indeed that it might be doubted that she was a
Marxist at all. Mr. Nettl rightly states that to her Marx was no

more than 'the best interpreter of reality of them all', and it is
revealing of her lack of personal commitment that she could write,
'I now have a horror of the much praised first volume of Marx's
Capital because of its elaborate rococo ornaments à la Hegel.'[3]
What mattered most in her view was reality, in all its wonderful
and all its frightful aspects, even more than revolution itself. Her
unorthodoxy was innocent, non-polemical; she 'recommended
her friends to read Marx for "the daring of his thoughts, the
refusal to take anything for granted", rather than for the value of
his conclusions. His mistakes . . . were self-evident . . . ; that was
why [she] never bothered to engage in any lengthy critique.' All
this is most obvious in *The Accumulation of Capital*, which only
Franz Mehring was unprejudiced enough to call a 'truly magnificent, fascinating achievement without its equal since Marx's
death'.[4] The central thesis of this 'curious work of genius' is
simple enough. Since capitalism didn't show any signs of collapse
'under the weight of its economic contradictions', she began to
look for an outside cause to explain its continued existence and
growth. She found it in the so-called third-man theory, that is, in
the fact that the process of growth was not merely the consequence of innate laws ruling capitalist production but of the continued existence of pre-capitalist sectors in the country which
'capitalism' captured and brought into its sphere of influence.
Once this process had spread to the whole national territory,
capitalists were forced to look to other parts of the earth, to
pre-capitalist lands, to draw them into the process of capital accumulation, which, as it were, fed on whatever was outside itself.
In other words, Marx's 'original accumulation of capital' was not,
like original sin, a single event, a unique deed of expropriation by
the nascent bourgeoisie, setting off a process of accumulation that
would then follow 'with iron necessity' its own inherent law up
to the final collapse. On the contrary, expropriation had to be
repeated time and again to keep the system in motion. Hence,

[3]In a letter to Hans Diefenbach, March 8, 1917, in Briefe an Freunde, Zürich, 1950.
[4]Ibid., p. 84.

capitalism was not a closed system that generated its own contradictions and was 'pregnant with revolution'; it fed on outside
factors, and its *automatic* collapse could occur, if at all, only when
the whole surface of the earth was conquered and had been de-
voured.

Lenin was quick to see that this description, whatever its merits
or flaws, was essentially non-Marxist. It contradicted the very
foundations of Marxian and Hegelian dialectics, which hold that
every thesis must create its own anti-thesis—bourgeois society
creates the proletariat—so that the movement of the whole process remains bound to the initial factor that caused it. Lenin
pointed out that from the viewpoint of materialist dialectics 'her
thesis that enlarged capitalist reproduction was impossible within
a closed economy and needed to cannibalize economies in order
to function at all . . . [was] a "fundamental error".' The trouble
was only that what was an error in abstract Marxian theory was
an eminently faithful description of things as they really were.
Her careful 'description of the torture of Negroes in South Africa'
also was clearly 'non-Marxist', but who would deny today that it
belonged in a book on imperialism?

II

Historically, Mr. Nettl's greatest and most original achievement is the discovery of the Polish-Jewish 'peer group' and Rosa
Luxemburg's lifelong, close, and carefully hidden attachment to
the Polish party which sprang from it. This is indeed a highly
significant and totally neglected source, not of the revolutions, but
of the revolutionary spirit in the twentieth century. This milieu,
which even in the twenties had lost all public relevance, has now
completely disappeared. Its nucleus consisted of assimilated Jews
from middle-class families whose cultural background was German (Rosa Luxemburg knew Goethe and Mörike by heart, and
her literary taste was impeccable, far superior to that of her German friends), whose political formation was Russian, and whose

moral standards in both private and public life were uniquely their own. These Jews, an extremely small minority in the East, an even smaller percentage of assimilated Jewry in the West, stood outside all social ranks, Jewish or non-Jewish, hence had no conventional prejudices whatsoever, and had developed, in this truly splendid isolation, their own code of honor—which then attracted a number of non-Jews, among them Julian Marchlewski and Feliks Dzerzhynski, both of whom later joined the Bolsheviks. It was precisely because of this unique background that Lenin appointed Dzerzhynski as first head of the Cheka, someone, he hoped, no power could corrupt; hadn't he begged to be charged with the department of Children's Education and Welfare?

Nettl rightly stresses Rosa Luxemburg's excellent relations with her family, her parents, brothers, sister, and niece, none of whom ever showed the slightest inclination to socialist convictions or revolutionary activities, yet who did everything they could for her when she had to hide from the police or was in prison. The point is worth making, for it gives us a glimpse of this unique Jewish family background without which the emergence of the ethical code of the peer group would be nearly incomprehensible. The hidden equalizer of those who always treated one another as equals—and hardly anybody else—was the essentially simple experience of a childhood world in which mutual respect and unconditional trust, a universal humanity and a genuine, almost naïve contempt for social and ethnic distinctions were taken for granted. What the members of the peer group had in common was what can only be called moral taste, which is so different from 'moral principles'; the authenticity of their morality they owed to having grown up in a world that was not out of joint. This gave them their 'rare self-confidence', so unsettling to the world into which they then came, and so bitterly resented as arrogance and conceit. This milieu, and never the German Party, was and remained Rosa Luxemburg's home. The home was movable up to a point, and since it was predominantly Jewish it did not coincide with any 'fatherland'.

It is of course highly suggestive that the SDKPiL (Social Democracy of the Kingdom of Poland and Lithuania, formerly called SDPK, Social Democracy of the Kingdom of Poland), the party of this predominantly Jewish group, split from the official Socialist Polish Party, the PPS, because of the latter's stand for Polish independence (Pilsudski, the Fascist dictator of Poland after World War I, was its most famous and successful offspring), and that, after the split, the members of the group became ardent defenders of an often doctrinaire internationalism. It is even more suggestive that the national question is the only issue on which one could accuse Rosa Luxemburg of self-deception and unwillingness to face reality. That this had something to do with her Jewishness is undeniable, although it is of course 'lamentably absurd' to discover in her anti-nationalism 'a peculiarly Jewish quality'. Mr. Nettl, while hiding nothing, is rather careful to avoid the 'Jewish question', and in view of the usually low level of debates on this issue one can only applaud his decision. Unfortunately, his understandable distaste has blinded him to the few important facts in this matter, which is all the more to be regretted since these facts, though of a simple, elementary nature, also escaped the otherwise so sensitive and alert mind of Rosa Luxemburg.

The first of these is what only Nietzsche, as far as I know, has ever pointed out, namely, that the position and functions of the Jewish people in Europe predestined them to become the 'good Europeans' *par excellence.* The Jewish middle classes of Paris and London, Berlin and Vienna, Warsaw and Moscow, were in fact neither cosmopolitan nor international, though the intellectuals among them thought of themselves in these terms. They were European, something that could be said of no other group. And this was not a matter of conviction; it was an objective fact. In other words, while the self-deception of assimilated Jews usually consisted in the mistaken belief that they were just as German as the Germans, just as French as the French, the self-deception of the intellectual Jews consisted in thinking that they had no 'fatherland', for their fatherland actually was Europe. There is, second, the fact that at least the East-European intelligentsia was multilingual—Rosa Luxemburg herself spoke Polish, Russian, German, and French fluently and knew English and Italian very well. They never quite understood the importance of language barriers and why the slogan, 'The fatherland of the working class is the Socialist movement', should be so disastrously wrong precisely for the working classes. It is indeed more than a little disturbing that Rosa Luxemburg herself, with her acute sense of reality and strict avoidance of clichés, should not have *heard* what was wrong with the slogan on principle. A fatherland, after all, is first of all a 'land'; an organization is not a country, not even metaphorically. There is indeed grim justice in the later transformation of the slogan, 'The fatherland of the working class is Soviet Russia'—Russia was at least a 'land'—which put an end to the utopian internationalism of this generation.

One could adduce more such facts, and it still would be difficult to claim that Rosa Luxemburg was entirely wrong on the national question. What, after all, has contributed more to the catastrophic decline of Europe than the insane nationalism which accompanied the decline of the nation state in the era of imperialism? Those whom Nietzsche had called the 'good Europeans'—a very small minority even among Jews—might well have been the only ones to have a presentiment of the disastrous consequences ahead, although they were unable to gauge correctly the enormous force of nationalist feeling in a decaying body politic.

III

Closely connected with the discovery of the Polish 'peer group' and its continued importance for Rosa Luxemburg's public and private life is Mr. Nettl's disclosure of hitherto inaccessible sources, which enabled him to piece together the facts of her life—'the exquisite business of love and living'. It is now clear that we knew next to nothing about her private life for the simple reason that she had so carefully protected herself from notoriety. This is no mere matter of sources. It was fortunate indeed that the new material fell into Mr. Nettl's hands, and he has every right to dismiss his few predecessors who were less hampered by lack of access to the facts than by their inability to move, think, and feel on the same level as their subject. The ease with which Nettl handles his biographical material is astounding. His treatment is more than perceptive. His is the first plausible portrait of this extraordinary woman, drawn *con amore*, with tact and great delicacy. It is as though she had found her last admirer, and it is for this reason that one feels like quarreling with some of his judgments.

He is certainly wrong in emphasizing her ambition, and sense of career. Does he think that her violent contempt for the careerists and status seekers in the German Party—their delight in being admitted to the Reichstag—is mere cant? Does he believe that a really 'ambitious' person could have afforded to be as generous as she was? (Once, at an international congress, Jaurès finished an eloquent speech in which he 'ridiculed the misguided passions of Rosa Luxemburg, [but] there was suddenly no one to translate him. Rosa jumped up and reproduced the moving oratory: from French into equally telling German.') And how can he reconcile this, except by assuming dishonesty or self-deception, with her telling phrase in one of her letters to Jogiches: 'I have a cursed longing for happiness and am ready to haggle for my daily portion of happiness with all the stubbornness of a mule.' What he mistakes for ambition is the natural force of a temperament capable, in her own laughing words, of 'setting a prairie on fire', which propelled her almost willy-nilly into public affairs, and even ruled over most of her purely intellectual enterprises. While he stresses repeatedly the high moral standards of the 'peer group', he still seems not to understand that such things as ambition, career, status, and even mere success were under the strictest taboo.

There is another aspect of her personality which Nettl stresses but whose implications he seems not to understand: that she was so 'self-consciously a woman'. This in itself put certain limitations on whatever her ambitions otherwise might have been—for Nettl does not ascribe to her more than what would have been natural in a man with her gifts and opportunities. Her distaste for the women's emancipation movement, to which all other women of her generation and political convictions were irresistibly drawn, was significant; in the face of suffragette equality, she might have been tempted to reply, *Vive la petite différence*. She was an outsider, not only because she was and remained a Polish Jew in a country she disliked and a party she came soon to despise, but also because she was a woman. Mr. Nettl must, of course, be pardoned for his masculine prejudices; they would not matter much if they had not prevented him from understanding fully the role Leo Jogiches, her husband for all practical purposes and her first, perhaps her only, lover, played in her life. Their deadly serious quarrel, caused by Jogiches's brief affair with another woman and endlessly complicated by Rosa's furious reaction, was typical of their time and milieu, as was the aftermath, his jealousy and her refusal for years to forgive him. This generation still believed firmly that love strikes only once, and its carelessness with marriage certificates should not be mistaken for any belief in free love. Mr. Nettl's evidence shows that she had friends and admirers, and that she enjoyed this, but it hardly indicates that there was ever another man in her life. To believe in the Party gossip about marriage plans with 'Hänschen' Diefenbach, whom she addressed as *Sie* and never dreamed of treating as an equal, strikes me as downright silly. Nettl calls the story of Leo Jogiches and Rosa Luxemburg 'one of the great and tragic love stories of Socialism', and there is no need to quarrel with this verdict if one understands that it was not 'blind and self-destructive jealousy' which caused the ultimate tragedy in their relations but war and the years in prison, the doomed German revolution and the bloody end.

Leo Jogiches, whose name Nettl also has rescued from oblivion, was a very remarkable and yet typical figure among the professional revolutionists. To Rosa Luxemburg, he was definitely *mas-*

culini generis, which was of considerable importance to her: she preferred Graf Westarp (the leader of the German Conservative Party) to all the German Socialist luminaries 'because,' she said, 'he is a *man*.' There were few people she respected, and Jogiches headed a list on which only the names of Lenin and Franz Mehring could be inscribed with certainty. He definitely was a man of action and passion, he knew how to do and how to suffer. It is tempting to compare him with Lenin, whom he somewhat resembles, except in his passion for anonymity and for pulling strings behind the scenes, and his love of conspiracy and danger, which must have given him an additional erotic charm. He was indeed a Lenin *manqué*, even in his inability to write, 'total' in his case (as she observed in a shrewd and actually very loving portrait in one of her letters), and his mediocrity as a public speaker. Both men had great talent for organization and leadership, but for nothing else, so that they felt impotent and superfluous when there was nothing to do and they were left to themselves. This is less noticeable in Lenin's case because he was never completely isolated, but Jogiches had early fallen out with the Russian Party because of a quarrel with Plekhanov—the Pope of the Russian emigration in Switzerland during the nineties—who regarded the self-assured Jewish youth newly arrived from Poland as 'a miniature version of Nechaieff'. The consequence was that he, according to Rosa Luxemburg, 'completely rootless, vegetated' for many years, until the revolution of 1905 gave him his first opportunity: 'Quite suddenly he not only achieved the position of leader of the Polish movement, but even in the Russian.' (The SDKPiL came into prominence during the Revolution and became more important in the years following. Jogiches, though he himself didn't 'write a single line', remained 'none the less the very soul' of its publications.) He had his last brief moment when, 'completely unknown in the SPD', he organized a clandestine opposition in the German army during the First World War. 'Without him there would have been no *Spartakusbund*', which, unlike any other organized Leftist group in Germany, for a short time became a kind of 'ideal peer group'. (This, of course, is not to say that Jogiches made the German revolution; like all revolutions, it was made by no one. *Spartakusbund* too was 'following rather than making events', and the official notion that the 'Spartakus uprising' in January 1918 was caused or inspired by its leaders—Rosa Luxemburg, Liebknecht, Jogiches—is a myth.)

We shall never know how many of Rosa Luxemburg's political ideas derived from Jogiches; in marriage, it is not always easy to tell the partners' thoughts apart. But that he failed where Lenin succeeded was at least as much a consequence of circumstances—he was a Jew and a Pole—as of lesser stature. In any event, Rosa Luxemburg would have been the last to hold this against him. The members of the peer group did not judge one another in these categories. Jogiches himself might have agreed with Eugene Leviné, also a Russian Jew though a younger man, 'We are dead men on furlough.' This mood is what set him apart from the others; for neither Lenin nor Trotsky nor Rosa Luxemburg herself is likely to have thought along such lines. After her death he refused to leave Berlin for safety: 'Somebody has to stay to write all our epitaphs.' He was arrested two months after the murder of Liebknecht and Luxemburg and shot in the back in the police station. The name of the murderer was known, but 'no attempt to punish him was ever made'; he killed another man in the same way, and then continued his 'career with promotion in the Prussian Police'. Such were the *mores* of the Weimar Republic.

Reading and remembering these old stories, one becomes painfully aware of the difference between the German comrades and the members of the peer group. During the Russian revolution of 1905 Rosa Luxemburg was arrested in Warsaw, and her friends collected the money for bail (probably provided by the German Party). The payment was supplemented 'with an unofficial threat of reprisal; if anything happened to Rosa they would retaliate with action against prominent officials.' No such notion of 'action' ever entered her German friends' minds either before or after the wave of political murders when the impunity of such deeds had become notorious.

IV

More troubling in retrospect, certainly more painful for herself, than her alleged 'errors' are the few crucial instances in which Rosa Luxemburg was not out of step, but appeared instead to be in agreement with the official powers in the German Social Democratic Party. These were her real mistakes, and there was none she did not finally recognize and bitterly regret.

The least harmful among them concerned the national question. She had arrived in Germany in 1898 from Zürich, where she had passed her doctorate 'with a first-class dissertation about the industrial development of Poland' (according to Professor Julius Wolf, who in his autobiography still remembered fondly 'the ablest of my pupils'), which achieved the unusual 'distinction of instant commercial publication' and is still used by students of Polish history. Her thesis was that the economic growth of Poland depended entirely upon the Russian market and that any attempt 'to form a national or linguistic state was a negation of all development and progress for the last fifty years'. (That she was economically right was more than demonstrated by the chronic malaise of Poland between the wars.) She then became the expert on Poland for the German Party, its propagandist among the Polish population in the Eastern German provinces, and entered an uneasy alliance with people who wished to 'Germanize' the Poles out of existence and would 'gladly make you a present of all and every Pole including Polish Socialism', as an SPD secretary told her. Surely, 'the glow of official approval was for Rosa a false glow.'

Much more serious was her deceptive agreement with Party authorities in the revisionist controversy in which she played a leading part. This famous debate had been touched off by Eduard

Bernstein[5] and has gone down in history as the alternative of reform against revolution. But this battle cry is misleading for two reasons: it makes it appear as though the SPD at the turn of the century still was committed to revolution, which was not the case; and it conceals the objective soundness of much of what Bernstein had to say. His criticism of Marx's economic theories was indeed, as he claimed, in full 'agreement with reality'. He pointed out that the 'enormous increase of social wealth [was] not accompanied by a decreasing number of large capitalists but by an increasing number of capitalists of all degrees', that an 'increasing narrowing of the circle of the well-to-do and an increasing misery of the poor' had failed to materialize, that 'the modern proletarian [was] indeed poor but that he [was] no pauper', and that Marx's slogan, 'The proletarian has no fatherland', was not true. Universal suffrage had given him political rights, the trade unions a place in society, and the new imperialist development a clear stake in the nation's foreign policy. No doubt the reaction of the German Party to these unwelcome truths was chiefly inspired by a deep-seated reluctance to re-examine critically its theoretical foundation, but this reluctance was greatly sharpened by the Party's vested interest in the status quo threatened by Bernstein's analysis. What was at stake was the status of the SPD as a 'state within a state': the Party had in fact become a huge and well-organized bureaucracy that stood outside society and had every interest in things as they were. Revisionism à la Bernstein would have led the Party back into German society, and such 'integration' was felt to be as dangerous to the Party's interests as a revolution.

Mr. Nettl holds an interesting theory about the 'pariah position' of the SPD within German society and its failure to participate in government.[6] It seemed to its members that the Party could

[5]His most important book is now available in English under the title *Evolutionary Socialism* (Schocken Paperback), unfortunately lacking much-needed annotations and an introduction for the American reader.

[6]See 'The German Social Democratic Party, 1890–1914, as a Political Model,' in *Past and Present*, April 1965.

'provide within itself a superior alternative to corrupt capitalism'. In fact, by keeping the 'defenses against society on all fronts intact', it generated that spurious feeling of 'togetherness' (as Nettl puts it) which the French Socialists treated with great contempt.[7] In any event, it was obvious that the more the Party increased in numbers, the more surely was its radical élan 'organized out of existence'. One could live very comfortably in this 'state within a state' by avoiding friction with society at large, by enjoying feelings of moral superiority without any consequences. It was not even necessary to pay the price of serious alienation since this pariah society was in fact but a mirror image, a 'miniature reflection' of German society at large. This blind alley of the German Socialist movement could be analyzed correctly from opposing points of view—either from the view of Bernstein's revisionism, which recognized the emancipation of the working classes within capitalist society as an accomplished fact and demanded a stop to the talk about a revolution nobody thought of anyhow; or from the viewpoint of those who were not merely 'alienated' from bourgeois society but actually wanted to change the world.

The latter was the standpoint of the revolutionists from the East who led the attack against Bernstein—Plekhanov, Parvus, and Rosa Luxemburg—and whom Karl Kautsky, the German Party's most eminent theoretician, supported, although he probably felt much more at ease with Bernstein than in the company of his new allies from abroad. The victory they won was Pyrrhic; it 'merely strengthened alienation by pushing reality away'. For the real issue was not theoretical and not economic. At stake was Bernstein's conviction, shamefully hidden in a footnote, that 'the middle class—not excepting the German—in their bulk [was] still

---

[7]The situation bore very similar traits to the position of the French army during the Dreyfus crisis in France which Rosa Luxemburg so brilliantly analyzed for *Die Neue Zeit* in 'Die Soziale Krise in Frankreich' (vol. 1, 1901). 'The reason the army was reluctant to make a move was that it wanted to show its opposition to the civil power of the republic, without at the same time losing the force of that opposition by committing itself,' through a serious *coup d'état*, to another form of government.

fairly healthy, not only economically but also *morally'* (my italics). This was the reason that Plekhanov called him a 'philistine'
and that Parvus and Rosa Luxemburg thought the fight so decisive for the future of the Party. For the truth of the matter was
that Bernstein and Kautsky had in common their aversion to
revolution; the 'iron law of necessity' was for Kautsky the best
possible excuse for doing nothing. The guests from Eastern
Europe were the only ones who not merely 'believed' in revolution as a theoretical necessity but wished to do something about
it, precisely because they considered society as it was to be unbearable on *moral* grounds, on the grounds of justice. Bernstein and
Rosa Luxemburg, on the other hand, had in common that they
were both honest (which may explain Bernstein's 'secret tender-
ness' for her), analyzed what they saw, were loyal to reality and
critical of Marx; Bernstein was aware of this and shrewdly remarks in his reply to Rosa Luxemburg's attacks that she too had
questioned 'the whole Marxist predictions of the coming social
evolution, so far as this is based on the theory of crises'.

Rosa Luxemburg's early triumphs in the German Party rested
on a double misunderstanding. At the turn of the century the
SPD was 'the envy and admiration of Socialists throughout the
world'. August Bebel, its 'grand old man', who from Bismarck's
foundation of the German Reich to the outbreak of the First
World War 'dominated [its] policy and spirit', had always proclaimed, 'I am and always will be the mortal enemy of existing
society'. Didn't that sound like the spirit of the Polish peer group?
Couldn't one assume from such proud defiance that the great
German Party was somehow the SDKPiL writ large? It took
Rosa Luxemburg almost a decade—until she returned from the
first Russian revolution—to discover that the secret of this defiance was willful noninvolvement with the world at large and
single-minded preoccupation with the growth of the Party organization. Out of this experience she developed, after 1910, her
program of constant 'friction' with society without which, as she
then realized, the very source of the revolutionary spirit was

doomed to dry up. She did not intend to spend her life in a sect, no matter how large; her commitment to revolution was primarily a moral matter, and this meant that she remained passionately engaged in public life and civil affairs, in the destinies of the world. Her involvement with European politics outside the immediate interests of the working class, and hence completely beyond the horizon of all Marxists, appears most convincingly in her repeated insistence on a 'republican program' for the German and Russian Parties.

This was one of the main points of her famous *Juniusbroschüre*, written in prison during the war and then used as the platform for the *Spartakusbund*. Lenin, who was unaware of its authorship, immediately declared that to proclaim 'the program of a republic ... [means] in practice to proclaim the revolution—with an *incorrect* revolutionary program'. Well, a year later the Russian Revolution broke out without any 'program' whatsoever, and its first achievement was the abolition of the monarchy and the establishment of a republic, and the same was to happen in Germany and Austria. Which, of course, has never prevented the Russian, Polish, or German comrades from violently disagreeing with her on this point. It is indeed the republican question rather than the national one which separated her most decisively from all others. Here she was completely alone, as she was alone, though less obviously so, in her stress on the absolute necessity of not only individual but public freedom under all circumstances.

A second misunderstanding is directly connected with the revisionist debate. Rosa Luxemburg mistook Kautsky's reluctance to accept Bernstein's analyses for an authentic commitment to revolution. After the first Russian revolution in 1905, for which she had hurried back to Warsaw with false papers, she could no longer deceive herself. To her, these months constituted not only a crucial experience, they were also 'the happiest of my life'. Upon her return, she tried to discuss the events with her friends in the German Party. She learned quickly that the word 'revolution' 'had only to come into contact with a real revolutionary situation to break down' into meaningless syllables. The German Socialists were convinced that such things could happen only in distant barbarian lands. This was the first shock, from which she never recovered. The second came in 1914 and brought her near to suicide.

Naturally, her first contact with a real revolution taught her more and better things than disillusion and the fine arts of disdain and mistrust. Out of it came her insight into the nature of political action, which Mr. Nettl rightly calls her most important contribution to political theory. The main point is that she had learned from the revolutionary workers' councils (the latter *soviets*) that 'good organization does not precede action but is the product of it', that 'the organization of revolutionary action can and must be learnt in revolution itself, as one can only learn swimming in the water', that revolutions are 'made' by nobody but break out 'spontaneously', and that 'the pressure for action' always comes 'from below'. A revolution is 'great and strong as long as the Social Democrats [at the time still the only revolutionary party] don't smash it up'.

There were, however, two aspects of the 1905 prelude which entirely escaped her. There was, after all, the surprising fact that the revolution had broken out not only in a non-industrialized, backward country, but in a territory where no strong socialist movement with mass support existed at all. And there was, second, the equally undeniable fact that the revolution had been the consequence of the Russian defeat in the Russo-Japanese War. These were the two facts Lenin never forgot and from which he drew two conclusions. First, one did not need a large organization; a small, tightly organized group with a leader who knew what he wanted was enough to pick up the power once the authority of the old regime had been swept away. Large revolutionary organizations were only a nuisance. And, second, since revolutions were not 'made' but were the result of circumstances and events beyond anybody's power, wars were welcome.[8] The second point was the source of her disagreements with Lenin during the First World War; the first of her criticism of Lenin's tactics in the Russian Revolution of 1918. For she refused categorically, from beginning to end, to see in the war anything but the most terrible disaster, no matter what its eventual outcome; the price in human lives, especially in proletarian lives, was too high in any event. Moreover, it would have gone against her grain to look upon revolution as the profiteer of war and massacre—something which didn't bother Lenin in the least. And with respect to the issue of organization, she did not believe in a victory in which the people at large had no part and no voice; so little, indeed, did she believe in holding power at any price that she 'was far more afraid of a deformed revolution than an unsuccessful one'—this was, in fact, 'the major difference between her' and the Bolsheviks.

And haven't events proved her right? Isn't the history of the Soviet Union one long demonstration of the frightful dangers of 'deformed revolutions'? Hasn't the 'moral collapse' which she foresaw—without, of course, foreseeing the open criminality of Lenin's successor—done more harm to the cause of revolution as she understood it than 'any and every political defeat . . . in honest struggle against superior forces and in the teeth of the historical situation' could possibly have done? Wasn't it true that Lenin was 'completely mistaken' in the means he employed, that the only way to salvation was the 'school of public life itself, the most unlimited, the broadest democracy and public opinion', and that terror 'demoralized' everybody and destroyed everything?

She did not live long enough to see how right she had been and to watch the terrible and terribly swift moral deterioration of the

---

[8]Lenin read Clausewitz' *Vom Kriege* (1832) during the First World War; his excerpts and annotations were published in East Berlin during the fifties. According to Werner Hahlberg—'Lenin und Clausewitz' in the *Archiv für Kulturgeschichte*, vol. 36, Berlin, 1954—Lenin was under the influence of Clausewitz when he began to consider the possibility that war, the collapse of the European system of nation states, might replace the economic collapse of capitalist economy as predicted by Marx.

Communist parties, the direct offspring of the Russian Revolution, throughout the world. Nor for that matter did Lenin, who despite all his mistakes still had more in common with the original peer group than with anybody who came after him. This became manifest when Paul Levi, the successor of Leo Jogiches in the leadership of the *Spartakusbund*, three years after Rosa Luxemburg's death, published her remarks on the Russian Revolution just quoted, which she had written in 1918 'only for you'—that is, without intending publication.[9] 'It was a moment of considerable embarrassment' for both the German and Russian parties, and Lenin could be forgiven had he answered sharply and immoderately. Instead, he wrote: 'We answer with . . . a good old Russian fable: an eagle can sometimes fly lower than a chicken, but a chicken can never rise to the same heights as an eagle. Rosa Luxemburg . . . in spite of [her] mistakes . . . was and is an eagle.' He then went on to demand publication of 'her biography and the *complete* edition of her works', unpurged of 'error', and chided the German comrades for their 'incredible' negligence in this duty. This was in 1922. Three years later, Lenin's successors had decided to 'Bolshevize' the German Communist Party and therefore ordered a 'specific onslaught on Rosa Luxemburg's whole legacy'. The task was accepted with joy by a young member named Ruth Fischer, who had just arrived from Vienna. She told the German comrades that Rosa Luxemburg and her influence 'were nothing less than a syphilis bacillus'.

The gutter had opened, and out of it emerged what Rosa Luxemburg would have called 'another zoological species'. No 'agents of the bourgeoisie' and no 'Socialist traitors' were needed any

---

[9]It is not without irony that this pamphlet is the only work of hers which is still read and quoted today. The following items are available in English: *The Accumulation of Capital*, London and Yale, 1951; the responses to Bernstein (1899) in an edition published by the Three Arrows Press, New York, 1937; the *Juniusbroschüre* (1918) under the title *The Crisis in the German Social Democracy* by the Lanka Sama Samaja Publications of Colombo, Ceylon, in 1955, apparently in mimeographed form, and originally published in 1918 by the Socialist Publication Society, New York. In 1953, the same publishing house in Ceylon brought out her *The Mass Strike, the Political Party, and the Trade Unions* (1906).

longer to destroy the few survivors of the peer group and to bury in oblivion the last remnants of their spirit. No complete edition of her works, needless to say, was ever published. After World War II, a two-volume edition of selections 'with careful annotations underlining her errors' came out in East Berlin and was followed by a 'full-length analysis of the Luxemburgist system of errors' by Fred Oelssner, which quickly 'lapsed into obscurity' because it became 'too "Stalinist".' This most certainly was not what Lenin had demanded, nor could it, as he had hoped, serve 'in the education of many generations of Communists'.

After Stalin's death, things began to change, though not in East Germany, where, characteristically, revision of Stalinist history took the form of a 'Bebel cult'. (The only one to protest this new nonsense was poor old Hermann Duncker, the last distinguished survivor who still could 'recall the most wonderful period of my life, when as a young man I knew and worked with Rosa Luxemburg, Karl Liebknecht, and Franz Mehring'.) The Poles, however, although their own two-volume edition of selected works in 1959 is 'partly overlapping with the German' one, 'took out her reputation almost unaltered from the casket in which it had been stored' ever since Lenin's death, and after 1956 a 'flood of Polish publications' on the subject appeared on the market. One would like to believe that there is still hope for a belated recognition of who she was and what she did, as one would like to hope that she will finally find her place in the education of political scientists in the countries of the West. For Mr. Nettl is right: 'Her ideas belong wherever the history of political ideas is seriously taught.'

PREFACE

WHEN I wrote the biography of Rosa Luxemburg, of which this is an abridged version, I intended to reconstruct the history of a person, a movement, and an epoch. Since 1917 the Marxist movement in which she spent her life has grown in power and extent to a world-wide phenomenon and dominates a large part of the developed as well as the under-developed world—although its form and ideology have changed almost beyond recognition. Indeed the analysis of the connection, if any, between Marx and those who act, write or merely shout in his name all over the world, and who quarrel bitterly among themselves, has become a major intellectual industry. Ph.D.s are to be had in it. The question of how relevant Rosa Luxemburg was to all this necessarily imposed itself on me. I answered it three years ago with a practical negative and an ethical affirmative. I now think I may still have underestimated it.

The Communism we know today has many forms. From rigid Stalinist uniformity imposed by Moscow it has become a polycentric movement. Soon each Communist country will have, or claim to have, its own version of Communism. In those countries where Communist parties are not in power the same right of autonomous decision-making over policy, adjusting to the particular conditions of each society, is being claimed. None the less, all these movements do have certain things in common and it is precisely these *common* elements which in turn differ strongly from Rosa Luxemburg's revolutionary concept.

For one thing almost all and every communist movement today is passionately concerned with problems and forms of organization (except perhaps the Cubans). Since no Communist movement has come to power by itself in a highly developed industrial country, the mass democracy which Rosa Luxemburg foresaw as the prime motor of socialist revolution has been replaced by a well-organized group of revolutionaries, acting on behalf of, or at least in the name of, the masses. They have seized power in relatively under-developed or non-industrial countries. Even in China, where the revolution may well be said to have achieved the highest rate of mass participation in the actual process of overthrowing the previous régime, the army, with all its emphasis on discipline and armed combat, played a vital part. The early Soviet concept of an élite of revolutionaries anchored in the organized urban working class has been replaced by very different social and strategic forms of revolution, ranging from a military—political resistance movement to imperialism with very strong nationialist overtones in Viet Nam to the bands of armed guerrillas in Cuba and Latin America. There are great differences—many of them elaborated theoretically—between all of these and the Bolsheviks; however, they all share with the Bolsheviks an even greater difference from the radical mass democratic revolution envisaged by Rosa Luxemburg. To make or to lead the revolution, there's the rub. The problem of democracy is a complex one; but certain it is that these modern movements, however democratic, differ substantially from the *type* of participant democracy in the revolutionary process envisaged by Rosa Luxemburg.

It is precisely the historical distance between her time and ours, the transfer of the action from the highly industrialized West to the underdeveloped Third World that in one sense has made it possible to do greater justice to the value of Rosa Luxemburg's ideas within the communist tradition—by taking out the constraints of ideological immediacy. As long as there was dissent, or even the possiblity of dissent, from the one central line of Soviet orthodoxy (and as long as it was agreed that there could only be one such orthodoxy, whatever it might be), the discussion of anyone who had disagreed with Lenin on major questions was necessarily taboo. In fact there was no such thing as 'mere' discussion; everything was struggle, everything had contemporary relevance. Only since the break-up of Stalinist orthodoxy—albeit with much hesitation and frequent reversals—has the discussion of Communist history become possible, and hence also more liberal. Communist historians are less interested in evaluating the mistakes of participants compared to the one and only Bolshevik orthodoxy, and in the process investing the Bolsheviks with the necessary seal of historical infallibility. Instead they are writing history with all its zigzags and blind alleys. Rosa Luxemburg has therefore benefited from the renewed interest in what happened, and particularly from the attention paid to the histories of the societies in which she was most active, Germany and Poland. The position she occupied for nearly a decade after her death has been restored; the Stalinist denigrations and lies rolled back. But all the same, this has been strictly a European restoration, limited in space as well as time. Though detailed discussion of her activities and evaluation of her position is still constrained, she has become a revolutionary heroine once more, instead of a tarnished minor figure, an early and largely mistaken revolutionary. To the historians and ideologists of Asian and Latin-American Communism she may be an interesting person but she has little immediate relevance—just as the pre-1914 history of Europe has only marginal importance. In Asia only the

Trotskyite party of Ceylon has shown any sustained interest in her work. As the following pages will show, Rosa Luxemburg's position is in one respect unique. Not only was she an ancestor of European, and to that extent, Soviet Communism, but the fact that she criticized Lenin acutely and repeatedly has provided ammuniton to right-wing socialists searching in a Marxism made toothless in long-term retrospection for ammunition against the Bolsheviks. These opposed yet continued claims of both Communists and anti-Communists to represent the true heritage of Rosa Luxemburg's ideas are shared only by Marx himself. In this case the conflict has been structured by overemphasis on the periodization of his work. The early humanist phase is opposed to his later preoccupation with economic matters and class; philosophy and sociology on the one hand against determinist economics and politics on the other. In Rosa Luxemburg's case there is the stress on democracy and freedom in her writings by Social Democrats against her personal commitment to social revolution emphasized by Communists. But the exclusive 'possession' of Marxist humanism by academic sociologists and philosophers (many of them Marxist 'deviants') in the West has recently been eroded by a renewed interest in both philosophy and humanism, coupled with the determination to give it concrete political, above all socialist, expression in a number of People's Democracies— Jugoslavia, Poland for a time, and recently Czechoslovakia. Similarly the emphasis on mass participation and democracy, on socialist legality and respect for persons, has stolen the exclusive insistence on these aspects of left wing socialism in the Second International on the part of con- servative, well-integrated reform labour parties in the West. Here, then, is the *prima facie* cause for a Luxemburgist revival in the People's Democracies. I say *prima facie* because any link between what has recently been happening in Jugoslavia and Czechoslovakia and Rosa Luxemburg's work was implicit rather than acknowledged; and because the first flush of freedom has produced at least as much petty bourgeois liberalism as left socialist democracy. The situation at the time of writing was ideologically as well as structurally in a state of flux.

It would be pointless to try to establish a direct intellectual link between the early Marx and Rosa Luxemburg (most of the early texts of Karl Marx were only published in the 1920s and some more recently). None the less, there is a fairly obvious connection in emphasis between Rosa Luxemburg's individualistic, creative Marxism as experienced in terms of struggle and friction, and Marx's concern in his early writings with alienation and with the subjective need for revolution. Both lived in an era when revolution was necessary; both were concerned with showing the intolerable nature of the society which was to be over- thrown. All this does not make Rosa Luxemburg more immediately relevant to the *problems* of the post-Stalinist People's Democracies today, but it does indicate a shift in priorities *towards* the problems with which she herself was mostly preoccupied. The gap between a revolutionary struggle to overthrow an imperialist form of capitalism and the attempt to make an established Communist régime more humane, more law-abiding, and more democratic, must remain very large. The liberalizers in Czechoslovakia and Jugoslavia control the machinery of the State. The problem is to make it capable of giving institutional expression to greater participation, to make the Communist party the leader and not the controller of—or substitute for—participant and democratic action. Though the pressures for change have come in part from the middle and lower sections of the party, the pace has none the less been set by established Communists themselves—by those in power. This is very different to Rosa Luxemburg's struggle from below against a party bureaucracy which itself had little power in society and no voice in the State—a barely tolerated institution of outsiders.

In short, the relevance of Rosa Luxemburg to socialist societies today is one of emphasis and not of precise application of her views. The study of her work highlights the attempt to grapple with problems that are again, or still, proving obstinately relevant in spite of revolutionary change in a socialist direction, in spite of the establishment of socialist or Communist governments. In established socialist societies she is essentially a historical figure, though an important and sparklingly brilliant one. Ironically, it is precisely in the Western parliamentary democracies that Rosa Luxemburg's programmatic writing has suddenly achieved a dramatic, almost lurid importance. I must confess that when I first studied her ideas and life, it was abundantly clear that what she had to offer was above all an extreme and unsurpassed critique of the industrial society in which she lived. If ever a revolt against the intolerable nature of bourgeois society had to be undertaken—irrespective of whether this was merely the personal decision of a single individual or the organized and collective determination of a party or class—then Rosa Luxemburg's ideas would truly come into their own. But such a radicalization of attitudes towards what is often called modern or even post-modern society seemed very unlikely. The very shift of Communist revolution from the industrial West to what are today labelled underdeveloped countries, and the resultant transformation in the meaning of Marxist socialism from a post-revolutionary 'rationalization' of fully industrial society into a political economy *of* industrialization itself, have shifted the whole arena of revolutionary relevance away from the industrialized democracies. In recent years these have become an island of piecemeal reform and socio-economic adjustment in a sea of revolutionary upheavals in the rest of the world. Though her own philosophy and way of life was firmly anchored in the industrial West Rosa herself actually played a considerable part in predicting and facilitating the eastward shift of revolution from the West to Russia. Admittedly, in her view, this involved no change in the basic meaning of Marxist revolution. She did not regard Marxism as a philosophy of industrial development: quite the contrary, her evaluation of revolutionary Russia in 1905–6 was that it was ready (or at least readier than had hitherto been supposed) for revolution in a Western sense. As I have strongly underlined in my analysis, her contrast of the positive Russian revolutionary spirit with German dogmatism and organizational conservatism was essentially cultural rather than socio-economic. It was the same type of revolution that was at stake, only the Russians were setting about it better. In many ways Stalin always remained faithful to this concept—though it was essentially a concept of the Second International. There was still, according to him, only one type of universal validity—even if he inverted the primacy of the revolutionary experience by assigning the Bolsheviks absolute and universal priority. Whatever the means, parity with the West was his unswerving aim.

Yet the irony of history will have it that it is as a philosophy and political economy of industrialization that Soviet Communism and the Bolshevik tradition has the greatest interest today—one, moreover, that is increasingly being accepted and studied as unique, incapable of replication elsewhere. The very determination to search for individual ways to socialism in many of the People's Democracies and among Communist parties in the West implies a recognition of the uniqueness of the Soviet experience. Among many Communists the Soviet Union is today regarded as conservative—conservative in Western eyes for its refusal to loosen the established and institutionalized control of the party beyond the Khrushchev reforms and liberalization; conservative in Chinese and Cuban eyes because of its national self-regard, its unwillingness to take revolutionary risks, its preference for sophisticated means of defending the national territory instead of supporting and undertaking a strategy of revolutionary offence in developing countries. It may well be that the post-Khrushchev economic reforms in the Soviet Union will eventually bring in their train a shake-up of the still rigid political structure, but this is beyond our present concerns. The fact is that the Soviet Union is no longer a model for the People's Democracies or left wing parties in the Western parliamentary democracies.

But my implied prognosis that little revolutionary change could be expected in the latter has proved false indeed. Rivulets of dissatisfaction and protest as yet inchoate, hardly institutionalized, and still bereft of ideological conviction (except in a sense of pure negation), show signs of joining up into a powerful stream of almost revolutionary discontent. Not, to be sure, based on the working classes—that motor of social transformation which Marx increasingly stipulated for the role of the proletariat; the dispossessed and alienated revolutionary vehicle of his early writings, which later became defined and analysed into the collective worker who 'owned' nothing but his labour power—chains rather than assets. In the event, the working class actually came to fulfil most of the optimistic prognoses of liberal thinkers; they have become largely 'socialized' through access to privilege, consumption, organization, and voting participation, as well as obtaining massive social benefits. They have become supporters of the *status quo*—not vociferous perhaps, but tacit approvers and beneficiaries none the less. The ferment today comes from sections of the community to whom political and social thought has never hitherto assigned any specific role; who have hitherto never developed specific political institutions of their own: youth, mostly students; racial minorities, a few dissident intellectuals—these form the new 'proletariat'. The basis of their dissatisfaction is not necessarily and always an objective level of deprivation but rather a mixture of relative deprivation—consciousness of possibilities and of the blockages which prevent their attainment—and above all an articulate dissatisfaction with the society around them. There is no good reason why such groups should not form, and act like, a proletariat in a perfectly Marxist sense. The economic causality collapses; the analysis of a decaying bourgeois society and the determination to overthrow it remain.

Rosa Luxemburg was a perfectly orthodox Marxist in stressing the ineluctable relationship between economic exploitation and proletarian (working class) class consciousness. She frequently used, as did many of her contemporaries, the phrase *petit bourgeois* as a rag-bag concept for the shifting forces on the fringe of the socialist movement—sometimes progressive, sometimes revolutionary, but never reliable as allies. To Communist ideologists in the Soviet Union and many of the Peoples Democracies, the dissident forces in the West come into the same *petit bourgeois* anarchist category. At times they are to be used, but they are not socialists or even potential socialists. In the setting of fifty years ago, therefore, the present protesting groups—had they existed—would have met Rosa Luxemburg's disapproval.

Today's conditions are in fact very different. The Communists have in large measure failed in this respect to bring their analysis of bourgeois society up to date—especially Soviet Communists. With a sleepy, often servile, and almost everywhere ministerially-minded Social Democracy, with Communist parties still struggling to free themselves from the Stalinist strait-jacket and unable to give a clear lead, almost the sole movement of basic negation and revolutionary protest comes from these hitherto unrecognized strata. If, therefore, we assume the presence of a Rosa Luxemburg today, evaluating the present situation and aware of all that has happened in the last fifty years, the problem of her attitude cannot be simply and categorically solved with a 'no'.

In Europe at any rate the search for an ideological foundation assigns Rosa Luxemburg quite an important place, particularly among the students. Their leaders in Germany have specifically rejected Soviet Communism; elsewhere its relevance as a model has hardly arisen. Their ideology, unformed as yet but in the process of crystallization, appears to be a mishmash of authorities as diverse as Lenin, Mao, Castro, Sartre, Marcuse, and Rosa Luxemburg. Any serious student of Marxism would regard these as incompatible if not downright contradictory. How could a single group of founding fathers range from the leader of the cultural revolution in China to the elderly professor of Philosophy in America, from the military Latin-American revolutionary with his highly personal and idiosyncratic rule to the Polish-Jewish intellectual of mass democracy? Yet they do all have a number of things in common. They all agreed on the fact that their own pre-revolutionary societies were or are intolerable. Above all, almost all stressed action; the essential component of personal commitment as a base of experience from which a superstructure of organization and strategy would follow. The growth of revolutionary fervour in individual participants and its spread to ever wider sections of the population must primarily be the result of struggle itself, not the distillation of thought or the prescription of correct ideology by others.

At times it has been necessary to do violence to Lenin's doctrines in order to cull an absolute primacy of action over correct ideological formulation and a correct organization; and violence to Mao's doctrines in order to drown in a passion of revolutionary fervour his very real policy of revolutionary uniformity, if not mass homogeneity. But today's dissidents are not interested in textual exegesis or intellectual logic. They take what they need and adapt it freely. The difficulty of applying Maoist and Fidelist precepts to German universities or American negro ghettoes is a scholastic rather than an action problem. No doubt much of this citation of authority is ephemeral and will disappear—or rather be reorganized into an adequate ideology based more and more on their own experience as and when this develops. The reason why these names presently serve as markers and inspirers is clear enough.

Rosa Luxemburg's presence among them is significant for one special reason. She more than any of the others was concerned with active struggle in a society closely approximating our own. She was the prophet *par excellence* of the uninstitutionalized revolution. She preached the primacy of action and the relationship between a revolutionary situation and the participation of growing masses of the 'proletariat'. Having no experience of the post-revolutionary socialist state and of the problems of continued alienation which this has been seen to entail, her focus was primarily on the evils of the present society and the necessity of transforming it. She knew better than any how close must be the relationship between personal commitment and action, between action and class-consciousness, between class-consciousness and revolution. Every student who demonstrates against the police in Britain and the United States and evaluates the lessons of this experience in terms of future tactics and strategy is in this sense much closer to Rosa Luxemburg than the tightly organized and controlled demonstrators who clashed with equally controlled and organized police forces in, say, Paris in the early 1950s. The difference is that between social revolution on the one hand, and paramilitary trials of strength on the other. This is where Rosa Luxemburg's arguments with Lenin in 1904 and her critique of the Bolshevik revolution, which I shall discuss at some length in this book, have their current significance. For revolutionary changes in parliamentary democracies will never come about by the action of paramilitary professionals.

Finally events in both parliamentary and People's Democracies have thrown up in very different ways interesting problems about the status and role of intellectuals at the present time. Here, too, Rosa Luxemburg represents an important example of the intellectuals' claim for status in the transformation of society. As guardians of culture, as articulators of ideology, above all as describers of the vision to be achieved and struggled for, intellectuals are an essential component of revolution—and nowhere more so than in the Marxist as well as the Leninist, Maoist, and Fidelist traditions. If the twenties and the Stalin era in the Soviet Union was increasingly the period of the organizer, the era of Communist *ouvrièrisme*, the break-out from physical and intellectual strait-jackets in Jugoslavia, Poland, and Czechoslovakia has been primarily the work of intellectuals. We tend to think of intellectuals as being at the opposite pole to activists, but this assumption is quite incorrect. The real distinction is between intellectuals who want change and bureaucrats who don't—whose only vision of change is quantitative, more rather than better. The dissent from bureaucratic rule, whether based on a parliamentary-bureaucratic consensus or the omnipresent party governing and controlling in the Soviet Union, is almost by definition an intellectual process. There are indeed periods when the intellectuals and the activists are separated, when one or other is silent but no transformation of society can take place unless they march together. But if the recent changes in Eastern Europe have been mainly intellectually inspired, the growth of dissent in the West has not yet reached an adequate relationship between activists and intellectuals. The latter have so far been swept aside by the sheer radicalism of the activists, by the primacy assigned to action as such on the part of dissenters. That perhaps is why the activists cling to such an ill-assorted pantheon of authorities. The gap may in fact be due to a failure on the part of today's intellectuals. Some sociologists claim that they have at last been integrated into the munificent, apparently permissive society of total literacy, *ad hoc* cultures and mass communication; others wonder whether this obliteration by kindness spells the end of the classic type of intellectual for good. For the moment certainly the activists are well ahead of the intellectuals—unlike in Rosa Luxemburg's day when it was the other way about.

The relevance of Rosa Luxemburg here is simply the stress on the need for a close relationship between activists and intellectuals. She herself personified the unity of theory and praxis so strongly postulated by Marx himself. The intellectuals in Eastern Europe have pointed to the need for broadening the basis of power, for mass participation, for the development of criticism instead of uniformity imposed from above. Understandably they cite Rosa Luxemburg in support of these demands. The dissenters in the West point to the need for commitment and action; Rosa Luxemburg represents these qualities in their pantheon. In West and East two different but vital components of her philosophy also appear to be missing from the current situation. In the East it is the component of the masses, who have not yet been brought into action; in the West the intellectual specification of programme and ideology is missing. What is needed there is someone to universalize and structure present discontents.

The purpose of this shortened version of my work is to enable a wider audience to have access to her life and ideas. Her importance as an historical figure is beyond doubt; the original volumes were dedicated to it. Ironically it was a hostile reviewer in Poland who made me more aware of her wider and directly contemporary relevance. In contemptuously dismissing my book as anti-Communist, as intended mainly to prop up ideologically the naïve anarchists of Western protest whom, in comparison to the achievements of state socialism in Poland, he also described as 'a virulent form of anti-Communism', he made me realize that the relevance of the orthodox Marxist Rosa Luxemburg might be at least as great in non-Communist surroundings of protest as for the historical self-contemplation of established Communists. So I unashamedly address this edition to anyone interested in using this rich fund of ideas, this rich life of action and experience, for their own purpose. The reader will best judge the relevance of Rosa Luxemburg to himself.

Oxford, 1968.

ABBREVIATIONS

The following are used regularly:

Bulletin BSI   Bulletin Périodique du Bureau Socialiste Internationale.

D & M   Dokumente und Materialien zur Geschichte der Deutschen Arbeiterbewegung. (Bibliography Section III, anonymous collections.)

IISH   International Institute of Social History at Amsterdam.

IML (B)   Institut für Marxismus-Leninismus, Berlin (East). Party historical institute for the SED.

IML (M)   Institut Marksizma-Leninizma, Moscow. Party historical institute for the CPSU.

LV   *Leipziger Volkszeitung.*

NZ   *Neue Zeit.*

PSD   *Przegląd Socjaldemokratyczny.*

SAZ   *Sächsische Arbeiterzeitung.*

SM   *Sozialistische Monatshefte.*

SDK   *Sozialdemokratische Korrespondenz.*

ZHP   Archiwum Zakladu Historii Partii, PZPR, Warsaw. (Archives of the party historical institute, Polish United Workers' Party, Warsaw.)

Parties

CPSU   Communist Party of the Soviet Union (from 1952 onwards).

KPD   German Communist Party.

KPR (B)   Communist Party of Russia (Bolsheviks) (from 1918–25). (Known as All Union Communist Party (Bolsheviks) from 1925–52.)

PPS   Polish Socialist Party.

RSDRP   Russian Social-Democratic Workers' Party (from 1898–1918).

SDKP   Social Democracy of the Kingdom of Poland.

SDKPiL   Social Democracy of the Kingdom of Poland and Lithuania.

SED	Socialist Unity Party (following on the amalgamation of the Communists and Social Democrats in East Germany in 1946).
SPD	German Social-Democratic Party.
USPD	Independent Social-Democratic Party of Germany.

CREDO

COMMUNISM is in reality nothing but the antithesis of a particular ideology that is both thoroughly harmful and corrosive. Thank God for the fact that Commmunism springs from a clean and clear ideal, which preserves its idealistic purpose even though, as an antidote, it is inclined to be somewhat harsh. To hell with its practical import: but may God at least preserve it for us as a never-ending menace to those people who own big estates and who, in order to hang on to them, are prepared to despatch humanity into battle, to abandon it to starvation for the sake of patriotic honour. May God preserve Communism so that the evil brood of its enemies may be prevented from becoming more barefaced still, so that the gang of profiteers . . . shall have their sleep disturbed by at least a few pangs of anxiety. If they must preach morality to their victims and amuse themselves with their suffering, at least let some of their pleasure be spoilt!

Karl Kraus in *Die Fackel*, November 1920; reprinted in *Widerschein der Fackel* (Volume IV of *Selected Works* of Karl Kraus), Munich 1956, p. 281.

ROSA LUXEMBURG

I

ROSA LUXEMBURG—WHO,

WHAT, AND WHY?

WHY a biography of Rosa Luxemburg at this time? Many people actually know Rosa Luxemburg's name, but its associations are vague—German, Jewish, and revolutionary; that is as far as it goes. To those who are interested in the history of Socialism she emerges in clearer focus, as the spokeswoman and theoretician of the German Left, and one of the founders of the German Communist Party. Two aspects of her life seem to stand out: her death—which retrospectively creates a special, if slightly sentimental, interest in a woman revolutionary brutally murdered by the soldiery; and her disputes with Lenin in which she appears to represent democracy against Russian Communism. The translator and editor of her works in America has seen fit to put out an edition of her polemics against Lenin under the title *Leninism or Marxism*, presumably because he too thinks this neatly sums up her position.[1] To many casual readers in the West she has therefore come to represent the most incisive defender of the democratic tradition in Marxism against the growing shadow of its misuse by the Bolsheviks. For them, insofar as revolutionary Marxism can be democratic, Rosa Luxemburg stands at its apex. She has become the intellectual sheet-anchor of all those old, but ever young, radicals who think that Communism could have been the combination of violence and extreme democracy. In their frequent moments of nostalgia it is the name Rosa Luxemburg that they utter.[2] Her death in action ended any possibility of giving

---

[1] Bertram D. Wolfe (ed.): Rosa Luxemburg, *The Russian Revolution* and *Leninism or Marxism?*, Ann Arbor (Michigan) 1961.

[2] Sometimes in the most improbable places. 'I remember sitting up [with some girls in Los Angeles who had a 'strange set-up with some football players' from College] one night and trying to explain patiently, I mean without patronizing them or anything, how the Third International might never have gone off the tracks if only they had listened to Rosa Luxemburg. I would have liked to have known, for instance, just what Radek and Bukharin felt when Rosa said her piece about over-centralization. . . . [The girl] seemed to think about [all] this at least as seriously as when one of the USC football boys asked her whether she preferred the quick-kick punt or a quarter-back sneak. . . .' (Clancy Segal, *Going Away* (2nd edition), New York 1963, p. 46.)

Quite a number of English and American poets and painters find a continuing source of artistic protest in Rosa's life.

effective battle to the Bolsheviks and also sanctified her views with the glow of martyrdom. But the difficulty is that these same Bolsheviks and their followers, whose ascendancy she is supposed to have resisted, have also claimed her for their own. In spite of her alleged mistakes and misinterpretations, they see her ultimately committed to Communism in its struggle against Social Democracy; had she lived she would have made the choice even more decisively than in the confusion of 1918. Once again the date of her death is crucial—as well as its form. Communist tradition can no more afford to ignore a martyr than any other embattled faith—and so someone who later might well have been buried with all the obloquy of a renegade, today still retains her place in the official pantheon, by dying early and by dying hard.

So the first reason for Rosa Luxemburg's importance in the history of political Marxism is the unique moment of her death. She and Karl Liebknecht were perhaps the only Marxists who committed themselves to the Bolshevik revolution in spite of fundamental criticisms which are as old as that revolution itself. What makes Rosa Luxemburg's case especially interesting is that her debates with Lenin on certain fundamental Marxist problems date back to 1903—they are central to her philosophy. Others in Russia had departed from or quarrelled with Bolshevism long before 1917—quite apart from those who were never within sight or sound of sympathy with Lenin. These had nothing to contribute to orthodox revolutionary Marxism after 1917. An even more important group came to differ from Leninism as it evolved into Stalinism; they opted out of the charmed circle of Communist politics. Trotsky and his followers, and all those purveyors of a precise conscience who orbited on the periphery of revolutionary Marxism from the 1920s onwards, suffered from the same two major disabilities: lack of a disciplined mass following to compensate for the organized support of Soviet power, and the ideological distress of having suddenly to prise themselves loose from their inheritance of the October Revolution. The awful alternative was either to deny the validity of the original event— the revolution—or to claim that it was those in power in Russia who deviated from some purely intellectual norm set by the dissidents. Rosa Luxemburg, however, could neither be brushed aside as irrelevant before 1917 nor denounced as a traitor afterwards. When she died she was a critical supporter; in her own words, 'Enthusiasm coupled with the spirit of revolutionary criticism—what more can people want from us?'[1]

But there are also good reasons why the relevance of Rosa Luxemburg's ideas should be greater today than at any time since the 1930s. With the death of Stalin, Communist theory has ceased to be merely the

---

[1] Adolf Warski, *Rosa Luxemburgs Stellung zu den taktischen Problemen der Revolution*, Hamburg 1922, pp. 6–7.

iron-clad accretions and deposits of the dictator's own notion of Marx-ism–Leninism. The bands have burst and with them a lively, if uneven, froth of speculation has broken out. In Jugoslavia a new participatory, in part even competitive, version of Marxism has emerged in the last decade; in Czechoslovakia there has been a compressed war-revolution more recently, with much the same results. In Poland there are demands for a further, more radical instalment of the 'Polish October' of 1956. In the Soviet Union, too, there have been profound changes since the death of Stalin. The impetus came from the top—but was taken up and carried forward from lower down.

This leads straight to the large-scale Marxist excavation which, in the 1960s, blaringly accompanied the Russo–Chinese conflict. And it did not take long for the digging to reach the revisionist controversy—one of the great watersheds of Marxism (though the thesis of this book is in part an attempt to shift its impact to a different time and a different dispute). No one spans these great issues more comprehensively than Rosa Luxemburg. The whole problem of revising Marx—which is none other than the problem of capturing the only authoritative interpretation of Marxism—was of great concern to Rosa Luxemburg. She expended some of her most important political analysis on the difference between Marxism and revisionism and on the difference between abandoning Marxist fundamentals like revolution on the one hand and mere cate-gories of analysis limited in time on the other, like the 'progressive' nation-state. The contrast between *postulating* revolution and *being* revolutionary, which today agitates the Russians as much as the Chinese, was precisely the central issue which Rosa Luxemburg tried to emphasize for the first time in her much neglected polemics against Kautsky in 1910. In addition, the inevitable confrontation, not of alternative philosophies but of the two different worlds of socialism and capitalism, was central to Rosa Luxemburg's thesis just as it is the mainspring of the Chinese attack on the Soviet Union. Placid and well-fed capitalism leading to an equally placid and well-fed socialism was as much Rosa Luxemburg's bogey as it is that of the Central Committee of the Chinese Communist Party.

But if the current interpretation of the new line in Communist countries comes from the top, the pressure for it comes diffusely from below. The areas of free expression in Russia and the People's Demo-cracies have suddenly become much larger. Though transgression of the limits is still a serious offence against Communist discipline, there is at least more room for manœuvre. The notion that art is not the completely disciplined tool of political will but a spontaneous expression which merely requires a censor's check in the light of stated political needs; that art needs social control but need not stem from controlled social inspiration, is slowly seeping its way upwards through the Russian

Communist Party. Here again the whole notion of art as *conforming*, as being analysed for good or bad content, corresponds much more closely to Rosa Luxemburg's conception than Stalin's idea of a disciplined expression of social purpose.

Rosa Luxemburg was not alone, out of her time, in the expression of ideas. Some things she said were exclusive to her, the emphasis often particular; but there was a whole consensus of similar views and aspirations. The relevance Rosa Luxemburg has re-acquired with recent changes in the complexion and emphasis of Communism applies equally to others. But few covered the ground as thoroughly and vivaciously, as totally as she. Rosa Luxemburg had much of that vital quality of immediate relevance which she praised so highly in Marx himself—often to the detriment of his actual arguments. She made Marxism real and important in a way which few contemporaries were able to achieve. Though there are hardly any Luxemburgists, in the way that there were Stalinists and still are Trotskyites, it is almost certainly true that more people at the time found their early way to revolutionary Marxism through *Social Reform or Revolution* and other writings of Rosa Luxemburg than through any other writer. And justly so. The very notion of Luxemburgism would have been abhorrent to her. What makes her writing so seductive is that the seduction is incidental; she was not writing to convert, but to convince. It was not only the quality of her ideas, then, but the manner of their expression: the way she said it as much as what she said.

The bitter tug-of-war for Rosa Luxemburg's heritage was a struggle for the legitimacy bequeathed by an important Marxist and an even more outstanding exponent of revolutionary Marxism. Social Democracy of the 1920s, particularly the German Social-Democratic Party (SPD), thought that it could see in her an ardent advocate of democracy who sooner or later was bound to come into conflict with oligarchical and arbitrary Bolshevism. Such an interpretation was cherished particularly by the many Communists who left the party in the course of the next thirty years. They found in Rosa Luxemburg's undoubted revolutionary Marxism, combined with the frequent use of the words 'masses', 'majority', and 'democracy', a congenial lifebelt—to keep them afloat either alone or at least on the unimportant left fringe of official Social Democracy. Nearly every dissident group from official Communism— German, French, or Russian—at once laid special and exclusive claim to the possession of Rosa Luxemburg's spirit, and it is significant that Trotsky, whose relationship with Rosa Luxemburg had been impersonal and hostile for a decade, claimed her spiritual approval for the Fourth International from the day of its foundation.[1]

---

[1] L. Trotsky, *Rosa Luxemburg et la quatrième Internationale*, Paris 1933.

The Communists were in no way prepared to let her go. However, to answer Social Democracy and their own dissidents it became necessary to interpret her work in such a way that those items and quotations on which the enemy based its case could be knitted together into a whole system of error. It no longer sufficed to shrug these off as so many isolated mistakes, and in due course Communist theorists constructed for and on behalf of Rosa Luxemburg a system called Luxemburgism— compounded from just those errors on which Social Democracy relied. The person became increasingly separated from the doctrine—rather like the English notion that the Crown can do no wrong. The fiercer the Communist struggle against Luxemburgism, the greater the attachment to the revolutionary personality of Luxemburg, stripped of its errors. As we have seen, this delicate surgery made Rosa Luxemburg unique in Communist history.

Beneath the caricature of 'Luxemburgism' and its 'spontaneity' there can be seen a consistent set of principles with which Rosa Luxemburg hoped to arm nascent Communism in Germany. She never set out to produce a comprehensive or even logically cohesive system of her own. Almost invariably her ideas found expression in the form of criticisms or polemics against what she considered to be errors. Out of this negative aspect of her own correction (and often over-correction, like Lenin's 'bent stick' of orthodoxy), we have to construct the positive content of her intentions. While it would therefore be wrong to construct a 'true' system in place of the false one—and no such attempt will be made—certain dominant ideas remain. The strong emphasis on action as a prophylactic as well as a progressive social impulse is deeply rooted in Communism today—deeply enough for its specific reincarnation in China because of its allegedly formal abstraction in Russia— and this was Rosa Luxemburg's most important contribution to the Marxism of her time. What has usually been ascribed to Lenin's peculiar genius for action, asserting itself against the bureaucratic and cautious hesitations of his closest supporters in 1917, was no more than the specific and longstanding recommendation of the German Left, most ably expounded in Rosa Luxemburg's writings. For most of her life revolution was as close and real to her as to Lenin. Above all, she sensed and hammered home the difference between theoretical and real revolutionary attitudes long before Lenin was aware that such differences could exist in the SPD. Modern revolutionary Marxism is thus peculiarly her contribution even though the debt may not be acknowledged.

The German Communist inheritors of Eastern Germany have never quite succeeded in obliterating the real image of Rosa Luxemburg with a false one and thus reducing the actual person of Rosa Luxemburg, as it were, to the pages of Socialist history. The whole ideology of the

Socialist Unity Party in East Germany has been permeated by its inability to digest the Communist role in the German revolution of 1918–19 and get it out of its system. East German ideology from 1945 to 1965 can most suitably be described as Marxism plus a bad conscience. Under the pressure of Stalinist orthodoxy, the old failure was measured by the extent to which the Bolshevik example was not followed, step by irrelevant step. Where *Spartakus*, the precursor of German Communism during the First World War, differed from the Bolsheviks it was always wrong; where these differences were substantial—separation from the body of Social Democracy at a much earlier date than 1918 or even 1914, organizational self-sufficiency, weakness in turning opposition to the war into social revolution, etc.—they provide the direct cause of the revolution's failure in Germany. Since 1953 party history in Russia has at last been catching up with itself a little, after slumbering so long. But in East Germany today the 1918 revolution was still being fought all over again. Every posture against West Germany had its parallel in 1918, its historical significance—just as every act by the German Federal Government could be and immediately was compared with the doings of the counter-revolution after the First World War. In such an atmosphere Rosa Luxemburg was perforce very much alive. Too 'alive', in fact, to permit a standard biography to be written and published so far—a privilege long accorded to intellectually lesser figures like Mehring and Clara Zetkin. Only discussions and articles on particular issues, and brief newspaper eulogies on special days of remembrance, have appeared. But a full collection of her works and a full-scale biography are said to be in preparation at last (1968).

Next, Rosa Luxemburg's revolutionary Marxism may yet conceivably become a specific political doctrine in its own right—intellectually, Trotskyism in the West today is really Luxemburgism. Trotsky pre-empted the devotion of all Marxist revolutionaries who opposed Stalin because of his enormous prestige, and the majestic tragedy of his political defeat in Russia. His person and his polemics drew nearly all anti-Stalinists into his orbit for a while. By identifying every opponent as an ally of Trotsky and using the vast and disciplined slander-factory of the entire Soviet state to discover Trotsky behind every real or imagined plot, Stalin helped to divide the world of revolutionary Marxism into two camps, and only two—orthodox Communists and Trotsky-ites, with the latter presented as the Marxist allies of counter-revolution. Yet the history of Trotskyism since 1930 is not a glorious rally of oppositional forces but a sad series of sectarian disputes. Trotsky's historical position as one of the chief architects of the October Revolution prevented him from developing a critique broad enough to generate an all-embracing anti-Stalinist movement, intellectually committed to proletarian revolution in all its Bolshevik ruthlessness—yet without

Stalin's narrow and fearful bureaucracy, itself terrorized and terrorizing. Instead Trotsky fell out with group after group of his non-Russian supporters over talmudic minutiae in the precise and dogmatic interpretation of Stalin's Russia as an example of valid Socialism. The Stalin/Trotsky antithesis, which both parties helped to make into an overriding and irrevocable division between revolutionary Marxists, actually subsumed all preceding arguments and pushed them into limbo. There was simply no room for anyone else. But Rosa Luxemburg, fervent supporter and at the same time profound and immediate critic of the Bolsheviks, would have provided just the rallying point for a broad rather than narrow opposition to Stalin: untainted by original participation—yet wholly revolutionary in its own right. Perhaps one day revolutionary—as opposed to reformist—Marxists will go back all the way to the beginning, to the primacy of highly developed capitalist countries in the calendar of revolutionary experience, to the 'enthusiasm coupled with the revolutionary criticism' of the pre-emptive October Revolution. It is admittedly improbable—and even less probable is any loosening in this direction within Russia or China, the established Communist giants, for all the present unravelling of Stalinism.

Finally, and perhaps most important of all, there is Rosa Luxemburg's position as an autonomous political thinker outside the context and organization of Marxism. Her ideas belong wherever the history of political ideas is seriously taught. Though she herself was fully committed to Marxism, the validity of her ideas transcends the Marxist framework. For hers was an essentially moral doctrine which saw in social revolution—and socialist revolutionary activity—not merely the fulfilment of the laws of dialectical materialism but the liberation and progress of humanity. Rosa Luxemburg preached participation above all, not merely the passive reward of benefits from the hands of a conquering élite. And participation is the problem that still occupies most political analysts and activists today, Marxist and bourgeois alike. Rosa Luxemburg's controlling doctrine was not democracy, individual freedom, or spontaneity, but participation—friction leading to revolutionary energy leading in turn to the maturity of class-consciousness and revolution. Though it is undesirable and meaningless to try and lift her writings one by one out of the context of Marxism (to which they most emphatically belong), the significance of her life's work and thought is not confined to Marxists alone—just like Marx's own achievements. The value of the few really original political thinkers cannot be tagged with the label of any school or group. Even the most orthodox disciples can become a burden; like barnacles they have to be painfully scraped away. The claim of universal validity beyond context is precisely what distinguishes the great from the merely partisan.

Yet all this is quite apart from any claim that can be made for Rosa

Luxemburg on purely historical grounds. Even without any present relevance she would be a figure of great historical importance, both in the Polish and the German Socialist movements. Her little-known role in the Russian movement, though not of first-rate importance, yet deserves mention and research at least as much as those of some of the very marginal figures who have benefited from the prevailing interest in the minutiae of Bolshevik history. It would be a distortion to base the excuse for this book entirely on the permanent relevance of all Rosa Luxemburg's views. This will be indicated where deserved. The bulk of what she wrote and did belongs to history. But what history? To more than a quarter of thinking people in the world today the period we deal with is the prophetic years, the Old Testament of the Communist Bible, without which the final incarnation of revolution has little meaning. In this context the history of any prophet is important, even if his vision was often cloudy and inaccurate.

What sort of person was Rosa Luxemburg? Small, extremely neat— self-consciously a woman. No one ever saw her in disarray, early in the morning or late at night; her long hair was carefully but simply combed upwards to add to her height. She had not been a pretty child and was never a beautiful woman: strong, sharp features with a slight twist of mouth and nose to indicate tension. Her appearance always commanded respect, even before she opened her mouth. Her dark eyes set the mood of the moment, flashing in combat or introspectively withdrawn, or— if she had had enough—overcast with anger or boredom.

The fastidiousness extended to her clothes right down to her polished shoes: plain but expensive, simple yet carefully chosen clothes, based on a precise evaluation of the image which she wanted to create; clothes that were never obtrusive or claimed an existence in their own right; accompaniment not theme. A hip defect acquired in early childhood was overcome completely in all postures but walking—and Rosa Luxemburg was a substantial walker precisely because of the difficulties of this exercise. She judged people—though with admitted humour—in accordance with their ability and willingness to walk; Karl Kautsky's physical laziness was one of the first black marks chalked up against him.

Her own appearance she viewed with slightly mocking contempt which never for an instant approached masochism or self-hatred. The imperceptible border between humour and bitterness was never crossed. Her long nose, which preceded her physical presence like an ambassador on permanent attachment, her large head which soured the lives of several milliners, all were captured in brief and flashing images of literary self-caricature. She called her self-portrait in oils, presented to Hans Diefenbach, *ein Klumpen von Lumpen* (an assortment of lumps). But such comments were reserved for intimates. In public her appearance was neutral; she did not use it to achieve any effect but was never inhibited by it either. The long imprisonment and the spells of ill-health during the war turned her hair white and lined her face, but it is only from the evidence of friends who saw her in prison or after November 1918 that we know it. In moments of crisis her body became an anonymous vehicle to achieve her purposes.

The only aspect of which she was always consciously aware was the fact that she was small. She admitted a penchant for tall and big-boned maids and housekeepers—'I would not like anyone to think that they had entered a doll's house'. Her domestic staff was subjected to the same demands of fastidiousness both in their personal appearance and in their work; breakages roused Rosa Luxemburg to fury and hatred. These were feudal relationships. Though she half-humorously complained to her friends about her involvement in the uninteresting private lives of her staff, she took on this task as manfully as any party assignment. There was a succession of such persons. The one to whom she was most attached was Gertrud Zlottko, who left for other jobs intermittently but somehow always returned. When her household had for all intents and purposes to be liquidated after her second arrest in 1916, a part of her personality went with it.

Her apartment was a faithful reproduction of her person: books carefully stacked in cases, manuscripts put away tidily in a desk, ornaments, paintings, and botanical collections all neatly labelled and instantly to hand. From 1903 onwards she had her own neatly embossed notepaper—for special occasions. Rosa Luxemburg could write for a book from province or prison, and secretary, housekeeper, or friend were able to lay their hands on it instantly. The favourite apartment was at 58 Cranachstrasse in Berlin—the red room and the green room, the old but well-preserved furniture, the carpets, the collection of gifts large and small which, once they had passed her critical taste in the first instance, were treasured for ever. She gave up this apartment in 1911, ostensibly because the city and its growing noise and traffic had engulfed it. More probably its associations had become too painful—the years of gregarious optimism. She then moved to the outskirts of the city at Südende, where she remained until 1916, and nominally to the end of her life. Her home, her privacy, were always sacred. Already in Switzerland her rooms near the University of Zürich had fulfilled an overpowering need for refuge and escape for those hours which so many of her contemporaries argued away in smoke-filled cafés. The closing of doors against all comers was always one of the pleasantest moments of her day. Though many people stayed with her, sometimes for long periods, it was always *her* home: her guests were welcome but the extent to which they could make themselves at home was carefully circumscribed. She entertained often but fastidiously. Unlike so many émigrés from Poland and Russia, there was nothing easy-going about her hospitality, and those who abused it were quickly shown the door. The English phrase 'make yourself at home' was unknown to her. In every respect she was as houseproud as any middle-class German; the German mania for cleanliness which as a symptom she held in such contempt was none the less discharged meticulously *chez* Rosa Luxemburg. Instead of making it a major subject of conversation, she employed others to carry out the work unobtrusively. No wonder that those of her students from the party school who were favoured with a Sunday invitation would sit hesitantly on the edge of the sofa and clutch the proffered plate of cake to their bosom for fear of dropping crumbs!

Such an establishment needed money and Rosa Luxemburg's problems in this regard were precisely those of any middle-class career woman, whose appetite for minor luxury constantly exceeds the supply of funds with which to meet it. Her private bank account—strictly to be distinguished from the party funds—was delicately balanced between credit and debit; most of the time projected income had already been pledged, if not actually spent. Apart from extraordinary sums needed to help close friends in trouble, an annual crisis centred round her summer holiday; Rosa Luxemburg always planned a year in advance and began to consider the possibilities the day after she returned from the current year's excursion. These holidays were mostly in the south—Switzerland in the early days to see friends, and particularly Leo Jogiches; later Italy whenever she could afford it. Always there was the mirage of a long trip farther afield—Corsica, Africa, the East. None of it—except Corsica—ever happened.

Among her closer friends she had the reputation of a spendthrift. Hans Diefenbach left her money in his will—strictly in trust: 'Her management of her personal economy is less sound than her knowledge of political economy.' Rosa's *fata Morgana* of ready cash was something of a joke with her German friends but a harmless one, since she was punctiliously correct about repayment and refused to borrow money from anyone if she sensed the slightest danger of distorting a relationship. When she went on holiday her funds were available to those who accompanied her. Again and again Konstantin Zetkin's pleas of penury were dismissed by the assurance that she would have enough for them both. There were periods when her journalistic work was largely inspired by the need to earn; the sense of urgency in her writing, which always suggested that she was bursting with things to say, was contradicted by private admissions that she had not the slightest notion what to say until she actually sat down to write it. Touchy, then as ever, for fear of letting money dominate her relationships, generous to a fault with friends, unable by nature to save and quite uninterested in trying, she was one of those secure in the knowledge that, if not God, at least her own abilities would always provide. The only evidence of meanness was in her dealings with shopkeepers and printers. To her these were a special class of twisters whose every account had to be carefully checked and with whom negotiation and much oriental bargaining, though she would never entertain it in other spheres, was a necessary and sensible proceeding. Rather than be cheated, she was prepared to engage in endless guerrilla warfare; her staff was taught—sometimes tearfully—to do the same. She would bow only to the ultimate deterrent of legal action. 'In the last resort,' she wrote to her housekeeper, 'it doesn't suit me to have a court case over a baker's bill—even though I am bound to win.'[1]

The whole problem of money, the need to relate earning in some way to spending, was something that, as an objective aspect of the human condition, came to Rosa Luxemburg relatively late in life. As long as she was living with Leo Jogiches in Switzerland, his own substantial remittances from home—he came from a wealthy family—were enough for them both. But money played a curiously symbolic role in their relationship right from the start. Rosa Luxemburg, who in the last resort would not defer judgement about her own opinions and actions even to Leo Jogiches, almost eagerly seized on money as a symbol of total deference. Whenever she was away from him she accounted at length and in detail for every penny, and craved indulgence for her often imaginary extravagance—while he in turn played out his part in the mannered comedy by scolding her soundly. On this subject his word was law; to borrow or not to borrow, to take from the German executive or to ask for support from home—he developed an absurd stinginess as part of the role of comptroller. And Rosa, who would circuitously but firmly reject his criticisms of her policy in Germany after 1898, when she went to live in Berlin, who berated him for his clumsy proof-reading of her doctoral thesis and much besides, none the less beat her breast under his financial strictures. This continued as long as their personal relationship itself.

Rosa Luxemburg was never an easy person to get on with. Her passionate temperament, of which she was aware and very proud, generated a capacity for quick attachment but also an unpredictable touchiness which acted like trip-wire to unsuspecting invaders. Her rigid standards of behaviour were partly the moral superstructure of her philosophy of life. But, though rigid, they were not constant; she deliberately adjusted them to what she thought was the capacity of the other person. A man like Parvus, who had a strong temperament himself, was granted more latitude than most run-of-the-mill members of the German party. Devotion and a willingness to please were no use by

[1]Rosa Luxemburg to Gertrud Zlottko, 1913, IISH, Amsterdam.

themselves. Anyone servile or self-pitying, anything routine, above all anything *mechanical* started at a disadvantage; so did self-satisfaction and a display of public virtue—German qualities all, but English too; Rosa Luxemburg's private hell was Anglo-German. Other Nordic nations suffered too, more by ethnic generalization than personal dislike since she had few Dutch or Swedish acquaintances. Henriette Roland-Holst, a close friend for a time, was specifically exempted; Rosa's 'blonde madonna' was the exception to prove the rule. The Russians came off best. There was always an innate sympathy for Russians—in a German context; against their own background they were at once judged more severely. Her friends in the Russian and Polish movements always appeared much more attractive among Germans than they were when compared with their own compatriots. One aspect of Rosa's internationalism was to prefer the foreign.

To make things more difficult, as her standards rose the closer people were to her; her demands for privacy became more exacting. Those admitted to the inner circle of friends were always in danger of trespassing on areas which were totally 'off limits'. Part of the reason for the chronic difficulties with Franz Mehring was due to the stop-go attitude which he adopted, the rapid change from intimate friendship without reservations to complete rupture and back again, with the additional risk that all the fruits of intimacy would be used as public ammunition during the next stormy period. Following her initial experience of Mehring after her departure from the editorship of *Leipziger Volks-zeitung*, she was determined not to leave valuable parts of herself in pawn to him again, and it was not until the war that their relationship once more became suffused with any genuine warmth. Close friends also had to have some measure of intellectual strength—she was incapable of intimacy with a stupid person. In spite of her close attachment to Clara Zetkin, the disparity of their intellectual capacities obstructed the friendship. It was only Clara Zetkin's acceptance of Rosa's primacy and her agreement with nearly every view propounded by Rosa on important questions that enabled the latter to put up with Clara's personal obstinacies and her political sentimentality.

There were a few people whom Rosa Luxemburg disliked beyond all reason. This was connected only marginally with politics. Kurt Eisner, an intelligent, sensitive, and kind-hearted person, was anathema to her. The few letters she wrote to him were couched in a tone of outstanding pettiness. 'Oh, anxious ethical colleague,' she began an epistle in 1905, 'may you drown in the moral absolutes of your beloved *Critique of Pure Reason.*'[1] Similarly Trotsky, whose intellectual and personal characteristics were very similar to her own, was always referred to like

---

[1] From a private collection of letters in Israel.

an enemy in whom she could find nothing creditable. Where personal dislike cut across political alliance, dislike predominated: one of the most curious examples of Rosa Luxemburg's personal attitudes in the German party was her ferocious dislike of Karl Radek and her refusal to accept or even notice the contribution he was making to her cause—and this at a time when she badly needed allies, particularly intelligent ones who shared her views on imperialism.

One type that Rosa Luxemburg always disliked was the 'great man'. She resented Plekhanov's authority even before she attacked his views; as she wrote to Jogiches, one looked for opportunities to put out one's tongue at him. Much of her resentment against Kautsky was generated by his unchallenged supremacy in all matters of theory—a position she did not automatically accept even in 1898. Authority was a matter of present performance, not the capitalized glories of the past. Thus she denied Plekhanov, Kautsky, and Wilhelm Liebknecht, but never begrudged Bebel; even after they had fallen out openly in 1911 Rosa Luxemburg never attempted to belittle his role in the SPD. On the whole she was uncharitable in her personal judgement. Her letters to the few people with whom she was really intimate—Leo Jogiches and later Konstantin Zetkin—show that even those who considered themselves close friends or allies were not immune from sarcastic epigrams which played up their faults and gave them small credit for their virtues. The letters to Leo Jogiches from Germany shortly after her arrival in 1898 present the SPD leadership as a cabaret turn of caricatures. Of course she felt an outsider and to a large extent chose to remain one; she proudly differentiated her own attitude to life from that of the Germans. Yet she despised those whose opposition was merely the product of resentment, and had an unerring eye for *personal* weaknesses—just as Lenin could usually spot *political* weakness however well hidden or camouflaged.

But these judgements are not only evidence of her particular personality: they show a rare self-confidence which was not only psychological but also social, a product of the secure political group in which she was firmly anchored from 1893 until after the first Russian revolution. All those who have written about Rosa Luxemburg have seen only the personal aspect and have ignored the social one. Without it no portrait of these thirteen years can be complete; and even afterwards, when the original close-knit group began to disintegrate, its influence lingered on. The Polish Social Democrats (SDKPiL), that small body of intellectual activists who broke out of the main Polish Socialist Party (PPS) in 1893, a year after it had been founded, was much more than a mere doctrinaire sect. This Social Democracy of Poland and Lithuania was a group of intellectual peers long before it became a political party. It provided its members with all the attributes of a primary group, an association which all the other émigrés lacked—a family, an ideology, a discipline, in short a constant and reliable source of strength. This function is almost unknown and we shall examine it at some length when we come to discuss the creation and activities of the SDKPiL— in some respects as conspiratorial and tight a group as Lenin's Bolsheviks, but open and outward-looking in others. The discipline was largely voluntary and was confined to public action; for the rest, it left large areas of freedom and choice to the participants, even room for profound intellectual disagreements. That is why the comparison with the Bolsheviks is instructive and at the same time meaningless. Trotsky, with all his friends, admirers, and disciples, never had the benefit of a peer group; hence his difficulty in building a following before the revolution and the fragility of his political support after 1923.[1]

The leading members of the SDKPiL were people of singular intellectual distinction and ability—or, if not contributing themselves, at least sharing in the intellectual glory. Men like Dzierżyński, Marchlewski, Hanecki, and Unszlicht all achieved positions of importance in Bolshevik Russia. One of them, Dzierżyński, occupies a central place in the revolutionary pantheon. Marchlewski and Hanecki were too individualistic to fit into the tight party apparatus of the post-revolutionary period; they found their roles among that distinguished small circle of Lenin's *hommes de confiance* who could be entrusted with special missions outside the party routine. Adolf Warszawski was intimately associated with the Polish Communist Party of which he remained one of the leaders until he was liquidated in 1937 along with almost the entire Polish leadership—Stalin found the spirit and tradition of independence among the Poles too great for his comfort. Jogiches and Rosa Luxemburg played brilliant roles outside the Polish movement, particularly in the creation of the German Communist Party: the one an indefatigable organizer, the other a formidable debater and publicist. Nowhere in the Second International was a small group so brilliantly led; nowhere for that matter was any leadership shared between such brilliant individuals.

Rosa Luxemburg's relations with the rest of this group are a fascinating study in themselves. With the significant exception of Jogiches, she was not especially close to any of them. She criticized them all severely on occasions; both their views and their persons. But all the same she was attached far more profoundly to this group than ever to the German party. Her criticisms and comments are part of the intellectual elbowroom which the SDKPiL permitted, indeed almost forced on its

---

[1] A peer group is a sociological term denoting a latent relationship among a group of people of roughly similar age and outlook, whose opinion is of particular importance with reference to one's own. Thus it is intended both to express the concept of reference group as well as to convey a group source of ideological and moral strength.

members. In so far as the old-fashioned word 'companion' has any political meaning in a modern context, it applies to this relationship— more than ally yet less than friend: a connection more secure than personal sympathy but at the same time more colourful than any purely functional, political relationship.

Naturally Rosa Luxemburg's role in the SDKPiL cannot be understood except in terms of her special relationship with Leo Jogiches. In the eyes of the world they *were* for many years the SDKPiL. It is rare for an intimate personal relationship to be matched by a political one without one dominating the other. Yet here no political concessions were made for personal reasons, nor personal allowances for the sake of political harmony; there was no question of either one leading the other. In her letters the varied strands of their lives were so completely intertwined that the very distinction between personal and political lost all meaning. Only with Leo Jogiches did she ever achieve such fusion. This woman, whose personality was built out of concentric, increasingly impenetrable rings of which the last and innermost was the loneliness of absolute privacy, always needed one and only one person with complete access, someone from whom nothing must be hidden. Precisely because further access became proportionately more difficult for friends once they had passed from the antechamber of acquaintance into the living-room of friendship, precisely because Rosa Luxemburg found it so difficult to open the last doors of frankness and intimacy, she made a point of stripping herself almost ritually naked before the one person whom she loved. This was the meaning of love. Far from the usual diffuse glow, from the see-saw agony of ecstasy and despair, love was something clinical and precise to Rosa—complete frankness. Again and again she demanded ruthless honesty in return—it was the one quality of which her love would not permit the slightest diminution. To a man like Leo Jogiches—closely compartmented, secretive and reserved by nature, unwilling to commit and reluctant to communicate—Rosa Luxemburg's insistent demand for frankness posed a constant challenge. He was jealous, both of her success and of her person. The required frankness thus forced his jealousy out into the open—with the result that Rosa had often to make difficult choices and flout the wishes she had forced him to express. They clashed often and hard, especially during her early months in Germany, when her judgement was pitted against his remote control. But comments and instructions were anyhow not the full measure of frankness she demanded. He was open enough about her—it was with regard to himself that she had to insist on communication, often simply on scraps of information. 'Why have you not written?' was her constant complaint. By 1905 she suspected that some of the doors of access to him, which she had so painfully forced open for many years, were being closed against her once more; she rushed to

Cracow in September of that year just to 'look straight into his eyes', and the fear of losing him may well have been a contributory reason for her going to Warsaw in December 1905, in the middle of the revolution.

Her devotion to Jogiches ended brutally fourteen months later when she heard that some of the doors closed to her had been opened to someone else. Rosa Luxemburg saw only black and white in personal matters; the strain of maintaining constant political contact with someone whom she was now determined to shut out of her personal life proved enormous. None the less the relationship survived, fossilized for a time in the iron clamp of sheer political necessity. In the midst of the spiritual desert of the First World War, with many of her old friendships brutally broken off, the resurrection of the old comradeship with Leo Jogiches must have helped them both to survive. But it was furtive and unspoken—and has left almost no trace for historians. Touchingly, Jogiches spent valuable time in ensuring that she was supplied with the right food for her increasingly delicate and nervous stomach. During the last few months of their lives he was constantly at her side, advising, guiding, cheering. This man, who had set his sights at the personal leadership of both the Polish and the Russian parties, whom his opponents thought ambitious to the point of madness, was finally content to accept a subordinate role to the brilliant woman who had for all practical purposes been his wife. After her death he concentrated his own last months' efforts on the identification and punishment of her murderers, and on ensuring that her ideas should survive.

When she learnt of his betrayal in 1907 it was Rosa herself who insisted on her freedom. For a long time Jogiches would not let her go—and beneath the hectic political activities from 1906 to 1909 a dark and grotesque comedy was played. From those who knew of their relationship—and this was already a privileged minority—the carefully preserved front of political collaboration hid the vacuum that was now between them. The role of Rosa's unique confidant was transferred to another man—a young, sensitive, talented, and unhappy boy whose mother was one of Rosa Luxemburg's closest friends. Rosa herself described this touching interlude as straight from the pages of Stendhal's Le Rouge et le Noir. Rebound, loneliness, disappointment no doubt played their part. But there was more. Rosa Luxemburg's temperament was capable, in her own words, of setting the prairie on fire, her passion for life more than enough for two; one wonders how the young man's frail shoulders were able to bear the torrents of intellectual and emotional discharge which Rosa Luxemburg unleashed on those she loved. In the end it was too much: twice she sensed a restiveness which immediately made her withdraw the extended antennae of her personality as rapidly as she had at first extended them. Twice she released him and yet on each occasion she felt his need for her to be greater than his revolt. It was not until the war that she finally recognized the frailty of the vessel into which she had poured so much of herself. But the need in her which he had filled was still as constant and real as ever. So she promoted her devoted Hans Diefenbach to the privileged place instead. Her letters to him mark a tragic but profoundly moving inflation of a small personality into the needed image of a big one—yet shot through with flashes of sad irony at this very process of self-delusion. Again one wonders how uncomfortable she must have made pale, precise, fastidious, and reserved Hans Diefenbach, who worshipped Rosa Luxemburg and her exotic temperament. He died in the war, and then there was no one left. The errant, irrepressible warmth had to be shared out between faithful and deserving friends like Luise Kautsky and Marta Rosenbaum. No lover, no intimate confidant waited for Rosa Luxemburg to come out of prison. And when she did emerge there was no more time for the exquisite business of love and living.

'Civilized'—the epitome of Rosa Luxemburg's attitude to life. She was very much the product of her age and time, scion of a cultured international optimistic bourgeoisie which sat appreciatively at the pinnacle of many centuries of artistic achievement. Rosa Luxemburg did not so much deny the existence of a valid proletarian culture: even the notion of such a thing was utterly incomprehensible to her. She was quite oblivious of the self-conscious efforts in the SPD to produce workers' songs and poems, to create a deliberately 'popular' art. At the same time, however, the revolutionary new forms of expression that were breaking through in painting and music were lost on her. She went to a few of the exhibitions—when Diefenbach succeeded in dragging her along—but she did not enjoy them. The other Russian revolution of the first decade of the twentieth century, that of the painters Kandinsky and Jawlensky, the movements of the *Blaue Reiter* and the *Brücke* were as remote to her as the realities of the 1905 upheaval in Russia were to the German bourgeoisie.

Her tastes were conservative and classical. She liked the same music as any cultured *fin de siècle* citizen of Berlin—or, better, of Vienna. She had neither the pioneering disdain for convention of an aristocrat nor the self-satisfied and rather squat certainties of working-class realism; her sole demands were clarity and honesty of purpose, and a harmony of means. Imperceptibly, her judgement advanced from a basic series of 'doubts' to a selective approval of such art as stood her severe tests, an *agrégation* of merit. There was little instinctive about it. Any 'clever' appeal to the intellect, any romantic invasion of the emotions, any too obvious *purpose* in art—even social—meant automatic disqualification. Art was *sui generis*. It had above all to reflect the realities of its time, at most foreshadow the immediate future but never extrapolate into the distance; what made art timeless was not vision but quality. As a means of social change she preferred direct political activity. Yet in speaking of 'art' in general we are already doing Rosa Luxemburg a major injustice. She hardly used the word, and never generalized about it. It was as private and individual a sphere as politics were public—and as such not susceptible to systematic analysis. Rosa strenuously resisted the many attempts of her friends to get her to indulge in literary criticism, and only wrote an introduction to her translation of Korolenko with great reluctance at the insistence of her publisher.

The great classical names were her familiars—in music Mozart and Beethoven; Titian and Rembrandt as painters. Her favourite contemporary composer was Hugo Wolf and among her circle of close friends was Faisst, a well-known and enthusiastic performer of Wolf's songs. Cause and effect? The enthusiasm for Hugo Wolf is intriguing. Apart from any intrinsic merit in his music, he was perhaps the first composer of songs who really succeeded in balancing text and music into a composite whole instead of a limping dichotomy. Moreover, he set to music many of Rosa's favourite poems by Goethe and Mörike.

Her literary preferences were wider, for writing was her natural element. First the German masters—Goethe, Mörike, Lessing—then the great French classics. She did not like Schiller, partly because she had been spoon-fed on his *Geist* in the parental home but also because a worshipful legend was being woven around him by the literati in the SPD. Rosa Luxemburg and Franz Mehring campaigned against the attempt to make political capital out of Schiller as a potential revolutionary poet.[1] Yet what she denied Schiller she accepted from a much less important romantic poet. Rosa Luxemburg shared, with most of the German Left—Socialist as well as Liberal—the passion for quoting Konrad Ferdinand Meyer, particularly his poem 'Ulrich von Hutten' which contained a rather facile embodiment of the revolutionary mentality at its most romantic.

But this was used to make a political rather than a literary point—and for political purposes even Wagner was occasionally pressed into service. The promotion of Hutten, the Don Quixote of the German sixteenth century, into the literary ancestor of the Left probably had little to do with Rosa Luxemburg's private appreciation. She always had her Polish equivalent, Adam Mickiewicz, another half-political promotion, but at least 'Pan Tadeusz' could be quoted more fluently than 'Ulrich von Hutten'.

Undoubtedly the most important aspect of Rosa's interest in literature was her profound feeling for the Russian nineteenth-century writers. She was not the person to experience the sudden all-engulfing whirlpool

---

[1] For Rosa's articles, see *NZ*, 1904–5, Vol. II, pp. 163–5, and her elaboration in a more political context in *SAZ*, 9 May, 16 May, 22 May 1905.

of empathy which Lenin felt when he first read Chernyshevsky's *What is to be done?* No single literary figure blazed her moral trail. Instead a whole tradition, a discipline, had captured her admiration; not what they said but how they said it. Year in year out she preached the importance of the Russian novelists into German Socialist ears that were intermittently attuned but more often blocked—a philistinism which roused her to a grotesque fury.

In prison during the war she tackled a full-scale translation of Korolenko's *History of my Contemporary* and wrote a preface in which for once her views on literature in general and the Russian writers in particular were systematically set down. Almost unconsciously she established a general classification of merit which proved most revealing. Among other things it underlined the acute Russian–German dichotomy which played such a significant part in Rosa Luxemburg's life. For her this was the central axis of contemporary civilization—the achievements of western bourgeois culture tempered with the emerging Socialist future in the East. Just because Rosa Luxemburg made no artistic concessions to politics, it would be a mistake to suppose that art and politics were not related on the highest level of personal consciousness. There was no conflict here—conflict was only created by self-conscious attempts to manipulate art for political purposes instead of letting it play its own autonomous, possibly even superior, role. The greater the art, the more important its ultimate political effect—that of heightening civilization.

It is in this context that the fascinating interplay of German and Russian influences must be viewed. When Rosa first went to Germany in 1898 the political quality of German Socialism dominated her thinking. Much as she disliked place and people right from the start, this was on account of personal, psychological faults; the German contribution to political civilization was still predominant and the task of spanning West and East consisted in emphasizing German unity and self-discipline to the disorganized and inchoate Russians. In course of time all this changed. Closer acquaintance with Russian writers—in her home, self-consciously permeated with western *Kultur*, they had been relatively neglected—now opened up vistas of civilization from the East which made the German contribution look increasingly formal and unreal. Participation in the Russian revolution of 1905 accelerated the process. Not that she appreciated masters like Goethe less; it was rather their irrelevance to the German present, when compared with the immediacy of writers like Dostoievsky, which obsessed her. More and more the particular German virtues became so much debris in a torrent of social confrontation. The real hope of cultural as well as political salvation now seemed to lie in the East. A touch of the conscious Slavophil was there, though it did not come to the surface. The official criterion of excellence was the relationship of art to society, the inescapable concern for social questions in Russia which seemed so strongly to contrast with the dead weight of formal *Kultur* in Germany.

In the last resort Rosa Luxemburg shared the common misunderstanding about the real nature of the German virtues. It still exists today; understandable as they are, these misconceptions none the less carry a great share of responsibility for the tragedies of the last fifty years. And in a way the Socialists are most to blame. For it was they who took up the great cry against the patriarchal discipline, the authoritarian tradition of obedience in the Prussian-German empire—and in attacking these only reproduced them *chez eux*. But what they pilloried (and copied) as public 'virtues' were in fact poor compensations for a lack of them. German virtues were and are essentially private, lonely ones, a tradition of *Einsamkeit*, of deprivation, of seeking to compensate for loneliness. The real home of public virtue is England, with its team games, its group loyalties, its tradition of different faces in public and in private. *Kadavergehorsam*, or *Friedhofsdisziplin*, and all the other emanations of the German tradition on which Rosa Luxemburg laid such sarcastic emphasis, were in fact vices derived from a lack of public virtues, rather than consequences of public virtues themselves. She would have been astonished to think of the sheeplike obedient Germans as lonely and lost.

Throughout her life in Germany she remained a self-conscious Easterner. It was a difficult situation and she never tried to make it any easier. Germany was in no sense a refuge to be grateful for. Rather it was the duty of any progressive and advanced Socialist party to welcome foreign participants, while *their* duty, far from abstaining, was to involve themselves in the new domestic environment as thoroughly as possible. Rosa Luxemburg's allegiance was not to Germany but to the SPD. The frequent references to a fatherland were not merely a sarcastic caricature of a sentimental and chauvinistic phrase but a positive acknowledgement to the only real fatherland she knew or wanted—the proletariat in general and German Social Democracy in particular. She was not alone in this. It was an allegiance shared by many of the intellectual émigrés, mostly Jews, who deliberately renounced the attempt to find refuge in any particular nationalism of the present or future. The fight against Polish national self-determination carried out by a ferocious and highly articulate group in the Second International, for whom Rosa Luxemburg was the most prominent spokesman, cannot be understood merely in terms of a negation; it implied the superimposition of nationalist sentiment on to political and class ideology. The only attainable fatherland was the working class—or, more correctly, the proletarian revolution. This concept was not just a political abstraction or even an inspired tactical expedient; it had all the hidden strength of patriotic attachment. Why, after all, should the notion of patriotism be confined to arbitrary political or ethnic frontiers, and be based on the artifact of a nation state? This deeply shared attitude was one of the main links which bound our peer group and provided a cohesive factor for people who were otherwise individualist and often very egocentric. Some historians have been puzzled by their rejection of any form of national self-expression but have not understood the substitution function of Socialism in this regard. Yet without it the whole history of the SDKPiL makes little sense. From 1907 to 1914 the political differences between the PPS-Left, which had broken away from the open nationalism of Piłsudski, and the SDKPiL appear increasingly irrelevant to the historian. Apart from ventilation of personal spleen the polemics are incomprehensible—except that the difference between *playing down* existing nationalist sentiment and acknowledging a totally *different* fatherland is somehow enormous. Rosa Luxemburg's whole career in the SPD, the fact that she put up with the strongly anti-Semitic and anti-Eastern tinge of the criticisms levelled against her from within and without the SPD, was due to her insulation: she was genuinely impervious to anti-Semitism and the charge of national vagrancy. Why, after all, stay in a country that you admittedly dislike, and insist on participation in its political affairs, unless you deny the very basis of the opposition which your presence creates?

People like Rosa Luxemburg, Parvus, and Marchlewski brought into German politics a quality hitherto unknown. It was not a matter of different policy or original views, but was what Trotsky himself called 'the Russian method'—the idea that action was of a superior order to any other facet of political life, and that it was the one and only cure for social rheumatism. For those who felt like this, the ability to align themselves with German methods became a measure of their patience. Parvus, the most impatient and untrammelled of them all, gave up after fifteen years of intermittent attempts to galvanize the SPD and went to amass a fortune in Turkey until the war opened up new possibilities of action for him. Rosa Luxemburg was more self-disciplined. In spite of intense frustration, she pursued her efforts to influence events in Germany, though even she retired for lengthy periods. Besides, Rosa was more closely involved with Germany than any of the others—Parvus, Radek, Marchlewski, Jogiches; and her contribution as a revolutionary in Germany is therefore unique.

Behavioural scientists have a yearning to create types, while historians study and seek comfort in the unique—this is the greatest difference between them. This divergence in approach becomes relevant here as soon as we confront the history of Rosa Luxemburg with the general problem of the intellectual in politics, which has fascinated modern sociology. That we may have been approaching the possibility of some such generalization may well have become obvious. Yet the surface appearance of felicity in applying the general concept is deceptive. Some who have analysed the intellectual have seen his participation in politics as something which perverts his natural functions. Thus 'absence of direct responsibility for practical affairs' is the intellectual's hallmark—and so the intellectual is defined as a deviant product of modern capitalist industrialization.[1] How does someone like Rosa Luxemburg, whose primary interest was the analysis and amendment of these capitalist processes, fit into the category of unpractical? Schumpeter's definition clearly accents the cultural preoccupation of the intellectual. More recent analysis, specifically concerned with the intellectual in politics, provides little more help. He is either the propagator of chiliasm—the millennium on earth—or the apologist for hard-boiled and practical conspirators—*le trahison des clercs*—the scribbling admirer of Leninism seeking sublimation.[2] Perhaps the most accurate characterization is the purely negative one: 'he who innovates is not heard; he who is heard does not innovate'—though this sad verdict is the product of research into the limited and specific problem of modern bureaucracy.[3]

As we shall see, Rosa Luxemburg's tentative participation in the 'modern' bureaucracy of the SPD ended in failure and contempt—so far the analogy holds. Similarly the SDKPiL—Rosa's 'ideal' party—was deliberately orientated towards correct theoretical formulations, and practical problems were not, before 1905, allowed to restrict the preferred intellectual activity of the leading élite.

But Rosa Luxemburg's reluctance to participate in practical work was limited to the most obvious manifestations of bureaucracy; far from abstaining from practical affairs, she not only kept her writing strictly aligned to political immediacies but also participated in the highly practical events of revolution whenever the opportunity presented itself. To this extent the abstentional definition of intellectuals applies much less to her than to people like Plekhanov and Kautsky—a difference of psychological makeup rather than sociological category. Rosa Luxemburg accepted politics at their face value. Politics are analysed, not beautified; there is no apology for mud and blood. She recognized that revolutionary politics brought confusion and much personal unpleasantness; violence was necessary, an instrument—yet not a proper subject for cult worship as it was for Sorel, and even for the Bolsheviks, with

[1] See Josef Schumpeter, *Capitalism, Socialism and Democracy*, New York 1950, p. 147.
[2] See the collection of writings in G. B. de Huszar, *The Intellectuals: A controversial portrait*, Glencoe (Illinois) 1959.
[3] See R. K. Merton, 'The Intellectual and Modern Public Bureaucracy' *Social Theory and Social Structure*, Glencoe (Illinois) 1957.

their specific dialectical 'theory' of terror, alias the dictatorship of the proletariat. Rather than seek to define intellectuals according to some notional degree of involvement in, or commitment to, political and social action, it would be better to distinguish them as primarily concerned with *influence* as distinct from seeking to exercise routine legitimate or bureaucratic *power*. The contrast between influence and power which Rosa Luxemburg raised to a unique relevance, is not quite the same as that between men of action and pure theorists. The latter are rarely front-line casualties in battle.[1]

The politics of influence failed in the Second International—together with the whole International itself; power was still the centrepiece of all politics, whether reactionary, reformist, or revolutionary. The question was, who should wield it, and Leninism's most enduring lesson was that it should, and could, be wielded by intellectuals—not of course scribblers or apologists, but those political intellectuals like Rosa Luxemburg and himself whose choice lay between influencing those with power and displacing them. It is here that both Mao and the leaders of the new Afro-Asian countries traced their legitimate ancestry back to Lenin, and that Khrushchev's impressive bureaucracy had less to offer. Subversion is one thing, but positive revolution requires the fusion of ideology and power.

Rosa Luxemburg was the product of her times—the optimistic pre-war world of peace and progress. Her personality as much as her political ideas made her the champion of active revolution. Imperialism, with all its overtones of violence and inescapable confrontation of classes, was the hand-maiden of her obsession with the self-satisfaction and immobility of German Social Democracy. War was objectively inevitable but subjectively beyond imagination—and no one, except perhaps Lenin, was more surprised than she when one day it broke out and engulfed pre-war Social Democracy. For her, peace and progress were not the usual bourgeois notions of economic development and a growing liberalism, but a Socialism strong enough to withstand the impact of international war and reassert the fundamental necessity of class conflict against it. All this of course proved an illusion, in 1914 as in 1939; and when the illusion was exposed the basis of her world collapsed. Unlike Kautsky, Rosa Luxemburg was acute and revolutionary enough to realize that the collapse was final. She drew the consequences. But she herself had been too much part of this world. She survived the political collapse of Social Democracy, but the revolutionary requirements of the future, the kind of personality that built the modern

[1] For a lengthy analysis of intellectuals in modern society along these lines, see J. P. Nettl, 'Ideas, Intellectuals and Structures of Dissent', in Philip Rieff (ed.). . . .

Soviet Union, that created twelve years of the thousand-year Third Reich, even the socially inclined conservatism of England, France, and America—these were alien monsters to Rosa Luxemburg. Her brilliant and devoted efforts during the German revolution were still no more than an attempt to deal with the problems of a new world by using the best tools and precepts of the old. In the last resort the relevance of her ideas to the world of today must mean a return to the basically optimistic enthusiasms of the Second International.

Probably Lenin's single most remarkable achievement was his confrontation of the Socialist collapse of 1914. He saw it as a constructive beginning, not a sad end. In this he was alone. It does not make him very lovable, but it certainly made him great. He never had to look back, either in sorrow or in anger.

POLAND—THE EARLY YEARS

1871–1890

THIS story moves back and forth across the eastern half of Europe, from St. Petersburg to Berlin. But we must begin in the East, with the murder of Tsar Alexander II. His assassin, Ignacy Hryniewiecki, was a Pole, working for a Russian terrorist organization. The heart of the old kingdom of Poland had been incorporated in the Russian empire since the end of the eighteenth century. There had been several disastrous attempts to prise it loose, the last of which, the revolt of 1863–4, brought about an intense campaign of Russification in the intellectual and administrative life of Poland. In its dealings with the Poles the Russian government was never as efficient and thorough as that of Prussia, but it was more brutal and consequently much more notorious. The Russian autocracy was the outstanding target for liberal and left-wing European indignation, including Karl Marx's.

A combination of brutality and inefficiency creates effective opposition. For some of its subjects and for nearly all of Europe Tsarist Russia was, throughout the whole of the nineteenth century, the symbol of obscure, rigid, and ever less effective reaction. But it continued to be viable as a power factor in Europe, still enjoying the apparent loyalty of most of its subjects, especially when compared with the empires of China and Turkey with their stiff and ancient outer shell whose living inside was visibly rotting away. At least there were some changes and attempts at self-renewal in Russia. The second half of the nineteenth century brough a great revival of Russian studies in the whole of central Europe and this linked up with an intellectual fermentation in Russia itself. Some of the greatest writers of the age were working in Russia at this time, not only producing escapist and obscure literature but also social novels which described and took issue with the world in which they lived. In the 1860s the Russian government, under the impact of western ideas and of the buffets sustained in the Crimean War, put a more liberal policy into operation.

Russian Poland during this period benefited especially from this loosening of the reins. On the one hand there was intense Russification, the precautionary destruction of a national élite after the 1863–4 insurrection to ensure that there would never be another attempt. All the power was centred in the hands of the governor-general whose rule was more or less equivalent to permanent martial law. Russian became the official language of the country and a host of Russian officials moved into 'Vistulaland'—even the name of Poland was abolished. In 1869 the Polish university in Warsaw became a Russian one. Banks, clubs, and other manifestations of local economic and cultural life were either abolished or Russified. The Polish governing classes lost their jobs and with them the reason for existence.

However, Poland benefited more than proportionately from the economic boom in the Russian empire. The industrial development of Poland proceeded at a greater pace than that of Russia. As a refuge from the destruction of national aspirations, Polish industrialists and businessmen concentrated on the exploitation of the enormous Russian market, on increasing their ability to supply it. This development, at first unconscious, later a valued prerogative of Polish industry, was later analysed and explained by Rosa Luxemburg in *The Industrial Development of Poland* and became one of the main pegs on which those who had a vested interest against Polish independence could hang their views.

The economic development of Poland continued more or less steadily throughout the whole of the last quarter of the nineteenth century, necessarily affected by the periodic economic crises that shook Russia but always in advance of the rest of that country. Of course comparison with Russian conditions is one thing; with European conditions, particularly in those countries—Germany and Austria—that contained a settled Polish population, quite another. By the beginning of the twentieth century the average wage of an industrial worker in Russian Poland was still a quarter lower than that of a Polish coal-miner in Silesia, though he in turn was the lowest paid worker in Prussia, well behind the German workers.[1]

So the Polish workers in the mines of Upper Silesia or in the oilfields of Austrian Galicia were economically better off than their counterparts in Russian Poland. Industrial development is always relative, at least in its effect on the people involved; perhaps the difference between the economic situation in East and West Poland provided just the incentive to make Russian Poland the motor of industrial development in Russia. In many respects the industrial revolution in Poland had all the aspects of savage pioneering of England fifty years earlier; Łódź was justly called the Manchester of the East. And with economic development came a new form of pressure for social change, socialist rather than merely political or nationalist.

---

[1] J. Grabieć, *Współczesna Polska w cyfrach i faktach* (Contemporary Poland in Figures and Facts), Cracow 1911, p. 10.

In 1881 Tsar Alexander II was murdered. Already, in the latter part of his reign, his government had become disillusioned with the liberal experiment. His death brought a stronger reaction. The new Tsar, Alexander III, and his advisers, drew the most convenient conclusion from the death of his predecessor: force must be answered with force. The social forces of reaction were mobilized to assist the police repression of terrorist and revolutionary movements. This mobilization, coupled with the new emphasis on Russian national supremacy over the minorities in the empire and on the Slav 'mission', affected all the minority nations and particularly the most dispersed and vulnerable, the Jews. It was the beginning of the great period of Jewish emigration, of Zionism and Jewish socialism. Thus apart from any Utopia of independence, one of the answers to discrimination was a re-emphasis on the distinct character of these minorities, the demand for a greater means of national self-expression and the right to an equal, if distinct, life within the country. In the case of the Jews this trend was especially strong, since there was no possibility of national independence except by 'swimming'—away to Palestine. The hope of finding salvation within a better Russia was bound to be given special emphasis among them. Even before any specifically Socialist movement emerged among the Jews, there was a division between the Zionists and those who wanted to fight for improvement at home and who later became supporters of the *Bund*. The issue was quite sharp. While the great centres of Zionism were in Russia itself, the main centre of Jewish Socialism was Vilna, the capital of Lithuania, a mixed town where no single nationality dominated to the same extent as in Russia or Poland proper, though numerically the Poles were in a majority. The city was the centre of aspirations for a troïka of discordant nationalities, living together in uneasy harmony. Both Zionism and Socialism were ideologies perfected and polished abroad and brought back to Russia from the West. Meantime this nascent split in Russian Jewry was superimposed on the older issue of assimilation, and the conflict between *Khassidim* and *Maskilim*, between extreme religious orthodoxy and a more social and cultural revival.

From 1880 the opposition to the existing state of affairs became broader and more radical. Oppression was felt, no longer only as a national factor, but as a political and, by some, a social one; the remedy was general social change. Naturally enough it was this movement that was most susceptible to the 'evangelization' of Marxism.

Economic and political influences do not always move in step, either chronologically or geographically. The satisfactions of economic development and the consequent improvement in the standard of living in Russian Poland was one thing, and the frustration among all the politically articulate sections of the population in the last two decades of the nineteenth century was another. After the end of the liberal era, there was a feeling that only the overthrow of Tsarism could end the unsatisfactory system, that reform or persuasion was hopeless because the government was not amenable to agreed change.

In the 1880s the dominant revolutionary party in Russia were the Populists and a terrorist organization which grew out of it, the *Narodnaya Volya* (People's Will). Its ideas about the future—a form of national regeneration through the peasantry—were vague and, in Marxist terms, utopian. However, the terrorist organization relieved itself of the necessity of political and economic analysis by concentrating on the technical means of eliminating prominent members of the administration, as symbols of the hated Tsarist régime. For a time the reputation of the 'People's Will' was very considerable, a series of raids and assassinations gave it an aura of success, and the Polish social revolutionary movements of the time were glad to co-operate with it as closely as possible. In spite of this association, in which the Poles ceded seniority and supremacy to the Russian group, Polish groups like *Proletariat* as well as *Lud Polski*, the 'Polish People', wanted from the start to create a mass base instead of relying exclusively on individual terrorist achievements. The Russians had the simpler, more romantic notion that once you removed the hard crust of autocracy, which bottled up the natural development potential of human beings, the possibilities of liberty and a better life would emerge by themselves. Like most movements strongly tinged with anarchism, the 'People's Will' believed in the essential goodness of human nature once it was 'liberated'. Such idealism could not long survive the harsh continued impact of reality, but the very process of its disillusion and decay brought at least one famous recruit to Marxism, Georgii Plekhanov. The Poles were for once more sanguine from the start.

The *Proletariat* party was founded by Ludwik Waryński, a magnetic personality who travelled all over Poland (Russian as well as Austrian) and also spent some time in Switzerland, at that time the intellectual power station from which East European revolutionary movements were supplied. Waryński returned to Warsaw from Geneva in 1881, the year of Alexander II's death, and by 1882 had founded the *Proletariat* which can be described as the first Polish Socialist party.[1]

Waryński and his friends articulated, and took back to Poland with them, a predilection for economic rather than purely political thinking. Among this small band there was little time for or interest in the problem of Polish independence. But right from the start Waryński found himself up against the strong if inchoate force of Polish patriotism. To

---

[1] See M. Mazowiecki, *Historya polskiego ruchu socjalistycznego w zaborze rosyjskim* (History of the Socialist Movement in Russian Poland), Cracow 1904, pp. 54 ff.

buttress his own programme, he argued that the well-to-do classes in Poland, interested only in profits, were not revolutionary; in their absence there were no real revolutionary factors making for Polish independence. The workers, on the other hand, the only truly revolutionary group, were concerned primarily with their own state of subjection and were at least as much exploited by their own capitalists as by the Russian autocracy.

Simultaneously with the *Proletariat*, the 'Polish People' was organized by Bolesław Limanowski who deliberately took for his organization the name that had been used by the first Polish group tinged with embryonic socialist tendencies. This had been founded in Portsmouth in 1835, its members—mostly soldiers and intellectuals—having emigrated to England after the insurrection of 1830–31. Where Limanowski was an imaginative writer, an exciting personality, Waryński was a quiet and close organizer. Waryński played down the traditional romantic element in the aims of his *Proletariat* party. For the purpose of a revolutionary movement based on mass support, the workers had to be rallied round familiar, everyday problems. This precluded the appeal to national sentiment. For a workers' party, immediate betterment of conditions and rights was important, not the theoretical liberation of the human spirit or the liberation of an abstract 'nation'. Limanowski on the other hand gave greater priority to the national question. He believed that no Socialist development could take place as long as one nation oppressed another, as long as Russia was occupying and exploiting Poland. From the weakness of Russian populism, particularly from the writings of Peter Lavrov, he drew the conclusion that the Poles could not afford to rely too much on Russian revolutionary initiatives. Socialism and patriotism were anyhow not incompatible. Consequently the movement must comprise not only workers and peasants, but intellectuals as well, especially the younger generation. He expressed these ideas in a pamphlet published in Geneva in 1881.[1]

The ideas of both groups, *Proletariat* and 'Polish People', were embryonic; they were associations of people with ideas rather than parties with programmes—better still, they were followers grouped around an individual personality. None the less, the emergence of two different trends in Polish Socialist movements at this time is worth emphasizing, because here was foreshadowed in embryo the major difference between the two schools of Polish Socialist thought which would divide them until after the First World War. The problem of Polish independence was always to be the main bone of contention between the two Polish Socialist parties; it was present from the start.

In 1884 Waryński's *Proletariat* party in Poland and *Narodnaya Volya*,

---

[1] *Patryotyzm i socjalizm*, Geneva, 1881.

the Russian 'People's Will', actually signed an agreement. Waryński himself had been arrested in 1883 and the alliance with the 'People's Will' was carried through by his second-in-command, Kunicki. Conforming to the general—perhaps inevitable—tendency, all top decisions on theory, strategy, and organization were taken abroad, in this case in Paris.[1]

In this joint programme an autonomy of operational control was reserved to each party within its own territory, Russia and Poland. The *Proletariat* party accepted the Russian formula of 'economic in addition to political terror in various forms'. Both parties were to consider themselves under the tactical leadership of the Russian group—at least until after the revolution. Since there was to be free interchange of action between Poland and Russia and free movement of operatives, the division of responsibility became largely a matter of geographical accident. The main effort of the 'People's Will' was in St. Petersburg.[2] As a result of this flexible exchange of personnel a number of Polish revolutionaries remained permanently in Russia, and later figured among the membership of the more orthodox Socialist organizations.

The *Proletariat* party succeeded in organizing a series of strikes in Poland in April 1883, including a mass strike near Warsaw. The government used troops against this strike and, during the next two years, the new 'tough' policy of the authorities resulted in large-scale arrests. There had been several attempted assassinations of police agents and gendarmes, and with these assassinations as a particular excuse, many of the leading members of the *Proletariat* were imprisoned by court sentence or by administrative order. Four of the leaders—Bardowski, Kunicki (who had signed the agreement with the 'People's Will'), Ossowski, and Pietrusiński—were hanged on 28 January 1886 in the Warsaw Citadel, fortress and prison and the symbol of Russian domination. Waryński himself was sentenced in the same year to sixteen years' hard labour in the notorious Schlüsselburg fortress near St. Petersburg, where he died three years later in 1889.

---

[1] Paris and, to a lesser extent, London were and remained the traditional centres of nationalist emigration. For almost 100 years many of the Polish émigrés had found their spiritual homes there, and it is interesting to observe that some of the birth pangs of Zionism too, for instance the decision of Ben Jehuda never to speak another word in any language but Hebrew, took place in Paris.

In contrast, the main threads of Russian and Polish Socialist activity abroad came in the 1870s to be centred more in Switzerland, particularly Geneva and Zürich. There was naturally a certain amount of antipathy between these two centres of different revolutionary activity—apart from the inevitable disputes within each group itself. Later the Russian Socialist emigration became dispersed to France, Germany, Austria, and London, but Paris remained the traditional centre for nationalist emigration.

[2] For this programme see Feliks Kon, *Escape from the Gallows* (London 1933), Chapter 1; Res (Feliks Perl), *Dzieje ruchu socjalistycznego w zaborze rosyjskim* (History of the Socialist Movement in Russian Poland), Warsaw 1910, Vol. I, p. 42.

The arrests and trials, and the particularly savage sentences meted out, effectively broke up the *Proletariat* party. In spite of its wish, *Proletariat* had never succeeded in being a mass movement. Out of the remains of the membership, three small groups continued to function, the so-called 'Second *Proletariat*', the Union of Polish Workers, and the Association of Workers, the last an offshoot of the Second *Proletariat*, determined to break with the terroristic methods of the 'People's Will'. Unlike the national rising of 1863–4, the activities and destruction of the *Proletariat* party caused hardly a ripple on the surface of Polish life; indeed, most Poles outside Warsaw were probably unaware that it existed. The revolutionary vacuum, the political silence of Russia, now covered Poland as well; for a time the Tsar ruled his extended Empire in a hush of surface deference.

When Waryński was sentenced in 1886, a Warsaw student called Rosa Luxemburg, not yet fifteen years old and already connected with dissident student circles in Warsaw, was probably feverish with excitement and anger. She had been born on 5 March 1871, the youngest of five children, three boys and two girls. Zamość, province of Lublin, in the flat agricultural area of south-eastern Poland, was then a large town, but of declining importance, overshadowed by Lublin to the north. More than one-third of the town's population was Jewish, one of the highest proportions in the country.[1] But it was not the 'poverty-stricken place with a population of low cultural level' which Rosa's biographers describe.[2] In fact, Zamość had long been a town of importance under its local lords, the Zamoyskis, big landowners with great power and influence. Under Austrian rule (in the first partition of Poland) until 1809, the district finally became Russian in 1815. Zamość was thus at the cultural crossroads, and Russification was better resisted there than elsewhere in the north and east. Nor was Jewish life 'narrowly fanatic, out of the way, a backward world of resignation and greed, obscurantism, dirt and poverty, a rotting morass'.[3] On the contrary, Zamość had a Jewish community of great importance, a particular kind of Jewish middle-class atmosphere graced by a setting of architectural splendour—a majestic Town Hall surrounded by a late-Renaissance square complete with arcades.[4] It was a centre of the *Haskalah* movement, a reaction against the over-zealous fanaticism of the *Khassidim*; one of its most important writers was Yitskhak Leyb Peretz who was

---

[1] Compare the next highest figures, for Warsaw in 1876; 89,698 Jews out of a total of 307,451. *The Jewish Encyclopaedia*, Vol. XII, p. 472.

[2] Frölich, *Rosa Luxemburg*, p. 13. The other German biographers, Henriette Roland-Holst and Fred Oelssner, follow Frölich in this fallacy.

[3] Frölich, loc. cit.

[4] Y. L. Peretz, *Bei nakht oyfn altn markt* (At night in the old market place), in *Collected Works*, (*Ale Verk fun Y. L. Peretz*), Vol. VI, p. 181.

born and lived much of his life in Zamość. The Jewish community of this town was actually one of the strongest and most cultured in Poland.[1] But the Luxemburg family had little or no part in this life. They had already become assimilated in the time of Rosa's grandfather. Such assimilation was more common in Zamość than elsewhere, precisely because of traditional links with Western literature and learning, an improvement on the more usual and miserable alternative of having to fall back on a surrounding Polish community of much lower culture. Already in the 1860s Jewish writers in Zamość were protesting against people who changed their name and traditional habits; this tendency to assimilation actually encouraged the rigid *Khassidst* section of the community against the *Maskilim* enlightenment.[2] Rosa's parents thought and spoke Polish; her father especially took an interest in Polish affairs. According to one biographer, hers was 'one of those homes where Western culture, particularly German, was at home'.[3] They were moderately well off—'comfortable' in middle-class terminology. The Luxemburgs lived on the main square right opposite the magnificent Town Hall with its flamboyant curving sweep of staircase. It was—and still is today—an attractive Renaissance house, one of a row, over an arcade; but inside, the stone front still gives way to wooden landings and a small dingy courtyard with a fountain. But the comfort was intermittent. On one occasion Rosa recalled that the spill for lighting the lamp in fact turned out to be the last banknote in the house.[4] According to her friend Marchlewski, who knew her parents, the linen had to be pawned from time to time. But at best these were temporary and isolated instances. Rosa's father had himself been educated in Germany and managed the family timber business. He often travelled on business as far as Germany and frequently to Warsaw.

As they did not lead a consciously Jewish life, the family were thrown back largely on their own resources. There is no evidence that they had any close Polish friends. Rosa's elder brothers were educated at high school in Berlin and Bromberg (Bydgoszcz) respectively. German was spoken and read in the house, with the emphasis on German romantic writing which in those days was more common among Jews in Vienna and Berlin than in Poland. The children all had classical names— Maximilian, Josef, Anna, Rosa herself—which were as much German as Polish. The name in fact may have been Luxenburg at one time, since Rosa's first known letters use Luxenburg or Luxemburg somewhat

---

[1] There is a vast Yiddish and Hebrew literature about Zamość, summarized in Y. A. Klausner, *Studies on the life and work of Y. L. Peretz*, unpublished doctoral thesis, London 1958.

[2] Klausner, op. cit., p. 37.

[3] Frölich, p. 13. He exaggerates the German influence.

[4] Frölich, p. 15. Oelssner, *Rosa Luxemburg*, p. 10. She herself must have told this story.

indiscriminately and her brother, as late as 1929, was still using Luxenburg.[1] Rosa's father, Elias or Eduard Luxemburg, 'was sympathetic towards the national-revolutionary movement among the Poles, but was not politically active himself and he devoted his attention to cultural questions and particularly to the Polish school system. He was a man of considerable energy. His material wellbeing and his education had given him confidence. . . . .'[2] The Jewish community of Zamość at any rate did not approve of families like the Luxemburgs; it is significant that none of the children ever played any part in Jewish movements or affairs.[3]

Rosa herself spoke seldom of her youth, her home, or her parents. There are a few incidental references in some of her letters, and she had a propensity for mildly Jewish jokes and occasional Jewish expressions. But any self-consciously Jewish atmosphere grated on her at once. The attachment to her family, though considerable, was very private; her letters are singularly bare of any expression of sentiment.[4]

Even less is known about Rosa's mother, Line, born Löwenstein. Her brother Bernhard, Rosa's uncle, was said to have been a Rabbi.[5] Frölich says that she 'exercised considerable influence on the development of the children. She was a great reader, not only of the Bible, but also German and Polish classical literature, and there was almost a glut of Schiller in the house'. But there is no real need to grub too deeply among the literary tastes of the Luxemburg family to explain Rosa's interests; she was the type of person who would always want to fill out her knowledge of history and science with the perceptions of fiction. The only writer to whom she remained attached from early youth was Adam Mickiewicz, the major nineteenth-century Polish romantic poet. Though he was a propagandist of Polish independence, this did not diminish her admiration. Mickiewicz was to provide a rich fund of

[1] 'Unknown letters to Robert and Mathilde Seidel' (hereafter cited as 'Seidel letters'), Z Pola Walki, 1959, No. 1(5), p. 67.

[2] Polish sources give his name as Eliasz (Z Pola Walki, 1959, No. 1(5), p. 77, n. 33). Luise Kautsky gives Eduard (Gedenkbuch, p. 20), and so do the Okhrana entries at the time of her arrest in 1906 (ZHP). His original name may have been Abraham; Peretz refers to 'the only daughter, a hunchback, of A. . . . . L. . . . .' (Y. L. Peretz, Collected Works, Vol. XI, 'Mayne Zikhroynes', p. 73.) There is at least a suspicion of some 'adjustment' of Rosa's background. Frölich and Oelssner, both orthodox Marxists, would consider it progressive for anyone to 'overcome' an orthodox religious background. It was probably not quite as 'comfortable' or as assimilated as they make out. Rosa certainly knew a little Yiddish, though she refused to speak it. Frölich met at least one of Rosa's brothers personally in connection with his work on her literary remains; he thus had the opportunity to learn about her background at first hand.

[3] See J. Shatzky 'Der Bilbul . . .' (The Muddle), Yivo Bleter, Journal of the Yiddish Scientific Institute, Vol. 36 (1952), p. 331.

[4] For instance Letters to Karl and Luise Kautsky, pp. 80–1, dated September 1904; also Frölich, p. 15. She opened out only to Jogiches.

[5] Luise Kautsky, Gedenkbuch, p. 20.

quotations for much of her Polish writing—a sure sign of approval. There is no evidence that Rosa was interested in or read much Russian during her youth, though she mastered the language as a child.

Rosa's links with her family were maintained throughout her life. She remained on good, if not very intimate, terms with all of them; there was no deliberate renunciation like that of many Russian revolutionaries. A letter in which she refers to her father's death expresses a rather passive regret that she had not had the chance to see more of him in his last years; life and the Second International had all too rapidly gobbled up the years.[1] But in another letter she speaks of being 'completely knocked out' by her father's death, 'unable to communicate with a soul for a long long period from which I have only just recovered'. However, this letter was to an elderly lady, the mother of a close friend, with whom Rosa's communication was almost deliberately sentimental; she may perhaps have exaggerated the intensity of her feeling.[2] She certainly had a bad conscience. After her mother's death in 1897 her father—perhaps with a premonition that he too had not long to live—had announced his urgent desire to come to Berlin to see her. It was the summer of 1898. The Bernstein controversy was boiling up and Rosa's career depended on her contribution; besides, she wanted to meet Leo Jogiches who was still confined to Zürich. Reluctantly she temporized with her father and this visit never took place; though she spent a few weeks with him in Germany just before his death.[3]

But she repeatedly met all three of her brothers and her sister after she left Poland, and did not hesitate to use her elder brother's house and help during her illegal stay in Warsaw during the 1906 revolution. A niece, daughter of a brother who emigrated to England, stayed with her for some months in 1910. We know that until the war she was in correspondence, sometimes clandestine, with her family, though none of the letters exists. Up to the end of 1899, her first year in Germany, she sometimes asked for money and they sent what they could spare—often pathetically little. But they neither understood nor supported her political views and activities, even though they no longer attempted to dissuade her after she left home in 1889. In fact the relationship was a surprisingly easy one. They respected her evident success in her chosen career and her manifest talents—the respect any family pays to professional achievements. In return they were always sure of a welcome on their way through Berlin. It was a sensible middle-class relationship, a matter of arrangements and courtesies rather than passion or intimacy. Rosa's close attachments were elsewhere: with her close political friends and their wives, with the very few people whom she loved.

---

[1] *Briefe an Freunde*, p. 129: letter to Hans Diefenbach, 27 August 1917, from prison.
[2] Letter to Minna Kautsky dated 30 December 1900, in Kautsky Archives, IISH.
[3] Jogiches letters, *Z Pola Walki*, 1962, No. 1(17), pp. 178 ff.

Indeed, she rather despised those who muddled their private and political lives, like Krichevskii and her friend Adolf Warszawski.[1]

In 1873, when Rosa was two and a half years old, the family moved to Warsaw. It had always been her father's wish to move to the capital, partly to benefit from the more cosmopolitan life and business opportunities, partly to give his children a better education. The family fortune had varied in accordance with the periodic slumps and booms of the Zamość region, and a period of prosperity finally decided the move. At first things were difficult for them in Warsaw. They lived in an old apartment house where the outlook on the world was confined to a few high windows and the clatter of all the other tenants reverberated through the building.[2]

Shortly after arriving in Warsaw, Rosa developed a disease of the hip which was wrongly diagnosed as tuberculosis and as a result wrongly treated. She was more or less confined to bed for a whole year and used this period to teach herself to read and write at the early age of five. This illness resulted in a permanent deformation of the hip which caused her to walk with a slight limp for the rest of her life, though otherwise it did not prove a serious disability. As far as her elder brothers and sister were concerned, she was the invalid in the family and as such was treated with special care and consideration. Probably this same physical disability caused her interests to turn towards literature, and she is said to have translated German poems and prose into Polish at the age of nine. Her first literary attempts were sent successfully to a children's magazine in Warsaw. At least one other attempt is more interesting for posterity. In 1884, at the age of thirteen, she wrote a poem on the occasion of the visit of the German Emperor William I to Warsaw, half reverent and half sarcastic, which may have been as much a protest against her father's excessive fuss as evidence of any early anti-monarchical convictions.[3]

In 1884, at the age of thirteen, she entered the second girls' High School in Warsaw. This was one of the best establishments of its kind in Poland, patronized largely by the children of Russian administrators, who had first call on most of the available places. (The first High School was in fact exclusively reserved for them.) Admission for Poles was difficult, for Jews even more so; the latter were normally confined to a limited quota in specially designated schools. One of the rules of all secondary schools was that lessons and conversations should be entirely in Russian and the children were not even allowed to speak Polish among themselves.

---

[1] See below, p. 56.

[2] *Letters to Karl and Luise Kautsky*, p. 81, dated September 1904.

[3] The poem, originally written in Polish, is printed in German in *Gedenkbuch*, p. 26, and Roland-Holst, *Rosa Luxemburg*, p. 10.

The *Proletariat* party was at its zenith at the time; it was largely an intellectual affair confined to the main cities, but with considerable influence among senior pupils of high schools and universities. Students were always the best intellectual tinder. During her last few years at the school Rosa Luxemburg was undoubtedly in contact with a group of illegal revolutionaries. She was fifteen when the four death sentences on the gallows—the first since 1864—were carried out. In her last year she was known to be politically active and not amenable to discipline. Consequently she was not granted the gold medal for academic achievement which her scholastic merits had earned. But the girl who passed out top in the final exams was not only a class nuisance; by this time she was probably a fully-fledged member of one of the remaining cells of the 'Revolutionary Party Proletariat' which had escaped police detection, and which formed the nucleus of the Second *Proletariat*. Rosa herself wrote a form of posthumous self-criticism of *Proletariat* some years later, when she was about to enter the 'adult' Socialist world of German Social Democracy. She described it retrospectively as too centralized, and too much like *Narodnaya Volya* in its emphasis on terror. This marked a definite stage—Marxist self-criticism always does—in her self-conscious growing up.[1]

After the destruction of the original *Proletariat*, one of the few remaining personalities of the new *Proletariat* was Marcin Kasprzak who incidentally was also one of the very few workmen to rise to a position of authority in this largely intellectual party. Kasprzak came from Poznań in Prussian Poland. He was at that time working in Warsaw and bringing together in small clandestine groups those of the members of the previous *Proletariat* whom the police had not picked up. In the course of this work he met Rosa Luxemburg, and a strong personal connection was formed which was to continue until his own death on the scaffold in 1905, seventeen years later. But the police continued to be active. After two years of agitation among the students in Warsaw Rosa Luxemburg was herself apparently threatened with arrest. She was too young and inexperienced to have developed the conspiratorial mobility and secrecy of the real revolutionary. At that time she was still living at home and at the same time working openly for her revolutionary group.

There was in the years 1888–9 something of a renaissance of Socialist activity to which both the surviving *Proletariat* under Marcin Kasprzak and the Union of Polish Workers contributed. The latter had been founded at the beginning of 1889 by Julian Marchlewski, Adolf

---

[1] *Sozialistische Monatshefte*, 1897, Vol. X, No. 10, pp. 547–56. It was, incidentally, the only article she ever wrote for this journal, which was later to become the main vehicle of revisionism. After 1898 Rosa refused even to review books for it.

Warszawski, and Bronisław Wesołowski.[1] At the beginning, this group concentrated on the immediate needs of the workers and on purely economic demands, though later, just before it merged with other groups to form the PPS, the emphasis was once more on political activities.[2] Although Rosa Luxemburg was to form a life-long friendship with both Marchlewski and Warszawski, she probably knew them only casually, if at all, in Poland at this time. *Proletariat* and the Union of Polish Workers were separate organizations, and Rosa Luxemburg was firmly committed to the *Proletariat* movement.

The next three years saw a new wave of strikes and, more significant, the first recurring demonstrations on May Day. For political reasons, the government refused to let the employers grant wage concessions—it was a period of good business—and there were several clashes with troops. A further wave of arrests followed and almost completely wiped out the Second *Proletariat* as well. The leaders of the Union of Polish Workers went abroad, some to Switzerland, others across the border to Galicia, the Polish part of the Austro-Hungarian empire which enjoyed the most liberal and also least efficient of the foreign governments. By then, however, Rosa Luxemburg was herself no longer in Warsaw. In 1889, warned of the imminence of her own arrest, she was smuggled abroad with the assistance of her friend and mentor Marcin Kasprzak. There were regular routes of entry and departure from Russian Poland into the Polish parts of Germany and Austria; indeed the traffic of people, literature, and money was already becoming highly organized. Few people were caught on these border crossings which, as they do on frontiers to this day, required only the active participation of the population on both sides of the border. In Rosa's case some last-minute difficulties arose in the frontier village; presumably the organized means of transport had broken down. Kasprzak persuaded the local Catholic priest that a Jewish girl wished to be baptized in order to marry her lover, 'but owing to the violent opposition of her family, could only do so abroad'.[3] The priest, inspired by a mixture of national goodwill and religious duty, gave his assistance and arranged for her to be hidden under straw in a peasant's cart.

[1] Marchlewski wrote and was usually known under the pseudonym of Karski, Warszawski under the pseudonym of Warski, and Wesołowski as Smutny. For the next twenty years the first two particularly were referred to indiscriminately by their real names or by their pseudonyms. (Wesołowski was caught in 1894 and spent eleven years in Siberia.) It will probably be easier if, irrespective of the name used at any particular time, I confine myself only to the real name in each case. The same problem arises with many other Polish Socialists and the same principle will be adopted throughout. In those rare cases where a pseudonym came to be adopted exclusively—as with Radek or Parvus—I shall use it.

[2] O. B. Szmidt, *Socjaldemokracja Królestwa Polskiego i Litwy: Materiały i dokumenty 1893–1904*, Moscow 1934, Vol. I, Chapter vi.

[3] Frölich, p. 22. This story is substantiated by almost all sources and presumably originates from Rosa Luxemburg herself.

Certainly she had been only too willing to leave. Her first acquaintance with the writings of scientific Socialism, with the works of Marx and Engels, had been made during the two years after leaving High School in 1887. For anyone interested in becoming a fully fledged Socialist, a period of study was highly desirable. The universities of western Europe were a great deal more tempting than those of Poland or Russia. To absorb Socialism thoroughly, it was necessary first to study existing capitalist society, and modern economic and political teaching—quite apart from any study of Socialist thought—was not available in the Russian empire. Rosa must have known that she would find in Switzerland not only the institutions of learning of a free and more questioning society, but also the presence of some of the most distinguished Marxists. Switzerland also offered the additional attraction of universities which traditionally admitted men and women on an equal footing. Rosa never wanted either to claim women's privileges or to accept any of their disabilities. The possible danger of arrest may even have been a welcome excuse for departure, possibly to appease an anxious family. They offered to support her financially as best they could at least for a while, and off she went, looking forward to the freedom of a society nearer to the final stage of Socialism.

The path to the West was well trodden. The departure of actual or potential Polish revolutionaries for western Europe was an old, well-established tradition. Polish and Russian Socialists were only following in the footsteps of their nationalist and liberal predecessors. But there was another, more typically Polish tradition: émigrés, particularly from Poland, had always given their services to the revolutionary movements of their host countries. There had been Poles among the immediate followers of Fourier, of Saint-Simon; a Polish general had died on the barricades of the Paris Commune. Thus integration into foreign revolutionary movements was almost as well-established as émigré plotting for a new revolution at home. Rosa Luxemburg faithfully followed both traditions. She based her activities on the international character of scientific Socialism, but in effect her work in the SPD was in line with a Polish tradition much older than Marxism—and so was the resentment which it caused among the Establishment in the West.

While Rosa Luxemburg was embarking on the life of a young student émigré in Zürich, the Polish Socialist movement rapidly developed and crystallized during the next few years. After the police had destroyed the Second *Proletariat* as well as the Union of Polish Workers, an attempt was made to bring together the separate émigré groups into one Socialist party for the whole of Poland. In 1890 the anti-Socialist laws were lifted in Germany and at once a society of Polish Socialists was founded in Berlin which concentrated on organizing the workers in Prussian

Poland—Silesia, Posen (Poznań), and Pomerania. In 1891 this group began to issue a weekly paper called *Gazeta Robotnicza* (The Workers' Journal). With the rapid development of a strong German Social-Democratic Party, the incipient movement in the Polish-speaking areas of Germany soon came under its organizational wing and for at least ten years remained within the orbit of German Social Democracy, though not always in harmony with the SPD leadership. These Poles became a minor, though persistent, problem for the German party, a matter in which Rosa Luxemburg became intimately involved.

A year later, in 1892, the leaders of the Polish Socialist groups of Austrian Galicia and Prussian Silesia formed distinct and separate Polish parties in their territories. At once this posed the urgent problem of relationship with the big Socialist parties of the two dominating countries, Germany and Austria. Both within the new parties and outside, among the émigrés from Russian Poland, there developed a more nationalistic current, as a reaction to what was held to have been the main failing of the Second *Proletariat*, its excessive negation of nationalist desires and its consequent lack of popular appeal. In a confused way, the pendulum swung between nationalism and anti-nationalism in the Polish parties, sometimes a matter of faith and conscious choice but often a reaction to previous failures. In addition, the Polish Socialists in Galicia under Ignacy Daszyński always got on much better with the Austrian party than the German Poles succeeded in doing with the SPD. In an empire which contained a host of emergent and conflicting nations, the Austrian Social-Democratic Party had to have a workable policy on national questions, and always had a some-what federal character—in fact, if not yet in name. Indeed, perceptive members of the SPD in Germany ruefully came to envy their Austrian colleagues for their ability to manage the recalcitrant Poles. There was finally the important personal friendship between Daszyński and the Austrian leader Victor Adler, which ensured powerful support for Daszyński's party in the International and incidentally made Rosa Luxemburg an important and permanent enemy in the person of the Austrian leader.

On 17 November 1892 a congress of all Polish Socialists in exile was summoned under the joint aegis of Mendelson from the first *Proletariat* and Limanowski and the remnants of his 'Polish People'. The old differences in emphasis between the two major constituent groups had largely disappeared, and it was Limanowski who presided over the pre-congress meeting, which consisted of ten members of his group and eight members of the first *Proletariat*. Out of this congress was born the new united Polish Socialist Party (PPS), linking up with the existing organization in Galicia and Silesia, and covering, it was hoped, the whole of Poland. But no all-Polish organization was possible, for the very real borders between the occupying powers could not be ignored. Thus the new party, PPS, covered only the Russian territories of Poland. It was closely related to the other two parties, the Prussian Polish Socialist Party and the Polish Social-Democratic Party in Austrian Galicia; at international congresses the Poles appeared as one unit—at least until the foundation of Rosa Luxemburg's SDKP, and for some ten years a special body existed in London to co-ordinate PPS activities in all three territories, the Association of Polish Socialists Abroad (*Związek Zagraniczny Polskich Socjalistów*).

The new party on Russian soil accepted terrorist activities in part and temporarily as a necessary means of action—an inevitable consequence of illegality—but it subscribed firmly to the idea of a Socialist state based on the working class. Most important, the new party issued a declaration extending the hand of co-operation to all Russian Socialists, but only as separate and equal partners.

III

SWITZERLAND—STUDY AND POLITICS

1890-1898

ROSA LUXEMBURG arrived in Zurich towards the end of 1889. She settled into rooms at 77 Universitätsstrasse, on a hill above the stately complex of University and Technical High School. There was a distant view over the lake and the wooded hills to the north of the city. She was immensely proud of her rooms—well furnished, comfortable, and above all, cheap. Next year she enrolled at the University of Zürich in the faculty of philosophy and followed courses in the natural sciences and mathematics. Mathematics fascinated her particularly; she felt she had a natural gift for it, and always claimed that her contribution to economics was only an extension of her proficiency in higher mathematics. In the natural sciences botany and zoology were her main interests, and though not to be her life's work, these subjects always retained a strong and almost professional fascination for her. Later, especially in prison, she would periodically go back to the detailed cataloguing of a collector, and bombard her merely nature-loving friends with technical explanations and comments on plant life. Out of this knowledge grew a genuine feeling for the beauty and unreason of plant and animal life; she was not just the deep-breathing romantic nature-lover portrayed by some of her biographers.[1] Somewhat self-consciously she would react to moments of extreme political frustration by lamenting that it would have been better if she had stuck to botany altogether; at least plants responded more directly than human beings to their environmental and natural laws instead of denying and resisting them.

In 1892 she changed over to the faculty of law.[2] Little is known about her activities at the University. The law faculty in the University of Zürich, then as now—and in common with the academic practice on the Continent—included social studies, which were of particular interest to Rosa Luxemburg. Among her teachers, Professor Julius Wolf was the most distinguished and prolific.

He was fortunate—or unfortunate—enough to have in his class several budding Marxists from Poland and Russia, already impatient

---

[1] Especially in *Gedenkbuch*, and by Henriette Roland-Holst.
[2] Staatsarchiv, Zürich, U 105b.

with the fashionably liberal theories of the time and probably irritated by the constant academic emphasis on the need to be objective. Some of these youngsters combined to make the Professor's life difficult; they asked loaded questions and Rosa Luxemburg was the one who was usually chosen to expose the Professor's 'old-fashionedness' with her own quick repartee and love of arguing.[1]

Rosa's life was of course not confined to the University. As a member of *Proletariat*, one of the constituent groups of the future PPS, she came armed with introductions and with the right, as well as the desire, to participate in the work of émigré Socialism. Switzerland was at the time the most important centre of Russian revolutionary Marxism, and Rosa Luxemburg soon became absorbed in this acrid but stimulating atmosphere. The politics of these groups were heavily tinged with problems of personal relations. This atmosphere, highly charged with the energy of strong personalities and compressed by the narrowness of personal circumstances, played a vital role in shaping Rosa Luxemburg's political manners and outlook. Some of the friendships she made in these early years in Switzerland remained for ever, a few dissolved slowly under the impact of events; but she was always more constant in her enmities than her friendships and the feuds of this period made her some important, lifelong enemies.

At the head of the hierarchy of Russian Marxism was the enormous figure of Georgii Plekhanov. His Group for the Liberation of Labour (*Gruppa osvobozhdenie truda*) included distinguished revolutionaries like Pavel Akselrod and Vera Zasulich. Years before, in 1883, Plekhanov had finally become disillusioned with the Populists; since embracing Marxism he had used his great analytical and philosophical faculties to break entirely new ground. To the younger generation of Marxists in Russia as well as abroad he was the giant of his day. The task of bringing Marxism to Russia had fallen on his shoulders, or, better, had been placed there by no less an authority than Engels himself. Plekhanov was the authorized interpreter into Russian of all past and present wisdom from London. But he was also an extremely touchy, prejudiced person who never hesitated to use the full hammer of his authority on his opponents, even when the issue was trifling. For young enthusiastic admirers from afar, the first meeting with him was a stimulating and at the same time disillusioning experience, to which Lenin, Martov, and Jogiches all testified independently. It was actually through Jogiches that Rosa Luxemburg first found herself in head-on conflict with the sage of Geneva, an experience that was to make them enemies for life.

---

[1] Frölich, p. 25, apparently based on a story of Marchlewski's. See also Julius Wolf, *Selbstbiographie*, in Felix Meiner (ed.), *Die Volkswirtschaftslehre der Gegenwart in Selbstdarstellungen*, Leipzig 1924, p. 12.

Jogiches was the most dominant figure in Rosa Luxemburg's life.[1] Born in Vilna in 1867, Leo Jogiches came from a prosperous Jewish family which, like the Luxemburgs, had been largely assimilated into their surroundings, though his family was far better off than Rosa's. He arrived in Zürich in 1890 and met Rosa a few months later. He too had escaped to avoid arrest, though his crossing of the Russian border was less comfortable than Rosa's: instead of straw he travelled under clay.[2] But he was preceded—or perhaps accompanied—by an established reputation; he had been among the first to organize the Jewish workers in Vilna. He was even supposed to have had contacts with army officers, and an additional and pressing reason for his departure was the disagreeable threat of military service, possibly in a penal battalion where his agitational talents would have been wasted. Escaping from military service was a traditionally powerful propellent of Jewish emigration from Russia; in Jogiches' case desertion was to form one of the main counts in the indictment against him when he was captured during the revolution in 1906. As early as 1885, at the age of eighteen, he had founded a revolutionary circle in Vilna and several of the Jewish Socialist leaders who were later to form the Jewish *Bund* acknowledged him as one of the earliest and most active Socialists in the town.[3] He had already been arrested and imprisoned twice and had each time got away before escaping finally to Switzerland.

He had brought with him a considerable sum of money, partly his own and partly funds he had collected for the printing and distribution of Marxist literature. The classics—mostly translations from Marx, Engels, Bebel, and Liebknecht into Russian, and the works of Plekhanov —were essential primary fuel to the spread of Socialism. These were to be smuggled into Poland and Lithuania through the channels which his and other Jewish groups were laboriously opening up. Jogiches went straight to Plekhanov and proposed collaboration: his money and technique, Plekhanov's prestige and copyrights. When Plekhanov frigidly asked what basis he had in mind, the young man coolly proposed fifty-fifty and was promptly shown the door. Their icy differences were confirmed by letter.[4] Jogiches was unabashed. He decided to pirate some of the

---

[1] He was born Lev Jogiches in 1867. In Russian and Polish circles he most commonly used Jan Tyszko or Tyshka, under which name he is known to historians of the Bolshevik party; in Switzerland and later in Germany he also hid under numerous pseudonyms. Only Rosa's circle of close friends knew him by his right name—though even this upset him. I shall refer to him as Leo Jogiches throughout.   [2] Frölich, p. 27.

[3] The *Algemener Yiddisher Arbeter Bund*, which was founded in 1897 and was the first Social-Democratic mass organization in the Russian empire.

[4] See *Gruppa 'osvobozhdenie truda' iz arkhivov G. V. Plekhanova, Zasulicha i Deicha*, Moscow/Leningrad 1928, Vol. II, p. 310 (Plekhanov to Jogiches), p. 312 (Jogiches to Plekhanov). A hostile account of these first contacts, and an equally hostile character sketch of Jogiches, can be found in a manuscript draft of Akselrod's memoirs for this period in the Akselrod papers at IISH, Amsterdam.

Marxist classics for translation and distribution in Russia, and created his own publishing venture for this purpose, *Sotsialdemokraticheskaya Biblioteka*.[1] At this Plekhanov declared open war. His instant dislike of Jogiches turned into noisy and public hatred. Like Trotsky, Jogiches suffered from two unforgivable defects in Plekhanov's eyes: self-assurance aggravated by youth, and being Jewish. To Engels he described Jogiches contemptuously as 'une miniature Ausgabe de Nechaieff,' a miniature version of Bakunin's wildest and most reckless anarchist disciple.[2]

Rosa fell in love with Leo Jogiches very soon after they met, and she was at once transported into the thick of the fight. Their relationship was far too close for any possibility of her remaining neutral. At first she tried to exercise a moderating influence on Jogiches; for her, Plekhanov was first and foremost the great man and Jogiches obstinate and perhaps unreasonable, not willing to appreciate the stature of his opponent. But to no avail; no one ever changed Jogiches' mind by persuasion, and by 1894 she too was ready to cock a snook at the 'old man' whenever there was an opportunity.[3]

This quarrel with Plekhanov had important consequences. It isolated Jogiches in the Russian Socialist movement abroad to such an extent that effective participation became impossible, at least to a man of his driving temperament. For four years Jogiches obstinately went on trying to maintain an independent foothold in the publication of Russian material, aided by the fact that his distribution outlets in Vilna were superior to anything available to Plekhanov and Akselrod. In 1892 he snatched a collection of speeches made at May Day rallies in Vilna and Warsaw from under Plekhanov's nose, and published them in Polish with an introduction by Rosa Luxemburg—her first known publication.[4] Plekhanov then retaliated by putting the obnoxious couple in Zürich under interdict. The upshot was that Jogiches' publishing venture failed, in spite of the large funds at his disposal.[5]

Already in 1892, after his first dispute with Plekhanov, Jogiches had

---

[1] It lasted from 1892 to 1895. Its editions consisted of Karl Marx, *TheEighteenth Brumaire of Louis Bonaparte* (translated by Krichevskii) and a few other works of Marx, as well as Kautsky's *Das Erfurter Programm* and two popular works on English and Belgian working-class struggles. See *Z Pola Walki*, 1930, Nos. 9/10, p. 146, note 25.

[2] Quoted by Leonard Schapiro, *The Communist Party of the Soviet Union*, London 1960, p. 170. The Russian translation of the letter, dated 16 May 1894, is in *Gruppa 'osvobozhdenie truda'*, p. 318.

[3] John Mill, *Pionirn un Boir* (Pioneers and Builders), New York 1946, Vol. I, p. 102. See also Seidel letters, *Z Pola Walki*, 1959, No. 1(5), p. 71.

[4] *Historishe Shriftn*, p. 376. See R. Kruszyńska, *Święto Pierwszego Maja* (First of May Celebration), Paris 1892.

[5] *Historishe Shriftn*, pp. 371-2, and footnote. Plekhanov put the sum at 15,000 roubles, nearly £1,500, loc, cit., p. 319.

turned his interests and funds increasingly towards Polish affairs. Most people believed that this was due to Rosa's deliberate influence—and so it probably was, though Plekhanov, who if anything preferred the young woman to the man, still thought that she was trying to keep him on Russian paths.[1] From 1893 onwards he was active behind the scenes at Rosa's side in the breakaway Polish movement and became its chief organizer and convener, though his name hardly figures in the documents before 1900. By driving Jogiches out of any effective participation in the Russian movement, Plekhanov unwittingly rendered Polish Social Democracy a great service.

While Jogiches was struggling with the intransigent elders, Rosa Luxemburg and a small group of friends were fighting an equally bitter but more rigorously ideological struggle against the leading lights of Polish émigré Socialism. When the united Polish Socialist Party (PPS) had been founded at the end of 1892 all the émigré groups adhered to it. The creation of a united party and the adoption of a programme acceptable to all the various groups was a considerable achievement, of which the participants were justly proud.[2] The programme of the PPS met not only the vociferous demands of the representatives abroad, but also covered the aspirations of the groups inside Poland, though these were obviously not in a position to make their views heard as forcefully as the émigrés. Of necessity it was a compromise programme, neither rigorously Marxist nor particularly nationalist. Like those of most western Socialist parties, it offered a declaration of the full Marxist faith as its maximum programme as well as directives for more immediate tactics—the so-called minimum programme. But where the bigger Socialist parties in the West made organization their main field of operations and kept the party programme for flag days and parades, like a sacred symbol, the programme of the Polish party was its holy of holies, the only cohesive factor. Within a few months of its adoption it became the subject of an acute controversy. And there was no organizational structure to enforce discipline.

In July 1893 there appeared in Paris the first issue of *Sprawa Robotnicza* (The Workers' Cause). It introduced itself with a leading article setting out the purpose of the paper and the line that it would follow— strict adherence to the cause of the working classes in their struggle against the class enemy. The accent was on the struggle against capitalism, solidarity with the Russian working classes in their struggle against Tsarist absolutism, and on the international character of all working-class movements including the Polish.[3]

[1] John Mill in 'Vilna,' *Historishe Shriftn*, pp. 74 ff. For Plekhanov see below, pp. 49, 62.
[2] Op. cit., Chapter 1, p. 61.
[3] 'Od redakcji', *Sprawa Robotnicza*, No. 1, July 1893, reprinted in *SDKPiL : Materialy i dokumenty*, Warsaw 1957, Vol. 1, Part 1 (1893–7), pp. 1–3.

Sprawa Robotnicza was the creation of a small group of young Polish enthusiasts, mostly students abroad. Right from the start Rosa Luxemburg was one of its leading lights and in 1894 formally took over the editorship, under the pseudonym of R. Kruszyńska.[1] The finance was provided by Jogiches, and *Sprawa Robotnicza* took over many of the ideas and methods, with a particularly Polish accent, which Jogiches had hoped to fulfil in association with Plekhanov. But the paper received no support from the leaders of the PPS. The very first number announced the paper's independent and unusual line, particularly on the question of co-operation with the Russian working classes—a flavour which ran directly counter to the attempt of the PPS leadership to liberate itself from Russian tutelage. Moreover, there was not a word in the first issue about Polish independence. On the contrary, Socialist progress in Poland was presented as a mere part of the general development in Russia.

The timing of the first issue of *Sprawa Robotnicza* was no accident. The Third Congress of the Socialist International was due to take place in Zürich from 6 to 12 August 1893. The group associated with *Sprawa Robotnicza* now staked a claim for representation at the congress as part of the Polish delegation. Although the Polish Socialists, unlike the Russians, had succeeded in forming a united party, representation at the congress was still based on individual groups and newspapers without any of the discipline and block votes of such western parties as the German or Austrian. There was always some confusion over the mandates of those loosely associated groups which generally had to be adjudicated by the congress.[2] If the *Sprawa Robotnicza* group could show that it ran a viable newspaper, its *prima facie* right to be represented at the congress would be established. In order to make doubly sure, Rosa Luxemburg wrote a Polish minority report on behalf of the *Sprawa Robotnicza* group on the development of Social Democracy in Russian Poland between 1889 and 1893, the period since the last International congress in Paris.[3] Such reports to the International of domestic activity were normally provided by each party affiliated to the

---

[1] *Sprawa Robotnicza*, No. 7, January 1894; *SDKPiL: Materialy i dokumenty*, Vol. I, Part 1, p. 128.

[2] The proceedings of mandate commissions of the International Congresses, established after 1896, always provided a good example of the cohesiveness of the parties. The delegations of the well-organized parties of the Second International made little trouble, and most of the mandate commission's work was concerned with sorting out the disputes of loose groups like the Poles and the Russians, and 'split' movements like the Americans and French. As European Socialism became more organized, mandate disputes decreased in number and intensity.

[3] This document was written in German but no copies of the original report remain in existence. A Polish translation was included in the collection, *Kwestia polska a ruch socjalistyczny*, Cracow 1905, pp. 173–7.

International. But the document of the *Sprawa Robotnicza* group was an unofficial venture; the PPS leadership presented its own report and so there were before the congress two separate and very different documents both claiming to represent the Socialist movement of Russian or (as it was sometimes called) Congress Poland. The *Sprawa Robotnicza* report contained the ominous phrase that 'the socio-economic history of the three parts of the former Kingdom of Poland has led to their organic integration into three partitioning powers and has created in each of the three parts [of Poland] separate aims and political interests'.[1] This was a veiled negation of the whole case for any re-establishment of historic Poland; by emphasizing and relying on modern developments it indicated that any policy of Polish independence was nothing more than a clutching at the archaic straws of history. The activities of *Sprawa Robotnicza* were emerging as clearly separatist and potentially oppositional to the main Polish party.

The official Polish delegation of the Association of Polish Socialists Abroad reported to the Chairman of the Congress Bureau, the Belgian Socialist leader Vandervelde, that it was opposing one of the Polish mandates—that of Kruszyńska. The Bureau at first tried to preserve peace; in its report to the congress, it recommended acceptance of the mandate and Kruszyńska's (Rosa Luxemburg's) appearance as a member of the Polish delegation. Daszyński thereupon took the matter before the congress itself. He asked for the mandate to be quashed on the grounds that 'only one issue of the paper [*Sprawa Robotnicza*] has appeared, the mandate has no signature, no one even knows the editor who sent this delegate'.[2]

Rosa Luxemburg was the last person to refuse a public challenge. She jumped up at once. 'These facts are due to the peculiar situation in Russian Poland. The paper is a Social-Democratic literary venture and expresses the view of the Polish Socialist proletariat.'[3] Willingly or not, the congress had to listen to the conflicting arguments. Daszyński emphasized the unimportance of his opponents, while Rosa Luxemburg argued her case on basic differences of policy.

Emil Vandervelde, the Belgian Socialist leader, left a description of the scene:

Rosa, 23 years old at the time, was quite unknown outside one or two Socialist groups in Germany and Poland . . . but her opponents had their hands full to hold their ground against her. . . . She rose from among the delegates at the back and stood on a chair to make herself better heard. Small and looking very frail in a summer dress, which managed very effectively to conceal her physical

---

[1] Ibid., p. 176.

[2] *Protokoll, Internationaler Sozialistischer Arbeiterkongress in Zürich* (*Organizationskommittee Zürich*, 1894), p. 14.

[3] Op. cit., p. 15.

defects, she advocated her cause with such magnetism and such appealing words that she won the majority of the Congress at once and they raised their hands in favour of the acceptance of her mandate.[1]

Memory and chivalry—the Second International was not ungallant—may have deceived Vandervelde. After further tumult, during which Marchlewski and Warszawski spoke in her support, the congress in fact voted for the rejection of the mandate. Plekhanov threw his voice and votes behind the PPS; he had already pledged his support to his Polish friends in advance and saw here a splendid opportunity for getting his own back on the infuriating couple in Zürich.[2] The Bureau, however, queried the congress vote, which had taken place amid some confusion; the Polish delegation demanded a vote by national delegations, and these voted 7 for and 9 against the young girl's mandate, with 3 abstentions. Rosa left, with a red face, under protest. Her friend Marchlewski, however, remained, since no one had challenged his mandate.[3]

Though Rosa Luxemburg failed to maintain her position against the powerful opposition of Daszyński and the other Polish delegates, she personally achieved something of a moral victory. Then and later she gave the appearance of someone reluctantly forced to display personal dissensions in public; by hinting that the dispute was one of principle and that both sides represented different versions of Socialism, she gave the appearance that it was Daszyński and the PPS who were trying to suppress an inconvenient opposition with whose policy they disagreed. The Second International subscribed to the majesty of principles and most of its leaders hated personal polemics in public. By the time the next International congress met in London in 1896 the right of Rosa Luxemburg's group to be heard as representatives of a genuine if small section of Polish Socialism was already established beyond challenge. The congress upheld her mandate on that occasion and continued to do so until, after 1900, the PPS leadership gave up attempting to challenge it.

Now that war had been openly declared between the *Sprawa Robotnicza* group and the leadership of the PPS, there was little point in the opposition remaining within the PPS organization. Originally they had considered the formation of an oppositional group within the party, probably hoping to influence and persuade an increasing number of PPS members to adopt their own point of view.[4] But the attitude of the leadership at the Zürich congress and subsequent attacks in the PPS press against the splitters doomed any such hopes. It was decided to

---

[1] Quoted by Frölich, pp. 51–2. I have been unable to find the original description in Vandervelde's numerous works. It is not in his *Souvenirs d'un militant Socialiste*, Paris 1939.

[2] For Plekhanov's manoeuvres before and at the congress see *Perepiska G. V. Plekhanova i P. B. Akselroda*, Moscow 1925, Vol. I, pp. 74 ff., 143.

[3] *Protokoll, Internationaler . . . Kongress*, p. 15.

[4] See declaration in *Sprawa Robotnicza*, No. 2, September 1893.

form a new party altogether called *Socjaldemokracja Królestwa Polskiego* (The Social Democracy of the Kingdom of Poland—SDKP). The choice of name was Rosa Luxemburg's, and in itself defined the attitude of the new party; by deliberately adopting the geographical limitations of the Kingdom of Poland, even the suggestion of *Polonia rediviva* was carefully avoided. The policy organ of the new party was *Sprawa Robotnicza*, its only newspaper. The programme of the new party was based on the statement of editorial policy which had appeared in the first number of the paper in July 1893. This, together with the group's report to the Zürich congress, was formally adopted as a programme at the party's first congress in March 1894.[1]

In spite of all the public enthusiasm over founding a new party, there was a somewhat indefinable and well disguised element of sour grapes. Having recognized the impossibility of remaining in the PPS, Rosa made a somewhat half-hearted attempt to join the Russians—only to be scornfully rejected by Plekhanov, who gleefully reported the Polish disarray to Engels and characterized Rosa as Jogiches' female appanage.[2] Thus the SDKP was the product of as much disillusion as enthusiasm. From time to time Rosa would still sigh briefly for a united Polish party —based on her policy and attitudes, *bien entendu*.[3]

The SDKP saw itself as the direct successor to *Proletariat*—and turned sharply away from the compromise programme of unity around which the PPS had been formed. The immediate aim—the *minimum* programme which every Socialist party predicated in contrast to the *maximum* eventual aim of social revolution—was a liberal constitution for the entire Russian empire with territorial autonomy for Poland— that curious, half-federal solution which Rosa Luxemburg and her friends were to defend staunchly in the Russian party for many years, and which was to be the subject of so much acrimonious debate. The SDKP stressed the need for close co-operation with Russian Socialists, though there was no mention of any pre-eminence for the latter as there had been in the *Narodnaya Volya–Proletariat* agreement. Polish independence was now specifically rejected; in Rosa Luxemburg's phrase—'a utopian mirage, a delusion of the workers to detract them from their class struggle'.[4]

---

[1] See leading article by Rosa Luxemburg, 'Nowy etap' (The New Stage), *Sprawa Robotnicza*, No. 9, March 1894.

[2] *Gruppa 'osvobozhdenie truda'*, Vol. II, p. 320. Plekhanov called the *Sprawa Robotnicza* report to the Zürich congress a 'lying Jesuitical document'.

[3] 'I am sure these blows would be far less painful [the loss of a transport of illegal material] if only we were one united party.' Jogiches letters, *Z Pola Walki*, 1930, Nos. 9/10, p. 149, dated 10 April 1895.

[4] O. B. Szmidt, *Dokumenty*, Vol. I, pp, 55–60. The entire Protocol of the First Congress was reprinted in *Sprawa Robotnicza*, No. 10, April 1894 and also *SDKPiL dokumenty*, Vol. I, Part 1, pp. 174–91.

The tactical consequence of this position was that the Polish Socialists in each of the occupied areas would have to join—or at least federate with—the Socialist parties of the partitioning powers, German, Austrian, and Russian. It was hoped that a united Russian party would soon come into being to enable such co-operation to become effective. From the moment of its foundation, the SDKP piously called on the Russians to form the necessary united party. For the rest, the SDKP programme was modelled on the German Socialist Party's 1891 Erfurt programme, with its careful synthesis of immediate tasks and final revolutionary aim. But it recognized that conditions in Poland were one very important step behind Germany. Since no possibilities of open agitation and electoral propaganda existed in Russia as they did in Germany, a liberal constitution for Russia must be the immediate aim of all Socialists in the empire.[1]

The whole programme was above all a reaction to the PPS position and organization. Its possibilities of positive achievement at the time were small. There was no Russian Socialist party to join, no prospect of contributing significantly to any constitutional reform in Russia, little chance of carrying away a substantial part of the PPS membership or of influencing events at home. Though the first congress took place illegally in Warsaw—a matter of great pride to the new leadership, even though they were unable to participate in it—the party was visibly the product of an émigré split, and a typical result of eastern obduracy over principles.[2] The whole effort must therefore be seen as a self-conscious assertion of a generation of young revolutionaries opposing the more practical and compromising leadership of the PPS. None the less, the division was not purely personal. There were profound differences of policy which crystallized more and more round the question of Polish independence. For the next few years the SDKP leadership, and particularly Rosa Luxemburg, embarked on a theoretical underpinning of their position on this question, until the negation of Polish independence became a doctrine in itself. At the same time, the sharp polemics on this subject with the PPS periodically forced the latter also to re-examine its own position, and the original vague commitment to re-establishing Polish independence became much more specific and unequivocal. The Polish Socialist movement remained sharply divided on this issue. In spite of periodic shifts of opinion, these two opposing views remained distinct and dominated Polish Socialism up to the First World War, forcing the two parties into polarization on almost every other issue as well.

[1] O. B. Szmidt, loc. cit. See also Dziewanowski, *Communist Party*, pp. 24–5.

[2] The émigré breakaway, and the establishment of a separate organization in Poland, took place independently. The participants of the Warsaw congress only later united with the émigré SDKP.

The creation of an independent Social Democracy of Poland with a small though viable organization at home was a remarkable achievement, even though it broke up the brief existence of a united Polish Socialist movement. The new movement could easily have remained a small émigré sect without followers or significance, as so many Russian and Polish dissidents were to be in the future. That it flourished in spite of all setbacks and grew into a powerful nucleus which eventually swallowed the major part of the PPS to form the Communist Party of Poland, is largely due to the outstanding quality of its leadership. Still more remarkable is the fact that it was, for most of the time, an émigré leadership. In spite of inevitable police penetration of the membership in Poland, and the repeated defection of the most important party workers, the émigré leadership always managed to rebuild local organizations and never lost contact entirely with the clandestine movement at home.[1] Most of what is known of the SDKP is based on its policy record, expressed in publications and documents; no study of its sociology has ever been attempted. Yet this is important in a context far wider than the history of Polish Socialism, for many of the leaders abroad played an important part in other Socialist parties and some of them eventually made their name in the Bolshevik party after the October Revolution in Russia.

The nucleus of the leadership was formed between 1890 and 1893 in Switzerland. Rosa Luxemburg and Leo Jogiches had been installed in Zürich since 1890. In 1892 Julian Marchlewski arrived, after a year of imprisonment in Warsaw followed by expulsion.[2] Marchlewski was a somewhat patrician figure in this circle. His family lived in Włocławek, half way between Poznań and Warsaw. He was not Jewish—his father was Polish and his mother German—and there was no tradition at home of political dissent or under-privileged minority status; he had come to Marxism entirely by conviction. Though by nature an intellectual, interested in philosophical questions and expressing his thoughts in a heavy and somewhat indigestible style, he had deliberately 'gone to the people' in the best populist tradition, and had tried to absorb working-class ideology by seeking employment in factories as a weaver or dyer. There was always something self-conscious and sacrificial about Marchlewski's Socialism. He found personal relations difficult and, like Mehring, was extremely sensitive to personal slights; his happiest

---

[1] None of those present at the first party congress, with the exception of Bronisław Wesołowski, played a role of any significance in the SDKP. They either joined the PPS, were caught by the police, or went into exile where they played a secondary role. For a list of participants, see *SDKPiL dokumenty*, Vol. I, Part 1, p. 174.

[2] Marchlewski later used the party pseudonym of Karski on most occasions. In the official service of the Soviet Union after 1919 he reverted to his own name. He died in Italy in 1925 as a senior Soviet official. A recent biography is Feliks Tych i Horst Schumacher, *Julian Marchlewski*, Warsaw 1966 (German ed. Berlin 1966).

moments were devoted to writing his complicated analyses of social conditions. Though by no means fully in agreement with all of Rosa Luxemburg's ideas, adherence to the SDKP and complete acceptance of its programme was part of his self-denial—though his personal relations with Rosa Luxemburg were often edgy. Frequently he was the spokesman of the party on matters with which in his heart he did not fully agree. Rosa Luxemburg did not really like him for many years: he was important rather than desirable; neither she nor Jogiches trusted him completely, and when Rosa moved to Germany in 1898 she steered clear of him for a while, unjustifiably as it turned out.

Another co-founder of the SDKP was Adolf Warszawski.[1] He, too, had been prominent in the Union of Polish Workers. Warszawski was a Jew, an excellent agitator and speaker who could transform the complications of Marxism into easily comprehensible slogans and ideas for the masses. He had not the intellectual equipment of Rosa Luxemburg or Julian Marchlewski but was much more the type of revolutionary whose entire life was devoted to the complicated and unrewarding routine of small-scale persuasion. He was a grey person, without obvious inspiration but hard-working and completely absorbed by his task; as such he found the atmosphere of the later Bolshevik group in the Russian Social-Democratic Workers' Party (RSDRP) more congenial than some of the other Polish Socialists. But his commitment was particularly to the Polish movement. He was the only one of the SDKP leadership who played no part outside the Polish movement, whose entire life was to be absorbed by it and who remained faithful to it until his death.

These four people—Rosa Luxemburg, Leo Jogiches, Julian Marchlewski, and Adolf Warszawski—were the nucleus of the SDKP from the day of its inception. They were more or less of the same age, and all found in the movement a fulfilment of their personalities and talents impossible elsewhere. Yet they were very different people and by no means thought alike on every question. Their co-operation was based on a shared long-term objective and on a common revolutionary temperament; none of them sought immediate recognition in terms of power and status within the Second International—indeed, there was a certain personal impatience with the self-indulgence of an international rolling endlessly onwards. All of them were dissenters by personal conviction, outsiders rather than organized conspirators. They had boundless self-confidence, both in the development of a Socialist future as well as in the rightness of their particular analysis and tactic. Most important, their collaboration was based on an indefinable web of personal attitudes generating a sort of spontaneous and flexible con-

[1] He, too, adopted a party pseudonym, Adolf Warski, and retained it consistently for the rest of his life, most of which was spent after 1918 either in Moscow or illegally in Poland. He was finally a victim of Stalin's almost total purge of the Polish Communist Party in 1937.

sensus which had nothing to do with any discipline of organization or with doctrine or even charisma. Instead of being created or prescribed, consensus emerged. Though the party statutes called for a tight and conspiratorial centralism—Lenin, had he bothered, would have found in them a perfect model for democratic centralism—the actual procedures of the leadership during these early years were informal and personal rather than tight and official. Consultations on matters of policy were of a purely personal kind, generally by private letter between individuals, and none of the formalities which were typical of the German and Austrian parties were observed. Yet collaboration was such that no party congress was found necessary for six years; the second party congress took place only in 1900, to register the important constitutional changes caused by the adhesion of the Lithuanian group.[1] Precisely this lack of formality makes the historian's task difficult, for comments on events and people were usually made in a mental shorthand which is impossible for the uninitiated to decipher.

Round the nucleus of these four personalities there grew a larger constellation of brilliant activists, drawn in by the aims and methods of the SDKP. In the course of its history such names as Dzierżyński, Hanecki, Unszlicht, and Leder became associated with it. Some, like Dzierżyński, remained intimately connected with the movement until the great Russian Revolution swept them into its orbit; others died before the First World War (Cezaryna Wojnarowska); a few dissented early, like Trusiewicz; finally, an important group—Hanecki, Leder, Radek, and Unszlicht—revolted against the émigré leadership and broke out to form a dissident movement in 1911. But it is striking that the SDKP at various times contained such a galaxy of revolutionary personalities, whose enormous energy overflowed into the German and Russian Social-Democratic parties without prising them loose from the Polish party. None the less, it was only our four figures who really saw the movement through from its inception in 1893 to the formation of the Polish Communist Party in 1918, and they particularly set the tone and provided the continuity of its policy. Without being unjust to the many other interesting personalities who will appear in these pages, the SDKP, which later became the SDKPiL, was the particular creation of Rosa Luxemburg, Leo Jogiches, Julian Marchlewski, and Adolf Warszawski.

Rosa Luxemburg was the fountain-head of policy ideas. *Sprawa Robotnicza* was primarily her inspiration; she had written the dissident report to the International congress and the articles which were to form the basis of the SDKP programme. It was through her that the dissatisfaction with the PPS leadership was articulated and hers was the decision to bring the split into the open. Right from the start, therefore,

---

[1] See below, p. 67. Besides, the party was in dire straits in Poland between 1896 and 1900.

she played a prominent role in the SDKP—a role which was to diminish relatively as the years went by and a self-generating and broader leadership became established. *Sprawa Robotnicza* was published in Paris, and between 1893 and 1898 she went there frequently both in connection with party work and to pursue her studies in the Polish libraries. Indeed, her second visit to Paris in 1894 was something of a rescue operation for *Sprawa Robotnicza* from the uninspired hands of Adolf Warszawski; for months Rosa not only wrote (or rewrote) most contributions but argued with Reiff, the printer, over priorities and costs.

Similarly, 77 Universitätsstrasse was the intellectual centre of the SDKP. But because Rosa Luxemburg was always the public half of the partnership while Jogiches remained in the background, his role has been too much played down. Rosa thought and formulated, but the dominating trend was laid down by him, and many of the concepts she developed were originally his. Certainly everything she wrote was discussed with him, and could go no further without his approval. Above all, their personal relations with other Poles and Russians were laid down by him, and the question whether a junior colleague was a fool, a knave, an innocent dupe, or a cunning deceiver, was debated seriously back and forth.[1] Plekhanov for one considered Rosa merely as Jogiches' mouthpiece—though this was obviously one of Plekhanov's personal oversimplifications. Most of their contemporaries, however, were more clearly aware of the man's important role than later historians, and he had a substantial share in her triumphs as well as her vicissitudes.

As Rosa's international reputation grew, more visitors called and the second-floor flat became one of the points on the international Socialist circuit. John Mill, Jewish Socialist leader from Vilna and international gossip, visited her several times during his journeys from Russia to the West in search of support for the foundation of the *Bund*. Though he found both Rosa Luxemburg and Leo Jogiches resistant to his early appeals to them as Jews, and firmly opposed to any obligation to a specifically Jewish Socialist movement, he none the less saw them with an eye that at that time was politically and personally neutral, if not benevolent. His description of their lives and works in this period tells us more than that of close friends or committed enemies. He described his first meeting with Rosa:

She was of low build, with a disproportionately large head; a typical Jewish face with a thick nose . . . a heavy, occasionally uneven, walk, with a limp; her first appearance did not make an agreeable impression but you had only to spend a bit of time with her to see how much life and energy was in the woman, how clever and sharp she was, and at what a high level of intellectual stimulation and development she lived.[2]

[1] Jogiches letters. See for instance *Z Pola Walki*, 1930, Nos. 9/10, pp. 129 ff.
[2] John Mill, *Pionirn un Boier*, Vol. I, p. 167.

When it came to discussing political co-operation, however, John Mill found himself up against an outburst of intellectual disapproval. 'One cannot work with crazy political kids who only want to play at soldiers', was Rosa's reply when he tentatively touched on the question of arms. Nevertheless the Jewish leaders appreciated Rosa's lively pen and Jogiches' conspiratorial abilities; between 1895 and 1897 a certain amount of SDKP material was distributed through *Bund* channels. Whatever differences there were between the SDKP and the emerging *Bund* leadership, the latter preferred to collaborate with Jogiches and Luxemburg rather than with the PPS. Jogiches' terms were stiff: he insisted on handling his own distribution and in the end the committee in Vilna reluctantly agreed to act more or less as his agents. This situation continued until 1897 when the formal creation of the *Bund* closed this convenient distribution channel to Leo Jogiches.[1]

In these early years from 1893 to 1895, Rosa Luxemburg and Leo Jogiches were almost entirely isolated. The PPS leadership had put a *cordon sanitaire* around them and even sympathizers kept away for fear of reprisal. Rosa's exuberant personality and her predilection for expressing herself in print exposed her far more than Jogiches, who always kept out of the limelight. By 1894 she had become the bogey-woman of Polish Socialism. 'She had been so blackened by the PPS that she was considered unclean [*tref*].' Even the parents of Julian Marchlewski, a close political collaborator of Rosa's, were preoccupied by their son's association with the outcast in Zürich.

During this time Rosa was particularly associated with the group of Russians round Krichevskii and Akimov who had formed the Union of Social Democrats Abroad and were competing with Plekhanov and his Group for the Liberation of Labour for control of the emergent Russian movement. From 1892 onwards she corresponded regularly with Krichevskii, and the SDKP's assessment of developments in Russia was very similar to that of the Union of Social Democrats. Apart from their close contact in Zürich, they met regularly at International congresses and probably collaborated in the presentation of views on Russian affairs.[3] The friendship did not, however, survive the test of time and political developments. A further group of émigrés at the end of the century under the leadership of Lenin and Martov adhered

[1] *Historishe Shriftn* pp. 388–90.

[2] *Historishe Shriftn*, p. 391 (translated from Yiddish).

[3] The letters to Krichevskii are no longer in existence, unless immured in the archives of IML (M). They must have been available to Frölich who quotes extensively from one letter (p. 35). Krichevskii led the Russian delegation to the 1896 International congress in London—a role which later party history denied him, wrongly assigning the leadership of the Russian group, in retrospect, to Plekhanov. Plekhanov considered Jogiches to be the 'evil genius' of Krichevskii's group.

initially to Plekhanov and his group; together they drove Krichevskii and Akimov out of their influential position in the Russian party by identifying them—the first use of this technique by Lenin and Plekhanov —with the 'economist' movement, which subordinated political activity to the trade-union struggle. Krichevskii was no longer able to get a mandate to the second RSDRP congress that year, while Akimov led a tenuous existence on the fringe as an observer until the 1906 Stockholm congress. Consistent lack of success and the resulting personal humiliation were not marketable commodities in Rosa Luxemburg's polity; looking back in 1910 she recalled:

Poor Krichevskii in Paris [after 1900]—a wreck perpetually complaining about his debts, his children, his ailments. . . . He failed to keep up with me mentally and when I saw him again it was like being visited by a provincial cousin whom one had known ten years ago as a brisk young man and found now nothing but a worried provincial hick and *pater familias*.[1]

There is little material to illustrate the daily routine of these young Socialists in Zürich. They were all poor, though both Rosa Luxemburg and Leo Jogiches received intermittent help from their families. These émigré circles were riddled with personal feuds and Rosa Luxemburg made a deliberate effort to avoid the usual meeting places. Self-pity, aided by alcohol, was despicable in her eyes and the resultant wildness of some of the political speculations repelled her.[2] Polemical, exposed, and unmistakably Jewish, she attracted—then as always—the anti-Semitic outbursts which were never far below the surface of Polish and Russian life, and which many genuine revolutionaries unconsciously shared with their enemies. The SDKP leadership, containing a higher proportion of Jews than almost any other Socialist group at the time, had consistently to ward off attacks tinged more or less obviously with anti-Semitic bias. Rosa Luxemburg became the target for most of the abuse. She was 'the direct cause of the first wild outbreak of anti-Semitic fury on the part of the former radical and free-thinking "black hundreds".'[3]

---

[1] Letter to a friend in ZHP, Warsaw.

[2] John Mill, *Pionirn un Boier*, Vol. I, p. 168.

[3] John Mill, *Pionirn un Boier*, Vol. II, p. 182. One of the leaders of these 'black hundreds', Andrzej Niemojewski, identified Rosa Luxemburg particularly with the reprehensible Jewish efforts to seduce Polish workers: 'The Jews agitate among our workers to cause them to consider Socialism as the equivalent of hating one's fatherland. . . . What Rosa Luxemburg and her supporters feed the workers is nothing but the intoxication of scribbling. . . . The devilish work of destruction carried on by the Jewish excrement under the guise of defending the working class, turns out to be nothing less than the murder of Poland; as all Jews hate non-Jews, so Luxemburg's Social Democrats have a passionate hatred for Poland.' (Andrzej Niemojewski in *Myśl Niepodległa* (Independent Thought), November 1910, No. 153, p. 1599.

But the loose, comradely, yet stimulating association between the SDKP leaders provided its own ideological defence. Rosa Luxemburg always found attacks of this kind particularly stimulating. They gave her an excellent chance to show up her opponents without, in fact, touching her on any especially sensitive spot. Anti-nationalism was a source of pride, not a shortcoming.

For all intents and purposes Rosa Luxemburg *was* Polish Social Democracy during these years. Her writings were the ones that caused comment and reaction. The others only helped—or, according to her, hindered: Adolf and Jadwiga Warszawski with their need to earn a pittance on which to live, Marchlewski with his soupy style of writing which had always to be stirred by someone else, even Jogiches with his fuss and bother. Then there was a whole group of people who helped occasionally—or had to be helped—Ratyński, Olszewski, Heinrich. Rosa Luxemburg was frequently exhausted and disillusioned during 1894 and 1895, when she felt she was doing everything and yet, according to Jogiches, never enough—but their relationship, personal as well as political, was never for one moment in doubt. It was her great source of strength.

The SDKP was very small. For seven years, from 1893 to 1900, it was practically a head without a body. Though *Sprawa Robotnicza* bravely boasted of its substantial readership in Poland, visitors to Poland found that the SDKP organization was largely non-existent.[1] After his first visit to Zürich, John Mill was asked to take back an important letter from Rosa Luxemburg to an SDKP organizer in Warsaw called Ratyński, the son of a shopkeeper; he turned out to be the only self-confessed Social Democrat in the entire city. And even he soon found the strain excessive; he was arrested in 1902 and joined the PPS in exile in Siberia.[2] As to *Sprawa Robotnicza* and its readership, 'you could search everywhere with candles and fail to throw any light on it.'[3] The correspondence printed in the paper from time to time was often fictitious and turned out to have been written by the editors themselves in Switzerland. Visitors who told them the latest news from home were astonished to find that their stories appeared as readers' letters in the next issue. *Sprawa Robotnicza* itself eked out an increasingly precarious existence from the spring of 1895 onwards, when Rosa Luxemburg left Paris for Zürich. The intervals between issues became longer and in

---

[1] 'The Pioneer Epoch in the Jewish Labour Movement', *Historishe Shriftn*, p. 388.

[2] Ibid. See also *SDKPiL dokumenty*, Vol. I, Part 2, pp. 410–12 for a reprint of Ratyński's 'obituary' published originally in *Czerwony Sztandar*.

[3] *Historishe Shriftn*, p. 389. The particular phrase loses its savour in translation from Yiddish.

July 1896 it ceased publication altogether.[1]

Of course, this situation was not due to any internal weakness in the SDKP nor even peculiar to it. The PPS, too, suffered from the inroads of the police into its organization in Poland, and both Socialist movements were reduced to token forces in 1896. The pattern was always cyclical: a resurgence of interest and growing organizations followed by a reaction during which the police were able to clean up most of the revolutionary nests, until new ones could be formed once more. These tendencies were general throughout Russia and applied in all regions. It was not until the last three years of the century that there was a revival; during the period which saw the formation of both the *Bund* and the RSDRP, the Polish Socialist movement, too, benefited from a sudden and rapid accession of strength. With the end of *Sprawa Robotnicza* the SDKP was left without an organ. In view of the doldrums at home it seemed more important to project a sophisticated party image at the Second International than to translate international Socialism for the benefit of a rapidly declining Polish readership. In 1895 under the auspices of *Sprawa Robotnicza* Rosa's first pamphlet had appeared, under the pseudonym of Maciej Rożga.[2] It was her first cohesive statement on the national question. The theoretical implications were assumed; the main plank of the argument was immediate and political. Any emphasis on Polish nationalism must divert the working classes from the intensity and purity of their Socialism. She felt as strongly as she reasoned convincingly that the two were incompatible; instead of going together, as the PPS claimed, they would necessarily struggle with each other for supremacy; one must supplant the other. Although she maintained that the socialist factor was as progressive as the nationalist factor was backward-looking, she must have felt a definite fear of contamination; in a struggle between nationalist and socialist tendencies within a fairly unsophisticated working class, Socialism would probably be the loser. Nothing but fear added to conviction will explain her intensity, her willingness to fall out at one time or another with almost every Socialist of importance, from Liebknecht to Lenin, over this question. Rosa Luxemburg justified her anti-nationalist programme in political terms by showing that nationalism was the refuge of the middle

---

[1] The reason is not entirely clear. The last number to appear was No. 24 of June 1896, before the International congress. The organization in Poland had admittedly ceased to exist owing to police depredations. But material for futher numbers was already in the hands of the printer. Politically, the congress itself was at least a partial success for the SDKP (the PPS failed to get its resolution adopted). I suspect, from only indirect evidence, that Rosa and Jogiches may have quarrelled at about this time and he may have refused to provide further funds. The years 1896–7 are ill-documented anyway.

[2] *Niepodlegla Polska i sprawa robotnicza* (Independent Poland and the Workers' Cause), Paris 1895. This seems to be the original title, though sometimes referred to as '*Niepodległość Polski a sprawa robotnicza*' (*SDKPiL dokumenty*, Vol. I, Part 2, p. 137, note 3).

class, but that this same middle class had ceased to be a revolutionary factor in Poland. Consequently, any nationalist aspirations) on the part of Socialists would merely chain them hopelessly to a *bourgeoisie* itself politically impotent. In any case, nationalism was something which the middle classes would always be able to propagate more successfully than Socialists. Most important, however, was the fact that if the middle classes had finally to choose between getting Socialist support in order to gather momentum for a campaign for the independence of Poland, or abandoning this demand in order to co-operate with the autocracy against the spectre of social revolution, they would always plump for the latter.

At times the pamphlet's argument seems ingenuous, even naïve. Rosa overstated her case in trying to have the best of both worlds. Thus she argued that the working class, theoretically powerful enough to bring about the collapse of the Tsarist government, or even to overthrow the order of society, was actually *unable* to achieve national independence. 'History shows that the workers by their own hands and against the class opposition of the *bourgeoisie*, have never achieved national independence but . . . have [for instance] wrung out a constitution, first with the help of the *bourgeoisie* and then alone.'[1] The *bourgeoisie* thus had to play a double, even contradictory, role to satisfy Rosa, supporting nationalism in order to mislead and vitiate Socialism, but opposing it if the workers hoped to achieve Socialism through a programme of self-determination. The latter proposition already foreshadowed the later economic theory which postulated that Polish capitalists were better off within the Russian empire and knew it. Straight national aspirations were arbitrarily reduced to being only the desire of one small class, the confused *petite bourgeoisie!* This class was to serve Rosa as a convenient dialectical rubbish bin for many inconvenient or abstract absurdities in the future.

Whether one accepts it or not, the case against the resuscitation of Poland deserves careful consideration. In order to make her point, Rosa Luxemburg did not confine the argument either to Poland or the arena of debate to Polish Socialists. Part of the policy of combating the PPS, on the international plane, was to contrast its exclusively 'national' orientation with the virtuously international policy of her own party. The 'national–international' antithesis was a weapon of variable efficacy—but it was more than just a tactical trick; the same argument was to be raised against the leadership of the German SPD during the First World War.

This problem, with all the pent-up emotions behind it, burst like a bomb at the next International Socialist congress, due to meet in London on 17 July 1896 for its usual purpose of reviewing and discussing

---

[1] Op. cit., p. 53.

international progress. The PPS prepared a resolution well in advance asking the congress to set the stamp of its approval on Polish independence as a 'necessary political demand for the Polish and indeed the entire international proletariat'.[1] The proposed resolution was given the widest publicity in the PPS press. The Polish committee in London worked hard in public and behind the scenes to ensure that the nefarious activities of the Zürich group would now be crushed once and for all. It could not afford to leave Rosa Luxemburg's *Niepodległa Polska i sprawa robotnicza* unanswered; yet at the same time it was important for the PPS to appear as the injured party—badly done by rather than doing. Simultaneously with the secret assault on the SDKP inside the boundaries of Polish Socialism, the PPS leaders used their connections in the Second International to present an innocent and purely defensive face. They succeeded admirably. 'I am afraid that the unnecessary but *certainly harmless* Polish [PPS] resolution for London will certainly be blown up into quite an affair by her [RL].'[2] Victor Adler's view was shared by most of the International's 'establishment'; Plekhanov and his group, particularly, were pledged to unequivocal support of the PPS.[3]

The offensive was not confined to political polemics. Warszawski was singled out for personal indictment—as a secret agent of the Russian police; and conveniently Marcin Kasprzak, who had recently escaped from Poland, was also available to be smeared as an individual of dubious reputation and honesty. Such accusations against individuals recurred with miserable regularity in the Russian and Polish movements; out of the vast armoury available to these hardened champions of personal abuse, the accusation of working for the Okhrana was the nastiest and most destructive.[4] The PPS leadership could be well

---

[1] Reprinted in *NZ*, 1895–6, Vol. II, p. 461, Cf. S. Häcker, 'Der Sozialismus in Polen', *NZ*, ibid., p. 327.

[2] Victor Adler to Karl Kautsky, 13 May 1896, in Victor Adler, *Briefwechsel mit August Bebel und Karl Kautsky*, Vienna 1954, p. 207 (my italics).

[3] *Perepiska G. V. Plekhanova i P. B. Akselroda*, Moscow 1925, Vol. I, p. 156. See also the attempt to embroil the distinguished Antonio Labriola and through him the Spaniards and others: 'Correspondence B. A. Jędrzejowski–A. Labriola 1895–7', in *Annali dell' Istituto G. Feltrinelli*, 1960, pp. 226–63.

[4] For further accusations against Kasprzak, see below, p. 115. The meaningless buzz of this particular type of accusation effectively deafened everyone to the occasional reality. Exposures like Azev's in 1908 caused considerable shock (see Rosa Luxemburg's article in *Vorwärts*, 27 January 1909). Lenin indeed seemed remarkably impervious. He belittled the accusations against his friend Zhitomirskii in 1912 and took no notice when Malinovskii, one of his most trusted lieutenants, was similarly accused by his Menshevik opponents in 1914—though in both cases the accusation happened to be only too true. Suspicious as Lenin normally was, this apparently was too common a slander for him to take seriously every time.

satisfied with its preparations for a final reckoning with its opponents at the congress. But Rosa Luxemburg reacted with speed and precision. Shaped now for a more sophisticated and international readership, the arguments of her Polish pamphlet were repeated in a series of articles in *Neue Zeit* and *Critica Sociale*, the chief theoretical organs of the German and Italian Socialist parties.[1] The International as a whole and the German and Austrian parties in particular were now put on notice that the alleged objectionable nationalistic tendencies of the PPS were not confined to an incomprehensible squabble in the bosom of distant Russia, but were affecting and destroying the precious unity of theory and organization of the two great parties. For Polish nationalism was not an alternative Socialist policy at all, but the negation of one; chameleon-like, the PPS, according to Rosa, wore Socialist colours merely as a disguise in order to undermine the authority of the German leadership over the gullible unsophisticated Polish masses.

At the same time the SDKP leadership had to refute the personal accusations against Warszawski and Kasprzak. The accusation against the former was handed over to a committee of investigation, under the chairmanship of the impeccable and ancient Russian revolutionary Peter Lavrov, which after a few sessions cleared him completely—with Rosa personally importuning the old man.[2] The case of Kasprzak was more difficult since so little was really known about him. He was an old-fashioned type of revolutionary conspirator, a practical man with pistol and printing press, without any great intellectual claims—but a leader none the less. He had been Rosa's guide and mentor in the early Warsaw days, and though they were never personal friends she described him as 'a most intimate party colleague' and later worked closely with him in Germany. In order to avoid imprisonment or exile, he had feigned madness and been confined in a Warsaw lunatic asylum from which he managed to escape. On arrival in Germany he had been promptly arrested by the German police who then negotiated with the Russian

---

[1] 'Neue Strömungen in der polnischen sozialistischen Bewegung in Deutschland und Österreich' (New tendencies in the Polish Socialist Movement in Germany and Austria), *NZ*, 1895–6, Vol. II, pp. 176 ff., 206 ff.; 'Der Sozialpatriotismus in Polen' (Social patriotism in Poland), *NZ*, 1895–6, Vol. II, pp. 459 ff. The Italian one is 'La questione polacca al congresso internazionale di Londra', *Critica Sociale*, No. 14, 16 July 1896. The Italians, like all other outsiders, confessed to ignorance about Polish matters. But Turati, the editor of *Critica Sociale*, 'was impressed by Rosa Luxemburg's weighty arguments'; besides, 'we attach weight to Rosa Luxemburg's letters, in view of the fact that these appeared in *NZ*, i.e. the mouthpiece of scientific Socialism, which represents *the official opinion of German Social Democracy.*' Labriola notwithstanding, the Italians had been won for Rosa! *Annali*, op. cit., pp. 248, 244.

[2] Frölich, p. 52. For Rosa's own interview with Lavrov, who got real pleasure out of current disputes among the Russian émigrés, see *Z Pola Walki*, 1930, Nos. 9/10. pp. 145–6.

authorities with a view to his extradition. The SDKP leadership appealed to prominent German Social Democrats on his behalf, while the PPS attempted to scotch such intervention with the accusation that Kasprzak was an Okhrana spy. Rosa Luxemburg was active in Switzerland and appealed among others to Seidel to use his many German friendships and connections.[1] It was through this correspondence that an intimate friendship blossomed in the next few years.

On 12 July, *en route* for the congress five days later, Rosa descended on Paris like a hurricane—to finish off the next two numbers of *Sprawa Robotnicza*; to whip up local Poles like Warszawski and her friend Cezaryna Wojnarowska; above all, to get support for her own SDKP congress resolution and pledges against that of the PPS. She was very cheered by her reception. Allemane and Vaillant more or less promised support—and, more important, hoped to get that of Jaurès; Bernstein was reputed to be sympathetic; even Plekhanov was suspected of using his colleague Gurvich (Dan) to send an offer of reconciliation and co-operation with the Russian congress delegation.[2] This suggestion was contemptuously refused. Co-operation with Parvus and John Mill was also flourishing. Altogether Rosa felt much more self-confident than during the last Paris visit—and immediately behaved much more arrogantly: Wojnarowska was 'mad' because she queried Rosa's distribution of mandates; Krichevskii an ugly rag (*triapka*) who would come to a bad end (*shvartzem sof*) because he was too sick and too unconcerned either to fight or to write; even Jogiches was for once roundly abused: 'You dealt superbly with [our delegation's] report! You had a whole week and only now you begin to scratch about for material. . . . You should be ashamed of yourself; at least this one thing you could have arranged without me.'[3]

Rosa Luxemburg's activities and articles in *Neue Zeit* caused a storm. Plekhanov took it upon himself to reply personally on behalf of the PPS.[4] Karl Kautsky, the editor of *Neue Zeit*, who had agreed to publish the articles in view of their high standard and closely reasoned argument, disagreed with the conclusions and invested the debate with his own very considerable prestige by answering Rosa Luxemburg at length.[5] He asserted the revolutionary, anti-Tsarist potential of the fight for Polish independence, and threw in for good measure all the authority of

[1] See Seidel letters, *Z Pola Walki*, 1959, No. 1(5), pp. 66–7, dated 21 October 1895. Kasprzak's personality and exploits resemble those of Kamo (Ter-Petrosian), the Bolshevik Robin Hood. They even looked alike.

[2] Jogiches letters, *Z Pola Walki*, 1930, Nos. 9/10, pp. 153 ff. Rosa's suspicion that Dan's letter (reproduced in *Z Pola Walki*) was inspired by Plekhanov may have been unjustified. Plekhanov had earlier reported to Engels that it was Rosa who wanted to get closer to the Russians. And immediately after the congress he attacked her again in print.

[3] *Z Pola Walki*, ibid., p. 160. [4] *Vorwärts* 23 July 1896.

[5] 'Finis Poloniae', *NZ*, 1895–6, Vol. II, pp. 484, 513 ff.

Marx's and Engels's own views, which he had at his finger tips. He solemnly warned that opposition to this view could only give active assistance to the Poles' present oppressors, the Russian autocracy. The most violent reactions, however, came from the members of the PPS. *Naprzód* (Forward) reviewed her first article with contemptuous regret that 'any serious German paper should be taken in by Miss Rosa . . . who has even managed to bluff the good Swiss into believing that she represents somebody or something in Poland'.[1] Berfus, one of the leaders of the PPS organization in Germany, was offered space in the official German party paper to reply.[2] The debate went on right up to the eve of the International congress, with Rosa Luxemburg insisting on the right to reply both in *Vorwärts* and in *Neue Zeit*.[3]

At the congress itself she led the SDKP delegation, confronted by a powerful PPS group under the leadership of its emergent 'strong man', Józef Piłsudski. To make doubly sure that there would be no unpleasant surprises about mandates, she came fortified with two additional German mandates which were beyond anyone's challenge.[4] These had been obtained from under the noses of the German leadership; the provincial SPD leadership in Silesia was becoming acutely conscious of the activities of the local PPS organizations and appreciated the incidental services of Rosa Luxemburg's policy in keeping the Poles faithful to the SPD organization. But to most of the leaders of the Second International she was merely a quarrelsome young woman who insisted on pitting her considerable wits against wiser and better heads. Victor Adler, who led the Austrian delegation, viewed her existence and activities with unmasked hostility, from which he was never to deviate one iota. He considered her articles ill-timed and tactless:

She is trying to do our thinking for us [*Sie zerbricht sich unseren Kopf*]. . . . Above all I am scared of the effect on our Daszynski. *He* himself is *very* sensible, but has to deal with his—as we with our—lunatics. . . . I implore you to send me whatever more you get in before setting it in print—not for my comments, but to enable me to calm things down, and make up for all the damage this doctrinaire goose has caused us. To hell with all these refugees. . . .[5]

Wilhelm Liebknecht, the august co-chairman of the German party, had already expressed his disapproval in a strongly worded private letter, and entered the public debate shortly after the congress with a polemical article against her in *Vorwärts*.[6] Daszyński was incensed by the report on

---

[1] *Naprzód*, No. 20, 14 May 1896.   [2] *Vorwärts*, 15, 17 July 1896.
[3] *Vorwärts*, 25 July 1896, Supplement No. 2.
[4] *Volkswacht*, Breslau, 1 June and 21 July 1896; *Vorwärts*, 19 July 1896. See also *Z Pola Walki*, 1930, Nos. 9/10, p. 159.
[5] Victor Adler to Karl Kautsky, 13 May 1896, in Victor Adler, *Briefwechsel mit August Bebel und Karl Kautsky*, Vienna 1954, p. 207.
[6] For his letter, see Frölich, p. 53 and below, p. 66; for the polemic, see *Vorwärts*, 11 November 1896.

Socialist activities in Poland with which the SDKP had again insisted on belabouring the congress, and characterized Rosa as 'a pedantic and quarrelsome person with a mechanistic interpretation of Marxism'.[1]

With so much personal opposition, it looked as though Rosa would have a rough passage at the congress. Even some of her immediate party friends were reluctant to follow her into a head-on conflict with all recognized authority, and partially dissociated themselves from her intransigent attitudes—at least in private. Marchlewski, who was himself breaking into the hallowed pages of *Neue Zeit*, told Kautsky that his material should not be confused with the polemical shafts of Rosa Luxemburg:

My work is not concerned with striking attitudes on the 'Polish question'. This will have to be solved by our Polish workers in Warsaw and Łódź on their own behalf, and one can only hope that, to the dismay of the émigrés, this will happen soon. . . . I can imagine that the contribution of at least one of my Polish colleagues has made you wonder exactly what you let yourself in for when you agreed to tackle the Polish question in your paper.[2]

Yet, surprisingly, honours were remarkably even between the two Polish parties—or rather between Rosa Luxemburg and the PPS. She unexpectedly whipped out a motion opposing that of the PPS, in which the aim of national independence was specifically denied as valid for any Socialist programme. With the help of a furious personal onslaught on Rosa Luxemburg the PPS delegation succeeded in persuading the congress to reject it. To overcome stalemate, George Lansbury, on behalf of the congress commission charged with this intractable dispute, asked the congress to declare that

it supports the right to complete self-determination of all nations and sympathizes with the workers of all countries presently suffering under the yoke of military, national or other despotism. It invites the workers of all these countries to enter the ranks of class-conscious workers of the whole world, in order to fight with them for the overthrow of international capitalism and the attainment of the aims of international Social Democracy.

The congress gladly adopted this compromise which expressed the right of all nations to self-determination but made no particular mention of Poland either as an example or as a specially deserving case.[3] Naturally Rosa Luxemburg's right to appear, and the whole question of the SDKP's existence as a separate member of the International, was also duly

---

[1] Frölich, p. 53. For the report, see *Bericht an den Internationalen Sozialistischen Arbeiter- und Gewerkschaftskongress in London über die Sozialdemokratische Bewegung in Russisch-Polen 1893–6*, submitted by . . . *Sprawa Robotnicza* . . . and its delegates . . .Zürich (?) 1896.

[2] Julian Marchlewski to Karl Kautsky, 12 December 1896. IISH Archives, D XVI, 390.

[3] *Verhandlungen und Beschlüsse, Internationaler Sozialistischer* . . . *Kongress zu London*, 27 July–1 August 1896, p. 18.

challenged, but upheld by the congress. Right or wrong about nationalism, Rosa was established as a noteworthy contributor to the mainstream of Socialist ideas. Her party had earned its spurs—though as far as the International was concerned, it is probable that it found more recognition and acceptance as the projection of Rosa Luxemburg than as the vehicle which had sent her to the congress.

Naturally the congress decision on self-determination was a blow. Rosa Luxemburg was perfectly genuine in believing in the importance of the International, not merely as a confederate gathering of autonomous parties, but as a supreme law-making body for that growing section of the world which represented Socialism and the future.[1] This body had now enacted 'legislation' directly contrary to her own beliefs. She tried at various times, but without much conviction, to deflect and reinterpret the purpose of the congress resolution; she claimed that what the London congress meant was not so much agitation for self-determination under existing conditions of capitalism, but the hope of its achievement after the world-wide social revolution had taken place.[2] This, of course, was no more than a piece of cynical sophistry to which even Rosa Luxemburg was liable at times; for she herself frequently pointed out that under Socialist conditions self-determination was unnecessary.

The argument did not, of course, end with the 1896 congress; no argument about Socialism was ever ended by any congress until Stalin turned the secret police into party congress bailiffs for ideas as much as for men. Rosa Luxemburg had already transformed the arguments about self-determination from a purely Polish context into an organizational question for the German and Austrian Social-Democratic parties. Now she broadened the argument still further. Having tried to show that Russia was no longer the hopeless bastion of reaction, to be weakened in every possible way, Rosa Luxemburg completed the argument by showing that one of the bastions of defence against aggressive Russia—a viable Turkish state—was nothing but an illusion. Far from being artificially maintained, it and not Russia should be pressed to disintegration. The dead weight of Turkish rule was even incapable of *generating* capitalism—and thus, ultimately, Socialism; the

---

[1] The International as the government of her proletarian fatherland was the necessary corollary of her anti-nationalism. For a detailed examination of this view, see below, Appendix: The National Question.

[2] Explanatory references to the congress resolution are scattered throughout her Polish writing. The most comprehensive reinterpretation of the resolution into a 'particular method of by-passing the whole question' is in 'The question of nationality and autonomy', *Przeglad Socjaldemokratyczny*, No. 6, August 1908. See also below, Appendix: The National Question. The PPS, too, maintained that the whole resolution was the product of an unexpected change of agenda in an unrepresentative committee! *Annali*, op. cit., p. 255.

sooner it was destroyed and split up into its constituent national parts the better—and then this backward area might catch up with the normal processes of historical dialectic.[1] Turkey, then, was the exception that proved the rule. Nationalism, far from being a progressive modern factor, was merely the last resort for lonely fossilized pockets of resistance which history had passed by.

Responsible public opinion in the Second International took offence once more. Further polemics rained down on the daring author. Old Liebknecht again took up his pen, and so did the PPS—a whole team of PPS publicists worked in relays to deal with every one of Rosa Luxemburg's unpredictable appearances in print.[2] Rosa eagerly seized the chance to reply offered by the editors of *Sächsische Arbeiterzeitung*, the Dresden Socialist paper. She now had the distinction of being involved in public polemics not only with Kautsky but with Liebknecht as well.[3] She became known to a wider section of party workers in Germany than she realized; when she moved to Germany in 1898 she found that Rosa Luxemburg from Zürich was a familiar name to many officials in Saxony who had followed her argument with Liebknecht with sly sympathy, and ruefully agreed with her condemnation of separatist PPS tactics.

Though Rosa enjoyed these polemics, her friends were becoming anxious about the exposure to which this constant solo performance was leading. Leo Jogiches expressed his own doubts and those of party friends.[4] As we shall see, this unremitting opposition to self-determination, on which the SDKP increasingly relied to the exclusion of all else, was not by any means to the taste of all the members. One of them, Stanisław Trusiewicz, was the centre of a small group in Poland which began to dissent from the extreme attitudes of the leadership in exile.[5] Other voices were to be raised later. At the same time the limited opportunities of a Polish émigré movement were beginning to prove irksome to her. She longed for the chance to enter the main international field, or at least a movement with more scope than the SDKP. These articles in *Neue Zeit* and the continuing polemic in *Sächsische Arbeiterzeitung* and elsewhere, provided a launching platform for Rosa Luxemburg. The fact that she was at loggerheads with accepted opinion was

---

[1] 'Die nationalen Kämpfe in der Türkei und die Sozialdemokratie', *SAZ*, 8, 9, 10 October 1896.

[2] For Liebknecht, see *Vorwärts*, 11 November 1896; the PPS reply was given by Kazimierz Kelles-Krauz in a pamphlet in French entitled *Internationalistes!* a manuscript copy of which is in ZHP, Warsaw.

[3] *SAZ*, 25 November, 1 December 1896.

[4] Jogiches letters, *Z Pola Walki*, 1930, Nos. 9/10, p. 136.

[5] O. B. Szmidt, *Dokumenty*, Vol. I, pp. 177, 195, 230. For Trusiewicz's later dissents, see below, p. 346, note 2.

secondary; her views had been worth a detailed refutation by some of the most distinguished Socialists of the time.

From 1897 onwards a revival of Socialist fortunes took place throughout Russia. The Jewish organizations, the most developed and class-conscious section of the Russian proletariat, were united in the *Bund* in 1897, and a year later the Russians, shamed and galvanized by this event, created a united party of their own, the RSDRP.[1] Both Polish parties benefited from this resurgence. The SDKP, particularly, received an important reinforcement through the adherence of the Lithuanian Social Democrats under the leadership of Feliks Dzierżyński. This not only increased the membership substantially but provided the movement with one of its most powerful and active personalities. In 1898 Dzierżyński escaped from Siberian exile and returned home to Lithuania. The scene there mirrored that in Poland: two parties, one with Polish nationalist tendencies led by Koczan-Morawski, the other Trusiewicz's anti-nationalist Social-Democratic party. Both men desired fusion with the SDKP and brought it about in December 1899. Trusiewicz had already exerted some influence within the SDKP.[2] The new party now took the name of the Social Democracy of the Kingdom of Poland and Lithuania, SDKPiL for short.

Immediately after the fusion, Dzierżyński moved to Warsaw where he began to rebuild the almost defunct SDKP organization. Although he was soon arrested again, his organizational efforts continued to prosper. By 1900 the SDKPiL had spread to most major industrial cities of Poland and to the Dąbrowa coal-mining area, though its membership was still predominantly artisan rather than industrial.[3] Now that a Russian party had finally come into being, the SDKPiL emphasized the need for close collaboration with it and began to discuss the possibility of fusion. This, as much as any question of Polish independence, set it apart from the PPS at this time; the latter had by the turn of the century become increasingly anti-Russian in a Socialist as well as a national context. We shall see how the aspirations of the SDKPiL were translated into concrete efforts at unity with the Russian party.[4]

This growth of the SDKPiL added height to Rosa Luxemburg's stature. Though she still spoke only for a small minority, she had battled through to respectability, and was no longer the isolated and

---

[1] For the effects of the formation of the *Bund* on the creation of the RSDRP and their early relationship, see H. Shukman, *The Relations between the Jewish Bund and the RSDRP 1897–1903*, Oxford doctoral thesis (1960) soon due for publication.

[2] He used the pseudonym Zalewski, under which he was more generally known. 'Lithuanian' at that period carried geographical rather than ethnical connotations.

[3] Dziewanowski, *Communist Party*, p. 27.   [4] See below, pp. 184–192.

remote figure of two years ago.[1] Contributions from her pen could safely be solicited. The *Bund* asked her for articles and in 1899 reprinted her article in *Neue Zeit*.[2]

In the spring of 1897 she presented her thesis to the University of Zürich for the advanced degree of Doctor of Law. Its title was *The Industrial Development of Poland*.[3] Using hitherto unknown sources, she analysed the growth of Polish industry in the nineteenth century. It was indeed the first serious economic analysis on this subject.[4] She showed that, economically speaking, Russian Poland had become an integral part of the Russian empire, that the economic growth of Poland could not have taken place without the substantial Russian market, and that the economy of Poland made no sense in any other context. The argument was Marxist only by implication; its aim, to prove in economic terms what she had already argued politically and dialectically, namely, that any attempt to prise Russian Poland loose from the Russian empire and join it to the other occupied areas of Poland to form a Polish national or linguistic state was a negation of all development and progress for the last fifty years. The thesis served her and others as an important reservoir of evidence against the political demands of Polish nationalism. At that time it was an unusual distinction for a thesis on a subject other than the natural sciences to be published, and research students today can still obtain the benefit of an original piece of economic history, the value of which has not dated or deteriorated. It was the first of Rosa Luxemburg's major economic works, and already showed her particular gift for enlivening accurate economic history with striking illustrations—a combination of statistics and social imagery which was peculiarly hers. She hoped to use the work as a basis for a general history of Poland, on which she worked intermittently throughout her life but which she never completed and of which no traces remain.

At about this time the desire to capitalize on her growing reputation in a movement with more scope than the émigré leadership of the SDKPiL was finally transformed into a definite decision to move to Germany. Kautsky, the editor of the important *Neue Zeit*, looked to her as a regular

---

[1] John Mill, *Pionirn un Boier*, Vol. II, p. 250.

[2] 'Der sozialism en Peulen', *Der Yiddishe Arbeter*, No. 8, December 1899. See also 'Diskussie vegen unabhengikeit fun Peulen', ibid., No. 13, 1902.

[3] Her official degree was Doctor Juris Publici et Rerum Cameralium. The thesis was published (Leipzig 1898) under the title *Die industrielle Entwicklung Polens*. Information from state archives of the Canton of Zürich, reference U 105 b. 4.

[4] According to Adolf Warszawski, it was Rosa's researches in the Czartoryski Library in Paris and the Bibliothèque Nationale during the years 1894–5 that revealed an eighteenth-century Polish echo of the writing of the physiocrats in France. Marchlewski accepted her suggestion of this as a suitable subject for his own doctorate, qualifying with the thesis *Physiokratismus im alten Polen*, Zürich 1896.

correspondent on Polish affairs—preferably on less delicate problems than Polish independence.[1] The friendship with Robert and Mathilde Seidel introduced her personally to a wider German circle. Robert Seidel had emigrated to Zürich to escape a charge of sedition and had remained after the end of the anti-Socialist legislation partly because the indictment had never been withdrawn and also because of his growing absorption into the Swiss Socialist movement. He had become editor of the important Zürich Socialist paper, *Arbeiterstimme*, to which Rosa then became a contributor on Polish questions; in return, she helped him with his literary work—Seidel had artistic pretensions—and was a frequent and welcome visitor at the Seidel house.[2] It was no doubt partly Seidel's influence which decided her to go to Germany.

Her German had much improved by this time. She spoke fluently, though some of her early public appearances in Zürich had not been too successful since she tended to get excited and nervous.[3] Gradually she overcame this, but for some years remained more convincing in print than at a political rally and always preferred to write German rather than to speak it. Though not as a rule a diffident person, doubts about the correctness of her German continued to beset her for the rest of her life, in spite of the reassurance of friends and critics.[4]

Nevertheless, a move to Germany was a big step and Jogiches for one could not bring himself to advise her to go. She would necessarily become absorbed in German affairs and Polish Socialism would lose its best brain.[5] Besides, he was frankly jealous. He was not able to write himself into a state of euphoria, in fact he was hardly able to write at all, and even proof-reading for Rosa caused him hours of agony—and produced 'linguistic boa-constrictors'. He was an unhappy and intermittent student, who never took his degree. But all technical considerations apart, he feared to lose Rosa on his own account as well as that of the Polish movement. Her reports of the attention of men like Parvus, Bruhns (party secretary in Breslau), and Schönlank caused him agony. We do not know if he really tried to prevent her from going, but we do know that he disliked it. There were actually telling party reasons for her departure, on which she played hard: the rescue of the Poles in

---

[1] See her article on the middle classes in Poland in *NZ*, 1897–8, Vol. I, p. 164.

[2] For Seidel, see *Z Pola Walki*, 1959, No. 1(5), pp. 65–6 (Introduction). Seidel was a figure of some importance in the Swiss party and had extensive contacts in Italy, Rumania, Croatia, and Hungary. Probably because of these articles, Frölich claimed that Rosa Luxemburg 'was active in the Swiss working-class movement', of which there is, however, no evidence at all (p. 54). The Swiss government would not have permitted it, and Rosa herself repeatedly expressed ignorance of Swiss Socialist affairs in later years.

[3] John Mill, *Pionirn un Boier*, Vol. I, p. 175.

[4] *Letters to Karl and Luise Kautsky*, Introduction, p. 18. One suspects that some of this diffidence was a form of false modesty.

[5] Frölich, p. 56.

Silesia and Poznań from the clutches of the PPS, and the need to gain German sympathy for their cause. But these two were too close for effective pretence. The ambition which he feared was also her main propellent. She knew she could make a career in Germany—she knew it and would prove it, to the grey heads of the International, to the PPS, and to him. There was no need to prove it to herself.

Meantime, there was the difficulty of obtaining a residential permit. This was a crucial problem for Socialists. To most of the German provincial authorities Socialists were little better than criminals, and active foreign ones were not entitled to the courtesies customary in those days for resident foreigners. The only solution—again on advice from the Seidels—was marriage to a German national, and so Rosa hatched a plot with one of her friends, the Polish wife of Karl Lübeck, another German expatriate. Old Lübeck had fallen on evil days, a cripple who had to trade on old comradeships to place his writing in the German party press. Rosa helped him in this and probably wrote a number of his pieces. Her particular friendship was with Olympia Lübeck who was the exact opposite of her husband: young, thoroughly Bohemian—especially in matters of money.[1] Serious Germans had never been able to bring themselves to approve of Olympia Lübeck's antics. While still émigrés both Kautsky and Bernstein had several times lent their own scarce money to a starving family, only to find Olympia fraudulently converting these starvation loans to artistic purposes—a visit to a theatre, for instance, with a whole group of friends. The two women had been friends since 1890. Olympia helped to solve Rosa's problem by providing a suitable young man—her own son, Gustav. He was serious, undistinguished, and did not approve of the idea. He had already, in 1895, acted as a post office for communications between Rosa in Paris and Leo Jogiches in the East—and been roundly abused for his pains. He knew all about their relationship, and considered his intended role as fictional husband undignified and unlikely to be peaceful. But the whole family felt under an obligation to Rosa for the long hours she had put in with old Lübeck; in any case, his mother decided that a career as Rosa's husband was better than anything he was likely to achieve on his own account.[2] No objections could prevail against her breezy insistence, and the marriage took place in the spring of 1897 in Basle, shortly after the completion of Rosa's thesis.[3] The young couple parted company at once on the doorstep of the registry office. But it took Rosa another five years to obtain a divorce. She always felt a certain amount of good-natured contempt for her

[1] For the Lübecks see Karl Kautsky, *Erinnerungen und Erörterungen Materials for an Autobiography*, Amsterdam 1960, p. 447.
[2] Karl Kautsky, ibid., p. 445.
[3] Copy of the marriage certificate is in ZHP, Warsaw. See facsimile opposite p. 95.

husband, though in the end she was very relieved to be rid of him. 'Typical Lübeck' became a synonym for carelessness and unreliability. Even to complete the divorce, the Seidels had to be brought in to supervise and agitate, since Gustav proved incapable of dealing with any formalities on his own. None the less, Rosa always got a certain amount of amusement from her married name and gleefully signed hotel registers and postcards with a flourish as 'Frau Gustav Lübeck'.

After the formalities were complete, Rosa paid a last long visit to Paris in May 1897—probably with Leo Jogiches. She renewed contact there with her Russian friends who were urgently engaged on the preparations for the forthcoming congress of the Russian party. More important for the future, however, was her contact with prominent French Socialists. The Paris she had originally disliked, consisting as it did of noise, smoke, and distance—and far too many Poles—now offered its traditional seduction for the first time.[1] Rosa Luxemburg now got to know Jaurès, Jules Guesde, and Édouard Vaillant better. Jaurès she admired, Jules Guesde was an object of somewhat cold esteem and impersonal approval; it was Édouard Vaillant with whom she became particularly friendly.[2]

On 20 May 1898 she moved to Berlin—strange, friendless city with straight streets and stiff-backed people. She disliked the place from the moment she arrived; it suddenly made Zürich seem curiously comfortable and attractive. But these sentimental glances back into the past were unimportant compared with the vistas which now opened before her—serious Socialism in a cold climate. With her departure from Zürich, a new chapter opened in Rosa Luxemburg's career, and it was with German Socialism that she was to be primarily associated for the next twenty years. As luck would have it, the moment of her arrival in Germany coincided with a major thunderstorm in the German party, which shook the very foundations of its accepted ideology.

[1] Jogiches letters, *Z Pola Walki*, 1930, Nos. 9-10, pp. 111, 116. The early comments on Paris resemble the later ones on Berlin—the comments of a Swiss country lass!—but the judgement on people differed: Paris was full of beautiful women, Berlin of stiff-backed Prussians (see below, p. 85). But we know few details about her stay in Paris.

[2] *Letters to Karl and Luise Kautsky*, p. 176, dated 27 December 1915, just after Vaillant's death.

IV

FIRST BATTLES IN A NEW ARENA

1898–1899

THE Germany Rosa Luxemburg entered in 1898 was two different things: to a resident it was a new society; to a Socialist an old battle-field. Every Socialist had this bifocal vision of his own society—and attempted, to the best of his ability, to reduce the double vision to a single, consistent view. Before examining Rosa Luxemburg's particular effort, however, we must look at these two aspects objectively and in turn.

To the rest of the world, and especially to most of its own citizens, the German Reich at the turn of the century was the economic and political bastion of continental Europe. Bismarck had created, in the eyes of his contemporaries, a strong, rich, and growing empire out of a collection of German-speaking princely states. As little as forty years earlier, these had been pawns on the political chess-board of a Europe dominated for two centuries by the notion of a balance of power. The disciplined and ambitious Prussia of Frederick the Great had given way to a weak and vacillating monarchy, a mere appendage of Hapsburg conservatism. To its everlasting indignity—an indignity that both Conservatives and Socialists were unwilling and unable to forget and from which they drew their respective inspiration—Prussia, in 1849, had to be rescued by the Russian Tsar from its own abortive revolution, the belated attempt to establish democracy. Pregnant with revolution, Prussia's back had been stiffened with the rusty iron of Nicholas I's autocracy; by supporting the Prussian king, he had succeeded in stifling the revolution throughout Germany. Among other things, the events of 1848–9 had stimulated Karl Marx into taking up his dominant attitude of political disdain for German liberalism. Within fifteen years, however, Bismarck had changed all this. Austria had been evicted from the German concert and had to turn south and east to the Balkans for a substitute sphere of economic and political influence. French hegemony over western Germany and the revived pretensions of a Napoleon on the French imperial throne were decisively defeated in 1871. More import-ant still, the impetus for German unity, which had originally come from the Liberals and had in 1848 found expression in the hope of a demo-cratic, equal, and spontaneous fusion of all the various states of Germany, had been contemptuously vitiated and trounced by Bismarck. He had made an almost reluctant King of Prussia into the Emperor of Germany; with the support of all but the extreme and lunatic fringe of Prussian Conservatives, Bismarck had created German unity without the support of the Liberals and on his own terms—permanent Prussian hegemony in the new empire. The Liberals could either accept the situation and join the band-wagon of triumphant German unity, or they could go into permanent and ineffectual opposition against the illiberal domination of Prussia and Prussian ideas. They could in turn be either Nationalists or Liberals—in the event the party name, National Liberals, became the embodiment of a myth—but they could not be both. They plumped for Nationalism and Bismarck. Over the years, they tried spasmodically to push the Reich government in the direction of traditional Liberalism— free trade and more government support for the interests of the growing industrial and commercial community against the landed gentry, the Junkers. But it was hesitant and hopeless. It meant using the Reich government against that of Prussia, a patent impossibility. In this respect the Social Democrats saw clearly; whatever the trimmings, the Reich government could never act against the interests of Prussia, its backbone and most powerful constituent.

Apart from Conservatives and National Liberals, the bourgeois political spectrum of the German empire included a large Catholic (Centre) party, the historic counterweight of the new Reich's west and south against the Protestants of the north and east. Farther left was a group of small progressive parties which, as a result of the schizophrenia of the National Liberals, pre-empted the whole oppositional tendencies of the small man in a modern industrial society still encased in the structure of semi-feudal Prussia. Socially speaking, the Progressives were not merely *petit-bourgeois*, but radical in the French and English sense: the expression of essentially political and economic rather than social aspirations.

But the power of all these parties, as distinct from the number of their seats in the *Reichstag*, was limited. The legislature was only slightly more necessary for the conduct of government business than the Elizabethan House of Commons. The only legislative control was exercised through the budget, and then merely in the raising, not the spending, of revenue. From 1870 right through to 1914 Conservatives repeatedly pointed out that the Emperor could, at any time, send along an officer and ten men to disperse this rabble of self-important legislators, and that the best way of demonstrating his rights and powers was to do it. The *Reichstag* was there to facilitate government business, not to criticize or obstruct it.

In any case, the Reich government found it fairly simple to manipulate party differences in such a way that a grouping could always be found to support whatever policy the government was then putting forward:

either by combining Conservatives with National Liberals and Progressives against the Centre, or through a Conservative–Centre block
against the others. It would be quite wrong to equate German parliamentary life with that of contemporary England, even though the
Reichstag was elected by universal suffrage and the British House of
Commons was not. The Upper House of the German parliament, the
federal *Bundesrat*, was at all times a conservative factor. Its federal
structure ensured, as with the Senate in America, disproportionate
representation of the smallest and most conservative areas against the
populous urban centres. Moreover, many aspects of sovereignty
remained in the hands of the provincial governments. The system of
election to most provincial legislatures was much less democratic than
for the *Reichstag*, with the result that the provincial legislatures were
much more conservative than the *Reichstag* itself. Members of the
Reich *Bundesrat* were not appointed by the provincial legislatures but
by the provincial governments whose voice they represented at the
centre, and who, if anything, were more conservative still. Probably,
with its universally elected *Reichstag*, Germany looked much more
democratic than it really was; subsequent history has shown, as it often
does, that the realities of power worked against the constitution and the
apparent structure of institutions created by it.

By 1900 the course of imperial German history was becoming
established in a new pattern. The immediate boom after the Franco-
Prussian War had been followed by a crisis, as a result of which the
anti-Socialist laws had been passed. But the economy soon recovered;
in spite of Bismarck's departure and the end of the special legislation
against Social Democracy, Germany prospered politically and economically. It was a time of gradual but continuous boom throughout the
world, and there was a general atmosphere of stability and confidence.
Germany had been a latecomer into the colonial field, and had not
obtained what was considered to be her proper share. Bismarck had not
been interested in a forward-looking colonial policy; indeed, towards
the end of his career, he had tried to call a halt to the extension of
German colonial interests and the expansion of Germany's international
commitments, which he considered a rival to her primary European
concerns. Such restraint, however, did not suit William II, heir to a
vigorous, muscle-flexing empire. After Bismarck had gone, the German
government under the particular inspiration of the Emperor clearly
announced its intention of obtaining its proper share in all fields of
international activity, colonial possessions, naval as well as military
power, and a share in the minding of international business as befitted a
great European power, irrespective of whether its direct interests were
concerned or not.

Underneath all this political activity and economic progress, there had grown, like an enormous mushroom bed in the damp of a neglected cellar, the organized proliferation of Social Democracy. After 1890, when its activities were legal once more, the Social-Democratic Party increased by leaps and bounds, both as a directly political organization and through the development of its industrial branch, the Free Trade Unions.[1] Unlike England, where trade unionism preceded political Socialism by many years (without taking into account the much neglected false start of political agitation between 1820 and 1840) and deliberately created the Labour Party at the end of the century, German trade unionism was the creature of the political party and was never allowed to forget it.

The SPD had been a fusion of two trends in German working-class organization. One was that of Lassalle, which had purely political aims and had already appeared as a marginal force on the political horizon in the early 1860s. From this side came the tradition of political activity *within* the framework of the middle-class state; the need for representation and influence within the organs of state power. The other trend was Marxist and had been nurtured by Marx and Engels from the days of the First International and through the period following its collapse. The fusion between the two wings had taken place at a congress at Gotha in 1875 when the programme adopted had been largely Marxist, though not entirely to Marx's liking. The progress of the new party had been followed closely by the great man in London, and after his death Engels kept in regular touch with the leaders until he died in 1895. Marx had mistrusted the revolutionary understanding and intentions of the German leaders, and often criticized them savagely in private (a fact that was to remain a closely guarded state secret among a few top SPD leaders until after the war).

The first party congress after the end of the anti-Socialist laws took place in Erfurt in 1891 and adopted an up-to-date programme of principles and tactics which was to serve the party until the outbreak of the First World War; it was reprinted with German solemnity as a foreword to the report of every annual SPD congress. The programme pledged support for the Marxist view of the inevitable collapse of capitalist society. It foresaw the establishment, within a distant but foreseeable future, of a Socialist society in its stead. It spoke of collapse, but out of deference to the laws and their eager agents of enforcement

---

[1] We shall refer to the German Social-Democratic Party hereafter as SPD (*Sozialdemokratische Partei Deutschlands*). The Social-Democratic trade unions were known as the *Freier Gewerkschaftsbund*. The word 'free' was to distinguish them from two other competing organizations, the Christian Trade Unions which had some affiliation with the Centre party, and the so-called Hirsch-Duncker or 'yellow' Unions which were a Liberal organization founded in the 1850s, middle-class inspired—a kind of 'strength through self-help' organization without political affiliation or interests, and as such soundly hated by the Social Democrats.

there was no mention of revolution. At the same time, however, the party accepted the need to protect working-class interests in the present, and laid down certain minimal aims for which the party must strive all the time. The programme thus divided into the final maximum and the more immediate minimum objectives: two separate aspects of one whole. The Erfurt programme was a synthesis of aims which were not necessarily the same and which might come into conflict at times, thus necessitating a choice.[1]

The theoretical part of the Erfurt programme was the work of Karl Kautsky, then the best-known Marxist theoretician in Germany and a familiar of the 'old man' himself. He provided the theoretical link between Marx and his own close friend Engels on the one hand and the SPD leadership of Wilhelm Liebknecht and August Bebel on the other. But though Engels approved of Kautsky and his work, he misunderstood its nature, and the gap between himself and it, between genuine revolutionary feelings and popularized revolutionary postulates in the abstract. The spread of Marxist dialectics was Kautsky's life's work, and though his friends Victor Adler and Eduard Bernstein for many years pointed out to him in private and even in public that this dialectic could not in practice be accommodated within the party's tactics, he himself never faced up to the 'empty juxtaposition' of final aim and present tactic which he had himself created in the Erfurt programme.[2] Nor did anyone else, at the time; there was much heated debate at Erfurt about the party's tactics, none about the adoption of Kautsky's draft of first principles, the chute down which all tactics had to roll.[3]

On the face of it, however, this two-legged stance was necessary, even inevitable, for political Social Democracy. Any political party representing a group interest in a society made up of various groups or classes had to look after immediate interests. This was especially true in a

[1] See Carl E. Schorske, *German Social Democracy 1905–17: The development of the Great Schism*, Cambridge (Mass.) 1955. This is the best modern history of the immediate pre-war period. For recent work on the foundation of the SPD, see Roger Morgan, *The German Social Democrats and the First International 1864–72*, Cambridge 1965.

[2] See Erich Matthias, 'Kautsky und der Kautskyanismus' in *Marxismusstudien* Second Series, Tübingen 1957, p. 160. This is the best short analysis of Kautsky and his ideas. For greater detail and a more communist view, see the more recent study by Ernesto Regioneri, 'Regarding the origins of Marxism in the Second International', *Critica Marxista*, No. 5/6, 1965, pp. 1–127.

[3] A few of the great men of the Second International passed into long-lived oblivion with Kautsky after the First World War, especially those who, like him, remained faithful to a purely theoretical necessity of revolution—neither abandoning the concept nor attempting to turn it into practice. For this small group—and only for them—Kautsky kept his reputation. Thus Daszyński wrote to him on 28 October 1924: 'In my eyes you belong to the paladins of the new era of proletarian liberation. . . .' (Kautsky Archives, IISH, D VII, 336.) Two of Rosa Luxemburg's great opponents thus clasped hands in their twilight of political oblivion.

society like imperial Germany where political parties could have no expectation of power and were no more than interest-groups, nudging the permanent power structure of imperial government in their direction. At the same time, however, the SPD was a party which maintained that this same society in which it operated was inevitably doomed in the long run; its aim was precisely to help bring about this doom and inherit all power. That was the maximum programme once more. In this respect the SPD was something quite new, just as Marxism as a political philosophy was new. There had previously been many groups and associations aiming to overthrow a régime, offering future blessings in place of present evils. But such parties had always arisen from an act of will by a group of people, large or small; they had claimed virtue, power, even the word of God; but none of them had ever been able to claim historical inevitability, or produce an all-embracing philosophy which made their activities objectively necessary, as well as subjectively desirable.

Nevertheless, a combination of day-to-day activity with the aim of total destruction of the very framework within which this activity took place was never an easy, straightforward policy in practice—especially not for a mass party observing the forms of democracy. Every step of the leadership was public property, freely discussed at any time and voted upon at least once a year. The novelty, the uniqueness, of the party was accepted, indeed it was a matter of pride and faith; but there was much less understanding of the secondary, often ill-defined, problems that went with it. The SPD was a confident party; history was on its side, and with the irresistible force of history went a clarity of vision vouchsafed only to the party of the rising proletariat. But this clarity was blinding as well as illuminating. It lit up the gulf between *bourgeoisie* and Socialists, between organized society and organized Social Democracy, between 'them' and 'us', so that no confusion was possible; but it obscured the political and personal consequences of such a black and white image of life. Looking out at the harsh bourgeois world from their tower of shining isolation, as remote and virtuous as the Holy Grail, Socialists began to think of themselves as generically different from other men, immune from their political failings and social diseases. The deliberate earthiness of Marx the politician—as opposed to the philosopher—became a kind of device to keep reality at bay; the direct, open tone of Socialist speech seemed to complement pure and idealistic processes of thought. Things were held to be valid and true because they were continually repeated. Confidence, and the possession of the historical dialectic, thus proved an obstacle to clear political thinking. When problems began to manifest themselves, the SPD was ill-equipped to deal with them.

The isolation of the party was at the same time self-imposed, on principle, and forced on it by society. The attempt up to 1890 to legislate the SPD off the political map was not repeated, though the idea and certainly the wish spasmodically occurred to the imperial government and its conservative supporters. But the Emperor, who boasted of his personal ability to deal with the Socialist menace, always preserved a particular dislike for its political manifestation, the SPD. In the eyes of the comfortable and respectable citizen of the German empire, loyal to the imperial promise of a German place in the sun, the SPD was the pariah party, an outcast from the fatherland. Among the Liberals and the Progressives there were some, especially a few professors, who under-stood the social urge for recognition among the working classes and tried, as it were, to build a direct bridge between them and the imperial throne, on Lassalleian and Napoleonic foundations, spanning the Marxist chasm. But their attempt was doomed, both by William II's complete reliance on the political forces of conservatism and by the SPD's blank refusal to compromise its policy of formal abstention. At home it wore its isolation proudly—the consequence of its materialist dialectic philosophy; for foreign consumption all the talk of abstinence and revolution was sometimes replaced by the lament that the govern-ment refused to treat Social Democracy fairly.[1] The stronger the SPD became, the more the leadership reiterated the fierce old words of hatred for bourgeois society, root and branch; and the more difficult it became in practice to enforce such a policy on a mass party.

Isolated, then, deliberately or inevitably, not at one end of the political spectrum but right outside it, the SPD became more and more self-absorbed. Concern with internal affairs increased as its influence on society was reduced to insignificance. Elections were mere musters of support, attempts to bring the ever-growing, increasingly discontented and impoverished proletariat, spawned by capitalism, into the orbit of organized Social Democracy. Any increase in SPD votes was seen primarily as a negation of, and protest against, the existing system as a whole. There was little point in analysing the precise differences between Liberal and Conservative parties, in manœuvring between them, profiting from any of their disputes—which were temporary and unreal anyhow, dissolving in fright as soon as Social Democracy took a hand. In short the SPD was creating a world of its own. The main preoccupation was to enlarge this world as much as possible, so that ambitious Socialists would not have to look to bourgeois society to achieve any of their political or private satisfactions.[2]

From the start the SPD leadership was absorbed with problems of

---

[1] E.g. Theodor Barth, 'Kaiser Wilhelm II und die Sozialdemokratie', *Cosmopolis*, Vol. I (1896), No. 3, p. 873.

[2] See J. P. Nettl, 'The German Social-Democratic Party 1890–1914 as a political model', *Past and Present*, No. 30, April 1965, for a further discussion of the sociology of isolation.

administration and organizational growth, more so than any of the other parties in Germany who were merely associations or social-interest groups advocating their particular policies. Since political power in the Reich was never in their grasp, party life, other than that within the SPD itself, never took on structural form. Only the SPD, however, tried to be both highly organized and severely democratic at the same time. The party congresses always began with a report on the organizational state of the party, the budget, the growth and circulation of the party press, the number of registered members, and a report on the activities of the executive, the provincial branches, and the *Reichstag* delegation.[1] This was partly a reflection of the personality of August Bebel, who from 1875 onwards dominated the policy and spirit of the SPD. The organizational imprint of the party was largely due to him. What was not so well appreciated was his extreme astuteness as a politician and his eye for short-range party tactics—a somewhat bourgeois virtue of which he himself was possibly not even aware. In the eyes of his contemporaries he was, by 1891, the grand old man of the working class whose many uncompromising statements always culminated in total defiance: 'I am and always will be the mortal enemy of existing society', and 'Not a man nor a farthing for this system'.[2]

When Rosa Luxemburg joined the German party, the other dominant personality was Wilhelm Liebknecht, who had been a close colleague of Marx and Engels for many years, and had, indeed, been responsible for uniting Bebel and the SPD to the two London exiles. Liebknecht and Bebel together had organized the joint committee for fusion with the Lassalle organization, the *Allgemeiner Deutscher Arbeiterverein*, which came to fruition in a constituent congress at Gotha in May 1875 (Bebel was at that time in jail).[3] Liebknecht had been Bebel's teacher and inspirer, and had brought him within the orbit of Marixist ideas; he more than anyone had given the German working-class movement its international orientation and its pre-eminent status within the International. Liebknecht was a much warmer person than Bebel, something of a romantic and a moralist, with all the advantages and disadvantages of a visionary approach to politics. His approach to politics was through people rather than through ideas; unlike Bebel, who could overcome

---

[1] These distinctive features caused contemporary sociologists like Max Weber and Robert Michels with considerable acumen to regard the SPD as the first 'modern' political party and the possible model for the future. They were as much interested in its structure as in its ideology, and used the latter primarily as a contrast to the logic of the former.

[2] The first phrase was used at the party congress in Dresden: see *Protokoll des Parteitages der SPD*, 1903, p. 313. I have not been able to discover the origin of the second phrase, which may not even have been Bebel's—by 1900 it had become a party slogan, regularly quoted by all those who upheld the 'old principles'.

[3] At this congress, the united party adopted the name of *Sozialistische Arbeiter Partei* which only became *Sozialdemokratische Partei* in 1890 at the Halle congress.

personal antipathies for the purpose of political combinations, or at least keep them hidden, Liebknecht found it almost impossible to work with those he disliked. By the time Rosa Luxemburg came to Germany, the efficient civil servants of the SPD hierarchy were finding the old man's unpredictable sorties a trial, and his love of adulation a regrettable though useful farce. Auer, the SPD party secretary, somewhat indiscreetly told Rosa Luxemburg: 'When he comes to London or Paris, they produce an ovation—three men of whom two are police spies—and then he thinks he knows the mood of the country. Well, he's an old man. . . . Discussion with him is useless—as you learnt yourself. But he's not a serious obstacle . . . he can be got around.'[1]

The special legislation against Socialism—the *Ausnahmegesetz*—had of course not destroyed the SPD or even made its existence entirely illegal. But its activities were limited, especially propaganda and recruitment; the only permitted efforts were those directly concerned with *Reichstag* elections. This gave electoral affairs a quietly special place in party mythology, never to be eradicated even when the party returned to full legality. But the Erfurt programme of 1891 once more put the seal on the party's formal commitment to both electoral activity and uncompromising long term socialism within the framework of recently restored legality. On the basis of this new programme, the SPD went from strength to strength, undisturbed by any major controversies for eight years. Within the party there were no thorny issues in the last decade of the nineteenth century, at least not until 1898. The only controversy of importance concerned agrarian reform. From the beginning—and even today—the problem of the land was difficult for Socialists. It might be possible to produce sweeping agrarian changes in theory, but it was impossible to obtain much support or enthusiasm for them among peasants and small farmers—or, indeed, to bring the ideas of Socialism into the world of farming at all. From the start, the party programme called for the progressive elimination of smallholdings and for the creation of large landed estates in private hands which would, when the time came, fall like ripe plums into the lap of Socialist agriculture by the simple act of confiscation. This was one of the most obvious examples of historicist helplessness: the attainment of Socialism by helping capitalism rather than combating it—a particularly inflexible transposition of industrial Socialism into agricultural terms. But some members of the SPD were unwilling to leave agricultural labour and smallholders to the inexorable fate of historical materialism. In 1894 Georg von Vollmar, a south German, raised the problem in a practical form. In his speech to the party congress at Frankfurt that year, he called for a special SPD programme for agriculture. He did not

---

[1] Jogiches letters, 25 May 1898, *Z Pola Walki*, 1961, No. 3(15), p. 147.

accept the need for the peasant to become totally 'proletarianized' through the growth of large estates. Historical inevitability was no policy for a party that was interested in the welfare of human beings; immediate and thorough reforms were needed instead.[1]

As a result of this proposal, a commission was set up to examine the problem, and at the next party congress in 1895 a sweeping programme of reform was put forward as an executive resolution. However, the resolution was rejected. The party programme, with its emphasis on Socialism as a final aim, could not simultaneously contain reforms that might shore up or even improve the condition of capitalist society. By a considerable majority the congress upheld principles against expediency.

The argument over agricultural policy was not itself of great importance. But for the first time two distinct groups had emerged in the party. The supporters of the agricultural programme were not, as might have been supposed, deputies from Prussia and the Junker areas where conditions were most backward, but from the south of Germany where, if anything, political life was more sophisticated and tolerant. The south German wing of the SPD, which had representation in provincial legislature unmatched by local government in the north and east, now called upon the party for the first time to recognize a special set of problems in the south, and consequently the need for special policies. Their plea was turned down. The party was not to return to agricultural problems as a major issue until after the war. But at the same time as the argument over the land, there arose a parallel problem peculiar to the south which was to dominate party congresses and literature for the next ten years, a chronic source of recrimination. The SPD delegates to the provincial legislatures of Württemberg, Bavaria, and especially Baden, had, as early as 1891, voted the *Land* government budgets in the provincial legislatures—this at a time when party congresses every year solemnly reiterated the doctrine: 'Not a man nor a farthing for this system.' The SPD made a solemn ceremonial of each refusal to help the class-state tax the people for the upkeep of its tyranny; its deputies voted solidly against one Reich government budget after another. The government funds were necessarily used in part precisely for combating the SPD, by maintaining the police, the courts, and above all that last anti-Socialist resort, the army. The action of the south Germans was thus not a mild departure from formal party manners, but a blow to the vital principle of isolation, of total opposition.

As early as 1894 a resolution had been submitted to the party congress which baldly forbade SPD delegations in any parliament to vote for any budget. The south Germans fought this resolution; their spokesmen argued that for all practical purposes the importance of the SPD as a political factor in the south would be destroyed if the resolution was

[1] See *Protokoll . . . 1894*, p. 134.

passed. This time the orthodox resolution was lost. In 1895, at Breslau, a similar resolution was again lost. Bebel among others was none too happy about south German budget-voting. But as long as the fiction of special circumstances was preserved, and no specific inroad made on party principles, the urgent convenience of a number of distinguished south German comrades could be quietly suited. When old Engels protested from London that Vollmar was hardly a good Social Democrat, and possibly an outright traitor, Liebknecht had to write half apologetically to pacify him.[1]

Finally, we should take a look at the structure and organization of the party which Rosa Luxemburg was entering. On the ground the SPD was organized like a honeycomb, in accordance with the administrative divisions of Germany. The local organization corresponded to the area of a *Kreis*, roughly the extent of a rural or urban district council. Directly above this was the province, and at the summit the central party organization with a proliferation of committees and commissions which were to grow in number and importance as the years went by. The party *Vorstand* (executive) was the repository of executive authority, under the joint chairmanship of Bebel and Liebknecht, but it submitted its activities and indeed itself to party approval or criticism at every annual congress. This was not so much a parliament or Soviet as an annual constituent assembly, the expression of the party's general will— a very Rousseau-like concept. The constitution of the party was very democratic indeed. Everyone accepted, at least tacitly, that the party congress was the highest authority on all matters of administration, policy, and personnel. The activities of the executive, the main events of the year, the action of parliamentary delegations and their individual members were examined at considerable length and often in great detail. Anyone who had something to say could do so with a liberal allowance of time; if this was insufficient, he could reapply to speak on the matter and, under normal circumstances, was permitted to do so. A senior member of the executive or of the party generally introduced any major topic with a platform speech at some length, after which the discussion was thrown open to the floor. Particularly important matters, or those where there was some disagreement, were given two platform speakers.[2] The status of the party congress was precisely that of an all-

---

[1] Rosa Luxemburg, *Collected Works*, Vol. III, p. 13 (Introduction by Paul Frölich). See also Friedrich Engels to Wilhelm Liebknecht, 27 November 1894.

[2] This peculiar German system of the *Referat*, which has no exact parallel in England, was taken over in its most extreme form by the Bolsheviks in the Soviet Union, where it still provides the means for the 'tone setting' speeches, used frequently by Lenin and later by Stalin and Khrushchev. In America it exists formally in the keynote speech at party conventions. The English practice, that movers of a resolution shall have the chance to open the discussion (the procedure of the House of Commons), is not quite the same thing. The *Referat* is speaking to a theme, while the English habit is to elaborate on a resolution.

powerful last court of appeal which English Labour Party Conferences consistently strive for but never achieve. Until the First World War the SPD, unlike the Labour Party, always effectively controlled its *Reichstag* members.[1]

Great value was placed by sponsors, private or executive, upon getting the congress to adopt their resolutions. These then became party 'law' for at least a year, or longer if the party did not alter or revoke them. The history of the SPD was littered with plaintive pleas that party congress resolutions were being ignored or not followed; arguments as to right and wrong usually took the form of differing interpretations of congress resolutions, seldom of outright disagreement with them: hence the rather arid discussion one year as to what the party congress had really intended the year before; hence also the prevalence of lawyers, professional and amateur, to extract the meaning of resolutions from the actual words.

Appearance at the party congress was governed by mandates. The bulk of these were from *Reichstag* constituency organizations of the SPD. In addition the members of the party executive and control commission, as well as SPD *Reichstag* deputies, all sat *ex officio*. As the SPD grew, so did the size of its congress. However, the same nucleus of people appeared year after year and, like all well-versed parliamentarians, were able to benefit from the particular skills of congressmanship, which often made newcomers feel rather uncomfortable. But until the last few years before the war there was practically no 'fixing'; the debates clearly show that the party preferred to air its problems in public and have them reported sardonically in the bourgeois press. The occasional warnings that this public oratory could not improve the party's image were drowned by the moral answer: 'we are not as other parties are'. Rosa Luxemburg was a particularly strong advocate of public frankness: the greater differences the greater the airing. She had a real horror of secrecy: she considered it both immoral and undesirable, especially in the context of working-class politics, which she saw mainly as a process of continual clarification. For her, the masses were ever-present spectators at the congress; they, more than anyone else, were the important judges of what was openly displayed before them and this, for Rosa and other radicals, was the main, the only reason for the display.

Above and beyond the SPD party congress, like a vague benevolent presence, was the Socialist International, meeting at intervals of two to four years. This was the incarnation of the world's Socialist presence; not an instrument of precise policies, but an expression of the immense moral authority of free proletarian co-operation in an age of imperialism

---

[1] Far more so than its delegates to the provincial parliaments, thus producing a curious 'federal' effect in what set out to be a centrally directed party advocating a unitary republic.

and war. The Second International had been founded in 1889, to express the reality of which Marx's First International had merely been the pious hope—mass Socialism—and as the base for its irresistible future. These international congresses were a useful place for individuals to meet and exchange ideas; each national party could report on its situation, and from the public proceedings ran the guiding lines for Socialist behaviour everywhere. Whether these resembled the pious public expressions of goodwill of a World Scout Jamboree, with the real exchange of views behind the scenes, or whether the congress resolutions were mandatory acts of international jurisdiction, was neither asked nor answered. Some certainly believed the latter, and among them Rosa Luxemburg.

For the first years of its existence, the International was preoccupied with cleaning Social Democracy of the anarchists who, formally thrown out of the conference halls in Zürich (1893) and London (1896), kept making Punch and Judy interruptions through windows and balconies. The problems of the International were naturally those of the most important national parties, primarily the Germans and the French—though the size of the delegations was highly flexible and governed in the main by the cost of transportation. International Socialism was poor and needed to conserve its resources—for the Great Day, but also for more immediate rainy days.

As far as the German party was concerned, there was little danger of conflict between the international view and its own. Amid all the euphoria and the slogans of triumph at international congresses, great care was taken not to wound national susceptibilities, at least not until some of the French Socialists and the SPD met head-on in 1904. When Rosa Luxemburg joined the SPD her status in the International changed perceptibly, even though she always attended more as a Pole than a German; the indignities of 1893 and 1896 could not be repeated on someone who, from 1900 onwards, was a figure of importance in the German party.

Whatever the International might feel about squabbling Poles, or even disunited Frenchmen, the SPD was the envy and admiration of Socialists throughout the world. Its preoccupations automatically became the International's agenda. In fact the SPD more or less dominated all the International congresses before the war, and was well aware of the fact.

By the turn of the century, then, the German party was an organized, forward-looking, powerful expression of working-class will, bestraddling tactics and long-term strategy with apparent success, an irresistible force to its enemies, the envy and example of other Socialist parties—the perfect arena, in fact, for a young Socialist bursting with ideas and the will to join the heart of the international class struggle.

Rosa Luxemburg arrived in Berlin on 12 May 1898. Her first official acts were to register with the police—'no trouble here, the papers were found in order and they gave me my identity card at once'—and with SPD party headquarters.[1] Her mood was compounded of despair and determination, alternating violently as they always did. Berlin was both fabulous and strange; it was far larger than any city she had known, more orderly—and at the same time much more impersonal. The Germans made an instant impression on her: stiff, reserved, untemperamental creatures of routine. 'Berlin is the most repulsive place; cold, ugly, massive—a real barracks, and the charming Prussians with their arrogance as if each one of them had been made to swallow the very stick with which he had got his daily beating.'[2] The same sentiment appears in Rosa's letters to Jogiches. They established a derogatory shorthand; Germans became Swabians and intermittently all the troubles of a sorrowful world were cast off by sticking pins into a vignette of a typical German. Within a few days of her arrival she wrote:

My soul is bruised and it is difficult to explain exactly how I feel. Last night in bed in a strange flat in the middle of a strange city, I completely lost heart and asked myself the frankest question: would I not be happier instead of looking for adventure to live with you somewhere in Switzerland quietly and closely, to take advantage of our youth and to enjoy ourselves. . . . In fact I have a cursed longing for happiness and am ready to haggle for my daily portion of happiness with all the stubbornness of a mule.[3]

The first difficulty was to get a flat and this took almost a week's hard searching. They were either too expensive or not good enough. She did not want to move to the outskirts: 'The air may be better, but it is outside Berlin and [these are] really rather proletarian districts.'[4] Finally she found a flat in Cuxhavenerstrasse: 'Near the centre—as you see, in the most aristocratic part. . . . They have never seen a woman doctor.'[5] But it was more expensive than they had planned and Rosa apologized profusely for exceeding the agreed budget.

For once, her change of circumstances was so dramatic that she felt impelled to describe her daily routine in detail—like any pioneer in the jungle:

I wake up before eight, run into the hall, grab the papers and letters and then dive back under the bed clothes and go through the most important things. Then I have a rub down with cold water (regularly every day); I dress, drink a glass of hot milk with bread and butter (they bring me milk and bread every day) sitting on the balcony. Then I dress myself respectably and go for an hour's

[1] Seidel letters, *Z Pola Walki*, 1959, No. 1(15), p. 68, 30 May 1898.
[2] Ibid., pp. 69-70.
[3] Jogiches letters, *Z Pola Walki*, 1961, No. 3(15), pp. 138-9.
[4] Ibid., p. 136.   [5] Ibid., p. 140.

walk in the Tiergarten [Berlin's Hyde Park], daily and in any weather. Next I return home, change, write my notes or letters. I have lunch at 12.30 in my room —marvellous luncheons and very healthy! After lunch every day bang on the sofa to sleep! Around three I get up, drink tea and sit down to write more notes or letters (depending on how I get on in the morning) or I write books. . . . At five or six I have a cup of cocoa, carry on with my work or more usually go to the Post Office to collect and send letters (this is the high spot of my day). At eight I have dinner—do not be shocked—three soft boiled eggs, bread and butter with cheese and ham and some more hot milk. . . . Around ten I drink another glass of milk (it makes fully a litre daily). I very much like working in the evenings. I have made myself a red lampshade for my lamp and sit at my desk just by the open balcony, the room looks lovely in the pink dimness and I get all the fresh air from the garden. Around twelve I wind my alarm clock, whistle something to myself and then undress and dive under the bed clothes. . . .[1]

At SPD headquarters Rosa Luxemburg got a cautious but not unfriendly reception. To her surprise, she was known—the intrepid gadfly from Zürich who had buzzed persistently at Kautsky and Wilhelm Liebknecht. As soon as she said that she had German nationality the interest became practical, and turned to fervour when without prompting she offered to perform the muddiest job of all—agitation for the coming *Reichstag* elections among the Silesian Poles. She listened politely to a lecture on the situation by Auer, the SPD secretary, then replied:

'You've told me nothing I didn't already know, in fact I know a lot more about it than you do.'

Then we began talking 'frankly'!

'In the executive', said the SPD secretary, 'we regard the independence of Poland as nonsense . . . we finance *Gazeta Robotnicza* [a Polish paper in Silesia] under the strict condition that there will be no nationalism.'

So far so good. Auer soon became still more frank.

'We couldn't do the Polish workers a greater service than to germanize them, only one mustn't say so . . . I'll gladly make you a present of all and every Pole including Polish Socialism. . . .'

I retorted sharply and the man became apologetic . . . Marchlewski? They do not even know his name, merely that there is someone about whose name begins with an M.[2]

And off she went to Silesia. It was on the darkest fringes of party activity. The district secretaries in Breslau and farther south, in the industrial area of Upper Silesia, felt remote, neglected, and resentful— much like Russian pioneers in Siberia. It was difficult enough to work successfully among the German textile workers who were probably the lowest paid and least class-conscious in the Reich, and so the least receptive to Socialism. Among the Poles, who supplied the bulk of the

[1] Jogiches letters, *Z Pola Walki*, 1962, No. 1(17), pp. 168–9.
[2] Ibid., 1961, No. 3(15), pp. 148–50, dated 25 May 1898.

labour in the mines, it was even more hopeless. There was the insurmountable language barrier and the fact that the PPS was hard at work for its own purposes which did not fit in with those of the SPD, though it was difficult precisely to spell out why. In this stale situation the arrival of a first-class agitator who spoke well and who spoke Polish, who had distinct ideas of her own in fundamental opposition to the separatist tendencies of the PPS, was very welcome. Bruhns in Breslau wanted to retain her in that city, but Rosa travelled on into Upper Silesia, the heart of the Polish area. There at Königshütte (Królewska Huta) sat Dr. August Winter who already had a particular bee in his bonnet about integrating Poles in the German organization and whom the party executive had therefore found invaluable for a job that no one else would undertake. 'Winter is *persona grata* in the SPD. Generally speaking, as far as they are concerned, the Polish movement *means* Winter.'[1] Rosa Luxemburg and he entered into a working alliance right from the start and their co-operation, after many setbacks and difficulties, was to lead five years later to an almost complete victory for the integration policies of the SPD—and the emergence of the SDKPiL as orthodox adviser to the German party on Polish affairs, to the discomfiture of the local PPS leaders.

But the collaboration between Dr. Winter and Rosa Luxemburg was purely political. Rosa Luxemburg had well remembered the derogatory remarks of the chief party secretary, Auer, about Poles. She knew that the Germans made no real distinction between political integration and total assimilation. This she was, of course, determined to resist.

It was a deliberate part of her policy to put the SPD leadership under an obligation to her. She always described this and subsequent visits to Upper Silesia as her stint in the desert—at least to acquaintances like the Kautskys.[2] Rosa Luxemburg may well have come to consider this agitation among the Poles less interesting than her activities nearer the centre of the political stage in the SPD. But at the same time she began, soon after her arrival in Germany, to develop that particular and deliberate schizophrenia about German and Polish affairs which makes so many of her actions appear contradictory at first sight. Though she always remained loyal to the Polish movement, it soon became obvious to her that Polish and German activities could not be integrated into a harmonious whole; that they would have to be kept separate as much as possible. No doubt this decision to live two lives was largely forced on her by circumstances. But it meant that to her German friends Rosa either kept quiet about her Polish activities or prevaricated. The

---

[1] Jogiches letters, *Z Pola Walki*, 1961, No. 3(15), p. 149.

[2] Rosa Luxemburg to Luise Kautsky, 30 December 1899, 'Einige Briefe', *Bulletin IISH*, 1952, No. 1, p. 32. See also Adolf Warszawski to Karl Kautsky, 20 May 1903, IISH Archives, D XXIII, 63.

reasons are not far to seek. Only through whole-hearted commitment to the German movement was she able to do something for the Poles—the fact that PPS leaders in Germany like Berfus were openly and entirely committed to an exclusively Polish point of view made the German leaders discount their opinions more and more.

She made a considerable impression, not only on the people she met but particularly on the party officials. At election time public meetings in the Polish areas were prohibited by the police and the work had to be confined to individual agitation.

You have no idea what a favourable influence my first appearances had on them and on me. . . . Now I am positive that within half a year I shall be one of the best speakers in the party. Voice, temperament, tongue, everything stands the test. And, most important, I mount the platform as if I had been doing it for the last twenty years.[1]

Jogiches had been against the whole agitation in Upper Silesia just as he was against almost everything that she undertook without him. But Rosa knew very well that having offered the executive her help in the *Reichstag* election campaign, she had to put up with it or shut up; her success here was bound to lead to greater possibilities at the centre. She had made her position clear from the start. Her sex was irrelevant; she indignantly refuted the official suggestion that, like Clara Zetkin, she might find her natural habitat in the women's movement. During a train journey she met Schönlank, the influential editor of the *Leipziger Volkszeitung*, who had raised that paper from the very average level of provincial Socialist publications to the highest level of political and literary journalism. A lively correspondence between them started at once. Schönlank wanted her collaboration on his paper and they exchanged several letters a week on questions of philosophy and literature—it was clear that he was paying her court and that the intellectual capsule of their communication was no more than a cover for more human intentions. Rosa Luxemburg was both flattered and amused. She reported it all faithfully to Jogiches—only to receive a burst of jealous resentment which she had much difficulty in calming. Nor was Schönlank the only one.[2] Bruhns in Breslau tried the more orthodox line of the

---

[1] Jogiches letters, *Z Pola Walki*, 1962, No. 1(17), p. 153.

[2] Much of the correspondence with Schönlank was an extended commentary on the meaning and importance of Immanuel Kant—probably the sole occasion in history when this angular philosopher's work served as a vehicle for courtship. Rosa Luxemburg's interest in Kant's philosophy was not very positive—as she made clear to the unfortunate Kurt Eisner some years later when she trounced him for his intellectual devotion to that philosopher; a suitable interest for a retired gentleman but not for an active Social Democrat. 'See to it that you are sufficiently informed to lecture about Russia. Otherwise it would be better if you confined yourself to Saint Immanuel and stuck to regurgitating him.' (Letter to Kurt Eisner dated 22 April 1904 in a private collection in Israel.)

misunderstood exile, immersed in a dull routine of wife and family which quite stifled his evident talents. Altogether Rosa Luxemburg caused a flutter in south-east Germany, compounded of political, intellectual, and personal motives. The difficulty was to decide which friendships had to be nurtured and which to be cooled down. Winter was necessary for the SDKP's Polish policy, Schönlank essential for her own advancement; but both needed careful handling to ensure their continued support without indelicate personal involvement.

Back in Berlin, Rosa Luxemburg summed up the positive gains of her trip. A basis for engaging the PPS had been established. But she could not see much point in sharpening the open political struggle for the moment, at least until the German party had officially taken notice of the specific problem of PPS separatism.

What am I to do? For instance should I go to Poznań, deliver a speech there, create some sort of organization, let myself be elected as a delegate or something; or should I just go to the meetings there and start a public discussion? The devil knows. . . . What is the fight with the Morawskis [PPS leader in Silesia] for? Agreement? This is out of the question and could in fact prove very awkward. An open quarrel? What is the concrete advantage from it, that is the question? . . . The best thing is to work indirectly through [German connections like] Schönlank.[1]

As far as her German career was concerned, the results were wholly positive. After the summer she was besieged with requests for articles, not only from the *Leipziger Volkszeitung* but also from *Sächsische Arbeiterzeitung*, where Parvus was editor. He, too, corresponded with her fervently: party affairs enlivened by the overtones of his irrepressible personality. The *Sächsische Arbeiterzeitung* had recently gained unexpected prominence through Parvus's vituperative onslaught on Bernstein.[2] It was Parvus's discovery of a kindred spirit in her that was primarily responsible for her collaboration with *Sächsische Arbeiterzeitung* which was soon to lead to her appointment as editor.

The most important work of the summer was her own reply to Bernstein in the form of a series of articles for *Leipziger Volkszeitung*. Every spare moment not occupied with Polish immediacies was devoted to them. It was to be her dramatic entrance on to the stage of the current drama in SPD politics; she felt it in her bones. Her contribution to the revisionist controversy had not only to be good but also to be timed correctly; its appearance had to take place shortly before the party congress in September in order to serve as a basis of discussion there.

---

[1] Jogiches letters, *Z Pola Walki*, 1962, No. 1(17), p. 154.
[2] See below, p. 96.

One must work quickly: (1) because the whole work will be good for nothing if somebody gets in first, and (2) most of the time has to be spent not on writing but on polishing. Generally speaking I have tackled the work very well. Already those pieces written in Zürich are just of the right dough (of course not baked yet). If I only knew what to write, the appropriate form would come by itself, I feel it. I am ready to give half my life for that article, so much am I absorbed in it.[1]

This, of course, was the first half of what was to become the pamphlet *Social Reform or Revolution*, Rosa Luxemburg's most important contribution to the revisionist debate and the first of the great works of Marxist analysis on which her reputation rests.

This statement of intent illuminates not only the purpose of her coming to Germany but her intentions and activities on arrival. She was out to make a career for herself, and almost everything she said or did was tailored to this end. As with her efforts in Silesia, the demands of SDKP policy coincided with her attempts to win the attention of the SPD leadership. She used her success among the Silesian Poles to make the personal acquaintance of as many of the leaders as possible; several times that summer she tried to see Bebel and Liebknecht and got introductions to them from people she had already met.

At the same time, she was not interested in power for its own sake. A career in the German party was a means of spreading those ideas which she held to be correct and important. The power structure of the SPD, with its hierarchical organization, its tendency to more clearly defined institutional authority, did not attract her at all. She was interested in influence, not power. Essentially a lonely person, she was suspicious of people, particularly Germans—and expected them to be suspicious of her. Why should they trust a person whose only claim to existence is a few articles, albeit first class? A person moreover who does not belong to the ruling clique [*Sippschaft*], who won't rely on anyone's support but uses nothing but her own elbows, a person feared for the future not only by obvious opponents like Auer and Co. but even by allies (Bebel, Kautsky, Singer), a person best kept at arm's length because she may grow several heads too tall? ... I take all this with great calm, I always knew it could not be otherwise ... in a year or two, no intrigue, fears or obstacles will help them and I shall occupy one of the foremost positions in the party.[2]

Thus she deliberately set out to influence people for particular purposes and expected others to try to do the same to her. However much she talked of masses, persuasion was mainly a private, personal affair. She had no feeling for the organized, structural fellowship of a party like the SPD—the huddle and the artificial glow of comradeship that goes with the common but negative experience of being rejected, deprived by

---

[1] Jogiches letters, *Z Pola Walki*, 1962, No. 1(17), p. 162. For the issues and history of the revisionist controversy, see below, pp. 94 ff. and Chapter vi.

[2] Jogiches letters, *Z Pola Walki*, 1963, Vol. VI, No. 3(23), p. 150, dated 1 May 1899.

society. She took the formal German camaraderie for granted, and saw it as a hostile rather than a friendly force. As Briand put it some years later: 'Genossen, Genossen, j'en ai marre de ces genosseries.' Instead, individuals had to be prised loose from their web of immediate loyalties, by reason and influence, towards the policies which Rosa Luxemburg advocated. This attitude was to remain constant throughout her career in the SPD, even though her policies only crystallized as distinct and oppositional much later. 'I have no intention of limiting myself to criticism. On the contrary I have every intention and urge to "push" positively, not individuals but the movement as a whole . . . point out new ways, fighting, acting as a gadfly—in a word, a chronic incentive for the whole movement, the work that Parvus began . . . but left sadly unfinished. . . .'[1] She was never 'in' the SPD to the extent and in the manner in which she was 'in' the SDKPiL. Its people were not her people. In the Polish party she exercised a major influence in the creation of ideas which flowed outwards from the peer group at the top. In the SPD, however, right from the start she was pulling away from the establishment; she was competing in the creation of ideas, and her influence was projected towards the centre rather than outwards from it. Even from 1901 to 1905, when she appeared to speak for the party executive on many issues, she was always an outsider—by choice as well as by necessity. 'It is always like that with them, when they are embarrassed—to the Jews for help—and when it is over—away with you, Jews.'[2]

She learned to live with this situation. At the beginning, occasional loneliness assailed her unbearably and at such moments her correspondence with Jogiches in Zürich provided the only link with what she felt to be the one genuine reality of her life.

I cannot write much about my own person. I can only repeat what I have written to you before, but you will again not understand and will be angry. 'I feel cold and calm'; you understand the phrase with regard to your own self, but do not comprehend the fact that I am complaining about my condition which goes on and on. There is a lethal apathy in spite of which I act and think like some kind of automaton, almost as if someone else were doing it all. Explain to me what I can do. You ask me what is wrong. I am lacking some part of life; I feel as if something had died within me, I feel neither fear nor pain, nor loneliness, I am like a corpse . . . I seem to be an entirely different person from what I was in Zürich and I think of myself as having been quite different in those days. . . .[3]

---

[1] Ibid. The use of the word 'push' was Luxemburg shorthand for Jogiches' tendency to manoeuvre people behind the scenes rather than persuade or argue openly (see below, p. 257). They frequently argued about this; when he made futile proposals about her personal tactics in Germany, she called him an 'incorrigible diplomat' (p. 152).

[2] Ibid., p. 145. 'Jak bieda to do żyda, po biedzie precz żydzie.' Rosa Luxemburg used a slightly bitter Polish jingle which had become a common saying in a country with a long tradition of anti-Semitism.

[3] Jogiches letters, Z Pola Walki, 1962, No. 1(17), p. 156.

Here was the one person who could be told everything, without adorn-
ment or rationalization. But this brutal, incoherent frankness brought its
own penalties. Jogiches made a point of disagreeing with many of her
decisions and increasingly resented the implications of her growing
independence. Rosa Luxemburg satisfied him as far as she could by
explaining everything at great length and accounting in detail for
things like money and arrangements; but she found it impossible to
submit to his decision on the intellectual aspects of her work. In these
she knew that she was right. The break-through in Germany was hers
alone; the more Jogiches attempted to force it into the framework of
their partnership—in which he clearly predominated—the more Rosa
Luxemburg felt the need to assert her independence all along the line.
It is symptomatic of their relationship that when Rosa was offered the
editorship of *Sächsische Arbeiterzeitung* and proudly informed Jogiches
of the fact, she received a laconic telegram which instructed her to
'decline unconditionally'—and equally symptomatic that she took no
notice but went right ahead. Jogiches capitulated. He slipped quietly
away from Zürich and joined her in Dresden in her moment of triumph
—keeping, as always, in the background so that her fellow editors, with
whom she was soon to become embroiled in a struggle, were entirely
unaware of his presence.

To do justice to their relationship, we must document the moments of
euphoria as well as the disputes. Rosa Luxemburg celebrated her
twenty-eighth birthday in a good mood: 'things poured on her from a
veritable horn of plenty' from German friends and admirers, but the
most valued gift was Jogiches'—an edition of the works of Rodbertus, a
German economist. Her letter of acknowledgement is one of the most
touching personal documents she ever wrote.

I kiss you a thousand times for your dearest letter and present, though I have
not yet received it. . . . You simply cannot imagine how pleased I am with your
choice. Why, Rodbertus is simply my favourite economist and I can read him a
hundred times for sheer intellectual pleasure. . . .[1] My dear, how you delighted
me with your letter. I have read it six times from beginning to end. So, you are
really pleased with me. You write that perhaps I only know inside me that
somewhere there is a man who belongs to me! Don't you know that everything
I do is always done with you in mind; when I write an article my first thought
is—this will cause you pleasure—and when I have days when I doubt my own
strength and cannot work, my only fear is what effect this will have on you, that
it might disappoint you. When I have proof of success, like a letter from Kautsky,
this is simply my homage to you. I give you my word, as I loved my mother,
that I am personally quite indifferent to what Kautsky writes. I was only pleased

[1] For a rather different view of Rodbertus, see Rosa Luxemburg, *The Accumulation of
Capital*, London 1951, pp. 238 ff.

with it because I wrote it with your eyes and felt how much pleasure it would give you.[1]

. . . Only one thing nags at my contentment: the outward arrangements of your life and of our relationship. I feel that I will soon have such an established position here (morally) that we will be able to live together quite calmly, openly, as husband and wife. I am sure you understand this yourself. I am happy that the problem of your citizenship is at last coming to an end and that you are working energetically at your doctorate. I can feel from your recent letters that you are in a very good mood to work. . . .

Do you think that I do not feel your value, that whenever the call to arms is sounded you always stand by me with help and encourage me to work— forgetting all the rows and all my neglect! . . . You have no idea with what joy and desire I wait for every letter from you because each one brings me so much strength and happiness and encourages me to live.

I was happiest of all with that part of your letter where you write that we are both young and can still arrange our personal life. Oh darling, how I long that you may fulfil your promise. . . . Our own little room, our own furniture, a library of our own, quiet and regular work, walks together, an opera from time to time, a small—very small—circle of intimate friends who can sometimes be asked to dinner, every year a summer departure to the country for a month but definitely free from work! . . . And perhaps even a little, a very little, baby? Will this never be permitted? Never? Darling, do you know what accosted me yesterday during a walk in the park—and without any exaggeration? A little child, three or four years old, in a beautiful dress with blond hair; it stared at me and suddenly I felt an overpowering urge to kidnap the child and dash off home with him. Oh darling, will I never have my own baby?

And at home we will never argue again, will we? It must be quiet and peaceful as it is with everyone else. Only you know what worries me, I feel already so old and am not in the least attractive. You will not have an attractive wife when you walk hand in hand with her through the park—we will keep well away from the Germans. . . . Darling, if you will first settle the question of your citizenship, secondly your doctorate and thirdly live with me openly in our own room and work together with me, then we can want for nothing more! No couple on earth has so many facilities for happiness as you and I and if there is only some goodwill on our part we will be, must be, happy.[2]

Like all events in history which later turn out to be major watersheds, convenient dates for dividing one period from another, the revisionist controversy has been, if not over-simplified, at any rate compressed. All writing of history is compression, but the scale on which it is done varies considerably, becoming most intense where one period is thought to link up with the next. Revisionism gave its compact name to a widely differing series of attitudes and policies, as much on the part of the historians as of the original participants. The intellectual content of the original revisionist controversy has been sharpened and simplified

---

[1] For the letter in question, see below, p. 106.
[2] *Z Pola Walki*, 1963, Nos. 1/2 (21–2), p. 336, dated 6 March 1899.

considerably, to produce the required political sales appeal for different periods of Communist history. The result is that today it is exceedingly difficult to liberate the analysis of contemporary attitudes from the heavy burden of later imputation.

The revisionist controversy as such can be dated approximately from the beginning of 1898. Not that the problems were entirely new; they had recurred consistently since 1891 but had always been dealt with as isolated questions of tactics without giving rise to any general discussion of principles as the foundation of party policy.[1] Towards the end of 1896 a man called Eduard Bernstein in his typically leisured and peaceful manner had sat down and analysed the events of the preceding ten years of Socialist history. This broad survey took the form of a dialogue between reality and illusion, between the existing policy of the SPD and the one that appeared to him objectively desirable. It was a complex subject; one thing necessarily led to another and in the course of his investigation Bernstein tackled almost every major aspect of Socialism.[2] Bernstein himself was a distinguished figure in the German party—he was particularly well liked for his good nature and agreeable, restrained temperament. For a time he had been Engels's secretary and had always remained particularly close to him. He had shared the Swiss emigration with many important German leaders, among them Kautsky, to whom he was personally close. Then he had moved from Switzerland to London where he had remained—again on account of one of those mysterious and ever-pending indictments with which the imperial authorities belaboured Social Democracy and which would have led to a court case as soon as he put his foot on German soil. In the course of his stay in England he had developed considerable sympathy with English attitudes. In fact, Bernstein did not return to Germany until 1901. What he had to say, therefore, was treated primarily as the product of a well-known and respected mind. His peers unhesitatingly accepted Bernstein's right to speak on all these matters with authority.

The form which the great controversy was to take, and particularly the roles of Parvus and Rosa Luxemburg, cannot be understood without

---

[1] See 'The Roots of Revisionism', *Journal of Modern History*, 1939, pp. 334 ff.; also J. P. Nettl. 'The German Social-Democratic Party 1890–1914 as a political model', *Past and Present*, No. 30, April 1965, pp. 68 ff.

[2] It is not necessary to go at length into the problems examined by Bernstein and the solutions he put forward. Some of these will be discussed in due course. For a general discussion of Bernstein and his ideas, see Peter Gay, *The Dilemma of Democratic Socialism*, New York 1952. The most recent and best biography of Bernstein is Pierre Angel, *Eduard Bernstein et l'evolution du Socialisme allemand*, Paris 1961. Bernstein's series of articles in *Neue Zeit* were under the general title 'Probleme des Sozialismus' (*NZ*, 1896–8). These were later published in book form as *Zur Geschichte und Theorie des Sozialismus*. Bernstein also summarized his immediate conclusions and proposals in another, better-known, book, *Die Voraussetzungen des Sozialismus und die Aufgaben der Sozialdemokratic*, Stuttgart 1899.

a clear appreciation of the attitude of the fathers of German Social Democracy to Bernstein's articles. Kautsky found them 'extremely attractive'; he had, after all, accepted them in his paper. When the first criticisms appeared from Dresden, Bernstein interrupted his series to reply to Parvus, and Kautsky accompanied this reply in *Neue Zeit* with an editorial note to the effect that he had received 'a number of polemical comments on Bernstein's articles which we have to turn down for publication because they are based on a mistaken conception of Bernstein's intentions'.[1] He later described Bernstein as one of his closest friends, with whom he had been 'one in heart and soul'; a friendship which other people regarded as that between 'a kind of red Orestes and Pylades'.[2] Kautsky was not a man who formed intimacies easily. Later, when Victor Adler accused him of supporting Rosa Luxemburg beyond the bounds of political reason, he hotly denied that his political alignments could ever be governed by personal friendships—and cited his attitude to Bernstein in support.[3]

Vorwärts, too, welcomed any critical appraisal of Marxist theory on principle even though Bernstein's ideas could in part have given rise to 'misunderstandings'.[4] Even the controversial *Leipziger Volkszeitung* had at first nothing sharper to say than 'interesting observations which none the less terminate in a mistaken conclusion; something that is always liable to happen especially to lively and critical people, but there is no more to it than that'.[5]

In the spring of 1898, Bernstein was far from being odd man out; it was Parvus who was demonstrably behaving like a maniac. He was editor of *Sächsische Arbeiterzeitung*. The SPD party press had just begun to rise above its humble, purely agitational beginnings. Questions of theoretical interest were reserved by consensus to *Neue Zeit*; *Vorwärts*, the party's official gazette, had practically a monopoly of important official business, which it treated with ponderous and dull solemnity— much quoted and probably little read. The provincial papers suffered from a dearth of journalistic talent and also a lack of interesting material. The gutless state of party journalism had been obvious to Rosa Luxemburg from the day she arrived. 'I do not like the way party affairs are written up . . . everything so conventional, so wooden, so repetitive.'[6] Only Schönlank in Leipzig was creating a paper of wider range with a strong emphasis on culture; the traditional rivalry between the cities of

[1] Karl Kautsky in Felix Meiner (ed.), *Die Volkswirtschaftslehre der Gegenwart in Selbstdarstellungen*, Leipzig 1924, p. 135. Also *NZ*, 1897–8, Vol. I, p. 740.

[2] Meiner (ed.), *Die Volkswirtschaftslehre . . .*, p. 126.

[3] Victor Adler, *Briefwechsel*, p. 435; Karl Kautsky to Victor Adler, 18 October 1904.

[4] Paul Frölich, Introduction to Rosa Luxemburg, *Collected Works*, Vol. III, p. 17.

[5] Ibid.

[6] Seidel letters, *Z Pola Walki*, 1959, No. 1(15), p. 69.

Leipzig and Dresden was reflected in the struggle between their respective Socialist papers. Parvus, a man of impatient and scintillating temperament, was determined to make a revolution in *Sächsische Arbeiterzeitung*. It was a revolution in every sense: his articles had a polemical bite quite unknown to German party papers, and in addition he kept the administration of the paper in a constant state of flux. His decision to mount a noisy artillery barrage against Bernstein was therefore as much editorial policy as it was an expression of Parvus's own literary appetites. In seizing on Bernstein as a target, he succeeded beyond his wildest expectations in putting his paper on the political map. By the time the party congress assembled that year, people were already talking of 'taking a *Sächsische Arbeiterzeitung* line'.[1]

In fact Parvus cleared the editorial decks in Dresden and launched into a lengthy series of polemics against Bernstein beginning on 28 January and concluding on 6 March 1898. It was a prolonged upheaval which completely disrupted the work of the paper and greatly upset the staff. He began his series with the title 'Bernstein's Overthrow of Socialism', and almost every issue carried yet another instalment of fireworks.[2] The onslaught was such that Bernstein was compelled to interrupt his own series in order to reply. He took issue particularly with those of his critics who insisted on waving the Communist Manifesto as though it were the fount of all wisdom. 'Surely it is ridiculous to argue 50 years later with excerpts from the Communist Manifesto which are based on wholly different political and social conditions to those which face us today. . . . There is no genuine reason to assume that the basic considerations which motivated the party [in formulating the Erfurt programme] are necessarily those which Parvus thinks.'[3] The argument thus moved from history to politics, from the past to the present, and back again. By the time Rosa Luxemburg appeared on the scene, the problem of whether current social conditions justified Bernstein or Parvus had already been posed, and was replacing the academic exercise of discovering what Marx really meant.

[1] See *Protokoll . . . 1898*, also 'Einige Briefe Rosa Luxemburgs und andere Dokumente', *Bulletin of the International Institute for Social History*, Vol. VIII, 1952, p. 9.

[2] See *SAZ*, 1898, Nos. 22 to 54. In the course of these articles Parvus pursued every one of Bernstein's subjects at length: the concentration of industry, the specific statistics furnished by Bernstein in support, the forces of revolution, the peasantry, the social structure, tariff policy, the class system of the German Reich, the pre-conditions of social revolution, and finally the broader problem of Socialism and revolution. The choice of title for the series was deliberately based on an analogy with Engels's polemic against Dühring which had appeared twenty years earlier in *LV*, under the title 'Herrn Eugen Dührings Umwälzung der Wissenschaft'. (See W. Scharlau, *Parvus-Helphand als Theoretiker in der deutschen Sozialdemokratie, 1867–1910* (The role of Parvus–Helphand as a theorist in German Social Democracy), unpublished doctoral dissertation, Münster (Germany) 1960.)

[3] E. Bernstein, 'Kritisches Zwischenspiel', *NZ*, 1897–8, Vol. I, pp. 740, 750.

Parvus returned to the attack in increasingly personal terms. He did not take the factual range of discussion much further but he did raise the temperature by several degrees. Moreover, it was Parvus who now suggested that since factual argument with Bernstein was hopeless he could only be treated as a ridiculous deserter from Socialism. It was at this stage that Rosa Luxemburg took a hand.

There is consequently a clear difference between the personal attitudes of Rosa Luxemburg and Parvus right from the beginning of the revisionist debate, and the actual contributions they made to the important questions that had been raised. Parvus had forced the controversy on to the public conscience of the party by his uncompromising tone and the comprehensiveness of his dissent. Having earned notoriety for his paper and himself, he soon lost interest; as for Bernstein, systematic analysis was not really his line. But Rosa Luxemburg saw here an opportunity for short-circuiting the lengthy process of making an impact on the party. The situation of 1898 was a race for time: not only had she to throw her hat into the ring before the party congress, when the whole problem would be discussed by all the big guns before a critical audience, but she had to get her word in before her rivals. By the end of the year it became plain that Kautsky too could no longer keep quiet; an amusing race now took place for possession of a proof copy of Bernstein's new book. *Die Voraussetzungen des Sozialismus und die Aufgaben der Sozialdemokratie*, which was to put his case more fully to the party. Rosa Luxemburg was the first to review this book and tried to ensure that Schönlank would give her review absolute priority. Schönlank had his personal interests to protect; it was important that he should be the first to comment on it, before *Neue Zeit*.[1]

The party congress assembled in the first week of October 1898 in Stuttgart. Schönlank had persuaded Rosa Luxemburg that she too must attend—initially, as an expert on Polish questions. The Polish Socialist Party of Prussia, Rosa's local enemies of the PPS, might well raise the Polish question at the congress. Her mandates were provided from Silesia by Bruhns. In the event the Polish question was not raised, but Rosa was able to use her presence at the congress to participate in the much more interesting preliminaries of what was already beginning to be known as the revisionist controversy.

Parvus, who had no formal mandate, had been invited to attend and was anxious to use the assembly for a full discussion of the whole matter. His resolution, roundly condemning Bernstein and his views, was submitted by his friends representing the 6th electoral district of Dresden, but the party executive declined to support it. Bebel wrote to Kautsky on 3 September:

---

[1] Jogiches letters, *Z Pola Walki*, 1962, No. 4(20), p. 181.

Parvus's resolution is tactless. The man is eaten up by galloping personal ambition and his resolution shows that he doesn't at all understand our circumstances. To have the party congress solemnly declare that it stands for social revolution—that really would be all we need! Some time we will certainly get to another set-to about tactics but it is too soon to do it at Stuttgart. . . .[1]

Even Liebknecht, though he agreed with the array of Parvus's facts, criticized the manner of presentation; 'A tone more suitable for a school master than for a party comrade . . . definitely *de haut en bas.*'[2]

The speakers at the congress did not separate theory from practice, but they did try to keep personalities out of it as much as possible. The leaders considered that the immediate problem was to soothe the feathers ruffled by the two tactless foreigners—mainly Parvus, but also Rosa Luxemburg. In trying to shunt the whole argument off on to rails of 'mere' theory, they certainly gave some delegates the impression of tacit support for Bernstein and his ideas. Clara Zetkin, editor of the Socialist women's paper, *Gleichheit*, and chief of the German Socialist women's organization, had already been attracted by Rosa Luxemburg's contribution. She wrote to Kautsky on 29 September:

The fact that Bebel has stated what the tasks of the party congress are is already some improvement on the notion previously held that it exists only to expedite 'business', and hasn't any right to mess about with 'problems' . . . ah, if only our Engels were still alive to wake him [Bebel] out of his enchanted sleep [*Dornröschen-Vorsicht*]. God in Heaven, how he would have laid about him with blunt instruments against all this opportunist rubbish in our ranks.[3]

Kautsky's position, too, was equivocal. He was beginning to have doubts as to whether the Bernstein formulations were really as harmless as he originally thought. While disassociating himself strongly from Parvus, he made it clear that, theoretically speaking, he did not share Bernstein's views, though the congress should at least be grateful to Bernstein for having provided the opportunity for a lively discussion and much fruitful rethinking—a platitude that roused Plekhanov, who attended the congress as a fraternal delegate, to fury.[4]

Rosa Luxemburg spoke twice at the congress. Her criticisms were directed not at Bernstein, absent in England, but at Heine, one of Bernstein's most prominent supporters in Germany. He served as a convenient scapegoat. In the course of the *Reichstag* elections Heine had suggested that the party should concentrate above all on getting votes, and it was this fairly common and harmless suggestion that now drew Rosa's fire. Instead of playing down the revolutionary aspect of the party programme at elections, what was needed was its particular emphasis.

[1] 'Einige Briefe', p. 10.   [2] *Protokoll . . . 1898*, p. 133.
[3] 'Einige Briefe', p. 10.   [4] *Protokoll . . . 1898*, p. 126.

Our task can only be made comprehensible [to the voters] by emphasizing the closest possible connection of capitalist society as a whole with the insoluble contradictions in which it is enmeshed and which must lead to the final explosion, a collapse at which we shall be both executioner and the executor who must liquidate bankrupt society.[1]

She did not miss the opportunity of seizing on Bernstein's formulation about the relative importance of aim and movement and turning it upside down. 'On the contrary the movement as such without regard for the final aim is nothing, but the final aim is everything for us.'[2]

It looked at the congress as though the resentment against Rosa Luxemburg and Parvus would engulf the tentative doubts of many people about Bernstein. The executive besought everyone to go away and think more calmly. Who knew but that within a year the whole thing might not have blown over? The SPD leaders were good politicians; before they felt obliged to get involved in any party controversy, they provided every opportunity for it to die a natural death. Kautsky was still very reluctant to engage in public polemic against Bernstein, but had declared intellectual war against him in private, 'Our co-operation is finished. I cannot follow you any longer from this day on. . . .'[3] Bebel's own reaction was similar. He, too, wrote privately to Bernstein, not with the teleological certainties of Kautsky, but with quite unusual sorrow and diffidence. 'I write to you so outspokenly because I want to save you from disappointments and because only unmitigated frankness might conceivably make you reflect very carefully once more whether you are not after all in a blind alley.'[4] Like Kautsky, Bebel recognized that he and Bernstein did not differ merely about details. But unlike the 'Marxists', he still saw the difference as one of opinions, and attributed Bernstein's 'contradictions and many wrong conclusions' to the latter's naïve tendency to absorb local colour too easily—in this case in England. What made the whole thing important was not so much the views themselves as Bernstein's status as an old friend and comrade. He had chosen to go out on a limb—not for the first time: 'Vollmar may be with you, Schippel hardly, under no circumstances Auer, however he may like to play the diplomat and moderator.'

[1] *Protokoll . . . 1898*, p. 99.   [2] Ibid., p. 118.

[3] Karl Kautsky to Eduard Bernstein, 23 October 1898, in Victor Adler, *Briefwechsel*, p. 278. Kautsky's dislike for public polemic was genuine and not just fear. But since he was not consistent in his dislike, he always succeeded in giving the impression of tactical hesitation rather than genuine reluctance; he invariably entered controversies too late, at a time when the dice had already been loaded by others. His historical analogy of the wisdom of Fabius Cunctator in the tactical debate of 1910 can be taken to apply to himself (see Erich Matthias, *Kautsky*, p. 182). Kautsky always felt impelled to explain his public position with lengthy comments in private letters to his friends—a sure sign of moral uncertainty; e.g. Victor Adler, *Briefwechsel*, p. 382, dated 21 November 1901.

[4] August Bebel to Eduard Bernstein, 16 October 1898, in *Einheit*, 1960, No. 2, p. 226.

Bebel felt sorry for Bernstein, but not angry about a revisionism or reformism which he did not yet recognize as existing. The real pressure on the executive to intervene against Bernstein was mounted after the congress, in private as well as in public. Throughout October Rosa Luxemburg continued to publish polemics against the revisionists in *Sächsische Arbeiterzeitung*, of which she had now become editor.[1] Bebel was stung at least into private acknowledgements: 'I'll answer *Sächsische Arbeiterzeitung* as soon as the next article is out, and particularly [I'll deal with the question] why I—one of the old men— did not get right in there and fight at once.'[2] On 31 October Rosa Luxemburg wrote personally to Bebel in the most unequivocal terms.

I am surprised . . . that you and Comrade Kautsky did not use the favourable atmosphere at the party congress for a resolute and immediate debate, but instead encouraged Bernstein to produce [a further] pamphlet which can only drag out the whole discussion. If Bernstein is really lost to us, then the party will have to get used to the fact—however painful—that we have to treat him henceforward like Schmoller or any other social reformer.[3]

Similar communications flowed into the executive from other sources.

But perhaps the most significant pressure on the executive came from outside the German party altogether. The Russian Social Democrats in Switzerland, in the throes of founding their own united party at last, had followed the polemics with great interest from the start. Both Parvus and Rosa Luxemburg were well known to them. Plekhanov in particular saw in this debate the treatment of problems in which he had a vital and professional interest.[4] His natural counterpart in Germany was Kautsky and as early as May 1898 he had written to him suggesting joint and immediate action against Bernstein. Kautsky had pleaded preoccupation with his current book on agrarian questions and personal attachment to Bernstein.[5] At the Stuttgart congress itself the distinguished Russian Marxist had been an honoured guest and had witnessed the executive's equivocations. Plekhanov thereupon decided to attack Bernstein himself. In October both Bebel and Liebknecht thanked him fulsomely for his intervention. 'Keep hitting him good and hard', they advised. Liebknecht went on to blame Kautsky for the German failure

---

[1] See below, pp. 102 ff.
[2] Bebel to Kautsky, 12 October 1898, quoted in 'Einige Briefe', p. 12.
[3] IML (B). Reprinted in *Selected Works*, Vol. II, p. 728. Schmoller was a professor of economics and a prominent writer on social subjects. In propagating reform he was encroaching upon Social-Democratic preserves and was particularly disliked by Rosa Luxemburg.
[4] *Perepiska G. V. Plekhanova i P. B. Akselroda*, Moscow 1925, p. 205.
[5] *Literaturnoe nasledie G. V. Plekhanova: Sbornik—v borbe s filosofskim revizionizmom* 1938, pp. 261, 264; Plekhanov to Kautsky, 20 May 1898; Kautsky's reply, 22 May. However dilatory in action, Kautsky was always quick and punctilious as a correspondent.

to take issue with Bernstein more sharply. Theory, after all, was Kautsky's *ressort*. 'If I had been him I would have gone for Bernstein with gusto. If Kautsky had not hesitated from considerations of principle, there would never have *been* a Bernstein case.'[1]

The controversy could no longer be buried as just a little intellectual squall or the product of personal friction. The executive hoped to have at least twelve clear months before having to meet the problem once more at the 1899 congress. Meantime, the party officials at the centre did their best behind the scenes to relieve the pressure which always built up at the annual jamboree. Men like Auer, the party secretary, deplored the public airing of what were largely questions of individual conscience. He wrote to Bernstein: 'My dear Ede, one does not formally make a decision to do the things you suggest, one doesn't *say* such things, one simply *does* them.'[2] And Bernstein, essentially a practical person, got the point; he even felt able to vote for future resolutions specifically condemning revisionism. All that was needed was to add 'a grain of salt to his vote'.[3]

The whole thing was like a modern version of the great Galileo controversy three hundred years earlier. There, too, the trouble had been the inexorable result of public commitment to what were honest if personal conclusions—*et ruat caelum*. The only difference was that the sixteenth-century Catholic Church was far more adept in its public relations than the modern SPD; while the Papal advisers realized early on that the controversy could get out of hand, the SPD leaders for a long time believed that the revisionists could be silenced by sustained and superior public argument. But in the end they too came to accept the simple need for a guillotine on discussion. Who, then, was the guilty party—in the old controversy as much as the new: the irresponsible questioners or the organization pledged to maintain order and cohesion irrespective of scientific truth? Have men and women the right to question dogma in public and still call themselves members of the Faith? Who is the real disturber of the peace, questioner or suppressor—irrespective of whether the questioner is revisionist and the dogma revolutionary?

As it turned out, by the autumn of 1899 the personal element had indeed receded, but the practical questions had only become that much more urgent. The revisionist controversy simply could not be confined to abstract propositions in the pages of *Neue Zeit*.[4] For, unlike the

---

[1] *Literaturnoe nasledie G. V. Plekhanova* . . ., p. 269 (letter from Bebel), p. 271 (letter from Liebknecht).

[2] E. Bernstein, 'Ignaz Auer, der Führer, Freund und Berater' in *Sozialistische Monatshefte*, 1907, Vol. I, p. 846.

[3] Bernstein to Auer, quoted in the Introduction to Rosa Luxemburg, *Collected Works*, Vol. III, p. 20.

[4] Victor Adler, *Briefwechsel*, p. 435, dated 18 October 1904.

Galileo controversy, the issue here was abstract truth indeed, but also the livelihood and policy of a great mass party. The dilemma can best be illustrated by Bebel's own attitude. The master tactician of the party was always sensitive to the needs and feelings of the members. Four years earlier he had complained that, 'in the party press we have got out of the habit of expressing any kind of criticism or independence. All this namby-pambyness makes one shudder. The more I look the greater the faults and deficiencies I see in our party.'[1] But by 1900 he had had his fill of controversy. The new tendency for personal polemics was now a sign of deterioration in the party, and could not be deprecated sufficiently.[2]

At the end of September 1898, even before the party congress could meet, Rosa Luxemburg benefited from an entirely unexpected event. Parvus, editor of *Sächsische Arbeiterzeitung*, and his assistant editor, Rosa's old party comrade and doubtful friend Julian Marchlewski, were both expelled by the Royal government of Saxony. The blow fell on 25 September 1898 and the expulsion order gave them only a few days' grace before departure. They urged the local party press commission to appoint Rosa Luxemburg and cabled her to come at once. Marchlewski met her at the station and within a few days the appointment was confirmed by the press commission. The last doubts were overcome by the fact that both Parvus and Marchlewski made their future contribution to the paper conditional upon Rosa's appointment. By now the paper was an asset to the local party and Parvus's views could not be neglected.[3] Rosa Luxemburg took up her duties more or less at once while Parvus and Marchlewski, after being refused residence in various parts of Germany, finally settled in Munich. Rosa Luxemburg already attended the party congress as editor-elect; it was this which promoted her from a possible adviser on Polish questions to full participant with the right to speak on the main problems of the day.

In Dresden she inherited an administrative mess of the first order. Much of the resentment against Parvus's haphazard editorship spilled over on to her, and the exercise of authority needed to put it right was strongly resented in a woman.[4] At the same time she continued his assault on revisionism, though without the pointed extremes of his tone. She used *Sächsische Arbeiterzeitung* to winkle the executive from its protective neutrality. In the course of this campaign for clarification,

[1] August Bebel to Karl Kautsky, 3 December 1894, in 'Einige Briefe', p. 27.
[2] August Bebel to Karl Kautsky, 12 December 1900. By 1903, however, he had been roused once more; in the attempt to end the indiscipline of practising revisionism, he did not hesitate to pull out all the stops of personal invective—and encouraged his supporters to do the same.
[3] 'Einige Briefe', pp. 11 ff.; Jogiches letters, *Z Pola Walki*, 1962, No. 2(18), pp. 89 ff.; also Frölich, p. 57.
[4] Einige Briefe', *Bulletin IISH*, p. 13: Rosa Luxemburg to August Bebel, 31 October 1898.

Rosa Luxemburg took issue specifically with *Vorwärts*, the central organ of the party. It was a mixture of journalistic rivalry and genuine disagreement over policy, or—as she put it—dislike of the central organ's lack of policy. The general slanging-match soon found a more particular focus, in the person of Dr. Georg Gradnauer, one of Rosa's predecessors as editor of *Sächsische Arbeiterzeitung* and now an assistant editor of *Vorwärts* as well as *Reichstag* deputy for Dresden. Gradnauer was a prominent revisionist. With all the authority of a *Reichstag* deputy, he had written a series of articles in *Vorwärts* commenting on the Stuttgart congress. He blamed the executive and the radicals for having 'created' the controversy. This annoyed Rosa Luxemburg and she took him publicly to task in *Sächsische Arbeiterzeitung*. Gradnauer first replied in *Sächsische Arbeiterzeitung* itself, but his next attempt to defend himself met with the negative exercise of Rosa's editorial discretion. He then turned to *Vorwärts*—only too glad to get even with the provincial upstart. At the same time Gradnauer placed the issue before the Dresden party organization as a question of principle and discipline. He was after all the sitting member for Dresden, an important person to whom the local party paper owed respect—which was probably why Rosa Luxemburg chose to take him on in the first place. The dissatisfaction which had prevailed on the editorial board since Parvus's days now found a ready means of articulation, and three of her colleagues lined up with Gradnauer against her.[1]

Rosa Luxemburg offered to resign at a meeting of the press commission of the provincial party executive of Saxony on 2 November. She stated that she could not continue to serve as editor if her own colleagues did not support her and even attacked her in public. On 3 November a notice appeared in *Vorwärts* that Rosa Luxemburg had already resigned—clearly based on a slanted 'leak' from someone present at the meeting. The executive now decided to intervene. Under instruction from Berlin, the press commission forbade publication of Rosa Luxemburg's apologia; they would not even let her print a personal reply to the attacks. She approached her friend Bruno Schönlank at *Leipziger Volkszeitung*, only to find that Bebel had blocked this avenue of publication as well.

---

[1] Two of them later became allies once more. Heinrich Wetzker was one of the few personalities in Germany who joined Rosa Luxemburg in her battle against Kautsky in 1910, though his reasons were personal rather than political; he was if anything a 'radical revisionist', who carried on a chronic, subterranean feud with the entire leadership. He was an editor of *Vorwärts* from 1899 to 1905 and had to resign during the purge in November of that year.

Emil Eichhorn was politically much further to the left. He became a member of the opposition to the leadership during the war and was on the left wing of the independent Socialists, the USPD. As Police President of Berlin at the beginning of 1919 he was to play a significant part in setting off the events which led up to Rosa Luxemburg's death.

I do not know what her explanations are, but Rosa Luxemburg acted wrongly and without cause. . . . Her inconceivably tactless statement against her colleagues justifiably should remain unpublished. . . . If I were to meet her I would tell her my opinion in much stronger words. You may show Comrade Luxemburg these lines. I am especially annoyed that she has proved herself too much of a woman and not sufficiently a party comrade. I am disillusioned with her. It is a pity.[1]

Bebel and Schönlank did not get on—the classic rivalry between self-conscious *Kultur* and equally self-conscious 'calloused hands'—but the matter was too serious to be left to run its natural course. Schönlank did not reply to Bebel but he did show the letter to Rosa Luxemburg, who promptly sat down and wrote to the party chairman at length.

I prefer to reply directly to your letter of which a copy reached me through Comrade Schönlank. It is beneath my dignity to go into such matters as 'moral face slaps, unbelievable tactlessness' etc. . . .

. . . Since the days of Parvus conditions on the editorial board [of *SAZ*] have been so disrupted and untenable that there had to be a row sooner or later, the more so since my colleagues were all on edge after the long struggle with Parvus, and were determined to use the change in the editorship to get complete control of the paper. In this they had the support of the press commission who resented all the accusations against the unpleasant and vulgar tone of the paper. . . . For my part I consider it wrong to confine myself—as did Parvus—to the writing of tactical and polemic articles, and let everything else on the paper go to the devil. I considered it my first duty, after the discussion of tactical matters, to improve the state of this neglected paper, and so took an interest in a number of items which gave cause for new frictions with my colleagues. . . . You are of the opinion, then, that in all matters of substance the commission found for me. In fact, however, it turned down all my proposals and requests, it supported my editorial colleagues all the way, and if I had returned to the editorship—given the present conditions and the mood of the press commission—I would have had to give up my independence. Formally it may have appeared merely as a matter of altering my editorial manner but in effect I would soon have been unable to publish my articles—and, more important—Parvus's articles. I said to myself: if *that* is the commission's point of view, then I have nothing more to do here, then everything is *already* lost to us. If the commission intends to give me the necessary freedom of decision they can still tell me so, even after my resignation. Please note, I repeated ten times during the meeting of the commission that I was being *forced* to resign, that there was no way out—they smiled at this as an empty threat, the sort of gesture that Parvus used to make repeatedly. . . .

I hope that with these facts I have shown you that you have been a little hasty in your verdict on my actions.[2]

---

[1] August Bebel to Bruno Schönlank, 3 November 1898, 'Einige Briefe', p. 16.

[2] 'Einige Briefe', p. 17. The letter was never published, but was found among the Bebel papers at IISH.

The many enemies Rosa had made—all the seniors of the Second International who had been stung by the disrespectful young controversialist of Zürich—had watched her unexpected success in Germany with mixed feelings, however much they might admire her intellect. In Dresden she had laid down the law not only to her old opponents on the national question, but to the Germans—as well as the French, the Belgians, and any other party whose affairs came within the range of her interests. The editor of even a middling provincial party paper was a person of some consequence in the Second International. Thus Jaurès and Plekhanov and many others, as well as Victor Adler, were probably pleased that she appeared to have overreached herself. Perhaps now she would learn to serve by waiting a little. Certainly the feeling that Rosa's departure from *Sächsische Arbeiterzeitung* involved any matter of principle was entirely confined to herself.

So ended Rosa Luxemburg's first attempt to participate in the organizational structure of the SPD. She had taken on the editorship in order to project her influence in the party, but she fell victim to the truism that membership of a hierarchy necessarily involves limitations on personal freedom—particularly of public self-expression; that power and influence are sometimes parallel, but more often contradictory. Within the structure of the party her natural disadvantages—youth, foreign origin, sex, above all impatience and intellectual superiority—stood out glaringly. Collective responsibility and cohesion, the hierarchy's mutual self-protection against outsiders—which she despised and attacked—could not suddenly be invoked to her advantage. Her complaint to Bebel and to the press commission that her colleagues would not support her showed that the pressures of institutional cohesion were the same for her as for everyone else. She made one more attempt to 'belong' when she took on the joint editorship of *Leipziger Volkszeitung* after Bruno Schönlank's death. This, too, ended in failure. Henceforward Rosa Luxemburg would accept the implications of her temperament and remain an outsider seeking influence but despising power, attacking the hierarchy's inevitable efforts to cover up for its members, finally attacking the hierarchy—or 'ruling clique' as she called it—for its very existence.

V

THE DIALECTIC AS A CAREER

1899–1904

AFTER the fiasco in Dresden, Rosa Luxemburg moved back to Berlin. Although she now had a few friends—and a much greater number of detractors—there was an inevitable sense of anticlimax. She felt almost as lonely as when she had first come to the capital six months before.

The new rooms were at 23 Wielandstrasse, in Friedenau, a popular residential suburb in the western section of Berlin. Now she was only two streets away from the Kautskys. As a neighbour, she began to see more of them than of anyone else in the party. Their interests and political alignment were alike; close contact soon ripened into friendship. In 1899 she reported to her Swiss friend, Seidel:

The only people I meet here—Friedenau, near Berlin where I live—are the Kautskys, my neighbours, and from time to time Bebel, Mehring, Stadthagen, etc. Mostly however I prefer to sit at home at my desk, in my warm room . . . and read. I fear that more than ever I am able to make do without people, and withdraw more and more into myself. I suppose that this is abnormal, but I don't know—I seem always to have so much material to think about and live through, that I don't feel the vacuum.[1]

Within the year, her friendship with the Kautskys became much closer. The immediate impulse was Rosa's ostentatious gesture in refusing to do a commissioned review for *Sozialistische Monatshefte*, Bernstein's paper, and offering Kautsky first refusal of her piece instead. Impressed and flattered, he asked her to visit them more often: 'We Marxists are unfortunately thin on the ground in Germany, and the present revisionist crisis gives us every reason to stick closely together.'[2] The awe-inspiring sage Franz Mehring, too, had taken a firm liking to the self-confident young woman, almost to the latter's surprise: 'quite un-

---

[1] Seidel letters, *Z Pola Walki*, 1959, No. 1(5), pp. 77–8.
[2] *Letters to Karl and Luise Kautsky*, p. 55; Rosa Luxemburg's handwritten copy of Kautsky's reply is in Jogiches letters, *Z Pola Walki*, 1963, Vol. VI, Nos. 1/2(21–2), p. 333. The whole slightly machiavellian ensnarement of Kautsky had been forced on a reluctant Rosa by Jogiches, who was jubilant at the Kautsky connection—which rather embarrassed Rosa, who did not like political friendships.

deserved . . . friendship always seems to me something unexpected—a gift'.[1]

She did not like Berlin any better—even allowing for the distortion of all comparisons. 'You in Zürich, in that happy, blessed Zürich, have no idea what darkness there is in Berlin during the winter. I have to light my lamp at half past three to write a letter, and you know . . . how I long for sunshine.' This passion at least she shared with the German class enemy, for this was the period when northern Italy and the Mediterranean coast were being 'discovered' by refined, sensitive, middle-class Germans in large numbers; the pioneers of that Anglo-German myth about the soft, all-permissive, lemon-growing 'South', *das Land wo die Zitronen blühen*, constructed on no less respectable a base than Goethe. For Rosa, too, the only thing that could occasionally thaw out the rigid confrontations of the class war was—the sun.

In the summer of 1900 Jogiches had suddenly to leave Zürich, and joined her in Germany at last. At first they lived together in Cuxhavenerstrasse, a more suitable apartment, where she had moved some time in February 1899. But Jogiches did not stay in Berlin very long. The SDKPiL was still largely moribund once more; the movement in Poland had failed to take hold and, as with the Russians, the newly emerged local leadership had to go into exile. Jogiches, restless from the futility of an émigré command without troops—made all the more bitter by contrast with Rosa's successful participation in the SPD—took himself off at the end of 1901 to Algeria, where his brother was dying in a tuberculosis sanatorium. Leo Jogiches remained there for some months; what little party news there was could easily be supplied by Rosa Luxemburg in her frequent letters. He did not return until March 1902, by which time Rosa Luxemburg had finally found the ideal flat at 58 Cranachstrasse, still in Friedenau—the well-loved rooms in which she was to remain for almost ten years. She became very attached to this flat; even while imprisoned in Warsaw in 1906 during the revolution, she was more concerned that the rent payments should be kept up than with her own safety. The red and green rooms, the book-cases, the pictures—some of them painted by her—her cat Mimi; all constantly appear in her letters as the few anchors of an otherwise restless life.

What of the career, which had been driving Jogiches to jealous despair? By 1899 the revisionist controversy was coming to the end of its first, free-for-all, phase. The intellectuals—Kautsky, Parvus, Rosa Luxemburg on one side; Bernstein, Schippel, and Heine on the other—had fought each other to an inconclusive draw, as intellectuals on their

[1] Letter to Minna Kautsky, Karl's mother, 30 December 1900. IISH Archives.

own often do. But, though they had settled nothing by themselves, they had made sufficient noise to draw in the real powers in the party, the 'practicals', the leaders. During the intellectual onslaught on Bernstein, the south German SPD leaders had been singled out as revisionism's most skilful practitioners—and had hit back, not in defence of Bernstein at all, but for self-protection. Indeed, they carefully avoided all reference to Bernstein's ideas, confining themselves to personal tributes in which Kautsky and all the leaders generously joined; they did not intend to become involved in intellectual fireworks. If they had kept quiet, and lain low for a time, the whole thing might well have fizzled out as just another unreal *Wortstreit*, blown up by a few ambitious editors of the party press. As it was, they decided to counter-attack the noisy, irresponsible outsiders—foreigners, to boot—and so forced a reluctant leadership to turn its full slow wrath against them, and against Bernstein too. For the most practical manifestation of revisionism was indiscipline and disobedience, a door opened to centrifugal bourgeois influences. It is difficult to do justice to Rosa Luxemburg's role in this process of 'politicization'—turning an intellectual dispute into a political problem and mobilizing the political forces in the party against the revisionists. Apart from her various articles on particular aspects of revisionism, her most significant contributions were the two series of articles in *Leipziger Volkszeitung* and her support of Schönlank, its distinguished and influential editor. 'The gossip has gone round Kautsky, Mehring and Babel . . . that Schönlank's attitudes are largely due to my influence. Curious mud slinging!'[1]

She could claim with justification that her Bernstein pamphlet, more than any other, had provided an intellectual rallying ground for the opponents of revisionism. 'My articles and particularly my pamphlet have met with approval and are making their mark. They will put the seal on my right to participate in the discussion and you will see that even Bebel at [the coming party congress at] Hanover will simply repeat from my pamphlet, just as Clara Zetkin did [at her recent meeting in Berlin].'[2] She certainly received many letters of support and admiration.

Rosa Luxemburg's view of herself at this stage of the revisionist controversy was a curious mixture of profound scepticism about people, coupled with self-confidence and belief in the possibilities of exercising influence in the German party. However much she feared and disliked the attitude of the German 'establishment', which used people and then discarded them—particularly outsiders—she still felt

[1] Jogiches letters, *Z Pola Walki*, 1963, Vol. VI, No. 3(23), p. 142, dated 24 April 1899.
[2] Jogiches letters, *Z Pola Walki*, 1963, Vol. VI, No. 3(23), 1 May 1899. Rosa Luxemburg also maintained that Kautsky's current writing on the Bernstein question was merely a repetition of what she had said.

that the German party and the leadership were capable of greatness. She argued with Jogiches, whose tendency then as always was to advise personal, behind-the-scenes manipulation rather than open engagement.

As to your accusation that I am an idealist in the German movement, this is ridiculous and I don't agree. Firstly, there are idealists here also—above all an enormous mass of simple agitators from the working masses. Secondly, there are certainly idealists among the leaders as well, for instance Bebel. In the last resort none of this matters to me. The principle which I have adopted from my Polish and German revolutionary experience is this: be always completely indifferent to your surroundings and to other people. I definitely wish to remain an idealist in the German as well as the Polish movement. Naturally this doesn't mean that I want to play the role of a wide-eyed dreamer. . . . Certainly I want to achieve the most influential position possible in the movement but this really need not conflict one bit with one's ideals and does not require the use of any other means but those of my own 'talents', those that I know I have.[1]

If anything, the disillusion in Dresden had been a salutary lesson, and had proved that personal participation in a cliquish, élite-conscious movement was much less productive than the development of her natural talents. Dimly Rosa Luxemburg perceived even at this early date what her real contribution to Socialism was destined to be.

You know what I feel lately but very strongly? Something in me stirs and wants to come to the surface—naturally something intellectual, something to write. Don't worry, it is not poems or novels again. No, my dear, something in the brain. The fact that I have not used a tenth, a hundredth part of my real strength. I am already very fed up with what I am writing, I already feel that I have risen above it. I feel in a word the need, as Heine would say, to 'say something great'. It is the form of writing that displeases me, I feel that within me there is maturing a completely new and original form which dispenses with the usual formulas and patterns and breaks them down, and which will convince people—naturally through force of mind and conviction, and not just propaganda. I badly need to write in such a way as to act on people like a thunderclap, to grip them by the head—not of course through declamation, but by the breadth of outlook, the power of conviction and the strong impressions that I make on them. But how, what, where? I don't know yet. But I tell you that I feel with utter certainty that something is there, that something will be born.[2]

Bebel, Mehring, and Clara Zetkin were all urging her to capitalize on her new reputation with a speech at the SPD congress at Hanover. Jogiches from Zürich urged her to tie Bebel down to a formal commitment for a speech. This she knew was impossible; once more her very

---

[1] Jogiches letters, *Z Pola Walki*, 1963, Vol. VI, No. 3(23), p. 151, 1 May 1899.
[2] Ibid., p. 136. The remark about poems refers to the production of an early manuscript to commemorate the 1st of May 1892 for publication in *Sprawa Robotnicza*—in iambic verse—a performance which Jogiches for years feared she might repeat.

success would rouse the latent opposition of a jealous establishment. When Bebel wrote to her that she really must come to Hanover and discuss with him in advance a 'definite plan of campaign', she commented sarcastically: 'As soon as everything is clearly set to go well, he and Kautsky will quickly cool down and remove me from the agenda. I know this lot like I know my five fingers.' But to Hanover she went none the less; and speak she did. The congress lasted five days, from 9 to 14 October. It was a quiet congress compared with Stuttgart the year before; the executive had merely requested the participants not to engage in personal recriminations and to discuss problems rather than people. To Bebel and Auer, theory was still a useful safety valve which could not harm the political unity of the party.

In accordance with the official line, Rosa confined her speech largely to theoretical questions. None the less, her temperament soon got the better of her; attacking the validity of English analogies for German conditions, she referred to 'comrades with crazy ideas', and immediately her opponents, who had been waiting for just such an outburst, triumphantly called her to order. This was the opportunity for Fendrich, Peus, and all the other trade unionists to hand out punishment for the insult of 'the labours of Sisyphus', one of those gullet-sticking phrases at which Rosa excelled. On the whole it was Rosa Luxemburg who was on the defensive (Parvus, who had been merely an unofficial delegate at Stuttgart the year before, was not present at all this time), while the eminent 'practicals' took the offensive. Vollmar even paid her a back-handed compliment: 'Comrade Luxemburg has been surprisingly mild this time . . . in order to lay such a gaseous egg, was there really need for so much squawking?'[1] Several times the chairman of the congress had to protect her from the sarcasm of her opponents, and Rosa herself reminded them that they were not a discussion club where words carried no real weight, but an embattled party.

Encouraged by the increasingly firm stand of the executive against at least the theoretical conception of revisionism, Rosa returned to her attack on *Vorwärts*, an issue that had remained in suspense since the argument over the editorship of *Sächsische Arbeiterzeitung*. Her old enemy Gradnauer was still ensconced in *Vorwärts*, together with Kurt Eisner and other even more clearly defined revisionists. In September 1899, even before the Hanover congress, Rosa Luxemburg published an article in *Leipziger Volkszeitung* in which she roundly accused the party central organ of having no opinion of any kind. Such a wishy-washy policy could not, as Gradnauer claimed, be based on the party programme. 'The party needs neither a standing nor a lying but a forward-marching central organ, and it is to be hoped that the Hanover

---

[1] *Protokoll . . . 1899*, p. 215.

party congress will set it on its feet and give it a push.'[1] Gradnauer, with evident pleasure, replied in *Vorwärts* on 24 September 1899: 'Comrade Luxemburg should be the last to live under the illusion that it is her duty to lecture us on how to run a paper. She should not forget too quickly that her own attempt to head a party paper finished in the shortest possible time with the quickest possible push—for her; a tragi-comedy.'

This produced one of Rosa's sarcastic outbursts, after which there was little left to say. It was no use expecting *Vorwärts* to express an opinion; to express something, you must first have it. No editor of *Vorwärts* would ever walk out voluntarily as she had done in Dresden; questions of principle, of backbone, never arose there. 'There are two types of living organisms, those who possess a backbone and therefore walk, at times even run; the others, invertebrate, who either creep or cling.'[2] She developed an almost gallic gift for political epigram, which made her not only readable but quotable, that essential prerequisite for political influence.[3]

The support she had received from Wilhelm Liebknecht at the Hanover Congress brought about a *rapprochement* between her and the old man shortly before his death. Their differences had largely been over Polish questions, for Liebknecht, 'the secretary of all foreign parties in Berlin', had not only a sentimental attachment to the old Marxist ideal of Polish independence, but a voracious appetite for telling foreigners their business—or rather, suggesting it forcefully.[4] But the insistent and opinionated young woman was much less disagreeable when, in the revisionist debate, she used her Marx more literally—the right way up—and when her pen flashed in the same direction as his own. He was always willing to let bygones be bygones. When in September 1899 one of the editorial places at *Vorwärts* became vacant, he himself suggested Rosa Luxemburg. The executive wanted to put some life into the central party organ, but had difficulty in finding a suitable young man and had even cast about as far as Vienna for candidates.[5] However, Bebel, a more astute politician than Liebknecht, saw that Rosa's appointment could only lead to trouble: 'I shall advise Comrade Luxemburg to withdraw. I think she will have a tough time and would shortly leave on her own account. The editors admittedly made as if

---

[1] 'Unser leitendes Zentralorgan', *LV*, 22 September 1899.
[2] *LV*, 26 September 1899.
[3] She found an equally telling phrase for a press service started in 1904 by Friedrich Stampfer, in which well-known revisionists like Wilhelm Keil participated: 'an opinion factory for the confusion of working class brains'. Friedrich Stamper, *Erfahrungen und Erkenntnisse, Aufzeichnungen aus meinem Leben*, Cologne 1957, p. 94.
[4] Victor Adler, *Aufsätze, Reden und Briefe*, Vol. 6, p. 297.
[5] Adolf Hoffmann to Victor Adler, 23 October 1899.

she were welcome, but that is pure hypocrisy. I shall vote for Ströbel.'[1]
He bluntly told Rosa the same thing; the last thing he wanted was a
repetition of the Dresden scandel in the inner sanctum of the party
leadership.[2] Sensibly enough, Rosa herself wrote to the chairman of the
press commission briefly and formally, withdrawing her candidature.

After this incident and until Liebknecht's death in August 1900, there
was a pale autumnal friendship between them. Rosa was more upset by
his death than she herself expected. At the time she wrote:

Recently when I was at the *Vorwärts* office, the old man took me aside and
suddenly whispered in parting, 'I will always do everything I can for you. My
suggestion for you to become an editor was meant perfectly seriously and I
would have been glad to have you. Whenever you have something stirring to say
[*etwas fulminantes*] give it to me for *Vorwärts*; it does after all carry more weight
there than in the *Leipziger Volkszeitung*.' I promised to do so, and he extended a
warm invitation to me to visit him, saying that he and his wife would always be
glad to see me. A bagatelle, but I was glad to have parted from him in peace.[3]

At the end of December 1899 she was canvassing once more in the
Polish areas of Upper Silesia, whence had come her mandates for the
Hanover congress. The SPD was by now living in increasing discomfort
with the Polish Socialist Party of Prussia, founded in 1893 if not as a
completely separate and independent party, at least as a means of
miniature Polish duplication of all SPD functions, from local cell to
national party congress. For Rosa's purposes it was the Russo-Polish
PPS all over again. The Poles in Germany played hard on the SPD's
bad conscience about the underprivileged Poles, and on the peculiar
and incomprehensible nature of Polish politics. At first the question
was mainly one of organizational definition, so that the parties should
not get in each other's hair. From the beginning, the Poles got moral
support and advice from Daszyński across the Austrian border; his
ideal was the Austrian Social Democrats, a federated party made up of
independent national organizations. The Prussian Poles also received
SPD subsidies, especially for their paper, the *Gazeta Robotnicza*. But
with the appearance of Rosa Luxemburg in Germany, the latent
organizational friction was brought into the open by the question of
principle which she had brought, battle-scarred, from two international
congresses—Polish self-determination. As the controversy in 1896 had
shown, no important member of the SPD shared her theoretical platform
in public, though some agreed with her on the quiet. However, events
soon played into her hand. By constant hammering on the covert
emergence of a separate PPS organization in Germany, duplicating and

---

[1] August Bebel to Karl Kautsky, 24 November 1899; also August Bebel to Victor Adler,
27 November 1899, in 'Einige Briefe', p. 30.
[2] Jogiches letters, end of November 1899. IML (M).
[3] *Letters to Karl and Luise Kautsky*, p. 66, about 9 August 1900.

displacing that of the German party, Rosa Luxemburg touched the SPD on its most sensitive spot—not intellectual unanimity but organizational control. Gradually, under such iron-clad cover, she managed more and more to insinuate her ideas of principle into the minds of the SPD leadership, self-confessedly ignorant about Polish affairs. She did this with great tactical skill and forbearance, never overplaying her hand; indeed, it was the only tactical campaign of her life from which she emerged wholly victorious.

The first thing was to transfer the battle from Upper Silesia 200 miles to the north, to the politically hostile 'jungle' of Posen (Poznań). Here an old comrade-in-arms was installed. Marcin Kasprzak had remained in Prussia after his release from prison in 1896.[1] The Prussian PPS, which he had joined as political cover, had evicted him after the sustained campaign alleging theft and treachery which emanated from the leaders of the PPS in London. Already in 1898 she had tentatively inquired how he stood in regard to the questions she was currently agitating in Upper Silesia, and had received a characteristically curt but favourable response. Now Rosa Luxemburg, Kasprzak, and Gogowski —another Polish supporter of Rosa's—worked on the creation of a trade-union organization in Poznań, favourable to her principles of complete integration in the SPD.[2] Poznań was industrially one of the least organized areas in Germany, and the Polish workers supported the bourgeois Polish National Democrats. One of Rosa's friends graphically described the work to the sympathetic Kautskys four years later during the 1903 *Reichstag* election campaign. 'Our Rosa has gone into the desert and is now immersed in very hard, health-breaking work . . . and what a desert! Not a trace of modern culture, only clericalism and feudalism, everything has to be started from scratch. The worst of it is, I can't help her myself [not being a German citizen].'[3]

The PPS at first tried peace overtures. Rosa herself attended the fifth Prussian PPS congress at Easter 1900. 'Her supporters submitted two sharply worded resolutions against the "nationalist fantasies" of the Prussian PPS; indeed, the resolutions called for no less than complete dissolution of the Polish party and its absorption by the SPD.'[4] Rosa supported the resolutions with a pointed and polemical speech.[5] The

---

[1] See above, pp. 61 ff.

[2] Zbigniew Szumowski, 'Ruch robotniczy w Poznaniu do 1918 roku' (Labour movement in Poznań until 1918) in *Dziesięć wieków Poznania* (A millennium of Poznań), Vol. I of *Dzieje społeczno-gospodarcze*, Poznań 1956, p. 182; also *Protokoll des dritten Gewerkschaftskongresses 1899*, p. 23.

[3] Adolf Warszawski to Karl Kautsky, 20 May 1903, IISH Archives, D XXIII, 63. See also *Vorwärts*, 20 October 1899.

[4] *Vorwärts*, 3 April 1900; *Gazeta Robotnicza*, 7 April 1900.

[5] The speech was reprinted in *Gazeta Robotnicza*, 28 April, 5 May 1900, and also in *Vorwärts*, 18, 20 April, and other papers. It made a quite a stir.

party congress naturally resisted this attempt to make it vote its own dissolution, and Rosa—who probably had never expected that her resolutions would be adopted—cleverly withdrew them and offered a compromise: the creation of a press commission to be responsible for propaganda and for supervising the editorial policy of *Gazeta Robot-nicza*. The executive of the PPS apparently believed that this sudden change of direction could lead to the conversion of their bitterest opponent into a potential supporter, and even supported her election to this proposed press commission. However, Rosa merely used the opportunity, as might have been expected, to combat the ideas of the PPS from within it and to try to destroy the close connection between the PPS executive and its paper. When, later, the PPS tried to obtain her agreement to the idea of an independent Poland as a 'compromise solution', Rosa Luxemburg instantly took up in public her complaints against 'the destructive operations of the nationalists'. Within three months the artificial alliance had been exploded.[1]

At the next German party congress in Mainz, 17–21 September 1900, she again represented Polish constituencies in Upper Silesia and Posen, and spoke mainly on Polish questions. The congress had before it a resolution protesting against the Prussian government's measures to eradicate the use of the Polish language in schools and the general tendency to treat Poles as second-class citizens. Rosa, now on the offensive, wanted to augment this resolution, to adjure the Polish worker 'to give up national utopias, and to accept that his national interests are best taken care of by Social Democracy, and not by taking up a separate position as a Pole in the wake of nationalist parties'. One of the PPS speakers attacked Rosa Luxemburg, referring particularly to an article she had written in which she had used the objectionable words 'social nationalists' and 'social patriots'.[2] 'She would not have dared to rely on the words of Wilhelm Liebknecht if he had still been alive; one need only refer to the letter he wrote her shortly after the Hamburg congress in 1897.'

By this time the PPS had reached the stage of putting up Polish-speaking candidates against the official SPD candidates, thus splitting the working-class vote in the Polish-speaking areas. This was obviously news for the majority of the congress; when Rosa Luxemburg mentioned it there was a general disturbance. Most of the delegates, even the leadership, were unfamiliar with the problem, as they freely admitted. Rosa also pointed out that it had been her influence at the last provincial congress that had prevented the Polish organizations in Germany from authorizing an official Polish candidate to be put up against the SPD in Upper Silesia to spite Winter. But, in addition to separate parliamentary

[1] *Vorwärts*, 18, 20, and 29 April, 24 and 26 August 1900.
[2] *Protokoll . . . 1900*, p. 125. The article is in *Vorwärts*, 26 August 1900.

candidates, the *Gazeta Robotnicza*, German-financed but Polish-controlled, was now even calling for the establishment of exclusively Polish trade unions.

In the winter of 1900, at the insistence of Rosa, a 'summit conference' between SPD and PPS executives was at last organized; Dr. Winter, Gogowski, and she herself attended as consulting 'experts'. The Germans now took the offensive, accusing the PPS of nationalism, of irresponsible attacks against Kasprzak, an innocent comrade. They insisted that either he or Rosa must join the editorial board of *Gazeta Robotnicza*. When this was refused, the Germans withdrew their subsidy as of 1 April 1901. What annoyed them even more was their failure in the Posen by-election for the *Reichstag* in March 1901. The SPD executive had requested the PPS to support Kasprzak, their official candidate, or at least not to oppose him openly; instead, the Poles agitated loudly against him with the old accusations and nearly put up their own opposition candidate, as a result of which—or so it was held—Kasprzak obtained less than 3 per cent of the total poll.[1]

At the Lübeck congress (22–28 September 1901) the executive, despite the protest of several members, obtained the party's approval for its decision to withdraw financial support from the *Gazeta Robotnicza*. The official grounds for stopping the subsidy were slightly hypocritical: not the oppositional tendencies of the Polish Socialists, but the failure of the paper to achieve a circulation commensurate with the expenditure which the SPD executive had lavished upon it. The PPS supporters reverted once more to personal denigrations borrowed from the old PPS armoury. Biniszkiewicz told the Lübeck congress that Marcin Kasprzak 'had fled to the German party and pretends to be an honest man, but in reality it is because his existence in Poland has become impossible . . . we cannot work together with people like Kasprzak . . . some of the so-called Poles in Germany are not Poles at all, are born abroad, and do not even speak a word of Polish.'[2]

These harsh words were the product of defeat. Guided by Rosa, the SPD executive treated the PPS with increasing hostility. In doing so it obtained the support of what, for Rosa, were unfamiliar allies in the party—establishment figures like Auer who believed that organizational unity was sacrosanct, and that the reasonable interests of the majority must prevail against a minority, however vocal.[3] There were others who

---

[1] *Vorwärts*, 7 February 1901; *Gazeta Robotnicza*, 20 March 1901; also Florian Miedzyński, 'Marcin Kasprzak 1860–1905' in *Wybitni Wielkopolanie XIX wieku*, Poznań 1959, p. 436.

[2] *Protokoll . . . 1901*, p. 125. The executive in fact reported its investigations into the Kasprzak case at this congress. The PPS executive had formally accused him of treachery and various other things, which finally boiled down to the concrete complaint that he had stolen 60 marks deposited with him by Polish comrades. A commission of the SPD had looked into the charges and declared them groundless.

[3] Quoted by Wehler, *Sozialdemokratie*, p. 141.

simply felt that a big German party was not going to be dictated to by a small Polish one, especially one that big brother was financing. The whole concept of separate Polish organizations, even within the broader framework of SPD policy, was challenged in the course of the German counter-attack. And under such massive cover, Rosa and her friends infiltrated further into the PPS stronghold. In Posen a new Polish organization mushroomed out of the ground demanding sole recognition by the SPD authorities, 'now that relations between German Social Democracy and PPS had been totally broken off'.[1]

Now Rosa Luxemburg felt strong enough to come out openly once more for her own basic principles and against Polish self-determination, instead of taking refuge behind the organizational squabble. Whether this was deliberate planning or emerged in the heat of debate at the 1901 SPD congress at Lübeck was uncertain, though Rosa had by now acquired sufficient self-control to overcome the impulses of spontaneous anger. We may safely assume that her outburst was planned.

Meantime the PPS attempted to defy the German party openly. At a meeting at Auschwitz (Oświęcim) in Austrian Silesia on 13 July 1902, eight Polish opposition candidates were nominated to stand against the SPD. At the SPD congress at Munich on 14 September there was accordingly a more heated discussion than ever. Rosa and twenty-two German delegates submitted a resolution 'condemning the independent grouping of the PPS and their separate mandates as sharply as possible, and calling on them to dissolve their separate organization'.[2] Even Bebel mildly criticized Rosa Luxemburg's apparent intransigence—though it was the high point of their friendship and co-operation—and submitted a compromise amendment to her resolution. 'Comrade Luxemburg told me *privatim* a short while ago that if I was not prepared to go all the way with her point of view, there was in the end no point in her being restrained and sensible for once', at which everyone laughed, Rosa included. Yet the problem of the Polish population in Germany, quite apart from the 60,000 mine workers in the west German coalfields, was crying out for a solution, either a German or a Polish one. Bebel and the German executive began to think that perhaps they should not drive things to an extreme. Bebel sighed that relations with the Poles in Germany would be far better 'if only these were headed by a man of Daszyński's intelligence', which was no compliment to Rosa Luxemburg.[3]

The PPS was in dire financial straits, and also had second thoughts.

---

[1] *LV*, 30 May 1901; *Vorwärts*, 29 and 30 May 1901. For the PPS side, see *Sprawozdanie z obrad VI Zjazdu PPS . . . 1901 w Berlinie* (Report of Proceedings of the 6th PPS congress . . . 1901 in Berlin), ZHP.

[2] *Protokoll . . . 1902*, p. 148.

[3] *Protokoll . . . 1902*, p. 152.

A new unity conference took place in October 1902, shortly after the SPD congress, made up of the two executives, with a panel of experts consisting this time of Daszyński from Galicia, Rosa Luxemburg, and representatives from Posen and Silesia. The Germans presented their organizational demands, and Rosa contributed her own special theses: the Prussian PPS to become the 'Polish Social Democracy in Germany', with explicitly no self-determination in its programme; the Polish party executive and the board of *Gazeta Robotnicza* to be made up equally of representatives from Posen, where she was strong, and Silesia, where she was not.[1] How Rosa must have enjoyed sitting opposite her old enemy Daszyński, with all the weight of the great SPD behind her. She was at the height of her influence. When the PPS, after bitter argument, decided at its seventh congress to accept the German organizational conditions and in effect merge with the SPD, Rosa suddenly reappeared in print with a further demand—for the inevitable statement renouncing self-determination, though this thesis had not been insisted upon by the SPD at the October meeting; indeed, she had specifically withdrawn it there, since at one stage it had been the only obstacle to agreement.[2]

This was sheer bravado, but Rosa still retained the support of Dr. Winter and the SPD executive—as she had known she would. The latter went back on the word of their previous negotiator and insisted on further negotiations; also that Rosa and Marcin Kasprzak be formally invited to join the PPS. Even this slap in the face was accepted.[3] But the now thoroughly roused organizational fears of the SPD were still not allayed. Baulked on her question of principle, Rosa determined to push the complete destruction of separate Polish organizations down the throats of her opponents; they were not even to elect their own executive in the future, and were to sign a secret protocol 'not to pursue any separate policy demanding the re-creation of an independent Poland'.[4] And it was only through Bebel's intervention that the required undertaking was made into a secret instead of a public document, a device that Bebel was notoriously to use again later.[5]

But this time Rosa's determination to humiliate her opponents had gone too far. Infuriated more by the breach of faith than by the actual

---

[1] *Vorwärts*, 10, 11 October, 28 November, 28 December 1902. The PPS wrote an open letter to the SPD, a copy of which, in Rosa Luxemburg's writing, presumably noted from the original for propaganda purposes, is in ZHP.

[2] The new condition is discussed in *Vorwärts*, 28 December 1902, and in full in *Sprzawoz-danie z VIII Zjazdu PPS . . . 1905 r. w Katowicach* (Proceedings of 8th PPS congress 1905 in Katowice), pp. 8–12.

[3] *Vorwärts*, 1 January 1903; *Volkswacht*, Breslau, 12 January 1903; in general, see Wehler, *Sozialdemokratie*, p. 149.

[4] Rosa Luxemburg's note in *Open Letter*, p. 20 (see note 1, above).

[5] *Protokoll . . . 1903*, p. 280. See below, p. 298.

conditions, the PPS now withdrew all its consents and, on 14 March 1903, finally broke off negotiations. A temporary arrangement for the 1903 elections was nevertheless worked out at the last moment, though the SPD–PPS results in Silesia and Posen were disappointing.

The supporters of the PPS, especially Ledebour and Konrad Haenisch—there were many Polish labourers in the Dortmund area where the latter worked—attacked the methods of the executive at the Dresden congress of 1903. Ledebour made a point of pillorying the real initiator of these perfidies, Rosa Luxemburg. He disclosed that the paper published by her group, the *Gazeta Ludowa*, which the SPD was now subsidizing instead of the *Gazeta Robotnicza*, cost the executive 70 marks per subscriber, since the subsidy of 2,600 marks had to cover precisely 37 of them.[1] But by this time the executive and the party congress were tired of this question; Rosa wisely undertook to answer Ledebour's charges later and outside the congress, though she and Ledebour argued the toss intermittently for another two months in the hospitable but indifferent pages of *Vorwärts*.[2]

The history of the Polish problem in the SPD shows how Rosa Luxemburg was able to get her way in the end, at least on the surface. In spite of the commitment to offer all matters of importance for the judgement of the party congress, many of the day-to-day decisions in the SPD had to be taken by the executive, and these created a momentum of policy that was very hard to break—and especially in awkward, unfamiliar matters like the Polish sub-life in German Socialism. Rosa Luxemburg and her friends succeeded, between 1899 and 1903, in cutting the ground from under the feet of their opponents in the German party. By 1903 Rosa was the acknowledged authority in Germany on Polish questions. Requests to speak were incessant, sometimes in strange company with the danger of physical assault. 'I'm supposed to go to Posen to a meeting of the Polish People's Party to open the discussion, seeing that we can't have any meeting hall for ourselves. Nice prospect; in several such meetings our people have been beaten up and pretty thoroughly . . . I'm very curious whether I shall stop a few blows myself.'[3] Anyone in Poland who wanted something from the SPD executive, and especially from Kautsky or Bebel, was well advised to obtain her clearance first.

Of course the separatist movement among the Poles in the Reich was too strong to be reversed. The PPS programme of national restoration exercised a great pull; even the SPD executive could not prevent the PPS increasing its influence from its strong base in Austrian Poland. In

---

[1] *Protokoll . . . 1903*, p. 277.

[2] *Vorwärts*, 17 October, 5 December, 20 December 1903.

[3] Rosa Luxemburg to Franz Mehring, 1903(?) IML(M) Fund 201, No. 844, photocopy IML(B), NL2 III–A/18.

the process, relations between the German and Austrian Socialist parties became very strained—and Victor Adler and his lieutenants, at any rate, thought they knew exactly whom they had to blame for the SPD's uncompromising policies of integration. Though the revolutionary atmosphere of 1906 finally produced a German–Polish agreement—on SPD terms—by 1908 the Poles were back once more to separatist propaganda and activities. From 1906 till 1913 relations between the two parties oscillated between politely cool and very frosty. But by that time Rosa was herself preoccupied with the revolution in Russian Poland and SDKPiL policy in the Russian context; after her return from Warsaw she lost interest in the minutiae of party affairs and concentrated on broader aspects of policy. Finally, she fell out with Kautsky and Bebel; by 1911 she had lost much of her influence on the SPD executive in German matters and made no sustained efforts to mobilize German support against the new, far more nationalistic, executive of the PPS which had taken over from the old leadership of Berfus in 1905. Her direct attempts to influence and organize a Polish labour movement in Posen based on her ideas and those of her friends Kasprzak and Gogowski were in the long run also doomed to failure. In this area of agriculture and small industry the influence of clergy and middle-class nationalism was too strong. The *Gazeta Ludowa* with its 37 subscribers of 1903 finally folded up a year later; the last issue appeared on 1 July 1904 after the SPD had withdrawn financial support from it as well as from its PPS opponent.

As in 1898, Rosa Luxemburg's success with the German Poles earned her the respect of party headquarters, in particular that of the highly organization-minded Bebel. Organizational preoccupations were now generally to the fore in the party. The revisionist controversy had developed into an open power confrontation within the party, regional against central authority, trade unions against party, spontaneity against discipline. Bernstein and his analysis was nowhere. Not entirely with cynicism, Bernstein had subscribed to the vaguely condemnatory congress resolutions in 1898 and 1899 which asserted the continued, chronic validity of 'the good old principles'—and was to do so again when a much sharper resolution appeared in 1901. On this point there was apparently little left to argue about. But the cohesion and discipline of the party, the alignment behind the central executive of all the important publications and regional executives was still a very open question. Thus by 1901 the SPD executive—and Bebel in particular—were ready for a more taxing trial of strength with the practitioners of revisionism. They drummed up a crusade. Parvus was expressly summoned from a lengthy silence into a new outburst of polemics.[1] Fully aware of the

---

[1] 'Der Opportunismus in der Praxis', *NZ*, 1900-1, Vol. II, pp. 609, 673, 740, 786.

irony of this sudden courtship, he wrote to Kautsky, not without justi-
fiable sarcasm: 'Now by taking issue with me over my strong language,
and so keeping yourself at a careful distance from me, you can help to
defend our common point of view all the more ruthlessly. You are, as it
were, advancing under covering fire—whether you would have fought
so bravely without covering fire, I doubt.'[1] Rosa, too, was formally
enlisted for the Lübeck congress by the executive. 'Best regards to Rosa,
and tell her to put on her most shining armour for Lübeck.' Bebel himself promised to intervene actively. 'The next speech which I will fire at
[Bernstein] will be such a battering as he has never hitherto experienced.'[2]
For Bebel, a superb tactician, still found it advisable to flog his enemy
at one remove—through the convenient pelt of Eduard Bernstein;
another example of a technique adopted but not invented by today's
Communist leaders.

The general recommendation of fierceness was followed by precise
combat orders. 'I recommend that Rosa keep her eye firmly on the
Baden legislature [voting for provincial budgets]. Better still if a
resolution on this subject were put up—she can always refer to the
appeal by the party executive. . . .'[3]

At the congress itself Bebel pronounced a lengthy and powerful
indictment of the revisionists. Rosa's own contribution was limited,
partly because she had to leave before the end in order to appear in
court on a charge of sedition, arising out of her Polish pamphlet 'In
Defence of Nationality'. Her opponents, however, took the opportunity
of her absence to attack her as well as Parvus for their renewed polemics.
As Parvus had correctly pointed out, they were being used as scapegoats for the executive. The party membership did not know that the
sudden revival of the onslaught in the press against the revisionists was
in part officially inspired. Bebel himself admitted the equivocal nature of
their position.

. . . the articles [Parvus's 'Der Opportunismus in der Praxis'] are not in fact a
personal degradation of Vollmar and Bernstein but an objective if not always
correct criticism. But our sensitive brethren [Gefühlsmeier] who are always
opposed to anything personal, and who anyhow have Parvus stuck in their
throats like a fishbone, will certainly be all worked up [at the congress] and will
make our position difficult. You cannot imagine the animosity against Parvus
and also La Rosa in the party, and even if I am not of the opinion that we
should be guided by such prejudices we cannot at the same time afford to ignore
them completely.[4]

Other prominent party members had their piece to say in private as

[1] Parvus to Kautsky, no date (1901), 'Einige Briefe', p. 27.
[2] August Bebel to Karl Kautsky, 24 July 1901, 'Einige Briefe', p. 28.
[3] August Bebel to Karl Kautsky, 29 August 1901, 'Einige Briefe', p. 28.
[4] August Bebel to Karl Kautsky, 4 September 1901, 'Einige Briefe', p. 28.

well as in public about the tone of the polemics. Ignaz Auer wrote to Kautsky about 'all that noise down there from Rosa, Mehring, Parvus . . . who consider themselves to be the exclusive proprietors of the last and final truth . . . look round in our party, who cares about the rigid tactics preached by you [all]? Not a soul.'[1]

Both Rosa and Parvus appeared on the face of it to be much more isolated than they really were. The personal onslaught against them both at Lübeck made Bebel prevaricate once more about the tone of their polemics. It requires 'considerable tastelessness to present distinguished party comrades as it were in their bathing costumes to the public gaze', he now admitted.[2] Richard Fischer spoke of 'literary Teddy boys' (*Raufbolde*); one of the south German delegates spoke of the 'unpleasant tone in the party press produced by the male and female immigration from the East'. And it was Heine who had to be officially rebuked by the congress chairman for drawing the final conclusion—that Parvus's and Rosa's articles were positively correlated to the rising wave of anti-Semitism in Germany.[3] But the mood of the party had subtly hardened against the revisionists; their outcry was no more than the diversion of a rearguard. No one attacked Kautsky any more for supporting Rosa and Parvus. Even Victor Adler in Vienna, though still fulminating against Rosa's monstrous tactlessness, admitted that 'I can begin to understand these otherwise incomprehensible excesses when I consider my own discomfort at the spread of revisionism in all its various manifestations'.[4] The warmest support for Rosa and Parvus on this issue came from the Russians, especially Martov.[5]

On 30 October 1901 Bruno Schönlank died, and Rosa Luxemburg was invited to take over as joint editor of *Leipziger Volkszeitung*, in which she had published most of her work since her break with the Dresden paper three years before. Schönlank had made it perfectly clear that he wished his protégée to succeed him. By this time she was a national figure. When the news of her appointment was published, the Conservative *Kreuzzeitung* called on the police to extradite her; the *Vossische Zeitung* suggested that at least the party should get rid of her. Franz Mehring congratulated 'our young friend at the horror which the mere mention of her name called forth [on the other side]'.[6]

It was to be a co-operative effort between Mehring and herself as joint part-time editors—the most distinguished journalistic talent the SPD could muster. Rosa was still reluctant to move to Leipzig alto-

<hr/>

[1] Ignaz Auer to Karl Kautsky, 11 June and 9 December 1901, ibid.
[2] *Protokoll . . . 1901*, p. 165.
[3] *Protokoll . . . 1901*, pp. 191, 189, 195.
[4] 'Unmassgebliche Betrachtungen', *NZ*, 1900-1, Vol. II, p. 779.
[5] See Ignotus (Martov), 'The Lübeck SPD congress', *Zarya*, Nos. 2-3, December 1901, pp. 417-19.
[6] *LV*, 31 May 1902.

gether. To Clara Zetkin she wrote on 16 March 1902 that she still had 'so much unquenched thirst for education and knowledge; I am so strongly drawn to scientific, theoretical work. . . . You know as well as I do that conscientious editorship and scientific self-education don't go together. . . . Franz [Mehring] and I have specifically taken on the political direction and have a free hand to do as we like on the paper. We can carry out all necessary reforms, hire and fire collaborators, etc.'[1]

Mehring's congratulations were short-lived. In practice the day-to-day collaboration with Rosa did not work out happily. The details were not made public, but by the late spring of 1902 they had completely fallen out. Mehring complained about her to all and sundry; to Kautsky he wrote in his style of warped courtesy about 'the lady Luxemburg's power complex, her dirty power-grabbing attitude'—at a time when they were still officially collaborating![2] It is not hard to guess what happened. Rosa tried to emulate her distinguished predecessor Schönlank, to impose her will and policy on staff and collaborators alike; they, however, were not willing to accept from a young and rather aggressive woman what they had taken from the most distinguished journalist and editor in the SPD. Mehring, instead of helping, hindered and obstructed at every turn; he felt his own status to be at stake. It was the story of the *Sächsische Arbeiterzeitung* all over again, though this time there was not even any matter of principle involved.

After a few months Rosa left this post as well. Her departure was less publicized than the earlier one from Dresden, and the circumstances have never been entirely cleared up. Apparently the editorial board tried to put the new editor under firmer control and Rosa found this unacceptable. One of her biographers has suggested that she lacked staying power, that she was essentially a rolling stone as far as any administrative work was concerned, but the evidence suggests that her reasons for leaving Leipzig were more positive than this.[3] In the course of her departure she fell out with Mehring openly and completely, especially since it was he who now took over as sole editor. By October 1902 she had given up all collaboration with the paper. She claimed that too many of her articles found their way into the wastepaper basket, and that her successor would not defend her interests with sufficient vigour. Frölich speaks of 'an icy letter breaking all relations', which she is supposed to have written to Mehring.[4] Whatever the real issue of the quarrel, they were again on better terms the following year, after Rosa had defended him at the 1903 congress where he suddenly found him-

[1] Photocopy IML(B), NL2/20, pp. 46–7.

[2] Letter dated 5 January 1902, No. 162, IISH Archives.

[3] H. Roland-Holst, *Rosa Luxemburg*, p. 47. Rosa's own version in Jogiches letters, *Z Pola Walki*, 1965, No. 1.

[4] Frölich, p. 92.

self the subject of a highly personal and bitter attack for his anti-Socialist writings thirty years earlier.

The affair of the Leipzig editorship certainly helped to confirm Rosa's reputation as a cantankerous female, even among those who wished her well. An incidental result was that, as a regular contributor, only the pages of *Neue Zeit* now remained open to her, and she was only too well aware of the limitations which this imposed.[1] Bebel, at the moment kindly disposed towards her, warned her not to fall out indiscriminately with Left and Right by hitting out in all directions; this could only result in her complete isolation in the German party.[2] The warning was well meant—a politician must know how to close down his anger—but Rosa, stung by the monotonous attacks both within the SPD and in the bourgeois press, was roused to an excited defence of her position.

. . . If I were inclined to sulk, I would truly have had ample opportunity already —from the first moment of my appearance in the German party, from the Stuttgart party conference onwards. In spite of the peculiar reception which I and other non-Germans—comrades not *de la maison*—have had to put up with, I have not missed any opportunity to stick my neck out for trouble. It did not occur to me, quite apart from any question of sulking, even to withdraw to the much more agreeable safety of purely scientific study. . . .

. . . Since June I have been pushed out [of *LV*] step by step through Lensch [one of the editors], and if I have committed any sin, it is an excess of my almost cow-like patience, with which I have let myself be kicked around by too much consideration for personal friendships, instead of getting out on my own account and at once.[3]

'Cow-like patience' was perhaps going rather far, but Rosa had the Russian view of polemics—a necessary form of Socialist self-expression, in which people's names and to some extent even their personalities served as symbols in a political equation. Personal dislike as a political end in itself was alien to her; one should not attack people in public except for political purposes. To this extent her attitude was the exact opposite of her German colleagues' who deplored personal politics in public but respected private personal dislike. Rosa extended the area of politics well beyond the essentially bourgeois limits of the SPD—not in terms of attitude but of range. When she relaxed, wrote letters about botany or classical literature, took pity on a frozen beetle, she was not withdrawing from politics but fulfilling her concept of a wholly political life. This is what gives all those 'non-political' letters a slightly self-conscious, even unctuous tone, and the appearance of a theatrical performance; private life, perhaps, but always with a highly political basis. Rosa's real privacy was of a different and very secret order.

---

[1] Seidel letters, *Z Pola Walki*, 1959, No. 1(5), p. 86.
[2] 'Einige Briefe', p. 34.
[3] Rosa Luxemburg to August Bebel, 11 October 1902, ibid.

In any case these events did not seriously weaken her position. The executive had not yet finished with the Polish problem, nor with the revisionists. In the 1903 *Reichstag* elections the SPD made an important advance in voting strength, raising its *Reichstag* representation to eighty-one. Rosa contributed to this triumph in Polish-speaking Posen and in Chemnitz, the centre of the textile area, where she established her campaign headquarters for Saxony. Every day there were crowded meetings, in the open air, in beer halls—anywhere with enough space. Thousands came to hear her. The candidate she was supporting was none other than Max Schippel a well known revisionist. 'He would prefer no meetings, no handbills, no argument . . . he feared that his opponents might recall that Bebel had called him a rascal [at the 1902 party congress]. That of course was a jab for my benefit. . . .'[1] But when it came to fighting against the class enemy, it made no difference whether the candidate was *kosher* or revisionist. She strongly objected to the suggestion that any personal resentment would prevent her from supporting SPD candidates anywhere in an election: 'Right off the beam. To hell with it. I used to work for the worst revisionists; now I should let personal friction prevent me from helping my political friends!'[2]

This success at the polls encouraged the executive to make what they hoped would be a final reckoning with the revisionists at that year's party congress. The areas of permissible contact with bourgeois politics were at last tightly defined and limited. Rosa's direct participation was no longer required, since the executive was itself prepared to occupy the positions of the advance guard which it had pushed out in 1901. This was the high-water mark of Rosa's position and prestige. She attended the 1904 International congress at Amsterdam in a dual capacity, both as a German delegate with a mandate from Bydgoszcz (Bromberg), and as a Polish delegate with a mandate from the SDKPiL central committee in Poznań. For the first time there were no mandate challenges. She was one of the two German members on a congress committee to report on trusts and unemployment, and the Polish representative on the more important commission on international Socialist tactics. In the latter she brought an amendment to a resolution by the Italian Ferri, in which she reiterated that Socialist tactics could only be based on the total class struggle—her contribution to the general pressure on the French to achieve unity based on firm Marxist principles. She defended the right of the small delegations—Russia, Poland, Bulgaria, Spain, and Japan—to vote on the congress resolution on Socialist tactics, against

---

[1] *Letters to Karl and Luise Kautsky*, p. 70, dated 6 June 1903.

[2] *Briefe an Freunde*, p. 28: letter to Konrad Haenisch, 2 December 1911. The 'political friend' in question was Henke from Bremen, a Left radical and friend of Karl Radek, whom he had staunchly supported against the SPD executive and Rosa. See below, pp. 310–11.

the proposal by the Belgian Socialist Anseele that only the parties most affected should be allowed to meddle in such an important issue with its vital consequences for the important French party. 'We must not permit the congress to divide delegates into active and passive ones, to build a European concert of big powers who would be the only ones to decide the basic principles of international Socialism.'[1]

In a photograph taken at the congress, Rosa stands out as the only woman among so many old, mostly bearded and wise-looking men, significantly stuck between her old hero Vaillant and her enemy Victor Adler. The main achievement of the congress was in the victory of German principles over Jaurès, for which she had fought in so many printed pages and which she again demanded at the congress in a short, sharp speech, summing up her entire case against revisionism. And she contributed to the general feeling of euphoria—with French unity now in sight—by a small, personal gesture towards her great opponent Jean Jaurès, whom she never actually managed to dislike, while he had not even attempted to dislike her, respecting her talent and integrity in spite of the many bitter polemics. When he had finished his eloquent defence of his party's position, ridiculing both the stale, cheap theories of Kautsky—'sur demande'—and the misguided passions of Rosa Luxemburg, there was suddenly no one to translate for him. Rosa jumped up and reproduced his moving oratory: from French into equally telling German. It was the kind of gesture which the Second International loved (impossible to imagine in Stalin's Comintern). Amid general applause, Jaurès thanked her elaborately, and felt certain that this was evidence of a solidarity greater than all their surface differences.[2]

Rosa was well satisfied. Both the SPD and the International had, after much delay, finally voted the complete negation of revisionist ideas and tactics. The orthodox line had triumphed at the highest Socialist court of appeal. In private, Rosa at first placed no great faith in Jaurès's intentions of putting into practice the resolutions of the International; the centrifugal experiences of Poles and Russians did not set an encouraging example of self-denial.[3] But she was wrong. Her experience of conceptual wrangling with the German revisionists blinded her to the calibre, the attachment to international Socialism, of an individualist

---

[1] *Protokoll, Internationaler Sozialistenkongress zu Amsterdam . . . 1904*, Berlin 1904, p. 49.

[2] *Sixiéme congrès Socialiste internationale à Amsterdam, Compte rendu analytique*, p. 174. The German version of the congress protocol contains no reference to this incident— though not for any sinister reason; it is simply shorter.

[3] 'The fuss about unity in France is completely pointless, except to unmask Jaurès's hypocrisy. He who directly killed the principle of unity, now has to turn and twist to avoid it—a joke for the Gods!' (H. Roland-Holst, *Rosa Luxemburg*, p. 213, letter dated 27 October 1904.)

like Jaurès. This was the seamier side of Rosa's internationalism. For with the denial of all national solutions went a monochrome universality which even obliterated national distinctions. The great battle against revisionism had been won in Germany—won at least in the way in which Rosa Luxemburg still conceived of victory, with words on paper and in resolutions; for the moment the whole socialist world *was* Germany. It was Kautsky's conception but in public it had her full support. It appeared as though Socialism, after six years of struggle, had now been declared free of disease. The yellow flag of quarantine, all the sacrifices of the siege, could be lowered at last.

But Rosa's own dialectic was already at work, undermining the satisfactions of apparent triumph. While Kautsky's politics were essentially a chain of static situations, hers were a process; while he moved towards a given end, and then a new one, her ends were no more than a sophisticated means, chimerical postulates with which to whip the tired caravan onwards through the desert. The monochrome universality had come before the triumph, not with it; a means once more, not an end—the very triumph of Amsterdam actually bred dynamic disillusion. She wanted more action, not less. Instead of peace, the success at the International meant sharper struggle. The only problem was how, what, above all—against whom.

From the International congress at Amsterdam, Rosa returned to Germany—straight to jail. In July 1904 she had been sentenced to three months' imprisonment. The charge was insulting the Emperor, that same William II who prided himself on his inspired capacity to understand the problems of the German workers better than any Social Democrat. The authorities took exception to her remark in a speech during the 1903 *Reichstag* election campaign that 'a man who talks about the security and good living of the German workers has no idea of the real facts'.[1] The incident did not have much repercussion at the time because the SPD was more preoccupied with the big trial at Königsberg in East Prussia during the same month, in which a number of prominent Social Democrats, including Otto Braun, were indicted for helping to smuggle revolutionary literature into Russia. Rosa Luxemburg herself referred to this trial, and the happy result of acquittal of the major defendants.

Above all we ought to congratulate ourselves upon Königsberg. It is a real triumph, at least I feel it as such here, and I hope you feel the same where you are, notwithstanding the heat and the beauty of nature. [St. Gilgen in Austria,

---

[1] Frölich, p. 94; see also Jogiches letters, *Z Pola Walki*, 1965, No. 1(29), pp. 121–9. These were written from jail. I have not seen a record of the trial or whether she was sentenced in person or *in absentia*.

Kautsky's favourite holiday resort.] Great Scott, such a judgement of blood on both Russia and Prussia is still much more beautiful than any majestic mountains and smiling valleys.[1]

Rosa began her sentence at the end of August 1904 in the jail at Zwickau. 'Rest quite easy about me, everything is all right—air, sun, books, and good fellowship on the part of fellow human beings.'[2] First, she caught up with her correspondence. She followed party affairs closely from prison—her relations with Mehring had been re-established, and the thought that he might resign from the job of editor of the *Leipziger Volkszeitung* now caused her consternation, though it was a threat which Mehring repeated monotonously. The enforced idleness, however, gave her time for deeper reflections, which in Rosa's case invariably culminated in impatience with the existing state of things. From prison she wrote to Karl Kautsky:

So now you still have other battles to fight. I am quite happy about this for it shows that these dear people [the editorial board of *Vorwärts*] felt our victory in Amsterdam quite severely. That is why I am annoyed that you envy me the peace and quiet of my cell. I don't doubt that you will thoroughly hit out [at the 1904 Bremen party congress]. But you must do it with guts and joy, and not as though it was a boring interlude; the public always feels the spirit of the combatants and the joy of battle gives resonance to controversy, and ensures moral superiority. Certainly you will be quite alone; August [Bebel] will remain in the vineyard of the Lord until the last moment and both dear Arthur [Stadthagen] and dear Paul [Singer] will be 'elegiac' as you put it. Would that thunder and lightning struck them seven fathoms into the ground if they can still go on being 'elegiac' after such a congress [the last congress at Dresden]—and this between two such battles when one ought to be happy to be alive! Karl, this brawl is not just a forced skirmish, fought out in a listless atmosphere . . . the interest of the masses is on the move; I feel it even here penetrating through the prison walls. And don't forget that the International is looking at us with bated breath. . . . I am writing you all this not to stir you up to rebellion—I am not so tactless—but rather to make you happy for battle, or at least to transmit *my* joy to you, for here in cell No. 7 I cannot make much use of that commodity. . . .[3]

Instead of serving three months, Rosa was released—'or rather almost

---

[1] *Letters to Karl and Luise Kautsky*, pp. 71–2, dated end of July 1904. For a time the SPD had given official assistance to the RSDRP (Russian Social-Democratic Workers' Party) for their transport of revolutionary literature to Russia. A press had been housed in the cellar of the *Vorwärts* building. Later, afraid of the police, the SPD executive had requested its removal. In order to keep its official hands clean, it circularized for comrades willing to help in a private capacity. See Botho Brachmann, *Russische Sozialdemokraten in Berlin 1895–1914*, Berlin (East) 1962, pp. 40–52, for a summary and sources. The East Prussian SPD organization was naturally most closely involved, since the transport route passed across its territory. Karl Liebknecht was one of the defending counsel at this trial, his first major public appearance.

[2] *Letters to Karl and Luise Kautsky*, p. 77, dated 1 September 1904.

[3] Ibid, pp. 82–4.

thrown out'—after six weeks, on 15 October 1904: the usual amnesty at the coronation of a new monarch, King Friedrich August of Saxony. Rosa did not want to accept such forms of royal grace and favour, but she had no choice.[1] From her cell she went straight back to work in Berlin. Her impatience mounted. She expressed it most clearly in a letter to her Dutch friend Henriette Roland-Holst. The two women, totally dissimilar in origin and temperament, had formed a momentary friendship—and tried hard to convert an intellectual relationship into something more involved and human. The effort—and the friendship— did not last more than a few years, but for the moment Rosa was able to adopt a much more intimate tone than with Karl Kautsky, much less 'managed'; she could speak frankly.

With you I want to talk about our general situation. I am not in the least happy about the role which the so-called orthodox 'radicals' have played up to now. Chasing after each opportunistic hare, and yacking critical advice doesn't satisfy me; in fact, I am so sick and tired of this sort of activity that I would really rather keep quiet in such cases. I envy the certainty with which some of our radical friends merely find it necessary to lead back the strayed lamb—the party—into the safe domestic fold of the old principles [*prinzipienfestigkeit*] and don't realize that in this wholly negative manner we don't move forward one single step. And for a revolutionary movement not to move forward is—to go back. The only means of radical struggle against opportunism is to move forward oneself, to enlarge [the range of] tactics, to increase the revolutionary aspect of the movement. Opportunism is in any case a plant which only flourishes in brackish water; in any strong current it dies on its own. Here in Germany a move forward is an important and burning need! And how few people realize it. Some fritter their effort away in arguing with the opportunists, and others believe that the automatic mechanical growth in membership (at the elections and in our organizations) represents a move forward. They forget that quantity has to be turned into quality, that a party of three million cannot adopt the same flexible tactics as a party of half a million. . . . We must talk about this, otherwise this letter will turn into a leading article. . . . The problem is not just a German one, but an international one. The congress at Amsterdam made me very conscious of this. But German Social Democracy must give the signal and provide the direction.[2]

Nothing could be clearer than these two examples of pending disagreement between a party executive, which only a year earlier had finally measured up to her rigorous standards in the condemnation of opportunism, and Rosa Luxemburg, urgently looking for new and sharper weapons of struggle. She was constant in one thing only: the new tactic had to be found in Germany, where the victory over revisionism had been won.

---

[1] H. Roland-Holst, *Rosa Luxemburg*, pp. 210–11, letter dated 27 October 1904.
[2] Ibid., pp. 216–16, letter dated 17 December 1904.

These years from 1900 to 1904 marked a definite stage in the development of Rosa Luxemburg's personality. The youthful eagerness, the deliberate enthusiasms—playing it young—this was over. No more Don Quixote engagements with party bosses, or harmless practical jokes. Instead, a maturer acceptance of immobility as a political phenomenon which had to be fought with political weapons, and not just so many personal obstacles against which one could charge head on. What was needed was a broad revolutionary mass movement that would sweep these obstacles away, or at least sweep them along.

VI

REVISIONISM, MASS STRIKE
AND IMPERIALISM:
THE CONTRIBUTION TO THEORY

I: REVISIONISM

R EVISIONISM was all things to all men—supporters and opponents alike.[1] To Plekhanov, attending the 1898 Stuttgart congress of the German Socialist Party as a fraternal delegate, it was mainly a problem of philosophy and, as such, peculiarly important and fascinating. He found the lowly political concerns of the Germans unworthy and disagreeable. 'You say your readers have no interest in philosophy,' he wrote to Kautsky, 'then you must force them to take an interest; *"c'est la science des sciences"*.'[2] But philosophy did not mean abstraction or restraint. 'If you want me to write against Bernstein you must give me full freedom of speech. Bernstein must be destroyed [*anéanti*] and I will gladly undertake this task if you will let me.'[3]

This was an extreme position which tells us much about Plekhanov but little about German revisionism. It was shared by no one in Germany, and is therefore of little direct consequence to our analysis of the revisionist debate and Rosa Luxemburg's contributions to it. Paradoxically, Plekhanov's desire for a tough-minded philosophical campaign against Bernstein had specific political results—it shamed the German party leaders into taking a position against the revisionists

---

[1] For the purpose of this discussion, no attempt has been made to distinguish meaningfully between revisionism, reformism, or opportunism. In theory, and at the start of the 'troubles', revisionism was specifically identified with the body of speculation produced by Eduard Bernstein as a revision of the Marxist dialectic, and revisionists were those who accepted his analysis. Reformism was the more practical and particular aspect of achieving Socialism by reform without revolution. Opportunism was the most diffuse version—and also the pejorative one—of seizing tactical opportunities without any regard for principles. In the course of the events described, these words become largely interchangeable, though opportunism grew into a vast cesspool of a category which eventually included revisionists, reformists, and all your other enemies. I stick to revisionism wherever possible, use opportunism only in the broad cesspool sense, and reformism not at all.

The word 'revision' was first used in its present context by Bruno Schönlank at the 1895 Breslau party congress when he spoke of the proposals for agrarian reform being a 'revision' of the SPD programme.

[2] Plekhanov to Kautsky, 16 September 1898, D XVIII, 586, in Kautsky Archives, IISH Amsterdam.

[3] Ibid., 24 December 1898, No. 588.

earlier and probably more strongly than they would otherwise have done. For how could the spearhead of attack on revisionism—essentially a German matter—be left to the Russians who at that time had not even a united Social-Democratic party of their own?

We shall divide our analysis of the revisionist controversy into two parts, the question of theory and that of practice. These are different aspects of the same problem though in the first instance their analysis involves some rather arbitrary separation. As the revisionist debate proceeded—and in a sense it has never really ended—the emphasis changed increasingly from theory to tactics, from first principles to political immediacies, and then back again. But this chronology is the broadest of generalizations. In fact, it is more helpful to think of emphasis on theory and tactics, not as superseding each other in time, but as a dichotomous state of the system of each participant's interests, habits, and beliefs.

The Theory of Revisionism

Bernstein did not intend to produce any new political system, or to substitute his own ideas for the SPD's existing philosophy. Primarily he expounded what he thought he saw. Somewhat remote from the day-to-day struggle in Germany—he was still living in London at the time—Bernstein attempted to underpin his empirical observations with a set of causalities. None the less,.Bernstein did produce, if not a complete philosophical system, at least a fairly consistent critique of an existing one. Briefly he concluded that the evidence of the last few years showed serious weakness in Marx's prediction of capitalist collapse. Capitalism had a far greater potential for survival than Marx had realized—the evidence was based on the survival of the small capitalist against the predicted process of amalgamations and concentration, the use of credit as a means of evening out the excessive cycles of slump and boom, above all the factual absence of any crises for the last twenty-five years. Not that Bernstein abandoned the *aims* of Socialism. He was no more a liquidator, except in the eyes of his opponents, than all the Mensheviks were liquidators, except in the eyes of Lenin. He emphasized the moral content of Socialism, its importance as a means of redistributing income and opportunity. These ends would be achieved by pressure on and within the existing system instead of an unreliable utopian hope for its overthrow. The means of pressure were co-operatives of producers and consumers, and the trade unions. The role of the SPD would be that of a radical or reformist party using its electoral strength and opportunities to press for reform; Bernstein admitted the possibility of resistance and therefore the need for pressure, substantial at times. Nor did he demand a radical change from existing policy. What he recommended was in fact what the SPD was already doing; all that was needed was for the party to 'dare to appear as what it actually was: a democratic Socialist party of reform'.[1]

If anything, Bernstein had gone further towards a systematic demolition of Marxism than he actually desired.[2] He was concerned to bring practice and theory into a more positive relationship. By removing the arbitrary assumptions about revolution, he felt that he had corrected theory and brought it more closely into line with reality. 'I have no objection to the practical aspect of the Social-Democratic programme with which I am entirely in agreement; only the theoretical part leaves something to be desired', he replied to Kautsky's accusation of destructiveness.[3] Bebel himself had said years before that 'a correct tactic is more important that a correct programme'.[4] Consequently he neither expected nor desired a lengthy theoretical debate, particularly not the acrimonious onslaught of Parvus and Rosa Luxemburg: at most, an amicable discussion in the pages of Neue Zeit.

Rosa Luxemburg's articles in reply in Leipziger Volkszeitung were issued together in 1899 under the title Social Reform or Revolution.[5] She denied Bernstein's claim to be speaking for a well-developed, even dominant tendency in the party. Nor indeed could she do otherwise, for her whole argument was based on making Bernstein into the symptom of something new rather than the confirmation of something old. Throughout Social Reform or Revolution and all her other writings on revisionism, the emphasis was always on the need to defend established orthodoxy against unwarranted innovations. 'The proletarian movement has not suddenly become Social-Democratic, it has been and becomes more Social-Democratic every day . . . and what is surprising is not the emergence of opportunist tendencies but their weaknesses.'[6] Though Rosa Luxemburg did not use the phrase which was to emerge as the executive's slogan—'the good old tactic'—everything she wrote was in its defence. And when she did take up the phrase after 1906— as a mark of contempt and in order to belittle it—she never fully realized the extent to which she herself had contributed to making it the dominant philosophy of the party.

But Rosa Luxemburg's analysis was no mere reliance on traditional even if unspoken assumptions. In order to defend existing Social

---

[1] This very short summary hardly does justice to the full import of Bernstein's views, as expressed in his many writings. But, though short, I believe it to be a just summary. For a fuller discussion and a rather different interpretation, which makes Bernstein much more important, see P. Gay, The Dilemma of Democratic Socialism, New York 1952.

[2] Gay, Democratic Socialism, p. 232.

[3] Vorwärts, 26 March 1899.

[4] A[ugust] B[ebel], 'Zum Erfurter Parteitag', NZ, 1891/2, Vol. I, p. 33.

[5] Sozialreform oder Revolution, Leipzig 1899, reprinted in Collected Works, Vol. III, pp. 35–100, from which quotations are taken.

[6] Ibid., p. 99.

Democracy against Bernstein, she analysed its purpose and philosophy at considerable length. Her emphasis was twofold: first, the *importance* of theory; secondly, its *validity*.

What distinguishes [all the opportunist tendencies in the party] on the surface? The dislike of 'theory', and this is natural since our theory, i.e. the bases of scientific Socialism, sets our practical activity clear tasks and limits, both in relation to the *goals* to be attained as much as in regard to the *means* to be used and finally in the *method* of the struggle. Naturally those who only want to chase after practical achievements soon develop a desire to liberate themselves, i.e. to separate practice from 'theory', to make themselves free of it.[1]

The notion that any Social-Democratic activity could have meaning or validity apart from its causal relationship to theory was anathema to Marxism with its emphasis on the unity of theory and praxis. The distinction between bourgeois and Marxist politics was precisely that the former was practical in the sense that as it stood it had no systematic meaning, while the latter was practical only by being part of a theoretical necessity. Any attempt to relate practical activity only to its immediate purposes, and abstract it from the causal pressure of theoretical necessity, was an irrevocable step out of Socialism and into bourgeois politics. This in fact was the main basis for the accusation that Bernstein was no longer a Socialist. She countered his appeal for Social Democracy to recognize what it really was—a 'practical' party, according to his definition—by asking the party to get Bernstein to face a similar disillusionment and to admit that he was no more than a radical *petit bourgeois* democrat.[2]

Concurrently with the exposition of the need for theory went the proof of its validity. But to achieve this it was necessary to dismantle every one of Bernstein's assumptions about the nature of capitalism and the role of Social Democracy. This detailed critique of Bernstein is still part of the standard tradition of Marxism up to the present day and can be found in every textbook on Marxism; only a brief summary is necessary here. Credit did not reduce crises but accentuated them.

Instead of a regular series of minor crises you had an irregular series of greater ones, hidden but not alleviated by the development of banking finance. The small and intermediate capitalist was not an identifiable group of given size which must decrease and disappear before capitalism was ready for its final collapse. Instead it represented the most dialectic facet of capitalism. Such capitalists were getting fewer but they would never disappear altogether. Periodically they were 'mown down like so much ripe corn' and absorbed into larger concentrations; at the same time the actual victims were replaced by a new spawning of small

---

[1] Ibid., p. 96.   [2] Ibid., p. 100.

capitalist developments in the shelter of the periodic increases in the rate of profit following each depression.

On the political side the tendencies towards democracy, which Bernstein had hailed as a positive herald of change opening up exciting and objective possibilities for social reform, were dismissed as no more than the political manipulations of the *bourgeoisie*. Far from making revolution unnecessary, they provided the very factors which made it essential. As long as the situation of the oppressed class was a matter of formal law, such laws could presumably be changed—hence the partially legal character of all bourgeois revolutions. But wage slavery— the real basis of contemporary oppression—was not a matter of law at all.

Instead of resting on laws the level of wages is . . . governed by economic factors. . . . Thus the basic conditions of capitalist class domination cannot be altered by reforms of the law, like their original transformation into [the present] bourgeois conditions, since they had not themselves been brought about by such laws in the first place.[1]

The extra-legal nature of bourgeois domination was precisely the reason why revolution rather than reform was logically necessary. There could be no other way.

This particular aspect has been quoted at some length because it is the only point where Rosa Luxemburg departed from the more usual Marxist analysis of bourgeois liberalism as the legal and constitutional reproduction of bourgeois class domination. Instead of basing herself on the somewhat formal idea that bourgeois society was as much expressed by its laws as any other and that revolution was necessary because a change of the law would be resisted, she introduced the novel idea that it was the *particular* feature of bourgeois society that its main engine of oppression was extra-legal—and therefore incapable of being changed by law, even if such a thing had been politically possible. Unfortunately this interesting idea was not developed by her or anyone else and she herself reverted later to the more usual formulation. Its relevance to our own day will be immediately obvious; the struggle for legal recognition of racial equality in the United States and the long resistance to this for instance, followed more recently by the more revolutionary recognition that in this context, as in many others, changes in the law do not necessarily entail changes in the realities of power and domination. Even in her pamphlet the development of this idea was in any case not consistent. 'Democracy is essential not because it makes the capture of political power by the proletariat *unnecessary*, but on the contrary because it makes the seizure of power essential as well as uniquely possible.[2] The notion of democracy as a means, a Socialist tool, was much more usual.

[1] *Collected Works*, Vol. III, pp. 87–8.   [2] Ibid., p. 89.

Having demolished Bernstein's revisions of theory, Rosa Luxemburg went on to emphasize most strongly the essential relationship between *correct* theory and practice. Correct theory postulated revolution—and consequently everything that Social Democracy did or left undone must contribute to that end. In asserting the relationship between theory and practice, Rosa Luxemburg necessarily characterized practical activities in a way which reduced them to a secondary and contributory factor only, without any meaning or validity of their own. Her criterion of the relationship was qualitative, not quantitative.

The trade union struggle, thanks to the objective circumstances of capitalist society is like the labour of Sisyphus. This Sisyphus labour is of course essential if the worker is to receive the amount due to him in any given situation, if the capitalist law of wages is to be realized and the perpetually oppressive tendency of economic development is to be paralysed or more gradually weakened. Any notion, however, that the trade unions can reduce profits *pro rata* in favour of wages presupposes firstly a halt to the proletarianization of the middle strata and to the growth of the proletariat, and secondly an end to the increase in productivity. . . . In other words a return to pre-capitalist conditions.[1]

This description of trade-union work was to have rumbling political consequences. Although it followed directly from Marx's own, the striking phrase about the labours of Sisyphus gave great offence and was to be the symbol of the trade union's chronic enmity towards Rosa Luxemburg. But it is curiously ironic that this classical, if highly coloured, analysis of trade-union roles should have had far greater political repercussions than many of the really new and startling formulations she produced in the same pamphlet.

Consumers and producers, co-operatives and trade unions—this was the extent of Rosa Luxemburg's examples of practical activity. The argument was concerned with up-grading theory and expounding it; practical work was merely its executive arm, any elaboration of which was needed only to illustrate the relevance of theory, a simple diagram of how to apply it in practice. Rosa Luxemburg did not find it necessary to enlarge on party tactics in order to buttress her argument. She had established the conceptual framework between theory and practice. She had created a synthesis of the two modes of Socialism, a tightly-knit fugue. All that now remained was to use the fugal technique on the different melodies of the moment. But paradoxically, the great bulk of her writings on revisionism was in fact concerned with questions of practical policy. Since it is contradictory to demote a form of activity to secondary importance and then to upbraid people at length for performing it wrongly, she had to give positive content to the pattern of causality between theory and practice. This was the doctrine of class consciousness. It was built up into the lynch-pin of her causations.

[1] Ibid., p. 78.

Only by intense promotion of class consciousness was it possible to show that wrong practical action could affect, obscure, and indeed destroy theory.

The notion of class consciousness was of course not invented by Rosa Luxemburg. It springs from Marx's own analysis of epistemology and dialectic. Already half-way through the nineteenth century it had become the main justification for his political activities. Rosa Luxemburg was therefore not original in her reliance on this concept. She never explained it, since it was already known to be an essential part of the process for creating the conditions for revolution, a process to which the SPD was fully committed. In bringing it to the fore in the revisionist debate she was merely reiterating the fundamental necessities of the class struggle against the attempt to 'revise' it. By questioning the final aim of revolution. Bernstein was incidentally destroying the very need for any separate proletarian class consciousness and reducing it to the level of a narrow and sectional interest. Class consciousness was an integral part of the doctrine of totality; revisionism—here as in other things—broke up the totality into self-sufficient, limited, and therefore meaningless purposes—meaningless, that is, in terms of a general class confrontation.

Once we get away from the exclusive preoccupation with the improvement of the immediate situation of the workers—the need for which is common as much to the traditional purpose of the party as to the purpose of the revisionists —the entire difference becomes this: according to the traditional conception the Socialist purpose of trade-union and political struggle consists in preparing the proletariat for social upheaval, i.e. emphasis on the subjective factor. According to Bernstein the purpose of trade-union and political struggle consists in limiting capitalist exploitation, in robbing capitalist society increasingly of its capitalist nature and impressing a Socialist character upon it, i.e. to bring about the social upheaval in an objective sense. . . . In the traditional conception the trade-union and political struggle brings the proletariat to realize that it is impossible to alter its situation through such a struggle . . . and convinces it of the inevitability of its final seizure of political power. In Bernstein's conception we start with the importance of seizing political power in order to achieve a Socialist order as a result of the trade-union and political struggle.[1]

Rosa Luxemburg continued her analysis of developing class consciousness as the main purpose of Socialist tactics as follows: 'The great Socialist importance of the trade-union and political struggle consists in *socializing the knowledge*, the *consciousness of the proletariat*, in organizing it as a class.'[2] This sentence contained the essential sociology of Marx and its particular implications for that time in Germany; the

---

[1] *Collected Works*, Vol. III, pp. 61–2.
[2] Ibid., p. 62. My italics.

practical activities of Social Democracy, far from achieving any positive or objective results, could only serve to introduce a Socialist reality into the vacuum of alienation. 'Knowledge' (*Erkenntnis*) is the Marx–Weber term on which rests the entire modern sociological theory of knowledge; its use in this context was clearly intended to convey a frictional process of intervention in the mental vacuum of a proletariat oppressed by objective circumstances, unable as yet to appreciate the subjective requirements of its class interests.

It is at this point that we reach a fundamental statement about the nature of the class struggle which has been missed by most commentators. Here, for instance, was the real difference between her analysis and that of Lenin—which has usually been looked for in the polemics about organization in 1903. For these polemics, in spite of the rhythmic downbeat of 'first principles' throughout, were really concerned with derived phenomena rather than fundamentals. Both sides plugged their conflicting views about party *organization*; both sides insisted that the purpose of the party must be the creation and representation of proletarian class consciousness. But in *Social Reform or Revolution* Rosa Luxemburg went further than this. It was not the *existence* of the party— and even the best organization was only a manifestation of its existence, not a substitute—which helped to foster class consciousness, but the *frictions* from contact with society arising out of the tactical activities in trade-union and political work. Lenin, however, specifically denied the creative function of such conflict. In order to ram home the imperativeness of his organizational ideas, he claimed that trade-union and political activity could reproduce only a hollow echo of bourgeois consciousness in the working class—in other words a false and corrupt class consciousness.[1] Though the issue never arose clearly between them, they differed over the meaning and effect of alienation. The concept as such was not familiar or interesting to Lenin, and he saw the problem as a simple one: either revolutionary proletarian class consciousness or bourgeois infiltration, without any intermediate stage of 'emptiness'.[2] Rosa Luxemburg's notion of a vacuum—alienation without class consciousness—provided a more sophisticated version of Marx's doctrine of alienation. It allowed for the existence of self-

---

[1] Lenin, 'What is to be done?', *Sochineniya*, Vol. V, pp. 368–409, 442 ff.

[2] The secondary or incidental importance of the theory of cognition and class consciousness for Lenin is curiously illuminated by the hesitation and blank stares with which Soviet Communist theoreticians meet the question of Lenin's views on this problem. Alienation as a concept and problem figures large in the early Marx, before 1847 and the Communist Manifesto. Soviet Communist theory has concentrated on the late, class-focused Marx; insofar as it acknowledged Marx's early work at all, it treated it as immature. Mainly the Jugoslavs and the French, more recently a few bold spirits in Poland and Czechoslovakia, have taken up the early, 'Hegelian' Marx and most particularly the problem of alienation—even as applying to socialist societies.

instruction resulting from the small-change of Socialist activities, the legal aspect of the struggle which existed in Germany but could hardly exist in Russia. Instead of assuming a closed circuit in which only ruthless injection of proletarian principles under pressure could ever displace bourgeois consciousness, Rosa Luxemburg assumed an open-ended situation in which the routine activities necessarily had their effect and the problem resolved itself into one of *purpose*, i.e. the relationship between tactics and final goal; 'why' rather than 'how'. Only a deliberate misinterpretation of tactics *à la* Bernstein could cause the creation of a false bourgeois class consciousness; left to themselves (to the established principles of the party), daily activities must create correct class values. Lenin was innovating and already substituting; Rosa Luxemburg, in spite of her sophistication, was still rescuing existing and traditional analyses.

Rosa Luxemburg's analysis of class consciousness as a product of friction adumbrated a theory of action which was only to be developed a decade later. The hint in the one sentence quoted above was elaborated a few pages later:

Clearly the traditional Social-Democratic tactic does not consist of sitting down and waiting for the development of contradictions in capitalist society to their final point, followed by their dialectic resolution. On the contrary, once the direction is recognized, we only base ourselves on it [in theory] but use the political struggle to develop these contradictions as much as possible, this being the very nature of every revolutionary tactic.[1]

It is an odd paradox that, finding herself on the side of the majority in the SPD for the next few years, the implications of action as the creative factor of subjective class consciousness was largely lost in a welter of tactical debates and victories which led inexorably into a blind alley of immobility and self-satisfaction. If Rosa Luxemburg and Parvus had remained the extreme outsiders which they were at the beginning of the revisionist controversy in 1898, if the executive had turned against them in substance and supported Bernstein, the radical doctrine of action which Rosa Luxemburg developed after 1907 would probably have emerged much earlier. It was to be essentially the product of opposition to the would-be powers in the SPD, but could not emerge as long as she fought alongside the executive against the revisionists. We shall later examine the nature and implications of this alliance between Rosa Luxemburg, Kautsky, and the executive.

Rosa Luxemburg was well aware that in practice this vacuum was largely an arbitrary postulate and not a reality. Writing could never create social education—though, as Marx had shown by his example, it could facilitate the process by avoiding mistakes in understanding.

[1] *Collected Works*, Vol. III, p. 64.

She was as conscious as Lenin of the possibilities and dangers of perversion. Wrong tactics *à la* Bernstein would also produce a type of class consciousness in the proletariat, but a wrong one. As with Lenin, the alternatives were proletarian class consciousness versus bourgeois class consciousness. Rosa Luxemburg analysed Bernstein's views at some length and with much evidence as a substitution of bourgeois values for proletarian values. This in fact was the main purpose of her critique. Towards the end of *Social Reform or Revolution* Rosa Luxemburg outlined the issue at stake.

By letting off his sharpest arrows against the dialectic, what does Bernstein do but take issue with the specific mode of thought of the rising and class conscious proletariat? He attacks the very weapon which hitherto has helped the proletariat to break through the mists of its historical future, the mental weapon with which, economically still in chains, it has already defeated the *bourgeoisie* by recognizing its transitory nature and with which it has already carried out its revolution in the sphere of theoretical comprehension by recognizing the inevitability of its own victory. By saying goodbye to the dialectic and placing himself on the see-saw of 'on the one hand'—'on the other hand', 'if'—'but', 'more'—'less', he necessarily accepts the historically limited conception of the doomed *bourgeoisie*, a conception which accurately reflects the *bourgeoisie's* social existence and political activities. . . . The endless qualifications and alternatives of today's *bourgeoisie* are exactly like Bernstein's quality of thinking and the latter is nothing but the most refined and accurate symptom of a bourgeois consciousness.[1]

With increasing sharpness, Bernstein and other purveyors of opportunism were attacked not so much for their 'wrong' tactics as such (though these, too, were attacked, as we shall see), but as carriers of the bourgeois virus into the Socialist camp. Faced with the need to defend Social Democracy against an enemy who possessed such a substantial Fifth Column—and its real extent was only to emerge frighteningly in the next few years—all thought of an advancing tactic had to go by the board as long as the internal front was not secured. This was why the 'action' doctrine as a means of sharpening class conflict and thereby hastening the revolution was left hanging in the air at the time; a mere hint which could only be brought back into the sphere of practical immediacy, and developed, once the rescue operation was completed.

Having right from the start exposed Bernstein's theories as an infiltration of bourgeois values in Socialist fancy dress, Rosa Luxemburg soon discovered the secret transport route—and a fat nest of smugglers for good measure. There were at this time a group of radical and progressive bourgeois theorists—academic social scientists, mostly—who, while strongly denying the validity of Marxism, none the less accepted the need for substantial concessions by society to the working class. These prophets of social integration were Bernstein's link. They manned one end of the bridge in society while Bernstein manned the other in the Socialist camp. Like Bernstein, they were anxious to overcome the dialectic, to deny class conflict; they urged concessions on the government in much the same way that Bernstein urged concessions on the doctrinaires of the SPD. This complementarity was seized upon by Rosa Luxemburg.

Suddenly, all these good people, whose paid profession it is to combat Social Democracy with their theories from the lecture platform, found themselves, to their astonishment, transplanted into the middle of the Socialist camp. In Bernstein's theories—and those of his supporters—the platform Socialists, the 'subjectivists' who had lived, died and rotted away with their long and useless talk, who had buried themselves in words, suddenly found a new lease of life. . . .[1]

The more sophisticated and emphatic the plea for collaboration and social harmony, the more violent Rosa Luxemburg's denunciation. In a way, *Kathedersozialisten* (academic Socialists) like Schmoller, Sombart, Roscher, Konrad Schmidt, and Böhm-Bawerk were even more dangerous than Bernstein. They were outside Socialist jurisdiction and therefore could not be disciplined by expulsion which, it must be remembered, was still Rosa Luxemburg's final solution to the revisionist problem—at least until the end of 1899. If we think of bourgeois society and Social Democracy as two armed camps, then the siren sound of these academics was doubly dangerous since it came from society's camp; many misguided Social Democrats who would have shrugged Bernstein off as hopelessly utopian might well change their minds if they saw him supported and to that extent validated by sympathetic echoes from the other side. A steady tradition in the SPD had always maintained that the antithesis between Socialism and society was due as much to the latter's rejection and expulsion of the former as to any dialectic necessity.[2] Thus Rosa Luxemburg reached heights of bitterness and satire in her attack on these socially-minded Professors which far exceeded anything she wrote against the revisionists themselves.

Here we have the whole secret of the 'correct', 'realistic', 'historical' method. To fight against Social Democracy, to refute its programme?—Goodness no, how unmodern, how unrealistic, how unhistorical! Instead, precisely to accept the working-class movement, the trade unions and Social Democracy as well as class warfare and even the final revolutionary goal; to accept everything! Only—to give the trade unions a basis *in their own interest*, which is necessarily in contradiction to Social Democracy, to civilize Social Democracy *in its own*

---

[1] 'Hohle Nüsse', *LV*, 22 July 1899; *Collected Works*, Vol. III, p. 215.
[2] For an elaboration of this view for foreign consumption, see Theodor Barth, 'Kaiser Wilhelm II und die Sozialdemokratie', *Cosmopolis* (London), Vol. I (1896), No. 3, p. 873.

interest into a national Socialist party. . . . In a word, to break the neck of the class struggle in the interests of the class struggle—that is the secret![1]

An attack on Socialist agitators as an unnecessary luxury which the working class could well afford to discard in its own best interests, was accordingly answered in the most personal terms—as though Rosa Luxemburg were the incarnation of all agitators.

'How repellent, how wounding, how coarse' the tone of discussion in which they engage. So, Mr. Associate Professor, you want to rid the working classes of their 'caricatures' or 'political agitators'? And whom, pray, do you mean by this exactly? Is it the countless canvassers of Social Democracy that you have in mind, those lazy devils whose prison sentences under the anti-Socialist legislation added up to a millennium? How dare you, you economic scribbler, spending your whole life in the security of the academic lecture and drawing-room!

Or do you perhaps have in mind the modest editors of our small provincial papers, the people who address our meetings, who have worked themselves up from their proletarian origin with untold efforts, who have struggled to possess every ounce of knowledge and who through their own efforts have become apostles of the great doctrine of freedom? Are these the 'weak-minded, irres-ponsible firebrands' to whom you refer? You yourself are an irresponsible firebrand, fed since youth on the lukewarm platitudes and tautologies of so-called German science in order that one day, with the help of God and of right-thinking people, you might actually become a full Professor instead of merely an associate!

Or is it our countless and nameless canvassers, risking their very existence and that of their families at every moment, who never weaken in their un-rewarding work to instruct and enthuse the masses, who bring them a hundred and thousand times the old and ever new words of our Socialist faith—are these your 'caricatures of political agitators'? . . . You miserable caricature of a Lassalle, who can do no more than stammer like a parrot the ancient litany of bourgeois economics and the even older saws about the danger of Social Democracy! You dare not even shout your doctrine from the roof tops, but lisp and defame and sink your poison into the masses by counting on their *naïveté* and good nature.[2]

For, contrary to the claims of the *Kathedersozialisten* to be a real opposition to government policy, they were no more than the velvet glove occasionally but cynically pulled over the iron fist.

The German social scientists have always functioned as an extension of the police. While the latter act against Social Democracy with rubber truncheons, the former work with the weapons of the intellect . . . first by stupefying public opinion with the production of pot-bellied professorial wisdom . . . then through

---

[1] Rosa Luxemburg, 'Die Deutsche Wissenschaft hinter den Arbeitern', *NZ*, 1899–1900, Vol. II, pp. 740, 773; *Collected Works*, Vol. III, p. 237. The pamphlet under review and attack was Werner Sombart's *Dennoch. Aus Theorie und Geschichte der gewerkschaftlichen Arbeiterbewegung*, Jena 1900.

[2] *Collected Works*, Vol. III, p. 237.

polemics and slanders against Marx and his pupils, finally by creating a special bourgeois/Socialist concoction called academic wisdom.[1]

A special place in her pantheon of hatred was always reserved for social scientists in general and German social scientists in particular. There was first the established tradition of contempt of the positive doctrinaire for the neutral social scientists which Georges Sorel expressed so concisely: 'Autre chose est faire de la science sociale et autre chose est former les consciences.' Then there was the particular poverty of the Germany academic contribution, with its arid formulations divorced from real life. The tone is very reminiscent of Marx's attacks on some of the Young Hegelian philosophers.

It is no accident that Italy was the cradle of mercantilism, France of the school of Physiocrats, England produced the classic thinking on international trade, while Germany is the birth-place of the 'historical' school of Political Economy. Whereas these other great systems of national economy led and inspired the practical policy of the rising *bourgeoisie* with their broad ideas, it was precisely the fate of the German 'national' economists to furnish weapons to the bourgeois-feudal block against the rising working class.[2]

After 1906 Rosa Luxemburg was to contrast this with the social analysis provided by Russian literature—in favour of the latter.

But most significant of all was perhaps the paralysing feeling of intellectual inferiority which pervaded German Social Democracy—and which psychologically helped to produce the frenetic tone of aggression. The Second International had hardly any established academics in its ranks. A few, like Sombart, came close to Marxism but sheared off at the last moment. There was no German Labriola. The role of academic spokesman had therefore to be taken over by people like Rosa Luxemburg and Franz Mehring, academically qualified but not academically established. The SPD was quite content to leave its intellectual defence in their hands.

We may think of the SPD at the time of the revisionist controversy, therefore, as a fortress beleaguered by a hostile society. Suddenly an important Fifth Column was discovered, partly innocent carriers of a virus, partly deliberate purveyors of the enemy's ideas. To start with, an effort was made to distinguish between these two types. But soon, and ever since in the history of political communism, both were treated as conscious fifth columnists.

While the cleaning-up operation inside the fortress was being carried out, sorties against the enemy outside were out of the question. The weapons of offence were put into cold storage. In order to succeed in mopping up the internal enemy, it was necessary to put the citizenry

[1] Loc. cit.
[2] 'Im Rate der Gelehrten', *NZ*, 1903–4, Vol. I, p. 5; *Collected Works*, Vol. III, p. 249.

on its guard, and this led to the public witch-hunt against revisionism which Rosa Luxemburg conducted with such vigour for the next few years. Since, moreover, the proletariat was an international concern—the international aspect always preoccupied Rosa Luxemburg—the lessons of the domestic diagnosis were carried post-haste to other beleaguered fortresses in France, Belgium, and elsewhere, all equally sick with the enemy's virus of opportunism. In Polish Socialism the German experience made it that much easier to put the old enemy, the PPS, into quarantine with the same disease; no longer a particular enemy, but the local representative of the world-wide foe. But Rosa Luxemburg's main battles were still to be fought primarily in Germany, at least until 1903 when the citizens' delegates assembled at the party congress finally saw and heard the last of the lepers routed—or so it seemed. As in all beleaguered fortresses, the need for physical survival had to take precedence over civilized comforts like freedom of speech.

As in every political party freedom to criticize our way of life must have a definite limit. That which is the very basis of our existence, the class struggle, cannot be the subject of 'free criticism'. We cannot commit suicide in the name of freedom to criticize. Opportunism, as Bebel has said, breaks our backbone, nothing less.[1]

The Practice of Revisionism

Rosa Luxemburg's analysis of revisionist practice fell into two categories. The first and more important was its relation to class consciousness. This hinged, not on a variable of more class consciousness or less, but on the dichotomy of tending to *proletarian* or *bourgeois* class consciousness. The definition between them was absolute; not of degree but of kind. The second and less important category was concerned with judging the merit of any action by its practical results; the measure of efficiency.

(a) *Tactics and class consciousness.* Almost every discussion of tactics raised by the revisionist controversy was at once traced as a pattern in the magnetic field of class consciousness. In Germany two examples are of particular interest. First, the problem of elections for the *Reichstag* which was to prove the test and breaking-point of the SPD's role as a revolutionary or reformist party. Participation in elections, particularly with the system of the second ballot existing in Germany, raised the problem of temporary alliances and coalitions on every electoral occasion.[2] This gave tactical considerations a preponderant importance at

---

[1] *LV*, 14 September 1899, quoted in *Collected Works*, Vol. III, p. 175.

[2] Under this electoral system, one or two polls took place in each constituency. If no absolute majority was obtained by any candidate on the first vote, a second or run-off poll was taken a short time afterwards. This naturally gave the parties a chance to make arrangements by which those candidates who had no chance at all stood down in favour of the lesser evil. Thus a Progressive candidate might stand down in favour of a National Liberal in order to keep out the Conservative on the second vote.

certain times, and opened the door to a whole 'style' of politics very different from the SPD's traditional negative disdain. Elections were the party's Achilles' heel. Sensing this, Rosa Luxemburg uncompromisingly relegated the process of election—and indeed all activities in the *Reichstag*—to their primeval educational roles. This was the old (i.e. the correct) interpretation, corroded only by recent revisionist practices.

The old tradition of the party is disrupted. Not *mandates* but *education* has hitherto been the main object, and where Social Democrats voted for middle-class candidates in any second ballot it was a question of strengthening opposition. In Bavaria, however, [the pact] helped the most reactionary and dishonest of parties to obtain an absolute majority ... all manifestations of opportunism have in common *the simple attainment of immediate daily success at any cost*. . . .[1]

To the many implicit and open challenges against such a restrictive interpretation of Socialist members' freedom of action in the *Reichstag*, she replied head-on that their activities could have no other meaning within the walls of this 'talking shop'. Every speech, every gesture, every vote, had to be aimed at the masses outside. Socialist words spoken in the *Reichstag* must carry through the window—hence the well-established phrase 'durch das Fenster reden'. How alien this was to the reality of institutional common sense which pervaded the growing contingent of Socialist *Reichstag* deputies can most vividly be seen by the reaction of his colleagues to Karl Liebknecht, who tried to carry out this prescription literally. They thought he had gone mad.[2]

Even before the question became acute on a national scale—and this happened only after 1912 when the SPD became the largest party in the *Reichstag*—it had already arisen as an obstinate local problem in south Germany. Here Social-Democratic participation in the work of the state legislatures had always been greater than in the north. There was an established tradition- of co-operation and participation by the SPD in communal affairs, with the party providing its electoral quota of local government officials. Hence the plea for the recognition of special conditions in the south, which the party was expected to accept, instead of generalizing about revisionism. Again Rosa Luxemburg met the argument head-on. She repeatedly denounced the notion of special conditions. In this she was at first almost alone. For, whether justified or not, the famous special conditions did exist in the south. In all the thunder about discipline, unity, and cohesion put out by the executive after 1901, the analytical problem was swept aside, and never settled. On the surface Rosa Luxemburg had the last laugh when in 1910–11

---

[1] *LV*, 30 August 1899, reporting Rosa Luxemburg's speech in Leipzig on 29 August. My italics.
[2] See below, p. 395.

she was able to document the complementary nature of the 'exciting new vistas' after the coming *Reichstag* elections and the old but often condemned practice in the south. But it was this same laugh which turned sour when the logic of objective complementarity finally imposed itself on universal consciousness at the outbreak of war. For by this time the objective conditions had become much the same in north and south; but instead of leading to a reappraisal of party policy, it led to the acceptance of the situation in practice.

The second example was the long debate over Socialist participation in bourgeois government, brought to the fore by the Millerand case in France. This, too, Rosa Luxemburg treated throughout as a question of first principles.

In any case we are not concerned with judging the special case of the Waldeck-Rousseau cabinet, but with the establishment of broad rules. From this point of view the entry of a Socialist into bourgeois government must be seen as an experiment that can only harm the class struggle. In bourgeois society Social Democracy is confined by definition to the role of an opposition party; it can only appear as a ruling party on the ruins of that bourgeois society.[1]

This led to cross-referencing between France and Germany: since revisionism in Germany (except in the south) had been confined to words and intentions but in France had found startling application in practice, Rosa Luxemburg was led to conclude that France was to that extent behind Germany in the order of historical development.

In Germany we have just defeated—after a thorough difference of opinion—an attempt to destroy the balance between final aims and present movement, at the expense of the final aims. In France, through the union of the radical elements [in Socialism] the balance [between final aims and present purposes] has only just been established for the first time all along the line.[2]

But this exercise in comparative political sociology led her into a desert of abstract misinterpretations. She who loved France and knew the value of French revolutionary achievements, paradoxically was now obliged to demonstrate at great length the proposition that these achievements were partly mythical, that the French Republic was less 'advanced' than imperial Germany. This in turn meant denigrating the victory against reaction in the Dreyfus affair as ephemeral and meaningless— in direct contradiction to earlier analysis of the 'affair' undertaken before

---

[1] 'Eine taktische Frage', *LV*, 6 July 1899, quoted in *Collected Works*, Vol. III, p. 273.

[2] 'Die Sozialistische Krise in Frankreich', *NZ*, 1900–1, Vol. II, pp. 495, 516, 548, 619, 676; quoted in *Collected Works*, Vol. III, p. 282. The French 'radical union' was the attempted fusion of Vaillant's *Parti Socialiste-révolutionnaire* and Guesde's *Parti Ouvrier français* with Jaurès's *Parti Socialiste français* at Japy in the summer of 1899. The union never got under way; left and right split again almost at once.

the straight-jacket of revisionism had descended on her perceptions.[1]
Rosa Luxemburg's writings on France from 1898 to 1901 are among
the least creditable and informative of all her work. She carved through
the plea of special conditions with the same imperative negation as in
the case of the south Germans: 'In vain we [in Germany] continue to
look for anything significant to the country of "great experience".' [2]
The revolutionary experience of France was, for present purposes,
valueless; the new methods of which Jaurès was so proud were not new
but old, and certainly out-dated.

> He merely repeats monotonously the great slogans of the halcyon days of the
> Dreyfus affair.... Jaurès's melodies remind you of Verdi's good old arias,
> which flow from the lips of every black-eyed and happy apprentice in sunny
> Italy ... but which now grind out in distressing monotony like the lifeless
> mechanism of a barrel-organ. Tempi passati! And the organ-grinder himself
> looks on, bored and disinterested; it is only the practised hand which turns the
> handle; his heart is not in it.[3]

The contradictions are easy to see. If Jaurès's new methods were in
fact ancient, then revisionism, of which they were a symptom, must be
ancient too; in which case the plea for a return to the established and
hitherto unchallenged principles of Social Democracy became meaningless. Similarly, if the Dreyfus affair was merely an internecine quarrel
in the capitalist camp in which Socialists were not required to participate, then it was impossible to blame Jaurès for inconsistency—for he,
too, was interested in the continuation of his policy and did not consider
it superseded merely because the immediacies of the Dreyfus affair had
been settled. Occasionally there were flashes of reality in Rosa's analysis:
when she admitted, for instance, that the rigid attitudes of the most
'Marxist' group in France, led by Jules Guesde, far from being an ideal,
were a distorted compensation for the opportunism of Jaurès and the
right wing. This analysis of left-wing rigidity and extremism as an
excusable reaction to opportunism was new—and Rosa Luxemburg
made a general hypothesis out of it, using it later to explain Bolshevik
intransigence as the product of Menshevik opportunism. But these
were rare glimpses. On the whole, the elaborate treatment of French
affairs, starting with the Dreyfus affair right through the Millerand case
to the Amsterdam International congress of 1904, was a sad example
of the isolation and unreality induced by the towering earthworks

[1] Cf. 'Die Sozialistische Krise in Frankreich', written in 1900, with the series in SAZ in
1898, particularly 9 August, 18 August, 13 September.
[2] 'Der Absohluss der sozialistischen Krise in Frankreich', NZ, 1901–2, Vol. II, pp. 710,
751, quoted in Collected Works, Vol. III, p. 366.
[3] Ibid., p. 375. For 'Jaurès's melodies' see his speech (and Guesde's reply) made in Lille
in October 1900, reprinted in 'Les deux méthodes', Œuvres, Vol. VI, pp. 189–217.

thrown up by German Social Democracy as the result of the revisionist controversy.

(b) *The practical success of tactics*. Rosa Luxemburg would have her cake and eat it too, and her indictment of revisionist tactics was as often due to their lack of immediate success as to their confusion of principle. Her dispute with Parvus over south Germany was in part a simple question of fact: had the alliance with the Liberals succeeded in keeping out the much more reactionary Catholic Centre, or had it helped the Centre to carry off a greater election victory? In the French context, had Jaurès's alliance with the radicals and progressives kept reaction at bay or helped to advance it? But these debates were not empirical, fact-finding sessions. If the dubious 'arrangement' resulted beyond any doubt in a defeat for reaction—why, then, Rosa had a piece of decisive sleight-of-hand all ready: reaction's original threat must have been illusory! Perhaps the most significant example of Rosa Luxemburg's involvement with the practical consequences of tactics was Belgium; the alliance of Belgian Social Democracy with the Liberals to achieve universal suffrage. Here Rosa Luxemburg was at her most eclectic.

At first, judgement was left in suspense, pending the outcome of action. 'The Belgian labour movement now occupies its proper place as the most revolutionary force in a rotting capitalist state. What the morrow will bring we shall see after Philippi.'[1] Having fired off her usual theory-barbed arrows against alliances with bourgeois parties, Rosa Luxemburg for once was willing to let the results speak for themselves without pre-judging the issue. But the Belgian strike effort for suffrage reform failed to achieve the desired results, and Cassandra now wailed more loudly than ever. Here at last was a perfect example to illustrate the dual thesis that wrong tactics not only corrupted class consciousness but always failed to achieve their stated object as well. In a series of articles on the Belgian question Rosa Luxemburg re-created the German progression of revisionist causality; indecision leading to practical failure, treachery leading to corruption.[2] The reason for the intermediate stage of indecision and error *leading to* the full Bernstein treatment of treason and corruption was necessary since Rosa Luxemburg was dealing here with the official leadership of a substantial Socialist party, not merely with the reformist wing. In France Jaurès represented an important and independent group of Socialists, but Vandervelde was the acknowledged leader of the unitary Belgian party; neither of them could be dealt with like the dissident faction of German Social Democracy. Therefore the proof of ideological corruption, which made both

[1] 'Der dritte Akt', *LV*, 15 April 1902; *Collected Works*, Vol. IV, p. 330.

[2] 'Steuerlos', *LV*, 21 April 1902; also 'Das belgische Experiment', *NZ*, 1902–3, Vol. I, p. 105, quoted in *Collected Works*, Vol. IV, p. 337; 'Die Ursache der Niederlage', *LV*, 22 April 1902, quoted in *Collected Works*, Vol. IV, p. 334.

the *Parti Socialiste français* and the Belgian Social-Democratic party the direct equivalent of the German revisionists, could not simply be postulated from theory, but had to be proved in detail, from their policy and actions. Rosa Luxemburg's concern with tactical questions was partly nosiness, but above all a necessary step in creating the required theorem of international opportunist complementarity.

The analogy of a besieged fortress is particularly helpful if the consequences of the revisionist debate are to be grasped. Revisionism was not destroyed—rooted in reality, it survived continual condemnation by taking refuge in its grass-root origins. But after 1903 it ceased to be a debatable issue in the SPD as far as party principles or policy were concerned. All that remained was to attack its symptoms.

The decision of the party congresses of 1901 and 1903 and of the International congress of 1904 to condemn the theoretical basis of revisionism was not an automatic consequence of the debate about Bernstein's proposition of 1898. At first the debate about theory had been inconclusive. For two years the SPD executive avoided commitment by encouraging the theoretical aspect of the debate, in which it was not primarily interested. But the issue was not to be confined to a few intellectuals, especially once the latter had connected principles to practice and started their witch-hunt against the reformist practitioners. These were often distinguished and important comrades who stoutly defended their actions and eventually forced the executive to take sides. As we have seen, every disposition of personal friendship and loyalty pulled the executive towards the revisionists, while people like Rosa Luxemburg and Parvus were friendless outsiders. Why then did the executive come down so heavily against Bernstein and his followers?

Certainly it was not only sentimental attachment to the good old principles, but a far more practical and self-interested consideration. If Bernstein was right, then the exclusiveness of Social Democracy as a way of life and as an organization could not survive. The party leaders had made their careers out of total opposition to society, their supporters had re-created in the SPD a substitute for the society which had cast them out. Lights had been lit in the darkness. And after 1890 they had reaped their reward. By the end of the century the SPD was a state within a state and its legitimate rulers represented a powerful vested interest in the maintenance of this *status quo*. The accent on separateness went well beyond mere politics or even ideology; it was a profound moral differentiation which made Socialists regard themselves as almost a different species—a view shared, rather uncomplimentarily, by the rest of society. This deliberate, almost generic, distinction became so widely accepted in Germany that the discovery that Socialists had a good many 'normal' German traits, that they too said one thing and often did another, was considered a major sociological breakthrough. It took no less a man than Max Weber to point it out—and sociologists today still use Weber's 'discovery' that Social Democrats were human beings as evidence for showing that class- or caste-divided societies have as much in common as they have apart.[1] Any ambition to influence society directly and at once meant entering it, becoming like any other political party in Germany, a mere interest group without any pretensions to power then or later. The authority of the entire hierarchy must disappear in proportion to the achievement of reformist aims; for it was not only the authority of political leadership but of that acquired in substitution for the normal structure of society. As far as the party was concerned, reformist success was self-liquidating. As Socialist aspirations were fulfilled, so the proliferation of Social-Democratic organization, the position of the leaders as the autonomous government, must be weakened too. Their *raison d'être* was precisely the impossibility of achievement. Their presence filled the vacuum created by the abstention from political participation in society. They had not been elected to articulate policy within society but to create a new society which would take over after the collapse of its predecessor. The party's sole purpose was growth, and growth implied separation from the opposing camp. Participation in society could only delay the date of final collapse. In Marxist terms, the party was the bricks-and-mortar structure of alienation. This then was the fortress to be defended.[2]

It is obvious that all this did unintentional violence to Marxism—a dynamic and never static theory of social change. That is why 'Marxists' like Rosa Luxemburg, Plekhanov, Kautsky, and Mehring, honoured as they were, always thought of themselves as lonely and isolated, and periodically railed against the ignorant obtuseness of those around them. The fact that Kautsky, the most respected of them all, actually came to provide a theoretical validation of a state of affairs which was essentially static in an un-Marxist sense—and all in the name of Marxism—is one of the great ironies of Socialist history. It was not, as we shall see, without a logic of its own; not accidental or treacherous, but implicit and inevitable—and above all unconscious. That was to be why Kautsky remained the Communist bogeyman for many years, long after he had ceased to be important (his world ended when Social Democracy split and his failure to realize it confined him instantly and inexorably to the museum). That too explains why the Communists everywhere thought

---

[1] See the reference to Max Weber in Reinhard Bendix, 'Public authority in a developing political Community: the case of India', in *European Journal of Sociology*, Vol. IV, No. 1 (1963), 51, note 15.

[2] For a more detailed discussion of the SPD as a state within a state and the implications of its policy of abstention, see J. P. Nettl, 'The German Social-Democratic Party 1890–1914 as a political model', *Past and Present*, No. 30, April 1965, pp. 76–86.

of themselves as reconnecting directly with Marx rather than taking up from his Social-Democratic heirs.

What the revisionists proposed was to sign peace with the enemy, open up the fortress to him in return for a limited number of places in society. Where Rosa Luxemburg argued the Socialist case from strength, the executive implicitly agreed with her—from a position of weakness. They doubted their ability to maintain their position and authority in any but siege conditions.[1] Political exigencies therefore made Rosa Luxemburg the spokesman and ally of an executive whose real motives were vastly different from her own strict teleology. The executive was not interested in revolution but it was interested in the *status quo*—and if this involved a revolutionary postulate, then so be it. The momentary confusion between different motives is evident from the fact that Rosa Luxemburg and Kautsky managed to reach a common identity of views and that the executive used them both indiscriminately to propagate its case. As later events were to show, what the executive needed in effect was a strict separation of theory and practice, with the former merely brandishing its weapons to cover up and gloss over the exigencies of the latter. This was pre-eminently Kautsky's task; he performed it long, unconsciously, and well. His self-interest in the *status quo* was the same as that of the executive; in the words of Catherine the Great to Diderot, the theorist wrote on paper while the ruler wrote on men's skins—a much more sensitive and awkward parchment! There was no need for conflict or competition. But it was not good enough for Rosa Luxemburg.

Thus the maintenance of orthodoxy gave both the executive and Kautsky what they wanted. For Rosa Luxemburg, on the other hand, it was a blind alley, and the uncompromising and intransigent character of her opposition to the executive after 1907 was precisely the result of her own efforts in the revisionist debate. After 1907 she was backing up the long road which she had travelled between 1899 and 1904. Her whole later conception of the mass strike, followed by the far broader doctrine of imperialism, was a corrective to the self-satisfied isolation, the apotheosis of the *status quo* and its extrapolation *ad infinitum*, which she herself had so vociferously and ably helped to make possible. But what she saw first as a misunderstanding, then as a difference in policy (norms), and finally as a conflict of *Weltanschauung*

[1] The problem of cohesion among emerging social groups as well as among nations is very similar, and the relationship between the 'principles' of the SPD and the nationalism of present-day emergent or developing nations will now appear obvious. Nor is it merely due to the same pressures acting on different groups. In many ways the SPD in particular—and, for Rosa especially, international Socialism in general—was a nation, a fatherland, not merely a class-based political party. That is why the two situations are truly comparable. See also below, Appendix: The National Question. This problem is discussed fully in J.P. Nettl, *Political Mobilization: A Sociological Analysis of Methods and Concepts*, London 1967.

(values), had in fact altered the whole nature of the party over whose orientation the battle was to take place. With the emergence of self-sufficient, orthodox abstention in the party after the revisionist controversy, the function of party institutions imperceptibly changed. Ideology, the same old outward-going ideology of revolution, served more and more exclusively as a means of internal cohesion. With the continuation of 'practical' politics at all levels—participation in elections, trade-union activity, attempts to form blocs with bourgeois parties in the *Reichstag*—the gulf between theory and practice inevitably widened; hence increased ideological assertion became all the more necessary to sublimate the uselessness of practical politics—the uselessness which was all that was permitted. In turn, the lower echelons of party work became a desert in which one served to obtain one's promotion—instead of the grass-roots of a vital struggle; the party congresses ceased to be the law- and policy-making sovereign assembly and became an annual ritual where ideology was enthroned and from which participants dispersed full of moral satisfaction—to illuminate their comrades accordingly. The structure remained unaltered, except for the growth of the executive and its bureaucracy, but its functions, and with them the foci of power, underwent a considerable change.[1]

2: MASS STRIKE AND IMPERIALISM

As soon as Rosa Luxemburg left Warsaw for the comparative quiet of Finland in the summer of 1906, she became anxious to interpret the Russian revolution for the SPD. The fact that the Hamburg provincial organization of the SPD had commissioned a pamphlet from her provided an ideal opportunity. She outlined her task quite clearly at the beginning. 'Practically all existing writings and views on the question of the mass strike in the international Socialist movement date from the time before the Russian revolution, the first historical experiment on a bigger scale with this weapon. This explains why they are mostly out of date.'[2]

The first thing was to wrest the mass strike from its more or less

---

[1] For party congresses and their changing role, especially from 1905 onwards, see below, Chapter VIII, pp. 209–10 and note 1 on p. 210. For a discussion of the theoretical relationship between ideology and political effectiveness and the concepts of pragmatic and expressive ideologies, see R. K. Merton, L. Broom, and L. S. Cottrell (eds.), *Sociology Today, Problems and Prospects*, New York 1959, Chapter I; R. K. Merton, *Social Theory and Social Structure*, Glencoe (Illinois) 1957, Chapter 1; and Ulf Himmelstrand, 'A theoretical and empirical approach to depoliticization and political involvement', *Acta Sociologica*, 1962, Vol. 6, Nos. 1–2, pp. 91–5.

[2] 'Massenstreik, Partei und Gewerkschaften', Hamburg 1906. See *Collected Works*, Vol. IV, p. 410. References to this work will be made as 'Massenstreik' and are all taken from Vol. IV of *Collected Works*.

exclusive possession by the anarchists—at least in the eyes of its opponents. Rosa Luxemburg was well aware of the strong reservations in the German party on this account. Her rescue bid was based on two main propositions: (1) The development in the organization of the working classes which made them powerful enough to undertake mass strikes. The notion of the mass strike thus ceased to be a chimera of 'revolutionary romanticism', a compound of 'thin air and the mere goodwill and courage to save humanity', and became a *practical* proposition. (2) The increasing means of political as opposed to mere economic activity in Socialist parties. This was based on the confluence of the two trends, with the political aspect being definitely the higher form of struggle; wage strikes were no longer 'the only possible direct action of the masses and the only possible revolutionary struggle arising out of trade-union activities'.[1]

None the less, the mass strike was just one weapon—albeit a very important one—in the arsenal of Social Democracy, and definitely not the final act in the overturn of society. It was a political weapon, rather than a purely economic one with incidental or miraculous political consequences. Finally, since it was not an end in itself, it could not be 'planned' like an apocalyptic upheaval.

The proper conception of the mass strike—her own— was essentially the product of a recent historical experience, the events in Russia between 1905 and 1907. It began as a large-scale withdrawal of labour, which upset the stability of the economy and the society which depended on it. But the purpose of the strike was not the negotiation of better conditions; in fact it had nothing to do with conditions of work at all. Rather it was a pre-condition for further action. The negative act of ceasing to work drew into the pool of revolutionary reserves vast armies of people, whose energies were now available for a more direct revolutionary purpose. Rosa Luxemburg was not concerned with the technique of organizing or starting a mass strike—the how, when, how much, how long. These problems would settle themselves. It was sufficient to point to the mounting wave of industrial strikes in Russia from the turn of the century as generating the subsequent revolutionary period with its higher form of political mass strikes. As we have seen, Rosa Luxemburg was particularly concerned that the energies and thoughts of Social Democracy should not be expended on technical problems. She repeatedly emphasized that a mass strike was both a symptom and a typical product of a revolutionary period. Consequently mass strikes could never be 'made'. Neither the determination of the most powerful executive nor the greatest goodwill on the part of the masses could 'make' a mass strike—unless objective circumstances demanded it.

---

[1] Ibid., p. 414.

With this assertion the anarchists' miraculous act of will was left far behind. So was the notion of the mass strike as a lucky 'find' for the armoury of Social Democracy just at the moment when—according to Rosa Luxemburg's friend Henriette Roland-Holst—Socialist technology had been at a loss for new weapons. 'If the mass strike signifies not just a single act but a whole period of class struggle, and if such a period is the same as a revolutionary period, it will become clear that a mass strike cannot be conjured as an act of will even if the decision came from the highest level of the strongest Social-Democratic party.'[1]

The first problem was to integrate the mass strike into the wider process of revolution. Its inception and use marked a higher stage of action than the individual and unconnected strikes and actions that preceded it. The mass strike was essentially a collective noun for a whole series of activities—collective not only in terminology, but because the various processes and actions which the term covered were genuinely linked by intricate causalities. For the first time, hitherto separate forms of struggle were welded into one compact and unified whole.

The mass strike as we see it in the Russian revolution . . . reflects all phases of the political and economic struggle and all stages and periods of the revolution. Its use, its effects, its reasons for coming about are in a constant state of flux . . . political and economic strikes, united and partial strikes, defensive strikes and combat strikes, general strikes of individual sections of industry and general strikes in entire cities, peaceful wage strikes and street battles, uprisings with barricades—all run together and run alongside each other, get in each other's way, overlap each other; a perpetually moving and changing sea of phenomena. And the case of these manifestations becomes clear; they do not arise out of the mass strike itself, but from the political and social power factors in the revolution. The mass strike is only a form of revolutionary struggle.[2]

Rosa Luxemburg particularly stressed that this compound was greater than the sum of its components because the confluence took place at a stage of history higher than that in which the phenomena existed discretly. She called it 'a collective concept covering a period of years, even decades, in the class struggle'. But at the same time she did not merely move the arena of struggle from the economic to the political field. The mass strike was essentially a process of interaction between political and economic activity, with one fertilizing the other. 'Every political class action . . . tears hitherto untouched sections of the proletariat out of their immobility, and this awakening *naturally* finds expression in *stormy* economic struggles . . . since these are closest to hand.'[3] The emphasis, however, had to be on 'stormy'—that is, of equal weight with the new intensity of political action. There had to be

---

[1] 'Massenstreik', p. 443.
[2] Ibid., pp. 437–8.   [3] Ibid., p. 442—my italics.

a causal link between one and the other—not merely coincidence. Rosa Luxemburg thus neatly (and probably unconsciously) pre-empted the discussions between Plekhanov and Lenin on the one hand and the so-called 'economists' on the other. Instead of opposing pre-occupation with economic activity by emphasis on political struggle, she combined the two. The only criterion was causality and heightened intensity.[1]

So much for the 'input' into mass strikes. At the other end, 'output', their integration into the historical process of proletarian class struggle was made even more emphatic. Nothing was, or remotely could be, achieved by any mass strike on its own. In marshalling her Russian evidence, Rosa Luxemburg clearly indicated the presence of the next stage in embryo. Thus in December 1905 the third general mass strike had broken out in the Russian empire. 'This time the course of the action was quite different from the two previous occasions. The political action no longer gave way to an economic one as in January 1905 but equally it failed to achieve a quick victory as in October. . . . As a result of the logical and internal development of events, the mass strike this time gave way to an open uprising, to armed street fights and barricades in Moscow.'[2] The conclusion she drew from this was that the mass strike, even at its most pervasive and diverse, could achieve nothing if it were not hooked on to the next stage of the revolutionary process. Revolution had at least to be in the air even if it was not actually imminent.

It is obvious that all this was based on a particular view of Socialist revolution which differed sharply from the ideas put forward by almost everyone else at the time, not only in Germany but throughout the Second International, the Russians included. What was more immediately relevant was the role prescribed in all this to Social Democracy, the advance guard of the proletariat. It was this which was to be developed in the course of her battle with the leadership of the SPD during the next few years.

The leadership of a mass strike rests with Social Democracy and its responsible leaders in quite a different sense. Instead of racking their brains about the technical problems, the mechanics of a mass strike, it is Social Democracy that

---

[1] This did not mean that she regarded party and trade unions as being equally important. There was no fiercer opponent of trade-union parity than Rosa Luxemburg. But where Lenin equated trade unions with the economic struggle—who else was there to lead it?— and relegated both to the world of primitive politics, Rosa Luxemburg's experience of the essentially conservative German trade unions made her separate economic struggle from trade-union control. This important distinction was never made explicit.

[2] 'Massenstreik', p. 436. Rosa Luxemburg identified three different results from the three waves of mass strikes. In January 1905 the strikes following on the massacre of 22 January petered out into individual local and largely economic strikes. In October their renewed outbreak succeeded politically in the Tsar's manifesto. In December they led to the armed uprising in Moscow.

must take over the *political* leadership even in the midst of a revolutionary period. The slogans, the direction of the battle, the tactics of the political struggle have to be organized in such a way that every phase and every moment in the struggle is related to the existing and already realized achievements of the proletariat and that this is always taken into account when the plan of campaign is made so that the tactics of Social Democracy . . . must never fall *below* the level of the genuinely existing possibilities, but must always be in advance of them—this is the most important task of the 'leadership' during any period of mass strikes. And it is such leadership which automatically settles technical problems as well. . . .[1]

This statement was almost a complete preview of Rosa Luxemburg's later elaboration of the function of Socialist leaders, both in her criticism of the Bolshevik revolution and when she tried to apply her views in practice during the German revolution. But here again we should not look too far forward. Her definition of the tasks of Social Democracy was incidental; there still appeared every prospect that it might come to express the common consensus in the SPD and not merely the views of an isolated and increasingly disaffected outsider. We shall examine Rosa Luxemburg's ideas on the role of the leadership more closely as they developed in opposition to the practices of her German and Russian opponents.

This, then, was the mass-strike doctrine as it stood at the end of 1906, the 'pure' doctrine, still unadulterated by the special emphases of later polemics. Half way through the pamphlet, tucked away among a lot of explanation, came the crux—the purpose of the whole exercise.

The question arises how far all these lessons which can be drawn from the Russian mass strikes can be applied to Germany. The social and political circumstances, the entire history and nature of the working-class movement in Germany and Russia, are wholly different. At first sight the inner laws of the Russian mass strikes which we have elaborated often appear to be the product of specific Russian conditions which can have no bearing on the German proletariat.[2]

The rest of the work was precisely concerned with applying the lessons of Russia to Germany, in the form of general propositions about the nature of class war. Briefly, what were these lessons?

1. The indivisibility of the proletarian class struggle—which meant that by definition Russian lessons became applicable to Germany or anywhere else.

Clearly from any point of view it would be totally mistaken to regard the Russian revolution as a beautiful spectacle, as something specifically Russian. . . . It is vital that the German workers should regard the Russian revolution as

---

[1] 'Massenstreik', p. 445.
[2] Ibid., p. 446.

their own affair, not only in the sense of any international class solidarity with the Russian proletariat, but as a chapter of their own social and political history.[1]

2. The 'leapfrog' effect by which the demands and the achievements of the Russian proletariat caught up with, and even overtook, those of better organized working classes like the German. It should be noted that apart from postulating this leapfrog effect, Rosa Luxemburg at this stage specifically queried some of the assumptions of German 'superiority'.

The contrast [between Russia and Germany] becomes even smaller when we examine more closely the actual standard of living of the German working classes. . . . Are there not in Germany very dark corners in working-class existence, where the warming light of trade-union activity hardly penetrates; large segments which have not yet been able to raise themselves out of the most elementary slavery through the simplest forms of economic struggle?[2]

3. The inversion of the accepted relationship between organization and action. Rosa Luxemburg postulated the important idea that good organization does not precede action but is the product of it; organization grows much more satisfactorily out of struggle than in periods of peaceful disinterest.

A rigid mechanical bureaucratic conception will only recognize struggle as the product of a certain level of organization. On the contrary, dialectical developments in real life create organization as a product of struggle.[3]

The fact that she deliberately over-emphasized the element of the spontaneous was probably due as much as anything to the hope—this was 1906—of persuading leaders and members of the SPD to accept her analysis and above all prognosis of the situation. '[Spontaneity] plays as we have seen a very large role in all the Russian mass strikes without any exception, both as a forward-moving and also as a restraining element.'[4] This emphasis had a twofold purpose: to undermine the

---

[1] Ibid., p. 460. This was clearly a necessary step in any doctrine of permanent revolution. Rosa Luxemburg went at least part of the way with Trotsky. But Trotsky's internal causality—his scientific 'must'—remained for Rosa Luxemburg a strongly urged 'should' and 'ought'. She never passed from political analogy to scientific (and therefore obligatory) causation. As will be seen, she and most of her friends had strong reservations about the validity of the full doctrine of permanent revolution. I cannot agree with the assertion—stated but never analysed—of Trotsky's most recent biographer that 'Rosa Luxemburg, representing the Polish Social-Democratic party, endorsed the theory of permanent revolution' (Isaac Deutscher, *The Prophet Armed*, London 1954, p. 178)—even though Trotsky himself made the same claim, albeit long after the actual events (L. Trotsky, *My Life*, London 1930, p. 176).

[2] 'Massenstreik', p. 448. This critical examination of the validity of the claims of German working-class superiority will be examined in more detail later.

[3] Ibid., p. 453. This of course is the crux of the organization-as-process and spontaneity accusation against her.

[4] Ibid., p. 444.

trade-union bureaucracy and at the same time allay the fears that the carefully built organizations might be destroyed in the course of action. Hence the reference to the spontaneous element as 'both . . . a forward-moving and also . . . a restraining element'. Emphatically the party was still seen at this stage as synonymous with the masses; it was the party which had to provide the necessary spirit of movement to the static organization mania of the trade unions. Rosa Luxemburg went a long way to stress the difference of attitude between party and trade unions—which she condemned as 'German Social Democracy's worst fault'. In postulating the antithesis unions/party, she attempted no distinction *within* the SPD between leaders and masses. The word 'executive' appeared nowhere in the pamphlet, and all references to the party were simply made in terms of 'Social Democracy'. In 1906 spontaneity was thus shorthand for Social Democracy, while immobility meant the trade unions.

In view of later events, the terminology is important. This indiscriminate use of 'Social Democracy' and 'masses'—the former being no more than 'the most conscious advance guard' of the latter, but essentially part and parcel of it—contained the germs of future misunderstanding. Either Rosa Luxemburg's view could be taken literally—and must then lead to just that doctrine of confused spontaneity of which she was later accused by the heirs of Lenin's highly 'deliberate' Bolsheviks, for whom spontaneity really meant confusion—or a closer differentiation between leaders, party members, and masses would have at some stage to be made, distinctions which acknowledged, or empirically observed, differences and which could be underpinned with theoretical explanations. We shall see how the notion of spontaneity developed in Rosa Luxemburg's thinking; how the concept of party was broken down first into leaders and masses, and finally into leaders against masses; and how dissatisfaction with the leaders brought about a reliance on the masses which trapped Rosa Luxemburg in the terminological blind alley of spontaneity—a blind alley in which her later Communist detractors were only too willing to wall her up. But the trap was one of words, not meanings.[1]

---

[1] It might help if at this stage the difference between on the one hand the so-called doctrine of spontaneity as still attacked by the Soviet leadership and Rosa Luxemburg's formulation on the other, were made clear. The Communist notion of spontaneity implies that the 'spontaneous' appearance of wishes and ideas in the masses must prevail against and govern the rational policy of the party. This of course runs counter to the whole concept of party control on which the government of the U.S.S.R. is based and is as much anathema to them as ever. In 1958 Khruschev again declared roundly: 'Spontaneity, comrades, is the deadliest enemy of all' (speech to Central Committee of the CPSU, 19 December 1958; *Plenum Tsentralnogo Komiteta KPSU 15–9 dekabrya 1958 goda, stenograficheskii otchet*, Moscow 1958, p. 452).

But Rosa Luxemburg never propagated such a general doctrine of spontaneity. First she

One aspect of Rosa Luxemburg's historical argument was especially important and provocative. Her historical reference was largely Russian. The mass-strike lesson to be learnt was above all a Russian lesson. This was no accident. But the idea of putting forward Russia as a revolutionary example to Germany happened to constitute a complete dismantling of the natural order of things. It also meant a reversal of the widely accepted direction in which Socialist advice had hitherto always flowed.

It has already been emphasized that the SPD, with much justification, considered itself the most progressive party in the Second International. The German party leaders were very conscious of their international role, and dispensed advice in all directions. In this distribution service Rosa Luxemburg was an enthusiastic participant. Her letters and articles on Russian questions before 1905 all preached the German example of unity to the divided and cantankerous Russians and gave them the benefit of her experience of six years in Germany. Suddenly all this was changed. Russia had become the eye of the revolutionary storm, with Germany merely the periphery; the cyclone of cause and effect was blowing the other way about. Rosa Luxemburg now gave advice to the Germans based on her Russian experience. At first this was no more than a change on the revolutionary weather map, the centre of pressure moving from west to east. As yet no judgement on parties or policies was intended. But the 'leapfrog' concept of historical development implied that in some respects at least the Russian masses were in

---

postulated mass action as an essential feature of Social-Democratic activity. Nobody would quarrel with that. Later, when it became clear that the party leadership would not encourage mass action, she came to examine the *limits of the powers* of the leadership if opposed to the willingness of the masses to act. Her case for mass control and supremacy was based on the existence of unsatisfactory leaders—unsatisfactory in specific and fully documented ways. Third, and most important, the spontaneous power of the masses was limited to a special case, that of action. The argument is primarily about action, and only incidentally about sovereignty.

It might be argued that in that case all that had to be done was democratic removal of the leadership by the masses and replacement by leaders more in tune with the political tasks of Social Democracy. As we shall see, the full elaboration of Rosa Luxemburg's doctrine *in the German party* (the whole argument only makes sense in this context) coincided with the outbreak of the war, when party democracy was suspended. Rosa's effort during the war was specifically aimed at removing the membership from the control of the SPD executive.

In short, the concept of Luxemburgist spontaneity is an elaboration and extension by others of certain notions expressed by her. To some extent it is a misrepresentation. As we shall see, her ideas developed slowly on this point; as she became more disaffected with the policy of the SPD leadership, so she stressed the concept of the masses against it. But this concept was indissolubly wedded to action. In her view supremacy of the masses over the leadership made sense only when the former favoured action and the latter immobility.

It will be helpful if this analysis is borne in mind during the examination of Rosa Luxemburg's developing ideas both before, during, and after the war.

advance of their German brethren. Rosa Luxemburg did not suggest that this was due to the merits of Russian Social Democracy, or that the latter was in any way superior to the SPD, but equally she did not dissociate the Russian party from the revolutionary successes of the workers. In fact she deliberately avoided any reference to Russian party questions in her German writings at the time, probably to avoid causing embarrassment. Nevertheless the very idea of learning Russian lessons was greatly resented by the Germans, not only by the party authorities but even by fellow radicals like Ledebour. It was not only a matter of comparing the SPD and all its achievements with the notoriously disorganized and ineffective Russian Social Democracy. According to history, buttressed with innumerable quotations from Marx and Engels, Russia was the mainspring of European reaction—with Germany and its growing Socialist party unquestionably the centre of future revolution. When Rosa Luxemburg put forward her new interpretation in her mass-strike pamphlet the reaction of her readers varied from sceptical disbelief to nationalist outrage.

The extent to which Rosa Luxemburg reversed her political thrust as a result of the Russian revolution is crucially important. Most of her writings before 1905 were in defence of the SPD as it was—in her view—established: emphasis on the correct traditional tactic against various attempts to amend it; emphasis on unity and cohesion of doctrine against fragmentation by individual theories and local preferences. The accepted dogma in the Second International was that only a united, well-organized mass party could be a progressive spearhead of Socialism. It behoved small, divided, and disputing parties like the Russian to take example from the SPD. Now all this was turned upside down. Organization had become a potential hindrance, cohesion a factor of immobility, tradition a dead weight. And beyond the horizon of these slowly crumbling bastions there rose the new life force of Social Democracy— the physical masses on the move. As yet the change in Rosa Luxemburg's thinking was one of emphasis rather than polarity, but shifts of emphasis are often sharpened by opposition and controversy into mutually exclusive choices. Where previously discipline and tradition had served to eradicate errors, now only mass action could sweep them away. Thus organization and mass action, discipline and enthusiasm, unexpectedly became alternatives. Moreover, the action of the masses not only brought objective revolutionary benefits, but provided a subjective cure for internal party disputes and differences. The new doctrine of action thus pre-empted all the old debates on tactics and strategy in the SPD, just as the revolution had pre-empted the divisions in the Russian party.

Historically, the process by which Rosa Luxemburg thus came to the threshold of an analysis of imperialism is interesting and important. It was an outward-going process, a broadening of the discussion of party tactics rather than an attempt to find a defence against any genuine attack by society on Socialism. The preoccupation with imperialism and Rosa Luxemburg's developing ideas on this subject arose directly out of the mass-strike discussion, from the difficulties of making headway in the party. To get to grips with the problem of society at all it was necessary first to break the crust of self-absorption within which the SPD slept its leaden sleep. If the party could not be galvanized from inside then an outside stimulus had to be applied. Thus we have first a mass-strike doctrine, then a struggle for its application, next a dissatisfaction with party policy against a background of personal disenchantment, and finally the development of a doctrine of imperialism in order to overcome the party's recalcitrance. Just as Canning had once spoken of bringing in the New World to redress the balance of the Old, so Rosa Luxemburg brought in imperialist society to redress the balance in the party.

Rosa Luxemburg was not the only Socialist to develop a doctrine of imperialism, but her manner of approach and the purpose it was intended to serve were highly individual. Both Hobson and Hilferding believed that the phenomenon they were analysing was in some way unique, and looked for the signs and causes of this uniqueness. Both provided a definition of imperialism which distinguished it from any other form of society. Hobson stressed the peculiarity of colonial development and said openly that certain restraints and alterations of policy on the part of 'imperialist' powers could conceivably undo the evils of imperialism. Hilferding, a Marxist, made no attempt to provide a cure for imperialism but he too searched for the particular effects which distinguished an imperialist state from a normal capitalist one.[1] At the opposite end of the line was Lenin's work.[2] It was first written in the spring of 1916 in Switzerland, long after the others and partly in reply to them. Instead of a frontal attack on the problem—what and why—Lenin grasped it by the scruff of the neck—from behind. He was primarily interested in explaining the causes of the war and more specifically the lamentable failure of Social Democracy to resist it. As always, the conceptual tools mobilized were just sufficient for his purpose—no more, no less; as regards the economic complexion and build-up of imperialism, he largely followed Hilferding. But, like Rosa Luxemburg's, his purpose was mainly political; unlike her, theory had

---

[1] See J. A. Hobson, *Imperialism*, London 1902; and Rudolf Hilferding, *Das Finanz-kapital*, 1st ed. Vienna 1910.

[2] Lenin, 'Imperialism as the most recent stage of Capitalism', Petrograd, April 1917 (written in the course of 1916); later, 'Imperialism as the highest stage of Capitalism', *Sochineniya*, Vol. XXII, pp. 173–290. In 1920 this pamphlet was reproduced in German, French, and English editions.

always to serve these ends and never venture beyond them. The treachery of the Social-Democratic leadership thus became itself a factor of imperialism, which by definition differed from capitalism precisely because it succeeded in suborning a labour aristocracy to serve *its* interests and not those of Social Democracy. Imperialism's colonial aspect helped to mobilize new non-proletarian revolutionary forces— like the peasantry, temporary allies of the revolutionary proletariat. It all led straight to a new strategy—or rather to a justification of the strategy already adopted: in the stage of imperialism as defined by Lenin, the proletariat must look for allies outside its own class; the peasantry at home, and subject colonial peoples abroad. But more important still was the concept of imperialism as a weapon in the perennial struggle against opportunists. 'The most dangerous are those people who will not realize that the fight against imperialism can only be a hollow lying phrase if it is not combined with the fight against opportunism.'[1]

With one significant and substantial exception, Rosa Luxemburg did not theorize about imperialism. The problems Lenin examined in 1916 did not exist, or could not be seen to exist, before the war. Nevertheless, the political problem of imperialism already exercised Rosa considerably; indeed it became her central preoccupation after 1911.

She needed a theory of imperialism for political purposes and had to construct it from whatever raw materials were to hand. Before 1914 a general Socialist concept of imperialism was still in the process of creation; only the outbreak of the war provided the necessary fillip towards completing and sharpening it into a widely recognized doctrine. To this extent Rosa Luxemburg was a pioneer.

The earliest trace of Rosa Luxemburg's characterization of imperialism dates back to 1900, when she criticized the party's pusillanimous tolerance of German participation in the Chinese war. Rosa Luxemburg was then mainly concerned to avoid the impression that the SPD was a purely parliamentary party, but this was nevertheless the first occasion on which a specific act of aggression by the German government was singled out as calling for a general mass response by Social Democracy.[2] Similar comments were made from time to time, for instance during the first Morocco crisis in 1905. Looking back, it is not difficult to see during the revisionist debate the emphasis on the dual nature of the SPD—revolutionary and parliamentary—as the springboard for Rosa Luxemburg's theory of imperialist confrontation. Similarly, the discussions at the International congress of 1907 and the fight for a sharper resolution on war and militarism, theoretical as it still was, at least provided a framework which could later be filled out with more specific content.

[1] Ibid., p. 288. [2] For Rosa Luxemburg's speech, see *Protokoll . . . 1900*, p. 116.

The special concept of imperialism received a strong fillip during the second Morocco crisis in 1911. Once more it was the internal crisis in the party that provided the initial stimulus. During the following months she turned increasingly to a systematic examination and exposure of the society in which Social Democracy was encased. The bulk of her social reportage is thus significantly grouped round two main periods: the revisionist debate when it was necessary to prove that capitalism was not tamed, and the imperialist debate when society had actually to be shown on the offensive. The main difference between the two periods was in the conclusions which Rosa Luxemburg drew. From 1911 onwards every piece of evidence cited against society had to be 'lifted on to the shoulders of millions of proletarians and carried into battle'.[1]

The political manifestations of imperialism and their galvanizing effects on Social Democracy have been analysed in detail in their particular contexts. The compound of these various experiences became the totality of imperialism. But the generalization of experience, the creation of the totality, did not detract from the intensity of the evil. Imperialism was the primary, permanent, and overriding preoccupation of Social Democracy—at least Rosa Luxemburg intended to make it so. 'The questions of militarism and imperialism are the central axis of today's political life . . . we are witnessing, not a recession but an enormous boom of imperialism and with it a sharpening of class contradictions.'[2] More commonly she spoke of 'the great times in which we live' —and everyone knew what she meant. Rosa Luxemburg did not consider imperialism as the product of a specific feature or features in society—either new or unique. She only *described* imperialism itself on rare occasions, and then usually without mentioning the word. 'Militarism closely connected with colonialism, protectionism and power politics as a whole . . . a world armament race . . . colonial robbery and the policy of "spheres of influence" all over the world . . . in home and foreign affairs the very essence of a capitalist policy of national aggression.'[3] More often it was her anxious postulate of universality for any individual event or experience which related her analysis specifically to imperialism; that and the intensity of the fact or event described. It was the *effect* of these symptoms—themselves chronic and familiar— which constituted imperialism; the sharpening of class conflicts, the proximity of the two worlds, the need for a response. Thus imperialism differed from previous capitalism not by nature but by effect, not by what it was but by what it did—an almost utilitarian conception of imperialism. Indeed, politically imperialism could only be 'proved', not

---

[1] *Collected Works*, Vol. IV, p. 165.
[2] *Collected Works*, Vol. III, p. 527.   [3] *LV*, 6 May 1911.

from the existence or exaggeration of given symptoms in society, but from their specific effect on Social Democracy. This analysis of imperialism as a set of two-way responses is central and peculiar to Rosa Luxemburg's concept.

Thus Rosa Luxemburg's imperialism was essentially a general state of affairs—a state of acute conflict, moreover, not merely a general name for unconnected symptoms. Here was the conceptual method of the mass strike all over again. Moreover, her definition of imperialism was an equation of which both society and Social Democracy were essential functions; the social location of imperialism was the product, and confined to the area, of their collision. It was almost a constituent part of imperialism; without it the necessary heightened social conflict became impossible.

Just as imperialism was an advanced stage of capitalism, so was the Social Democracy in an imperialist country a higher form of Social Democracy—at least it should have been, and Rosa Luxemburg's whole thesis of imperialism was designed to make it so. The pressure under which her characterization of imperialism developed was not intellectual but political, not scientific but polemical. Lenin acutely put his finger on it when he referred to her 'self-flagellation', though he neither understood nor did justice to her achievement.[1] Rosa's main purpose was action. Each one of her comments on imperialism was immediately related to a particular precept for proletarian action in reply.

This becomes clear from the peculiar dual nature which Rosa Luxemburg postulated for imperialism. As foreshadowed in the mass-strike discussion in 1910, it was characterized as being both strong and weak at the same time. This paradox was the essential corollary of the Socialist tactic of simultaneous defence and attack which Rosa had elaborated in order to weld the party's half-hearted commitment to a defensive mass strike on to her own strategy of attack. Society was attacking Social Democracy and simultaneously defending itself. The economic features inherent in imperialism were an undeniable source of economic strength; that increasing armaments provided greater military striking power was evident. But in order to prise Socialist policy loose from the hypnotic paralysis induced by an ever more powerful imperialism, which had affected Bebel so noticeably during his last years, Rosa was now at pains to demonstrate the extent to which these signs of strength were also evidence of weakness. This was not just an example of classical dialectic technique according to which the perfection of imperialism necessarily predicated its final collapse. Rosa Luxemburg dealt with this aspect separately in *The Accumulation of Capital*. It was rather a demonstration that as the power of imperialism increased it also became more fearful and therefore more fragile.

[1] *Leninskii Sbornik*, Vol. XXII, p. 346.

This proud German militarism which according to Bismarck was afraid of God but nothing else, this militarism which is supposed to frighten us in the guise of a colossus of iron and steel bristling with armament from top to bottom —*this colossus shivers at the very thought of a mutiny of precisely twelve soldiers. The whole of the German Empire is seen as dissolving in ruins as a result of a Social-Democratic demonstration.*[1]

Rosa Luxemburg's apparently contradictory emphasis on the simultaneous weakness and strength of imperialism was the product of her particular time. It synthesized two prevalent but opposing Socialist moods—one optimistic and one pessimistic. The optimistic view was Kautsky's. Here imperialism had a purely economic, not a political connotation. His strategy of attrition was based on it—an ever-growing array of Social-Democratic forces which would peacefully overwhelm the shrinking and alienated supporters of society. As against this, the pessimistic view went with the burdens of organizational responsibility. It hung over the party leadership like a pall. Bebel had repeatedly confessed in private before his death that if the full might of imperial Germany were to be launched against the SPD, the party was powerless—and therefore would never risk any open confrontation. The extent of these fears was put to the test at the outbreak of war; while it is easy to show that the SPD leadership really wanted to collaborate with the German government for patriotic reasons, they dressed up their decision in the coy veils of helplessness. This pessimistic view thus gave full credit to imperialism; by implication it too enjoined the party to sit back and wait for the collapse of society predicted by the dialectic —and its foremost interpreter, Karl Kautsky.

Rosa Luxemburg differed from both these views. She emphasized imperialism as a special condition of society; as an aggravation—a necessary and inevitable one since she had never subscribed to the notion of a normal and more amiable capitalism of which imperialism was a temporary variant that could be contained. At the same time she refused to accept the implication of powerlessness. Apart from and because of the dialectic, imperialism was as weak as it was strong; every increase in strength brought a simultaneous weakening. Nor was she content with paradoxes alone. To the practical question of what could be done, she replied by emphasizing the initial strengthening of class consciousness along the whole line of confrontation with the imperialist state. Class conflict existed not only in the obvious battlefield of factory or political arena but for instance in the army where the soldiers—'proletarians in uniform'—confronted the officers. As soon as the soldiers could be made conscious of the fact that uniforms were

---

[1] Speech at Freiburg, 8 March 1914, *Rosa Luxemburg . . . gegen . . . Militarismus*, p. 102. The italics are those of the original stenographic report in the local paper.

merely a disguise and that wearing them and taking soldiers' pay could not get rid of the omnipresent class struggle, obedience—the whole basis of militarism—was eroded.

This then was Rosa Luxemburg's characterization of imperialism. It was consistent and broad enough to be called a doctrine, even though she never claimed any such title. As with the mass strike, the doctrine developed piecemeal; the product of polemic. For this reason her contribution to imperialism so far has deliberately not been described as a theory. To qualify for this any exposition has at least to be logically consistent and its component parts must be capable of substantiation. Her totality was comprehensive rather than structural—like the identicast used by police forces to catch criminals.

It is not at all surprising that Rosa Luxemburg's characterization of imperialism has almost completely escaped recognition, let alone acceptance. Both her critics and her sympathetic biographers have ignored it. But this is due only in small part to ignorance or unwillingness to reconstruct her views from difficult primary material. The main obstacle is *The Accumulation of Capital*, that curious work of genius which has overshadowed all her other work on imperialism.

In *The Accumulation of Capital* Rosa Luxemburg set out, not to describe, but to justify and analyse the basic causality of imperialism. The sub-title of the book was 'A contribution to the economic clarification of imperialism'. The emphasis throughout was on economics and she wrote to Konstantin Zetkin in November 1911: 'I want to find the *cause* of imperialism. I am following up the economic aspects of this concept . . . it will be a strictly scientific explanation of imperialism and its contradictions.' Rosa Luxemburg was teaching political economy at the time. The particular problem that excited her interest was a technical one concerned with Marx's economics, more specifically the problem of capitalist reproduction which Marx had begun to set out in Volume III of *Capital*. It is almost certain that her solution of this problem led to the discovery of what she took to be the theoretical cause of imperialism. Important as this obviously was, the discovery was clearly incidental. She was able to kill two birds with one stone and in the process discovered not only how compound reproduction in capitalist societies is possible, but how it must inevitably lead to imperialism and finally to collapse. In *The Accumulation of Capital* we thus have a *theory* which was lacking in her political writings—hence the reason why her followers and critics promoted *The Accumulation of Capital* at the expense of her other diverse and individually minor political writings.

The theory evolved in *The Accumulation of Capital* is in essence simple enough. Marxism postulates the collapse of capitalism under the weight of its economic contradictions. Marx himself went part of the way in underpinning this assertion with mathematical and empirical evidence.

Rosa Luxemburg believed that this evidence did not justify the conclusion—this was her specific problem. Failing to resolve the mathematical equation, she looked for an alternative outside cause of collapse.
This she discovered in the ability of capitalism to continue its existence
and growth (capitalism was essentially a growth process which could
not exist statically) just as long as there were pre-capitalist societies to
be captured and brought into the economic sphere of influence of the
capitalist colonial power. When the entire surface of the earth had been
drawn into the process of capitalist accumulation, then capitalism could
no longer grow and must collapse. But what had all this to do specifically
with imperialism, beyond explaining its logical (economic) necessity?

The answer is, very little. Paradoxically, her one major work on the
subject of imperialism took almost all the political implications for
granted. The question she asked was not 'what is imperialism' and
'how does it look', but 'why is it inevitable'. In more than 400 pages
of untidy and often highly polemical argument (against other economists) she tried to provide a neat and fastidious *economic* solution; far
neater than could be provided by any *political* discourse. There is no
logically necessary connection between the two. Rosa Luxemburg offered
no specific recommendations for policy; Social Democracy is not mentioned throughout the book in any political context—or for that matter
in any context at all. In fact, it was Rosa Luxemburg's only large-scale
essay in the theoretical social sciences.

If we are to relate this work to the rest of her writings on imperialism
—and the validity of such a relationship is by no means certain—then
one large step at least is missing. On the one hand we have a rigorous
economic causality of the enemy's being, on the other a series of pamphlets on tactical combat. How does the one become the other, how
was theoretical economic necessity transformed into the political
provocations which required specific Socialist action? Rosa Luxemburg
does not tell us. The two aspects of her work were kept in separate
compartments; she never referred her political readers to *The Accumulation of Capital* nor did she refer her economic readers to the political
conclusions of her newspaper articles. Indeed, she admitted that *The
Accumulation of Capital* was intended only for advanced students and
wrote a simplified commentary on it in prison during the First World
War in order to clear up the widespread misunderstandings to which
the book had given rise.

In spite of this, *The Accumulation of Capital* has been used as the
basis for criticizing Rosa Luxemburg's attitude to imperialism in all its
aspects. The foundation stone of this pyramid of criticism was laid by
Lenin. His chief criticism was fundamental: her thesis that enlarged
capitalist reproduction was impossible within a closed economy and
needed to cannibalize pre-capitalist economies in order to function at

all, he described as a 'fundamental error'.[1] This has provided the springboard for all later Communist criticism of a much more detailed and sophisticated kind.[2] From it has been deduced Rosa Luxemburg's allegedly 'objective' attitude to capitalist collapse which by implication almost completely destroys the role of Social Democracy and its leader-ship—the entire subjective element. From this in turn there developed the heresy of Luxemburgism, based on a theory of spontaneity which systematically negated the function of rational cognition, of will and of decision on the part of Social Democracy. In the words of Rosa Luxem-burg's most bitter opponent in Germany, whose views were one long campaign against her predecessor's heritage: 'The German party based its theory and practice in the main on Rosa Luxemburg's theory of accumulation, and this is the fount of all errors, all theories of spontaneity, all erroneous conceptions of organizational problems'.[3]

The most likely explanation is that Rosa Luxemburg did not attempt to relate *The Accumulation of Capital* to her immediate political purposes at all, that she saw no contradiction between a rigorous theoretical analysis of the economic causes of imperialism and her characterization of its political manifestations.[4] It is, however, possible to argue—a view moreover that has the advantage of consistency—that Rosa Luxemburg did indeed believe that her economic analysis provided the only feasible explanation of the transition from capitalism to imperialism. This would have meant that the militaristic phenomena of imperialism, resulting in more intense pressure on Social Democracy, were the direct consequence of the need to protect the vital under-developed economies within each national sphere of influence, without which neither economy nor society could survive. Such an interpretation need not necessarily alter her description of imperialism as a force to be combated at home. Then indeed we do have here a propensity to spon-taneity and objective automatism, only mitigated by the specific recom-mendations to action. But there is no positive evidence of this view at

---

[1] *Leninskii Sbornik*, Vol. XXII, p. 337.

[2] See N. Bukharin, 'Der Imperialismus und die Akkumulation des Kapitals', *Unter dem Banner des Marxismus*, Vienna/Berlin, 1925–6, Vol. II, p. 288. See also the summary in F. Oelssner, *Rosa Luxemburg*, Berlin (East) 1956 (3rd ed.), pp. 172–87.

[3] Ruth Fischer, *Die Internationale*, Vol. VIII, No. 3 (1925), p. 107.

[4] Cf. the similar methodological and analytical break between politics and economics in Rosa Luxemburg's portrait of capitalist society during the revisionist debate. Readers interested in the sociological context of this problem are strongly urged to read Talcott Parsons' remarkable but little known essay 'Democracy and Social Structure in Pre-Nazi Germany', *Journal of Legal and Political Sociology* (U.S.A.), Vol. I (1942), pp. 96–114. It is argued there that the analysis of capitalism presented a *special* problem for German intellectuals and social thinkers, because of the incongruence between the static social structure and the dynamics of rapid industralization. Much of the argument developed in the present chapter can profitably be considered within this wider context (not to mention the work of Max Weber).

all—such negative evidence as exists (her failure to relate her political and economic writings) points against this conclusion. In this connection it may be significant that Rosa Luxemburg developed no political policy for colonial countries, that she made no recommendations as to how colonial peoples might resist their exploitation and thus further hasten the collapse of capitalism. Nor did she recommend any specifically colonial policy to the SPD.

Why then the missing step? Was it oversight? Is there significance in the fact that Rosa Luxemburg did not emphasize or define the 'imperialist' features of her political ideas, but relegated them simply to being a sharpened version of an already existing class conflict? Perhaps the reason was political—a question of tactics. If applied to practical politics, her 'new' theory of imperialism outlined in *The Accumulation of Capital* might indeed have given rise to a 'new' theory of political inaction. By emphasizing imperialism merely as capitalism writ large and fierce, Rosa Luxemburg was more likely to get action— of a kind already familiar from the Russian revolution, not some new anodyne by ballot of the sort Kautsky was already advocating as his contribution to 'the great times in which we live'. In that case the separation of her economic from her political work was deliberate—to avoid the very spontaneity theory of which she was later accused.

Rosa Luxemburg's doctrine of imperialism was necessarily based on certain assumptions about democracy which we must now sketch briefly if we are to understand her whole theory of action. They will be examined in greater detail later in relation to the Russian and German revolutions. Mass action was never a purely formal concept. Rosa Luxemburg's longstanding emphasis on class consciousness predicated an important role for the 'conscious' or educated masses. The example of the first Russian revolution increased her estimate of this role even further. Thus the concept of mass action in Rosa Luxemburg's mind existed long before the development of a polarity between the leaders and masses after 1910. She never formalized the masses into an abstraction to the extent that many Bolsheviks did; nor was there any trace of a doctrine of substitution of party leadership for mass action. The role of the masses could never be assumed.

During the war, when a choice between secret organizational activity and mass propaganda under difficult circumstances had to be made, the *Spartakusbund* chose the latter. The reason for remaining in the party, for avoiding an organizational break, was again and always the need to keep open the channels of approach to the masses which they believed could only be done within the official organization of the SPD. Much incidental light is shed on this problem in Rosa Luxemburg's comments on the Russian revolution. One of the main reasons for acclaiming the Bolsheviks was that they had solved the problem of obtaining a majority.

Only through their dynamic and active policy had they built themselves up from being 'a small hunted and despised minority to the leadership of the revolution in the shortest possible time . . . and with this had solved the famous question of the "majority of the people", which has oppressed German Social Democracy from the beginning'.[1]

During the German revolution Rosa Luxemburg specifically emphasized that there could be no question of seizing power without the clearly expressed support of a majority of the people. There was therefore no contradiction but only the strongest dialectical connection between a revolutionary policy on the one hand and the resultant approbation and support by a majority on the other; a majority moreover that had to be real and could not merely be assumed.

What were these masses? Clearly not numbers trooping through voting booths to scribble on bits of paper. Equally not, as has just been explained, proletarians by definition with no choice but to support the party which spoke in their name. Rosa Luxemburg never explained the positive content of the word 'masses', but since she most frequently used it in connection with dynamic physical action it is probable that her view approximated to the sort of visible manifestation of mass support which Rousseau may have had in mind;[2] at least potentially, in a revolutionary situation or period.

Rosa Luxemburg's view of revolutions coincided perfectly with such a concept. Revolutions were long-term not short seizures of power. Like Mehring she was deeply anchored in history. Its revolutionary examples—the English seventeenth-century revolution and the great French revolution—always played themselves out over long periods of time; hence Mehring's phrase about revolutions having a very long breath. We shall see this doctrine applied in practice during the German revolution; here it concerns us particularly as a necessary consequence of Rosa Luxemburg's preoccupation with the masses and the question of majority.[3] Though she occasionally accepted the need for armed uprising, she saw this entirely as a further manifestation of mass action not as a coup by armed conspirators. This was her conclusion from the Moscow uprising of December 1905. In her analysis of the Bolshevik revolution of 1917 Rosa Luxemburg never investigated the technical seizure of power; the *ex post facto* majority support had clothed it in the necessary aura of legitimacy.

---

[1] *The Russian Revolution*, pp. 52, 54.

[2] Rousseau was probably the last political analyst who spoke of the people as a whole in terms of a demonstrable gathering—and even here it is not certain that he meant this literally. Later writers either used 'masses' or 'people' in a purely formal sense or broke it down into recognizable parts (classes, groups, demonstrators, voters).

[3] I prefer to use the word 'majority' rather than 'democracy' since the latter carries such strong connotations of a particular type of democracy which Rosa Luxemburg opposed.

The need for a majority was thus an essential part of Rosa Luxemburg's doctrine of imperialism and of revolution. This particularly has been the cause of an almost unique situation in which two utterly opposing Socialist camps continued mightily to document their claims on her allegiance. Such tenacity cannot be based entirely on fiction. The Communists emphasize the revolutionary aspect of her thought; the Socialists rely on her preoccupation with a majority—democracy, for short. Because of the deep division between them, both parties insist on their possession as exclusive; for the Communists her revolutionary determination precludes vulgar democracy, whilst for the Socialists her deep feeling for democracy would eventually have counteracted her impatience for physical revolution. In this respect the date of her death is important, for the choice—if indeed it is a choice—did not have to be made during her lifetime. But Rosa Luxemburg herself certainly did not see any exclusiveness in these two ideas, but believed them to be interdependent. Her Communist critics have never belaboured her for any excessive preoccupation with democracy. The theoretical attack on spontaneity carefully avoids any disagreement with her concept of democracy as such, and concentrates on the automatic and excessively objective features of *The Accumulation of Capital*. Lenin himself did not even mention spontaneity expressly or by implication in his summary of Rosa Luxemburg's errors in 1922.[1]

Rosa Luxemburg's view of democracy did for a short period in the 1920s assume critical importance. The German Communist Party was being disciplined to accept Russian control. Since she had specifically opposed the foundation of the Third International for that very reason, and had warned the new KPD in the few weeks before her death against importing the oligarchical traditions of the SPD, the prestige of her name was an important weapon for those resisting the Bolshevization of the German Communist Party. It was from that moment on that Rosa Luxemburg's views were subjected to an over-all systematic criticism. But even then there could be no overt disagreement with the concept of majority support as such. Her view of the masses as the repository of final authority was attacked as leading to indiscipline—an unnecessary inheritance from the bad days of the SPD. An attempt was made to identify such indiscipline with the failure of the SPD and its betrayal of the real cause of Socialism—leading to the absurd proposition that it was the SPD's inability to maintain discipline and cohesion which caused its failure in 1914. And out of this practical need to counteract Rosa Luxemburg's undisciplined influence eventually grew the onslaught on the more sophisticated notion of spontaneity which has already been discussed.

[1] Lenin, *Sochineniya*, Vol. XXXIII, p. 184.

Whatever the polemics against the doctrines of Rosa Luxemburg, however, they were never classed as reactionary. There was no attempt to make any specific identification of her writings with opportunism until Stalin's famous letter to *Proletarskaya Revolyutsiya* in which he brought his chorus of ancillary analysts to the point where the German Left was identified as its half unconscious and half deliberate ally. At the same time the criticisms of Rosa Luxemburg's ideas were knit together into the coherent doctrine known as Luxemburgism—national question, spontaneity, poor arithmetic, failure to understand opportunism in organizational matters; it is always easier to build on the ruins of a whole system than merely to contradict individual deviations from orthodoxy.

The final question remaining is the extent to which Rosa Luxemburg's theories as they developed between 1906 and 1914 add up to any coherent system. That she produced a coherent *theory* of imperialism and a consistent *policy* for Social Democracy cannot be doubted. But was this all? Her later Communist critics certainly credited her with a total system—Luxemburgism. To what extent was this an artifact for purposes of demolition and how much of it, irrespective of content can really be called a system?

No one in the Second International, and certainly not Lenin and his supporters, ever tried to work out a formula of government for the post-revolutionary state. In all this time there was only one article in *Neue Zeit* which even posed the problem, and then it dived away from all modern political contexts by analysing the various utopias of the past.[1] Speculation on this subject was frowned upon as romantic. Even the form and nature of the revolution which would usher in the Socialist future was not discussed except in a purely formal context and then strictly with relevance to present problems. After the Bolshevik revolution Lenin, an extremely empirical tactician, was therefore able to act without fear of counteracting any established doctrine. But then he was less bound by *tradition*—as opposed to Marxist *orthodoxy*—than almost anyone in the Second International.

Rosa Luxemburg followed established practice in avoiding any overt speculation about the future. Believing as she did in the creative force of mass action, she stated more and more specifically that the creative aspect of action would solve not only the immediate problems which had called it into being but also those that would arise as the revolution moved forward. This followed logically from the belief that organizations grew out of mass action, that class consciousness was increased

---

[1] Karl Kautsky, 'Zukunftstaaten der Vergangenheit', *NZ*, 1892–3, Vol. I, pp. 653–63, 684–96.

by it. If such organizations and consciousness grew in a healthy way, they would automatically be equipped to deal with the problems of revolutionary technology and the problem of power after victory. Her criticism of the Bolshevik revolution contained strong elements of this theory. This was one of the most important and at the same time disastrous criticisms of the Russian revolution—disastrous because she and those who looked to her for inspiration in Germany became burdened with an obstinate lack of realism with regard to revolutionary technology. We shall see how the consistent refusal to face up to problems of power, the postponement of these problems till they would be solved by action itself, ultimately helped to make *Spartakus* success impossible even if objective circumstances had been more favourable.

But even in her criticisms of others within or without the SPD, Rosa Luxemburg never tried to build one system in order to oppose another. More and more her answers to unsatisfactory systems were not alternative static systems, but movement—anti-system. She came to see systems as static and movement as dynamic, so that the very existence of an accepted system of society was already a fault. In her criticisms of Kautsky, a system-builder *par excellence*, she carried the distrust of complete panaceas to its furthest possible limit.

This applied not only to her refusal to construct a theory of Socialist government with which to confront society, but also to her unwillingness to meet the unsatisfactory system within the SPD by any alternative. Though she was one of the first to do so, she only recognized the systematic nature of German Social Democracy in 1912, deducing it from the party's excessive preoccupation with itself. Nearly all those who founded the *Spartakusbund* were strongly driven by their hatred for the SPD system. Rosa Luxemburg was by no means the fiercest opponent of party discipline as such; as her correspondence in 1915 with Karl Liebknecht shows, he went much further in his negation of discipline than she did.[1] None of these German left-wingers was ever able to envisage Socialism in static terms again or feel at ease in a static situation. This goes a long way to explain the constant fever among the *Spartakus* leaders, at least for the first twelve months after the war.

In the last resort Rosa Luxemburg was a critic, albeit profound and acute, rather than a political theorist. Through her writings we learn a great deal about society and about Socialism, but we do not see a coherent alternative system to the ones she was criticizing. Luxemburgism—if it exists at all—is at most a tendency, a way of thought, an attitude to existing societies. It cannot exist in a vacuum, in the rarefied air in which pure political speculation takes place. It needs strong meat

---

[1] *Unter dem Banner des Marximus*, Vienna/Berlin, 1925–6, Vol. II, pp. 416 ff. (see particularly p. 420).

on which to fasten its teeth. Rosa Luxemburg needed not only society and Social Democracy as humus for her thought but the specific society of imperial Germany and particularly the German Social-Democratic party that had grown within it. Once more we are back to the problem of the relationship between Socialism and society. To what extent did Socialism then and does Communism now need hostile societies within or without in order to survive and flourish? Rosa Luxemburg's Socialism is unthinkable except in terms of an imperialist society pressing closely upon Social Democracy.

And it is precisely this sense of continuous involvement with society in its widest context (rather than any retreat into internal party pre-occupations) which infused Rosa Luxemburg's Socialism with its strong glow of humanity. Unlike Lenin, she could not theorize about the First World War in abstract terms as History's contribution to revolutionary midwifery. Nor, like Mussolini and other Socialist ad-mirers of action first and foremost, could she welcome the war as a personal escape route from preaching into doing.[1] Hence the immensely painful contradiction of the first war years, the disorientation which Lenin was to seize on as a sign of weakness: society must indeed be transformed by revolution, but if millions bled to death in a holocaust of mutual butchery, there would be little left to transform. Society for Rosa Luxemburg always consisted of people first and foremost. They might, most of them, be playing the roles in which capitalism had cast them, but the whole point of social revolution was precisely to reallocate their roles. Rosa Luxemburg's whole notion of revolution can only be understood in this light—one that was steeped in humanitarianism.

---

[1] A good account of Mussolini's progress from radical socialist to fascist via an almost hysterical fascination for action is in Renzo de Felice, *Mussolini il rivoluzionario, 1883–1920*, Turin 1965.

VII

RUSSIANS, JEWS, AND POLES—
THE ÉMIGRÉ VIEW OF REVOLUTION
1898–1904

THE last few years of the nineteenth century witnessed one of those mysterious revivals of revolutionary activity in the Russian empire which periodically boiled up out of nowhere and ebbed away just as mysteriously a few years later. All the revolutionary parties benefited: Russian Socialists and Socialist Revolutionaries, the *Bund*, PPS, and SDKPiL. Polish Social Democracy got a special bonus when the Lithuanian Social Democrats under Dzierżyński and Zalewski joined the SDKP in 1899. This brought not only a new organization but several outstanding leaders into the party. Dzierżyński was active in Warsaw on behalf of his new party until the end of 1901, when he was arrested; his efforts resulted in a brief flowering of Social-Democratic activity in Warsaw and other industrial centres in Poland.

The ripples of Socialist activity emanating from the Russian empire pushed the émigré groups to make an effort to unite. In 1897 the Jewish organizations centred on Vilna had formally constituted themselves as the General Union of Jewish Workers, the *Bund*. They were the most active propagandists for all-Russian unity and possessed by far the biggest organization at home as well as the most efficient transport network between their foreign committee and the organization at home. For Plekhanov and the other Russians this was an example to emulate— but also a cause for jealousy and in some cases dislike. Within a year of the formation of the *Bund* the Russian Social-Democratic Workers' Party (RSDRP) came into being—though only after protracted argument and bargaining.

It had not been easy. Plekhanov and his *Gruppa osvobozhdenie truda* demanded a pre-eminent role in the new party, much greater than that of father-figure and fount of philosophical wisdom, which was all the constituent groups in Russia were willing to concede.[1] The matter was shelved rather than solved. Right from the start the Russian party was faced by an internal tug-of-war between the local organizations at home and the distinguished but somewhat remote leadership abroad. In addition, there was the status problem of the relationship with the Russian party's two precursors, the *Bund* and the SDKPiL—two

---

[1] V. Akimov, 'Pervii S"ezd RSDRP', *Minuvshie Gody No. 2*, 1908, pp. 129 ff.

snorting steeds whose impatience had helped to put the creaking Russian cart on to the road in the first place. Should there be one all-embracing party, or should they be separate but equal; and if not equal, who should predominate? Having succeeded in extracting substantial concessions from the other participants, Plekhanov asserted the same claim for primacy for the RSDRP over the *Bund* and the Poles. He was suspicious of the *Bund*—a suspicion which was fully reciprocated—and his relationship with Rosa Luxemburg's group had been bad for over seven years.[1] In addition, Krichevskii, Teplov, and Akimov, who were Rosa Luxemburg's and Leo Jogiches' closest Russian friends, were also Plekhanov's particular enemies. The auguries for Russian unity and friendly collaboration with their natural allies were not good.

Neither Rosa Luxemburg nor Jogiches took any part in these negotiations and exercised no influence on them at all. They had lost touch with Russian affairs since the London congress of 1896. 'What is your impression of the new Russian party? Exactly the same as mine no doubt. None the less the blighters managed to bring themselves to do it. They did not quite get the publicity they hoped for, they chose a bad moment. . . .'[2] Certainly the earlier enthusiasm for Polish participation in the Russian party had waned, even though the ideological commitment was still asserted. The leading Poles did not care much for the new Russian leadership; besides, Rosa's German affairs were flourishing and the outlook for Russian unity was still very uncertain. None the less, Rosa did not want to lose touch with the Russians altogether, and the occasion gave rise to one of her severely rational appeals against Jogiches' policy of all or nothing:

I find your whole attitude towards the Russians uncongenial and exaggerated as I have told you so many times already in Zürich. In the end one has to face up to the fact that constant criticism, demolishing everything but doing nothing oneself to improve matters, is a senseless form of behaviour. I never liked the way you rebuffed every Russian who tried to approach you. You can boycott or banish the odd individual or even a group of people but not a whole movement. Your behaviour befits a sourpuss like Krichevskii but not a strong and noble person [like yourself]. . . . I personally could not care less about the Russians; I merely thought that the contacts I have made might be of some use to you. The whole thing hardly affects me either way; though I don't agree with your views, it is not a big enough matter to bicker about. Your constant complaint that they have not invited you is ridiculous—as you must have realized yourself when you wrote it. You have spat in the face of everyone who has come near you. . . . Forgive me for writing all this; I know some of it is bound to hurt you and even make you angry, but just this once I must tell you the truth. If you

---

[1] John Mill's letters in *Bund* archives, quoted by H. Shukman, *The Relations between the Jewish Bund and the RSDRP 1897–1903*, Oxford D.Phil. thesis, 1960, p. 47.

[2] Jogiches letters, *Z Pola Walki*, 1962, No. 1(17), p. 158.

think about it you will surely admit that I am right. . . . [Your attitude] does not suit a man of your calibre. I myself prefer to praise everything other people do rather than criticize everything and yet do nothing myself. . . .[1]

The new upsurge of Socialist strength in Russia was short-lived—and so was the pressure for unity. The first congress of the RSDRP at Minsk in March 1898, at which the party had been effectively founded, had not been representative of all the interested groups. It had only been possible to hold it at all because the *Bund* made its technical facilities available and its leaders contacted the various groups and solicited the presence of their representatives. An attempt to hold a further congress or conference at Smolensk at the end of April 1900 had failed since most of the delegates were arrested on their way to it.[2] In the course of this year Lenin, Martov, and other important Russian Socialists went into emigration; this strengthened the quality of the leadership abroad but at the same time all the difficulties and disagreements of clandestine activity in Russia were simply transferred abroad —where they grew strong and resilient like weeds. Soon the leadership of the RSDRP polarized into two main factions: Plekhanov, Lenin, and the other young émigrés around *Iskra*, against the older Union of Social Democrats Abroad led by Teplov and Krichevskii—the villainous 'economists' of the very near future. Subsequent conferences in Russia were to represent this deliberate and emphatic alignment.[3]

Thus the years between 1897 and 1902 were a period of unproductive isolation. Both Russians and Poles were absorbed in their own internal party affairs; contacts between them were precarious and insignificant. In addition to internal difficulties, they suffered from an effective police counter-offensive. Large-scale arrests took place, clearly helped by inside information; those who escaped arrest or custody were forced to flee abroad. By the beginning of the new century the importance and numbers of émigrés had grown considerably, though the organizations at home were once more in a precarious state. In Poland, where police vigilance was sharpened by the fear of a nationalist revival, the SDKPiL was hardly able to maintain effective contact with its groups in various cities. Even the fight against the PPS was flagging. As for the Russian leadership, its primary concern was to rid itself of *Bund* tutelage; concurrently with the attempt to demolish the power of the Union of Social Democrats Abroad, Plekhanov and his new allies prepared an

[1] Jogiches letters, *Z Pola Walki*, 1963, Vol. VI, Nos. 1/2(21–2), pp. 314–15, dated 15 January 1899.

[2] *Nasha Zarya*, 1913, No. 6, p. 31.

[3] For instance the congress or conference at Bialystok in March 1902 and the subsequent Pskov conference in November 1902. See *KPSS v rezolyutsiyakh i resheniyakh*, Vol. I, pp. 28–35. For the Union of Social Democrats' version of its activities and negotiations, see *Minuvshie Gody*, 1908, No. 7, pp. 279–96.

attack on the *Bund*. All this was to be achieved at the coming congress to which Plekhanov, Lenin, and all the others now devoted their energies. It was in connection with this great event that the Poles were to be drawn once again into the orbit of the RSDRP.

For Rosa Luxemburg the period which began with her departure from Zürich to Germany and ended with the outbreak of the Russian revolution of 1905 can be divided into two distinct parts. For the first two years, until Leo Jogiches joined her in Berlin at the beginning of 1900, she was almost as little concerned in Polish affairs as in Russian, and her entire energies were devoted to the new and splendid career in the SPD. Leo Jogiches, trying half-heartedly to complete his studies in Zürich, was still for all intents and purposes the boss, but he was more concerned with giving Rosa good advice on how to live and act in Germany than in keeping her up to date with SDKPiL events—such as they were. Rosa Luxemburg did not take kindly to this Polish intrusion into her new and very special German territory.

You are a little ass. Where dozens of publications and hundreds of adult people take part in a discussion, it is quite impossible to have a single 'direction'. In fact I often wanted to write to you about the way you seem to think that it is possible to export the methods of our Russian-Polish stable—in which a glorious total of 7½ people are working—to a million strong party. To you everything depends on 'pushing'; this person has to be persuaded, that one pushed, a third has to be made a bit more active, etc. I held exactly the same view till my last visits to Kautsky and Bebel. Now I see that it is all rubbish. Nothing can be done artificially. One has to concentrate on one's own work, that is the secret and nothing can be done by puppetry behind the scenes.[1]

At first sight all her expectations of the glorious SPD had been fulfilled, and she was only too eager to adapt herself to the new surroundings. But in fact there was to be no real change in Rosa Luxemburg. It had always been her particular task to 'influence', and right from the start her *milieu* had been the international Socialist movement much more than the manipulation of the membership of the SDKP. She kept a tight, suspicious rein on her enthusiasm for Germany, as we have seen. None the less, the challenge of a million card-carrying minds to influence—instead of seven and a half obstinate arguers—was too exciting to be denied.

The exclusion of Poland did not last very long. By 1900 she was already engaged in a new battle in the PPS in Prussia under the auspices of the SPD—and thus returned with enthusiasm to the familiar Polish problems and methods. From then until 1911 she always engaged in German and Polish activities simultaneously. The only concession to

---

[1] Jogiches letters, *Z Pola Walki*, 1963, Vol. VI, No. 3(23), p. 139, dated 21 April 1899.

the different methods required was her rigid separation of the two lives; only Jogiches knew the full extent of her activities, and no one in Germany got more than a foot inside her Polish door. This rigid separation was convenient, suitably conspiratorial—Jogiches insisted on conspiracy—and, most important of all, suited Rosa's highly developed sense of privacy. But, as we shall see, the division was not just functional, or even a matter of applying the different methods she had advocated; what was at stake was no less than two different ideologies—or perhaps two entirely different relationships between ideology and practice. For the moment it was useful to keep the two activities in distinct and self-contained compartments. This was why Rosa Luxemburg did not figure as one of the official SDKPiL leaders on documents and proclamations. None the less, from 1900 onwards her Polish work increased in extent and importance once more. Between 1900 and 1904 her role in Polish Social Democracy was crucial.

What kind of a party was the SDKPiL? The accession of the Lithuanian Social Democrats and their leaders had brought new blood to the little group of intellectuals who had first broken loose from the PPS in 1893. By now Rosa Luxemburg had emerged from her quarantine as an international scapegoat; her activities in Germany and her writings on the Polish question had secured her a place among the recognized names of the Second International—if not yet in the front rank with Adler, Liebknecht, and Plekhanov. To a man like Dzierżyński, whose entire experience had been in clandestine agitation and organization, the chance of joining such a leadership abroad was a matter of great pride—and for him the greatest moment came when he met and spoke to Rosa Luxemburg, an event to which he had been particularly looking forward.[1] Even Dzierżyński's friend, Jacob Firstenberg (Hanecki), who had arrived in Germany at much the same time, felt this sense of elation —though such a shrewd and devious conspirator was much less inclined to starry-eyed romanticism.

The SDKPiL leadership—since the fusion of the Polish and Lithuanian parties and the subsequent emigration of its most important local leaders—thus enjoyed an importance and stature out of all proportion to the size of the party at home. It is very difficult to judge the latter accurately. The arrests had made great inroads on the party; and by the beginning of 1902 there was again hardly anyone of importance left in Poland. Even Rosa Luxemburg wrote of the 'last of our Mohicans'.[2] Then, however sharp the propagandist warfare between Social Democrats and the PPS abroad, no such clear separation existed among the

[1] Feliks Dzierżyński to Cezaryna Wojnarowska, 10 August 1902, reprinted in *SDKPiL dokumenty*, Vol. II, pp. 100–1.

[2] Rosa Luxemburg to Cezaryna Wojnarowska, 17 January 1902, *SDKPiL dokumenty*, Vol. II, p. 10.

members at home. Distinct SDKPiL groups existed only in the big towns (the most important were Warsaw, Łódź, and Białystok); yet even here the respective spheres of influence and control were often confused. A number of Social Democrats were in close touch with the PPS, and the evidence indicates some drift away from the SDKPiL to the PPS during these years. This seemed especially to apply to those who were arrested; PPS influence with exiles in Siberia must have been particularly strong.[1] Though the PPS was not without its dissidents, some of these preferred to form a separate splinter group rather than join the Social Democrats, with their extreme rigidity on the national question. The picture of things at home varies considerably according to the person reporting it: Dzierżyński was always optimistic—with success just around the corner; Hanecki much more cynical. This difficulty over an accurate party census was to raise its head during the negotiations for joining the Russian party in 1903. Hanecki was preoccupied with the fear that acceptance of the Russians' conditions and the need to fuse local committees with those of the *Bund* would expose the fictitious claims of SDKPiL strength, whose many local committees existed largely on paper.[2]

This situation did not deter the leadership in the least. The first generation of émigrés had now been abroad continuously since the first years of the previous decade. Their interests were international. Almost all were active in parties other than the Polish: Marchlewski in Germany, Warszawski in Munich since 1897 and especially close to the Russians, Cezaryna Wojnarowska closely connected with the French Socialists in Paris. Most important, Rosa Luxemburg had established a reputation in German Socialist circles which, in the eyes of her contemporaries, had dwarfed her Polish importance. When she became involved in a public controversy with Lenin in 1904 she was acting, and considered by all spectators to be acting, as a representative of German Social Democracy rather than as a Pole. This state of affairs was to continue until the 1905 Russian revolution.

Rosa Luxemburg's international stature fitted perfectly into the political concepts of the SDKPiL leadership. Internal party matters, and organizational problems in Poland itself, had traditionally taken second place to the creation of the party's international image. Then, as now, the public relations effort was beamed more at the leaders of the Second International—'public opinion' in the Socialist world of the Second International—than at the membership at home. Rosa Luxemburg was superbly equipped for just this task. She had the connections and the talent to put the SDKPiL case consistently and

---

[1] See *Czerwony Sztandar*, August 1903, No. 8, pp. 4–5.
[2] See below, p. 187.

uncompromisingly before the intelligent reading public of the Second International. The leadership of the SDKPiL naturally reflected these priorities of purpose; influence before power, intellectual standing before size. It was more of a pressure group in international Socialism than a political party—and its organization and methods faithfully reflected the fact. Though a formal hierarchy and respectable party statutes had been established at the very first congress of 1894, this evidence of outward respectability—borrowed as it was largely from the German model, in particular the Erfurt programme, with some concession to Russian circumstances—in practice remained words on paper.[1] This myth naturally produced tensions of its own. When they functioned, the committees in Poland occasionally protested against the unilateral decisions of the Foreign Committee—but these protests were more formal than real. It was a situation that was understood to be inevitable, chronic, and part of the penalty for having such distinguished leaders. Not yet familiar with the informal manner in which the SDKPiL was really run behind a façade of formal rules, Dzierżyński began his career as an émigré in 1902 by agitating for conferences to put things right—'weed-pulling conferences . . . to tighten organizational procedure', as he called them.[2] But though one of his conferences did in fact take place, it brought about no significant change; it merely provided an opportunity for some harmless ventilation of steam.

The system also had its advantages. Central control was loose enough to permit those whose ideas on organization differed from the élite consensus to do what they pleased in their particular territory. When Dzierżyński returned to Cracow at the beginning of 1903 to manage and distribute the party's paper *Czerwony Sztandar*, he took the oppor-

---

[1] For the party statutes, see *SDKPiL dokumenty*, Vol. I, Part 1, pp. 174–96, 225–30. The ideas and principles came largely from Germany but the formation of a Foreign Committee (*Komitet Zagraniczny SDKPiL*), as liaison and occasional lifebelt for the Central Committee (*Zarząd Główny*), was borrowed from previous bitter Russian and Polish experience. The Central Committee, equivalent to the later Russian Central Committee, was the over-all authority in the party between congresses; the Foreign Committee a permanent body to represent the exiled leadership and to deal with all questions affecting foreign parties. In the SDKPiL, with its special emphasis on international relations, the Foreign Committee largely dominated the Central Committee from the start. Most of the time a nucleus of the same people served on both. Thus the Central Committee established at the third SDKPiL congress in 1901 was for all intents and purposes soon declared moribund owing to arrests at home; at a meeting of the Foreign Committee in December 1902 new informal rules for managing the party were drawn up. (See IML (M) Fund 163, No. 47, enclosed with a letter from Dalski to unknown party members.) Compare this with the long struggle in the Russian party to overcome the predominance of the foreign organizations and to weld the leadership into a proportionate representation of foreign and local organizations in Russia.

[2] *SDKPiL dokumenty*, Vol. II, p. 100.

tunity of creating what he proudly called 'a new type of organization with no rights but to work, to carry out the instructions of the Foreign Committee, to educate itself, to distribute literature, etc. This section shall have no voice at all or any right of representation in the party; its aim simply is to become Social-Democratic and to be at the beck and call [usługa] of the Foreign Committee.'[1]

It could hardly be otherwise. The Polish leadership of the SDKPiL was always scattered geographically. Rosa Luxemburg was in Berlin with only short interruptions from 1898 onwards. Jogiches, the main organizer, remained in Zürich until the end of August 1900 and then went for some months to Algeria to visit his brother who was in a TB sanatorium there. Such organizational problems as arose as a result of his absence were simply settled in correspondence between them. When he returned, Jogiches joined Rosa Luxemburg in Berlin. After his eviction from Dresden, Marchlewski finally settled in Munich where he remained until he returned to Poland in 1905, running a precarious publishing venture with Parvus which finally went bankrupt because the latter's hand was firmly ensconced in the till. Warszawski remained in Paris only until 1897 when he too established himself in Munich, close to the new Russian leadership after 1900. Wojnarowska was based in Paris throughout. It was largely her fortuitous residence in that city which won her the job of representing the Polish party in the International Bureau in Brussels until Rosa Luxemburg took over in 1904. The other members were highly peripatetic. Such dispersion made for informality, for letters of persuasion and opinion rather than resolute instructions. To a large extent each member of the élite acted on his own initiative and in accordance with his own predilections and habits. Orders were rare indeed; apart from exceptional cases like the Russian negotiations of 1903, communication was a matter of dispensing rabbinical shades of opinion. Dzierżyński was horrified at this laxity and saw it as evidence of deterioration. 'No policy, no direction, no mutual assistance . . . everybody has to cope on his own.'[2] In these circumstances success depended on personal initiative and ability—and of course it was here that Rosa Luxemburg excelled. 'Only Rosa Luxemburg has energy and brilliance which is wholly admirable—she works enormously for us.'[3] What Dzierżyński failed to realize was that this condition was not an accident but provided precisely the *milieu* in which Rosa Luxemburg's peculiar genius could flourish. The type of party organization he

[1] Feliks Dzierżyński to Cezaryna Wojnarowska, 13 February 1903, IML (M), Fund 76, No. 25. The letter and the whole concept is very typical of Dzierżyśnki and his 'revolutionary self-denial'.

[2] Feliks Dzierżyński to Cezaryna Wojnarowska, about 15 June 1903, IML (M), Fund 76, No. 26.

[3] Ibid.

had in mind would have been unacceptable to most of the Polish leaders. Bolshevism, then or later, was unthinkable.

After members, the scarcest commodity was money. Here again a comparison with Lenin is interesting. Little specific effort to raise funds was made; it was up to each individual to find a means of earning as good a living as possible (mostly by his pen). He was then expected to finance his local party activities from his own earnings. The party treasury was almost always empty. As a result, the most successful groups were those run by people with earning power—and this again meant Rosa Luxemburg with her writings and Jogiches with what little remained of his private funds. Closely connected with this was naturally the problem of transporting literature to Poland. Over and above the organized transport facilities, which never reached the efficiency of Lenin's, Jogiches and Rosa Luxemburg utilized private contacts for this purpose. 'Kasprzak is supposed to have a friend engaged in smuggling alcohol, etc. Officially [this friend] is in the fruit business. He will require 45 roubles per *pud* in advance because he is a business man and does not want to risk his own capital (though he is making some contribution). Let us try it once and see how it goes.'[1] But these extra activities of Kasprzak, however useful, did not meet with high-minded Rosa Luxemburg's approval: 'A nice lot these smugglers, I must say!'[2]

Far from being an accidental lacuna in the party's administration, this informality was deliberate and jealously guarded. At some stage a formal party decision was reached that Rosa Luxemburg should not concern herself with organizational matters at all, that she should not participate in any of the official conferences or congresses; in public, at least, Rosa Luxemburg ceased from 1901 to have any official standing in the party at all![3] Not that she relinquished for one moment her say in matters of importance. On the contrary, she continued to formulate the party's strategy and much of its tactics, and it was her pen that provided the vivid and uncompromising presentation of its case. It would hardly be an exaggeration to say that the primary preoccupations of the SDKPiL between 1901 and 1904 were those dictated by Rosa Luxemburg's particular interests—the destruction of PPS influence in Germany and the International, and the attempt to force the PPS into

---

[1] Jogiches letters, 19 May 1903, IML (M). Not even a close party friend like Kasprzak could be forced or instructed!

[2] Ibid.

[3] I have been able to find no formal resolution to this effect. However, her correspondence repeatedly refers to such a decision whenever anyone asked her for information, or solicited her views on problems of organization. 'Others will communicate with you regarding the conference. . . . Naturally I did not take part in it because as you know it has been established as a principle once and for all—at least in our Russian/Polish organization—that I do not participate in congresses. . . . None the less I am up to the ears in [private] meetings.' Rosa Luxemburg to Cezaryna Wojnarowska, 18 August 1902, IML (M), Fund 209, No. 925.

openly anti-Russian attitudes by testing the arguments about the general principle of self-determination in the specific crucible of relations with the Russian party. The SDKPiL's situation was unique, unimaginable either in the Russian party or in the SPD—or in any other Socialist party for that matter. Only in this context was it possible for the outstanding personality of the party to have no official function at all. And nothing shows more clearly the orientation of the SDKPiL as a pressure group, exercising influence on other parties rather than power in its own back-yard. Where both the Germans and Russians automatically referred to their 'party', members of the Polish élite preferred to call themselves a 'society' (*Stowarzyszenie*)—at least in private communication to each other.

Yet these people were in no sense merely a group of Bohemian *literati*. Theirs was not so much a deliberate blindness to the necessities of organization as the patient self-assurance of prophets waiting for preordained events in the dialectic calendar to fall due. As these events approached, they would surely settle the relatively minor problems of mass membership and organization. Though no one expressed themselves in such Messianic terms, it is very clear that what was at stake was a philosophy of life; once discovered, it imposed itself obligatorily on the chosen few who would in turn become the chosen many when the time was ripe. Far better to hasten on these events by clear and public thinking—they all had enormous faith in the power of the written word—than to grub about in sectarian cells and pretend that such artificial creations could be a substitute for or even help to bring about the coming social upheaval. It is here that we find the great difference between these Poles and Lenin's Bolsheviks, and the background to the dispute between Lenin and Rosa Luxemburg in 1904. Though technically she confronted Lenin in German, the cognitive experience had a strong Polish accent—as did all Rosa's work.

As a model of organization, the SDKPiL has left no direct heirs. It was swamped on the one hand by the Bolshevik imperative which preempted attention after the October revolution and on the other by the combination of formal democracy and oligarchy which Social Democracy adopted as a necessary condition for participating in bourgeois parliamentary life. In Poland particularly these ideas left no roots; they had been developed by Poles but not on Polish soil. But they did greatly influence the development of the future German Left under Rosa Luxemburg's direction. As we shall see, a similar élite or peer group was to emerge after 1914 out of the atomized opposition. In many ways the personal relationships, attitudes, and ideas about life and work, which evolved in the *Spartakusbund*, were all directly, if unconsciously, modelled on the SDKPiL. In Germany they were to create a tradition which Russian Bolshevism and its German supporters like Ruth Fischer and Thälmann had to work hard to eliminate. In Germany, too, the basic orientation was to be that of a pressure group which required the existence of a larger party or parties on which to operate—organizationally a parasite, but intellectually supreme. In the *Spartakusbund* as in the SDKPiL there was great reluctance to squander effort on organization: let others create the infra-structure for the apostles to 'capture'. The analogy extends even to personal relations: a group of leaders who co-operated through informal contact, united against outsiders but retaining all the personal liberties and quirks of distinct and highly individualistic intellectuals. Below them, in the SDKPiL as much as the *Spartakusbund*, was a group of less privileged activists whose job it was to collect money, distribute literature, and generally be of service to the leadership—without the glitter. No one contributed more decisively to creating this political environment than Rosa Luxemburg, with her curious combination of an essentially public orientation for her activities with a jealous autonomy in her private life and views.[1]

Since the beginning of 1902 the new Russian leadership in exile had been making strenuous efforts to call a general congress which would finally create the real unity which had hitherto been lamentably lacking. After the foundation of *Iskra* in 1900, the editors constituted themselves as an organizational nucleus for the coming congress and an Organizing Committee was formed to negotiate with the various factions inside and on the fringe of the Russian party. These managers were new people, unknown to the Poles; there is no evidence that anyone had already picked out Lenin as the coming man. If one man emerged as the architect of the impending congress in Polish eyes, it was Yurii Martov. But what particularly attracted the Poles was the new look in the Russian party, and the apparent relegation of Plekhanov to being merely *primus inter pares*. From the beginning of 1903 Warszawski in Munich was officially delegated by the Polish Foreign Committee to negotiate with the Russian Organizing Committee about Polish participation in the congress and SDKPiL adhesion to the Russian party. The Poles were not interested in or familiar with the complicated manœuvres of the *Iskraists* within the Russian party; there is no evidence that anyone read Lenin's *What is to be done?* and certainly no comment on it was made by the Poles. As far as the SDKPiL was concerned the main

---

[1] The respective roles of Rosa Luxemburg and Leo Jogiches in the SDKPil in many respects follow the pattern of leadership emergence in small groups in accordance with the theories of modern social psychology. Thus optimally 'a solidarity and group morale leader and a [different] task leader' appear; a general definition which fits the different roles of the two leaders very well. See P. E. Slater, 'Role differentiation in small groups' in A. P. Hare, E. F. Borgatta, and R. F. Bales (ed.), *Small Groups*, New York 1955, pp. 498–515. See also bibliography in Josephine Klein, *Working with Groups* (2nd ed.), London 1963, pp. 116–18.

object of the congress was to deal with the baleful dominance of the *Bund* and if possible relegate that organization to its proper place as an autonomous sub-group. The Polish party's relationship with the *Bund* was crystallizing into hostility, much like the Russians, even though the *Bund* itself was on far better terms with the SDKPiL than with the PPS, who advocated complete Jewish integration in Polish society and would not admit the need for any separate organization at all.[1] At the *Bund's* third and fourth congresses the pursuit of Polish independence was roundly condemned and with it its chief supporters, the PPS.[2] None the less, the SDKPiL, though admitting the *Bund's* right of autonomous organization with limited powers, gradually convinced itself of the latent nationalism of the Jewish party. 'There is no doubt that the *Bund* definitely holds up the progress of Social Democracy . . . with its everlasting and ubiquitous stress on its Jewishness.'[3]

This apprehension was not unmixed with jealousy: 'The *Bund* has a better organization than anyone, good propaganda and much revolutionary enthusiasm . . . but a regrettably nationalist tendency and these obstinately separatist ideas in matters of organization.'[4] The Poles realized full well that *Iskra's* intention was to isolate the *Bund* at the coming congress and to make its adhesion to the Russian party impossible —unless the *Bund* accepted conditions of organizational integration which were both destructive and humiliating. Hence the Russian emphasis on the coming congress not as a constituent assembly but merely as the second in a consecutive series. Although it was clear to all concerned that a 'new' party must in fact emerge, the insistence that the congress was the second in an orderly series, that the party was being reorganized rather than created, thus gained genuine constitutional significance: 'The *Bund* will not be able to appear as a separate constituent group helping to create a federal relationship.'[5]

---

[1] Though the SDKPiL would not think of using this as an argument, for obvious reasons, the PPS attitude to the *Bund* is perhaps the best 'proof' of the former's latent nationalism—far more conclusive than some of Rosa Luxemburg's Procrustean arguments. For one of the features of nationalism is that it is simultaneously assertive—of its own national identity—and denying—of the identity of sub-groups; the more it asserts the more it denies. Examples are legion. Compare Bavarian nationalism with the denial of a Franconian identity within it, and the present attitude of Ceylon to the Tamils and the Sudan to its black, Christian, south. The PPS in fact suggested that there was no racial discrimination in Poland except insofar as it had been 'imported' by the Russians.

[2] M. Rafes, *Ocherki po istorii 'Bunda'*, Moscow 1923; p. 45.

[3] Feliks Dzierżyński to Cezaryna Wojnarowska, June 1903, *SDKPiL dokumenty*, Vol. II, p. 324.

[4] Adolf Warszawski to Karl Kautsky, 20 May 1903, IISH Archives, D XXIII, 63.

[5] Adolf Warszawski to the SDKPiL Foreign Committee, mid-June 1903, *Z Pola Walki*, 1929, Nos. 7–8, p. 171. The Russians hammered this point home to such an extent that Warszawski willy-nilly incorporated the word *kolejne* (consecutive) every time he wrote to Berlin about the congress.

The recognition of these tactics was not due to Warszawski's particular perception; the Organizing Committee made its position very clear and hoped to have Polish support for its ultimatum to the *Bund*. '*Iskra* admits that the Poles have a special common interest with it as regards the *Bund*.'[1] Rosa Luxemburg and the other leaders agreed by silence and implication; they were not apparently concerned by the obvious fact that all the arguments used against the *Bund* could equally well be applied to the Poles. In their self-satisfaction the Poles probably thought they were the acknowledged exception to the Russian rule about federation—or else that all this talk of general principles was only intended for particular application to the *Bund*; when they had announced their plans for a Russian Social-Democratic party reconstructed on federal lines two years earlier, *Iskra* had published the Polish proposals in full—without comment![2] Probably a number of Russians were willing at first to grant the Poles—this distinguished group formed as long ago as 1893, and with some claim to have been pace-setters—the right to claim a special interest; though, as we shall see, the Polish notion of their 'special interest' differed radically from what *Iskra* supposed. But for the moment all seemed straightforward enough. Dzierżyński, who never believed in half measures, told Liber, one of the leading *Bundists* and at the time Dzierżyński's brother-in-law, that the Poles had formally committed themselves to supporting *Iskra* against the *Bund*.[3]

The actual negotiations in the early summer of 1903 between Russians and Poles were delicate and protracted. The Poles pressed for a formal and unconditional invitation to the congress while the Organizing Committee claimed that it did not have the necessary power; only the congress as a whole could issue an invitation. However, it was clearly intimated to Warszawski that if the Poles met *Iskra*'s conditions an invitation could be informally guaranteed. Thus the SDKPiL must acknowledge itself as a member of the RSDRP: 'Our letter giving this adherence to the general party would *not* however be published but only submitted to the relevant authorities in the Russian party.'[4] But the Poles refused to accept these conditions and stalled for time on the excuse that the comrades in Poland had to be consulted. In fact, Rosa Luxemburg and Leo Jogiches wanted more time to think and above all to call their own Polish congress to discuss the matter in more detail.

[1] Ibid.

[2] At the Polish third congress in the summer of 1901 (Protocol in IML (M), Fund 164, No. 2). See *Iskra*, August 1901, No. 7, pp. 5 ff.; *Przegląd Socjaldemokratyczny*, March 1902, No. 1, p. 7.

[3] See report of conversation in Kirshnits, 'Bund un RSDRP', *Visnshaftlikher Iohrbikher*, Vol. I, p. 72.

[4] Warszawski to SDKPiL Foreign Committee, *SDKPiL dokumenty*, Vol. II, p. 319.

In the end Jogiches sent a letter to the editorial board of *Iskra* in which he admitted that the Poles considered themselves 'ideologically and politically belonging to one party with the Russians though temporarily not incorporated in one single organization—a situation similar to that appertaining to all the other Russian Social-Democratic groups'—a typically brittle and artificial Jogiches formulation.[1] Words were being stretched to disguise meanings, but there was still goodwill on both sides.

The hurriedly assembled Polish congress took place in Berlin between 24 and 29 July 1903.[2] The congress decided that negotiations with a view to Polish membership of the new Russian party were desirable and appointed two delegates for this purpose, giving them the right to negotiate with 'carte blanche within the framework of the congress resolution'.[3] The outline of the negotiators' instructions was almost certainly penned by Rosa Luxemburg herself—though she did not personally attend the congress—and was accepted by the meeting 'without much discussion'.[4] The delegates were to be Hanecki and Warszawski. From the Polish point of view, the difficulty of joining hinged largely on the form of organization demanded by the Organizing Committee of the Russian party: a firm Russian refusal of federation and instead, some kind of limited autonomy, which would make the Central Committee of the RSDRP the ultimate governing body of the Polish party as well. Most of the SDKPiL leaders preferred federation in substance if not in name; they were reluctant to forgo the cohesion and autonomy of the Polish leadership and let the Russian Central Committee deal directly with their own local organizations in Poland. This was partly an unwillingness to dismantle the existing organization and to diminish a leadership which considered itself at least as distinguished, if not more so, as any Russians; in addition, there was the real fear that the Russians would soon discover that the SDKPiL was in fact like a South American army—all generals and few soldiers.[5]

[1] Declaration of SDKPiL to the editorial board of *Iskra* for the Organizing Committee, 26 June 1903; *Z Pola Walki*, 1929, Nos. 7-8, p. 174. Jogiches' authorship is establised in *SDKPiL dokumenty*, p. 321, note 1.

[2] The official report of the congress is printed in *SDKPiL dokumenty*, Vol. II, pp. 351-62. Only two commentaries on the congress were published. One was by Rosa Luxemburg, *Przegląd Socjaldemokratyczny*, August 1903, No. 8, pp. 284-96, in which she defended Polish intransigence at the Russian congress by stressing the superiority of the Polish organizational concept (p. 293). The other was Hanecki's and appeared 30 years later when not to have been a Bolshevik in 1903 was a grave demerit. See J. Hanecki, 'The SDKPiL Delegation at the Second RSDRP Congress', *Proletarskaya Revolyutsiya*, No. 2 (1933), pp. 187-200.

[3] *Sprawozdanie ze Zjazdu IV SDKPiL*, 24-29 July 1903, 2nd day, p. 4, loc. sit.

[4] Hanecki, *Proletarskaya Revolyutsiya*, p. 189.

[5] See particularly *Z Pola Walki*, 1929, Nos. 7-8, pp. 180-2, letter from Hanecki to Dzierżyński. For the Polish claim of superiority see Rosa Luxemburg, 'The IV SDKPiL Congress', *Przegląd Socjaldemokratyczny*, August 1903, No. 8, pp. 292 ff. The article was of course written after, and in justification of, Polish withdrawal from the Russian congress.

These questions had loomed unspoken behind the earlier correspondence between the Organizing Committee and the Foreign Committee of the SDKPiL, but had been obscured by the phraseology about the right to attend at all.

On Monday 3 August the two Polish delegates arrived at the Russian congress in Brussels hotfoot from their own congress. Two days earlier, on Saturday 1 August, the Russians had formally invited two Polish delegates to come to Brussels with the right to speak but not to vote. Even this had produced considerable discussion, and had been voted against the wishes of Lenin, Martov, and the other *Iskraists*, who maintained that the Poles had missed their chance.[1] Warszawski led off with a prepared speech which combined the general Polish desire to join with the particular Polish conditions for joining. The speech had been written in Berlin, once again almost certainly in close collaboration with Rosa herself.[2] After some perfunctory applause, negotiations began at once on the Polish minimal conditions: the SDKPiL to be the exclusive representative of Polish Social Democracy in the Russian party, and to maintain its organizational and control structure intact. In addition, the Poles asked for stricter definition and clarification of paragraph 7 of the provisional Russian statutes, which dealt with the national question, and also for clear condemnation of the 'Polish social-patriotism of the PPS'—though these were *not* part of the bed-rock conditions. The managers of the Russian congress, and the *Iskraists* in particular, were anxious not to fall out with the Poles now that they were there; their main fire was reserved for the *Bund*. The Polish negotiations were accordingly removed to a special commission out of the glare and heat of full congress discussion. Here, in relative privacy, the Poles were first asked whether they insited on autonomy or federation and were told that only the first could be considered. They were then asked to define autonomy. The discussion continued inconclusively for some days.[3]

Whether the Polish conditions would have been met and an autonomy that was really federation achieved can now only be a matter of guess-

---

[1] *Protokoly, vtoroi ocherednoi s"ezd RSDRP, izdanie tsentralnogo komiteta*, Geneva 1903, pp. 47–54, 375.

[2] Hanecki, *Proletarskaya Revolyutsiya*, p. 191. Against too definite an assignment of responsibility to Rosa, it must be stated that by 1933 all the surviving Polish participants were finding it convenient to lay as much at Rosa's door as possible.

[3] The Polish report of the proceedings is given at length in the documents printed in *Z Pola Walki*, 1929, Nos. 7–8; particularly Hanecki's letter to Dzierżyński quoted above. See also the Russian congress protocol, pp. 135 ff. The Polish case was later published by Warszawski himself in 'The Polish Delegation to the Second Congress of the RSDRP' in *Przegląd Socjaldemokratyczny*, 1904, No. 1, pp. 25–41. Some of the relevant Polish material is reprinted by S. Krzhizhanovskii, 'The Polish Social Democracy and the Second Russian Congress' in *Proletarskaya Revolyutsiya*, No. 2 (1933), pp. 111 ff.

work. Probably not; the Polish demands ran counter even to the basic concepts of organization which were shared by Lenin and Martov and which a large majority of the congress insisted on imposing on the *Bund*—who in due course gave up and packed up. Like the *Bund*, the Poles were not willing to make many concessions in this field, even if a new and quite unexpected issue had not suddenly arisen at the end of July which put all other questions in the shade.

The July number of *Iskra* carried an article by Lenin on the subject of the Russian attitude to the national question. In this he asserted once again the need for the Russian party to support self-determination for subject peoples as both theoretically just and tactically necessary. The RSDRP programme, accordingly, 'in no way prevented the Polish proletariat from making a separate and independent Poland their slogan, even though there might be little or no chance of realizing such a thing before the coming of Socialism itself'.[1] The article was not meant to raise difficulties or to annoy the Poles. Lenin had nothing very new or startling to say on the national question; self-determination was an integral part of the RSDRP programme—there for all to see—and Lenin went out of his way to explain that this was in no sense to be interpreted as support for nationalism in general or the PPS in particular. But the effect in Berlin was of a bombshell. Although the Poles knew from the draft statutes worked out by *Iskra* that national self-determination was part of the Russian programme, they had considered this merely as a formal catechism. Their interpretation of Russian attitudes was based on a previous article in *Iskra* by Martov, which put much less emphasis on self-determination; a statement of the position to which they could at a pinch subscribe.[2] Suddenly the official Russian attitude appeared quite different—just when the tricky organizational problems were under negotiation. Suspicious by nature and experience, frightened perhaps at the thought of being played like salmon, Rosa Luxemburg and Leo Jogiches reacted violently. The delegates were summarily instructed to tell the Russians forthwith that in view of the *Iskra* article the negotiations 'now hung by a thread [*na ostrzu noża*]. . . . It is very advisable that you tell the Russians that following this article the moral value of joining the Russians [as a weapon against the PPS] practically disappears and it was only the moral aspect that interested us in the first place. If they are not willing to alter paragraph 7 [of the

---

[1] Lenin, 'The National Question in our Programme', *Iskra*, No. 44, reprinted in *Sochineniya*, Vol. V, p. 346.

[2] Yu. Martov, 'Za sorok let', *Iskra*, No. 33, p. 1. Warszawski in his correspondence with the Polish leaders had repeatedly referred to this article as an indication of Russian attitudes. The Russians had also supported Rosa Luxemburg's anti-PPS efforts at integrating the German Poles into the SPD during 1902–3. See 'Organization and Nationality', *Iskra*, 1 April 1903, No. 37, pp. 3 ff.

statutes, which embodied the right to self-determination emphasized
in the *Iskra* article] we will have to break off the [intended] affiliation.
Tell Zasulich that after the *Iskra* article I [Rosa] am not in the least bit
interested in affiliation and that I have advised that no further concessions be made.'[1]

Warszawski had asked for instructions on the organizational question
as well, and though Rosa Luxemburg was mainly interested in the
national question, detailed orders and comments on all the problems
under negotiation were now supplied. To the demand that the Russians
should have representatives in the Polish Central Committee, Rosa
Luxemburg replied negatively. To the demand that the Poles should
form joint committees with the *Bund*, she said yes, but not for the moment. And so on. In each case Warszawski was given his answer, and
had his diplomacy predigested as well. Rosa Luxemburg not only gave
the leadership's decision but also supplied detailed argumentation with
which to defend it. Finally, she came back to the national question again.

If they try to persuade you that in view of their willingness to maintain our
point 3 [that no other Polish organization can belong to the general Russian
party] the *Iskra* article has no real practical significance for us and the PPS is
anyhow kept the other side of the door, then you must reply that for us the
whole problem of affiliation has less practical than moral importance as a
permanent demonstration against nationalism.[2]

Warszawski conveyed all this to the committee but was obliged to
report to Berlin that the congress would not budge on paragraph 7;
they intended to confirm it and its recent interpretation by Lenin.[3]
Rosa Luxemburg and Leo Jogiches now made a last attempt to strengthen
their delegates' hands. In a telegram—probably on 6 August—they
emphatically repeated their point of view and insisted that a refusal to
eradicate the right of self-determination from the Russian programme
meant nothing less than the abandonment of the class struggle in
Poland and the alienation of the Polish working classes. It was the sort
of fanfare that was clearly meant to be trumpeted under Russian noses.
Warszawski now had no choice but to add the question of self-
determination to the list of Polish minimum demands—it had not
figured there before the appearance of the *Iskra* article. The Russians
naturally refused to accept the demands of the Polish ultimatum on
the spot; indeed the commission had no power to do so. Lenin held out
little hope to Hanecki. As instructed, the Polish delegates thereupon
deposited a declaration of their position with the committee and with-

---

[1] Original letter in IML (M), Fund 209, No. 435, reprinted in *SDKPiL dokumenty*,
Vol. II, pp. 368–73. Also Krzhizhanovskii, op. cit., p. 121. Rosa Luxemburg to Adolf
Warszawski, probably 5 August 1903.

[2] *SDKPiL dokumenty*, p. 372.   [3] *Z Pola Walki*, 1929, Nos. 7–8, p. 189.

drew. By the next day, 7 August, it was all over. The congress itself hurriedly left Brussels to escape the over-anxious Belgian police and moved *en bloc* to London. There the *Bund* withdrew as well—as had been planned; in due course Lenin and Martov fell out over their respective drafts of paragraph 1 of the party statutes and the congress aligned itself into the now famous Bolshevik and Menshevik factions and ended up more divided than ever. The Poles, however, did not participate in any of this; their delegates had forlornly remained in Brussels when the Russians scurried away.[1]

The end of the negotiations and the manner of their ending none the less caused a minor flurry in the Polish party. No one bothered to inform the Polish membership officially about the negotiations or why they had failed; even some of the leaders, particularly Julian March-lewski and Cezaryna Wojnarowska, had to rely on information from the Russians or gossip from Polish visitors to find out what had happened. There was the blatant discrepancy between formal SDKPiL thinking on organizational problems, allegedly the main purpose of the negotiations in the first place, and Rosa Luxemburg's private assessment that the main purposes of joining had been for moral aid and comfort against the PPS. All the business about organization now appeared as so much stuff and nonsense. Rosa and Leo Jogiches had apparently decided the issue off their own bat and had laid down fundamental priorities which might indeed be theirs but were not necessarily anyone else's. Some members were unaware of her reasoning and continued to see in the organizational questions the insurmountable obstacle. Others considered even these as an insufficient ground for failing to achieve that unity with the Russians which Rosa herself had preached for so long. Nothing shows more clearly than these negotiations and their failure to what extent an unofficial leadership dominated the official structure and procedures of the SDKPiL and how much of the policy of that leadership was made by Rosa Luxemburg herself.

Surprisingly, it was Cezaryna Wojnarowska who openly took issue with Berlin. She used the breakdown of the Russian negotiations as an excuse for expressing a generally critical view of SDKPiL policy. There was the formal discrepancy between the instructions of the fourth party congress to their delegates and their actual stand. There was further the domination of policy by the Foreign Committee—euphemism for Jogiches and Luxemburg. Finally, and most important,

---

[1] The quirk of timing thus kept the Poles from any commitment in the original Bolshevik/Menshevik alignment. Consequently, they escaped being classified for ever by later Communist history—a fate that befell all those who happened to be present and participated in the voting. No one has ever 'solved' the question whether the SDKPiL were initially Bolshevik or Menshevik in accordance with the imperative of later Communist history—though not for want of trying.

there was the everlasting and obsessive preoccupation with the PPS which in fact made Polish Social Democracy into a purely negative anti-PPS organization with little positive contribution of its own. The Foreign Committee distributed her letter to its members and solicited replies. The result was a general drawing together; all the members agreed that the criticism was unjustified and that the Poles had no cause to 'capitulate' before the Russians. They refused to call a conference to deal with the problem——'for technical and financial reasons and on account of the pressure of party work'—and also refused to nominate new representatives to continue the efforts to join the Russian party.[1] Hurriedly a new organizational statute for the Foreign Committee was worked out and submitted to the members (and only the members); all wrote in to give their agreement. Cezaryna Wojnarowska, feeling herself censured, resigned her post as the representative of the SDKPiL in the International Socialist Bureau and from then until her death in 1911 played only a minor role in the party. Her place on the Bureau was taken by the obvious candidate—Rosa Luxemburg.

But even though the ruling group had managed to draw together against the attack of one of its members and had prevented her from carrying out her threat to take her issue into the party, the whole thing could not be entirely hushed up. No attempt had been made to remove the genuine confusion in the party about the real reasons for starting and subsequently breaking off the negotiations. The SDKPiL committee in Warsaw took the opportunity at its next conference to issue a resolution calling for an early re-establishment of a Central Committee, to be based on Poland rather than abroad, and censured the Foreign Committee for calling the fourth congress 'without adequate local representation'.[2] Even the publication of an official commentary on these events by Warszawski and Rosa Luxemburg herself did not settle the problem entirely; as Warszawski ingenuously admitted, his article was necessited only by the publication of the official Russian minutes of the congress.[3]

For all practical purposes Rosa forgot about Russian Social Democracy for the moment. But there was no forgetting Russia—on the contrary, new and exciting possibilities were appearing on the eastern horizon. The Russo-Japanese War had broken out and, like the RSDRP, the Polish Social Democrats speculated on the possible

[1] See draft of a resolution of the Foreign Committee, 22 October 1903, IML (M), Fund 163, No. 65. These decisions were communicated to Cezaryna Wojnarowska with some glee by Dzierżyński on 5 November 1903.
[2] See resolution of conference of SDKPiL activists in Warsaw on 27 December 1903, *SDKPiL dokumenty*, Vol. II, p. 537.
[3] A. Warszawski, 'The Polish Delegation to the Second Congress of the RSDRP', *Przegląd Socjaldemokratyczny*, 1904, No. 1, p. 25.

revolutionary consequences. But to start with, these were abstract and general rather than particular and immediate; certainly there was no prediction of any revolutionary outbreaks. Rosa Luxemburg confined herself to general remarks about the internal weakness of Tsarism which did not differ substantially from the standard analysis of the preceding years.[1] When it came, the revolution of 1905 took the Poles as much by surprise as it did their Russian colleagues. And then the reaction was not for Socialist unity but entirely the opposite—even sharper differentiation from the PPS. For Rosa Luxemburg, unity among the squabbling Russians was one thing—there was nothing of substance to quarrel about, beyond personal intransigence; in Poland, on the other hand, the division was fundamental, between Socialists and pseudo-Socialists. Unity could come only if the PPS capitulated and went out of existence. No one in the SDKPiL seriously disagreed with her. The Luxemburg tradition was firmly embedded.

The break-up of the second Russian congress and the subsequent hair-raising polemics between Bolsheviks and Mensheviks echoed unsympathetically in the German party. The SPD leaders were not interested in or familiar with Russian questions but the tradition established by Wilhelm Liebknecht of solving other people's problems made recourse to their judgement and good offices almost inevitable. Both Mensheviks and Bolsheviks made every effort to draw authoritative German opinion into the dispute on their own side. The Mensheviks were better known and better connected—especially once Plekhanov had aligned himself with Lenin's opponents. Accordingly, throughout 1904, Martov, Akselrod, Potresov, and Dan solicited their German acquaintances for their views—and above all for contributions to *Iskra* which they now controlled. 'The question is how to beat Lenin. . . . Most important of all, we must incite authorities like Kautsky, Rosa Luxemburg, and Parvus against him.'[2] Contributions were readily forthcoming. When Lenin attempted to counter this critical support for the Mensheviks by sending Lyadov to explain the Bolshevik case, Kautsky told him frankly: 'Look, we do not *know* your Lenin. He is an unknown quantity for us, but we do know Plekhanov and Akselrod very well. It is only thanks to them that we have been able to obtain any light on the situation in Russia. We simply cannot just accept your contention that Plekhanov and Akselrod have turned into opportunists all of a sudden.'[3]

---

[1] 'War', *Czerwony Sztandar*, February 1904, No. 14.

[2] *Sotsial-demokraticheskoe dvizhenie v Rossii, Materialy* (edited by Potresov and Niko-laevskii), Moscow/Leningrad, 1928, p. 124.

[3] M. Lyadov, *Iz zhizni partii v 1903–7 godakh (Vospominaniya)*, Moscow 1956, p. 16; also O. Pyatnitskii, *Zapiski bolshevika*, Moscow 1956.

Thus Bebel, Kautsky, and the others were naturally predisposed to support those whom they had known so long rather than a new upstart recently arrived from Russia. They were primarily concerned with healing a split which they did not really understand; as in the dispute among French Socialists a few years earlier, the Germans reluctantly heaved themselves into action through the formal procedures of the International Socialist Bureau. In private they had nothing` but contempt for such squabbles. '[These differences] are all bunk when one considers what is involved in practice and how much [really important] work remains to be done.'[1]

Only two people in Germany really knew some of the issues involved —Parvus and Rosa Luxemburg. She for one was well aware that Kautsky's contribution to Russian problems would at best be general and theoretical—he knew nothing of the particulars. 'Karl does not understand these things in detail. His attitudes are largely based on my attitudes. If people start talking to him he may easily lose the firm ground under his feet and . . . get himself all tangled up.'[2] The Mensheviks thus knew very well what they were doing in concentrating their solicitations on Parvus and Rosa Luxemburg. Willy-nilly, she found herself drawn back into Russian affairs, not as a Polish candidate for membership of the Russian party, but as German expert and arbiter between the disputing factions.

Parvus did not want to be drawn into taking a definite stand. His position in the German party was precarious. He thought the Russian quarrel unnecessary and exaggerated and in his private letters criticized and advised moderation to both sides. Rosa Luxemburg on the other hand was more easily mobilized for a firm commitment. The Menshevik leaders were no close friends of hers, quite the contrary; but she had a more recent score to settle with Lenin on account of the national question. More important still was the fact that she had taken Cezaryna Wojnarowska's place in the International Bureau and this institution had now formally been saddled with the difficult question of re-uniting the Russians. She was the German party's main expert on Russian, as much as on Polish, questions. Consequently at the beginning of 1904 she took the somewhat belated opportunity of looking into the issues that had been raised after the Polish departure from the second Russian

---

[1] August Bebel to Victor Adler, 28 December 1904, in V. Adler, *Briefwechsel*, p. 446. For a discussion of German attitudes to the split in the Russian party, see D. Geyer, 'The attitude of German Social Democracy to the split in the Russian party', *International Review of Social History* (1958), Vol. III, pp. 195–219, 418–44.

[2] Jogiches letters, IML (M), mid-October 1905. Kautsky in fact contributed to the current controversy on 15 May 1904 in *Iskra*, No. 66: 'A sermon on the virtues of tolerance and the need to respect one's leaders'. (J. L. H. Keep, *The Rise of Social Democracy in Russia*, London 1963, p. 145.)

congress, and so happened inevitably upon Lenin's *What is to be done?*
Her own negative reaction to Lenin's organizational propositions thus
coincided with Potresov's request for an article in *Iskra*; she killed two
birds with one stone by writing a long article for *Neue Zeit* which she
offered the Russians for translation.[1]

In her article Rosa Luxemburg took issue not so much with Lenin's
detailed prescriptions but with the underlying philosophy. She seized
on his characterization of Social Democracy—'Jacobins joined to a
proletariat which has become conscious of its class interest'. The notion
of Jacobins led directly to the notions of Blanqui and Nechaev—both
highly sectarian bogey-men to the adults of the Second International
and their mass concepts. 'Social Democracy is not joined to the organization of the proletariat. It is itself the proletariat . . . it is the rule of
the majority within its own party.' Instead of an all-powerful central
committee whose writ ran 'from Geneva to Liège and from Tomsk to
Irkutsk, the role of the director must go to the collective ego of the
working class. . . . The working class demands the right to make its
mistakes and learn in the dialectic of history. Let us speak plainly.
Historically, the errors committed by a truly revolutionary movement
are infinitely more fruitful than the infallibility of the cleverest Central
Committee.'[2]

Lenin's analogy of factory discipline as being a useful school for a
revolutionary party caused Rosa Luxemburg not only to attack this
particular—and perhaps unfortunate—simile but to attack Lenin's
preoccupation with discipline as a whole. The sort of leadership that
could create and direct a disciplined party was much more likely to
hold the working class back than to push it forward:

The tendency is for the directing organs . . . to play a conservative role. The
present tactical policy of German Social Democracy is useful precisely because
it is supple as well as firm. This is a sign of the fine adaptation of the party, in
the smallest detail of its everyday activity, to the conditions of a parliamentary
régime. The party knows how to utilize all the resources of the terrain without
modifying its principles. If there was inertia and over-emphasis of parliamentary
tactics in Germany, this was the result of too much direction rather than too

---

[1] Rosa Luxemburg, 'Organizational Questions in Russian Social Democracy', *NZ*,
1903–4, Vol. II, pp. 484–92, 529–35; also 'Organizatsionnye voprosy russkoi sotsialde-
mokratii', *Iskra*, 10 July 1904, No. 69, pp. 2–7. It has been suggested that the use of the
word 'russkii' (ethnic) rather than 'rossiiskii' (geographical), which was in the official title
of the RSDRP, was a derogatory hint at Polish-Russian discord, thus calling in question the
all-Russianness claimed by the RSDRP (E. H. Carr, *The Bolshevik Revolution 1917–23*,
London 1950, Vol. I, p. 36). One wonders, however, whether this inflection, if deliberate,
was Rosa Luxemburg's or Potresov's. Quotations are taken from *Leninism or Marxism?*
(edited by Bertram D. Wolfe), Ann Arbor (Michigan) 1961. For Rosa Luxemburg's
comments to Potresov, see *Sotsial-demokraticheskoe dvizhenie v Rossii*, pp. 129 ff.

[2] *Leninism or Marxism?*, pp. 84, 89, 108.

little, and the adoption of Lenin's formula would only increase rather than thaw out such conservative inertia. How much worse would be such a strait-jacket for nascent Russian Social Democracy on the eve of its battles against Tsarism.[1]

Opportunism—against which, according to Lenin, a centralized organization would serve as a bulwark—was not an alien ingredient blown into the Russian party by western bourgeois democracy, by debased intellectuals looking for careers in Social Democracy. (Did Rosa take this as a reflection on herself?) It was due in the Russian context to the 'backward political condition of Russian society'—a natural and inevitable condition which only time, work, and experience could heal.

But the debate should not be seen—though it usually is—as a collision between two fundamentally irreconcilable concepts of organization, or even revolution.[2] First, Rosa Luxemburg's knowledge of Russian conditions was in fact more limited than might appear; her competence was substantial only by comparison with other people in Germany. She was arguing from the German experience to the Russian. She extolled the German virtues rather more forcefully than her belief in them warranted—or than she would have done in any context but the Russian. Certainly she never made such a contrast between Polish and German conditions, though it would have been just as valid. Secondly, as we have noted, her own attitudes in the Polish party hardly bore out such demands for more 'democracy'; instead of controlling local organizations, she simply ignored them altogether. Jogiches, on the other hand, later tried to institute a system of control as tight as Lenin's, even if he did not choose to expound a philosophy of centralization. We must always make allowances for the fact that the angles of the argument were made more acute by the particular polemic—just as we must for Lenin. In this particular instance, moreover, Lenin took the unusual step of admitting this openly.

We all know now that the Economists bent the stick to one side. To make it straight again it had to be bent to the other, and that is what I did. I am sure that Russian Social Democracy will always be able to straighten the stick whenever it has been bent by any kind of opportunism and that our stick will consequently be always at its straightest and entirely ready for action.[3]

Rosa Luxemburg, too, was usually willing to make allowances for excessive rigidity where genuine revolutionaries were concerned—as in

[1] Ibid., p. 93.
[2] Western liberal and socialist tradition has coupled Rosa Luxemburg's article with her later comment on the October revolution, and it is significant that the American editor of her work has published these two articles in a separate book as indicative of a consistent and fundamental critique of Bolshevism (see above, Chapter 1, p. 1).
[3] *Vtoroi s"ezd RSDRP, Protokoly*, Moscow 1959, p. 136; also *Leninskii Sbornik*, Vol. VI, pp. 220–49.

Guesde's case—but she would make no such concessions to Lenin; indeed, she was careful to give her article as unpolemical an appearance as possible, as though her statements represented the minimum that was reasonable.

There is no escaping the conclusion: throughout the Russian negotiations and in her argument with Lenin Rosa Luxemburg showed a deviousness, a sophistry, which in her German context she would have stigmatized as beneath contempt. There are traces of it in much of Polish–Russian life, particularly where the PPS was concerned. It is almost as though we were dealing with two different people. The careful, secretive compartmenting was not merely convenience, a difference in procedures and methods according to the kind of people with whom she had to deal, but a substantive clash of attitudes, mutually incompatible, which had to be kept separate. To some extent Rosa was always aware of this; she lectured Jogiches about it but without realizing the extent of her own schizophrenia. Her own objective evaluation of the needs of her two different worlds, and the responses they called for, was perceptive enough, but there is a more fundamental issue here which goes beyond national differences. The difficult relationship between ideology and pragmatic action has been identified as a continuing problem for all political parties, *irrespective* of their ideology—but the more intense the ideology, the greater the difficulty. Where does the relevance of ideological assertions for practical politics end, and mere functional symbolism or ritual for the purpose of ensuring unity or legitimacy begin? The problem becomes acute in any assessment of Lenin's political actions and programmes—and is still the most difficult question in dealing with the Soviet Union or China today. In Rosa Luxemburg's case, how much of the famous unity with the Russian proletariat, of the democratic criticism of Lenin, was genuine ideological commitment and how much symbolic rhetoric?[1] Most important of all, was it the recognition that dissonance between preaching and practice was the prevailing style in the SPD that made her reconcile her own tactics almost puritanically to her expressed ideology? Probably so, in which case her (and Lenin's) highly personal polemics were an unconscious concession to the primitive, still highly personal, politics of the East. There the need to assert ideological unity was foremost, while in Germany a stage had been reached in which choices of policy and of the means to implement them already predominated.

But Rosa Luxemburg was never one to polemicize to order or to express any view that was not sincerely held. Her call for broad popular

---

[1] In sociological terms, the difference is between the *pragmatic* and the *expressive* function of ideologies. For an analysis of the Soviet Union in such terms, see Z. Brzezinski, *The Soviet Bloc—Unity and Conflict*, Cambridge (Mass.) 1960.

participation in Social-Democratic activity was partly due to an excessive transplantation of idealized German conditions into the Russian context, just as Lenin's conditions were far too narrowly Russian to have general validity. Underlying this, however, was a more fundamental question. This concerned, not organization at all, but class consciousness—its nature and growth. Lenin believed that without the active tugging of a revolutionary élite, working-class consciousness was doomed to a vicious circle of impotence, that it could never rise above the economic level of trade-union activity. This had been the stuff of his battle with the 'Economists' (who in fact would have agreed with many of his propositions; as so often, Lenin's analysis was sharpened by attributing an extreme view to his opponents which bore little relation to reality). But he really did see the growth of class consciousness in terms of a critical minimum effort not unlike that of modern economists with regard to growth 'take off'; a volume of effort injected into the system greater than it would normally be capable of generating itself. Rosa Luxemburg, on the other hand, believed class consciousness to be essentially a problem of friction between Social Democracy and society. Friction was thus the main function of class consciousness. The more closely Social Democracy was engaged with bourgeois society on all fronts—economic as well as political, industrial as well as social, mental as well as physical —the greater and more rapid the growth of class consciousness. It was not a tangent but a continuum. Her solution was always more friction, more close engagement; a confrontation of eye to eye and fist to fist— rather than any specific and peculiar injection of energy from some élite. She proved from her own experience and way of life that élites were necessary; but that they should be allocated a specific function in Marxist theory or strategy was another matter altogether. She was neither analyst nor practitioner of power but of influence; instead of a dynamo which drove the whole Socialist works, an élite should be a magnet with a powerful field of influence over existing structures—a magnet, moreover, whose effective intensity grew as more friction stepped up the electric current. Friction once more was the source of all revolutionary energy—an analysis already indicated in her pamphlet *Social Reform or Revolution* and elaborated, as will be seen, with great sophistication after 1910.

The fact that this problem never directly emerged in her polemic with Lenin is no doubt due to the given organizational context of the argument (see only the title of her article), and the polemical rather than exploratory orientation. Like Lenin, she saw the dispute as a contest between opportunism and the application of consistent principles; they differed only over which was which. When dealing with Lenin's concept of opportunism she immediately put on her German spectacles—and promptly the peculiar Russian circumstances which had produced his concept in the first place were blotted out; all Rosa saw was the familiar Bernstein version which she had already dealt with in *Social Reform or Revolution.*

We thus have three separate factors to consider. First, the Polish–Russian background and style of the debate, the use of Russian rather than German *techniques* on both sides. Second, the real philosophic difference between Lenin's élite effort and Rosa's élite influence—due to a difference in the ontological appraisal of class consciousness. Third, the conscious and unconscious evocations of *experience* on both sides which simply do not match: the centrifugal Russian individualism and indiscipline which Lenin knew, and Rosa's defence against a German assault on the validity and meaningfulness of Marxist theory in favour of reformist pragmatism. These three factors are different in kind but are exceedingly hard to separate. Yet, having identified them, it is possible to see them quite dramatically separate in action. Thus the following passage shows the tension between the pressure of the philosophy of class consciousness and the partly restrictive framework of the Bernstein context, with its dichotomy of means and ends. The kink in the argument is quite clear. First, class consciousness:

For the first time in the history of civilization the people are expressing their will consciously and in opposition to all ruling classes. But this will can only [in the end] be satisfied beyond the limits of the existing system. Today the mass can only acquire and strengthen this will in the course of the day-to-day struggle against the existing social order—that is, within the limits of capitalist society.

Then, instead of directing this argument specifically against the Leninist concept of class consciousness, Rosa Luxemburg suddenly returned to the 'German' relationship between end and means, between revolution and reform, which really had no place in the present polemic.

On the one hand we have the mass; on the other its historic goal, located outside existing society. On the one hand we have the day-to-day struggle; on the other the social revolution. . . . It follows that this movement can best be advanced by tacking betwixt and between *the two dangers by which it is constantly being threatened.* One is the loss of its mass character, the other the abandonment of its goal. One is the danger of sinking back to the condition of a sect, the other the danger of becoming a movement of bourgeois social reform.[1]

Lenin's thesis was fitted into the German revisionist debate by very procrustean means; he simply became the opposite extreme to the Bernstein evil—sectarianism instead of reformism, and both leading to the divorce of social revolution from day-to-day activities. The argu-

---

[1] *Leninism or Marxism?*, p. 105. My italics; the reference is directly to *Social Reform or Revolution.*

ment is ultimately circular. Both extremes lead to failure; only the central and correct position leads to success. The real issue—essentially one of means, since Lenin was not one whit less revolutionary than Rosa Luxemburg—was forgotten.

Confronting two sets of ideas is never an easy problem, even when they are causally related in a specific polemic. The same obscure dissonances recur in the other, later, Lenin–Luxemburg disputes, the national question, the October Revolution, imperialism—and not only with Lenin, of course. The present elaboration will warn the reader against facile and over-simplified confrontations. There is more at stake than democracy versus authoritarianism. And then there is the whole host of latent *agreements* which do not even surface through this polemic; the most important of them is the joint commitment to revolutionary action, as the events of 1905–6 were to show. The distinction between doing rather than talking, which ultimately brought Luxemburg and Lenin together on the same side, did not even appear to exist in 1904. Nor did the accusation of spontaneity, with its assumption that if you promote the importance of mass action you proportionately demote the function of leadership. In analysing the clash of ideas, historical hindsight is fine—provided it is declared at the border, and not smuggled in with the pretence that it has a right to belong and can justly be required of the original participants.

Of all the foreign contributions to the Menshevik cause, only Rosa Luxemburg's really went home—even though Martov had expected the great Kautsky's intervention to be their most effective deterrent. Lenin was stung by her article into a curious and typical reply which he offered to *Neue Zeit*, but Kautsky refused to publish it; in fact Rosa Luxemburg, to whom it first came for comment, contemptuously brushed it aside as 'prattle'.[1] It is significant that Lenin treated Rosa Luxemburg, not as a Pole, an opponent-in-kind who for ten years had been within the orbit of Russian Social Democracy, but as a distinguished foreign commentator clothed in all the majesty of the SPD. 'We have to be thankful to the German comrades for the attention which they devote to our party literature and for their attempt to disseminate this literature in German Social-Democratic circles.' Nor would he give battle all along the front; the more she wanted to discuss first principles, the more Lenin chose to argue about discrete facts. 'Rosa Luxemburg deals in absolutes and ignores relative truths. For instance she completely missed the purpose of our wish for centralized control so preoccupied was she with

---

[1] See *Letters to Karl and Luise Kautsky*, p. 91, letter dated Summer 1905. Lenin's article is called 'One step forward, two steps back (An answer to Rosa Luxemburg)', first reprinted in *Sochineniya*, Vol. VII, pp. 439–50. The article was drafted by Lenin in Germany with the assistance of an unknown friend.

the horrors of that control itself.'[1] He carefully analysed the voting at the congress—he was really the first scientific psephologist of Marxism; had the congress not given his ideas the approval of a clear (Bolshevik) majority? But above all, the article was defensive. He had learnt his lesson; in future, fringe groups would be kept out of his party, or at least confined to the periphery. He would not risk public confrontation again. It was a lesson he remembered even after 1906, when the Poles began to play a significant part in the RSDRP; this time he dealt with them not as Germans but as with any Russian opponents. Meantime he prepared for the next congress at which there would be no Poles. In the event, the third congress of the RSDRP was dominated by the Bolsheviks, and it politely refused the German offer to arbitrate in the Russian party dispute.[2]

Rosa Luxemburg's effect on the actual Bolshevik–Menshevik dispute was therefore slight. Lenin might be stung by foreign comment, but he would not accommodate his policy one whit.[3] Only the Russian revolution temporarily submerged the quarrel; but when it was over the confrontation between Bolsheviks and Mensheviks emerged once more, sharpened by a new post-revolutionary bitterness which put even the previous arguments in the shade. It was not until much later, after Rosa Luxemburg's death, that her isolated comments on the organizational problems of Russian Social Democracy were resurrected and used as building blocks in the new technology of constructing political legitimacy out of historical alignments for or against Lenin.

[1] Ibid., pp. 439–41.

[2] *Tretii s"ezd RSDRP, Protokoly*, Moscow 1959, pp. 339–40. The congress took place in April–May 1905.

[3] Throughout 1905 Lenin trailed before his readership a number of derogatory references to what by this time had already become concretized as a special but fallacious Marxist theory of organization—Rosa Luxemburg's 'organization-as-process'. Most of these described her views as 'little else but defence of a lack of principles', and 'something not to be taken seriously' (see for instance *Vpered*, 14 January, 14 February, 21 February, 1905). Naturally the opportunity of lumping Rosa Luxemburg with Akselrod and other Mensheviks was not to be missed. The most recent summary of the literature of issues can be found in Luciano Amodio, 'The Lenin–Luxemburg Confrontation on Party Organization', *Quaderni Piacentini*, Vol. IV, No. 21, January–February 1965, pp. 3–20.
This controversy has of course left its mark in subsequent polemics, and Rosa Luxemburg's critique of Lenin has been used many times as evidence—from an impeccably revolutionary Marxist source—of Lenin's basically bureaucratic and dictatorial tendencies. Elaborate reference is made in the following major works: F. Dan, *Proishchozdenie Bolshevizma*, New York 1946; N. Valentinov, *Mes Rencontres avec Lénine*, Paris 1964; Bertram D. Wolfe, *Three who made a Revolution;* see also Amodio, op. cit., pp. 9–10, note 10.

VIII

REVOLUTION OVERTAKES THE

REVOLUTIONARIES,

1905–1906

1: GERMANY

IN the eyes of contemporaries the Russian revolution erupted dramatically on 22 January 1905. An act of specific violence on the outskirts of St. Petersburg was followed by repercussions so intense and widespread as to justify the sacred word revolution, a continuous and above all an interconnected process with enormous if unforeseeable consequences. Only later, in the search for perspective, were the earlier warning signs identified and appreciated; at the time the chief feature of the Russian revolution was its marvellous unexpectedness. Surprise was universal—for the Tsarist government with its palate jaded by years of hair-raising police reports; for the distant Germans for whom nothing but squabbles, chaos, and terrorism ever came from the East; but most of all for professional revolutionaries like Martov, Lenin, and Rosa Luxemburg. The fact that she later worked out a connection between the wave of strikes which began in the last years of the previous century and the events of 1905 is evidence only of her sense of history and not of any special contemporary perceptions.

Rosa Luxemburg at once moved into high gear. She intensified her activities in both her roles: the postulation of tasks for the Russian and Polish proletariats and the translation of these revolutionary events for the benefit of German Socialists. Though the importance of the Russian revolution was great enough to call for detailed blow-by-blow reportage, Rosa Luxemburg always translated the lessons from these events into a German context. Emphasis and selection were deliberate. She was sufficiently aware of the difference between the two societies, and between the two Socialist movements in Russia and Germany, to realize that such pointing up was necessary; the lessons would be lost if they were indiscriminately reported. Rosa Luxemburg was probably the only person able to carry out this dual task; and during 1905 she devoted almost all her effort to it—the most burning problem of the time. 'The connection of political and social life among all capitalist states is today so intense that the effects of the Russian revolution will be enormous throughout the whole so-called civilized world—much greater than the effect of any bourgeois revolution in history.'[1]

Though the revolutionary events in Russia were not matched by any similar outbreak in Germany, there were some surface indications of ferment. Germany, too, was in the grip of heightened tension, a fever which swept through the best-fortified regions and across national borders like the plague. In 1905 the number and extent of strikes in Germany reached a new peak; both trade unions and employers reported a hardening of attitudes and the language of the class conflict crept insidiously into the most routine confrontations. The events in Russia gave these economic clashes a self-conscious political character. At the same time, the first real movement for Prussian suffrage reform crystallized into the political peg on which to hang the new militancy; the political orientation of Social Democracy focused on this issue. The interaction between political and economic dissatisfactions—which Rosa Luxemburg was later to elevate into a peculiar feature of a revolutionary period—was clearly at work in the early months of 1905. None of this was caused specifically by the Russian revolution, but events in Russia were widely discussed in the German press and this certainly raised the temperature. German Social Democracy developed a distinct feeling of solidarity with the proletariat in Russia; here and there even muted calls for emulation could be heard.

Since the years 1905–6 not only made their immediate contribution to the development of SPD policy but later became a rich source of recrimination and misunderstanding in the party, the general effects of the Russian revolution on German Social Democracy must be summarized briefly. The party as a whole undoubtedly moved left—the executive and those elements in the SPD which produced as well as interpreted the consensus: left, it should be said, not into the arms of 'foreign revolutionary romantics' like Rosa Luxemburg and Parvus, but in their willingness to discuss positive action and to work out tactics accordingly. The idea of the general strike was much in vogue. Already in 1904 *Neue Zeit* had opened its pages to contributors on this subject, and had actively encouraged discussion of tactics as well as wider implications. The anarchists and syndicalists who had previously been driven underground by orthodox Social Democracy now rose to the surface like mushrooms on the periphery of the SPD; when it came to something resembling 'their' general strike they felt they were close to legitimacy once more. For the first time for years anarchist speakers appeared on provincial Socialist platforms by invitation. The orthodox party press led by *Vorwärts* was much more cautious; but it, too, gave pride of place to Russian events and for the first few months abstained from wagging blunt and cautious fingers over the difference between

---

[1] 'Reflection of Revolutionary Flames', *SAZ*, 29 April 1905 (special May Day issue).

Russian chaos and German order. Here was 'good old somnolent *Vorwärts*', that 'creeping object without a backbone', in the van of salutation for the Russian workers.[1] In more practical terms, the Russian representatives in Germany, living in their opaque world of illegal circles and pseudonyms, found sudden interest and sympathy among their hosts. The puzzled, *petit-bourgeois* attitudes of benevolent indifference among the German comrades quickly thawed out into spontaneous demonstrations of goodwill and offers of practical assistance; Russian and German students discovered all at once that they had much in common.[2] Even more important in creating solidarity was the negative aspect of common persecution; the German authorities now clamped down all the more ruthlessly on all Social Democrats suspected of furthering the discomfiture of the Emperor's imperial cousin in Russia.

All over Germany meetings were held in support of the Russian revolutionaries, with inflammatory speeches from members of the executive followed by collections to provide more practical backing. Money was, as always, the staple export of the rich and well-organized SPD. The year 1905 was one of agitation on a new scale—not being an election year the agitation was free of the limiting necessities of cadging votes. The atmosphere in Germany during 1905 had a new tang: at the top, a predisposition to more radical thinking and planning; at the bottom, a new militancy in pressing the routine economic and political confrontations between Socialism and society. In itself this year of heightened expectations left little positive trace either at top or bottom, but it did leave memories on which a further wave of agitation five years later could self-consciously build. And in the minds of a small left-wing group the events in Russia and in Germany planted a seed of practical revolution which was never entirely to be uprooted. It was they who hammered home 1905 as a German as well as Russian precedent that would not be denied, even though they magnified the importance of German revolutionary sentiment in the process. This was the group for which Rosa Luxemburg provided the intellectual leadership and personal example; for nearly a decade she became almost the sole embodiment of the validity of this experience. Karl Radek's later statement that 'with [Rosa Luxemburg's] *Massenstreik, Partei und*

---

[1] For the coverage of the revolution in the German press, Left as well as Right, see the exhaustive collection, '*Die Russische Revolution von 1905-7 im Spiegel der Deutschen Presse*', Vols. 2/III to 2/VII in the series *Archivalische Forschungen zur Geschichte der Deutschen Arbeiterbewegung*, 2nd Series, Berlin (East), 1955-61.

[2] See M. Lyadov, *Iz zhizni partii v 1903-7 godakh (Vospominaniya)*, Moscow 1956, particularly p. 16, and O. Pyatnitskii, *Zapiski bolshevika*, Moscow 1956, p. 38. But neither of these books does justice to the sudden *frisson* of Russo-German solidarity in 1905; both were written with all the hindsight of many years of Communist indictments of German Socialist *embourgeoisement*.

Gewerkschaften begins the separation of the Communist movement from Social Democracy in Germany' may have been elliptical but it was not untrue.[1]

When the Russian revolution broke out the SPD had only recently emerged from its long tussle with revisionism. After the 1903 congress the executive considered itself victorious, and its theory-conscious allies were on top of the world. Kautsky and Rosa Luxemburg in close partnership had carried the colours of the Germany victory over revisionism into the International, and had brought home an even more resounding triumph from Amsterdam. The articulate defenders of revisionism were silent at last. The attack on revisionism in practice had been carried right into the southern camp—into the stronghold of the so-called special and all-permissive conditions. The German party leaders had every reason to be pleased with themselves, and Kautsky was in his most optimistic mood. With revisionism apparently out of the way, he could now devote his intellectual energy to the formulation of a more aggressive strategy for a once more united party.

But the unity was more apparent than real. The trade-union leaders, pragmatists all, had kept relatively silent during the spate of words about revisionism; they had resisted only when directly attacked, when intellectuals—particularly foreign ones—had claimed authority to speak on organizational matters with a competence which they clearly did not possess. The debate about the general strike, however, which had begun in 1904 in the relatively remote sanctum of *Neue Zeit*, was now spilling over on to the shop floor. The constituency parties—in Germany, as in Britain, among the most radical elements in the party—seemed possessed by the mass-strike devil, and claimed the right to interfere in local trade-union affairs. As the debate moved dangerously forward as far as consideration of when and how, the trade-union leaders were forced to come out into the open. Not only were the usual agitators currently going the rounds and peddling their utopian mass strike, but even revisionists like Bernstein and Dr. Friedeberg, who saw the strike purely as a deterrent, were actively engaged in the discussion. The question was no longer whether the mass strike was feasible but the extent to which the party executive could keep its finger on the strike button. The trade-union leaders were already disturbed by the current rash of

---

[1] *Rosa Luxemburg, Karl Liebknecht, Leo Jogiches*, Hamburg 1921, p. 15. For a brief analysis of the effects of the Russian revolution on official SPD thinking, see H. Schurer, 'The Russian Revolution of 1905 and the Origins of German Communism' in *The Slavonic and East European Review*, Vol. 39 (1961), pp. 459–71.

A thorough examination from German official archives of the effect of the revolution on Germany as a whole, on the SPD, the bourgeois parties, on Reich as well as provincial governments, is in '*Die Auswirkungen der ersten Russischen Revolution von 1905–7 auf Deutschland*', Vols. 2/I and 2/II in the series *Archivalische Forschungen zur Geschichte der Deutschen Arbeiterbewegung*, Berlin (East) 1955–61.

industrial strikes. As early as January 1905 the miners' leaders had attempted to prevent a large-scale stoppage in the Ruhr. Their colleagues on the Central Council did their best to stop it from spreading into other industries. When it came to deliberate extension of strikes for purely political purposes, like Prussian suffrage, the union leaders took fright. At the triennial Trade Union Congress in Cologne in May 1905 they faced up squarely to the problem; indeed, they moved over to the offensive. Here no clever party scribblers with their taunts and puns were present, no SPD executive to preach party solidarity. This was the platform on which the particular interests of the unions could be stated —untrammelled by any outside considerations. Speech after speech reflected the trade-union leaders' preoccupations; the unions were not strong enough for 'experiments'—at least not until the success of the experiment had become a certainty! What about the highly practical problems of feeding and clothing the strikers' families? And who would prevent the employers' profiting from the disarray with lockouts and reduced wages—while union members spent their strength in political battles with which they were but marginally concerned. Surely the answer was still more and better organization and above all peace and quiet in which to build it. 'Let us have no more talk of mass strikes . . . general strikes are general nonsense.'[1]

The union leaders thought they could identify their main enemy quickly enough—the same waspish Rosa Luxemburg who had downgraded their decades of splendid work into futility with the Sisyphus metaphor. The foreigner, the woman, the greenhorn was stumping the country preaching revolution, praying for chaos in civilized, sophisticated, and secure Germany—all the chaos and misery of backward Russia. Otto Hué, the miners' leader, concluded an article in the July number of his union paper with some return advice.

In Russia the struggle for liberty has been raging almost a year. We always have wondered why our experts on the 'general strike theory' don't take themselves off speedily to Russia, to get practical experience, to join in the battle. In Russia the workers are paying with their lives; why don't all those theoreticians, who anyhow come from Poland and Russia and now sit in Germany, France and Switzerland scribbling 'revolutionary' articles, get themselves on to the battlefield? High time for all those with such an excess of revolutionary zeal to take a practical part in the Russian battle for freedom, instead of carrying on massstrike discussions for summer holiday resorts. Trying is better than lying, so off with you to the Russian front, you class-war theoreticians.

The revisionists joined in the chorus. Here was a chance to get even

---

[1] For the Cologne Congress see K. Kautsky, *Der Politische Massenstreik*, Berlin 1914, pp. 117 ff. The statement itself is attributed to Auer, the Party secretary (see *Protokole SPD 1906*, p. 246).

with their main adversary without raising any problems of principle which might have brought down the wrath of the party executive on their heads once more. *Sozialistische Monatshefte* sarcastically referred to her as an imitation Joan of Arc. The spectre of real revolution made the affairs of the SPD the urgent concern of the Liberal press as well. They had already begun to talk about 'bloody Rosa' and, delighted as always with any disagreements within the Socialist camp, they joyfully took up the cry of the sensible miners' leader. 'Excellent words', wrote Friedrich Naumann in *DieHilfe*; 'let her tell us why she isn't sufficiently "international" all of a sudden to go off to Warsaw.'[1]

Rosa Luxemburg returned the compliment. For the first time she openly identified the trade-union leaders as the most dangerous current vehicle of revisionism within the party. In speeches throughout the year she compared the heroic deeds of the Russian workers with the chicken-hearted policy of contentment in the German trade unions. The 1st of May in Russia and Poland, traditionally the occasion for working-class demonstrations, had produced proportionately significant outbreaks of strikes and protests in this year of revolution. Rosa Luxemburg analysed the May events in great detail in the German press and was given pride of place in *Vorwärts*. The allusion to an example to be followed in Germany, where the May Day spirit had never really taken hold, was thinly veiled.[2] After the Cologne trade-union congress she reviewed its debates and decisions first as a renunciation of the new revolutionary spirit in Germany, and secondly as a trade-union declaration of independence from party supremacy. The Cologne decision amounted to a total misconception of the profound social requirements which had produced the mass-strike phenomenon in the first place. Worst of all, it was parochial: in order to escape the inexorable demands of social revolution the trade-union leaders shut themselves up in an arrogant German self-sufficiency which was merely a larger national version of south German particularism.

Belgium isn't worth studying ... a latin, an 'irresponsible' country, on which the German trade-union experts can afford to look down. Russia, well Russia, that 'savage land' ... without organization, trade-union funds, officials—how can serious, 'experienced' German officials possibly be expected to learn from there ... even though precisely in Russia this mass-strike weapon has found unexpected, magnificent application, instructive and exemplary for the whole working-class world.[3]

Her allusion was prophetic—even though it escaped the notice of the

---

[1] Quoted by Rosa Luxemburg in her speech on 21 September 1905 at the Jena party congress, *Protokoll ... 1905*, p. 269.

[2] See *Vorwärts*, 3 May, 4 May, 6 May, 7 May 1905.

[3] 'Die Debatten in Köln', *SAZ*, 31 May 1905.

party leadership at the time: by the following year, while Rosa Luxemburg was in Warsaw, party and trade-union leaders had to face a constitutional crisis over their respective authority and mutual relationship. By that time the SPD executive, too, had had enough of revolution. In their agreement with the trade-union leaders of February 1906, the latter were officially accorded autonomy in all trade-union questions and the party in practice abdicated any right to enforce political policy on the unions without the latter's full consent. The fact that the agreement was secret proved its departure from recognized and established practice. With this, the executive's participation in the revolutionary atmosphere of 1905, already breathless and failing, had finally come to an end.

But Rosa Luxemburg was more than just the most daring exponent of official party policy. Already by the end of 1904 she had perceived the difference between defensive measures inside the party and a more positive tactic in relation to society as a whole. The expenditure of energy in 'pursuit of particular opportunist boners' was showing less and less marginal return; the party as a whole had to move left and not confine itself to whipping the reformists back into Social-Democratic 'normality'.[1]

Though Rosa Luxemburg was clear enough in her own mind where she differed from official party attitudes, little sign of these differences appeared in public. There could be no question of any open opposition to the leadership. No doubt the main considerations were tactical; the atmosphere of 1905 was entirely different from that of 1910 when opposition seemed inevitable and hence desirable—and the penalties of conforming greater than the risks even of a one-woman campaign. More basic was the hope that the logic of the situation, the pressure of events in Germany and the influence of the Russian revolution, would themselves move the SPD in the required direction of greater activity—and keep it there. Meantime the task of those who wanted a more radical policy was not to oppose their own conception of tactics to that of the leadership, but to spread the Russian news before the public and to hammer away at the analogy with present events in Germany—to turn the executive's declared intentions into actual performance.

This then was Rosa Luxemburg's policy. When Bebel in the name of the SPD executive published an open letter on 9 April 1905, calling on all German Socialists resident in Poland or Russia to join the organized Social-Democratic parties of those countries, Rosa Luxemburg persuaded the SDKPiL Central Committee to reprint this appeal under their own aegis. It was useful as a propaganda weapon against the PPS

---

[1] Letter of Rosa Luxemburg to Henriette Roland-Holst, 17 December 1904, Henriette Roland-Holst, *Rosa Luxemburg*, p. 215, and see above, p. 172.

in the Polish context, but it also served to underline the intimate connection between Social Democracy in Germany and Russia. Similarly Rosa Luxemburg seized upon the executive's cautious preoccupation with the mass strike as proof of official legitimation. Authority for the use of this weapon was now beyond dispute; the only question remaining was how and when and on what scale it should be used: Rosa Luxemburg carried the discussion into every possible area, in speech and letter and print. Throughout the year she travelled all over the country to address meetings and initiate discussion. 'In spite of an overload of literary and organizational work for the Polish revolutionary movement, and in spite of poor health, she unleashed a quite extraordinary spate of agitational work in Germany.'[1] She pulled every string in order to get invitations to speak—her position as leader of a party directly involved in the Russian revolution and the help of friends like Clara Zetkin enabled her to make appearances even on a few trade-union platforms, like that of the metal workers who had some strongly radical branch organizations in the provinces.[2] These activities rose to a crescendo in the second half of the year. But throughout, the accent was on elaboration and interpretation of official SPD policy; Rosa Luxemburg was careful to give the impression that her speeches had official blessing. What was new was not the policy (nor did she lay claim to any originality); it was the situation that had changed and the new line was merely the SPD's dialectic adaptation to circumstances. The fact that her interpretation of official policy was not challenged by anyone except the trade-union leaders was due to the general atmosphere of revolutionary speculation which the executive certainly did nothing to hinder. The discretion given to individual party speakers and journalists to interpret party policy was still very wide in those days; only after 1910 did greater attention have to be paid to the official line.

On 17 September 1905 the annual SPD congress met at Jena to review, discuss, and resolve as usual the events of the year. Traditionally this was the occasion when differing interpretations of party policy could confront each other and if possible be resolved. As always at party congresses, the latent conflict between ideology and pragmatism, to which a party like the SPD was prone, came out into the open. The executive always tried to avoid too sharp and clear an assertion of ideology over the practical and self-perpetuating requirements of policy. The party congress was never confronted openly with any attempt to belittle ideology (as opposed to theory); instead, congress resolutions were usually watered down later in their practical application. Thus on

---

[1] *Collected Works*, Vol. IV, p. 387 (Sectional introduction by Paul Frölich).
[2] Ibid., p. 118.

the one hand the executive mobilized its supporters to prevent too sharp a deviation from its traditional middle path—and was usually able to kill heavily partisan resolutions. On the other hand it accepted the tone established by the 'sense of the congress' and did not fly in the face of predictable majority opinions. This was the measure of its difficulties. In this revolutionary year of 1905 the tone was sharp—and the executive made little direct attempt to soften it.[1]

Rosa Luxemburg had pushed the analogy of the Russian experience and the discussion of the mass strike further than anyone else—to the final limits of the permissible. The congress would, as always, help to define these frontier areas, would approve her conquest of any new territory or leave her isolated beyond the pale. The immediate issue was the mass strike; everyone waited keenly to see which way Bebel would jump in this matter and how far he would go. His address, over three hours long, was radical in tone, in its general outline—but, as so often in both past and future, his practical recommendations were 'practical' indeed: wait and see if our class enemies act against us, we shall certainly know how to reply. The first move was specifically left to them. Within this scheme of things the mass strike had a place, though a defined and limited one. 'Since he saw revolution as a defensive act, so he recommended the mass strike primarily as a defensive weapon . . . against an attack on either universal suffrage or the right of association—the two prerequisites for the pursuit of the Erfurt tactic.'[2] The importance of Bebel was never in what he said but how he would later allow it to be interpreted; textual exegesis and interpretation was the occupational disease of German Social Democracy.[3] To a large

---

[1] No doubt there was a gradual change in the function of party congresses between 1890 and 1905. What had originally been a policy-making body was gradually turned into an increasingly formal festivity, a symbol of ideological assertion which helped to counteract the dispersal and frustrations inherent in permanent opposition. This new saliency of ideological assertion was particularly noticeable at the 1905 congress. The party congress had become 'an expressive function of ideology' whose purposes were to 'increase the loyalty of party members . . . to the given ideology and to the party holding this ideology'. (Ulf Himmelstrand, 'A theoretical and empirical approach to depoliticization and political involvement', *Acta Sociologica*, 1962, Vol. 6, Nos. 1–2, p. 91. See also R. K. Merton, *Social Theory and Social Structure*, Glencoe (Illinois) 1957, Chap. I.) For a discussion of this problem in the particular context of German Social Democracy in the present period, see Günter Roth, *The Social-Democratic Movement in Imperial Germany. A study of class relations in a society engaged in industrialization*. Totowa (NY) 1963; also J. P. Nettl in *Past and Present*, loc. cit.

[2] Carl E. Schorske, *German Social Democracy 1905–17*, p. 43.

[3] And still is in Communist countries. Stalin both wrote the texts (highly equivocally) and enforced the interpretation; Mao too ('Let a hundred flowers bloom' and the substantial analysis of permissible deviation, e.g. 'On the Historical Experience of the Dictatorship of the Proletariat', *Jen-min Jih-pao*, 5 April 1956.) One of the abiding hallmarks of the Khrushchev revolution in the Soviet Union and elsewhere is the virtual abandonment of this exegetical dimension of all discussion relating to action.

extent the fierce tone was a substitute for clear thinking and this fundamental prevarication forced his critics into a similar dichotomy between
public support and private criticism. This same uncertainty is clearly
reflected in Rosa Luxemburg's private comments. To Jogiches she
wrote immediately after the congress:

I was once more in the vanguard of our movement, something which you
could never guess from the *Vorwärts* report [of the congress] because they have
falsified it completely. The truth is that the whole congress was on my side,
Bebel agreeing with me at every moment and Vollmar sitting next to him
almost getting apoplexy. On the whole Jena is a great victory for us all along
the line.[1]

Within a few days the atmosphere of symbolic participation in the
congress had dispersed and more critical evaluation prevailed. To her
friend Henriette Roland-Holst in Holland, Rosa Luxemburg described
the congress far less optimistically. She and her friends already looked
like a 'far Left opposition'. The agreement with the executive, far from
being genuine, was largely tactical; a necessary alliance against the
revisionists. If there was a revolutionary consensus, Bebel's submission
to it was reluctant and unconscious, not deliberate.

I entirely agree with you that Bebel's resolution deals with the problem of the
mass strike very one-sidedly and without excitement [*flach*]. When we saw it in
Jena, a few of us decided to mount an offensive during the discussion so as to
nudge it away from a mechanical recipe for defence of political rights, and
towards recognition as one of the fundamental revolutionary manifestations.
However, Bebel's speech put a different complexion on things, and the attitude
of the opportunists (Heine, etc.) did even more. On several other occasions we,
the 'far left', found ourselves forced to fight, not against him, but with him
against the opportunists, in spite of the important differences between Bebel
and us. . . . It was rather a case of joining with Bebel and then giving his
resolution a more revolutionary appearance during the discussion. . . . And in
fact the mass strike was treated, even by Bebel himself—though he may have
been unaware of it—as a manifestation of popular revolutionary struggle—the
ghost of revolution dominated the whole debate, indeed the whole congress.[2]

At the congress itself Rosa Luxemburg saw her task as twofold: to
be the spearhead of the attack on the trade unions, and to do her utmost
to maintain the revolutionary frontiers against Bebel's conservative
demarcation. The more personally her opponents went for her, the

[1] Jogiches letters, end of September 1905, IML (M).
[2] H. Roland-Holst, *Rosa Luxemburg*, p. 218, letter dated 2 October 1905. The unconscious
contradiction in tone between the beginning and end of this extract are evidence not only of
the objective difficulty in interpreting the verbose but slippery Bebel, but also of Rosa
Luxemburg's own capacity for writing herself into a state of relative euphoria (or pessimism); her mood was always more sharply defined at the end of any letter than at the
beginning.

broader the form of her reply; to all detailed and practical criticisms of the mass-strike concept and the validity of the Russian experience she opposed the broadest amalgam of revolutionary activity.

Anyone listening here to the previous speeches in the debate on the question of the political mass strike would really be inclined to clutch his head and ask: 'Are we really living in the year of the glorious Russian revolution, or are we in fact ten years previous to it?' (Quite right.) Day by day we are reading news of revolution in the papers, we are reading the despatches, but it seems that some of us don't have eyes to see or ears to hear. There are people asking that we should tell them how to make the general strike, exactly by what means, at what hour the general strike will be declared, are you already stocked for food and other necessities? The masses will die of hunger. Can you bear to have it on your conscience that some blood will be spilt? Yes, all those people who ask such questions haven't got the least contact or feeling for the masses, otherwise they wouldn't worry their heads so much about the blood of the masses, because as it happens responsibility for that lies least of all with those comrades who ask such questions.[1]

Already the dispute over the new revolutionary boundaries was overshadowed by an utterly new approach to class conflict. Action came first, the creator of strength and organization—and not, as had been traditionally held in Germany, an optional but risky dividend. This analysis in fact turned German thinking upside down; more galling still was to be its justification, the supremacy of the Russian experience which at one blow threatened to sweep away years of German progress and with it the SPD's claim of revolutionary primacy within the Second International. The latent action doctrine of 1905 would in the next nine years grow stronger and more systematic in proportion to Rosa's alienation from SPD orthodoxy. All this, however, is historian's hindsight. To most participants at the time it seemed no more than a misunderstanding, a matter of emphasis and tone, an excess perhaps of revolutionary excitement. Bebel half humorously summed up the congress's tolerant surprise at Rosa Luxemburg's fervour:

The debate has taken a somewhat unusual turn. . . . I have attended every congress except during those years when I was the guest of the government but a debate with so much talk of blood and revolution I have never listened to. (Laughter.) Listening to all this I cannot help glancing occasionally at my boots to see if these weren't in fact already wading in blood. (Much laughter.) . . . In my harmless way I certainly never intended this [with my mass-strike resolution]. . . . None the less I must confess that Comrade Luxemburg made a good and properly revolutionary speech.[2]

1 *Protokoll . . . 1905*, p. 320.
2 *Protokoll . . . 1905*, pp. 336, 339.

And a month after the congress he repeated his mild protest at a private meeting:

August accused me (though in a perfectly friendly manner) of ultra radicalism and shouted: 'Probably when the revolution in Germany comes Rosa will no doubt be on the Left and I no doubt on the Right,' to which he added jokingly, 'but we will hang her, we will not allow her to spit in our soup.' To which I replied calmly, 'It is too early to tell who will hang whom.' Typical![1]

Rosa Luxemburg could look back on the congress with considerable satisfaction. Even if the frontiers had been staked out more narrowly than she liked, they had at least been moved forward sufficiently to embrace the mass strike once and for all. For years to come Rosa Luxemburg would come back to the mass-strike resolution of the 1905 congress as a precedent, as indestructible proof that the mass strike had been officially incorporated into the tactical armoury of German Social Democracy and that no reinterpretation or explanations could ever again exorcise it. Later, as the executive moved to the Right, Rosa Luxemburg stood pat on this one issue—all the way into opposition; simultaneously with the desire to interpret the real meaning of the mass strike went the need first of all to hold the executive to its commitment. Thus Rosa Luxemburg's revolutionary interpretation of the Russian events was always coupled to a formally conservative, almost legalistic, emphasis on precedent.

The executive regarded the congress above all as a legitimation of its four-year-old battle with the revisionists and used the new revolutionary atmosphere primarily to complete the defeat of the revisionists within the party. One of the last bastions of revisionism was *Vorwärts*, Rosa Luxemburg's longstanding nightmare, peopled by sparring partners like Gradnauer and Eisner. At the pressing request of the Berlin regional organization of the party, who looked upon *Vorwärts* as primarily their paper, the Berlin Press Commission decided in the autumn of 1905 to carry out a purge. First the executive tried quietly to 'feed in' two radical assistant editors, but the resultant indignation and solidarity of the editorial board led to more thorough action. Six revisionist editors went and a new team took over. At the particular request of August Bebel, Rosa Luxemburg now joined the *Vorwärts* editorial board.[2] *Tempis mutandis*—this was the job that he had advised her to refuse in 1899.

---

[1] Jogiches letters, second half of October 1905, IML (M).

[2] The evicted editors were Kurt Eisner (later prominent in the first phase of the Bavarian Soviet Republic in 1919), Wetzker, Gradnauer, Kaliski, Büttner, Schröder; the newcomers were Rosa Luxemburg, Cunow, Stadthagen, Ströbel, Düwell. Thus the old team of six was replaced by a new team of five. This purge gave *Vorwärts* a radical outlook which it was to keep right up to the first months of the war. Most of the editors became 'Centrists' and supporters of Kautsky; Cunow had a cataclysmic conversion to patriotism and joined

The purge had already been in the air during the summer and Rosa Luxemburg was aware of some impending change, though not of the intention to appoint her. She was pleased to have the opportunity of putting forward her views in the central organ of the party, but was immediately sceptical as to the extent of her influence and powers. At the end of October, even before her participation was certain, she played down the significance of the change. 'It will consist of very mediocre writers, with their hearts in the right place; they'll all be *kosher* enough. This is the first time since the world began that *Vorwärts* has an entirely left-wing government on the premises. Now they've got to show what they can do. . . .'[1] None the less, she began to contribute regularly to *Vorwärts* in the last week of October, particularly on Russian questions; from the 25th of that month she had practical control of the Russian desk. At the beginning of November she was formally installed and her comments on the Russian revolution appeared almost daily, though in anonymous form. By 3 November the extent of her powers had already become clear—and with it the first impact of disillusion:

As you correctly deduced, *Vorwärts* is no better than *Sächsische Arbeiterzeitung*. What is worse, I am the only one who understands this problem and partly Karl Kautsky: the editors are no better than indolent oxen. There is not one journalist among them, apart from the fact that Eisner & Co. with the whole bag of revisionists are carrying on a determined campaign against us in the press and all we can get to reply on our behalf are August (!) or Cunow and similar gentlemen (!!). I am limited to the Russian section although I write the leader every now and then and go round dishing out good advice and praise for initiative which is then carried out so terribly badly that I can only throw up my hands. . . . I remarked to Ströbel that his answer to Calwer [a revisionist] is even worse than if Eisner had written it, that we did not come to *Vorwärts* just to wag our tail and cover up our traces, that we have to write sharply and clearly. To which he proudly replied next day: 'Now I shall do better and you will be pleased with me.' And today I see in the current number some horrible bleating about 'revolutionary lightning'—a mish-mash of senseless phrases and radical chatter. . . . We shall fall into such disgrace that I am truly fearful and I see no way of escape because we simply haven't the people . . . I am alone . . . tormented by my current preoccupations.[2]

Lensch and Haenisch in the coterie which was to form round Parvus on the *Glocke*. Stadthagen died in mild opposition in 1916 before the foundation of the USPD. When Rosa Luxemburg resigned from *Vorwärts* at the end of December, her place was taken by Hans Block, another of Kautsky's supporters, whose presence and attitude as editor of the *Leipziger Volkszeitung* in 1913 was to precipitate the foundation of the oppositional *Sozialdemokratische Korrespondenz* under the editorship of Rosa Luxemburg and Julian Marchlewski.

[1] Jogiches letters, end of October 1905, IML (M). Parts of the letter have been published in *Collected Works*, Vol. IV, p. 386.

[2] Jogiches letters, 3 November 1905, IML (M).

None the less, for the two months of November and December Rosa Luxemburg blazed out one fiery comment on Russian events after the other. The period coincided with the last great upheaval in Russia— the preparations for the Moscow rising, the general strike in St. Petersburg, and the sympathetic events in Poland. On 17 October (or 30 October in the West) the Tsar had issued his manifesto and amnesty, but then declared martial law a few days later. The country was in chaos. All this flowed through the pen of Rosa Luxemburg—and though her task was mainly foreign reportage she drew the analogy for Germany whenever possible. Inevitably the official attention of the government was insistently drawn to her activities, and the right-wing parties in the *Reichstag* called for action against this homeless agitator and purveyor of hate. Rosa Luxemburg, *dénaturée* and *dépaysée*—two major crimes in an essentially traditionalist society—was undermining the proud stability of efficient Prussia. Could nothing be done to stop her?[1] It fell to Bebel to defend her as the commanding general of her party and—at least vis-à-vis the class enemy—as her personal friend. In the *Reichstag* he identified himself completely with his difficult ally— as tradition demanded.[2]

Unexpectedly, her enemies, inside the party and out, who had been crowing about revolutionaries in secure places egging on others to spill their blood, were made all at once to eat their words. Rosa Luxemburg suddenly decided to leave for Warsaw forthwith—abandoning the newly conquered commanding heights at *Vorwärts* and the whole discussion of the German mass strike. Her reasons were 'Polish', valid and urgent —nothing less than the fear of being left out of the most exciting moment in the life of 'her' SDKPiL. We shall see more precisely why she went when discussing the Polish side of her story. Throughout the second half of 1905 she had shivered with intermittent nostalgia at the thought of the real revolution in the East; after the Tsar's manifesto in October the flow of exiles back to Russia only made her longing more acute. These were all friends—or at least fellow émigrés—and their return left her increasingly isolated. Even though Jogiches was not likely to be sympathetic, she complained that '[the news of Martov's and Dan's return to St. Petersburg] agitates me; my heart is gripped by a sense of isolation and I long to get away from the misery and purgatory of *Vorwärts* and to escape somewhere, anywhere. How I envy them.'[3]

To her German friends her decision seemed capricious, incompre-

[1] *Stenographische Berichte ... Reichstag*, 11th Legislative Period, II Session 1905-6, col. 359 ff., 15   1905.

[2] Loc. cit., col. 2638 ff., 5 April 1906. Another tradition that was to be overthrown after the outbreak of the war.

[3] Jogiches letters, end of November 1905. IML (M).

hensible—yet also typical of her impetuous courage. They never knew how deeply she was attached to the Polish movement and to what extent she had always been involved in the SDKPiL's affairs—Rosa Luxemburg herself ensured that they should not know. They did their best to dissuade her. Bebel and Mehring insisted on elementary prudence—just as they had warned Parvus in October of the personal risks he was running.[1] In Rosa's case their preoccupations were greater still. She was a woman—though pointing this out to her merely made obstinacy more certain; there was also the horrifying and all too recent execution of Kasprzak to serve as an example. The Kautskys pleaded that she would be abandoning their joint campaign to radicalize the SPD at the very moment when success was near. The place of the intellectual was at his desk—another reason to spur her on rather than make her desist.

On the morning of 28 December 1905, immediately after the Christmas holidays, a small group of people assembled on the platform of the Friedrichstrasse Station, Berlin's railway terminus to the East. The Kautsky's and a few others were seeing Rosa Luxemburg off, to 'go to work'.[2] They loaded her with gifts—useful things like shawls and mufflers for the Russian winter—as well as good advice on how to keep warm. To a family whose physical adventurousness was confined to an annual holiday at a mountain spa, the idea of travelling to Warsaw in the mid-winter of revolution was lunacy, if not masochism—even though they had to admit to a sneaking admiration for Rosa Luxemburg's extraordinary courage. Finally, with a defiant whistle-blast, the train moved off—and Rosa Luxemburg, well-known German writer and intellectual, became Anna Matschke, the anonymous Polish conspirator falsely decked out as a minor journalist.[3] As the train moved eastwards into the gathering dusk Rosa Luxemburg in her third-class compartment prepared joyfully for the coming experience.

2: POLAND

The Russo-Japanese War and the ignominious Russian defeat first brought the possible collapse of Tsarist autocracy into the range of the most optimistic revolutionary vision. Together with the other parties in Russia and Poland, the SDKPiL worked out a programme of minimum demands which the revolutionary parties could press on a weakened government should the occasion arise. Naturally enough, it was Rosa Luxemburg who wrote it. The evolution of her ideas from 1904 to 1906

---

[1] Parvus, *Im Kampf um die Wahrheit*, Berlin 1918, p. 9.
[2] *Letters to Karl and Luise Kautsky*, p. 96.
[3] Rosa Luxemburg took the name and papers of Anna Matschke, who was a real person. This borrowing of identity was the usual manner of illegal infiltration into Russia.

reflected not only the widening revolutionary perspectives but the corresponding sharpening of Social-Democratic demands and evaluations.[1] In the process the Social-Democratic programme evolved from very general statements of principle to more precise demands. To begin with there was little beyond the need to destroy the autocracy and replace the government by a popular republic. More immediately relevant was the evidence of the government's weakness and to the dissemination of this most of Rosa Luxemburg's Polish writing in 1904 was devoted.

As yet it still amounted to little more than occasional rhythmic accompaniment to the prevailing melody of struggle with the PPS. As we have seen, even the negotiations with the Russians had ultimately been dominated by the dictates of this one and everlasting battle. As defeat followed upon Russian military defeat in the course of 1904, the oppositional groups in Russia attempted to work out some practical form of collaboration. In October 1904 a conference was called in Paris by the representatives of the various revolutionary organizations. Since invitations were issued to all potential allies including middle-class opponents of Tsarism, the decision to accept or refuse became a critical test of attitudes in Socialist ranks; confrontation with the government took second place to the sharp ideological divisions within the revolutionary camp. The Socialist Revolutionaries and the PPS accepted the invitation, while the Bund, SDKPiL, and RSDRP declined. The PPS gave wide publicity to their participation as evidence of their willingness to collaborate with anyone pledged to weaken Tsarism—and this at once drew a spate of Social-Democratic criticism of such 'opportunistic kow-towing to bourgeois parties, the mistaken emphasis on terror and bloodshed instead of the mass strike'.[2] In the PPS the influence of Piłsudski and the activists was at its height. They saw their opportunity in the creation of what was to be in effect a second front in the Russo-Japanese conflict, and negotiated with the Japanese for help and assistance to promote a new national Polish uprising. As yet there were no signs in Russia or Poland of any revolutionary activity with which the SDKPiL could oppose the PPS policy of purely national secession. The Polish Social Democrats were on the defensive and confined themselves to reiterating general Socialist principles.

All this changed dramatically on 22 January 1905. The bloodshed in St. Petersburg and the wildfire response throughout the Russian empire

---

[1] See 'Czego chcemy?' (What do we want?), first published in Przegląd Robotniczy, Zürich 1904, No. 5, pp. 1–21, and 1905, No. 6, pp. 1–40; finally expanded into a brochure of the same title published in Warsaw in January 1906. See below, pp. 229 ff, for a fuller discussion of this programme.

[2] O. B. Szmidt, SDKPiL dokumenty, 1893–1904, Vol. I, p. 568; also appeal by SDKPiL Central Committee, ibid., p. 562.

signalled the outbreak of revolution.[1] The Poles came out five days later on 27 January in spontaneous response to the events in Russia and with fully equal fervour. A state of emergency was proclaimed and there were clashes and casualties, but the repression was sporadic and the heightened momentum was maintained for several months. It was a period of extreme confusion. Economic and political demands leap-frogged over each other; whatever the cause, the articulate dissatisfactions of the middle classes in Russia as well as in Poland found themselves carried along on a heaving base of working-class action. The Social Democrats were in a quandary. They had not predicted such events and were in no sense responsible for them—yet at the same time the masses had spontaneously come into action precisely in accordance with the most optimistic prognosis of Social-Democratic theory.[2] Moreover, the connection between Poland and Russia had been formally established for all to see; far from a separate and anti-Russian movement in Poland, the workers of both countries behaved as if no ethnic frontier existed between them.

In the first phase of the Russian revolution, which reached its height in June, all the Socialist parties tried to adjust themselves to events, to mesh into the moving wheels of history and to align their policy to the action of the masses as best they could. 'The influence of the political parties on the development of the events of January and February could hardly be felt. Neither SDKPiL nor PPS nor the *Bund* was ready as yet to direct such great masses in action either politically or organizationally. At that time their political propaganda had barely begun to penetrate the masses and influence the character of their actions.'[3]

In this first phase a curious contradiction in party alignment took place. At the bottom, on factory floor or local cell, the often hazy distinction between PPS and SDKPiL seemed to lose all meaning in action; control by the two parties was anyhow negligible and only the disci-

---

[1] The PPS traditionally dated the outbreak of the revolution in Poland from a fracas in the Plac Grzybowski in Warsaw on 13 November 1904—thus anticipating Russia by two months. In SDKPiL eyes this was a minor, purely nationalist, affair. See 'Jak nie należy urządzać demonstracji' (How not to arrange demonstrations), *Czerwony Sztandar*, December 1904; J. Krasny (ed.) *Materialy do dziejów ruchu socjalistycznego w Polsce*, Moscow 1927, Vol. II, pp. 43–7.

[2] Róża Luksemburg, 'Przykład do teorii strajku powszechnego' (Example of the theory of the mass strike), in *Wybuch rewolucyjny w caracie*, Cracow 1905; pp. 37–40. This was a reissue of an article in *SAZ*, 3 March 1905.

[3] Stanisław Kalabiński and Feliks Tych, 'The Revolution in the Kingdom of Poland in the years 1905–7' *Annali dell' Istituto Giangiacomo Feltrinelli*, Year 5, 1962, p. 198. This summary of research on the revolution in Poland is the most modern and comprehensive account. No satisfactory history of the 1905 revolution in Russia or Poland as yet exists. The quotation is especially interesting in view of the fact that it represents the official thinking of party historians in contemporary Poland.

plined action groups of Piłsudski stood out sharply. This confusion in practice—in spite of all the years of intellectual caterwauling—was to have profound consequences for the PPS. The party was soon forced to choose between the masses and the armed fighters, between joining the Russian revolution or keeping separate from it. In March 1905 a national conference was called against the wishes of Piłsudski and his friends—and constituted itself as the seventh party congress. A new Central Committee was elected and Piłsudski lost control over the political direction of the party. However, he did retain control over the military organization which he had been largely instrumental in building up—a fact which separated him even more from the new leaders of the party.[1] At the top, however, and particularly abroad, the differentiation between PPS and SDKPiL became sharper than ever—and the Social Democrats did their best to keep it so. The relatively simple alignments produced by the conference of October 1904 shivered into a newer and more delicate kaleidoscope, particularly as the differences between component parts of the Russian party began to emerge more clearly. Partly through the good offices of the Foreign Committee of the SDKPiL, a conference of Russian revolutionaries was arranged to take place in Zürich in January 1905. Both the SPD and the Austrians were to participate, partly in order that their authority might help to unite the squabbling Russians, partly also to commit them to moral and financial support for the Russian revolutionaries. The conference came to nothing—and Rosa Luxemburg privately did her best to see that it should not. She wrote to Akselrod:

Bebel is so little informed about the issues and the whole thing so ill-prepared, that nothing can go right. How you can agree to take part in a conference with Adler, that specialist in supporting opportunism, a man moreover who gives every aid and comfort to federalism, terror, nationalism and co-operation with the liberal nationalist block which we have already refused, how you could agree to invite the Polish terrorists—all this is surprising and quite incomprehensible.[2]

Even though the PPS was not invited, the fact that Adler was to be present came in her view to much the same thing. However insistently Rosa might preach Russian unity, she resisted to the utmost every attempt to create a similar unity among the Poles—even though the Germans, guided by a spectator's clear-cut logic, did not always appreciate the subtle difference.

Though Rosa Luxemburg was little concerned with the practical

[1] See Introduction, pp. 1–11, to *PPS-Lewica 1906–18, Materiały i dokumenty*, Warsaw 1961, Vol. I, 1906–10.

[2] Rosa Luxemburg to Pavel Akselrod, 9 January 1905 (Russian dating), in *Sotsial-demokraticheskoe dvizhenie v Rossii, Materiały*, Moscow/Leningrad 1928, p. 150.

problems of the revolution, she was as always the spearhead of her party's intellectual and policy formulations. As she saw it, the overriding need was intellectual clarity—more than ever in this period of real revolutionary activity. 'If we don't want to forgo our advantage which has been enhanced more than ever as a result of the May [general strikes and demonstrations], we must now unleash a veritable shower of publications.' Accordingly she would write 'until her eyes fell out with tiredness'.[1]

Who was she writing for? Who were the youngsters and intellectuals to whom she kept referring in her correspondence?[2] In this revolution, as in Germany thirteen years later, clarity of vision and a widening of intellectual horizons were essential concomitants of revolution—as though both the revolutionary mind as well as the revolutionary will were capable of infinite expansion under the pressure of events. The two processes of growth were complementary and interdependent— without a growing intellectual appetite the whole moral and self-liberating purpose of revolution was largely destroyed. Mere will was nihilistic.[3] This was an essential part of Rosa Luxemburg's philosophy. Her programmatic writing always had this twofold purpose, the postulate of higher goals both as practical slogans for political action and as internalization of new experiences and wider perceptions. The revolutionary proletariat must not only know what to do but how and why it has to be done. The SDKPiL in 1905 gained thousands of new recruits,

---

[1] Jogiches letters, 20 May 1905, *Z Pola Walki*, 1931, Nos. 11–12, p. 211.

[2] A comparison with the stresses of Bolshevik propaganda during the same period is interesting. The Russian material is well documented in the substantial collection *Revoliutsiya 1905–7 gg. v Rossii: dokumenty i materialy* (ed. A. M. Pankratova, Moscow 1955 onwards). An interesting analysis of this material in terms of stress distribution of issues in accordance with regional and social divisions among the recipients or addressees of propaganda in Russia, is undertaken by D. S. Lane, *The 'Social Eidos' of the Bolsheviks in the 1905 revolution: A comparative study*, University of Birmingham, Centre for Russian and East European Studies, Discussion papers, Series RC/C, No. 2, October 1964. Although no similar statistical comparison is possible for Poland since a complete documentary collection of leaflets and other material has not been published, my own impression of a sample of such material in ZHP, Warsaw, suggests that SDKPiL propaganda was addressed more to intellectuals and so more inclined to stress the ideological totality of Marxist revolution than the equivalent Bolshevik material. The only exception was the repeated and strong emphasis on the national question in the struggle against the PPS—a stress absent among the Bolsheviks. Naturally this applies particularly to Rosa Luxemburg's work; none the less, the general intellectual tone of SDKPiL material compared with that of the Bolsheviks is striking.

[3] Readers familiar with classical political philosophy will catch the echo of one of the oldest problems in the world of philosophical speculation: but how to reconcile this with Marxist materialism? It might be argued that for Rosa Luxemburg the final and self-liquidating apotheosis of materialism, the capacity for such self-enlargement, was the *process* of revolution, not the consequence of its successful achievement. For elaboration of this thesis, see above, pp. 151 ff.

or at least supporters—people swept freshly into the revolutionary process by events which the party had neither created nor controlled. These newcomers had to be offered intellectual stimulation, all the more brilliant and startling for having to be compressed into such a short space of time: the long, solid German experience had to be predigested. Rosa Luxemburg offered the newcomers not only the new meat and drink of Marxism, but tried to answer in advance the sort of problems that must trouble an emerging class consciousness still befogged by ignorance and prejudice. At the same time they had to be assured that they were not alone; instead of building on their national prejudices, Rosa Luxemburg offered them the wider reassurance of solidarity not only with Russians but with their German fellow proletarians.[1]

This then was Rosa Luxemburg's answer to the problem that Lenin characterized in more down-to-earth terms. 'Young strength is required. My advice is simply to shoot those that say there are not enough people. There are many people in Russia, you only have to go wider and be bolder, bolder and wider, and once again bolder if you want to attract the youth. This is a time of war. . . . Break with all the old habits of immobility.'

By the summer of 1905 Rosa Luxemburg began to feel increasingly restive. Her comrades were closer in Cracow to the events in Russian Poland and to that extent more concerned with the immediacies. 'I feel as though I were in an enchanted circle. This perpetual current stuff . . . prevents me from getting down to more serious work and seems to have no end', she wrote to Jogiches on 25 May.[2] Sitting far away in Berlin, at the dim end of the party's efforts, she felt that she was ill-equipped for snappy, up-to-date journalism.

Today particularly I was struck by the complete abnormality of my Polish work. I get an order to write an introductory article about autonomy (or about the constitutional assembly)—okay. But for that, one has to read the Polish and Russian publications to keep up to date with what is happening in society, to have regular contact with party matters. Otherwise all you will get from me are pale formulas or schemes. I cannot score bull's-eyes everywhere and the times have long gone when you simply reeled off the party's old and set line

---

[1] See, for instance, Rosa Luxemburg's pseudonymous dissertation on the problem of religion, so important in this context: Jósef Chmura, *Kościól a socjalizm*, Cracow 1905—a curious piece of historical sophistry designed to show the distortion of Christianity from its early just and egalitarian principles in the hands of the systematizing hierarchy of the church. The sophistry was necessary because Rosa Luxemburg opposed the church but would not attack religion. This pamphlet has had a curious echo—in present-day Ceylon, where the substantial Trotskyite party has made it into something like an official text.

[2] Jogiches letters, *Z Pola Walki*, 1931, Nos. 11–12, p. 214.

with a little agitational dressing. Today every single question comes straight from the front line. To limit this war purely to fighting the PPS in the old manner is an anachronism. If I am to write about autonomy I have to mention not only the PPS but the National Democrats and the Progressive Nationalists, etc. Each and every movement has to be taken into account. And how am I supposed to do this when I never see any Polish publications, neither the legal ones nor the underground literature . . . and when all I get from time to time is a bundle of isolated cuttings?[1]

This was not merely the accidental handicap of geography. Rosa Luxemburg became obsessed with the idea that she was being deliberately put on ice, that the easy logic which kept her safe and sound in Berlin—post office, letterhead, and contact woman—was part of Jogiches' deliberate plan to reduce her influence. In the spring of 1905 all the important SDKPiL leaders had made their way to Cracow to join Dzierżyński and Hanecki; these two then went clandestinely to Warsaw while Jogiches, Marchlewski, and Warszawski unfurled the banner of the Central Committee in the old and elegant cathedral city. It was left to Rosa Luxemburg in Berlin to pick up the fag-end of the work, to represent the party in the International Bureau and to manipulate and influence the Germans.

What finally made her sense of isolation and impotence boil over were the Russian events of October 1905. The government's concession of an advisory Duma, the so-called Bulygin Duma, had been denounced by all the Socialist parties in Russia and Poland as a farce, though some of the liberal constitutional opposition had been willing to participate. At the beginning of October the printers came out on strike in Moscow and again a wave of general strikes spread throughout the empire. On 25 October the vital railway workers joined in and communications were practically paralysed. At first the authorities had tried to play it tough; instructions were issued to take the sharpest possible measures including the use of arms. But the strikes merely became more intense and unexpectedly the Tsar capitulated. He issued his manifesto on 30 October (new style), promising a constitution and a new, more effective Duma. At the same time he granted an amnesty for political prisoners and émigrés. Now vital decisions had to be taken quickly. The long, illegal struggle could suddenly come into the open. What should the new tactic be? At the end of November the SDKPiL held a full conference which included not only the leaders in Cracow but also those who were now released from prison—Dzierżyński, arrested in Warsaw during the summer, and even Bronisław Wesołowski, Marchlewski's old friend who had been exiled in Siberia since 1894. The only important person missing was Rosa Luxemburg. She sat in Berlin and

---

[1] Jogiches letters, end of October 1905. IML (M).

chafed while the stream of Russians flowed past her back home to Russia from Switzerland and from France and England—many of them passing directly through Berlin. The revolution had reached a new level of success and excitement in the second half of 1905, and inevitably Rosa Luxemburg's impatience and frustration mounted apace. Though eleven days after the manifesto a state of siege was declared which in practice revoked many of the Tsar's promises, the wave of enthusiasm would not be stemmed. Above all, most of the revolutionaries had at last succeeded in joining 'their' revolution.[1]

Finally there was the purely private element, the link with Jogiches. It was close but it could never be taken for granted. Rosa's present isolation had its personal penalties too. She had come to Cracow at the end of July 1905 for four weeks—against his wishes; his dissuasions were met with the brutal brevity of a telegram—'I am coming to Cracow'.[2] And now the chips were down. What could previously—with goodwill and imagination—be explained by the needs of the situation and a necessary division of revolutionary labour between them, was now plainly a deliberate attempt to keep her at a distance: plain at least to Rosa Luxemburg, if not yet to friends like Adolf Warszawski and his wife. Jogiches' peremptory tone, his refusal to explain or even provide information about party activities, was jeopardizing their whole relationship; so much so that Rosa Luxemburg dashed off to see him again in September immediately after the Jena congress—and to the devil with the exploitation of her German victory. 'I didn't like the look in your eyes and I want once more to look straight into them.' Still nothing was settled, and after her return to Germany she renewed her demands for her share of information and consultation. 'In spite of my work on *Vorwärts* I insist on being kept *au courant* with our work. Don't be childish and don't try to push me out by force from Polish work by depriving me of all information and news.'[3] But it was all to no avail; whatever personal assurances Jogiches may have given her in Cracow, silence punctuated only by curt instructions had become his routine. Rosa Luxemburg wrote bitterly at the end of October in one of her last letters before Jogiches himself went to Warsaw and thus out of any safe postal orbit: 'I am good enough for scribbling anything and

---

[1] The only major Russian Socialist who did not go at all was Plekhanov. Akselrod was ill and did not get beyond the frontier until early 1906. The majority, however, took immediate advantage of the amnesty—particularly the main Bolshevik and Menshevik leaders. Parvus, impatient as always, had already gone in early October while Trotsky of course had been in Russia since February—the first of them all.

[2] Telegram of 10 July 1905: 'Ich komme nach Krakau', Jogiches letters, IML (M). For her stay, see also *Letters to Karl and Luise Kautsky*, pp. 93–4, 10 August 1905. To the Kautskys Rosa pretended that it was her whimsical idea of a holiday.

[3] Jogiches letters, end of September and early October 1905. IML (M).

everything but not for the privilege of knowing what goes on.'

There was nothing for it but to throw up her German work and go to Warsaw herself. Even before the amnesty, the SDKPiL leadership moved *en bloc* from Cracow to Warsaw. The opaque curtain round Rosa Luxemburg now shut her off from them completely. When they heard of her intention to come, both Dzierżyński and Warszawski warned her strongly against it. Her German friends tried even harder to retain her. But she ignored the latter; while the suspicious protests of her Polish colleagues served only to make the journey more urgent. All the news from the East indicated that a new confrontation between the government and the revolutionaries was imminent—the last, though neither side realized it yet. The virtual retraction of the manifesto's promises goaded the revolutionaries to a huge new effort: on 15 November another general strike in St. Petersburg, followed by the arrest of the leaders of the Soviet; in Moscow, preparations for the armed uprising. In Warsaw, too, plans were made for a sharper reply to the government, backed up by arms this time, to turn the latest strike into something more effective. Objectively and subjectively, for revolutionary as much as personal reasons, Rosa Luxemburg knew that she must go now or never.

The high excitement of her departure on 28 December almost immediately fizzled out like a damp squib—by courtesy of the railway company. Trains on the direct line to Warsaw were not running owing to the strike and Rosa Luxemburg had to make a big diversion through Illovo in East Prussia, whence she reported her first Russian experience —a good meal of *Schnitzel* at the railway restaurant.[1] Next day, however, she smuggled herself aboard a troop train—the only civilian and certainly the only woman; the metaphor of a Trojan horse was not lost on her keen sense of humour. Finally, on Saturday 30 December (new style), she arrived at her destination, frozen stiff from confinement in an unheated and unlit train which had to proceed at snail's pace for fear of sabotage from the striking railwaymen. 'The city is practically dead, general strikes, soldiers wherever you go, but the work is going well, and I begin today.'[2]

Warsaw was under a heavy pall of anxiety. The general strike in St. Petersburg was now known to have failed; the frantic efforts of Parvus to reform the Soviet after the arrest of Trostsky and most of the other leaders, and to call out the transport workers in a renewed strike, were meeting with little response. Similar news came from Moscow—though here the final confrontation had been a bang rather than a whimper: the Bolshevik-controlled Soviet had ordered, indeed

[1] *Letters to Karl and Luise Kautsky*, p. 97.
[2] Ibid., p. 98.

attempted, armed uprising in the city. By mid-January it was clear to the Polish leaders in Warsaw that for the time being the revolutionary drive in Russia had slackened off. No one knew whether this was temporary or permanent, but the Polish leaders saw the present ebb as a *reculement* which they must use for a further and better leap forward, and as soon as possible. Rosa Luxemburg wrote to the Kautskys on 2 January 1906 (new style):

To characterize the situation in two words (but this is only for your ears), the general strike has just about *failed*—especially in St. Petersburg where the railwaymen made no real effort to carry it through. . . . People everywhere are hesitant and waiting. The reason for all this is simply that a *mere general strike by itself* has ceased to play the role it once did. Now nothing but a general uprising on the streets can bring about a decision, though for this the right moment must be prepared very carefully. The present period of waiting may therefore continue for a while unless some 'accident'—a new manifesto from the Tsar—brings about a stupendous new surge.

On the whole the work and the spirit are good; one must explain to the masses *why* the present general strike has ended without giving any visible 'results'. The organization is growing by leaps and bounds everywhere and yet at the same time it is messy, because everything is naturally in a state of flux. In Petersburg the chaos is at its worst. Moscow stands much more firmly and the fight in Moscow has indeed opened new horizons for the general tactic. There is no thought of leadership from Petersburg; the people there take a very local point of view in a ridiculous manner (this by the way is clear from the argument developed by D[eutsch] when he asked for help for Petersburg alone). From their standpoint this was very ill-advised as I had to tell him myself afterwards: in St. Petersburg alone the revolution can never succeed; it can only succeed in the country as a whole. . . .

. . . My dear it is very nice here, every day two or three persons are stabbed by soldiers in the city; there are daily arrests, but apart from these it is pretty gay. Despite martial law we are again putting out our daily *Sztandar*, which is sold on the streets. As soon as martial law is abolished, the legal *Trybuna* will appear again. For the present the production and printing of the *Sztandar* has to be carried out in bourgeois presses by force, with revolver in hand. The meetings too will start again as soon as martial law is ended. Then you will hear from me! It is savagely cold and we travel about exclusively in sledges. . . . Write at once how things are faring in the *V[orwärts]* and whether August [Bebel] is furious.[1]

Uncertainty did not mean hesitation. By now both Polish revolutionary parties had caught up—at least intellectually—with the fullness of revolutionary possibilities. The PPS was splitting ever more visibly down the middle; the dissatisfaction with the military and exclusively anti-Russian efforts of the Piłsudski wing had been reinforced by an open letter from Daszyński in Cracow in which he called for a clear

---

[1] *Letters to Karl and Luise Kautsky*, pp. 98-100. Rosa Luxemburg's italics.

separation of the Polish struggle from that of the Russian; the latter had failed, the former must be free to succeed on its own. Specifically Daszyński opposed the continuous wave of strikes which only ruined the economy of the country without furthering any visible revolutionary ends.[1] The SDKPiL had also begun to appreciate the insufficiency of strike movements as such—at least for the purpose of driving the revolution forward.

For the moment the situation is this: on the one hand it is generally felt that the next phase of the fight must be one of armed *rencontres* [following the example of the recent events in Moscow]. I have learnt much from this *and all of it more encouraging than you can imagine.* . . . One may for the moment regard Moscow as a victory rather than a defeat. The entire infantry remained inactive, even the Cossacks! There were only minimal losses on the part of the revolutionaries. The whole of the enormous sacrifices were borne by the bourgeoisie—i.e. the people who had no part in the affair inasmuch as soldiers simply fired blindly and destroyed private property. Result: the entire bourgeoisie is furious and aroused! Money is being contributed in quantities for arming the workers—among the *leading* revolutionaries there was hardly a casualty in Moscow.[2]

That the prolonged strike movements were causing great misery could not be denied, especially now that the government had mounted a counter-offensive. The employers, previously only too anxious to come to terms with their striking workers, were now stiffening their attitude and locking the workers out.

The sore spot of our movement . . . is the enormous spread of unemployment which causes indescribable misery . . . *voilà la plaie de la révolution*—and no means of curbing it. But there has alongside this developed a quiet heroism and a class consciousness of the masses which I should very much like to show to our dear Germans. . . . Here the workers *of their own accord* make such arrangements as for instance setting aside a day's wage each week from the employed to the unemployed. These conditions will not pass over without leaving their marks for the future. For the present the work accomplished by the revolution is enormous—deepening the gulf between the classes, sharpening conditions and clearing up all doubts. And all this is in no way appreciated abroad! People say the struggle has been abandoned, but it has only gone down into the depths of society. At the same time *organization* progresses unceasingly. Despite martial law, trade unions are being industriously built up by Social Democracy . . . the police are powerless against this mass movement. . . .[3]

The theoretical transformation of the mass strike into the next stage

[1] See 'Open letter', *Naprzód*, 3–5 January 1906. Rosa Luxemburg's answer is in *Czerwony Sztandar*, 16 January 1906 (No. 44) and 27 January (No. 48).
[2] *Letters to Karl and Luise Kautsky*, pp. 102–3, dated 11 January 1906. Rosa Luxemburg's italics.
[3] Ibid., pp. 110–11, dated 5 February 1906.

of armed uprising was a vital problem which Rosa Luxemburg attacked head on in her usual manner. The 'young intellectuals'—that postulated readership to which her most important writing was addressed—now expected a dialectical analysis in which the process of mass strikes was meshed accurately and historically into the next stage of armed uprisings. First, Rosa Luxemburg analysed the three general strikes of January, October, and December 1905—each representing a stage of growth and intensification. She defined these stages as follows:

In the first phase of the revolution the army of the revolutionary proletariat assembled its forces and brought together its fighting potential. In the second [and third] phase this army achieved freedom for the proletariat and destroyed the power of absolute rule. Now it is a question of removing the last shreds of the Tsarist government; to get rid of the rule of violence which hinders the further development of proletarian freedom.[1]

It was very important to differentiate her concept of armed uprising from that of the PPS. The latter's was an act of desperation, the consequence of the totally wrong analysis which claimed that the mass strikes had failed and that the spirited action of a few armed men could be a substitute for the unsuccessful efforts of the whole proletariat.[2] The armed uprising Rosa Luxemburg had in mind, on the contrary, would be carried out precisely by the same participants as those who made the mass strikes—only more of them and more determined. It would be the masses themselves who would call for this action; dimly the antithesis masses/leaders emerged for the first time as a justification for venturing on a path which the naturally prudent leadership might otherwise hesitate to follow.

In a word, the course of the last strikes has proved not that the revolutionary cause is retreating or weakening but on the contrary that it is moving forward and growing more intense; not that the Socialist leaders are beginning to lose influence over the masses but that the masses as usual at any turning point of the battle only push the leaders spontaneously to more advanced goals.[3]

Lenin put it in very similar terms when he analysed the extent to which the Social-Democratic leaders measured up to their situation. 'The proletariat understood the development of the objective circumstances of the struggle, which demanded a transition from strike to uprising, earlier than its leaders.'[4]

---

[1] *Z doby rewolucyjnej: co dalej?*, Warsaw 1906, p. 12. This pamphlet was an enlargement and elaboration of the analysis of 1905 under the same title. (See *Czerwony Sztandar*, April 1905, No. 25, and the first version of the pamphlet itself reprinted from it a few months later in Cracow.)

[2] See 'Blanquism and Social Democracy', *Czerwony Sztandar*, 27 June 1906, No. 82.

[3] *Z doby rewolucyjnej: co dalej?*, p. 14.

[4] 'Lessons of the Moscow Uprising', *Sochineniya*, Vol. XI, p. 147.

These were days of great expectations—and efforts to live up to them. Rosa Luxemburg was writing at a rate which even she, with her enormous capacity for concentration, had never achieved hitherto: analysis, exposition, writing, printing, distributing—the process of revolutionary cognition and its transformation into theory and tactics for Social Democracy. The whirlwind rush of taking the manuscript down to whatever printers could be inveigled or forced into producing it, the surveillance of the printing, the checking, the distribution, and finally once again the mental work of digesting new impressions and ideas from the political process and committing them to paper—all this was pre-eminently Rosa Luxemburg's task. At the same time there was the renewed contact with the leadership, the clandestine meetings and discussions, the possibility of clarifying the Central Committee's policy with her own sharply etched views—above all, the knowledge that at this moment of crisis she was close to the man she loved and admired; no wonder that these few weeks provided the high-water mark of her life for many years to come. We do not know how her colleagues first received her. It is possible that Jogiches may have resented her presence and that their co-operation, however fruitful politically, may have been ringed with a sour edge of personal tension. The bacillus which was to lead to the inward death of their relationship a bare twelve months later may have already been at work in their collaboration.[1] But this was not the moment for personal resentments. For the first time the SDKPiL was at work—in just the circumstances for which it had always prayed: an atmosphere of intellectual clarity and optimism welding together a group of professional revolutionaries long accustomed to each other, men known outside only by their brief and pithy pseudonyms, coming and going mysteriously on their revolutionary business, each one knowing only a part of the whole so that in case of capture the loss would be minimized. And in between all this, the curious interstices of a normal life—at least for Rosa. We often forget that revolutions rarely last twenty-four hours a day—people sleep and talk and eat; they visit relatives and Rosa Luxemburg had a family in Warsaw whom she had only met briefly in transit abroad for the last sixteen years. They were determined to make the most of her return. 'Personally I do not feel quite as well as I should like to. I am physically weak although this is now improving. I see my brothers and sisters once a week, they complain bitterly about it, but *non possumus*.'[2] Beneath the superstructure of

---

[1] See below, pp. 256–9. The evidence for the cause of their break is based on events that relate strictly to the period after Rosa Luxemburg's departure from Warsaw and Jogiches' escape from prison at the beginning of 1907. But I cannot overcome the suspicion—based on some of the doubts and worries expressed in Rosa Luxemburg's letters of the second half of 1905—that the root cause for the failure of their relationship was already inherent at that time.

[2] *Letters to Karl and Luise Kautsky*, p. 103, dated 11 January 1906.

revolutionary excitement, the mundane necessities and arrangements
of life could never be entirely ignored. Even in January 1919, when
Rosa Luxemburg was on the run and armed bands of soldiers were
searching for her all over Berlin, she could still write calmly to her
friend Clara Zetkin that it would be wiser to postpone her visit for a
little while until things had quietened down.

The SDKPiL had entered the revolution at its start in January 1905
with a bagful of ideas which bore little relation to what was actually
happening. Its membership had consisted at the most of a few hundred
secret activists. By February 1906 the party had some 30,000 members,
artisans and proletarians, in spite of the fact that its activities had been
plunged once more into illegality after a brief fortnight of open agitation.[1] In addition, its influence extended over large numbers of workers,
directly or indirectly exposed to its ideas—the wildfire of strikers looking
for intellectual *points d'appui.*

Having rapidly caught up with the revolution, the SDKPiL tried to
turn from following to leading. It was agreed that armed insurrection
was the next step and at the beginning of 1906 Julian Marchlewski was
sent to Belgium to purchase arms.[2] No one knew when, or even whether
the moment for this initiative would ever come; it certainly could not
be dictated by the party but could only take place once the revolutionary
vehicle was driven forward again by the masses. Rosa Luxemburg had
been clear and specific about this all along; only a new wave of action
could provide the necessary stimulus. How then to create the necessary
atmosphere? This was Rosa Luxemburg's task and we must now examine
how she dealt with it.

First, the clear enunciation of a programme. The uniqueness of the
moment and its dialectical possibilities had to be identified and captured.
The programme, always a dynamic instrument, had to exploit these
possibilities to the full and yet lead directly beyond them to the next
stage. It had to be neither utopian nor slack—tension at full stretch was
required. The party had always stood for the destruction of the Tsarist
autocracy as its main revolutionary task. Her analysis of the revolution
was very similar to that of the Bolsheviks—autonomous advance-guard
action by the proletariat to achieve what was essentially a bourgeois
revolution; maintenance of proletarian supremacy to ensure that the
bourgeois beneficiaries of this revolution, fearful of the new proletarian
spectre, did not slip back into the bear-hug of the autocracy. Though

---

[1] Kalabiński and Tych, 'The Revolution in Poland', *Annali . . . Feltrinelli*, p. 247. In
1907 the official figure given to the fifth Russian congress in London was 25,654; see M.
Lyadov, *Itogi londonskogo s"ezda*, St. Petersburg 1907, p. 84.

[2] Feliks Tych i Horst Schumacher, *Julian Marchlewski*, Warsaw 1966, p. 145. See also
Letters to Karl and Luise Kautsky, p. 111, dated 11 January 1906.

the working class must be the motor of these achievements, it did not claim correspondingly exclusive privileges; its action was for the benefit of society as a whole.[1] Here the analysis began to differ sharply from that of the Bolsheviks. There was no talk of any dictatorship, either in words or by implication. Instead, the achievements of the working classes on behalf of society as a whole would provide the conditions for the necessary growth of working-class consciousness out of which the confrontation of the next stage could emerge—proletariat versus *bourgeoisie*, like the situation that existed in Germany. 'These struggles are vital for raising the level of the workers. . . . The political struggle serves primarily to defend the interests of the proletariat and to extend its influence on the legislature and the politics of the state as a whole.'[2] Rosa Luxemburg sharply defined the allocation of roles between the working class as actor and nascent bourgeois society as benefactor:

When it is a case of establishing the political order,' that is a task for the whole people, but when it is a matter of strangling energetically and boldly the remnants of reaction and safeguarding the aims of revolution, that is the task of the class which is the very soul of the struggle, which has brought political maturity and consciousness to the people as a whole—i.e. the sovereign proletariat.[3]

The precise political demand was for a constituent assembly for the whole of Russia, freely elected and with the necessary powers to decide the republican constitution of the state. This constituent assembly would be the new field of battle in which Social Democracy—the organized and most conscious section of the proletariat—would carry out a struggle on two fronts: the final dispatch of reaction, fighting a rearguard battle, and the preparation for the coming assault on the politically maturing *bourgeoisie*. Rosa Luxemburg characterized this struggle in three steps: first, the achievement of the constituent assembly; second, forcing the *bourgeoisie* to remain loyal to the revolution; third, the workers' provisional government to hold the fort until the democratic constitutional forms emerging from the constituent assembly could take effect. Presumably the workers' provisional government would then be replaced and would resign its temporarily arrogated power into bourgeois-republican hands. This of course was the logical consequence of commitment to the step-by-step dialectic which postulated capitalism prior to Socialism and turned the thrust of working-class action away as yet from any specifically proletarian aims—the unsatisfactory impasse from which Trotsky and Parvus tried to break out with their notion of a chain reaction or permanent revolution leading

---

[1] *Czego chcemy? Komentarz do programu SDKPiL*, Warsaw 1906, p. 29.
[2] Ibid., p. 14.
[3] *Rzecz o konstytuancie i o rządzie tymczasowym*, Warsaw 1906, pp. 13–14.

direct to a Socialist solution without a lengthy capitalist 'pause'.[1]

The constituent assembly would then give concrete form to the all-Russian republic which the SDKPiL was already demanding as the programmatic minimum. In addition, all nationalities would be emancipated, with the assurance of freedom for their own cultural development, national systems of education, freedom to use their native language, and autonomy for each ethnic region. The elections would be secret, based on universal, equal, and direct suffrage. Towns and villages would be self-governing and the same electoral prescriptions would apply to urban and rural self-government. Rosa Luxemburg did not allocate any governmental role to Soviets (nor did anyone else) though she was well aware of their significance; these were spontaneous instruments of the struggle but were not to be incorporated into the permanent institutional structure. This conception of Soviets as a means rather than an end still dominated the early thinking of the *Spartakusbund* in Germany twelve years later, and it was not until the *Spartakus* leaders had to face the unwelcome demand of the majority of the SPD for a constituent assembly that they allocated a more positive and permanent role to the workers' and soldiers' councils—inspired by a Russian example itself already out of date![2]

The elective principle ran right through the SDKPiL programme, applying to judges as well as officials at all levels. For the rest, the programme was the impeccably orthodox application of the rights of man as articulated in the French Revolution: equality of all before the law, inviolability of the person, freedom of speech, press association, and assembly; freedom of conscience, and full emancipation of women. To this were added the fruits of recent Socialist discussion in Germany: 'The abolition of a standing army and the creation of an army of the whole people—that is the best guarantee of a country's peaceful development and the best means of facilitating the final liberation from the yoke of capitalism.'[3] From the same source came the demand for compulsory and free education; the abolition of customs tariffs and indirect taxes and their replacement by a progressive tax on income, property, and inheritance; and finally a spread of attractive labour legislation. The influences are clear: the old 'Russian' demand for abolishing the autocracy, the essence of bourgeois legality and equality taken from the classic example of bourgeois revolution in France, and finally the German preoccupation with direct, as opposed to indirect, taxation and a people's militia—with all the contradictions and difficulties inherent in these demands.

---

[1] A detailed comparison with Bolshevik and Menshevik views will not be attempted here. For the latter, see L. Schapiro, *The CPSU* (an anti-Leninist view), and J. L. H. Keep, *The Rise of Social Democracy in Russia*, Chapter VII.

[2] See below, pp. 443, 447–53.   [3] *Czego chcemy?*, p. 47.

Rosa Luxemburg devoted special attention to the problem of autonomy since it was the most touchy subject in Poland and the main point
of opposition to the PPS. The constituent assembly would be all-
Russian; and the basic constitutional forms for the new state must be
centrally decided by one all-Russian body. 'But each country is a
separate entity within Russia, it has a distinct cultural life and its social-
economic forms are different from those of the rest of the country.'[1]
There would accordingly be a *sejm* or national assembly in Warsaw as
well, concerned with those problems which were justifiably and distinctly Polish. Thus the *sejm* would deal with all matters affecting
schools, courts of law, local government offices, and all matters relating
to the national culture. Its authority would be delegated by the Russian
centre and limited to these specific fields; the big political questions
would be settled in Russia—though, of course, the Poles would be
represented proportionately in the central government together with all
other minorities. The fully federal solution propagated by some Liberals
—quite apart from any extreme demands for total independence—was
a bourgeois trick to forestall adequate working-class representation; by
supporting it the Polish workers would only support their class enemies
who played on nationalism as a means of diverting revolutionary energy
into safer channels.[2]

As Rosa Luxemburg had insisted in 1905, the SDKPiL had to take
issue not only with the PPS, its immediate class competitor, but with
the bourgeois parties who had entered the ring of apparent opposition
to Tsarism. The most important of these were the National Democrats
—and the attack on federalism was in effect a reply to Dmowski's compromise solution of the national question. Thus Rosa Luxemburg had
to tread carefully between two contradictory programmes, the PPS and
its demand for revolutionary independence—to be answered by breaking
up the juxtaposition of revolution and independence as mutually incompatible—and the National Democrats' non-revolutionary or reformist federalism, a concession which they hoped to gain from Tsarism—
which in turn had to be denounced by showing that the interests of the
Polish and Russian *bourgeoisie* were identical, and so called for a similar
and joint response on the part of the two working classes. The path was
tortuous, the argument necessarily sophisticated; only Rosa Luxemburg's
skill enabled her to steer between the Scylla and Charybdis of mutual
contradiction. But once again she came up against the old problem of
overstating her case, which had already arisen in 1895; if Polish independence was really so *démodé*, how to make this paper tiger into a
snarling menace? If neither the *bourgeoisie* nor the masses really wanted

---

[1] *Czego chcemy?*, p. 23.
[2] *Rzecz o konstytuancie* . . ., pp. 16–18, 31–3.

independence, then who did? Rosa Luxemburg promoted the general scapegoat of latter-day Marxism for this purpose, the hidden solvent of all difficult class equations—the *petite bourgeoisie*.[1] For years the intellectuals of the Second (and Third) International went on treating the lower middle classes as a dispensable walk-on in their dialectic productions, until in the end this forgotten class suddenly developed its own terrifying strength and extorted a grim revenge from its detractors—in the guise of Fascists and National Socialists.

Though the revolutionaries hardly realized it, the intensification of their efforts in the first three months of 1906 lagged behind the course of events. Precisely at the time Rosa Luxemburg was showering pamphlet upon article to create an intellectual and political framework for the inchoate revolutionary movement, the tide of that movement itself was ebbing fast. The last great efforts of December and early January were followed by only limited ripples which were no longer capable of generating the mass support of workers in Poland or Russia. In 1906 a total of 1,180,000 workers were out on strike, compared with 2,863,000 the year before. Alongside industrial action the persistent, if inarticulate, peasant pressure split up into individual, local acts of terrorism and destruction. For some time the SDKPiL clung to the hope that the pause was merely longer than had been anticipated. At their fifth congress, which assembled in the Galician resort of Zakopane from 18 to 23 June, the delegates agreed almost unanimously that a resumption of the revolution could shortly be expected. Accordingly, new measures were planned to provide better organizational control over the next mass action, to point it more sharply at the heart of the government's defences. The struggle had to become more political, better organized, above all more disciplined and effective. Since the SDKPiL had now officially joined the newly reunited RSDRP, special emphasis was laid on the all-Russian unity struggle. Though both Rosa Luxemburg and Leo Jogiches were inevitably absent, Julian Marchlewski opened the congress and the crucial report on revolutionary achievements was presented by that most eminent practitioner of agitation and discipline, Feliks Dzierżyński.

Soon, however, the ebb of the revolution had to be recognized even by the optimists. The Tsarist authorities had gone over to a counter-offensive in March 1906—the first for over a year. A wave of arrests swept over the cities, sometimes followed by summary executions. The police redoubled their efforts to penetrate the revolutionary organizations with their spies. Frequent appeals were issued to the army to collaborate closely with the civil authorities. At the same time the growth

---

[1] *Rzecz o konstytuancie* . . ., p. 37. See also *Program federacji, czyli PPS w błędnym kole*, Warsaw 1906, pp. 10–13.

of trade unions, though intended to increase and organize the revolutionary potential of the workers, in fact diverted their energies from
political action into more immediate economic demands. Thus the
efforts of the SDKPiL to keep the newly emerging unions 'political' to
a large extent failed, so much so that when trade unions were later
made legal by the government the Social-Democratic leaders had become sceptical of their value; Rosa Luxemburg for one saw no point in
re-creating in Polish conditions and with the blessing of the authorities
precisely those self-centred and undisciplined trade-union figures with
whom she had been bickering in Germany since 1900. In any case, the
strongest influence in the new trend for industrial organization did not
come from either Socialists or Social Democrats but from the National
Democrats, who formed their own trade unions to compete with the
Socialists. By now this party, with its programme of compromise and
concession, began to exercise a growing influence on the exhausted and
somewhat disillusioned workers. It stood for consolidation of the benefits
obtained and limited co-operation with the authorities as long as they
remained in a mood for concessions—and long after. The unemployment
and hardship—'la plaie de la révolution'—was taking its toll; there were
lockouts rather than strikes, culminating in the great struggle at the
Poznański works in Łódź at the end of 1906.

The SDKPiL would not—indeed could not—admit formally
that the revolution was coming to an end, they observed the disintegration of mass action into fisticuffs with considerable concern. They too
had lost much of their leadership to the police drag-net—Rosa Luxemburg and Leo Jogiches immured in the notorious Pavilion X, Marchlewski arrested but not recognized and shortly released, Leder also
arrested and awaiting trial. The Central Committee withdrew to
Cracow in the spring, leaving its most experienced conspirators Hanecki
and Dzierżyński in Warsaw. The battle against the authorities had
degenerated into costly clashes with the militant supporters of the
National Democrats, and the leadership was obliged to advise against
what they described as pointless brawls—both between the two Socialist
parties and between the workers organized by the Socialists and Liberals
respectively.[1] The practical period of the revolution was over; the time
had come for digestion—and theoretical analysis. Once again it was
Rosa Luxemburg's turn to move to the centre of the stage. But for the
moment there was the bare and brutal question of her survival.

At the end of January 1906 Rosa Luxemburg had written to Karl

---

[1] *Czerwony Sztandar*, 11 June 1906, No. 76, and 19 June 1906, No. 77. The appeals have
the suggestive titles 'Walka ideowa zamiast walki na pię ści' (Fight with ideas instead of
fighting with fists), and (Walka rewolucyjna czy rewolucyjne awanturnictwo?' (Revolutionary struggle or revolutionary hooliganism?).

Kautsky that 'Luise is a thousand times right in wishing me back in Berlin. I would take off at once for that destination were it not for the fact that I must first finish several things here and then go to St. Petersburg for the "family celebration" [party congress].'[1] The news from Berlin, with the report of mass strikes in Hamburg and the counter-offensive by the German trade-union leaders, made Rosa feel restless. Once more the revolutionary grass began to seem greener in the other valley. She planned to return to Berlin in mid-March. Her colleagues thought the situation more dangerous for her than ever in Warsaw and she had anyhow magnificently fulfilled her immediate tasks of exposition and propaganda. Accordingly, Rosa Luxemburg got her German journalist's pass visa'd for her return journey and began to make definite arrangements for departure.

But the axe fell too soon. Sunday 4 March (new style) was a mild, muggy day which broke the winter with a slushy thaw. A police raid on the house of one Countess Walewska flushed two unexpected lodgers out of bed, German journalists whom the police suspected of being Polish revolutionaries—though they flourished papers with the names of Anna Matschke and Otto Engelmann. It seems that the certainty of Rosa Luxemburg's presence in Warsaw had finally been obtained by press reports from Germany; the right-wing papers carried denunciatory stories about Russian revolutionaries in Germany at the time.[2]

The two, man and women, were hauled off to the Town Hall loudly maintaining aliases and innocence. Armed with definite suspicions, the police raided the home of Rosa's sister and soon uncovered photographs. Pretence was no longer possible. Jogiches did better; his alias was broken only at the beginning of June, again perhaps through identification from Germany. The German government certainly did everything possible to collaborate with the Russian police.

Rosa Luxemburg accepted her lot with fatalistic irony.

This way will have to do just as well. I do hope you won't take it too much to heart. Long live the Re . . . and everything connected with it. In some respects I even prefer sitting here to arguing with [my German trade-union opponent] Peus. They caught me in a pretty undignified position, but let us forget about that. Here I am sitting in the Town Hall where 'politicals', ordinary criminals and lunatics are all crowded together. My cell is a veritable jewel; with its present ornaments (an ordinary single cell for one person in normal times) it now contains 14 guests, fortunately all of them political cases . . . I am told that these are really conditions approaching paradise, for at one time 60 people sat together in one cell and slept in shifts. . . . We are all sleeping like kings on

---

[1] *Letters to Karl and Luise Kautsky*, p. 108.

[2] The connection is suggested by Frölich, p. 136. He attributes the identification of Rosa Luxemburg as Anna Matschke to an article in the conservative *Post*. I am informed by Dr. Tych that there is documentary evidence that the police action was triggered off by the *Post* article.

boards on top of each other, next to each other, packed like herrings, but we manage nicely—except for the extra music provided; for instance yesterday we got a new colleague, a mad Jewess, who kept us breathless for 24 hours with her lamentations . . . and who made a number of politicals break out into hysterical sobs. Today we finally got rid of her and there are only three quiet *meshuggene* left. . . . My own spirits are as always excellent. For the present my disguise is still working, but I suppose it won't last long. . . . Taken by and large, the matter is serious, but we are living in serious times when 'everything that happens is worth the trouble'. So cheer up, and don't worry. Everything went *excellently* during my lifetime . . . my health is quite all right. I suppose I shall soon be transferred to a new prison since my case is serious.

1. Pay my rent, I shall pay back everything promptly, and with many thanks.

2. Send an order for 2,000 Austrian *kronen* at once to Mr. Alexander Ripper at the printing press [a Warsaw address supplied] giving as sender Herr Adam Pendzichowski. Leave *all further possible demands* from that quarter unheeded. . . .

4. Pay out no money apart from this, *without an order from me*, unless perhaps upon demand by Karski [Marchlewski] otherwise not. . . . Dear Karl, for the time being you must take over the representation of the Social Democracy of Poland and Lithuania in the International [Bureau]. Send them official word to this effect; eventually travel to meetings will be refunded. . . . News of my arrest must not be published until the complete unveiling [the breaking of Rosa's alias]. After that, however—I will let you know when—make a noise so that the people here will get a scare. I must close, a dozen kisses and greetings. Write me direct to my address: Frau Anna Matschke, Town Hall Jail, Warsaw. Remember I am [here as] an associate editor of *Neue Zeit*. But of course write carefully. . . .[1]

Whatever fate might await her, there were practical details to attend to both for the party and for herself. Only in such moments of stress did Rosa tackle her financial problems with calm efficiency!

Conditions in the Warsaw jails were truly chaotic. Each police razzia brought in more prisoners to the already overcrowded jails and the task of identification and questioning was at first carried out haphazardly. The whole thing was run in the classic Tsarist tradition, brutality combined with inefficiency. After a few days Rosa was moved from the Town Hall to Pawiak prison, and then on 11 April to the notorious Pavilion X of the Warsaw Citadel outside the city on the banks of the Vistula. This was the fortress for dangerous political criminals—the place where the nationalist revolutionaries of 1863 and the first members of *Proletariat*, all major public enemies, had at one time been incarcerated. The government saw little point in sophisticated distinctions between revolutionary opponents. Soon Rosa's family obtained permission to visit her, and found their sister encased 'in a real cage consisting of two layers of wire mesh or rather a small cage that stands

---

[1] *Letters to Karl and Luise Kautsky*, pp. 113–15, dated 13 March. The letter must have been smuggled out.

freely inside a larger one so that the prisoner can only look at visitors through this double trellis work'. Rosa Luxemburg recalled the scene many years later—when she was trying to cheer up the wife of another convict, Karl Liebknecht.

It was just at the end of a six-day hunger strike in prison and I was so weak that the Commanding Officer of the fortress had more or less to carry me into the visitor's room. I had to hold on with both hands to the wires of the cage, and this must certainly have strengthened the resemblance to a wild beast in a zoo. The cage was standing in a rather dark corner of the room, and my brother pressed his face against the wires. 'Where are you?' he kept asking, continually wiping away the tears that clouded his spectacles.[1]

Her family naturally set to work at once to get her out. Their first suggestion was an appeal for clemency to Count Witte, the Russian premier. This Rosa refused out of hand. The next problem was the establishment of her German nationality. This had to be proved and not merely asserted; there were agonized letters to Berlin and endless but inevitable delays in reply.[2] Her family intended to couple this with an appeal to the German Consul for intervention on her behalf, which Rosa Luxemburg again resisted; but they approached the German authorities regardless. At the end of June her brother briefly visited Berlin to complete the most important part of the release formalities— the raising of money for bail or ransom.

Rosa Luxemburg's crime against the state was one of the most serious, and her friends were well aware of it. Henriette Roland-Holst badgered the Kautskys for news, and so did Clara Zetkin and the Mehrings. Bebel asked for good wishes to be conveyed and assurances of help if possible. Kautsky transmitted all these messages to his acquaintances in the SDKPiL.[3] In return he begged Warszawski for the latest news, but the latter was unable in good conscience to allay the fears in Berlin. Money was still the most helpful alleviator of tension with the Russian bureaucracy.

Some news of Rosa, as I promised. . . . Matters are very bad. The threat of a court martial was real enough. We decided to force the issue with money. First thing was to get the indictment changed to another paragraph. This succeeded. . . . Next, it will probably come to an amnesty, but one from which Rosa will be excluded. We are doing our best to get things moving, so that only those paragraphs are listed [in the indictment] which would not exclude Rosa [from

---

[1] *Letters from Prison*, Berlin 1923, p. 17, dated 18 February 1917.
[2] See letter from Rosa Luxemburg's brother to Arthur Stadthagen, 26 June 1906, *Briefe an Freunde*, p. 34. It appears from this exchange that the telegraphic code of the Luxemburg family business in Warsaw was 'Luxemburgeois'—an ironic address for a revolutionary Socialist.
[3] Correspondence in Kautsky Archives, IISH.

an amnesty]. Perhaps tomorrow or the day after tomorrow I may be in a position to send better news.[1]

His warnings had the required effect in Berlin and Josef Luxemburg was able to collect 3,000 roubles, the sum demanded as bail, when he appeared in person. The money almost certainly came direct from the SPD executive, though Rosa probably did not know this at the time.[2] She was as always determined to maintain her revolutionary posture to the last and ask for no help, either from the German authorities or from the party. The SDKPiL leadership supplemented their financial persuasion with an unofficial threat of reprisal; if anything happened to Rosa they would retaliate with action against prominent officials.

Though her spirit was high, Rosa's health was rapidly deteriorating and the prison doctors could easily justify an official release on bail for reasons of health. The reaction of many months of feverish activity had taken its toll. Her hair began to turn grey, a medical commission reported in June that she was suffering from 'anaemia, hysterical and neurasthenic symptoms, catarrh of the stomach and dilation of the liver'. Though these reports were probably greased into exaggeration, she herself reported to her friend Emmanuel Wurm that she looked 'yellow' and felt 'very tired'.[3] The discipline of Social Democracy causes revolutionaries to cast almost identical shadows in the sun; but once immured in prison and darkness their peculiar personality takes unhindered charge. Parvus in the Peter-Paul fortress in St. Petersburg merely lamented his fate; he was unable to think or write one word, as though paralysed. Trotsky in a cell near by simply abstracted himself from reality and used the welcome opportunity of solitude to complete his processes of revolutionary digestion. The theory of permanent revolution was worked out in its full logical implications in jail—as though he had enjoyed the seclusion of an Oxford college. Rosa, having to share her cell, was unable to think quietly for long enough to write more than scraps of manuscript which were smuggled out of jail. But for the rest, she talked and preached and diffused revolution to the immediate circle

---

[1] Adolf Warszawski to Karl Kautsky, 15 May 1906, IISH Archives, D XXIII, 64.

[2] The evidence for this is circumstantial but I consider it conclusive. Certain suggestions were to be made from time to time about her ungratefulness when she developed her open oppositional tendencies after 1910. The reference was clearly to some special obligation on her part to the SPD leadership. When in 1907 Bebel formally offered her a sum of money on behalf of the executive to restore her depleted finances, she refused the idea of 'further payments' as she did not want to be 'kept' by the executive. (Luise Kautsky's statement to Werner Blumenberg in Amsterdam.) Finally, and most important, Bebel wrote to her peremptorily after her release in July and ordered her back to Berlin. Clearly he was in a position to justify such a command. See *Letters to Karl and Luise Kautsky*, p. 122; also Frölich, p. 139.

[3] *Briefe an Freunde*, p. 41, letter dated 8 July 1906.

of her fellow inmates, and her letters show an aggressive and determined cheerfulness which, broken only by a few desperate moments, she was to maintain throughout the long and much drearier imprisonment during the First World War.

On 8 July 1906 she was finally released, the result of threats and pleas to the authorities, the medical diagnosis, and most of all the charm of money. She was free—but not allowed to leave Warsaw. There was not much work for her to do. The revolution had receded and the main body of the leadership had moved back to Cracow. A few articles for *Czerwony Sztandar*, polemics against Dmowski, and advice to the workers—the last parting shots of a party fighting a rearguard action.[1] Her main concern now was to get out of Warsaw altogether. The public prosecutor in Warsaw to whom her file had been handed was still having difficulty with her German nationality. Frequent calls at the dispersed offices of an inefficient bureaucracy brought some of the informal contact which exists even under the harshest government; a gossipy Russian official gleefully told her that even if the Russians let her go, the German police had already asked for her expulsion at a specific point on the border. A prosecution was now pending against her in Germany for seditious remarks at the Jena congress a year before.[2] But the main hurdle had been overcome with her release from prison; she was out of the clutches of the police and the rest was a matter of time and formalities. Finally, on 8 August (new style) she was allowed to leave Warsaw with instructions to report to the police in Finland, whither she was bound. By now her programme had crystallized: a month or so in Finland close to the Russian revolutionary leaders gathered there, and the preparation of a considered analysis of the events she had witnessed—for the benefit of German readers. For it was now clear that the next important step must be her return to Germany in time for the next party congress. Germany was once more to be the centre of her activities—her impact heightened by the lessons she would be able to impart to her staid but fascinated hearers.

Rosa Luxemburg had missed the SDKPiL congress of June 1906 and, perhaps more important still, the great unification congress of the Russian party at which the SDKPiL had finally pledged its adherence. The gathering of the clans originally intended for St. Petersburg in February had never taken place; owing to police pressure, neutral Stockholm had been judged safer. A new feeling of unity and co-operation appeared to have swept through the RSDRP. It was the ideal moment for Rosa Luxemburg to exercise her influence on the Russian leaders. Above all, she wanted to see what these Bolsheviks, with their

---

[1] See *Czerwony Sztandar*, 30 August 1906, No. 102, pp. 1–2.
[2] *Letters to Karl and Luise Kautsky*, p. 126, letter dated 11 August 1906.

nearly successful Moscow rising, were really like.

At the outbreak of the revolution the leaders of the SDKPiL, and Rosa Luxemburg in particular, had been orientated towards the Mensheviks. The personal breach with Plekhanov was never repaired, but Rosa Luxemburg had managed for a time to achieve polite and reasonably friendly relations with Akselrod, Dan, and particularly Potresov. But throughout 1905, as Menshevik policy developed, Rosa Luxemburg became increasingly critical of the new Menshevik *Iskra*; in private her comments were couched in a tone of increasing asperity. But as long as there was still hope of persuading Martov, Akselrod, and Potresov of the errors of their ways it was better not to polemicize against them in public. 'I am all for not making it excessively difficult for them to come over to us by too sharp a polemic—merely for the sake of words. I would rather try and get their agreement for the wording of the resolution.'[1]

Above all, Rosa Luxemburg was determined not to be drawn into the whirlpool of Russian party squabbles, and tried to prevent Kautsky and other prominent Germans from becoming involved. Whenever she was called upon—and even when she was not—she advised caution and diffidence towards the emissaries of both Russian camps who were now beginning to solicit Berlin for sympathy and particularly for material help. She warned the SPD against placing too much credence on the boastful assertions of each of the Russian factions that they alone represented the party as a whole; when the Bolsheviks held a conference at Tammerfors in Finland and claimed the authority of a full party congress, she warned the Germans that the conference resolutions should not be republished in Germany at their face value.[2]

If anything, Rosa Luxemburg was anti-Lenin rather than pro-Menshevik. Her criticism of the Mensheviks certainly did not make the Bolsheviks any more attractive. *Bolszyństwo*—as it was known in the Polish party—was still a synonym for narrowness, obstinacy, and unreason; any trace of it in Polish attitudes was to be deplored and eradicated.[3]

When Rosa Luxemburg reached Warsaw and discussed the December

---

[1] Jogiches letters, mid-October 1905, IML (M).

[2] *SAZ*, 20 June 1905.

[3] Once approval of the Bolsheviks had come to be the touchstone of orthodoxy, the attitude of Rosa Luxemburg and the Polish leaders towards the Russian faction became the subject of detailed Communist study and commentaries. See Introduction by A. Krajewski to Jogiches letters, *Z Pola Walki*, 1931, Nos. 11–12, p. 178: also 'The SDKPiL in the revolution of 1905–7', ibid. For a modern view of the same old problem, see Jan Sobczak, 'The anti-Menshevik position of the SDKPiL in questions of the intra-party struggle in the RSDRP in the period between the fourth and fifth RSDRP congresses', *Iz istorii polskogo rabochego dvizheniya*, Moscow 1962, pp. 58–102; also the polemics between Roman Werfel and Julian Hochfeld in *Po Prostu*, February–March 1957, reprinted in Adam Ciołkosz,

events in both St. Petersburg and Moscow with her colleagues, she found quite a different attitude. Criticism of the regrettable tendency to overrate Russian liberalism, which had already caused some minor if sharp squabbles with the Mensheviks in 1905, now turned into something close to condemnation of Menshevik pusillanimity in St. Petersburg and corresponding admiration for the Bolshevik Soviet in Moscow. Things looked quite different in Warsaw than in Berlin. The Bolsheviks had at least attempted armed insurrection and the Polish Social Democrats had also committed themselves to this essential next stage. Rosa Luxemburg purveyed the December events in Moscow to Polish readers with sympathy and enthusiasm.[1] More significantly, the Poles accepted the Bolshevik version of events in both Moscow and St. Petersburg supplied by Lenin's emissary who passed through Warsaw on his way to Berlin.

Why this rapid change? By the beginning of 1906 both Bolsheviks and Mensheviks had worked out their version of revolutionary strategy; Lenin with his slogan of democratic dictatorship of proletariat and peasantry, the Mensheviks with their more orthodox support for a bourgeois revolution. Lenin particularly had given much thought to immediate tactics, and in one of his most clear-cut articles had contrasted his own prescription with that of his opponents.[2] The Poles largely agreed with the Bolsheviks—though they themselves did not work out a slogan of their own in reply until 1908. The main difference between Bolsheviks and Mensheviks was largely over the function of the proletariat in the current revolution, which—both sides were agreed—could only reach the limits of a bourgeois-democratic one. Plekhanov allocated the proletariat a secondary, supporting role to the *bourgeoisie*, who at the present state of history must still be the main spearhead of attack against the feudal remnants of absolutism; for Lenin and Rosa Luxemburg, on the contrary, the proletariat would—indeed must—be the prime mover in the creation of a bourgeois capitalist society, liberal democracy within which the proletariat could then go on to develop its anti-capitalist struggle.

But what was at issue here was not in the last resort only a question of sophisticated Marxist interpretation. The SDKPiL decided that the Bolsheviks had shown themselves as the activists of the Russian revolu-

---

Róza Luksemburg a rewolucja rosyjska, Paris 1961, pp. 233–56. But today the Poles have consigned the problem to history and the historians. See the mere passing reference to this question in official ideological evaluation of the SDKPiL. e.g. Feliks Tych, 'On the 70th anniversary of the foundation of the SDKPiL', *Nowe Drogi*, July 1963, No. 7(170), pp. 25–37.

[1] 'Armed revolution in Moscow', *Czerwony Sztandar*, 3 January 1906, pp. 1–2.

[2] 'Two tactics for Social Democracy in the democratic revolution', *Sochineniya*, Vol. IX, pp. 1–119.

tion and therefore became the natural allies of the equally active Poles. At the fourth, or unity, congress of the RSDRP in Stockholm in April 1906 the Bolsheviks unrolled the red carpet for the Poles. They in return helped the Bolsheviks to obtain a majority on several important matters before the congress. Representatives of the SDKPiL, as the only Poles admitted to the congress, now joined the Central Committee of the Russian party. Informally, a curious parallelogram now came into being: on one side SDKPiL and Bolsheviks, on the other Mensheviks and PPS-Left—though the latter were outside the Russian movement. This alignment, at first the incidental product of similar attitudes and programmes, was soon reinforced by more specific support. Beneath the formal appearance of unity both Russian factions retained their separate existence and organization, especially the Bolsheviks; both looked for allies and the two sets of Poles, too, were keen to have formal Russian support for their unceasing polemics against each other. But this was yet to come. For Rosa Luxemburg and her colleagues one of the most important achievements of the revolution in the year 1906 was the formal embodiment of party unity at the Russian congress—a unity which they would fight hard to maintain in the coming years and which in the last resort was even more important to them than any alliance with the Bolsheviks.

Rosa arrived in Finland in the second week of August. The revolutionary leaders had established themselves at Kuokkala, in the comparative safety of Finland but within easy reach of St. Petersburg. Their life followed a curious routine—stealthy visits to the capital during the day and then, after the evening return to quiet Kuokkala, the long, smoke-shrouded sessions into the early hours. Rosa Luxemburg spent much of her time with Lenin and his immediate Bolshevik circle. She had met him personally only once before, during 1901 in Munich, through the good offices of Parvus who, in the early halcyon days of *Iskra*, had been the only contact with German Social Democrats which Russian conspiratorial caution had permitted. Now at last, after polemics and dislike at a distance, they got to know each other well. Evening after evening she sat in Lenin's ground-floor flat in the house of the Leiteisen family in Kuokkala and talked over the Russian revolution at length with Lenin, Zinoviev, Kamenev, and Bogdanov.[1] She made a considerable impression on them; 'the first Marxist who was able to evaluate the Russian revolution correctly and as a whole'.[2] A personal sympathy between Lenin and Rosa Luxemburg—based, like all Lenin's friend-

---

[1] N. Krupskaya, *Memories of Lenin*, p. 112. From memory Krupskaya wrongly gave the date as June and the place as St. Petersburg.

[2] See G. Zinoviev, *Zwei grosse Verluste* (speeches at the session of the Petrograd Soviet, 19 January 1919), Petrograd 1920, p. 18.

ships, on mutual intellectual respect—was born at this time and was to survive for six years until party differences drowned it once more in the froth of polemics. Even then a spark of personal sympathy always survived the renewed hostilities.

Fascinating though they were, these discussions were secondary to Rosa Luxemburg's main purpose in Finland. The Hamburg provincial organization of the SPD had commissioned her to write a pamphlet on the Russian revolution in general and the mass strike in particular. This was to serve as a text for the forthcoming SPD congress at Mannheim at which Rosa Luxemburg planned to make her dramatic reappearance in the German party. It was also to be Rosa's considered verdict on the great events of the past year. Most of her time in Finland was devoted to this work. She stayed in the country house or *dacha* of a woman painter and party comrade—close to but not immersed in the endless Russian discussions and their meetings and committees; a little haven of peace and quiet all to herself and highly conducive to intellectual activity. With her interest focused more and more on the coming return to Germany, she pressed the Kautskys for copies of the most important German newspapers, to help her research and to make her familiar once more with the scent of German circumstances. What she read failed to please her—naturally enough; but all the same she was bursting to get back into the familiar fray. Her health was rapidly recovering and with it her usual state of mind returned—an increasing impatience to be back at work. She was impatient also to get news of the impending prosecution against her; she had no wish to be put 'behind bars preventatively as soon as the tip of my nose smells royal Prussian liberty (as you know with me the nose always projects before anything else)'.[1] But it was difficult for her friends to give her the required information; the case was still pending and the public prosecutor, undisturbed by her thirst for knowledge, was still considering proceedings against Bebel as well as Rosa Luxemburg.[2]

The prospects she was leaving behind in Russia seemed politically bleak. Even Warsaw was better than St. Petersburg—'where no one in the street seems to be aware of the fact that there is such a thing as a revolution any more'.[3] But though she might claim to 'itch' to get back

[1] *Letters to Karl and Luise Kautsky*, p. 119, dated 7 April 1906.

[2] Jena, where the 1905 congress had taken place, was in Thuringia and the case was therefore the responsibility of the provincial authorities. The public prosecutor was advised by his Reich superiors that there was no hope of obtaining a conviction against Bebel but every prospect of one against Rosa Luxemburg. Report of Dept. of Justice (*Reichsjustizamt*) to Reich Chancellor, 17 October 1905, in *Archivalische Forschungen*, Vol. 2/I, *Die Auswirkungen . . . auf Deutschland*, p. 140. The authorities were visibly determined to 'get' Rosa once more.

[3] *Letters to Karl and Luise Kautsky*, p, 135, dated 26 August 1906.

to Warsaw, the pull was personal rather than political—and in any case such a journey was out of the question. Her family had reported that police were everywhere; friends and relations were in 'real danger of their lives at every step'. The fate of her fellow prisoners was a solemn warning. Some of them were dealt with by administrative decree, but Jogiches for one was to be put on trial. It had taken months to establish his identity, but once the police had broken his alias—in spite of Rosa's efforts to help preserve it with German affidavits—he had to face not only charges of 'plotting to overthrow by armed violence the monarchical form of government as laid down in the constitution' but even the ironical addition of 'trying to obtain the independence of Poland'. The military command of the Warsaw district was not interested in fine distinctions between different types of revolutionaries. His trial eventually took place in January 1907. The indictment covered Rosa Luxemburg as well, though of course she refused to appear in person. Jogiches refused to plead or even to speak; he remained contemptuously silent throughout the three-day trial. He was convicted of high treason as well as military desertion—like thousands of other émigrés of every political complexion, he had evaded military service in 1891 by going abroad. The sentence was harsh—eight years' hard labour in Siberia and lifelong enforced residence there. But like Parvus and Trotsky he escaped, actually just before the departure of his transport; an escape which Hanecki had helped to organize by bribing a policeman.[1] By this time Rosa Luxemburg had been back in Germany for some months.[2]

She left Kuokkala on 14 September 1906. There was still no certainty about her own situation in Germany—whether the Prussian police would meet her off the boat with a warrant for her arrest. Now she no longer cared—to hell with ever-cautious lawyers who advised her to await the endless procrastinations of the imperial judiciary. The people in Hamburg urged her to stay for a few days in order to look through the proofs of her manuscript which she had sent them two weeks earlier. Her reading of the German press in recent weeks had already produced a welcome sense of combat; its mealy-mouthed tone made her 'feel ill at Plevna' like the Tsar at the prospect of the Turks—a sure sign that Rosa Luxemburg was fighting fit once more:[3] for her no question of further rest, no slow and complicated theoretical regurgitation of experience. The next and important phase of her work already beckoned impatiently—the German party congress. Clara Zetkin had begged her

---

[1] See J. Krasny, *Tyszka*, Moscow 1925, pp. 18–19.

[2] 'Regarding a sentence of fifteen years' hard labour passed on me, no official notification has reached me from the Military Court; consequently I am in no position to confirm or deny with certainty the truth of this report.' Rosa Luxemburg's letter to *Vorwärts*, 22 January 1907, No. 18, Supplement 1, p. 2.

[3] *Letters to Karl and Luise Kautsky*, p. 132, dated 22 August 1906.

to come to the 'Rhenish music festival at Mannheim'—'you bet I will be there', Rosa sang in reply.

The Russian revolution was the central experience of Rosa Luxemburg's life. The vague dissatisfactions with German party policy—previously felt but not fully analysed—were now to be converted into a definite doctrine by the Russian experience. First she tried to sell it to the German leadership, then to the party as a whole; finally she set up in opposition to the entire SPD establishment and plugged her lesson from her small base year in and year out to all who cared to listen. Significantly, many of her main allies were those who had shared the Russian experience, Marchlewski and the unacknowledged Radek. Clara Zetkin, devoted follower and friend, was able to substitute belief for what she could not evaluate through experience or cognition. By the time the war came Rosa Luxemburg had a fire-tested doctrine of opposition to hand round, to which all those who could not swallow the capitulation of the leadership were able to rally.

But with all her gifts and efforts, Rosa Luxemburg's contribution to the revolution on its Polish home ground was not destined to leave any significant mark. The next step she envisaged was never to be made: the broad proletarian action leading to a democracy in which the proletariat would force both the *conditions* for its inevitable confrontation with capitalism and that confrontation itself. The next step was either a tenuous liberalism without the proletariat, or Lenin with the proletariat-peasantry combination; either an independent Poland or the Stalinist solution to the nationality problem. Neither was welcome to her—especially not in isolation, without a corresponding German upheaval. For anyone reading her Polish articles and pamphlets of 1905–6 the feeling of utopian optimism, all the perceived reality of mass upheavals incarcerated in an arbitrary and often unreal system of beliefs, is overwhelming. The postulated open-endedness of mass action, for ever growing in size and intensity, was exaggerated. No provision was made for the necessary extra push by a disciplined and determined group of leaders, an élite, to overcome the armed resistance of existing society. The basis of mass support from a revolutionary urban proletariat was admittedly greater in Poland than in Russia, the relative land hunger and strength of the peasantry less significant; nevertheless the achievement of a successful social revolution by 'more of the same'—on which Rosa Luxemburg based her whole concept—was clearly out of the question. What was more, her solution of the national question was an extrapolation of highly abstract arguments which had been born and bred from factional squabbles in emigration; in spite of all her sophistication and persuasiveness, the attempt to apply them to a real revolutionary situation proved hopeless. Though for three months she gave herself completely to Polish work and believed profoundly in what she was doing, she herself provided perhaps the most accurate evaluation of her work—when she applied its conclusions elsewhere than in Russian Poland.

The proper place was and continued to be Germany. It was here that the experiences of the Russian revolution were to give birth to a doctrine that was viable and could be tried out in practice. Only in Germany did the social objectification of a participatory mass proletariat really exist, a class which made her social orientation feasible. The concept of masses and leaders as different and conflicting could have meaning only in the German context. All that was needed was a 'Russian' situation in Germany, a 'Russian' will to act, and this Rosa Luxemburg now set about creating—or at least teaching people to recognize it when it existed. For what she brought back from Russia was not in the last resort analysis or knowledge, but the enormous prophylactic of revolution as a state of mind. Irrespective of policy, it was this state of mind which mattered, the moral liberation of doing rather than planning, of participating rather than teaching. Believing this beyond all need of proof or demonstration, Rosa Luxemburg's prescriptions of 1906 should not be judged too harshly in terms of their practical content. They served her as a trial run, not for a successful Russian revolution, but for Germany, for the transposition of Russian action to German circumstances. Rosa Luxemburg summed up the essence of her doctrine simply enough: 'The revolution is magnificent, and everything else is bilge [*quark*].'[1]

---

[1] *Briefe an Freunde*, p. 44, dated 18 July 1906.

IX

THE LOST YEARS,

1906–1909

ON the way back from Finland in early September 1906, Rosa Luxemburg spent a few days in Hamburg with the publisher of her pamphlet on the mass strike. She already knew what she would find.

The people in Hamburg are, according to what they write . . . not at all satisfied; *Vorwärts* goes round the whole problem [of the mass strike] like a cat round its milk. This is of course August Bebel's instruction; he is always calling on others to be restrained, only in order to burst out like a hurricane himself. Only one never knows in which direction that particular thunderstorm will discharge.[1]

Once she had arrived in Hamburg, the new atmosphere of restraint made itself apparent in a curious and significant incident. She had sent her manuscript from Kuokkala a month or so earlier so that it might be ready in time for the Mannheim congress, and now expected merely to read through the proofs. But the SPD executive had put its spoke in at the last moment; the original had to be withdrawn, the printing blocks destroyed—this was a normal precaution against police raids—and a toned-down version issued instead. The object was to avoid disturbing the new balance of relationship with the trade-union leaders. But the provincial organization of the party, who had commissioned the pamphlet—the most forceful strikes of 1905 had taken place in Hamburg—was resentful of this interference. The delay cost Rosa a few anxious days.[2] More important, it meant that the pamphlet could not now circulate as a radical brief for the delegates.

The surf at Mannheim from 23 to 29 September proved in the event to be merely the foam of a fire extinguisher—and most of the participants knew what to expect. 'The brief May flowering of the new revolutionary spirit is happily finished, and the party will again be devoting itself with all its strength to the positive exploitation and expansion of its parliamentary power', the organ of the revisionists had

---

[1] *Briefe an Freunde*, p. 37, from Finland, dated end of August 1906. For a detailed discussion of this pamphlet, *Mass Strike, Party and Trade Unions* see above, pp. 151–60.

[2] *Collected Works*, Vol. IV, p. 389 (Introduction). *Briefe an Freunde*, p. 38, to Arthur Stadthagen, dated 20 September 1906.

written with obvious relief.[1] In such an atmosphere Rosa's revolutionary enthusiasm, fresh from Russia, was painful to behold.

The first thing that struck her disagreeably was the strong aura of secrecy about the arrangements between the trade-union leaders and the party executive. No one at the congress knew their precise nature—except those who had participated in making them; even their existence was a matter only of strong surmise. But how else could one interpret the sudden extraordinary attempt on the part of the executive to claim now that the resolution at the Cologne trade-union congress early in 1905, which had declared the political mass strike unmentionable and had been criticized by the party at the time, was actually a confirmation of the party's mass-strike resolution at Jena later in the year? That resolution had seemed flat enough to Rosa at the time; now it was to be further vitiated by a monstrous reinterpretation. But mass strike apart, what was this new haggling on the quiet between trade-union and party leaders?[2]

Throughout the congress she kept coming back to the specific and most important question of the relationship between party and trade unions.[3] Much play had been made by both executive and trade-union leaders with the dangers of anarchosyndicalism—that old bane of Marxist Social Democracy; in the facile echo of opposition to anarchism a ready means of euthanasia for the whole mass-strike idea could always be found. But by tying the party executive to the support of the trade unions against anyone they chose to label as anarchist, the party was really resigning its political primacy and its independent judgement.

I fear that the relationship of the trade unions to Social Democracy is developing like that of a peasant marriage contract, in which the woman says to the man: 'When we agree, your wishes will prevail, when we disagree, then my wishes will be carried out.' . . . If we kick out the anarcho-socialists from the party, as the executive has proposed, we shall merely set a sad precedent for always finding energy and resolution enough to set clear limits on the left, while leaving the doors wide open to the right. . . . Anarchism in our ranks is nothing else but a left reaction against the excessive demands of the right. . . . At least remain faithful to our old principle: nobody is evicted from the party for his views. . . . Since we have never kicked out anyone on the far right, we do not now have the right to evict the far left.[4]

Rosa Luxemburg sensed that the trade unions were the new factor behind this change; for the first time since 1898 she openly attacked their institutional influence, not merely the attitudes of a few leaders. This followed naturally from her preoccupation with the strike question. The decision and organization of strike movements was in the first

---

[1] SM, 1906, Vol. X, No. 2, p. 914.   [2] Protokoll . . . 1906, p. 261.
[3] Ibid., p. 315.   [4] Ibid., p. 316.

instance a trade-union prerogative; though Rosa strenuously denied that such dependence on union decisions was justified, she none the less followed the bait right into the den where the dragon lived. For the next few years the trade unions were her special target.

It might seem as though this was merely a new symptom of the old battle against revisionism. But this was not how it appeared to Rosa Luxemburg. Trade unions were *sui generis*; they were not interested in the theoretical exposition of their attitudes and, unlike Bernstein, could not be attacked with the two-pronged pitchfork of theory and practice. The trade unions were a far more elusive and yet substantial enemy, well dug in and organized. The only way to deal with them was to impose the supremacy of the party on them from above, and later to assert the more revolutionary view of mass action from below. It was a pincer movement of short duration, for it assumed what in fact proved illusory—the willingness of the party to impose its concepts on the unions, or even, indeed, the existence of more revolutionary concepts in that party. The next few years witnessed a shift of emphasis. The party arm of the pincers withered away, while that of the revolutionary masses developed increasing blood and muscle.

For the moment, however, the best way to get at the trade-union leadership was still by pushing the party executive as the supreme fount of all authority and wisdom. In 1906 this still seemed possible, in spite of a temporary setback. But it required tact. It was no use just contrasting her Russian experiences with the new negative attitude of the German party, merely preaching the example of Russian enthusiasm against the organized conservatism in Germany. Rosa Luxemburg was sensitive enough to the atmosphere to alter her approach between her first speech and her closing remarks four days later. By that time it seemed that she was really defending the executive against the encroachments of wrong-headed and malignant robots from the trade unions.[1]

A personal participant in the great events in Russia, she was naturally in great demand at local public meetings. At one meeting in Mannheim the crowd brushed aside the formal agenda with shouts of: 'Tell us about Russia.' Before this enthusiastic audience there was no need to adjust to the finer questions of internal party relations. These were the crowds, the masses who would ultimately make and unmake the party's policy. And what they wanted to hear was precisely what Rosa really wanted to talk about—the lessons of Russia.

What I have learnt from the Russian revolution is this. As soon as one believes it to be dead, it rises up again. I had intended to stay in bed today as I am not well, but I decided to appear and say a few words about the revolution, in so far

---

[1] 27 September 1906, *Protokoll . . . 1906*, p. 316.

as my strength allows me. My immediate predecessor called me a martyr at the end of his speech, a victim of the Russian revolution. I must begin, therefore, with a protest against this. Those who don't merely study the Russian revolution from afar, but participate in it, they will never call themselves victims or martyrs. I can assure you without exaggeration and in complete honesty that those months spent in Russia were the happiest of my life. Rather I am deeply saddened by the fact that I had to leave Russia and come back to Germany. . . . Abroad the picture created of the Russian revolution is that of an enormous blood-bath, with all the unspeakable suffering of the people without a single ray of light. That is the conception of the decadent middle classes but not of the working classes. The Russian people have suffered for hundreds of years. The suffering during the revolution is a mere nothing compared to what the Russian people had to put up with before the revolution, under so-called quiet conditions. . . . How many thousands have died of hunger, of scurvy, did anybody ask how many thousands of proletarians were killed at work, without any statistician bothering in the slightest? . . . Compared to this, the present sacrifices are very small.

Now the other side of the coin. While previously the Russian people lived on without the slightest hope of escaping their terrible misery, they now know why they are fighting and why they are suffering. . . . Today the middle classes are no longer at the head of our movement, and the proletariat has taken over the leading role. It knows full well that the introduction of Socialism overnight is not possible, that nothing other than a constitutional bourgeois state can be created. . . . But the very fact that this state will have been created by the efforts of working men's hands will give the proletariat an understanding of its own role and the benefits it must derive from it . . . it is not fighting with the illusions which still beset working classes in 1848, it is fighting for its rights within a bourgeois state, precisely in order to use these rights as weapons against the middle classes in the future.

In conclusion, Rosa drew the essential parallel between East and West.

The Russian events prove that, in line with the general situation, we in Germany must get ready for battles in which it is the masses who will have the last word. The Russian proletariat must be our example, not for parliamentary action but by its resolution and daring in putting the political aims just as high as the historical situation permits. If we are to get anything out of the Russian revolution it must not be pessimism but the highest optimism.[1]

If the SPD congress would not listen to what Rosa Luxemburg had to say about the Russian revolution, at least the people did. For the first time she was appealing to the masses in Germany as a relief from the party leadership's lack of interest.

If Bebel had been angry over her Polish escapade, he was so no longer. He offered her a moderate sum of money to set her on her feet again, since her limited resources had all but disappeared during her activities

---

[1] *Redner der Revolution*, Vol. XI, *Rosa Luxemburg*, Berlin 1928, pp. 26–30. The speech was also reported in *Vorwärts*, 29 September 1906.

in Poland and the subsequent efforts to get her out of jail. But Rosa refused all financial help. She felt she had already accepted too much for her own independence. 'I will not be kept by the executive.'[1] Besides, she had seen the attitude of the executive at Mannheim and was unhappy about it; all the more important to avoid being under any political obligation. Bebel never quite forgave her for her refusal; their relationship became more mistrustful. He was further offended at an incident that took place early in 1907. Rosa and Clara Zetkin had been for a walk on Saturday morning and were to meet Bebel for lunch at the Kautsky's house. They had lost count of the time and arrived late; when Bebel said jokingly that he had feared they were lost, Rosa turned on him with a sour half-smile and said: 'Yes, you can write our epitaph: "Here lie the last two men of German Social Democracy".'[2] Bebel had always had a sneaking admiration for Rosa Luxemburg, but these gadfly attitudes destroyed his small fund of benevolence and made the political fracas a few years later all the more credible. Henceforth Bebel still turned his charm on Rosa from time to time, but always for precise political purposes—and Rosa knew it full well.

Rosa had no precise plans for the future, but there was the beloved flat in Cranachstrasse—the red and the green rooms, the books—and there were the Kautskys, who had so valiantly acted as a communication base during her absence. What a welcome they must have given her, safely returned from the well-reported, but personally quite unimaginable dreadfulness of revolutionary Russia! This should have been the high point of the three-cornered friendship and for some months it was, before Rosa's awful disillusion began to set in with the SPD in general and K.K.—as he was known—in particular. But for the moment she again frequented the Kautsky home and took part in the Sunday sessions when a walk through the fields with Luise Kautsky or Clara Zetkin before lunch would be followed by long discussions with visiting Socialists from all over the world. It was at this time that she met Trotsky, though the meeting did not lead to friendship; Rosa never had a good word to say for or about him. Their situations at the time were somewhat similar, their character and political thinking too individualistic for any chance of intellectual collaboration.[3] More important was

---

[1] This incident was reported by Luise Kautsky to Werner Blumenberg at IISH Amsterdam. I have gratefully to acknowledge my thanks to the late Herr Blumenberg for much background information about Rosa Luxemburg and for illuminating a number of specific incidents—he spoke repeatedly and at length to Luise Kautsky during the Second World War in Amsterdam. Further references to this source will be listed as 'Blumenberg'.

[2] This remark has been variously quoted as being made at some official function. In fact, the information comes from Luise Kautsky via Blumenberg. Like so many of Rosa's epigrams, it became something of a saying in the SPD.

[3] The similarity of *character* is stressed, indeed overstressed, by Deutscher in *The Prophet Armed*, p. 183.

the fact that Rosa much preferred Lenin, with whose faction the SDKPiL was closely collaborating at this time.

At last in November 1906 came the long-awaited holiday in the beloved south with Luise Kautsky; there was all too little time before the coming trial at Weimar in December for her speech at the Jena congress the year before—a whole revolution away. The possibility of this prosecution had dogged Rosa throughout her stay in Warsaw and Finland. Also the *Reichstag* elections for 1907 were in the offing, with an intense bout of campaigning due at the end of December and in the first weeks of the new year. A change and a rest in the sun were essential —the two ladies alone: all the appurtenances—Karl, the children, Granny—were left behind. Perhaps for the last time in her life Rosa let herself go like a child. 'Forgive that crazy Rosa if the whole thing is illegible', Luise wrote at the head of a postcard to her eldest son which Rosa had all but ruined with her surrealist interstices between the lines.[1]

The pale Indian summer of weather and mood did not last long, either personally or politically. In mid-December Rosa took the train back north over the Brenner with a heavy heart, to stand her trial at Weimar, the capital of Thuringia. The Jena speech earned her two months, due to begin the following summer. Meantime there was a lot of work to be done. The government of von Bülow dissolved the *Reichstag* and went to the country on a colonial and nationalist issue which later became known—especially among Social Democrats—as the 'Hottentot elections'. It was a direct, specific attack on the SPD as the permanent internal enemy of Germany's greatness, linked for the occasion with the fortuitous enemy of the moment, the Catholic Centre, which of late had been more than usually critical of the colonial policy of the government.[2] The appeal to nationalist sentiment, coupled with skilful mass agitation copied from the Social Democrats themselves, succeeded beyond all expectations. The SPD won only forty-three *Reichstag* seats instead of the previous eighty-one; all the other parties combined against it.[3] This electoral defeat was to preoccupy the SPD leadership morbidly for the next seven years, as a measure of its apparent image among the electorate; the hitherto progressive successes at each election had been taken for granted as part of the 'inevitability' of Socialism. Now the revolution would have to wait, at least until the lost electoral ground had been recovered; 'easy does it', especially on revolutionary phraseology, now became the official line.

Rosa had been as active as ever in the election campaign, speaking in Berlin and in the provinces. She was now one of the star speakers of the SPD, with an unrivalled grasp of social conditions which she was able

---

[1] Text and partial facsimile in *Briefe an Freunde*, pp. 198–201, dated 5 December 1906.
[2] Prince Bernhard von Bülow, *Imperial Germany*, New York 1914, pp. 208–47.
[3] Schorske, *German Social Democracy*, pp. 60–61.

to translate into clear and striking phrases for popular consumption; moreover she, unlike anyone else in Germany, could speak of revolution at first hand. For the purposes of such an election, a complete truce was declared among factions in the party; revisionists and radicals fell over each other's feet and for a short while the issue simply became Social Democracy against the entire existing régime and all other political parties. This was particularly true at this election, where the government was in effect asking for a vote of confidence for its imperial policy. Henceforward imperialism played a major part in Socialist propaganda, and continued to do so until the First World War.

But the internal party truce did not survive electoral defeat, and for many months to come radicals and revisionists belaboured each other with their respective analyses of the failure. The party executive, though officially neutral and merely distressed by the internal discord, had subtly moved against the radical tactic even before the Mannheim congress. The danger of 'Russian' disorder and fear for the precious, well-built organization of party and trade unions put the dampers on more firmly. Bebel himself, whose attitude had already shocked Rosa Luxemburg at Mannheim—the more so for his having been absent during the early months of 1906 when the change had taken place—now shed almost all his usual equivocation. Rosa was not among those who, like Liebknecht and—unexpectedly—Kurt Eisner, concentrated their fire specifically on imperialism and German militarism, but she still played an important part in defending the radical case in general. She too had her particular angle at this moment—the mass strike as a means of broadening popular support for Socialist policies and keeping Social Democracy on the move. It was left to Kautsky to produce a broad and subtle analysis of the general failure. The *petit-bourgeois* floating voter who had hitherto supported the SPD at elections as a radical democratic party had now deserted it; but he saw this as a consequence of economic trends, as a reaction to the fear of growing Social Democracy—a sharpening of the final line-up of classes—not as a hurricane of straight nationalistic emotion which could temporarily blot out the dialectic process in any society: such a simple explanation was too crude for the fine-toothed Marxist equipment of his mind.[1]

Rosa Luxemburg did not entirely agree, but she reserved her own comments for her close friends—for they went well beyond her public doubts about the party's tactics. 'German party life is nothing but a bad dream, or rather a dreamless leaden sleep', she wrote impressionistically on 20 March 1907, and to Clara Zetkin she wrote at greater tactical length:

Since my return from Russia I feel rather isolated . . . I feel the pettiness and the hesitancy of our party régime more clearly and more painfully than ever before.

[1] *NZ*, 1907–8, Vol. 1, pp. 590–5.

However, I can't get so excited about the situation as you do, because I see with depressing clarity that neither things nor people can be changed—until the whole situation has changed, and even then we shall just have to reckon with inevitable resistance if we want to lead the masses on. I have come to that conclusion after mature reflection. The plain truth is that August [Bebel], and still more so the others, have completely pledged themselves to parliament and parliamentarianism, and whenever anything happens which transcends the limits of parliamentary action they are hopeless—no, worse than hopeless, because they then do their utmost to force the movement back into parliamentary channels, and they will furiously defame as 'an enemy of the people' anyone who dares to venture beyond their own limits. I feel that those of the masses who are organized in the party are tired of parliamentarianism, and would welcome a new line in party tactics, but the party leaders and still more the upper stratum of opportunist editors, deputies, and trade union leaders are like an incubus. We must protest vigorously against this general stagnation, but it is quite clear that in doing so we shall find ourselves against the opportunists as well as the party leaders and August. As long as it was a question of defending themselves against Bernstein and his friends, August & Co. were glad of our assistance, because they were shaking in their shoes. But when it is a question of launching an offensive against opportunism then August and the rest are with Ede [Berstein], Vollmar, and David against us. That's how I see matters, but the chief thing is to keep your chin up and not get too excited about it. Our job will take years.[1]

Here was the left-wing tactic in embryo for the next seven years. Why did Rosa, never given to reticence or fear of publicity, not come out with all this in public, as she did in 1910? Possibly she thought the reaction against the revolutionary mood of 1905 temporary. Kautsky and she were still friends and allies; maybe he advised her against it and she deferred to him yet again. In any case she was now to become curiously remote from German affairs for three years. What she had to say did not fit at all into the current notions of tactics in the party; the leadership was more concerned with the re-establishment of a position believed to have been weakened at the elections than with any attempt to move into sharper conflict with society. To protest one needs *some* echo, either from friends or at least from the imagined support of anonymous masses 'outside', as Karl Liebknecht had in 1916, and Rosa herself in the three years immediately preceding the outbreak of the war.

But at least the partnership with Kautsky in *Neue Zeit* was still flourishing. The two editors took themselves off to Lake Geneva at Easter 1907 for a working holiday to hammer out the policy of the paper in the latest situation and also to give Rosa a further chance to rest and recover her health.[2] As it turned out, this trip with Kautsky was the

---

[1] *Illustrierte Geschichte der deutschen Revolution*, Berlin 1929, p. 62. The letter must be dated the beginning of 1907. Extracts from the letter are quoted by Frölich, pp. 148–9.
[2] *Letters to Karl and Luise Kautsky*, p. 137.

start of Rosa's disillusionment with the personality of her friend. It was the first time they had been alone together for any length of time and she found him 'heavy, dull, unimaginative, ponderous'; his ideas 'cold, pedantic, doctrinaire'. Worst of all, he was old—a great intellectual sin: 'I had no notion that [Kautsky] already requires so much rest, I took him to be much younger.' Rosa's ideal routine consisted of hard concentrated work followed by a brisk walk, but it was only with great difficulty that Kautsky could be persuaded to join her and she soon gave up trying. Though the disillusion is clear from letters written at the time, she only realized afterwards that this was in fact the beginning of the long decline in their relationship.

She was particularly busy with Polish affairs and continued to be for the next four years; this also helped to make her participation in German affairs sporadic. But in politics silence often means regression. Where she had stood at the centre of things before her departure for Warsaw, she now suddenly found herself on the fringe. Hence she hardly realized the extent of the changes that were taking place in the party leadership, changes of attitudes, of people, and even of institutions. The new opposition was 'official', tame and polite. It preferred to act behind the scenes, 'politically' (which meant diplomatically)—the war-time centre in the making. The building of a real opposition had to begin entirely from scratch.

Now that the drama of the revisionist controversy had petered out, the whole tone of the discussion had altered as well; the tacticians pure and simple were taking over the leadership of the SPD. There were no great issues. The trade-union leaders exercised a quiet but constant pull on the executive, and this was much less easily singled out for attack than the public declarations of a Bernstein or a Max Schippel. Most of the time, the trade-union attitude to controversy was a shrug of the shoulders, *lasst schwätzen* (let them drivel), while they got on with their work.[1] Noske made his first prominent appearance at the 1907 congress at Essen as the party spokesman on national defence and the army—a direct result of the executive's wish to keep that party in tune with the more nationalistic mood shown by the electorate.[2] As usual, the executive's attitude was not of course called 'new'; solid quotations were available to show a tradition of patriotism in the SPD— but then, if one wished to dig for them, quotations were available for almost any attitude. In this atmosphere Rosa Luxemburg, fresh from Russia, was like a fish out of water—and until 1910 there was no specific item on which she could fasten her combative teeth.

[1] *Protokoll . . . 1913*, p. 295, speech by Gustav Bauer, deputy chairman of the Trade Union Commission. Are not all unions the same?

[2] *Protokoll . . . 1907*, pp. 230 ff. Also Gustav Noske, *Erlebtes aus Aufstieg und Niedergang einer Demokratie*, Offenbach/Main 1947, p. 28.

Rosa 'sat out' her jail sentence of two months in June and July 1907. Unlike the time so proudly and impatiently served in 1904, she now was depressed and uncommunicative. There were no bristling, scintillating letters—only silence. She even failed to obtain a mandate to the 1907 SPD congress, for the first time since 1898 (though as the guest of the government she had missed the 1904 congress). The affairs of the Polish and Russian parties, and the International, predominated. From prison she went almost directly to the International congress at Stuttgart on 18 August 1907. There was thus hardly any time for the constituency work needed for a mandate. In any case, since the setback in the *Reichstag* elections, it was becoming uphill work for unattached radicals to get constituency support, unless they were firmly anchored to a local party organization, like Clara Zetkin in Stuttgart.

But political reasons alone cannot account for Rosa Luxemburg's silence and withdrawal. Adversity never depressed her; on the contrary, it usually stimulated the saliva of political controversy.

At the beginning of 1907 a major upheaval took place in her private affairs, perhaps the most important in her whole life. Her relationship with Leo Jogiches underwent a complete change and with it her entire outlook on life and people.

When Rosa Luxemburg left Warsaw for Finland after her release in July 1906 her relationship with Jogiches was intact. As far as she knew he was still in prison and due to be tried; she was extremely anxious about him and her correspondence with Polish friends hints at her anxiety on Jogiches' behalf. In February 1907 Jogiches escaped and lived in hiding for a short while in Warsaw, and then in Cracow, before travelling through Germany in April on the way to London for the Russian party congress in May of that year. During this time he seems to have been helped and looked after by a woman comrade in the Polish party, possibly called Izolska (Irena Szer-Siemkowska). The precise nature of this relationship is not known, though apparently there are some letters in Moscow from her to Jogiches which indicate that, though brief, it was close.[1] It is also not clear how all this came to Rosa Luxemburg's knowledge. The time interval between Jogiches' escape and his appearance in the West was no more than six to eight weeks; a highly conspiratorial person, it is hardly likely that his relationship with Izolska—if indeed it was she—would have been notorious. Most probably he himself wrote to Rosa Luxemburg about it from Cracow,

---

[1] According to my information, these letters are probably in IML(M). The details and dates of Jogiches' escape are in J. Krasny, *Tyszka*, Moscow 1925, p. 19—a very brief but the only reliable account. Krasny (a pseudonym, real name Józef Rotstadt) was himself a colleague of Jogiches and for a short time after 1916 a member of the SDKPiL Central Committee and a leading personality in the early Polish Communist Party.

but since none of the letters received by her survives there is no means of confirmation.

Rosa Luxemburg at once broke off all personal relations. She refused to meet Leo Jogiches or to communicate with him; as a man he was dead for her—though not of course as a party leader. The distinction was clear enough to Rosa, but incomprehensible and unacceptable to Leo Jogiches. They did not meet again until the Russian party congress in London in mid-May 1907, to which they travelled separately. The congress, with its highflown discussions and conspiratorial asides luridly revealing the hidden menace of the meetings between Leo Jogiches and Rosa Luxemburg, was like one of those unexpected emotional precipitations in Dostoievsky's *The Idiot*. In addition to everything else, one of Rosa Luxemburg's brothers who lived in England invited them both to a slap-up dinner during the congress. As Jogiches walked in with her past the potted plants in the entrance to face the smiles and all the food laid out on little tables, he whispered: 'As soon as this dinner is over I shall kill you'—'and this terrible moment was instantly sponged away with laughter and handshakes all round, though not for me'.[1] In the course of this battle of two strong wills, all of which took place *sotto voce* in the swirling atmosphere of a Russian party congress, Rosa succeeded in making three brilliant speeches about the Russian revolution and putting forward the analysis of the SDKPiL.

Whatever Leo Jogiches may have done himself after his escape when en route to Siberia, he was determined not to let Rosa go. Love is an anodyne word; we owe it to two such sharply defined characters to be more specific in our judgement of their relationship. In Jogiches' case— and we have to rely largely on Rosa Luxemburg's interpretation of his motives—jealousy and possessiveness played a large part. Rosa was 'his' and he repeated to her again and again that she could never now be 'free' of him—and indeed she never was, though he later tightened the hold of party discipline more and more as her personal life moved increasingly beyond his horizon. Rosa knew well that she was being punished, and accepted things for that very reason. It is not too fanciful to attribute to his highly personal struggle some of the obstinacy and arbitrariness with which Jogiches later drove an important section of the SDKPiL into secession.

On her side the chief factor was obviously pride. All her life Rosa instantly ruptured any relationship which she felt had been compromised or taken too much for granted. Several times in the next few years she would do so again. In this respect her moral standards were absolute. She had a passion for clarity in personal as well as political relationships: 'I want you to see me as clearly as I can see you', she wrote—knowing

---

[1] Letter to Konstantin Zetkin, May 1907.

full well that clarity is blinding, and can be the most destructive element of all in human relations.

Thus the end of what to all intents and purposes had been her marriage was instantaneous. By one of those coincidences which are normally a novelist's stock-in-trade, a young friend was sitting in Rosa's flat in the Cranachstrasse at the time she heard the brutal news from Jogiches, and she instantly rebounded head over heels into love with him. This was none other than the 22-year-old son of her close friend and colleague, Clara Zetkin. He was full of admiration and already extremely attached to her; as so often, her own unhappiness turned affection into passion. By the end of April they were lovers—a relationship that Rosa quite correctly described as straight out of the pages of Stendhal's *Le Rouge et le Noir* and from which she derived the enormous satisfaction of being lover, mentor, and friend. Perhaps it was not entirely a coincidence. Rosa Luxemburg was one of those people who was able to keep a certain unbridgeable distance from all her friends, political and personal, only because she always had at least one total intimate but one only—a symmetry that is more common in the lives of people with temperament than is usually realized. Passion is curiously exclusive and the need for it irresistible, while promiscuity is passionless —a mere collector's obsession. If it had not been so Rosa, who had temperament enough for ten, would possibly have indulged in the generalized and partial confidence which most people deal out indiscriminately and for which they continually suffer the boomerangs of betrayed confidence.

Jogiches sensed that he had strong cause to be jealous. He still had the keys to the flat that he had once shared with Rosa, and apparently for reasons of political convenience in their work insisted on retaining them. He was able to call at any time during the day and night—and exercised the discretion to the full. He captured one of her letters to Konstantin Zetkin—unaddressed—and the threat to kill her now became a double threat to kill them both. For the next two years he would dash after her during her journeys abroad and in Germany in order, as she thought, to surprise her with her lover. Rosa's purchase of a revolver mentioned by Luise Kautsky was no more than self-protection. Balanced on this razor edge, the situation continued more or less unchanged for the next eighteen months.

In these circumstances Rosa struggled hard to break off all but the most essential party contact with Leo Jogiches and to liberate herself from his incessant demands. 'I am only I once more since I have become free of Leo. . . .' To achieve this liberation it was necessary to come to a satisfactory arrangement about the flat and to ensure that his visits would take place only by arrangement. 'I cannot support this constant shoulder rubbing', she informed him in September 1908. From 1907 onwards her letters are impersonal—wherever possible in the passive or third person without address or salutation. Eventually a satisfactory *modus vivendi* was achieved. And, however much she disliked him personally, she never lost her judgement or her respect for his talents. In July 1909 she wrote to encourage someone who had despaired of his ability to express himself on paper:

Leo for example is totally incapable of writing in spite of his extraordinary talent and intellectual sharpness; as soon as he tries to put his thoughts down in writing he becomes paralysed. This was once the curse of his existence . . . especially since he had to leave the practical work and organization in Russia [on his departure from Vilna in 1890]. He felt completely rootless, vegetated in constant bitterness, finally even lost the capacity for reading since it seemed anyhow pointless to do so. . . . Then came the revolution and quite suddenly he not only achieved the position of leader of the Polish movement, but even in the Russian; in addition the role of leading editor of the party fell into his lap. As before, he doesn't himself write a single line but he is none the less the very soul of our party publications.

And certainly as far as the great bulk of party comrades in the Polish and German parties were concerned—it must be remembered that only the leaders of both parties knew that there had ever been a personal relationship between Rosa Luxemburg and Leo Jogiches in the first place—the two names continued to be spoken in unison.

The break with Jogiches affected all Rosa's relationships. Indeed, it is a watershed in her whole approach to people. She had always been highly critical, but now it became even more difficult to gain her friendship without reservations: 'I am determined to bring even more severity, clarity, and reserve into my life', she wrote in 1908. The immediate effect was to believe nothing of anyone (*'niemandem nichts'*). This scepticism was as much political as personal. Yet, curiously enough, with the halo of the returned revolutionary over her head, she was much in personal demand. Parvus almost besieged her after his own escape from Russia: 'He comes as often as my changeable mood permits'—perhaps too often, for he becomes so 'fiery that I get scared'. But Rosa did develop a soft spot for him and an increasing regard for his intellect. At the end of 1906, as a Menshevist relic, he had still been a 'windbag'; in 1910 she praised his latest book, 'although I am beginning to think that the man is mad'—which with Rosa was an admission of temperament and by no means uncomplimentary.

Apart from Parvus, there was a regular and faithful group of men offering flowers, tickets to the opera, and rides in that new-fangled invention, the motor-car. Gerlach, Kurt Rosenfeld—like Parvus, a friend who had with delicate force to be prevented from turning into a suitor—and of course Hans Diefenbach. In the emotional upheaval of her private life at the time, the latter's quiet and even temperament sometimes grated on her: 'It has long been clear to me that Hans [Diefenbach]'s intelligence has very distinct limits and his pale face and perpetual pessimism is capable of diminishing even the sunniest day in the country.' Diefenbach persevered—whether oblivious of his mixed reception or in spite of it—and earned his reward during the war.[1] Then there was Faisst, 'the master', pianist and special interpreter of Hugo Wolf, who first introduced Rosa Luxemburg to his most fastidious of composers. The point about them was that in one way or another they were all interesting. They made Rosa laugh or weep; if they bored her she soon ceased to be available; and yet they altered nothing of her basic loneliness, compounded from the convolutions of her most intimate private life, the political isolation, and her concentrated work for the party school. Every now and then she wished them all to the devil, only to open her doors once more a week or two later.

She also saw her family intermittently. One of her brothers met her in London in 1907 and another—her favourite—in Italy two years later. The elder sister, severely arthritic, spent some weeks with Rosa at Kolberg on the Baltic. Seized by sudden remorse, Rosa was determined to make her sister's stay outstandingly pleasant and, since she was almost immobile, accompanied her everywhere. The long break before the revolution was now made good. Her family in general and this sister in particular never did manage to understand fully what Rosa's political convictions were or what her party work was about—but they respected both.

[My sister] knows very little about scientific socialism but in her good nature complains bitterly about my brothers who are cowards and have given up all faith in the revolution. She at least believes in it as firmly as I do. At the same time she is foolish enough . . . to want to take the current number of *Przegląd Socjaldemokratyczny* which is lying on my table with her to Warsaw in her pocket and raised her eyebrows in disbelief when I refused.

In the midst of her stay in 'that hole' Kolberg, surrounded by her sister's buzz about her health, and with the lukewarm water of the Baltic lapping at her feet, Rosa wrote the complicated and polemical articles on the national question for the Polish review which represented the quintessence of her thoughts on this subject. No one but Rosa Luxemburg could have produced a highly complicated and theoretical article in such funny-postcard surroundings.[2]

---

[1] According to Luise Kautsky and Blumenberg, Rosa's closer circle of friends believed that after the war she would marry Diefenbach. I have found not a scrap of positive evidence to support this; it may have been mere wishful thinking on the part of her friends —most people like the lives of their friends laid out in simple geometry.

For a period, Rosa's niece Jenny from England (the daughter of the brother who had

The political discomfort of Germany since her return was matched—indeed partly inspired—by a wave of irritation with all things German, one of a series which had kept breaking into Rosa's consciousness since 1898. It seems that she could hardly go abroad without feeling a sense of anticlimax on her return, and the longer she was away the stronger it was. She encouraged her friends to learn Russian, 'which will soon be the language of the future'. To Konstantin Zetkin she wrote repeatedly that he should not take the German situation too seriously; since he was not himself German (he was Russian on his father's side) he could never be contaminated by the political dullness of the Reich. At the end of 1910 she had a chance discussion about Tolstoy with Karl Korn, a Socialist intellectual and critic; the latter's pedantic insistence that Tolstoy was not 'art' roused her to tremendous fury; 'There he stands in the street like a pot-bellied public lavatory [pissrotunde]. . . . In any Siberian village you care to name there is more humanity than in the whole of German Social Democracy. A longing to live somewhere else seized her once more. It was not possible, of course, in spite of—or because of—the unsatisfactory state of the German party; at least not until 'all accounts were settled'—a state of affairs as distant as judgement day. The only means of overcoming her depression was to 'throw myself into the thick of the fight and to drug my suffering heart with a real political set-to'. These words were written in the summer of 1910; the mass-strike agitation, quite apart from its effects on German Social Democracy, had its own stimulating and prophylactic effect on Rosa herself, and she was determined never again to stand outside political controversy.

Did she really enjoy the practical work of agitation and public speaking? Her judgement of the success of any public meeting was often as formal as her view of the 'masses'. The enthusiasm of the audience, the feeling of response, pleased and stimulated her, but all too frequently she translated these reactions into concrete political evidence to justify her policy. At the same time these meetings cost her much nervous energy; she would dash from place to place, spending all day travelling and then conduct her meetings in the evening, sometimes taking the train home at 2 o'clock in the morning after a post-mortem with the local party leaders going on right up to the station platform. She complained of 'leaden headaches', 'a skull bursting with tiredness', especially in the summer, complete inability to eat. At some moments she hated the whole thing: 'As usual I feel sick at the contact with this coagulated

emigrated to England a few years earlier) spent some time in Berlin and was a frequent visitor to Rosa's home. Rosa reports the engagement of this niece in 1912 to a 'nice young man' but without name. It may therefore well be that the last descendants of the Luxemburg family are living somewhere in England.

mass of strange people.' Perhaps the facts should speak for themselves more than her own hurried statements which necessarily varied with her mood and state of health. After 1910 her determination to return to regular agitation was in practice maintained right until the end of her life, except when she was in prison. No doubt there was an element of duty here, but the scale of her efforts exceeded the minimum demands of party obligation, especially since she was in opposition to the party authorities and therefore owed no duty to anyone but herself and her own conscience.

In the summer of 1907 Rosa Luxemburg spoke repeatedly of chucking up everything: 'I would move instantly to the south and away from Germany if I had the slightest notion how to earn a living', she wrote to a friend. But the recipient did not take this too literally and neither should we; it was a recurring theme engendered by impatience, frustration, and the temperamental hatred of Germany and German attitudes which was never far below the surface. The disgust with German organization, though real enough, was also culturally fashionable; it was this which lent the Latin—or even Swiss—south the unmerited attraction of simply being different, above all for someone who really believed that she had fallen 'straight out of the Renaissance by mistake' into a most unsuitable century!

Suddenly, on 1 October 1907, all such talk came to an end, dispelled by an exciting new job which was to keep her busy for at least six months in every year. In 1906 the party had decided to found a Central Party School in Berlin in order to strengthen the work of the existing *Arbeiterbildungsschule*. This dilapidated institution carried on a form of general adult education for Socialist workers and its limited efforts since 1891 had been supplemented by party lecturers who continually travelled the provinces and gave circuit courses. The new creation was to be more of an élite school, to train suitable candidates from constituency organizations and trade unions who would in turn become teachers or activists themselves. Once more the SPD spawned a mirror image of a national function—higher education—the benefits of which Socialists had been unable to share adequately; the state within the state now extended its activity to this field too, as indeed it had to sooner or later.

The idea had been first mooted early in 1906: 'The Russian revolution released the . . . flood of energy and mobility . . . and the desire for discussing fundamental questions, and . . . the resolutions at party congresses for planned measures of theoretical education increased accordingly', according to Heinrich Schulz, the SPD's educational expert.[1]

1 *NZ*, 1907–8, Vol. II, p. 883.

The executive was perfectly happy with the propagation of theoretical revolution in a school as long as no one advocated it in practice. If you can't do, teach; this applied as much to revolutionaries as anyone else and would satisfactorily absorb the surplus froth of radical energy. In the autumn of 1906 a party educational commission was formed, consisting of seven members including Franz Mehring and Clara Zetkin; on 15 November 1906 the new school officially opened its doors. The whole plan was thoroughly debated at the party congress in Essen in 1907, after the first six months' course had taken place.

Luise Kautsky had first written about it to Rosa while the latter was still in Finland, as part of the gossip about the current SPD scene with which she kept her friend supplied. Rosa had sniffed suspiciously: 'What is it? Who is behind it?' At first, to her chagrin, there was no place for her, though she was too proud to push her own candidature when Bebel went through a list of possible activities for her at the end of 1906.[2] Yet she took an interest in its activities from the start. During the first season she persuaded her friend Clara Zetkin, a member of the supervisory body, to suggest to her colleagues that a course in the history of Socialism be included, which had not been intended in the original programme.[3] The idea caught on at once. The course was taught by Franz Mehring who, with Schulz, was the main luminary of the new school.

But the Prussian police rendered Rosa an unwitting service. Hilferding and Pannekoek, two of the lecturers at the party school, were both foreigners: Hilferding an Austrian, and Pannekoek—the Astronomer, as he was known—a Dutchman. The police presented the two foreign Socialists with an ultimatum just before 1 October 1907 when the party school was due to reopen for its second season—any further participation would be followed by immediate expulsion. Both Hilferding and Pannekoek accordingly withdrew and Rosa Luxemburg was engaged on the recommendation of Karl Kautsky. He himself was unable to teach as he felt he had insufficient time. 'In Rosa Luxemburg you will be getting one of the best brains in Germany', he told Schulz.[4]

Rosa was, or pretended to be, reluctant, probably because she was only invited to fill a gap: 'The whole school interests me very little and I am not the type to act as a school ma'am.' Besides, the school might prove to be a dull and official affair, executive-inspired. Nevertheless she accepted; the income was, according to her, 'a magnetic attraction'. At short notice, therefore, she plunged into a spate of teaching. She held

---

[1] *Letters to Karl and Luise Kautsky*, p. 133.

[2] From Werner Blumenberg.

[3] Dieter Fricke, 'Die Parteischule', in *Zeitschrift für Geschichtswissenschaft*, Germany (East) 1957, Vol. V, No. 2, p. 237.

[4] Kautsky Archives, IISH.

courses in political economy and in economic history, and taught 50 hours a month.

Though the only woman on the staff, she soon established a reputation and in addition found that she enjoyed the work thoroughly. As a rule the courses lasted from 1 October until the end of March or April, except in 1910 when Rosa ran off early in March to fan the flames of the suffrage agitation, and for two months after Christmas 1911 when *Reichstag* elections were taking place and staff as well as students issued forth like shock troops to help. Each course consisted of 30 members who were given an intensive programme during their time at the school. Altogether in seven courses 203 students passed through the party school at Lindenstrasse. The one thing upon which they were all agreed was the benefit they had received from Rosa Luxemburg's classes. She was a natural and enthusiastic teacher, clarifying the most complicated philosophical issues of Marxism with lively similes and illustrations, making the subject not only real but important. She took trouble with each one of the students and was prepared if necessary to carry on individual tuition after hours. A few became regular visitors to her flat and reliable supporters. The testimonials to her success were not confined to left-wingers. Wilhelm Koenen, until his death a senior civil servant in East Germany, recalled his own experiences at the school as a student in a letter to Dieter Fricke.[1] But similar praise came from a later right-wing member of the SPD, Tarnow.[2]

Apart from anything else, her work at the school provided a regular and steady income of 3,600 marks per course, which by Socialist standards was a lot of money. In 1911 Mehring retired from active teaching for health reasons and Rosa took over part of his course in the history of Socialism as well. The school kept Rosa physically and intellectually busy until the war; the many references in her letters during this period are evidence of her absorption and interest. While the school was in session Rosa lectured for two hours every day; very often teachers' conferences or extra work with the students went on into the afternoon. Otherwise Rosa would be home at lunchtime, somewhat exhausted and able to resume her own work or receive friends only after a rest or a brisk walk. The intensity of her teaching at the school is best shown by the fact that there were weeks on end when she and Mehring or Schulz

---

[1] Fricke, op. cit., p. 241.

[2] *Vorwärts*, 2 December 1909. Rosa herself wrote to Clara Zetkin about this young man: 'Tarnow is the most gifted student, and has sloughed off a lot of the revisionist influence from which he was suffering. I don't want to cede him to the unions, where he could eventually become a menace to us . . .' (IML(B) NL 2-20, p. 85 (end 1908)). Rosi Wolff-stein, later Rosi Frölich, wife of Rosa Luxemburg's biographer, who is still alive, was also a pupil of the school in the season 1912–13. She has given me the benefit of her lively recollections of the party school and Rosa Luxemburg's courses.

met only in corridors or on official occasions and found it impossible to exchange two words in private.

Out of her work at the school eventually came two major works of Marxist analysis. One was the *Introduction to Political Economy*, the substance of her lectures turned into a first draft for a book which she was able to finish only in prison during the First World War.[1] For nearly four years she worked on it whenever she could, and made every effort to avoid other engagements. 'I have sworn by the beard of the prophet not to give a single lecture until I have my "Introduction to Political Economy" ready for the printers', she wrote to Pieck in 1908, again turning down a request from her recent ex-pupil to lecture in Bremen, where Pieck was party secretary.[2] Then in the autumn of 1911 one puzzling aspect of the large subject suddenly engaged her whole attention and grew to full proportions in its own right. This, a study of imperialism, began as an attempt to clarify for herself certain technical contradictions in the construction of Marxist economics, and in the end became *The Accumulation of Capital*, Rosa Luxemburg's most important book and the one for which she is most widely known. Undoubtedly the constant polishing of ideas before her students helped Rosa greatly to clarify her own mind on the basic propositions of her political faith; 'only by sharpening the subject matter through teaching was I able to develop my ideas'.

The party school was not without its enemies, and these became more vociferous as the success of the school was assured. In fact attendance at the course did not appear to impose any particular attitudes on its students. Some of them later became Communists (Pieck—perhaps Rosa's most important student—Wilhelm Koenen and Jacob Walcher) but others, like Winnig and Tarnow, were to be prominent right-wingers. None the less, the revisionists in the party, particularly those from south Germany, sensed in the school an institutional means of popagating radical doctrines in the party. An attack was mounted on the whole concept in 1908. 'The school should go to the masses, not an élite creamed off into the school in Berlin', Kurt Eisner wrote in *Vorwärts*.[3] Moreover, the trade unions did not care for the programme of the school and never filled all the ten places allotted to their nominees.

The whole question was dragged into the open at the party congress at Nürnberg on 13–19 September 1908. Two views were represented. One held that the school was there to help raise the general level of education among workers, the other that it should be an advanced

---

[1] *Einführung in die Nationalökonomie*, first published by Paul Levi as part of Rosa Luxemburg's literary remains in 1925.

[2] Rosa Luxemburg to Wilhelm Pieck, 1 August 1908, Henke papers, SPD Archives, Bonn.

[3] *Vorwärts*, 22 August 1908.

teachers' and agitators' training college. The executive was anxious that Rosa should defend the school, and got her a mandate for that purpose. Bebel wrote to her twice to make sure of her attendance.

Rosa Luxemburg in a restrained and dignified speech admitted that she too had had doubts about the project at the beginning, 'partly from natural conservatism (laughter), partly because a Social-Democratic party must always aim at the widest mass effect in its agitation'.[1] However, her doubts had been largely dispelled. She admitted that there was plenty of room for improvement with regard to the selection of students, the type of course given, and so on. Then there was the question of what happened to the students after they returned to their local organizations.

What has been happening is that party organizations have sent students to the school like scapegoats into the desert, have not bothered any more about them, have not given them any worthwhile jobs when they come back. On the other hand there is also the danger that too much is being demanded from students when they do get a job. Comrades say to them 'You have been to the party school, now show us instantly what you can do'. The students of the party school cannot fulfil such expectations. We have tried to make clear to them from first to last that they will not get from us any ready-made science, that they must continue to go on learning, that they will go on learning all their lives. . . . There is, therefore, plenty of room for criticism against the party school, but such criticism as Eisner has been making has no justification at all.[2]

Rosa exposed as tactical humbug the excessive respect for the sciences shown by the critics of the party school—should complicated subjects be popularized for the sake of giving party members a smattering of learning? This was absurd deference to the hated bourgeois academics. What they were really getting at in their demand for practical teaching was to debase the party school into a mere guild institute. The contrast between theoretical and practical learning was for Rosa as bogus as the contrast between strategy and tactics. The school existed precisely to fill a gap by teaching something that the normal school of practical life could not provide. By insisting that the party school should teach practical matters they simply ignored the capacity of workers to learn from their daily activities; in other words denied the whole basis of growing class consciousness as postulated by Marxism.

They have not the slightest conception of the fact that the working classes learn 'their stuff' from their daily life, in fact absorb it better than Eisner does. What the masses need is general education, theory which gives them the chance of making a system out of the detail acquired from experience and which helps to forge a deadly weapon against our enemies. If nothing else has so far convinced

<hr/>

[1] *Protokoll . . . 1908*, p. 230.   [2] Ibid.

me of the necessity for having a party school, of the need to spread Socialist theory in our ranks, the criticism of Eisner has done it.

No doubt Rosa hoped that the students of their own volition would become a bastion against revisionism in the party. In this she was disappointed. In the course of 1910/11 a big debate was organized under her and Franz Mehring's auspices to discover the opinions of the students on party policy. That particular course contained a large proportion of right-wingers, and both Franz Mehring and Rosa were very shocked by the vigorous defence of the whole revisionist position from a section of the students. They all deplored Social Democracy's isolation and lack of influence. Surely the real value of education and agitation was to gain concrete concessions and as quickly as possible? Rosa Luxemburg said to Franz Mehring afterwards that 'in that case I wonder whether the whole party school has really any point?'[1] None the less, she enjoyed working there and had every intention of carrying on for the foreseeable future. The closure of the party school during the war left a significant gap in her life.[2]

In Rosa's calendar the chief political event of these years was the congress of the International at Stuttgart on 18–24 August 1907. It was a great occasion, a fitting successor to Amsterdam. For the first time the magnificent SPD was host on German soil. Rosa stayed with her friend Clara Zetkin; they spent much of the time together at the congress. She introduced her friend to Lenin who had come from Finland to head, with Martov, the delegation of the RSDRP, newly—and temporarily—united at the Stockholm congress the year before. The Russian revolution, and the long talks in Kuokkala, had brought Lenin and Rosa Luxemburg close together.

Rosa Luxemburg and Julian Marchlewski represented the Polish Social Democrats. She was therefore at the congress as one of the loosely united Russian group, and not on behalf of the German party. This made it easier for her to take a stand against the official German resolution, and to speak against Bebel as a foreign equal and not as a German subject. The German delegation was heavily loaded with trade unionists; membership of this delegation, with the usual German discipline of block voting, would have imposed an unwelcome strain on her.

But probably the most significant debates in committee and in the plenum were those on militarism and war. There were three major positions. The German delegation, led by Bebel, did not really want to discuss the question at all, and certainly saw no need for any new resolutions. Already in March 1906 the SPD had failed to persuade the

[1] Fricke, 'Parteischule', p. 246.
[2] Briefe an Freunde, p. 73, to Hans Diefenbach, 1 November 1914.

International Bureau to keep anti-militarism off the congress agenda. The whole problem was closely connected with the sensitive issue of the mass strike—the only weapon of the proletariat that was deemed to be effective if war broke out—and it was opposition to the irresponsible propagation of that tactic which then and until his death governed Bebel's thinking. The majority of the French, under pressure from a vociferous syndicalist wing, believed in the mass strike as a panacea, and wanted a resolution to harness the lumbering cart of anti-militarism to their fast mass-strike horse once and for all. Some of the leaders, for instance Jaurès and Vaillant, saw the need for some concessions to this view; already at the French Socialist (SFIO) congress at Limoges the year before, the party's policy had been packaged into one of those crisp French epigrams: '*Plutôt l'insurrection que la guerre.*' This then was the second view, heavily coloured by Jaurès's belief that Socialists would anyhow be able to prevent war, or soon stop it if it came, without too much detailed prescription beforehand. He could not accept what he considered to be Bebel's negative pessimism. 'It would be a sad thing indeed if one could not say more than Bebel does, that we anyhow have no specific means of preventing strife and murder between nations; sad indeed if the ever-increasing power of the German working class, of the international proletariat, does not extend further than this.'[1] Beneath the differences of opinion on tactics was the old Franco-German rivalry; enthusiasm against discipline, action against concepts, epigrams against formal theses—a clash sharpened in public by temperamental antagonism.

Rosa Luxemburg spoke on Wednesday, 21 August, in the name of the Russian and Polish delegations. Lenin, who spent a lot of time with her at Stuttgart, had realized early on that his position was much like hers, and that she could represent it with greater experience and chance of success. He was therefore quite content to remain silent himself and even offered her a Russian mandate for the voting committee.[2]

When I heard Vollmar's speech, I said to myself, 'if the shadows of fallen Russian revolutionaries could be present, they would all say, keep your tributes but at least learn from us'. I have to disagree completely with Vollmar and regrettably with Bebel as well, when they say that they are not in a position to do more than they are doing at present [about mass strikes]. ... I am a convinced adherent of Marxism and precisely for that reason consider it a great danger to give Marxism a stiff and fatalistic form. ... We cannot just stand with our arms crossed and wait for the historical dialectic to drop its ripe fruit into our laps. ... Jena [the SPD congress of 1905] showed the SPD to be a revolutionary party by adopting a resolution to use mass strikes in certain circumstances. ... True this was not intended as a weapon against war, but to achieve general suffrage. ...

---

[1] *Protokoll . . . Internatiaralen Sozialistenkongress . . . Stuttgart 1907*, p. 89.
[2] Ibid., p. 101.

[Therefore] after Vollmar's and Bebel's speech we have decided that it is necessary to sharpen the Bebel motion. . . . In part we actually go further than the amendment of that resolution by Jaurès and Vaillant; our agitation in case of war is not only aimed at ending that war, but at *using* the war to hasten the *general collapse of class rule*.[1]

The influence of Lenin was clear in the ending.

Her amendment was adopted. The final resolution was therefore a composite one, made up of parts of the resolutions submitted by the Germans, by the moderate sections of the French and of the deliberate sharpening of both resolutions by the Luxemburg-Lenin addition. The amendment was adopted in the teeth of Bebel's opposition. It was not so much a compromise resolution as a compound one. It read as follows:

The Congress confirms the resolutions of previous International congresses against militarism and imperialism and declares anew that the fight against militarism cannot be separated from the Socialist class war as a whole.

Wars between capitalist states are as a rule the result of their rivalry for world markets, as every state is not only concerned in consolidating its own market, but also in conquering new markets, in which process the subjugation of foreign lands and peoples plays a major part. Further these wars arise out of the never-ending armament race of militarism, which is one of the chief implements of bourgeois class-rule and of the economic and political enslavement of the working classes.

Wars are encouraged by the prejudices of one nation against another, systematically purveyed among the civilized nations in the interest of the ruling classes, so as to divert the mass of the proletariat from the tasks of its own class, as well as from the duty of international class solidarity.

Wars are therefore inherent in the nature of capitalism; they will only cease when capitalist economy is abolished, or when the magnitude of the sacrifice of human beings and money, necessitated by the technical development of warfare, and popular disgust with armaments, lead to the abolition of this system.

That is why the working classes, which have primarily to furnish the soldiers and make the greatest material sacrifices, are natural enemies of war, which is opposed to their aim: the creation of an economic system based on Socialist foundations, which will make a reality of the solidarity of nations.

The Congress holds therefore that it is the duty of the working classes, and especially their representatives in parliaments, recognizing the class character of bourgeois society and the motive for the preservation of the opposition between nations, to fight with all their strength against naval and military armament, and to refuse to supply the means for it, as well as to labour for the education of working-class youth in the spirit of the brotherhood of nations and of Socialism, and to see that it is filled with class consciousness.

The Congress sees in the democratic organization of the army, in the popular militia instead of the standing army, an essential guarantee for the prevention of

[1] Ibid., p. 97.

aggressive wars, and for facilitating the removal of differences between nations. The International is not able to lay down the exact form of working-class action against militarism at the right place and time, as this naturally differs in different countries. But its duty is to strengthen and co-ordinate the endeavours of the working classes against the war as much as possible.

In fact since the International congress in Brussels the proletariat, through its untiring fight against militarism by the refusal to supply means for military armament, and through its endeavours to make military organization democratic, has used the most varied forms of action, with increasing vigour and success, to prevent the breaking out of wars or to make an end to them, as well as making use of the upheaval of society caused by war for the purpose of freeing the working classes: for example, the agreement between English and French trade unions after the Fashoda incident to ensure peace and to re-establish friendly relations between England and France; the intervention of the Social-Democratic parties in the German and French parliaments during the Morocco crisis; the announcements prepared by French and German Socialists for the same purpose; the joint action of Austrian and Italian Socialists who met in Trieste to prevent a conflict between the two states; further, the emphatic intervention of the Socialist trade unions in Sweden to prevent an attack on Norway; finally the heroic, self-sacrificing fight of the Socialist workers and peasants in Russia and Poland in opposition to the Czarist-inspired war, to stop the war and to make use of the country's crisis for the liberation of the working classes.

All these endeavours testify to the growing strength of the proletariat and to its power to ensure peace through decisive intervention; the action of the working classes will be the more successful the more their minds are prepared by suitable action, and the more they are encouraged and united by the International. The Congress is convinced that pressure by the proletariat could achieve the blessings of international disarmament through serious use of courts of arbitration instead of the pitiful machinations of governments. This would make it possible to use the enormous expenditure of money and strength which is swallowed by military armaments and war, for cultural purposes.

In the case of a threat of an outbreak of war, it is the duty of the working classes and their parliamentary representatives in the countries taking part, fortified by the unifying activity of the International Bureau, to do everything to prevent the outbreak of war by whatever means seem to them most effective, which naturally differ with the intensification of the class war and of the general political situation.

Should war break out in spite of all this, it is their duty to intercede for its speedy end, and to strive with all their power to make use of the violent economic and political crisis brought about by the war to rouse the people, and thereby to hasten the abolition of capitalist class rule.[1]

---

[1] Copied from the Appendix to James Joll, *The Second International*, pp. 196–8. This is based on the official German text printed in the congress protocol; a French text with insignificant variations was printed in Carl Grünberg, 'Die Internationale und der Weltkrieg', *Archio für die Geschichte des Sozialismus und der Arbeiterbewegung*, Vol. I (1916), pp. 12–13. The Luxemburg-Lenin addition consisted of the last two paragraphs.

In forcing the amendment, and particularly by lumping Vollmar and Bebel together as representing much the same point of view, Rosa Luxemburg had issued a veiled declaration of war on the German leadership. For her the issue was still no more than the re-establishment of the 1905 position, now by authority of the International congress. The regressive, prohibitive interpretations of the 1905 resolution, current since the SPD's congress of 1906, were in her view now reversed by higher authority. Far from something new, the position she adopted was essentially conservative, a return to known principles already stated. She would hold to this resolution as a meaningful expression of intent and disregard the realities out of which it had arisen, as would Lenin, even though she soon realized, as Lenin did not, that the 'good old tactic' was a myth, and a return to it undesirable. This was because Rosa ascribed an almost mystical sovereignty to the International—and a practical one too, the capacity for enforcing its decisions. But for once her vision was cloudy, there was no 'it'; the International at best could not be more than the sum of its constituent parts, of whose weakness she was well aware. When the war broke out, betrayal of the International thus became in her eyes the first and major crime of the main Socialist parties of Europe.

It is easy to write off the Stuttgart declarations against war as self-stupefying rhetoric. And indeed it was a stew produced by several cooks with widely different tastes, cancelling each other out. Bebel's growing pessimism and fear, French optimism that any crisis would produce its own solution—both helped to nudge the congress into the merest statement of good intentions. The Socialists of the Second International were curiously legalistic—no resolution, no commitment. Lenin noted with surprise and shock what Rosa already knew, that 'this time German Social Democracy, hitherto the invariable representative of the revolutionary conception of Marxism, wavered and even took an opportunist stand. . . . Bebel's resolution, submitted by the Germans . . . suffered from the defect that all emphasis on the *active* tasks of the proletariat was missing. This made it possible to view the perfectly orthodox formulations of Bebel through opportunistic spectacles. Vollmar immediately turned this possibility into a fact. For this reason Rosa Luxemburg and the Russian Social Democrats brought in an amendment to Bebel's resolution. . . .'[1] Lenin was mistaken in differentiating thus sharply between Bebel's intentions and Vollmar's misuse of them. He did not fully understand the process of change in the SPD—indeed he never understood the SPD at all. All he saw was an isolated lapse which, flavoured with an excellently contemptuous comment by Engels about the endless German capacity for becoming Philistines if not kept

[1] *Proletarii*, No. 17, 20 October 1907, in *Sochineniya*, Vol. XIII, p. 64.

up to the mark by the French, he merely reported to his Russian readers.[1]
The attitude of the International—and indeed of the various national
parties—to war remains incomprehensible unless it is realized that in
1907 world war was a concept to Socialists but not a reality. There
were wars in the Balkans from 1912 onwards, campaigns against Africans,
skirmishes between colonial powers. There were several major incidents
in the years after 1905 which are nowadays served up by historians as
the inevitable *hors-d'œuvre* to the First World War. All this had only
begun in 1907. In the same year as the International Socialist Congress,
a conference met at The Hague to civilize future war by international
agreement; behind the technicalities loomed a real consensus to regulate
war out of existence. The millionaire philanthropist, Andrew Carnegie,
attending on his own behalf and at his own expense, felt sure that he
was preaching the supreme importance of peace to sympathetic ears,
including the Kaiser's. Among the ruling classes there was optimism—
and if Socialists mocked this assurance in public and referred to The
Hague conference as a 'robbers' feast', it was an expression of disdain
for all bourgeois governments rather than a gloomy prognosis of actual
war.[2] In fact war was much like social revolution to the members of the
Second International, the inevitable by-product of capitalist society,
requiring constant postulation to generate protest but also capable of
indefinite postponement as a physical event.[3]

The period 1907–10 was one of retrenchment and disillusion, not
only for Rosa Luxemburg but for German Social Democracy as a whole.
The imperial government had a splendid *Reichstag* coalition, the Bülow
bloc, from which only Catholics and Socialists were excluded; between
such bedfellows there was no basis for joint opposition. Baffled in its
probe for soft spots in the hostile face of society, the SPD concentrated
on internal reorganization. The caricature of a pedantic bureaucracy,
against which the French had railed whenever they were faced by the
disciplined and united German contingent at International congresses—

---

[1] 'Calendar for all for the year 1908' in *Sochineniya*, Vol. XIII, pp. 67–8. In his evaluation of the work of the congress he relied largely on Clara Zetkin's articles in her women's paper *Gleichheit*, to which Rosa had drawn his attention. But this again did not lead him to any profound analysis of events. Kautsky understood better what had happened when he said that the SPD had resigned its primacy in the International. As long as it was a matter of resolutions, Kautsky was sensitive enough to any manifestations of weakness or compromise.

[2] The remark was made by an Englishman, Quelch, at the Stuttgart congress, and he was promptly expelled by the provincial government of Württemberg for his pains. *Protokoll Internationaler Sozialistenkongress . . . 1907*, p. 32.

[3] Many modern historians consider that war was at least a 'probability' to the congress at Stuttgart (Schorske, *German Social Democracy*, p. 84) and that the famous resolution was a 'compromise of inaction' (Joll, *Second International*, p. 138). I have gone into this question at some length because I believe both points of view are wrong.

united at least when it came to voting—was fast becoming reality. Organization was striking firmly downwards from the centre into the remotest roots. The strengthening of the central party organizations after the 1905 Jena congress, especially the accession of additional secretaries, led to the operation of Parkinson's Law: with the new administrators came paid sub-officials and gadgets like telephones and typewriters.[1] When the party congress voted the necessary authority for this apparatus, most of the Left were keen enough; for them the SPD was then still the party of the 1905 mass-strike resolution, only awaiting the next revolutionary period. Organization was synonymous with more effective advance. Yet there were warnings. The great Max Weber said in a lecture:

One must ask which has more to fear from this [tendency to bureaucracy], bourgeois society or Social Democracy? Personally, I believe the latter; i.e. those elements within it which are the bearers of the revolutionary ideology. . . . And if the contradictions between the material interests of the provisional politicians on the one hand and the revolutionary ideology on the other could develop freely, if one would no longer throw Social Democrats out of veterans' associations, if one would admit them into party administration, from which they are nowadays expelled, *then* for the first time serious internal problems would arise for the party. Then . . . it would be shown not that Social Democracy is conquering city and state, but on the contrary, that the state is conquering Social Democracy.[2]

But Marxists were more politically than sociologically minded (and still are today); provided the policy was right—and it was up to the annual congress to supervise the executive on this point—they could see no conflict. The notion of a bureaucracy developing a will of its own and *for its own benefit* was unthinkable. In the Soviet Union it has been drowned in the multiple wails over the personality cult and more effectively in frequent purges the People's Democracies have only become conscious of this problem in the last ten years—but with a vengeance; as for the West, the 'managerial revolution' and all the literature about bureaucracy is simply ignored by Soviet analysts. So we cannot blame the SPD for not having our modern insights. And later the shocked and furious radicals were not wholly wrong when they rather narrowly put the blame on particular people and not on any general trend. The men who ran the party from 1907 onwards, men like Molkenbuhr, Ebert, Scheidemann, and Braun, were efficient, down-to-earth—and completely unrevolutionary. For them revolution merely meant self-

---

[1] For this organizational development see Schorske, Chapter V, pp. 116–45, and quoted sources.

[2] Address to the Verband für Sozialpolitik, 1908, quoted in Schorske, pp. 117–18.

destruction, both functionally and personally—and they knew it.[1]

This did not imply that democracy disappeared in proportion to the rise of the bureaucracy. Ebert has been called the German Stalin and so he was—at least as far as mentality and outlook were concerned, though he was not a cruel man. Nor was the deliberate maintenance of democratic forms a farce. The process was much more sophisticated. A multitude of minor but in the end significant decisions took place mostly in the interstices of party life which the congress did not touch, the manifold minor matters affecting local administration and control. At the top, congress resolutions continued to be binding; no one before 1914 would have ventured to suggest that these were a mere formality. Often the executive had to exercise all its skill to get its majority, as in 1911. But the strong tradition of supporting the executive, unless there were very cogent reasons of conscience or principle, usually prevailed; a tradition, moreover, of voluntary discipline, of conviction. There were no three-line-whips in the SPD, and little sense of compulsion. In short, a classic example of Max Weber's notion of routinized charisma.

In fact there was no apparent conflict between the tasks of the Social-Democratic Party and its administration. Only when the whole atmosphere changed during the war and the role of the party with it, was the foundation of the SPD finally found to rest not—as Rosa Luxemburg supposed—on the masses, but on a concrete structure of bureaucracy and leadership. If the situation of August 1914 had by some miracle taken place in 1900, there would have been confusion followed by a genuine realignment of opinions. By 1914, however, it was considered natural for the leadership to propose and for the party on the whole to follow. This was not, of course, equivalent to adopting the Communist tactic of deliberately pre-empting and manœuvring members' wishes; the attitude of the SPD during the war was possible only because the bulk of the members supported the leadership. The acceptance of legitimacy in the existing structure of control is in itself a positive expression of intent, just as much as if the policy adopted had been the result of a referendum. There was no question of blind, Nazi-type obedience.

Rosa Luxemburg took little part in the debates of these years. She was quite uninterested in problems of organization. It fell to Karl Kautsky to knead the listless dough of these years in *The Road to Power*.[2] This book probably represents the height of Kautsky's dialectic achievements, since it combined a complete negation of practical revolution with a strict emphasis on revolutionary attitudes. He faithfully reflected the

---

[1] For an analysis of party structure and its effect on the role of the SPD, see J. P. Nettl, 'The German Social-Democratic Party', *Past and Present*, No. 30, April 1965, pp. 74–86.

[2] *Der Weg zur Macht*, Berlin 1909.

current mood; indeed, he seized on the general disillusionment, not only within the SPD but throughout imperial Germany. There was constant talk of scandals in the Emperor's circles, and in the political life of the main parties.[1] Kautsky took the moral decay of society and elevated it into a revolutionary factor. As society itself decayed, the Social Democrats had only to grow in strength and to remain firm to their revolutionary principles of uncompromising hostility—and simply take over at the given moment when the existing structure collapsed. The only provision was that the SPD remain true to its principles, and keep itself clean from the corruption around it. In effect the doctrine of *The Road to Power* was nothing more than Kautsky's arguments against revisionism, decked out in a new outward-looking and more revolutionary form. Instead of being an internal party matter only, doctrinal purity and the resultant combat-readiness of the party now had greater relevance to what was going on outside.[2]

Kautsky saw the revolution as self-generating; it needed no physical action of the type envisaged by Rosa Luxemburg in her mass-strike doctrine. The necessary conditions for revolution were that confidence in the existing régime be destroyed, a majority of people be decisively opposed to it, and that there should be a well-organized party in opposition to harvest this discontent and speak for it, and to provide as a substitute for the ruling régime a visible focus round which the loyalties of the population could gather.[3]

To contemporaries *The Road to Power* appeared as a revolutionary document—the word 'revolution' appears in it much more frequently than in any previous writing—and the SPD executive certainly had strong reservations about it. It is hard to reconcile the statement from one scholar, that 'the activity of Kautsky cannot be separated from that of Bebel . . . Bebel, the unquestioned political leader of the party, and Kautsky, its leading ideologist, were always in agreement about the basic tendency of their views, in spite of occasional differences of opinion',[4] with the irritated and censorious letters that passed between the executive and Kautsky when his book was in proof. Thus Kautsky wrote to his friend Haase: '. . . Things are getting more and more extraordinary . . . either the executive must tell me once and for all which bits it insists I

---

[1] One of these rumours was that the Kaiser had been for a number of years in the hands of a crazy and irresponsible *camarilla*. See Johannes Ziekursch, *Politische Geschichte des neun deutschen Kaiserreiches*, Frankfurt 1930, Vol. III, pp. 190–2. Similar rumours had, of course, circulated for years about the Tsar in Russia and were a normal accompaniment of all court rule, particularly where the Crown had arbitrary power and the court had influence. Even in recent times such rumours appeared with regard to the Dutch royal family, and the English, too, are not always immune.

[2] Karl Kautsky, *Der Weg zur Macht*, pp. 107–18.

[3] Ibid., p. 64.

[4] Matthias, *Kautsy*, p. 172.

should alter, or else they must leave me alone to publish as I think fit.'[1]
In the end the executive did insist on the removal of certain offensive
passages—the same fate that had befallen Rosa Luxemburg's very
different mass-strike pamphlet.

We have no evidence of any reaction by Rosa Luxemburg to *The
Road to Power*. It is even more likely that Rosa never read it at the time,
at least not until her controversy with its author the following year.
Since Easter 1907, when Rosa Luxemburg and Karl Kautsky had sat
together on the shores of Lake Geneva planning the forthcoming issues
of *Neue Zeit*, the whole basis for Rosa's co-operation with Kautsky had
crumbled completely, leaving only the outward appearances of the old
relationship and the false intimacy of addressing each other '*per du*'. It
was part of the critical dislike with which Rosa Luxemburg viewed all
things German. By 1908 she began to find the Sunday lunch sessions
and occasional evenings at the Kautskys' house a bore: 'Newspaper
gossip at table, Jewish jokes by Bendel [Kautsky's son Benedikt] and
far too much gluttony by all concerned.' On 27 June 1908 she wrote to
a friend: 'Soon I shall be quite unable to read anything written by Karl
Kautsky.... It is like a disgusting series of spiders' webs ... which can
only be washed away by the mental bath of reading Marx himself ...
however wrong-headed his views on Hungarians, Czechs, Slavs, etc.'
Was it the comparison with Marx himself, a confrontation which so few
Marx commentators have been able to survive, which began to show up
the quality of Kautsky's writings to a sharp critic like Rosa Luxemburg,
full of recent revolutionary experience? In her search for lecture material
she was re-reading Marx and Engels's literary remains, and particularly
the articles in the *Neue Rheinische Zeitung*; her comment: 'A lot of
nonsense and much out of date, but what courage in making independent
judgements ... what concrete facts ... compared with the boring,
featureless constructions of history in the abstract which one finds with
Karl Kautsky...' By the summer of 1909, when Kautsky came to join
her in Italy, Rosa was reaching down into the animal kingdom for
metaphors to apply to her friend—he had become a beast of burden,
a donkey.

Beneath the political discussions and party gossip in the Kautsky
household there was a lot of private matrimonial tension and Rosa, to
say the least, was not a mere spectator. The pre-conditions for a row
thus already existed before 1910. The venom with which the party
argument was to be conducted on both sides was charged with all these
personal matters. When the explosion came in 1910 the apparently solid
structure of twelve years' close collaboration just collapsed. To mutual
friends and colleagues in the SPD, who had not been aware of the

[1] Karl Kautsy to Hugo Haase, no date [1909], C432, IISH Archives.

changes in their personal relationship behind the scenes or of Rosa's disillusion with Kautsky's status as writer and thinker, the polemics of 1910 could only be explained by Rosa's poisonous temperament—and Kautsky himself was not going to disturb this assumption.

In the summer of 1909 Rosa Luxemburg made an unusually long trip to the south. She spent some time in Swiss libraries working on her history of Poland, a project that she had not touched for many years.[1] From there she moved to Italy, breaking through the barrier of the Alps 'on to the sunny and superb Italian plains'.

Here I am in *Genova superba* as the city calls itself, while the people of Tuscany have a different opinion and say that all one finds here are *mare senza pesce, montagne senza alberi, uomini senza fede e donne senza vergogna* [seas without fish, mountains without trees, unfaithful men and shameless women]. I agree with the Tuscans, with only this difference: I also find the *uomini senza vergogna*, at least in the shops where they always cheat and always manage to smuggle a few false coins into my change.[2]

Rosa had now discovered the south with a vengeance, and with the same uncritical joy as so many generations of Germans. The Goethe myth of the south has penetrated deep into their romantic attitude to Italy; what was outrageous and unacceptable in Germany—patent dishonesty, inefficiency, irresponsibility, even the loss of Rosa's valuable mail—were noted but excused in the Italians, for it was but a small penalty for so much sunshine and song. Rosa had all the northern optimism of transalpine acceptance. She stayed in Italy for nearly three months and became determined to visit Corsica the following year.[3] Her letters were long, amused, and strangely uncritical. All the old-fashioned Victorianism of a great Socialist and revolutionary on holiday abroad came to the fore.

First of all the frogs. As soon as the sun sets, frog concerts, such as I have never heard anywhere, begin on all sides. . . . Frogs—all right as far as I am concerned, but *such* frogs. . . . Secondly the bells. I love church bells, but to hear them ringing every quarter of an hour . . . it is enough to drive anybody crazy . . . and thirdly—thirdly Karl, when you come to Italy, do not forget to take a box of insect powder with you. Otherwise it is wonderful here.[4]

These letters from Italy are a curious testimonial to Rosa's moral stamina, for their gaiety was more artificial than real. While she was

---

[1] *Letters to Karl and Luise Kautsky*, p. 141, dated 1 May 1909.

[2] Ibid., pp. 142–3.

[3] The plan to visit Corsica with her friend Konstantin Zetkin was put off each year with increasing determination to carry it out the next; in the end Rosa went alone (probably 1912). Even in prison during the war Rosa was once more planning to go with Sonia Liebknecht.

[4] *Letters to Karl and Luise Kautsky*, p. 153.

writing to the Kautskys about the joys of sunny Italy, she was heart-breakingly releasing her friend Konstantin Zetkin from his relationship with her because she suspected that it was stifling him. The task of Rosa Luxemburg's biographers is made so much harder by this rigid self-discipline which kept friendships in strictly divided compartments and never let the affairs of one relationship spill over into another, either between person and person or between person and politics.

X

DAVID AND GOLIATH,

1910–1911

BY the end of 1909 the cold anti-Socialist front in German politics was breaking up. The Bülow bloc began to fall apart on the question whether to introduce direct taxation to meet the growing bill for armaments. Most of the chauvinistic assertion, which had overwhelmed Social Democracy at the 1907 elections, had dwindled away two years later. In addition, for the first time since 1905 the Prussian suffrage question had come up again, and a parliamentary attack on the three-class system of elections in Prussia was being mounted in the *Landtag*. The two problems were connected. The Conservative leader in the *Reichstag* stated that his party would not vote for financial reform and direct taxation because they did not wish to 'surrender the power of taxing property in such a broad way . . . into the hands of a parliamentary body elected by equal suffrage'.[1]

The revisionist section of the SPD, which had hammered on the defeat of 1907 as a warning against political impotence, now saw in the break-up of the Bülow bloc an opportunity to re-establish Socialist influence in the *Reichstag*. The merger in March 1910 of various middle-class progressive groups into the new *Fortschrittliche Volkspartei* (Progressive People's Party) was held to be a sign of good times, the focus for a bourgeois radical party such as existed in France but had hitherto been sadly absent in German politics. Here finally was a coherent ally for the SPD, or at least for such of its members as believed in alliances.

The issue now facing the SPD was a complicated one: on the one hand, an alliance with the emerging middle-class opposition to the government in order to agitate jointly for direct taxation and suffrage reform; on the other, the continued refusal on principle to support any official measure proposed by the imperial government, and thus indirectly to vote for the continuation of the hated system of indirect levies on consumption. To vote with the arch-conservative Junker interest, or to vote with the equally hated government? Either way the party was ensnared. The radicals, foreseeing and accepting the dilemma,

---

[1] *Reichstag debates*, 1909: CCXXXVII, 9323.

put forward the slogan of 'No new taxes, but reduction of armaments'—
the old stand on opposition for opposition's sake, on all fronts.[1] They
felt that propaganda, the magical solvent, must make it clear to the
people that in refusing to support the government measures, the party
was not accepting responsibility for the old system of taxation; in calling
for a reduction of armaments it was attacking imperialism at its most
sensitive point. Paul Singer, joint chairman of the party who spoke
against his own executive on this occasion, felt that the SPD would
thus be kept free from involvement, with its principles unimpaired—
just as Kautsky had stipulated in *The Road to Power*.[2] *Neue Zeit* pitched
in on the side of Liebknecht and the radicals; even Parvus's radical but
rusty pen was dipped into fighting ink once more—and for the last time.
But the executive feared that the SPD would lose in popularity at the
next elections if it did not support a change in the system of taxation,
and with Bebel's written blessing from Zürich its view as usual prevailed.[3]

Thus the break-up of the Bülow coalition in 1909 reopened some of
the fundamental issues of Socialist policy, of which the fiscal question
was only a part; it raised the whole problem of co-operation with potential bourgeois partners—and, indeed, of engaging in 'politics' at all.
Given that co-operation was possible, could other old Socialist aims,
like suffrage reform in Prussia, also be achieved by such an alliance? It
was the same situation that had faced Belgian Socialists in seeking
collaboration with the Liberals six years earlier, when Rosa Luxemburg
had castigated them mercilessly. Indeed, it was the old revisionist
question posed in a new and more seductive way, now that Kautsky
had formulated his doctrine of subtle decay in a society which ten years
earlier had still seemed unshakeable.

The taxation crisis, though unresolved, brought about a change of
Chancellor and government. Bethmann-Hollweg replaced Bülow, and
the new government now relied on a coalition of Conservatives and
Centre, with both Liberals and Progressives in opposition together with
the perennial wallflower, Social Democracy. Hopes were strong that
the new Chancellor would himself make proposals for Prussian suffrage
reform. In Hessen a new suffrage bill was introduced into the provincial
diet but this unexpectedly turned out to decrease rather than improve
working-class representation. The first public SPD protests against it
brought into action sympathetic movements in Brunswick, which also
had a three-class suffrage system. Next came Bremen and Mecklenburg.
A ring of agitation had already been formed around Prussia when the

---

[1] *NZ*, 1908–9, Vol. II, pp. 838 ff.

[2] *Protokoll . . . 1909*, p. 364.

[3] Partly for health reasons, the elderly Bebel now spent an increasing amount of time in
Zürich, centre of the former SPD emigration, where his married daughter lived.

Prussian SPD called a provincial congress at the beginning of January 1910.[1]

Following the spirit of co-operation with the Liberals which had pervaded the party congress in 1909, Bernstein and his friends prepared a careful campaign to guide the tactic at the Prussian congress in the same direction.[2] But unexpectedly the Prussian spirit was much more militant. The idea of collaboration with the Liberals for a parliamentary suffrage campaign was unceremoniously thrown out. Instead the congress called, not for a parliamentary campaign, but for a 'suffrage storm'.

How, the radicals asked, could a successful campaign in parliament be launched when that parliament itself was so heavily and unfairly weighted against Socialist representation? Already the National Liberals were showing their hand; far from supporting a major campaign for equal manhood suffrage, it appeared that they were not even prepared to vote for such a measure if proposed in the legislature. The hopes for a 'popular front' following the break-up of the Bülow coalition had quickly faded, perhaps they had been an illusion all along; almost before the potential partners realized it, the usual polarization had again taken place. The middle classes turned sharp right, and the SPD more sharply to the left. This time the executive found itself almost alone. Instead of adopting the middle-of-the-road position of the old revisionist controversy, a majority of the executive—though the co-chairman, Paul Singer, was with the radicals—had to be taken in tow by the revisionists. And there were good reasons for it. So many previous debates had taken place over theoretical concepts, but this time there was a live issue and a very real threat of action to get something done. It was 1905 all over again, but the centre of the storm was now in Germany. The executive was forced to look to its defences, not only to its theory.

The dates are important. On 4 February 1910 the government published the Bethmann-Hollweg draft for Prussian suffrage reform. It satisfied no one. It tinkered with the system but did not alter it; the main provision was that a few groups—particularly academics—were moved up slightly from the bottom to the middle section of voters. Social Democrats and a few Progressives protested violently. *Vorwärts* rummaged in its arsenal of revolutionary phrases and called the bill a brutal and contemptuous declaration of war.

Almost immediately demonstrations broke out in Berlin and the Prussian provinces. On 10 February the Chancellor and Prussian Prime Minister—the offices were vested in one and the same person—spoke in the Prussian *Landtag* in support of his proposals and was greeted by '*pfui*'—that most expressive of German epithets—from the benches on

---

[1] Schorske, *German Social Democracy*, p. 172.
[2] *SM*, Vol. XIII, No. 3, pp. 1655–71.

the Left. But even his half-baked measure did not pass into law unscathed. After some political bargaining the *Landtag* passed the bill on 16 March, but it was amended in the upper house (*Herrenhaus*) and the two houses became locked in disagreement. Thereupon the government withdrew the bill altogether, and things were right back at the beginning again.

Meantime the Socialist demonstrations went ahead. Each Sunday there were visibly more people in the streets than the week before. On 13 February the Berlin police president, von Jagow, threatened reprisals in a brusque edict in which he made the old-fashioned comment that the streets were exclusively reserved for traffic. There were clashes, and in Frankfurt on 27 February the first casualties. On 6 March the SPD scored a bloodless prestige victory by announcing a 'suffrage promenade' in sarcastic conformity with police instructions. Having drawn the forces of law and order to a park on the outskirts of Berlin, the promenade in fact turned into a massive gathering right in the centre of the town, with the police arriving breathlessly only at the end of the proceedings.[1] The Conservatives, however, took the incident very seriously, and called for reprisals.

Coinciding with these demonstrations were a series of strikes, trials of strength organized by the trade unions in the mining and building industries. It was never quite clear who was on strike and who was locked out; the fact remains that the year 1910 had nearly 370,000 workers involved in stoppages.[2] The two movements began to overlap in March, and the demonstrations were swelled by half-day strikers giving their open support to the suffrage campaign. Clashes became more frequent in Berlin and in the provinces. It was what Rosa Luxemburg had defined as a typically revolutionary situation: interaction of economic and political movements, a spirit sufficiently aggressive among the workers to need large-scale troop movements in the coal-mining areas, and here and there the demand for a showdown. The lessons of 1905–6 had apparently not been wasted after all, and demands were being made for the use of the mass strike as incorporated into the Social-Democratic programme at the 1905 Jena congress.[3]

For Rosa Luxemburg the dog days were over in an instant. She was more than ready to take up her pen in support of a movement which conformed so precisely to all her predictions. Not only her pen; for the

---

[1] The incident is described at length by Paul Frölich in Rosa Luxemburg, *Collected Works*, Vol. IV, pp. 496–8, and *Vorwärts*, 6–8 March 1910. In due course it became a landmark in the SPD's calendar of its own revolutionary past, a sad yet comic German anniversary to match the 22nd of January 1905 in Russia. The SPD acutely felt the lack of a truly heroic chronology.

[2] Schorske, p. 180, note 32.

[3] See Heinrich Ströbel's article in *Vorwärts*, 5 January 1910.

next three months she spoke continuously all over Germany in support of the suffrage campaign. She was so much in demand that at one stage she had to suspend her course of lectures at the party school.

... From the 'war front'. . . . Day before yesterday, Tuesday, the 15th March, 48 evening meetings were arranged [all over Berlin] with the clear intention of providing some sort of action on the morning of the 18th. The speakers were all fourth and fifth rate, mostly trade-union officials! What is more, *Vorwärts* put out an advance prohibition on all street demonstrations after the meeting. I heard by accident at the party school on the 12th that they were short of a speaker in the fourth electoral district, I accepted at once, and so made my speech that same evening. The meeting was bursting at the seams (about 1,500 people), the mood excellent. Of course, I let fly good and proper, and this got a storm of agreement. Hannes [Diefenbach], Gertrud [Zlottko], Costia [Clara Zetkin's son] and Eckstein were all there; the latter, so he told me, had become converted to my view since yesterday.

Today got a telephone invitation from Bremen, a written one from Essen, to address meetings on the mass strike. Am seriously wondering if I should not chuck the school and move out into the country, to stoke up the fires everywhere.[1]

Next she toured the south. On 10 April she was back in Frankfurt to speak to a very large rally on 'the Prussian suffrage campaign and its lessons'.[2] From there she moved to the Ruhr and spoke in mid-April in Essen and Dortmund under the aegis of Konrad Haenisch, a frustrated radical editor seething in one of the remoter outposts of Social Democracy. This embattled meeting led to friendship and further collaboration.[3] Everywhere it was always the same theme: the suffrage struggle and how best to fight it. No wonder doing began to seem so much more exciting than teaching. All her letters testify to large crowds, enthusiasm, a universal desire to act. But at the same time she was murkily conscious of the restraining hand of the executive. This was to be the crucial question in the later polemics. We do not know exactly what evidence she had, only that it left her convinced that the executive was secretly sabotaging the demand for action as early as the end of February.[4] By the end of April she was back in Berlin.

In February, before she set off, she had written a challenging article which she called 'What Next?' ('Was Weiter?'). She analysed the confluent sources of radicalism in the present movement and proposed the

---

[1] Rosa Luxemburg to Luise Kautsky, 17 March 1910, in 'Einige Briefe', IISH *Bulletin*, 1952, Vol. VII, pp. 41–42.

[2] *Der Preussische Wahlrechtskampf und seine Lehren.* This speech was re-issued as a pamphlet under the same title (Frankfurt 1910).

[3] *Briefe an Freunde*, p. 24.

[4] 'During my journey to the Rhineland I got hold of a marvellous document about the famous gag on the discussion . . .', Rosa Luxemburg reported to Leo Jogiches. At the same time she repeated that 'the party executive is doing its best to kill the entire discussion'.

next steps to be taken by the leadership. These consisted in encouraging the growth of the nascent mass-strike movement as much as possible, while launching, on the political side, an agitation for a republic; this would help to radicalize the masses further and sharpen the impending conflict between Socialism and society. In view of the subsequent controversy it is important to remember that this was never intended to be a practical demand capable of achievement, but simply a means of keeping the spring-loaded agitation fully taut. She always believed that it was the duty of Socialist leadership to set the agitational tasks just higher than the immediate practical possibilities. This, rather than any organizational function, was the leadership's role in Social Democracy. It was the same principle that she would try to make effective in the German revolution during the last three months of her life.

Vorwärts sent the article back to her on 2 March with the following comment: 'We have regretfully to decline your article since, in accordance with an agreement between the party executive, the executive commission of the Prussian provincial organization (of the SPD), and the editor, the question of the mass strike shall not be elaborated in *Vorwärts* for the time being.'[1]

The mass strike was the central theme of the moment and Rosa wanted the article to appear in the SPD's *journal officiel*. She sent it next to *Neue Zeit*, where she knew that she had a pre-emptive right to the statement of her views. Kautsky took the article. He described it as 'very attractive and very important', but he also reserved the right to disagree with its conclusions and announced that he would do so publicly in due course, having no time just then. However, he refused absolutely to publish the section dealing with republican agitation. For a start, this 'set out from a wholly mistaken premise [*Ausgangspunkt*]. There is not a word in our [party] programme about the republic.' Though he constantly reiterated that there was no point in going over the well-known Marxist objections to any specifically republican agitation, he nevertheless took the trouble of writing several pages on the subject, quoting the warnings of both Marx and Engels against the distortion of dialectic totality through any over-emphasis on a limited and purely political aim.[2]

But Kautsky did not publish the article after all, and thereby loosened

---

[1] 'Die totgeschwiegene Wahlrechtsdebatte', *LV*, 17 August 1910. The correspondence relating to these events gradually emerged in the course of the polemics, as both Kautsky and Rosa Luxemburg began to publish selected chunks of their private correspondence. As so often in the past, *Vorwärts* was unable to maintain its attitude unequivocally in the face of later criticism. In the supplement of 9 June the editors complained that 'all the talk of a ban on discussion of the mass strike and of the concept of the republic is [nothing but] ill-informed gossip'.

[2] 'Die Theorie und die Praxis', *NZ*, 1909–10, Vol. II, pp. 566–7.

the first stone of an avalanche of recrimination between himself and Rosa Luxemburg which was to bury their long and friendly collaboration under an impenetrable mountain of abuse and misunderstanding. The exact reasons for his refusal never did emerge—at least in a version on which everybody could agree. Kautsky claimed that he would have published the article, possibly after some delay, but in the meantime decided to return it to her for reconsideration. 'I hesitated for quite a time . . . but left Comrade Luxemburg in no doubt that I thought the article a mistake. . . . The thought of publishing [it and my polemical reply] for the delight of our numerous common enemies was repugnant to me . . . I tried to get her to renounce the appearance of her article.'[1] Whether he acted on his own or under pressure from the party executive is not clear either. Rosa was convinced that the 'higher powers' of the party were behind it all, and that Kautsky merely applied their orders 'in his own sphere of power, the *Neue Zeit*'. Kautsky's letter to Rosa Luxemburg, with which he returned the article, has never been published—if indeed there was such a letter.[2]

Subsequent polemics clearly show that he was astonished by the unexpected fierceness of Rosa's reaction to his return of her article. Never before had Rosa written with such fury about a fellow Socialist and former friend: '[Karl Kautsky] this coward who only has courage enough to attack others from behind, but I'll deal with him.' She continued for some months in this vein. The personal issue began to flag only in the following year, and Karl Kautsky was removed to the flaccid pantheon of Rosa's political opponents, to be pitied as much as condemned. 'One should feel sorry for him rather than be angry with him, after all he is only trying to defend himself in an extremely messy situation.' None the less, echoes linger; the name Kautsky could still on occasions rouse her to vituperation as few others could.

In any case Rosa Luxemburg was determined not to be silenced, either in speech or in print.

Everything is going splendidly; I have already had eight meetings and six are yet to come. Everywhere I find unreserved and enthusiastic agreement on the part of the comrades. Karl's article calls forth a shrugging of shoulders; I have noticed this especially in Kiel, in Bremen, in Solingen with Dittmann. . . . Tell him that I well know how to estimate the loyalty and friendship involved in these tricks, but that he has put his foot into it badly by so boldly stabbing me in the back.[3]

Though greatly stimulated by personal pique, there was definite political purpose in Rosa's attitude. 'Let us hope that the whole dis-

[1] Ibid., pp. 335–6.
[2] Rosa Luxemburg, *Collected Works*, Vol. IV, p. 502; *NZ*, 1909–10, II, 336.
[3] *Letters to Karl and Luise Kautsky*, pp. 156–7, dated 13 April 1910.

cussion and its continuation at Magdeburg [the party congress in September 1910] will stimulate our friends and needle them into keeping on their toes against the "powers that be" [*Instanzen*]. In any case I considered it my duty to the party to proceed with ruthless openness.'[1]

When she received her article back from *Neue Zeit*, she had at once sent it elsewhere. The bulk went to Konrad Haenisch, who published it in his paper under the original title 'What Next?' on 14 and 15 March. She accompanied the manuscript with a summary of the situation as she saw it.

The party executive and the General Commission [of the trade unions] have already gone into the question of the mass strike and after long negotiations [the party] had to give in to the position of the trade-union leaders. In view of this the party executive naturally believes that it has to take in its sails, and if it had its way, would even forbid any *discussion* of the mass strike! For this reason I consider it urgently necessary to carry the topic into the furthest masses of the party. The masses should decide. Our duty on the other hand is to offer them the pros and cons, the basis of argument. I count on your support and that you will publish the article immediately.[2]

The article was no less than the beginning of a totally new—at least in the eyes of the executive—policy for German Social Democracy.

Our party must work out a clear and definite scheme how to develop the mass movements which it has itself called into being. . . . Street demonstrations, like military demonstrations, are only the start of a battle . . . the expression of the whole of the masses in a political struggle . . . must be heightened, must be sharpened, must take on new and more effective forms. . . . If the leading party lacks determination, [and fails to provide] the right slogan for the masses, then at once there will be disappointment, the drive disappears and the whole action collapses.[3]

For the first time Rosa Luxemburg openly advocated a new role for the party leaders—not as rulers, not as a party government, but genuinely as *leaders*, as the 'advance guard' of the proletariat in Lenin's sense, but without the Jacobin element of control. Once more it was precisely the policy that Rosa Luxemburg was to follow when she found herself in a leading position after the German revolution.

The means with which she proposed to intensify mass action was, of course, the mass strike. In her anxiety to avoid the appearance of propagating an anarchist panacea—the particular bogey of both party and

---

[1] *Briefe an Freunde*, p. 27.

[2] *Briefe an Freunde*, p. 26, to Konrad Haenisch. The letter clearly refers to the offer of the original article and is therefore wrongly dated by the editor as Summer 1910, when it should be approximately 10 March 1910.

[3] 'Was Weiter?', *Dortmunder Arbeiterzeitung*, 14 March 1910.

trade-union leaders—she over-emphasized the spontaneous element, thus going back to some extent on her previous insistence on the role of the leadership in guiding the movement. 'Even within the class party of the proletariat every great and decisive movement must stem, not from the initiative of a handful of leaders, but from the determination and conviction of the mass of party members. The decision to carry to victory the present Prussian suffrage campaign . . . "by all means"— including that of the mass strike—can only be taken by the broadest sections of the party.'[1]

Two factors thus determined Rosa Luxemburg's attitude. On the one hand there was the need to push the party authorities by applying pressure from below, a pressure moreover that was objectively justified by events. In her article, and throughout the next few months, she pointed again and again to the fact that radical pressure was at the bottom of the party hierarchy, among the masses—a direct application of the Russian lesson of 1905–6 as expressed in *Mass Strike, Party and Trade Unions*. The other factor, which again led to emphasis on the membership as opposed to the leaders, was the need to distinguish between her conception of the mass strike and the old anarchist idea of it as an exercise planned by the *illuminati*, a once-for-all panacea to be applied at the word 'go'. She was never able to make the distinction valid in the eyes of her contemporaries, and even later commentators have all too readily identified Rosa Luxemburg's notion of the mass strike with anarchosyndicalism.[2]

After this and other articles on the same theme, there followed a two months' break while Rosa stumped up and down western Germany making speeches and 'stoking the fires'. While she was away Kautsky exercised his option of disagreeing with her.[3] He analysed the general situation quite differently from Rosa Luxemburg. 'The excitement of the masses is not nearly sufficient for such an extreme course . . . but it was certainly great enough for the stimulus provided by Comrade Luxemburg to produce isolated attempts, experiments with the mass strike which were bound to fail.'[4]

Unwilling to criticize a tactical proposal without benefit of a theory to cover the facts, Kautsky—for such was his way—went on to produce a doctrine to suit the occasion. He took as his model the Roman general, Fabius Cunctator, who had defeated Hannibal, and from this example he evolved a modern version of the strategy of attrition (*Ermattungs-stragie*). Let the street demonstrations go on by all means, but at the

---

[1] Ibid., 15 March 1910. For an analysis of this 'spontaneity' and its importance, see above, pp. 167 ff.

[2] For instance: 'Her politics were animated by a species of syndicalistic romanticism . . .', George Lichtheim, *Marxism. An Historical and Critical Study* London 1961, p. 319.

[3] 'Was nun?' (What Now?), *NZ*, 1909–10, Vol. II, pp. 33–40, 68–80.   [4] Ibid., p. 336.

present level; for the moment there was no excuse for driving the move-ment artificially forward into a head-on clash with society. Instead let the party turn its mind to the coming *Reichstag* elections, where the fruits of the present radical sentiment could better be harvested—in terms of a greatly increased vote. Sooner rather than later the SPD would get that absolute majority which Kautsky had postulated as one of the conditions for what he called revolution. 'Such a victory must result in nothing less than catastrophe for the whole ruling system.'[1]

Rosa replied as soon as possible after her return with a major piece of theoretical delineation between herself and Kautsky.[2] What had become of Kautsky, 'the theoretician of radicalism', the man who had only very recently written that, 'since the existence of the German Reich the social, political and international contradictions have never been stronger and might . . . very possibly create conditions under which a mass strike with the support of the unions could topple the existing régime'? Was it merely the desire for an empty victory—over unimpor-tant anarchist illusions about the mass strike, the 'hollow trumpetings of Domela Nieuwenhuis, which no one took seriously'? It was not her or anyone else's agitation that had produced the call for mass action, but the situation itself. And why was Kautsky speculating about Roman history in the middle of a proletarian mass action? Caution was if any-thing the job as well as the besetting sin of the official leadership; not the task of a distinguished and respected Marxist thinker. 'As a brake, Comrade Kautsky, we don't need *you*.' For many weeks, the polemic dragged on in the pages of *Neue Zeit*, becoming ever more personal.[3]

Then in the summer a new element entered the debate. The southern SPD leaders, particularly Wilhelm Keil in Baden, took advantage of the disarray in the hitherto solid radical front. Having been the party scapegoat for so many years, they now at last went over to the offensive. Either reform or revolution, they wrote mockingly; but don't dither, choose.[4] They themselves naturally opted for reform with wicked pleasure. The SPD executive in Baden, already notorious in the party for its annual support of the provincial government's budget, now issued a public declaration to the effect that this policy would continue

---

[1] Ibid., p. 77.
[2] 'Ermattung oder Kampf?' (Attrition or Collision?), *NZ*, 1909–10, Vol. II, pp. 257, 291 (27 May, 3 June 1910).
[3] The summary of Kautsky's polemics was in *NZ*, 1909–10, Vol. II: 'Was nun?', pp. 33–40, 68–80; 'Eine neue Strategie', 332–41, 364–74, 412–21; 'Zwischen Baden und Luxemburg', 652–67; 'Schlusswort', 760–5. Rosa Luxemburg's polemics against Kautsky, *NZ*, Vol. II: 'Ermattung oder Kampf', pp. 257, 291; 'Die Theorie und die Praxis', pp. 564, 626; 'Zur Richtigstellung', p. 756. Mehring's polemic, *NZ*, Vol. II: 'Der Kampf gegen die Monarchie', p. 609, 29 July 1910 (though Rosa was not mentioned by name) and Rosa's reply, 'Der Kampf gegen Reliquien', *LV*, 9 August 1910.
[4] Wilhelm Keil in *SM*, Vol. XIV, No. 3, p. 1186.

come what may. This was grist to Kautsky's mill. Instead of arguing with Rosa Luxemburg and struggling with the delicate and difficult question of revolutionary action, he could revert to the old euphoric state of concern with internal affairs, with maintaining the purely conceptual purity which he held to be so important. In a Social-Democratic 'government' whose power depended on the maximization of exclusiveness and of abstention from society, Kautsky was the Home Office's Public Relations Officer *par excellence*. In July he suggested to Rosa Luxemburg that their debate might conceivably be put back—and he hoped forgotten—in order to 'avoid anything that appears as a quarrel in the Marxist camp . . . [in view of the Baden declaration] it is the duty of all revolutionary and really republican-minded elements in our party to stand together and push aside our differences in order to make a common front against opportunism.'[1]

Rosa Luxemburg refused. She was no longer interested in the dreary pleasures of beating frayed and dusty southern carpets when far more important issues were available. This refusal to join in the southern witch-hunt produced a further spate of acid comments. Kautsky elaborated his disappointment in an article wittily entitled 'Between Baden and Luxemburg', in which he accused Rosa Luxemburg of insisting on polemics about her own second-rate preoccupations when there was vital internal work to be done.[2] It was the most important of Kautsky's polemical formulations of the period, for it exposed the real difference between him and Rosa, which was to carry them into bitterness and contempt for each other right through the war. 'When we look at the Duchies of Baden and Luxemburg on the map we find that between them lies Trier, the city of Karl Marx. If from there you go left across the border, you come to Luxemburg. If you turn sharp right and cross the Rhine, you reach Baden. The situation on the map is a symbol for the situation of German Social Democracy today.'[3] By implication Kautsky's own centre position was identified with that of Marx. He never for one moment gave up the belief that his views were the only orthodox expression of Marxism. It was this central location of Marx more than anything that eventually earned him the lasting and lively hatred of the Bolsheviks, who had long ago carried Marx off to the left.

But Rosa was not the one to cede vacant ground to her opponents. She was perfectly willing to bring the situation in south Germany within the scope of her argument. But unlike Kautsky she did not think of Prussia and Baden as two separate problems with only a decision of priority to be made between them. For Rosa Luxemburg the whole Baden question was not only a chronic drug-resistant symptom of the

---

[1] *NZ*, 1909–10, Vol. II, p. 564.   [2] *NZ*, 1909–10, Vol. II, pp. 652–67.   [3] Op. cit., p. 667.

old revisionist disease, but was linked directly to the more interesting question of a static or an advancing party tactic. It was no use merely to condemn or weep over breaches of SPD discipline when something much bigger was at stake. For the situation in the south, far from being an isolated evil, was causally connected with the state of the party as a whole.

When does the party bother with what happens in the south? When a world-shaking scandal takes place in the matter of the budget—but the party as a whole *never* bothers with the daily activities of the party leadership, of the caucus in the provincial parliament, of the press in the south. . . . For twelve years already the party has been on the defensive against all revisionist tendencies and merely plays the role of the night watchman, who only appears and sounds the alarm when there is a disturbance in the street. The results show that by these means the evil cannot be removed. . . . Not through formal prohibitions or through discipline, but only by the maximum development of mass action whenever and wherever the situation permits, a mass action which brings into play the broadest masses of the proletariat . . . only in this way can the clinging mists of parliamentary cretinism, of alliances with the middle classes, and the [rest of such] petit-bourgeois localism be got rid of.[1]

Relations between Rosa and Kautsky were now so bad that she no longer wrote to *Neue Zeit* directly, but used her young friend Hans Diefenbach to act as an intermediary; the unfortunate but loyal youth wrote a series of stiff and awkward notes to Kautsky to inquire whether further replies on her part would be published or not.[2] As far as Rosa Luxemburg was concerned, the great pillars of SPD ideology had turned out to be nothing but a heap of sophistries attractively glued together, which had now fallen apart under the pressure of the suffrage campaign. The whole concept of revolution, indeed the very use of the word by Kautsky, proved to be meaningless; it had only to come into contact with a real revolutionary situation to break down into its constituent syllables, so many daring sounds without real meaning. Rosa never quite recovered from this eye-opener. For behind the particular failure lurked a more general one: if the leadership were not serious about this, how much more of the whole programme of defiance would prove to be merely words? So the contrast between leaders—individuals with evident human failings—and the happily anonymous and solid masses, was sharpened by the experience of the suffrage campaign and its consequences. The greater her disillusion with the definable 'establishment', the more she emphasized the prophylactic role of the conceptual masses —until in 1914 they too let her down, and she had to resort to a concept of the masses in its own way almost as arbitrary as Lenin's very different concept of the proletariat.

---

[1] 'Die Badische Budgetabstimmung', *Bremer Bürgerzeitung*, August 1910.
[2] Hans Diefenbach to Karl Kautsky, no date (presumably Autumn 1910), IISH Archives, D VII, 425.

The break with Kautsky also meant that Rosa's main supporter in the party had become her enemy. Bebel could now count on Kautsky for his assistance in keeping the wretched woman quiet. 'Dear Rosa must not be allowed to spoil our plans for Magdeburg . . . I shall see to it that the dispute will be relegated . . . to obscurity.'[1] Victor Adler rejoiced. He had 'sufficiently low instincts to get a certain amount of pleasure from what Karl was suffering at the hands of his friend. But it really is too bad—the poisonous bitch will yet do a lot of damage, all the more because she is as clever as a monkey [blitzgescheit] while on the other hand her sense of responsibility is totally lacking and her only motive is an almost perverse desire for self-justification. Imagine', he wrote to Bebel, 'Clara already equipped with a mandate and sitting with Rosa in the Reichstag! That would give you something to laugh about, compared to which the goings on in Baden would look like a pleasure outing.'[2] Mehring, too, supported Kautsky. He saw nothing in Rosa's suggestions but a confusion of tactics; anchored in his knowledge of the Marxist texts, he agreed with Kautsky that by raising the issue of the republic, the Socialist aims of the revolution would be forgotten.[3] Rosa did not hesitate to polemicize against Mehring as well; the result was that she once more fell out with the old man, and this breach was not repaired until his severe illness eighteen months later.[4]

Such support as Rosa had came from an odd and motley group, and not always because they fully agreed with her proposals. Clara Zetkin was completely loyal as always; Konrad Haenisch found this an excellent way of baiting the local bureaucracy in the Ruhr which he so hated. In Bremen Pannekoek and Henke gladly threw the local organization behind any radical agitation. Her friend Marchlewski, who had again taken up his German party activities after his return from Poland, supported her whole-heartedly. But now drawn up on the other side were all the radicals of 1909, the entire editorial board of Neue Zeit, including Rosa's friend Emmanuel Wurm (henceforth to be degraded to Würmchen), her colleagues at the party school, and of course the executive and most of the bureaucracy of the party. Rosa Luxemburg's role was the loneliest of all in any self-regarding political party—that of an individual! The fact that freedom of expression was a cherished right only made her loneliness more obvious.

---

[1] August Bebel to Karl Kautsky, 6 August 1910, IISH Archives, D III, 140.

[2] Victor Adler to August Bebel, 5 August 1910, in Victor Adler, Briefwechsel, p. 510. But Bebel was not going to eat humble pie before any 'we told you so' from Vienna. 'All that "Rosary" isn't as terrible as all that [compared to the] unbridled opportunism of the south Germans . . . with all the wretched female's squirts of poison I wouldn't have the party without her', he replied tartly. Bebel to Adler, 16 August 1910, ibid., p. 512.

[3] NZ, 1909–10, Vol. II, p. 610.

[4] 'Der Kampf gegen Reliquien', refused by NZ and published in LV, 9 August 1910. See also below, p. 311.

Abroad, too, the majority of Socialists supported Kautsky; the Austrians, the PPS, and the Belgians sent him letters of encouragement. Even the Bolsheviks, of all the principal parties of the International the most likely to back Rosa Luxemburg, expressed non-committal surprise. For Lenin, Karl Kautsky was still the fountain-head of Marxist orthodoxy. Leo Trotsky, self-appointed broker among the Russian factions and with his own sources of information in each group, wrote to Kautsky at the end of August 1910:

A few words about your polemic with Rosa Luxemburg. In this matter, as in everything else, the Russians are split in their view. The Mensheviks declare themselves perfectly in agreement with you, but are trying to interpret your point of view as a 'change' from your previous tactical intransigence to ... Menshevism! According to my friend Kamenev who has just come to see me from Paris, the Bolsheviks, or more correctly Lenin (no one else speaks for them), are of the opinion that you are quite right in your judgement as to the present political situation, but that the nature of the agitation which Lux [sic] is carrying on could be both very useful and important for Germany. In order to get unqualified approval for your point of view, Lenin suggests that you put up a motion at the next party congress demanding sharp agitation and pointing to the unavoidable nature of revolutionary struggle [in the future]. I at any rate have not met a single Comrade—even among the Bolsheviks—who has come out openly for Luxemburg [der sich mit Luxemburg solidarisch erklärt]. As far as my humble self is concerned, I think that the governing tactical factor with Luxemburg is her noble impatience. This is a very fine quality, but to raise it to the leading principle of the [German] party would be nonsense. This is the typical Russian method. . . .[1]

Trotsky was perfectly right. It was the Russian method, openly advocated only since 1906.

Kautsky was not above accepting other people's formulations which fell conveniently into his lap. He may have used this one to develop another of those attractive antitheses when he came to analyse, in 1912, what was then already known as the Marxist 'Centre'. The middle position was the only correct position for the German party. On each wing he saw two distinct types of impatience, both disastrous. On the left there was rebel's impatience (as suggested by Trotsky, though Kautsky never acknowledged any debt for the phrase). This meant pre-empting the natural development of the revolution everywhere, and bringing about the catastrophe he had predicted in The Road to Power by artificial and premature means. Interestingly, Trotsky was also the first to identify the 'Russian' origin of Rosa's attitude. It goes back beyond that date of course—to 1898; her whole style of argument, her passion for action, was always more Russian or Polish than German. Was this the clue which Kautsky and his friends picked up at the beginning of

[1] Leo Trotsky to Karl Kautsky, 21 July 1910, IISH, D XXII, 68.

the war, when they accused Rosa of being pro-Russian?

Diametrically opposite on the right wing of the party was the 'states-man's impatience' of the revisionists, which also wanted action but of a different kind—action *in* society and not against it. Kautsky recognized that the source of these two kinds of impatience was identical even though the objects were different. Both sprang from an inability to find satisfaction within a static and isolated Socialist world. There was a strong if unconscious element of self-defence in Kautsky's attitude. He was the intellectual king in a Socialist world which had become real only through the organization of the SPD, through the power and policy of the executive and its local bureaucracy. Without organized isolation Kautsky's importance as a theoretician would be finished; there would no longer be anyone to whom his formulations applied. And so it happened. After the war, with the SPD executive absorbed into society, Kautsky found himself relegated to the role of a has-been without ever really knowing why. Ironically, it was only the hatred of Lenin and the Bolsheviks for their former hero Kautsky, echoed by the German Communist Party, that kept him alive.

'Very well, alone.' Rosa Luxemburg did not possess the nexus of political friendships which had always kept Bernstein within earshot of the power centre even after the party had condemned his views. To the large majority of German Socialists she seemed an extremely quarrelsome female who did not hesitate to round on former friends if they dared to disagree with her. But she was stimulated rather than put off. Since 1907 she had become much more self-sufficient. If need be she would dispense with political friends altogether. There would be no more compromise; she could raise her standard much higher—only those who measured up to it would be admitted to the inner circle of friends.

At the same time she was back in the maelstrom of politics after an absence of nearly three years. Her barn-storming in the early months of 1910 produced a flood of invitations to address meetings, which she accepted or refused according to her mood and the time available. She disliked too many interruptions to her teaching courses at the school, to which she had, of course, returned. Her health, too, troubled her intermittently. But for any important subject she was always willing to give up weekends to address meetings. Any suggestion that Social Democracy was likely to be misrepresented by unsuitable speakers always brought her hotfoot on to the scene.[1]

---

[1] Thus she was anxious to accept an otherwise most inconvenient invitation to a fraternal meeting in Leipzig with Guesde and Vaillant, representing the French Socialists, during the 1911 Morocco crisis. About a series of such meetings in Berlin she wrote indignantly that 'it is a scandal that all we get from France are representatives of the anarchists instead of the real Social Democrats'.

The standard of public speaking in the SPD was weighty but dull. Local party officials had difficulty in obtaining interesting visitors from Berlin; members of the executive were usually busy and exceptionally pedestrian as speakers. Rosa Luxemburg had the reputation of drawing large crowds and always created an atmosphere of excitement and euphoria which was becoming the rare exception at party meetings. As a result she benefited from a curious political symmetry: as she lost her influence with the executive and the party leaders, she was more than ever in demand at the periphery of party life. Did this situational facility contribute to the development of her 'democratic' views? But the enthusiasm of local officials and members was deceptive; Rosa frequently mistook the response of her audience for genuine radical fervour. Her trade-union critics were right when they accused her of being totally unfamiliar with organization and its peculiar problems; she really had no conception of the dullness and routine in the lives of people like Dittmann in Solingen, Henke in Bremen, or Haenisch in Dortmund, and of the warm welcome which local branches extended to any interesting or distinguished speaker, especially a woman who could speak of revolution at first hand.

Nearly all her meetings struck her as 'grandiose'; if such was the spirit then it was high time to make up for her fallow years. 'I have promised myself in future to agitate far more than in the last seven years', she wrote in the summer of 1910. In typical Luxemburg style she was determined to carry the war right into the enemy's camp. In August 1910 she attended in person the Baden party congress at Offenburg—at which the offensive decision to support that year's state budget was taken. When Adolf Geck—another radical lost in a desert of revisionism—offered her a series of public meetings she accepted enthusiastically. She addressed four of these and only interrupted her tour reluctantly to attend the International congress at Copenhagen. As soon as this was over she returned for a further six meetings, until she had to flee to Berlin to recover from an 'excess of strange hands and faces'.[1]

The SPD executive viewed these activities with a jaundiced eye, not to speak of the Baden party leadership who considered Rosa their particular enemy. Bebel, whatever his private views, was far too skilful a politician to be influenced by personal considerations. In 1910, when he wanted something from her, he could still be *'zuckersüss'* (sweet as sugar); he confessed, at least in private, that he would rather put up

---

[1] Her original attempt to get Merker, the Baden party secretary and a young disciple, to organize meetings had foundered on his gloomy prognostications of failure. The invitation from Geck was an unexpected windfall. She left Merker in peace until in 1913 she returned to the attack and he actually organized a number of meetings for her which nearly ended his party career.

with her than any revisionist. But a year later a further incident took place which for all practical purposes ended the personal contact between Bebel and Rosa Luxemburg for good. 'From then on Comrade Bebel could only hear with his right ear', according to Rosa's own medical aphorism.[1]

In the summer of 1911 another international crisis suddenly blew up, the most serious to date. Under the personal direction of the Emperor, the German Foreign Office was anxious to flex its muscles in order to intimidate France. What Palmerston had been able to do with impunity for England in the middle of the nineteenth century, the German government now copied—was Germany after all not entitled to parity? On 1 July 1911 the cruiser *Panther* was sent to Agadir in Morocco to 'protect' local German interests. Camille Huysmans, the secretary of the International Socialist Bureau, sent a round-robin to all member-parties asking for their reaction to the impending crisis; these differed considerably except for a general desire to play it cool. Some favoured a general conference of delegates to the International Bureau, others a meeting of the representatives of the countries immediately involved; the rest failed to suggest anything.[2]

In Germany the correspondence was dealt with by Herman Molken-buhr, a senior party official. Bebel was again in Zürich, now his second home. In his reply to Huysmans, Molkenbuhr stressed the factors tending to peace, and pointed out that mutual class-interests made a war between two capitalist powers unlikely. These arguments served to disguise the fact that the SPD's preoccupations were elsewhere—with the forthcoming *Reichstag* elections. The executive was strenuously concerned to make good the defeat of 1907, to prove Kautsky's theorem that votes were more effective than mass strikes. In these circumstances Molkenbuhr's letter was reasonable, though lacking in sophistication.

If we should prematurely commit ourselves to such an extent, and allow the Morocco question to take precedence over matters of internal policy, so that effective electoral weapons can be used against us, the consequences will be unforeseeable. . . . We must not allow internal developments—fiscal policy, agrarian privileges, etc.—to be pushed into the background. But that is precisely what would happen if we preach the Moroccan question in every village. All we would achieve is merely to strengthen the counter-tendency.[3]

Towards the end of July England officially took a hand in the crisis and this produced just the chauvinistic reaction in Germany which Molkenbuhr had feared. Bebel wrote to Huysmans that if necessary a

---

[1] Reported by Freidrich Stampfer, 'August Bebel' in *Die Grossen Deutschen* Vol. III, Berlin 1956, p. 559.

[2] The correspondence with the various national parties was reprinted as an appendix to the protocol of the SPD Congress: *Protokoll . . . 1911*, pp. 464 ff.

[3] Ibid., pp. 466–7.

meeting of the Bureau might well be called if things should really reach an extreme state. But the executive admitted later that, if at all possible, it preferred to avoid a special meeting of the International Bureau on this issue.

In the party itself there was a certain amount of spontaneous reaction to the crisis. Meetings were called, especially in Berlin, and were well attended.[1] The crisis moved on towards its climax in the last week of July without any very resolute indication of policy from party headquarters.

Suddenly a lurid light was thrown on the matter from a totally unexpected quarter—Rosa Luxemburg. As representative of the SDKPiL in the International Bureau, she had received Huysmans's letter as well as a copy of Molkenbuhr's reply. On 24 July, at the very height of the crisis, she published the latter, together with a stinging attack on Molkenbuhr's arguments. The internal views and attitudes in the SPD executive were now public property—precisely what Rosa Luxemburg desired. For primarily she was not concerned with the international crisis at all.

It is possible to maintain different points of view regarding the necessity or otherwise of a conference of the International Socialist Bureau as a result of the Morocco affair . . . but the attitude of the German party to the Socialist-sponsored efforts in other countries clearly has not been exactly encouraging. Therefore it is all the more interesting to examine the reasons which have brought our party to take this line. Improbable as it may seem, these are once again—consideration for the impending *Reichstag* elections.

She admitted that it was probable that government circles and the right-wing parties would use the Morocco affair to whip up nationalist sentiment. For that very reason it became all the more necessary to counter this with widespread agitation to 'expose to the masses the miserable background and dirty capitalistic interests which are involved'. Success or otherwise in terms of votes was of secondary importance. 'The real purpose of the *Reichstag* elections is to enable us to spread *Socialist education*, but this cannot be achieved if we narrow the circle of our criticism by excluding the great international problems, [but rather we must] advance condemnation of capitalism to all corners of the world. . . .' The favourable situation in which the SPD was entering the *Reichstag* elections was not a political accident, but 'the fruit of the entire historical development inside and outside Germany, and the advantage of *this* situation can only be lost if we continue to regard the entire life of the party and all the tasks of class struggle merely from the point of view of the ballot slip'.[2]

[1] *Vorwärts*, 4 July 1911.
[2] All in *LV*, 24 July 1911.

It all sounded extremely self-confident, almost brazen, coming from someone who only the year before had apparently been cut down to size. Yet on the day after the article had gone off to the *Leipziger Volkszeitung*, Rosa wrote to a friend that 'she had no idea if she had done right' in sending it. While she had no doubt that her view was correct, the self-confidence of the style was more apparent that real. There was after all no one now whose advice she could seek.

This eruption was followed a month later by a specific criticism of the agitational leaflet on the Morocco crisis which the SPD had finally issued, more to calm the critics than to raise any substantial public protest.[1] This time Rosa did not hesitate, for she had found out that the official appeal had been written by none other than Karl Kautsky. Once more the party was treated to a Kautsky–Luxemburg polemic with Rosa now wearing the jousting colours of the *Leipziger Volkszeitung* and Kautsky as the official spokesman of the party in *Vorwärts*—for the first time since 1905.[2]

At the beginning of August Bebel came back from Zürich in a fury. The executive knew that this time there was no diverting the discussion into soothing generalizations about future policy. A sharp personal conflict was inevitable, and the executive decided to turn defence into attack by launching a personal campaign against Rosa Luxemburg just before the congress, so that this aspect should be uppermost in people's minds. A circular was sent to all delegates in which the executive's case on Morocco was repeated, with a respectable batch of documents annexed; Rosa Luxemburg was accused of indiscretion, disloyalty, and breach of party discipline. Bebel coolly evaluated the prospects of conflict. 'Probably I shall have an argument with the Lux. at Jena. No doubt you will be pleased', he remarked to Victor Adler.[3] And at the congress he performed superbly, in a tone of simple, homely confidence, conjuring up an atmosphere reeking of old comradely loyalties which went far deeper than the present discontents, and which Rosa and her like were subtly precluded from sharing.

Yes indeed, comrades, some of you seem discontented with your government and find that it has not done what it should and ought, that the fires will have to be stoked to drive it forward . . . it is nothing but a sign of vitality when the party bestirs itself and shows its dissatisfactions. . . . But on the whole you have generally been satisfied with us; after all you have always re-elected us. . . .[4]

---

[1] 'Unser Marokko-Flugblatt', *LV*, 26 August 1911. The executive's manifesto is in *Vorwärts*, 9 August 1911.

[2] Rosa Luxemburg, 'Um Marokko', *LV*, 24 July 1911; 'Friedensdemonstrationen', *LV*, 31 July 1911; 'Die Marokkokrisis und der Parteivorstand', *LV*, 5 August 1911; 'Unser Marokko-Flugblatt', *LV*, 26 August 1911; 'Wieder Masse und Führer', *LV*, 29 August 1911; 'Zur Erwiderung', *LV*, 30 August 1911. Karl Kautsky in *Vorwärts*, 4 August, 5 August, 29 August, 30 August 1911.

[3] Victor Adler, *Briefwechsel* p. 539.   [4] *Protokoll . . . 1911*, p. 173.

As far as the International was concerned, 'if there is one nation—and I say this without wanting to offend any other—which has always done its damnedest for the International at all times and as a matter of priority, then it is the German party'.

. . . It is clear that Comrade Luxemburg committed a serious indiscretion when she published Comrade Molkenbuhr's letter in *Leipziger Volkszeitung*. . . . If negotiations are ever to reach a successful conclusion, then discretion is a matter of honour for all concerned. Moreover, Comrade Luxemburg seriously misled other comrades by publishing Molkenbuhr's letter without its first sentence, and by claiming that the letter expressed the opinion of the party executive.[1]

In the best British tradition, Cabinet solidarity was being sacrificed under pressure and some of the blame at least was allowed to fall personally on Molkenbuhr's shoulders, but not a quarter of what Bebel unloaded on to him in private.[2]

The tactic now was to annihilate the political person of Rosa Luxemburg.

Now you know what to make of the fighting methods of Comrade Luxemburg. She did the same thing to Kautsky last year. I told him then, when he let himself be dragged into a public debate: 'you would have done better to have put your pen away for the duration.' Comrade Luxemburg did not hesitate to publish Kautsky's purely private letters. From that moment on I swore—not so much to cease writing to Comrade Luxemburg, which would be impossible—but never to write anything of which she might later be able to make use. . . .

He rounded on her directly at the end—for the rules of debate at SPD congresses were none too strict in requiring speakers to address the Chair. 'That is the result of your behaviour. You have managed to get us to agree with the opinion which the International Socialist Bureau has of you. It was I, as I said, who advised them against their original intention [of not sending you any more correspondence].'[3]

Rosa Luxemburg conducted a spirited defence of her own position, and counter-attacked strongly on the question of principle. There was little difficulty in answering the charges of misrepresentation. By quoting Bebel's own words she showed that his version of favouring a Bureau meeting could not be substantiated. 'If my eyes do not deceive me

---

[1] Ibid., p. 216.

[2] When Adler wrote to Bebel that as far as he could remember, Molkenbuhr's letter had been very sensible, though obviously not intended for publication, Bebel replied that 'things would never have got so far if Molkenbuhr were not a miserable hack. . . . I made things clear enough to him, but what is the use if one is far away, and only hears of things much too late, and when one's answers and suggestions are bound to be overtaken by events.' Adler to Bebel, 7 August 1911; Bebel to Adler, 9 August 1911, in Victor Adler, *Briefwechsel* pp. 538–9.

[3] *Protokoll . . . 1911*, pp. 216–18.

[these quotations] show a negative intention, but I never dare not to believe anything which the party executive asserts; as a faithful party member I accept the old saying *credo quia absurdum*—I believe it precisely because it is absurd.'[1]

The question of indiscretion, though less important, had to be pursued at greater length.

I do not only dispute the fact that it is an indiscretion on the part of a party member to take issue in public with the activities of the party executive in the interests of the entire party, but I go further and declare: the party executive has been guilty of neglect of duty, of not putting the whole case before us. It was its duty to publish the correspondence and to submit it to the criticism of the party. Quite honestly we are not dealing simply with formalities, but with a big question; whether the party executive has been guilty of neglect or not, protest actions against Imperialism or not. . . . If Molkenbuhr's conception [of what was to be done] was not that of the party executive—and I accept this in view of the latter's statement—then I ask what was it that induced you to do nothing in the meantime when something should have been done. . . . In closing I want to say that in the entire Morocco affair the party executive is not the prosecutor, but the defendant, the one who has to justify itself for the sins of omission. (Quite right.) Its unhappy situation could not be made clearer than in the statement of Comrade Müller. In my whole life I have never seen a picture of such pathetic confusion. (Laughter—Bebel: 'Take it easy'.) This is why I did not take your accusations badly, I forgive you and offer you the fatherly advice . . . (Bebel: 'Motherly advice'—great amusement), do better in future![2]

Having dealt with the personal side, Rosa tried to speak next day on the broader international question. The executive had followed the government's official line in ascribing the seriousness of the crisis mostly to Lloyd George's intervention in a purely Franco-German clash of interests. 'But this is quite irrelevant. On the contrary, I maintain—and I think everyone with me except perhaps Molkenbuhr—that it was not this or that speech by an English minister, but the fact that a cruiser was sent by the Germans to Agadir, that is to say the factual interference of the German Empire in the Morocco affair, which should have been the moment for us to develop our protest action against the Morocco danger.'[3] Here for the first time then was the germ of the notion that the main enemy is at home, a view which was to be developed during the war and immortalized by Liebknecht in his famous slogan.[4]

But it would have been too much to expect the personal aspect to be settled on the first day. As the congress went on, Rosa Luxemburg and Bebel got more and more in each other's hair. To his reference regarding their future correspondence, she replied: 'This precaution is quite unnecessary. You, Comrade Bebel, know as well as I do that the letters

[1] *Protokoll . . . 1911*, p. 204.   [2] Ibid.
[3] *Protokoll . . . 1911*, p. 247.   [4] See below, p. 394.

we write to each other are not normally fit for public reproduction. (Great amusement.)' Finally Rosa Luxemburg brought out the weapon which circumstances had placed in her hand the year before.

I have had at least one satisfaction. During your speech, Comrade Bebel, did you perhaps notice from where you got your great ovation? (Laughter.) The applauding hands were all Bavarian and from Baden. (Great disturbance. Shouts—'Is that so bad?' 'Cheek, unbelievable.' 'That is what we call party unity.') . . . I don't grudge you your laurels from the south, you have richly earned them. (Applause and hisses.)

And hisses were rare in the fraternal SPD!

This time, however, Rosa Luxemburg was not alone. Moral sentiment ran deep where militarism and war were concerned. Apart from her various newly-won friends of the year before, many future centrists and friends of *Neue Zeit*, and even some right-wingers like Eisner and Frank, leapt to her defence. Ledebour, the cross-eyed Don Quixote who strongly disliked her person and her policies, for once defended her vigorously.

No one has to answer here except the executive. As I prophesied a snare has been prepared for Rosa Luxemburg out of the publication of her letter. All this is merely being used to disguise the real heart of the matter. Comrade Luxemburg and I have often been in conflict; as I know Comrade Luxemburg—and as I know myself—we shall be in conflict many times yet, in the course of a long and fruitful career for the party—I hope. . . . Such mass demonstrations against war and warmongers as have taken place are not the achievement of Müller and the executive . . . the main credit must go to Rosa Luxemburg for her criticism and to her alone.[1]

The row did not stop in the German party. Under pressure from the SPD executive, the International Socialist Bureau examined the implications of Rosa Luxemburg's action. Huysmans had been in Berlin on 30 July, where he had again received Bebel's views on the unlikelihood of war (according to Bebel, 'the only war over Morocco will break out at home'[2]) and on the evil behaviour of Comrade Luxemburg. Persuaded that the status of the German party was at stake, Camille Huysmans rather unwisely suggested that Rosa Luxemburg might be barred from access to private correspondence, other than that which concerned the Polish party directly. He did not realize that his private musings would also become public property, for Bebel did not hesitate to use such useful ammunition. Rather unctuously he pointed out that it was only due to him that this prohibition was not put into effect—and thus in turn committed his own breach of confidence.

The suggestion of sanctions against Rosa Luxemburg in the Inter-

---

[1] *Protokoll . . . 1911*, pp. 212–13.   [2] Victor Adler, *Briefwechsel*, p. 539.

national Bureau was a pure red herring; the Bureau was not entitled to take such action, and Rosa Luxemburg knew it perfectly well. 'Huysmans is the employed secretary of the International Bureau who carries out our work and has hitherto done so splendidly. The decision as to who gets copies of information from the International Bureau is not within his competence, but is a matter for the Bureau itself, of which I am a member—and I would like to see the Bureau that would dare to cut me off from its information.'[1] As to Huysman's statement that Rosa Luxemburg had committed an indiscretion, and not for the first time, this was ironed out at the meeting of the International Socialist Bureau in Zürich shortly after the congress on 23 September 1911. Rosa Luxemburg asked him sharply if he had really said all this to Bebel. He awkwardly admitted it, but stated that the proceedings of the Jena congress, which he attended, had convinced him that he had expressed himself badly because of his poor command of German. All he had wanted to say to Bebel was that indiscretions had indeed taken place but were not necessarily all due to her.[2] This unexpected involvement in the factional struggles of the SPD was painful and bewildering. The *Leipziger Volkszeitung*, which had carried Rosa's articles, also had a position to defend and published a cutting reply to Huysmans's awkward attempt to extricate himself.[3]

The official last word on the matter was spoken in a communiqué by the International Socialist Bureau. 'After the agenda had been dealt with, a few questions of a private nature were raised. In particular it was decided that all communications from the Secretariat to the members of the Bureau must be treated as confidential, except those published by the Secretariat itself.'[4] So honours were even. The motion of censure on Rosa Luxemburg in the International Socialist Bureau had been officially withdrawn, while she conceded to the majority that she had sinned in form and in future would not publish private correspondence relating to BSI affairs. Both Lenin and Plekhanov were among those in favour of maintaining discipline.

The Jena congress was one of those rare occasions when an event outside the party shook groups and individuals out of their usual alignment. The issues were profound and emotional: bureaucracy against membership, executive against democracy—but all overlaid with the issue of war and peace. Many of those who supported Rosa did not subscribe either to her activities the year before, or to her oppositional tactics in the coming years. By raising the issue himself, Bebel had perhaps performed a useful service; many of the accumulated resent-

---

[1] *Protokoll . . . 1911*, p. 205.
[2] *Vorwärts*, 27 September 1911.
[3] *LV*, 28 September 1911.
[4] *Bulletin Périodique du BSI*, Brussels 1912, No. 8, pp. 129 ff.

ments in a party with great hopes but little immediate prospects could be shaken out and everybody disperse feeling better. An occasional explosion was salutary as long as it could be contained; the SPD was not yet ready for a straight-jacket.

XI

IN OPPOSITION,

1911–1914

IN between the resounding phrases at the Jena congress about the forthcoming victory of Social Democracy, there were tucked away the executive's tactical proposals for the *Reichstag* elections. They were put forward mutedly, with some hesitation, seeing that they called for electoral co-operation with other parties. Even Bebel had expressed his doubts whether the party would accept them, particularly as it would mean putting a temporary damper on the class aspect of agitation, which was always popular locally.[1] But the congress had been so absorbed by the spectacle of the party executive getting into trouble over Morocco that the election proposals had passed by virtually without challenge. Bebel's worries had proved unjustified—another incidental bonus for the executive.

Internal debate in the party was always put aside for the duration of the campaign. Radicals and revisionists alike swarmed forth to agitate and canvass. Fears expressed by Rosa's friends, that the acrimony of recent disputes might affect her willingness to speak, were scornfully dismissed.[2] But though the atmosphere at the actual meetings was again 'grandiose', this time the whole paraphernalia of the election left her cold. She could not even bring herself to register any pleasure at the party's victory, substantial though it was. The Socialist vote increased from 3,250,000 to 4,250,000 as compared with 1907, and their deputies from 43 to 110. This made the SPD by far the largest political party in Germany. It received more than twice as many votes as the Catholic Centre, its nearest rival, who obtained 91 seats. Everyone was jubilant—revisionists, executive, Kautsky and his friends. The prognostications of *The Road to Power* and the policy of peaceful attrition were triumphantly justified. Or so it seemed at the end of January 1912.

But the elections produced a curious aftermath. In accordance with the decision taken at the congress the year before, the SPD had in fact formed an electoral alliance with the Progressive party for the run-off

---

[1] Philipp Scheidemann, *Memoiren eines Sozialdemokraten*, Dresden 1928, Vol. I, p. 109.
[2] *Briefe an Freunde*, p. 28, to Konrad Haenisch, dated December 1911.

elections.[1] As usual in a system of single-member constituencies, the first poll had penalized the smaller parties. The National Liberals won only four seats, while the Progressives, who had received a total of 1,500,000 votes, held none at all. The executive saw an excellent chance of strengthening still further the anti-reactionary coalition. The alliance between SPD and Progressives in the second and last poll would ensure a strong anti-blue-black (Conservative-Catholic) alliance by getting the most promising candidate elected, whether Liberal, Progressive, or Socialist.[2]

In the event, however, the Progressive voters did not obey the guidance of their leadership. While the Social Democrats and their disciplined organization delivered to the Progressives all the constituencies they had undertaken to deliver, they received very little help from their allies. 'The Progressives in fact owed their continuation as a political party to the electoral policy of Social Democracy and to the discipline of its voters.'[3] The recriminations in the SPD naturally began at once, with Rosa Luxemburg among the earliest and most outspoken critics.

Already the year before she had warned against the illusion that the two middle-class parties would prove genuine allies against the Right. 'Both of these parties hit out against the Left, and fall over towards the Right, and the few party leaders who retain a little of their Liberal conscience make hopeless attempts . . . to pull back the chariot of Liberalism from the bog of reaction.'[4] Now at the end of February 1912 she examined the policy and its results in detail. Before going on to the question of principle, she compared the expectations with the actual achievements, and so blatant was the failure that she, who had always affected to despise 'practical' politics, was able to write sharply: 'A practical arrangement demands in the first instance to be judged on its practical results.'[5] It did not require a sophisticated electoral analysis to show that the Socialists had given what they promised and had received in return less than a quarter of what they were entitled to expect. 'It is hard to read the details of the arrangement without blushing from shame and rage at the Progressive attitude.' . . .

There is a very simple conclusion. The old lesson of Marxist historical materialism, to the effect that *real class interests are stronger* than any 'arrangements'.[6]

---

[1] According to the German electoral system, a second poll was taken in those *Reichstag* constituencies where the first poll did not produce a clear majority for the candidate of any one party. Imperial Germany had single-member constituencies, i.e similar to the English system rather than to any system of party lists.

[2] *Protokoll . . . 1912*, pp. 27–28; see also Paul Hirsch and Bruno Borchardt, *Die Sozialdemokratie und die Wahlen zum deutschen Reichstag*, Berlin 1912, pp. 24–25.

[3] Schorske, *German Social Democracy*, p. 231.

[4] *LV*, 16 June 1911.

[5] 'Unsere Stichwahltaktik'. *LV*, 29 February 1912.

[6] *LV*, 1 March 1912; 2 March 1912.

It was far better, she declared, to act *on* Progressives, and possibly even Liberals, then to act *with* them, to fight them rather than to appease them, to defend one's own class interests solely and exclusively instead of compromising them for non-existent benefits. 'A little less effort in parliamentary scene-shifting, less naïve belief in any "new era" on all and every occasion that the policy seems to drift to left or right; instead more quiet steadfastness and a long view in our policy, more calculation of distance for the great and decisive factors of class struggle—this is what we need in the great times in which we live.'[1]

And in due course the political alliances in the *Reichstag*, on which the SPD executive had placed so many hopes, proved as ephemeral as the electoral one. An attempt to give institutional significance to the SPD's primacy in the legislature by making Scheidemann vice-president of the *Reichstag* was undone after a few weeks by National Liberal defection. The party executive certainly did its best to appease its potential partners. On military questions, so dear to the National Liberals, the SPD introduced resolutions designed to improve pre-military training in the schools, and incidentally to procure for the SPD's co-operatives a chance to compete in the tenders for army supplies.[2]

In her running battle against the combinations in the new *Reichstag*, Rosa Luxemburg received the unexpected support of Franz Mehring, who had originally approved of the electoral alliance, but now turned strongly against it.[3] As we shall see, this unexpected alliance between Rosa Luxemburg and Franz Mehring was to provide the kernel of the new Left, leading first to the foundation of the *Sozialdemokratische Korrespondenz* and later providing a base around which *Spartakus* was able to rally.

The internal history of the party from 1911 to 1914 is confused and contradictory—and not nearly as schematic as recent historians have attempted to show. For one thing, membership of different groups within the party was far more variable and erratic than might be supposed. The realignment after the earthquake of 1914 undoubtedly had its roots in pre-war events, but the shock of the war was so great that for many people it brought about a complete change of attitude. The deep division which the war did bring to the surface, and at the same time helped to obscure for a while, was not the threefold one between revisionists, centre, and left, but the deeper antithesis between theoretical and practical revolutionaries.[4]

---

[1] *LV*, 4 March 1912.   [2] *Protokoll... 1912*, pp. 141–2.   [3] *NZ*, 1912–13, Vol. I, p. 628.

[4] For a carefully documented discussion of internal party affairs in these years, see Schorske, pp. 197–285. I must emphasize again that this treatment is too schematic and suggests group cohesions within the party which the evidence of private letters and documents generally contradicts—as opposed to the public writings and speeches on which the author excessively relies.

Two events require emphasis. In the spring of 1911 Paul Singer, co-chairman of the party and fairly consistent friend and supporter of the left wing, suddenly died. The election of a replacement caused a lengthy discussion about the composition and policy of the executive. The following year, with the added impetus of the Morocco affair, an attempt was made to reorganize the executive. Those who had opposed it in 1911 now hoped to make that body more radical, more sympathetic to its own policy. But the cohesion of the Left proved ephemeral, and this time the attackers were quietly routed. The executive was not enlarged, as they had proposed; the number of paid officials remained as it was—an increase in full-time bureaucrats was still seen as a radical measure at that time; on the other hand the party Control Commission, on which there was a sympathetic majority (Clara Zetkin was one of its moving spirits), had its functions reduced as a punishment for failing to support the executive over the Morocco question. The only bright spot was that the new co-chairman was another left-winger, Hugo Haase, but as he continued his law practice he was never able to devote the same amount of time to the work of the executive as full-time officials like Ebert and Scheidemann.

All the same, everyone was well satisfied with Haase's election. For Kautsky, soaring in his balloon of optimism, one of the last obstacles to whole-hearted collaboration with the executive was now removed.

In the last years it [the executive] had become the laughing stock of the whole world. But it is not, however, everyone's province to delight in its decrepitude in public like Rosa. Few people will not be encouraged by your election. . . . The only proper remedy is not to drive it into something of which it is not capable, but to get people on to it who can make a competent body out of an incompetent one.[1]

While Kautsky thus became reconciled to the executive after 1912, Rosa Luxemburg was pushed into total disillusion by the elections. In her private correspondence she described the resultant activities and attitudes as 'scandalous', 'hopeless', 'incredible'; she wrote the whole thing off as an event of no consequence. Even during the *Reichstag* campaign she could not resist an occasional opportunity of scoring at the expense of the executive at election meetings. The executive naturally took its revenge. From 1912 onwards the radicals were increasingly cut off from effective participation in the life of the party, and confined to protests; the executive kept the machine and the power. In this method of neutralizing opponents, the SPD reflected the policy and moods of society, its unwilling host; in the last two years before the war organized Social Democracy became almost the image of imperial Germany.[2] The

---

[1] Karl Kautsky to Hugo Haase, IISH, no date, C 436.

[2] For a comparative analysis of this similarity, see Gerhard Ritter, *Die Arbeiterbewegung in Wilhelminischen Reich*, Berlin 1959, pp. 52 ff.

moods of the country permeated the party. A wave of *Reichsverdrossenheit* (imperial disillusion), which the Chancellor of the time recalled in later years, was matched by *Parteiverdrossenheit*.[1]

The other development in the party which must be emphasized was the increasing importance and self-assertion of the SPD parliamentary group. This was a development many historians have missed altogether. Yet the crystallization of the parliamentary group of deputies as a factor in the party was natural enough. SPD *Reichstag* representation more than doubled in 1912. The new legislators, instead of being a small and lonely outpost of Social Democracy in the alien stronghold of society, had now become the largest group within it. Without realizing it they were corroded by institutional loyalty, by the atmosphere and tradition which all such bodies foster, particularly when entrance to the 'club' can only be achieved by the efforts and risks of public election. *Homme élu, homme foutu.* All important members of the executive had traditionally become *Reichstag* members, though there was nothing in the party statutes to that effect. It is interesting to speculate what would have happened if members of the executive had been automatically disbarred from sitting in the *Reichstag* or if, as in the RSDRP, the illegal nature of the party had forced the leaders to reside abroad. The dangers were not lost on western Communist parties after the war, who made elaborate arrangements to subordinate their parliamentary delegates to the party leadership outside.

In any case the concentration of the party's political effort into elections made for inevitable improvement in the status of the successful candidates. To be a deputy became important—in other people's eyes and in his own. Rosa Luxemburg herself saw evidence of this in her immediate circle. 'It is laughable how being [a member of the *Reichstag*] suddenly goes to all those good people's heads.[2] The left-wing contempt for self-sufficient parliamentary activity could only be heightened after 1912. No one was yet aware that power was shifting from the executive to the parliamentary faction (or better, that the executive was making its power felt through the parliamentary faction and not through normal party channels)—this only hit the eye after 1914 when the parliamentary delegation openly took over the party. But the universal pride in the party's greatly increased representation was matched by the increasing scorn of the radicals for the whole parliamentary mystique.

---

[1] Theobald von Bethmann-Hollweg, *Betrachtungen zum Weltkrieg*, Berlin 1919, Vol. I, p. 95.

[2] Some interesting points are made by Eberhard Pikart, 'Die Rolle der Parteien im Deutschen Konstitutionellen System vor 1914', in *Zeitschrift für Politik*, Vol. IX (1962), No. 1 (March), pp. 12–32. Among other things Pikart shows that the role of parties was more important in the constitutional life of imperial Germany than is often supposed and that there was a real feeling among deputies that they were close to the centre of power. Obviously this must have exercised a particularly strong pull on members of the SPD.

Rosa Luxemburg now began to cast about for a concrete alternative to elections and parliament. Criticism of official mistakes alone was no longer good enough. Since 1906 reliance on a return to the correct tactic —'the good old days'—smelt stale and artificial. Even the emphasis on a forward-looking tactic based on the masses, which was the essence of the mass-strike doctrine, no longer seemed sufficient; the mass strike was still an isolated phenomenon, which could only become meaningful during a revolutionary period. By 1912 Rosa Luxemburg recognized that a much more radical alteration of Socialist thinking in Germany was necessary. 'The eternal posturing against opportunism which only relies on phrases about our "old and tried tactics" is out-of-date . . . quite the contrary; we have to make a mighty push forward . . . I am giving considerable thought to this whole problem and the formulation of a completely new tactic.'

With all official ears now firmly stopped, the development of any new tactic was necessarily confined to personal discussions and elaboration in the press—but circumspectly. There was no question of organizing any internal opposition. A tentative attempt in this direction was made by Ledebour and some of those who had rallied against the executive in 1911; the party majority contemptuously labelled it the *Sonderbund* and unleashed a hailstorm of disapproval on the 'splitters'.[1] But there was evidence of a more subtle and unofficial co-operation between like-minded individuals and local organizations. These were necessary measures of self-defence. Like other extreme radicals, Rosa Luxemburg found it harder than before to obtain mandates for the party congress. Of the last five congresses before the war she attended only three; both in 1909 and in 1912 she failed to obtain a mandate and at Magdeburg in 1910 her mandate was actually challenged. This made it all the more necessary to nurse the districts which supported her and particularly the local leaders. In July 1911 she wrote to Dittmann: 'Even though I already have one from Hagen, I am reluctant to renounce the Remscheid mandate. I don't want to lose touch with that constituency and anyhow dislike the idea of appearing at every party congress with a different mandate.'[2]

Radical self-help was especially effective in the personal field. Rosa Luxemburg used her friendship with Clara Zetkin and Luise Kautsky to promote suitable friends and ex-students from the party school. She

---

[1] *Sonderbund* was the name used in 1847 by a group of Swiss cantons, who set themselves up in opposition to the Federal Union. The SPD had a curious devotion to history, particularly when it came to terminology and epithets.

[2] Rosa Luxemburg to Wilhelm Dittmann, 28 July 1911, Dittmann papers, SPD Archives, Bonn. Remscheid was the capital of Dittmann's parish in the Ruhr. The Hagen mandate was probably the result of some speeches she made there in the autumn of 1910 on the mass-strike question.

put herself out to get for Wilhelm Pieck, who wanted to leave his post as party secretary in Bremen, the job of assistant business manager of the party's cultural committee.[1] She recommended Thalheimer first to Haenisch at Dortmund and then to Lensch at Leipzig.[2] She tried hard to get Konstantin Zetkin a post at the party school in Berlin or some job in which his radical right-mindedness and ability—seen through eyes of affection—could be of use to the party; more use than as factotum on his mother's *Gleichheit*. It was this same radical self-help organization which caused the temporary and disastrous move of Radek first from Berlin to Bremen and then to Göppingen in Württemberg, to help out on the local *Freie Volkszeitung* while the regular editor was on holiday.

The importance of these activities must not be exaggerated. Not even later Communist historians, looking hard for traces of an emerging left-wing organization before the war, were able to make any case for the existence of an organized radical group. By temperament as much as by necessity, Rosa Luxemburg acted as an individual and on her own behalf. Previous disappointments with political friends made her very chary of entering into alliances. During 1911 she formed a working partnership with Lensch, the editor of *Leipziger Volkszeitung*, who seems to have admired her greatly and who visited her to discuss party affairs whenever he came to Berlin. He placed Rosa under contract to write regular articles, a commission which she accepted only after some hesitation—and largely for the sake of the fee. But even this collaboration with Lensch was sometimes stormy. And when he went on holiday in 1912 his deputy Hans Block, to whom Rosa Luxemburg referred as 'that animal' (*das Vieh*), proved far less co-operative.[3] She threatened to give up her work for *Leipziger Volkszeitung* altogether but withdrew her resignation when Lensch returned and apologized profusely. But he continued to try and cut out the most polemical passages from her articles. This collaboration with *Leipziger Volkszeitung* continued until Block finally took over from Lensch altogether in 1913 and the board of editors soon became locked in irreconcilable conflict with Rosa Luxemburg.

To many of her political supporters Rosa's uncommunicativeness and passion for privacy were largely incomprehensible. In September 1911 Konrad Haenisch complained that 'no one has seen anything of Rosa; though she sent a very kind sympathetic letter to Mehring, with whom she had broken completely . . . which confirms again . . . that she is in

---

[1] *Letters to Karl and Luise Kautsky*, p. 166, 9 January 1913.

[2] *Briefe an Freunde*, p. 25, to Konrad Haenisch, 24 March 1910.

[3] Block had taken her place at *Vorwärts* in December 1905 when she went to Warsaw and at the time she thought highly of his 'fresh and revolutionary outlook' (see above, p. 214).

the last resort not at all a bad person in spite of everything.'[1] But only a few days later he too threw up the sponge. 'Rosa has become utterly irresponsible', he wrote sadly to his correspondent.[2]

Konrad Haenisch was not perhaps a very good judge of people or situations. He was much agitated and distressed by an incident which in many ways was typical of Rosa Luxemburg. He tried to publish a defence of her at the Jena congress, pleading that any present misdeeds must be excused in view of all the loyal and devoted service she had always given to the party.[3] Moreover he had hinted—fatally—that she was entitled to special consideration as a woman. At once the full load of Rosa's fury was discharged on his head. First she sent a telegram to Henke, the editor of the Bremen paper: 'Suppress cretinous [*lümmelhaft*] article Haenisch.' When the red-headed knight errant wrote to inquire hesitantly what had caused this outburst he got the following reply:

Of course I was livid with you, because you simply would get it into your head to *defend* me, though in fact with your absurd strategy you succeeded in attacking me from behind. You wanted to defend my *morality* but instead conceded my *political* position. One could not have acted more wrongly. My morality needs no defence. You will have noticed that since 1898 . . . I have been continually and vulgarly abused especially in the south, and have *never* answered with so much as a line or a word. Silent contempt is all I have for this sort of thing. [Why?] Because—apart from personal pride—of the simple political belief that these personal denigrations are merely a manœuvre to avoid the political issue. It was clear before Jena that the party executive, who were in a mess, had no choice but to carry the dispute over into the area of personal morality. It was equally clear that all those who thought the matter important should have countered this manœuvre by not letting themselves be dragged into the area of personality. You however did just this, in so far as you concentrated on my person and gave away my position in substance . . . you may not even be aware of the impression that your article has made: a noble fearful plea for extenuating circumstances for someone condemned to death—enough to make anyone burst when one is in as important and favourable a tactical position as I was in Jena. . . . So much for the matter in hand. My 'anger' has long been forgotten and I really have other worries than to carry around all this rubbish in my head. So let that be the end of it![4]

Henke, too, got a taste of Rosa's touchiness. At the end of 1912 he

---

[1] 'Aus den Briefen Konrad Haenisches', in Carl Grünberg, *Archiv für die Geschichte des Sozialismus und der Arbeiterbewegung*, Vol. XIV (1929), p. 470.

[2] Loc. cit., 18 September 1911.

[3] *Bremer Bürgerzeitung*, 7 September 1911.

[4] *Briefe an Freunde*, December 1911. In spite of these explanations, Konrad Haenisch was quite unable to grasp her point of view. His comment was that of a spurned suitor: 'I have fallen out with all the radicals here on her account (especially with the people on *Vorwärts*), I have had the bitterest arguments with Mehring, I am on bad terms with Kautsky and Eckstein, all because I always stuck up for her—and now I get a kick in the pants from her as well.' (Grünberg, op. cit., p. 481.)

asked her to start writing for the *Bremer Bürgerzeitung* again after a two-year silence, only to discover that she would have nothing to do with him because he had stuck up for Radek.[1] Rosa was carrying out with a vengeance her determination never again to compromise with anyone.

But this intransigence had its compensations. Her attack on the party's policy in the run-off elections of 1912 brought her one entirely unexpected ally—Franz Mehring. That relationship had been going through a period of jealousy and indifference for the last five years, and had not been improved by Mehring's support of Kautsky in 1910. Then at the end of 1911 Mehring himself had trouble with the executive. He had attacked the party's electoral policy even before the elections, and after the victory received an official snub—a fact that was an open secret in the party.[2] In April, after various manœuvres, Kautsky succeeded in edging him out as leader writer of *Neue Zeit*. In future the leading articles, with the well-known diagonal arrow, were to appear no more; Mehring had to confine himself to reviews and other less politically sensitive work in the *Neue Zeit* supplement.[3]

As soon as she heard that Mehring had decided to throw up all collaboration with *Neue Zeit* she pleaded with him urgently.

Every decent person in the party who is not simply the slave of the executive will take your side. But how *could* you have let all this induce you to chuck such an extremely important position? Please do keep in mind the general party situation. You too will surely feel that we are increasingly approaching times when the masses in the party ̶ꜰꜰᴍ need energetic, ruthless and generous leadership, and that our powers-that-be—executive, central organ, Reichstag caucus, and the 'scientific paper' without *you*—will become continually more miserable, smallminded and cowardly. Clearly we shall have to face up to this attractive future, and we must occupy and hold all those positions which make it possible to spite the official 'leadership' by exercising the right to criticize. How few such positions there are, and how few people understand the situation you know better than I. The fact that the masses are none the less behind us and want different leaders has been shown from the last general meeting in Berlin, indeed from the attitude of almost all the party associations in the country. This makes it our duty to stick it out and not to do the official party bosses the favour of packing up. We have to accept continual struggles and friction, particularly when anyone attacks that holy of holies, parliamentary cretinism, as strongly as you have done. But in spite of all—not to cede an inch seems to be the right

[1] Rosa Luxemburg to Alfred Henke, 15 November 1912, Henke Papers, SPD Archives.

[2] Rosa wrote: 'Mehring has got a slap from the executive [*einen Rüffel erhalten*] over his article in *Neue Zeit* criticizing our parliamentary cretins. That is what our new "radical" executive looks like! Pity that this is not more widely known. People in the country need to know what goes on behind the scenes.' (9 December 1911.) Dittmann papers, SPD Archives. See also Schleifstein, *Mehring*, p. 57.

[3] See Schleifstein, *Mehring*, pp. 57–60.

slogan. *Neue Zeit* must not be handed over entirely to senility and officialdom. Laugh at these pathetic insults, and continue writing in it so that we can all take joy from what you write.[1]

He ignored the advice. 'One can only wish that he would not always take things so personally . . .', she sighed to her friends. They were very different people—both sensitive, but one personally and the other politically. Rosa had toughened enormously in this respect. Twelve years earlier, in Dresden and Leipzig, she had resigned over a very similar issue—and could still be tempted to threaten resignation by some of her present disagreements with Lensch. But Rosa Luxemburg was now rapidly developing the thesis of continuous battle, without retreat and at whatever personal cost and humiliation. This was to lead directly to the war-time principle of 'sticking to the masses at all costs' and once more explains why an organizational break was entirely unthinkable.[2]

As a result of this *rapprochement* with Mehring, Rosa Luxemburg went to some trouble with both Henke in Bremen—the Radek case was still only on the horizon—and with Lensch in Leipzig to secure Mehring's collaboration for both papers. To Lensch she suggested that Mehring be asked to write regularly, if necessary alternating with her. By June 1912 the last traces of Mehring's presence had been exorcized from *Neue Zeit*. But the Leipzig collaboration lasted hardly a year. In the summer of 1913 Lensch left *Leipziger Volkszeitung* and was replaced by Block. At once both Mehring and Rosa began to have difficulty in getting their stuff published as freely as hitherto. A number of articles were refused altogether and others had their sharpest stings drawn—a practice that always roused Rosa to fury.[3]

The final impetus for the creation of the first independent left-wing paper, *Sozialdemokratische Korrespondenz*, was, as so often in the history of radical self-assertion in the SPD, as much a personal as a political reaction. Hans Block, now editor of *Leipziger Volkszeitung*, was on holiday. Marchlewski, living in Germany on the edge of illegality, and therefore unable to risk any public controversy, was temporarily in charge of the paper at the beginning of September 1913. It was a curious

[1] Rosa Luxemburg to Franz Mehring, 19 March 1912, IML (M).
[2] It is interesting to note that Communist historians have not picked up the implications of this attitude. Schleifstein adds his share of criticism of Mehring's personal attitude and withdrawal. At the same time official historiography in East Germany continually laments the unwillingness of the German Left to organize itself outside the SPD before and during the war. The Leninist point of separate organization was, indeed must be, based on withdrawal from the mother party for a start.
[3] Rosa Luxemburg's articles on the prospects of the 1913 party congress at Jena appeared only on 11 and 18 September ('Die Massenstreikdebatte', 'Die Massenstreikresolution des Parteivorstandes,' *LV*, 11, 18 September 1913). Her comment on the congress itself, written immediately afterwards, never appeared at all and was published only in 1927 (*Die Internationale*, 1 March 1927, Vol. X, No. 5, pp. 147–53).

arrangement, for Marchlewski was an unwavering left-wing radical, who yet managed to retain the confidence of the SPD leaders and partly took Rosa's place as adviser on Polish affairs. Kautsky particularly had a soft spot for the bearded, academic-looking figure. He considered him 'above faction'—though why is not entirely clear.[1]

To Marchlewski's surprise his colleagues at *Leipziger Volkszeitung* suddenly refused to print any more articles by Rosa Luxemburg though they had previously been commissioned and Marchlewski himself had already accepted them. The press commission of the *Leipziger Volkszeitung* tried to resolve the conflict by compromise but its proposal proved acceptable to no one. Once again Mehring was in favour of dignified and hurt withdrawal.

Rosa Luxemburg took a different view on the advisability of breaking off relations. A series of meetings between Mehring and Marchlewski took place in her flat, and finally both men, whose temperaments were so similar, convinced her that pre-censorship by the editorial board must really kill any effective expression of views. After some discussion between them, Marchlewski wrote formally to Block on behalf of himself and his two colleagues:

What is at stake here is this: we three, and particularly I—which I want to emphasize—are of the opinion that the party is undergoing an internal crisis much much greater than at the time when revisionism first appeared. These words may seem harsh, but it is my conviction that the party threatens to fall into complete stagnation [*marasmus*] if things continue like this. In such a situation there is only one slogan for a revolutionary party: the strongest and most ruthless self-criticism.[2]

Within eleven days of this letter, on 27 December 1913, the first number of the *Sozialdemokratische Korrespondenz* appeared. The editorial offices were located in Marchlewski's flat, for money was short. In each weekly number there appeared as a rule a leading article each by Rosa Luxemburg and Franz Mehring, and an economic survey by Marchlewski. The idea was not so much to achieve broad circulation, but to syndicate the short and pithy essays to other papers. It had little

---

[1] Kautsky and Marchlewski were in friendly correspondence up to 1912. The first rupture between them came when Kautsky refused to accept an article by Marchlewski in *Neue Zeit* on the Jagiello mandate in Warsaw, a question agitating the Poles as well as the Russians at the time (see below, p. 358, note 2). Kautsky's unwillingness to publish was simply due to his exhaustion with Russian and Polish affairs. He turned down Warszawski on the same question for the same reason. Indeed, one of the advantages of his rupture with Rosa Luxemburg was that the pages of *Neue Zeit* were free of these everlasting disputations. The correspondence is in Kautsky Archives, IISH.

[2] Ernst Meyer, 'Zur Loslösung der Luksradikalen rom Zentrum in der Vorkriegszeit', *Die Internationale* 1927, Vol. X, No. 5, pp. 153–8. Julian Karski (Marchlewski) to Hans Block, 16 December 1913.

success in this regard; no more than four local papers ever reprinted any of the articles at any one time, and often whole issues appeared without any echo. The paper survived until after the beginning of the war, but from November 1914 onwards the leading articles were given up and only the economic survey continued to appear.[1]

The year 1913 was one of general disillusion: with the Empire among its supporters, and with the achievements of Social Democracy within the SPD. Since the SPD could not 'play' at politics there was nothing obvious to be done with the large number of seats. They could neither be used destructively as the radicals wanted nor constructively as the revisionists hoped—for all intents and purposes they were worthless.

That year Bebel died, and with him an era—for this cold, shrewd man had generated such an aura of achievement that the fortunes of the SPD were largely associated with his person. It is an aura which has clung obstinately to his memory even to the present day. Communist historians have torn the old SPD apart, shred by revisionist shred, but the value of Bebel's role was little denigrated—and is again on the rise. He was buried in Switzerland, where he died, and many genuine tears flowed in the long procession. Rosa spoke, among others, and she too seemed affected by the undeniable stature of the man; henceforward she never spoke of him with disapproval.[2] His successor, Ebert, was a much greyer man, but one who was to play a role which Bebel never dreamt of, Chancellor of Germany and inheritor of much of the imperial power.

Meantime the party trooped back to its perennial preoccupations. At the 1913 congress the mass strike was up for discussion yet again, not as fearful or joyful a weapon as before; 'not with any sense of victory, but out of sheer embarrassment'.[3] Something was needed to combat the sense of malaise. There was silent but widespread agreement when Rosa Luxemburg said that 'there is no doubt about the now considerable and deep dissatisfaction in the ranks of our party members.'[4] She too had nothing new to contribute. She spoke of the need for 'fresh air in our party life', the dissatisfaction with 'nothing-but-parliamentarianism as the sole panacea'. Perhaps for the first time since she attended SPD congresses, Rosa laid this directly at the door of the executive in general and Scheidemann—who spoke for the executive at the congress—in particular. But against the faulty tactic, against the manifold symptoms of rampant imperialism—economic crisis, higher defence budgets, opposition to suffrage reform—she could only offer her own 'clear, sharp and revolutionary tactics to stiffen the courage of

---

[1] See below, pp. 371, 378.
[2] The only report of her speech is in a long quotation by Dittmann in *Die Freiheit*, 22 February 1920.
[3] *NZ*, 1912–13, Vol. II, p. 559.   [4] *Protokoll . . . 1913*, p. 289.

the masses'.[1] To the delegates this was nothing but painful rhetoric. The whole tenor of the debate can be summed up by 'nothing new'. The right words and the right atmosphere which could create new things were noticeably lacking in Germany, in the Reich as much as in the SPD. Even Kautsky had to admit frankly that 'there is general discomfort here, an uncertain search for new ways, something must happen . . . [but] even Rosa's supporters cannot answer the question what. . . .'[2]

With Bebel gone, the gloss faded from the executive's tactics, leaving just the power nakedly exposed. Radek's case was a typical example of the new harshness on the part of the executive and of the political confusion on the Left. It was a complicated and obscure case which did not even begin in the SPD but was handed to the executive by the leaders of the SDKPiL.[3] As far as the German executive was concerned, however, the accusations against Radek did not meet with neutral justice, much less with sympathy. The executive was dealing with a nuisance, someone who had annoyed them greatly by exploiting the built-in friction between grass-roots, province and centre. Like Stalin, Ebert and Scheidemann disdainfully passed beyond Bebel's merely verbal annihilations; they spoke less but acted more.

Radek had taken over temporary editorship of a small and struggling left-wing paper in Württemberg, the *Freie Volkszeitung* at Göppingen. Short of money, and a thorn in the flesh of Keil's right-wing provincial political machine, the editors of the paper had appealed in their financial plight to the central executive of the SPD. By so doing they hoped to avoid the provincial organization's price for continued existence—a change of editor and a change of tune. Into this situation Karl Radek moved from Bremen on temporary assignment and immediately beat the drums of left-wing righteousness against what he maintained was a hidden alliance between the provincial and the central leadership. It took Radek little time—with his sharp pen and characteristic blend of secrecy and revelation, always containing the hints of further mysteries to be unveiled—to create a scandal of national proportions. Radical papers everywhere took up the case of the misunderstood and maltreated *Volkszeitung*. Unjustifiably accused—on this occasion—of collusion with the revisionist provincial organization, the executive decided to deal with the troublesome Radek. According to established bureaucratic practice they first called for the files to have a closer look at this unknown individual, and they soon discovered that

---

[1] Ibid., p. 290.

[2] Karl Kautsky to Victor Adler, 8 October 1913, in Victor Adler, *Briefwechsel*, p. 582.

[3] For a fuller explanation of the Polish aspects of the Radek case and its effects on German attitudes, see below, pp. 354–6.

there was some doubt as to his status in the German party. In addition to which there was a serious Polish complaint against him.

At the 1912 congress the question of Radek's status in the German party had already been inconclusively discussed; whether he had ever qualified as a dues-paying member and whether his apparent failure to pay dues had disqualified him from membership. His able work for the radical cause earned him the personal support of the Bremen radicals Knief and Pannekoek; even Henke, the local party boss, was inclined to back him but did so whole-heartedly only after a meeting of the members in the constituency had come out decisively for Radek. Meantime, at the end of 1912 and in the first few months of 1913, the Central Committee of the SDKPiL were pressing the Germans for a decision on his case; Rosa Luxemburg was their go-between. The German executive now decided that it could bypass the question of Radek's status in the German party altogether. At the Jena congress in 1913 it presented a report on his Polish situation. The executive asked the congress to pass two resolutions: first, that any Socialist who had been formally evicted from another party for valid reasons could not be a member of the SPD; and secondly, that this general rule should be specifically and retroactively applied to Karl Radek.

The congress passed both resolutions, though a wave of bad conscience swept through the party afterwards. Neither the votes at the congress nor the later reaction followed the 'normal' divisions; as in the Morocco crisis of 1911, the usual political alignments disappeared almost entirely once a moral issue was at stake. There had recently been a right-wing case of expulsion, and grave doubts were expressed equally from left and right about the moral state of a party that could deal with its members in such a summary fashion.[1] There was still a vocal body of members who considered that the *raison d'être* of the SPD was as much moral as political; on moral issues Liebknecht and Eisner, Mehring and Heine, tended to vote together against the executive—however different the particular remedies proposed. Morality is always more cohesive as a reaction *against* than as an instigator *of* policies.

Rosa Luxemburg's position was difficult. As a member of the Polish executive which had condemned and evicted Radek from the SDKPiL, she could hardly do other than use her influence in the German party for pursuing the demand for expulsion which she had formally requested

---

[1] See Ernst Heilmann, 'Parteijustiz', *SM*, XIX, No. 3, pp. 1267–72. This was only one of several articles on the subject which appeared in the party press at the time. The expulsion of a right-wing personality, Gerhard Hildebrand, by a provincial organization that happened to be radical, had been criticized by left-wingers like Mehring and Laufenberg; similarly Heilmann and Heine, who were well-known for their right-wing views, criticized the eviction of Radek.

in the name of the Polish party. At the same time she was not the person who would ever let a party decision overcome deeply felt personal convictions to the contrary. She disliked Radek intensely. In April 1912, before the Polish party court had even been convened, she was advising her German friends to keep clear of him. 'Radek belongs in the whore category. Anything can happen with him around, and it is therefore much better to keep him at a safe distance', she warned the Zetkins. When Radek and her friend Thalheimer (the official editor of the Göppingen paper, whom Radek had replaced while he was on holiday) made a desperate visit to Berlin in June in order to solicit at least the moral support of well-known radicals, Rosa Luxemburg received them coldly. After the meeting she referred contemptuously to the delegation as a 'pathetic collection of people' (*traurige Gesellschaft*). She claimed that Radek ruined whatever he touched; if it had not been for him the radicals would have done better at the party congresses in 1912 and 1913.

It is difficult for us to disentangle the attitude of Rosa Luxemburg as a prominent member of the SDKPiL from her 'German' view. She was clearly unfair to Radek. The fact that his views on imperialism as they appeared in *Neue Zeit* and the Bremen paper were closer to her own than anyone else's in Germany was entirely lost on her. Far from welcoming a vigorous recruit for the radical cause, she saw only scandal and ill-repute. There is no evidence that she even read his work. The opportunity to bait the executive was wholly ignored. On occasions Rosa had her completely blind spots, and Radek was perhaps the most important. Yet, ironically, her condemnation of Radek for putting his nose into things that did not concern him was precisely what Kautsky, Adler, Bebel, and so many others in the SPD resented in her.

At the 1913 Jena congress Rosa Luxemburg spoke about the Radek case only in terms of general principles. One of the solutions proposed by Liebknecht and many others was for the German party at least to review the evidence on which the Polish condemnation was based, so as to avoid a blind and retroactive expulsion. Though at first the SDKPiL executive had refused to let the SPD reopen their case, Rosa persuaded her Polish associates that this intransigence could only harm the Poles, who more than ever needed good relations with the SPD at this moment when they had a domestic party revolt on their hands. Almost at the end of the proceedings she offered, on behalf of the Polish executive, to hand over the entire documentation to enable the Germans to review the case if they wished.[1]

However, one wonders whether the refusal of the congress to accept Rosa's suggestion really caused her much distress.

During the long spell of unsatisfactory political weather, Rosa con-

[1] *Protokoll . . . 1913*, pp. 543–4.

centrated once more on her intellectual interests. Still at work on her political economy treatise, she suddenly became fascinated by one particular problem towards the end of 1911—the nature of capitalist accumulation. It all began with the difficulty of reconciling Marx's unfinished mathematical analysis of compound accumulation with her own observations. Trying to resolve this problem, she was swept away into what she modestly claimed was a 'wholly new and strictly scientific analysis of imperialism and its contradictions'. The problem fascinated her so much that in the following year she gave up a projected holiday in Spain and abandoned everything but the most immediate political duties—the elections of 1912 and the contracted articles for *Leipziger Volkszeitung*. By the middle of 1912 the work was finished and in the hands of the publishers. Although not completed in 'a four-months continuous session', as she later claimed, it was nonetheless a remarkable achievement, an intellectual eruption which stands as a monument to Rosa Luxemburg's tremendous powers of concentration.[1] In the long run the influence of *The Accumulation of Capital* sprang from its theoretical model of accumulation and imperialism, but at the time most of the reviewers were less interested in her theory than in evidence of Rosa Luxemburg's unorthodox political attitudes. She felt that much of what she wrote had not been understood, so that she later used her war-time prison leisure to answer her critics by going over the same ground again in simpler terms and with easier illustrations.[2]

Politically, the book merely enhanced her reputation as a brilliant *enfant terrible*. Within the SPD, close association with her became the political kiss of death. Her threatened visit to the south in the summer of 1913 was enough to put several local organizations in a stage of frenzy. Yet in another sense Rosa's isolation in the SPD was an arbitrary act of her own contrivance. The SPD in the last few years before the war was much more than a political vehicle whose only motor was policies; it was a world, a state of mind, an ideological protest against society— and from this Rosa never for a moment contracted out. When she became caught up in the treadmill of the imperial courts, she was hailed as a party martyr; no one could have guessed from the tone of the Socialist press that Rosa Luxemburg was anything but the party's darling. And this applied just as much to the executive, so long the focus of her criticisms. However difficult her relationship with the SPD leadership about current policies, she still had easy access to them on

---

[1] 'Do you know that I wrote the entire 30 galleys in one go in four months—incredible performance—and sent it off to the printer without so much as a further glance through. . . .' (*Briefe an Freunde* p. 105, to Hans Diefenbach, 12 May 1917.)

[2] See a very critical review by Eckstein in *Vorwärts*, 16 February 1913 (literary supplement); also Marchlewski in *Münchener Post*, Nos. 24–25, January 1913, and Marchlewski and Mehring in *LV*, 21 February 1913.

Polish matters and never ceased throughout this time to deal with them both formally and informally on behalf of the SDKPiL. No one in Germany knew much about the Poles, and many intrepid explorers like Ledebour had burnt their fingers. Kautsky's efforts to promote March-lewski never succeeded. 'If you want anything sensible about Polish history', Ryazanov, himself no friend of Rosa's, informed Kautsky, 'you either have to go to Rosa or else to a bourgeois historian.'[1] Rosa in turn was careful not to abuse this position and warned her Polish friends on several occasions that it would not do to abuse the confidence of the German executive.

Since 1910 Rosa had been trying to move out of the flat in Cranach-strasse. It reminded her too much of Jogiches, who still came and went with his own keys, never surrendered. Rosa was no longer so young; the house was noisy, there were too many children now, and she was far too accessible to visitors. With the school work on the one hand and the concentration required for her economic writing, she did not want her flat to be the centre of constant informal meetings. It was not easy to find what she wanted and for nearly a year she searched the newer suburbs of Berlin, until in the second half of 1911 she finally moved to Südende, 2 Lindenstrasse. Here there were green fields and only the more determined of her visitors would troop all that way to see her. The hope of solitude proved an illusion; most of her friends still came and so did a flood of Poles, refugees from the lost battle against Lenin in Paris. The entire Warszawski family billeted themselves on her for several long spells. Finally there was the little group of dissident intel-lectuals in the SPD; the decision to found the SDK was taken at her flat.

There are many glimpses of high human comedy from this period, quite at variance with all the political complaints; Rosa's first visit to a cinema, in the company of her enthusiastic housekeeper, and a visit by a Socialist worker from Denver, Colorado, who had raked together enough funds to make a personal tour in Europe.

I had a visit from Miss Twining . . . all these old girls [*Schachteln*] from England and America really are straight out of the zoo. This one asked me if I did not think Germany was *a very small country* and whether it would not be better for the movement if Germany were bigger! She also asked me whether Bebel was *a great man* and whether Lafargue *was also a great man*.[2]

Middle age had eroded her enthusiasm though not her passion. Rosa was instinctively conscious of her age. She had no use for young-old personalities who, like Karl Liebknecht, unbecomingly bounced

[1] Kautsky Archives, IISH.

[2] The phrases in italics were written in English by Rosa. Lafargue was Marx's son-in-law, a tourist attraction for Socialist visitors from overseas.

into and out of causes like a shuttlecock. Increasingly she valued privacy and self-restraint. But she still despised the humdrum, the colourless, the impersonal. Rosa Luxemburg was proud of her own strong temperament—it was the essential component of any satisfactory political personality—but she channelled its evanescent aspects into more disciplined and permanent attitudes. The impressionistic mirror which she had at one time held up to all the personalities in the German party was replaced by more reasoned judgements; inevitably she also accepted the existence of institutions and continuity in German party life with their own particular ideology. With a few significant exceptions like Kautsky, she was now less concerned with peculiarities of this or that personality, but thought about the 'executive' or the 'congress' or even the 'party as a whole'. Even her dislike of Germany became conceptualized; she felt increasingly out of touch with what she contemptuously described as the 'German mentality'. Is not this replacement of personalities with institutions, this judgement of the general rather than the particular, itself evidence of the extent to which the critic had become an outsider?

And then, suddenly, hers was no longer a voice crying in the wilderness. The first six months of 1914 saw a distinct revival of industrial as well as political unrest in Germany, and in Russia too. Disillusion was swept away like cobwebs. Rosa Luxemburg anxiously tried to broaden the discussion as much as possible, to take the mass strike not in isolation—as at the 1913 congress—but as part of the general confrontation with imperialism. The economic struggles, too, must be brought into the general movement. 'Will the strikes succeed? A useless question. The struggle itself is a victory for the workers' cause.'[1]

In 1914, sensing the change of air, she spoke and wrote on this subject as often as she could. The mass strike had now become a practical proposition once more. Even *Vorwärts* sounded belligerent: 'the second stage of the suffrage campaign begins', it trumpeted.[2] Rosa was still sceptical of the official attitude; she had been bitten by just this dog in 1910. 'Clearly we would make ourselves ridiculous with friend and foe ... if we allow the masses to get the suspicion that behind our battle slogan there are no serious intentions of acting. ...' If resolution was lacking at the centre, then the initiative 'in a truly democratic party like ours must come from below, from the periphery'.[3]

It was no longer a case of persuading or even forcing the leadership with resolutions. Scepticism of the executive's intentions expressed in leading articles was one thing; when it came to addressing the masses such caution was pointless. For all practical purposes Rosa Luxemburg

---

[1] 'Märzenssturme', *Gleichheit*, 18 March 1912.
[2] *Vorwärts*, 24 May 1914.
[3] *SDK*, 6 June 1914.

now ignored the leadership. The only way to achieve results, to ensure that the failure of 1910 would not be repeated, was to get the masses moving and to hope that they would truly sweep the leadership along. Two days after her strongly worded resolution at a Berlin meeting had been passed by acclaim, she emphasized again the need for mass pressure on the leadership.

Whether the trade-union leaders want to or not, the unions *must* get into battle sooner or later [in defending the right of economic association]. This is a much greater menace to the unions than it is to the party organizations . . . but if we really form our columns for the Prussian suffrage campaign, we can undoubtedly count on enthusiastic support on the part of every trade-union member. For they too are involved. '*Tua res agitur*—it is your cause that is at stake.'[1]

Not only pressure on the political leadership, but interaction of all related efforts into one—that was the struggle against imperialism.

It was not platform theory alone. Rosa Luxemburg had become involved with the problem of imperialism directly and personally. On 16 September 1913 'there was a large and magnificent meeting at Bockenheim [near Frankfurt] in which Comrade Dr. Luxemburg made a speech', which lasted for nearly two hours.[2] Nor was this an exceptionally long time; the members came to be inspired with all the receptive discipline of seventeenth-century Presbyterians—and the comparison is not fanciful. 'Step by step she described the form of the capitalist class state with all its barbarism and the hopeless prospects for the working population. . . . Accompanied by strong applause, the speaker paid tribute to Comrade Bebel for his systematic and critical emphasis on the maltreatment of soldiers and then came to speak about the mass strike.'[3] In the course of developing her argument, Rosa Luxemburg 'touched on the question whether we would permit ourselves to be dragged helplessly into a war. After shouts of "Never" in the body of the hall, she is supposed to have said, "If they think we are going to lift the weapons of murder against our French and other brethren, then we shall shout: 'We will not do it'." '[4] This phrase formed the basis of the Public Prosecutor's charge against Rosa Luxemburg under paragraphs 110 and 111 of the Criminal Code, in that she called for public disobedience of the laws.

The trial took place in Frankfurt on 20 February 1914. Conviction was certain, but at the end of the trial Rosa made one of the greatest speeches of her life. It was neither self-defence nor any plea for mitigation of sentence; in accordance with Socialist practice in the courts, the accused's opportunity to speak on his or her own behalf was used

[1] *SDK*, 16 June 1914.
[2] *Volksstimme* Frankfurt (Main), No. 227, 27 September 1913.
[3] Ibid.
[4] *LV*, 21 February 1914.

to make a political assault on the prosecution, the law, and the whole of society.[1]

She was sentenced to a year in prison. As usual the appeal procedure took many months. Predictably, the superior Reich court dismissed her appeal on 20 October 1914, after the outbreak of the war.[2] Execution of sentence under war-time conditions was due at any moment and without warning. Notice to serve the sentence was in the discretion of the authorities. As we shall see, Rosa Luxemburg tried to put it off as long as possible, partly for health reasons, but in the end she was seized and taken off to prison without any warning at the beginning of 1915.

The nature of the charge and the spirited quality of her defence were widely reported and brought her much sympathy and support.[3] The case was remembered for many years and Rosa Luxemburg's speech became a minor classic in SPD history, even at a time when she had long and unequivocally renounced her allegiance to the party—just as the unconverted citizens of Tarsus, who had no interest in the ambulant disciple, long remembered Saul.

Military questions were much to the fore in the first half of 1914. The SPD had always fought against the harsh disciplinary tradition of the Prussian army, an issue which, like other causes, rose and fell in intensity in mysterious cycles; 1914 was a peak year. Rosa Luxemburg had blundered into the controversy only by accident and by courtesy of the authorities; militarism as a *special* problem had never caught her interest. Now it brought her into closer contact with Karl Liebknecht whose special preoccupation it had been since 1906. The official party line—better conditions for recruits, the idea of a militia—had not been entirely to her liking, since the suggestion, openly put forward by Bebel and Noske at the 1907 congress, that better treatment for recruits would improve the quality of the imperial army, did not seem designed to hasten revolution. In the present head-on collision such nuances were lost—it was precisely the sort of general confrontation Rosa Luxemburg had always prescribed as the only medicine for revolutionary atrophy. She was fully aware of the repercussions of the proceedings in Frankfurt; every further push could only sharpen the dialectic.

Immediately after the trial in February 1914 Rosa wanted to embark on a whistle-stop tour of west Germany—as in 1910. This again was established practice; convicted party members, like martyrs on display, were always treated to mass demonstrations of solidarity. An immediate mass protest was organized in Frankfurt itself on the day sentence was pronounced. Similar protest meetings took place in Berlin the following

---

[1] *Vorwärts*, 22 February 1914.

[2] *LV*, 23 October 1914.

[3] See *LV*, 21 and 28 February 1914; also Clara Zetkin in *Die Gleichheit* 4 March 1914. The 'official' commentary was in *Vorwärts*, 23 February 1914.

Sunday. Reading the reports, it is difficult to remember that both the *Leipziger Volkszeitung* and *Vorwärts* had barred Rosa Luxemburg as a contributor and condemned her more than once as a disruptive element in the party. *Vorwärts*, which would not accept a sentence in Rosa Luxemburg's hand, reproduced at length both her speeches in court and her address to the protest meeting outside. As with Lenin, polemics must not be taken too literally as evidence of irreconcilable hostility.

Rosa was in excellent form and delighted her audience from the first word.

A severe criminal stands before you, one condemned by the state, a woman whom the prosecution has described as rootless. Comrades, when I look at this assembly my joy to find here so many men and women of the same opinion is only dimmed by the regret that a few men are missing—the prosecution and the judges of the court in Frankfurt. . . . I clearly have better and more solid roots than any Prussian prosecutor.[1]

Flanked by her friends and defence counsel Paul Levi and Kurt Rosenfeld, Rosa Luxemburg made a triumphal procession through south-west Germany. On her return to Berlin she addressed several well-attended meetings—still on the subject of militarism. Once a subject was revolutionarily in vogue, it was good sense to keep on with it. Here too the words of Rosa Luxemburg now met with full approval. Nothing shows the extent of public interest better than the lengthy reports of the case and of the subsequent meetings, not only in the Socialist but also in the Liberal and Conservative press.[2] In the areas where Rosa Luxemburg spoke, meetings called by the National Liberals and right-wing parties strongly condemned the 'inactivity' of the authorities in the face of the 'scandalous behaviour of Rosa Luxemburg . . . the German people insofar as they do not paddle in the wake of the Socialists, are unable to understand why an end is not put to the impertinent behaviour of this female.'[3]

Such reactions did not pass unnoticed by the authorities. After the Frankfurt trial, the Prussian Minister of the Interior instructed local authorities to take greater care in ensuring that official stenographic reports of Socialist meetings were available, particularly in the case where 'the agitator Luxemburg' was speaking.[4] Her subsequent speeches were all carefully analysed by the Public Prosecutor's office and finally they found what they wanted. This time it was the Minister of War

---

[1] Speech at Freiburg, 7 March, 1914, reported in *Volkswacht*, Freiburg, 9 March 1914.

[2] See for instance *Frankfurter Zeitung*, 21 February 1914. For summary of right-wing press see *Vorwärts*, 22 February 1914.

[3] *Vorwärts*, 2 April 1914, reporting a resolution of a National Liberal meeting in Württemberg.

[4] *Rosa Luxemburg im Kampf gegen den deutschen Militarismus*, Berlin (East) 1960, pp. 60–61, extract from Deutsches Zentralarchiv, Merseburg.

who asked for an indictment 'in the name of the entire corps of officers and non-commissioned officers of the German army'.[1] Honour had been besmirched by Rosa Luxemburg's allegation that maltreatment of soldiers was routine in the German army. There was some doubt as to whether this prosecution could be made to stick, but the Minister of the Interior fully supported the proceedings requested by his colleague at the War Ministry. In his appreciation of the situation, the Minister of the Interior stated that it was necessary to ventilate yet again the whole problem in law of the right to call publicly for strikes and demonstrations.[2] As a test case, the proceedings were to take place in Berlin rather than in Freiburg where the offending speech had been made.

Rosa Luxemburg was delighted; such a charge could only lead to the widest publicity—worth months of agitation. 'I can't tell you what pleasure the thing gives me . . . not a *lapsus linguae*, a bit of stupidity or clumsiness on the speaker's part which is on trial, but fundamental truths, essential component of our political enlightenment.'[3]

Her defence counsel now enlisted the entire organizational resources of the SPD. An appeal was published for defence witnesses to come forward and testify; anyone who could give evidence of maltreatment of recruits. It was hoped that the many instances brought to light by the Socialist press would make it possible to flood the court with witnesses.[4]

The trial took place in Berlin from 29 June to 3 July 1914.[5] The defence blanketed the court with requests for witnesses and even offered to extend the scope of the investigation from the Prussian army into the German armed services as a whole. Throughout the trial the Socialist press, realizing the effect of the testimonies, was celebrating the rout of the prosecution. On 3 July the prosecution requested that the case be adjourned, hoping to have it transferred to a military court. This was strenuously resisted by defence counsel and by Rosa Luxemburg herself, who had polished another assault for delivery after the verdict. It was never made. The judge granted the adjournment, against the wishes of the defence; but no provisions were made for transfer to a military court. The Socialist press, with *Vorwärts* most fiercely in the

---

[1] *Vorwärts*, 14 May 1914. The offending sentence of the speech at Freiburg read: 'One thing is clear, the recent attempt at suicide by a recruit is surely just one of many innumerable tragedies which take place day in and day out in German barracks, and it is all too rare for the groans of the sufferers to reach our ears.' (*See Volkswacht*, Freiburg, 9 March 1914.)

[2] *Rosa Luxemburg . . . gegen . . . Militarismus*, pp. 135–6.

[3] Rosa Luxemburg to Franz Mehring, 22 May 1914, IML (M), Fund 201; photocopy IML (B), NL2 III-A/18, p. 74.

[4] See the appeal in *Vorwärts*, 25 June 1914.

[5] Details of the speeches and testimonies are in *Rosa Luxemburg im Kampf gegen den deutschen Militarismus*, pp. 142–206.

van, was able to announce a complete victory, while the right-wing papers lampooned the government for its incompetence.[1] Nothing more was heard of this indictment.

By July 1914 Rosa Luxemburg could justifiably feel that her policy, so painfully evolved in opposition for the last four years, was at last coming into its own with a vengeance. The mass-strike discussion was once more under way. Instead of having to commune with unsympathetic party leaders, her point of view was making its impact directly on the masses. The meetings in the capital applauded her and, what was more important, voted for her resolutions. A particularly sharp resolution had been adopted in Berlin on 14 June 1914, against executive warnings. This agitational effort in Berlin in 1913 and 1914 brought its full rewards during the war; Niederbarnim was to be the base of *Spartakus* activities and the information bulletin issued by the leadership of that constituency became the foundation of the famous *Spartakus* letters. The efforts of Rosa Luxemburg and her friends in the 4th Berlin Constituency made it the Berlin headquarters of the *Spartakusbund* and even provided a secure nucleus for the KPD after the war. At the same time her preoccupation with militarism and the two trials rallied masses of comrades all over the country. Her name was more widely known in the summer of 1914 than ever before. After her trial at Frankfurt she had given notice that 'we look upon it as our duty to use the coming weeks as far as possible in order to hasten the next step of historical development which will lead us to victory'.[2] At the time this intention seemed entirely capable of fulfilment.

'Fist to fist, and eye to eye.' At last the boring preoccupations of internal party affairs were left behind; a general sharpening of conflict appeared inevitable. Even physically she felt better. A group of like-thinking radicals had crystallized out of the pressure of events: Liebknecht, Mehring, Marchlewski, Pannekoek—and friends like Stadthagen, Levi, and Rosenfeld. In no sense was this a new party, but a comradeship—that mixture of personal and political relations so congenial to Rosa Luxemburg, which she had brought with her from the early days of Polish Social Democracy.

A few days after the triumphant end of the Berlin trial Rosa took the train for Brussels, where the long-planned meeting of the International Socialist Bureau on the Russian question was to take place. She left Berlin in high spirits; a possibility at last of an SPD congress which might support a tonic assault on the executive, and set the seal of approval on large-scale actions. The International was to meet at Vienna

---

[1] *Vorwärts*, 5 July 1914.
[2] *Volkswacht*, Freiburg, 9 March 1914.

in the autumn, not only to register the recent Socialist successes against militarism but to crown the efforts to unite the Russian party in which Rosa Luxemburg had played so prominent a part. Brussels would be hot and full of talk, but Rosa was looking forward to it; fresh from her successes in Germany, she felt certain that her policy would prevail, even against the obstinacies of Lenin and his Bolsheviks.[1]

But all these hopes and plans were washed away, with those of millions of other people. While she was in Brussels the international crisis brought on by the murder at Sarajevo sharpened significantly. The weakness of the Socialist International in the face of threatened war had already been exposed, at least to the participants at the hastily assembled meeting in the last week of July, if not yet to the world at large. By the time Rosa Luxemburg returned to Berlin, war had become almost certain; all the hopeful signs of a confrontation with imperialism disappeared as though they had never been. The world that ended in August 1914 was essentially Rosa's world as much as Bebel's, Victor Adler's, and the Emperor's. Protest, even negation, had always been based on understanding of the essential processes of that world, had been a part—if an extreme part—of it. The Lenins, the Hitlers, with their tight ideological blinkers, had been in it but not of it—but they inherited the future, together with that blindly durable anonymity, the capitalist middle classes. For a brief moment the flame of revolutionary potential from the Second International flickered on, in post-war Berlin, to be for ever extinguished by bourgeois reaction and Communist efficiency.

[1] See below, pp. 360–1.

XII

POLES AND RUSSIANS,

1907–1914

THE Russian revolution, which had burst so unexpectedly into the red face of the unprepared revolutionaries, was now ebbing away almost as fast. From the spring of 1906 onwards, apart from a few major factory lockouts and some peasant outbreaks, the manifestations lost their spontaneous mass character. Small groups of conspirators were still active—the armed squads of Piłsudski in Poland and the Bolshevik raiding parties in the Caucasus. Reaction advanced fast on retreating revolutionary heels, and a wave of police counter-terror began. Each one of the émigrés had friends or family to worry about. Rosa Luxemburg knew nothing of Jogiches' fate until January 1907, when he was finally put on trial; she was indicted alongside him but naturally refused to appear. No doubt she was kept informed through party channels of the sentence of forced labour passed on him as a deserter and a revolutionary leader, and of his subsequent escape; no official notification seems to have reached her with regard to her own sentence *in absentia*.[1] But personal anxieties were a continuing feature of the next few years. Her own family was not molested though she feared for them until 1908; none the less, many SDKPiL members were captured and suffered from that particular blend of cruelty and neglect which characterized the Okhrana. One particular case roused her to a desperate flurry of activity; someone whose survival she described as 'a vital piece of my own life', who was sick and, as she feared, unlikely to survive imprisonment. As in her own case two years earlier, the security of the Russian state could, on medical advice, be satisfied by a cash transaction. Rosa bombarded her German friends for loans to supplement the pathetic resources of the boy's own family, after pledging all her liquid cash. And she succeeded, for a month or so later 'her own boy' was in Berlin, safe and sound.[2]

[1] See above, p. 244, note 2. Some of the court documents relating to her own case are in a special Rosa Luxemburg file in Zaklad Historii Partii, Warsaw.

[2] This incident has been pieced together by isolated references in various unpublished letters, i.e. to the Zetkin family, and Faisst. The identity of the young man was never revealed; apparently her friends were familiar enough with the story and name of Rosa's protégé. Possibly it was Leder, for whom Rosa always had a high regard and whose known circumstances—illness, imprisonment, release against payment—fit these facts. If so, he repaid Rosa with a slashing attack on her in 1912. See below, pp. 351, note 2; 353.

These personal tragedies, the inevitable aftermath of failure, took place in an atmosphere of disillusion in Russia and indifference abroad. The German Socialist leaders, after their early enthusiasm, had already lost interest by the summer of 1906; revolution in Russia was a fine foreign venture, but strictly to be deplored if liable to catch on at home, and the imperial authorities contributed their own warning. There was even talk—baseless as it turned out—of supporting the Romanov cousin with arms. In Russia itself hopes for legal agitation dimmed as Duma succeeded Duma with a progressively restricted franchise, and in June 1907 the Social-Democrat deputies were arrested en bloc—*pour décourager les autres*. With very few exceptions, all the SDKPiL leaders got away during 1907. Dzierżyński and Hanecki helped Jogiches to escape; they themselves were caught and deported to Siberia several times between 1907 and 1909, but managed to escape on each occasion. Marchlewski, whose alibi had not been broken during a short period of arrest, was with difficulty dissuaded by Jogiches from returning to Poland after the 1907 International congress and finally settled in Germany once more. By the end of the year even Finland was no longer safe, and the Bolshevik leaders split into little groups and flowed away westwards to Paris. By 1908 the pre-war revolutionary pattern was re-established: the leadership in exile, a hard core of militants underground, and rapidly dwindling membership. Police activity did not end at the border. They penetrated the émigré organizations with their own agents disguised as revolutionaries and tried to catch the couriers and delegates as they crossed the frontier. The existence of a legal Socialist delegation in the Duma made the police task of identification much easier, though all the Socialist parties, Polish as well as Russian, tried hard to keep the legal organization as watertight and separate from the clandestine groups as possible. The nervous awareness of successful police penetration at almost every level made the leadership abroad suspicious and intransigent; opponents in the party were all too quickly labelled as police spies or at least as their unwitting tools. After 1907 the party atmosphere abroad, in the SDKPiL as much as in the RSDRP, deteriorated to one of extreme nervousness and irritation. Unable to influence events at home, all the considerable energy of the leaders was concentrated once more on internal party affairs. Every dispute was pursued to the bitter end. For the next seven years the history of both parties, jointly and severally, is only comprehensible within this atmosphere of suspicion and disillusion. None the less, the effect on the two parties was very different. The SDKPiL split up, while the RSDRP was torn apart.

Active participation in revolution was now replaced by elaborate post-mortems. The returned revolutionaries threw themselves into this important Marxist task with zeal. As usual it was a battle on two fronts— for all Marxist analysis is essentially a battle, a creative contribution to the very struggle which it is supposed to analyse, for analysis is struggle, and criticism even more so. On the one hand there was the relationship between proletariat and society, the broad confrontation of classes; on the other the struggle for a correct tactic against opponents within the party. This latter aspect was especially important in Russian and Polish Socialism, where the division between Bolsheviks and Mensheviks, between SDKPiL and PPS, was sharp and permanent. In practice the two elements of struggle were closely connected, and Rosa Luxemburg was particularly well qualified to concentrate on this continuing two-variable analysis. Her writing for the next few years brilliantly formulated the SDKPiL view, both on intra-party tactics as well as on the Socialist confrontation with resurgent Tsarism. In addition to these two aspects, we have to disentangle the specifically Polish from the general Russian context. At the fourth or unity congress of the RSDRP at Stockholm in 1906 the SDKPiL had at last become an autonomous member party of the reunited RSDRP; following the fifth congress there were two Polish representatives on the Russian Central Committee and one on the central party organ, *Sotsial-Demokrat*. For the next three years Rosa Luxemburg wrote as freely and frequently on Russian as on Polish affairs.

The first major post-mortem on the revolution was staged at the fifth Russian congress in London from 13 May 1907. It was a more sober, practical affair than its predecessor at Stockholm the year before. The old alignments were hardening once more and, though the congress was representative of all the groups, there were continuous caucus meetings of the factions behind the scenes. The Bolshevik 'Centre' within the officially united RSDRP which had been formed in great secrecy at Stockholm in April 1906 was now agitating actively for support among the uncommitted delegates—the *Bund*, the Poles, and the Letts—all of whom had joined the Russian party as separate groups at Stockholm. Rosa Luxemburg, Jogiches, and Marchlewski attended the congress as Polish delegates; Warszawski and Dzierżyński, who represented the SDKPiL on the Russian Central Committee, did not. The Bolsheviks negotiated with these outstanding personalities individually as well as with the Poles as a group. Rosa Luxemburg had at least two conspiratorial encounters on the day before the congress and on the opening day, at an address which proved to be a dubious public-house in the East End. It was raining outside and wraiths of smoke pervaded the sleazy public rooms; a backdrop which corresponded with Rosa's alternating mood of depression and excitement.[1]

---

[1] From unpublished letters written from the congress, in Zaklad Historii Partii, Warsaw. We do not know whom she met there.

The convening of the congress itself had been largely inspired by the Bolsheviks who hoped to marshal a majority and thus gain control of the reunited party. There were no major problems before the delegates, many of whom grumbled that the whole effort was a waste of time and money.[1] The actual congress showed up once again the sharp edges of the split between Bolsheviks and Mensheviks; while the latter believed in the prophylactic properties of public discussion and reason—like the SPD—the Bolsheviks pulled their hidden strings, and reaped mysterious rewards in the voting. With one significant exception, they achieved small but consistent majorities during the meetings. *Sotsial-Demokrat*, the party central organ, now passed into the hands of the Bolshevik majority and Warszawski was voted on to the new editorial board as the representative of the SDKPiL. He also took one of the two Polish places in the newly elected Russian Central Committee together with Dzierżyński, while Jogiches, Marchlewski, Małecki, and Hanecki became candidate members.[2] All were personally known to Lenin; the qualities of Hanecki, Warszawski, and Dzierżyński had already been noted for future reference. At the congress the Poles supported the Bolsheviks fairly consistently, since they had begun, in return for support against the PPS, to identify themselves increasingly with Lenin's policy and with opposition to the Mensheviks after the last major flare-up of the revolution in January 1906.[3] But this support was not total or automatic. The big exception was the overwhelming adoption of the Menshevik resolution condemning armed raids and expropriation of captured money—in general terms, though only the Bolsheviks could be affected. Jogiches as well as Rosa Luxemburg voted against Lenin who obtained only 35 votes against 170, with 52 abstentions which included such prominent Bolsheviks as Zinoviev.[4] As far as Lenin was concerned, Polish support was invaluable in view of the almost even balance of the factions; but he resented his dependence on a group over which he had no control and for whose goodwill he had to negotiate on each occasion.

The official Polish position on the internal questions of the RSDRP was expounded by Rosa Luxemburg in two long speeches. Russian

[1] L. Schapiro, *The Communist Party of the Soviet Union*, p. 95.

[2] *Protokoly, Londonskii s"ezd RSDRP, Izdanie Tsentralnogo Komiteta*, Paris 1909, p. 786.

[3] For a summary of SDKPiL support of the Bolsheviks between the fourth congress of 1906 and the fifth in May 1907, see Jan Sobczak, 'Antimenshevistskaya pozitsiya SDKPiL po voprosy vnutripartiinoi borby v RSDRP v period mezhdu IV i V s"ezdama RSDRP' (The anti-Menshevik position of the SDKPiL in questions of the intra-party struggle in the RSDRP in the period between the fourth and fifth RSDRP congresses) in *Iz istorii polskogo rabochego dvizheniya*, Moscow 1962, pp. 58–102.

[4] *KPSS v resolyutsiyakh i rezheniyakh s"ezdov konferentsii i plenumov Ts. K*, Moscow 1954, Vol. I, p. 109; *Protokoly*, pp. 609–10.

congresses did not suffer from the need of the annual SPD congress to get through a heavy agenda quickly so that the delegates could return to their normal duties. The Russians had no 'normal duties' and Rosa, like all the others, held forth at length. There was no PPS delegation; the SDKPiL had adhered in 1906 on the condition that it should be the sole representative of the Polish proletariat. Rosa thus spoke in the exclusive name of the most advanced, prosperous, and revolutionary area of the Russian empire. In addition she spoke for herself; she was now a distinguished figure in her own right whose writings were known to many of the delegates. An obscure Caucasian Bolshevik and disciple of Lenin's, sitting quietly at the back of the hall, found Comrade Luxemburg's speech 'especially impressive' and noted with pleasure that she, as the fraternal delegate of the SPD as well as a leader of the SDKPiL, 'fully supported the Bolsheviks in the most important tactical problems of the revolution'. Her formulations were sufficiently striking for the young Stalin to reproduce some of them *verbatim*.[1] But though Rosa Luxemburg always spoke for herself, her analysis was also that of her Polish party; it had been discussed with Jogiches before the congress, in spite of the harrowing difficulties of their relationship.

The Poles supported the Bolsheviks particularly in their emphasis on the primary and self-orientated function of the proletariat in the revolution. Rosa Luxemburg's analysis of class roles corresponded exactly to that of the Bolsheviks—the achievement of constitutional democracy but *through* the self-conscious action and determined primacy of the proletariat. Instead of pressing (or, worse still, begging) the liberals for efforts to screw democratic concessions out of the autocracy, the proletariat had to achieve these by itself, dragging the reluctant liberals in its wake even though the latter would be the immediate and prime beneficiaries. According to Rosa Luxemburg, Liberalism was defunct, not only in the East but in the West as well, in Germany, in France, in England. This meant far brighter proletarian perspectives for revolution in the West than had hitherto been supposed—not because the liberals were strong and therefore an effective barrier to dialectical change, but because they were weak and Socialism could therefore leapfrog a whole stage of the dialectic.[2]

Now this analysis in its world-wide context was far too broad and arbitrary. It ignored the real strength of the *bourgeoisie* in France and England, and in Germany the very existence of the class which would come to political power by inheriting the tradition of state authority and strength—the lower middle class. It was admittedly early days for this—in a Germany still flushed with imperial strength. But was it too

---

[1] Stalin, *Sochineniya*, Vol. II, pp. 63–64.
[2] For this view elaborated in the German context, see above, pp. 304 ff.

much to ask that those who anyhow claimed to see collapse as an integral function of such great strength should also see the realities of that collapse? Was not the *Reichstag* election of 1907 a clear warning? What was clear to Trotsky twenty-five years later was already stated by Rosa Luxemburg in 1907; the German, like the Russian, classical *bourgeoisie* had neither past nor future—but in Germany the lower middle class had. These latter would turn their backs on the liberal attempt of their unsuccessful ancestors to restrict the power of the state, and use that power, even increase it, for their own ends till they reached the super-states of Nazi Germany and Fascist Italy. As far as England and France were concerned, however, the *bourgeoisie* did have the capacity for sur-vivial, but at the cost of their own liberalism; a conservative and no longer a liberal force. Thus the Bolshevik–Polish view, crude as it was, was also not wrong; its very crudity saved it from the later Stalinist–Trotskyite failure to understand fascism. But to any Englishman or Frenchman listening to this exposition, which arbitrarily insisted on sweeping in their own societies, the picture of the democratic rulers blotted out as a spent force must have sounded strange and foreign indeed.

Where Rosa Luxemburg's analysis and that of the Polish party differed from the Bolsheviks' was in the evaluation of armed uprising. This part of the speech naturally earned the ungrudging applause of Plekhanov and Akselrod. In fact the Poles were in a quandary here. Apart from their reluctance to accept the validity of Lenin's concept of organization—the only way a revolutionary situation could sensibly lead to armed uprisings—it was difficult to find a consistent argument for supporting the Bolsheviks on the one hand while strenuously and violently opposing the armed raids of Piłsudski's Revolutionary Fraction on the other. A choice had to be made—and the SDKPiL decided that its primary duty lay in emphasizing mass action as against armed up-rising; in taking a stand against Polish opponents even though this must mean disagreement with the otherwise more acceptable wing of the Russian party.[1]

Rosa Luxemburg attended the London congress not only as a Pole but as a German. She was the German fraternal delegate and her opening speech was entirely devoted to an analogy between German and Russian conditions. For the first time before a Russian audience the primacy of the Russian revolution over developments in Germany was openly admitted—part of the same reversal of the flow of experience

---

[1] 'The Polish comrades and I do not share the point of view of the Bolshevik comrades . . . as regards the so-called armed uprising.' (*Protokoly*, p. 288.) Though Rosa Luxemburg spoke against the Bolsheviks on this point, she voted with them for a watered-down resolution. Hence the confusion about her attitude (cf. L. Schapiro, *The CPSU*, pp. 106–7.)

and advice since 1905 which had already been demonstrated in the mass-strike pamphlet.[1] She refused categorically to admit any longer that German conditions were more 'advanced'. On the contrary, she went to considerable historical trouble to show that the weakness and unreliability of the Liberals was the same in Germany as in Russia. The recent *Reichstag* elections illustrated this—at least in Rosa's mind; neither she nor Kautsky nor anyone else would admit that the class war could even temporarily be exorcised by a wave of nationalist sentiment; that there was one appeal which was irresistible to all classes if made strongly enough—to the radical lower middle classes who had hitherto supported the SPD, to the workers themselves if it came to the crunch of war. To see the Liberals scurrying away from the Left and towards the Right was simpler and more convenient. Part of her opening speech at the Russian congress was reported in the German press; it is doubtful whether the SPD executive enjoyed the interpretation of its fraternal delegate and her evaluation of the status of German Socialism vis-à-vis the Russians.[2]

Her self-confident tone and the easy and on the whole consistent flow of ideas successfully covered up the extreme turmoil of Rosa's private life during the twelve days she spent at the congress (the congress itself went on from 13 May until 1 June, by the western calendar). She had not seen Jogiches since they were taken away to the Warsaw Citadel. The relationship round which Rosa's life had effectively revolved— though in closely guarded secrecy—had now collapsed. Though the physical presence of the man she had loved so intensely frightened and probably disgusted her now—and particularly the obstinacy with which he continued to press his claim—Leo Jogiches was the acknowledged party leader, and Rosa accepted this role without question. Her letters show that the need to confer, to appear smiling together in public, was painful for her. Her public performance at the congress thus bears witness to the strength and discipline of her intellect. But the applause was wasted; she longed to be away, though twice she was obliged to put off her departure. London had never pleased her less. And this paradoxical relationship with Jogiches, personal antagonism and party subservience, dominated not only Rosa's own role in the SDKPiL for the next few years, but also that of Jogiches. His strength and blindness were to be firmly imprinted on the history of the Polish party.

Though Rosa Luxemburg personally stood outside the Russian organization and had no direct voice in its policies or feuds, her contact with the Bolsheviks and particularly with Lenin was not confined to public speeches of support. The consensus reached during the long sessions with him, Zinoviev, and Bogdanov at Kuokkala in the summer

---

[1] *Protokoly*, p. 290.   [2] *Vorwärts*, 16 June 1907, 1st Supplement.

of 1906 were confirmed by the meetings in London and at the International congress at Stuttgart the following August. Their collaboration at Stuttgart culminated in the Luxemburg–Lenin amendment to the congress resolution on war. Lenin displayed enough confidence in her —a rare event—to leave the draft entirely to her, and armed her with a Russian mandate in the commission on militarism. In return Rosa proudly displayed Lenin to close friends like Clara Zetkin. Lenin's wife, Krupskaya, who knew how tactical Lenin's friendships were and in her memoirs rarely allowed any personal qualification to warm up the dry procession of names and dates, none the less admitted that 'since Stuttgart Rosa Luxemburg and Vladimir Ilyich had become very close'.[1] On their way to Paris in January 1908 Lenin, registered as a Finnish cook, passed furtively through Berlin and one of his few evenings was spent with Rosa.[2] But Lenin was none the less careful not to put all his Polish eggs in one basket. He also nursed his friendship with Dzier-żyński and Hanecki, both of whom were to prove so valuable to him in 1917. Warszawski, too, was favoured by his attentions, and did his stint for the Bolsheviks up to 1911.

For the moment Lenin hoped to have gained in her a permanent recruit for Bolshevik causes. He commissioned an article for the new Bolshevik paper *Proletarii* in which Rosa Luxemburg denounced the current 'Left' deviations in the party (otzovism and ultimatism).[3] In writing to thank her for the article, he half-humorously upbraided her for not devoting more time to the RSDRP and its publications; her tendency to relapse all too easily into the fleshpots of the SPD was understandable but a matter of regret all the same. 'We were all very pleased with your articles. . . . Pity that you are writing so little for the Russians, that you prefer the rich German Social Democracy to the poor Social Democracy of the Russians. None the less, all the best. Greetings to Tyshka [Jogiches]. A handshake.'[4] A joke of course; but meant to be taken seriously like all Lenin's infrequent jokes. Certainly they were close collaborators during these years, and much of their mutual respect was to survive even their renewed political enmity.

How far was all this a personal compliment to Rosa Luxemburg, and how far Polish—or for that matter Lenin's—policy? The jockeying for position inside the RSDRP was already rocking the flimsy craft of unity, but only reached and surpassed the pre-revolutionary level of savage recrimination in 1909, when it came to apportioning money. SDKPiL

---

[1] Nadezhda Krupskaya, *Memories of Lenin 1893–1917*, London 1942, pp. 120–1.
[2] Ibid.
[3] *Proletarii*, No. 44, 8 April 1909 (Russian dating). Just as the Poles solicited Russian articles for their press, so the Russians turned to the Poles; apart from Rosa Luxemburg, Marchlewski, Warszawski, and Leder all contributed to *Sotsial-Demokrat* and other papers.
[4] *Sochineniya*, Vol. XXXIV, p. 347, dated 18 May 1909.

policy was to support the Bolsheviks *within* the Russian party; that is, on all issues save those which patently led to organizational disintegration—the much feared split.[1] Polish attitudes to the re-emerging factions in the RSDRP were not left to any 'spontaneity'; they had to be cleared with Jogiches. Rosa accepted the discipline; when she was asked by Gorky and Bogdanov to lecture at the new party school in Capri, which was opened in the teeth of Bolshevik hostility, she at once consulted Jogiches. 'Will this, do you think, affect party policy in view of the dispute between the colony in Capri and . . . Lenin?'[2]

In the Polish movement itself Rosa's position was of course much more important. The revolution had greatly increased the strength of the SDKPiL, both absolutely and relatively, in relation to the PPS. The latter was now split into two mutually hostile camps, the unashamedly nationalist 'Revolutionary Fraction' dominated by the granite figure of Piłsudski, and the more Socialist majority of the PPS-Left. The latter had undergone a considerable transformation since 1906, when it first evicted the fighting squads. Having specifically rejected them as well as their emphasis on Polish independence, the PPS now occupied a middle position. But the uncompromising pressure towards polarity in Polish Socialism necessarily brought it closer to the SDKPiL. There was as little organizational or intellectual room for any consistent middle position in Polish Socialism as in Russian, with all the available no-man's-land long absorbed by one or other of the competing extremes. The undermining of a viable middle position was inherent in the attitude and policy of the SDKPiL, as it was in that of the Bolsheviks in the RSDRP—the creation of a separately organized and intolerant Left in the same year as the foundation of a united party absorbed, aggregated, and articulated all potential opposition to the main party leadership. Where in other countries—Germany, France, Italy—a distinct and coherent Left was precipitated gradually and painfully out of a variety of opposition groups within the party (this was to be especially noticeable in France), and only achieved an autonomous separate existence after the October revolution, the Poles and the Russians had their Left ready-made—the former even before the latter. The PPS-Left in some respects resembled the later USPD in Germany as a doomed attempt to establish a middle position—though the analogy must not be carried too far. Its life (1906–18) was longer and more robust than that of the USPD (1917–22), partly because splits were

---

[1] For a discussion of SDKPiL policy within the RSDRP see Jan Sobczak, 'Z dziejów udziału SDKPiL w życiu wewnętrznym SDPRR w latach 1909–10' (From the story of the participation of the SDKPiL in the internal life of the RSDRP in the period 1909–10), *Z Pola Walki*, 1963, No. 4 (24), pp. 40–57.

[2] Jogiches letters, 10 July 1909, IML (M). For the school, see Schapiro, *The CPSU*, p. 111.

anathema in Germany and common in Poland, and partly because of the split within the SDKPiL in 1911. Besides, Piłsudski's rape of the nationalist cause was far more brutal and obvious than the flirtation and humble courtship of the German revisionists; the circumstances of 1906 in Poland which brought about the creation of the PPS-Left were reproduced in Germany only after 1914.

In this way Rosa Luxemburg fought a curious war on two fronts between 1907 and 1911: against Piłsudski—*Frak*, as the Revolutionary Fraction was known—and against the PPS-Left. The former was an obvious task for the SDKPiL's chief propagandist and theorist; in her eyes *Frak* now became part of the bourgeois alliance against Socialism, together with Dmowski and his National Democrats—*Endecja*—all of them more or less conscious agents of Tsarism.[1] More important and obscure was the attitude towards the PPS-Left. Personal antagonism still ran deep between the respective leaderships, which made each interpret the other's motives as unfavourably as possible. Such almost spiteful dislike prevailed right into the First World War, though by that time it had become meaningless in terms of policy.[2] Rosa, too, obtained visible pleasure from the difficulty of the PPS-Left in establishing its proper orientation and programme in the changing circumstances since the revolution. For someone who could claim with justice a consistency which the PPS had previously always belittled as sheer blind pig-headedness, it was now gratifying to watch former opponents crawling towards one's own interpretation, with regular, painful reviews of the party line.[3] Whatever possibilities of co-operation might have existed, Rosa Luxemburg certainly extended no encouragement to the PPS. And it was not mere personal pique but the agreed SDKPiL party line on the subject.

Mere *Schadenfreude* might be suitable for popular propaganda in *Czerwony Sztandar*, but the differences between SDKPiL and PPS-Left went deeper than this, and it was Rosa's particular task to articulate them. At the instance of her party leadership she set out to do this in a long article in February 1908, which appeared in the party's important theoretical review.[4]

---

[1] See for instance 'Czarna Karta rewolucji' (The revolution's Black List), *Przegląd Socjaldemokratyczny*, July 1918, No. 5, p. 369.

[2] See letter from H. Stein (Kamieński) to J. Hanecki, 3 October 1915, IML (M), Fund 486, No. 79; for information on war-time relations between the Polish groups, see F. Tych, 'La participation des partis ouvriers polonais au mouvement de Zimmerwald', *Annali dell'-Istituto Giangiacomo Feltrinelli*, 1961, Vol. IV, pp. 90–125.

[3] 'Czwarty program—"na razie"' (The fourth programme—for the moment!), *Czerwony Sztandar*, 25 February 1908. An anonymous article attributed to Rosa Luxemburg in *Z Pola Walki*, 1961, No. 1(13), p. 72.

[4] 'Likwidacja'. (Elimination), *Przegląd Socjaldemokratyczny*, 1908, Vol. III, No. 1, pp. 46–62; Vol. IV, No. 2, pp. 112–31.

Every revolution is an epoch of political elimination . . . promoting healthy and virile foci of success, sweeping aside all relics of the past and all ideological fictions . . . like social patriotism. In three years of revolution a party of numerous workers, intellectuals and writers, a party rich in material resources, unlimited energy and perseverence has been ruined.[1]

Out of this ruin had grown two bastards, one the old uncompromising Pilsudski 'fraction', the other an opportunist party which, like Bernstein's or Jaurès's followers (but Rosa did not draw the parallel), tailored their unprincipled policies to every political boom or slump as it appeared. For the departure from the commitment to Polish independence was not from one principle to another, but into an opportunist void. In the process the 'reconstructed PPS has become neither one thing nor the other, neither fish nor fowl'. Rather than this, Rosa Luxemburg almost preferred Pilsudski who at least had a programme and not merely a bundle of tactics.[2]

But worst of all, the renunciation of nationalism was false. Though it was not part of the minimal programme, Polish independence was still the ultimate PPS solution.[3] The underlying assumption of this article, which was to be repeated in the future by Rosa Luxemburg and her colleagues, thus was that nothing had fundamentally changed in the PPS; that the eviction of *Frak* was but a little step compared with the big one across to the camp of genuine SDKPiL Socialism which the PPS-Left was not willing to take; that the PPS leadership was still wedded to the evil traditions of Daszyński and the London congress of the International. More serious, however, was Rosa Luxemburg's refusal to see a new, younger, and more radical leadership emerging behind the old stalwarts, one which represented aspirations that really did approach those of the SDKPiL. When the time came the operation of merging Centre with Left actually proved easier than in any other country and took place far earlier; the Communist Party of Poland was quickly welded together out of these hitherto inimical components before the last year of the war had ended, two whole years before similar operations could be carried out in Germany and France. But then Warszawski, representing the SDKPiL whose former leaders were now scattered between Berlin and Moscow, was able to put his back into the effort—so much so that he was accused of going too far to meet the PPS-Left leadership.[4]

---

[1] Ibid., quoted from *Wybór pism*, Vol. II, p. 7.

[2] Ibid., *Wybór pism* pp. 59, 63, 37. Compare a similar preference for the 'honest' conservative Right (Graf Westarp) over the 'dishonest' Social-Democrat Centre in German conditions, below, p. 409.

[3] See for instance *Myśl Socjalistyczna*, Vol. I, No. 1; also H. Walecki, *Przyczynek do programu PPS* (Comment on the PPS programme), 1908.

[4] See his article in *Nasza Trybuna*, 13 December 1918; see also below, pp. 362–3.

All these are valid if extraneous reasons. There was one fundamental but specific factor which made any collaboration between the existing SDKPiL and PPS-Left well-nigh impossible. The PPS-Left had gone a long way in abandoning Polish patriotism, but they did not accept the SDKPiL's own very different patriotism, that of the international proletariat.[1] This Socialist fatherland was as real to Rosa Luxemburg as Poland was to Piłsudski, a substitution of references not a denial of concepts. It was the cement of the SDKPiL peer group, binding together such diverse personalities as Rosa Luxemburg, Marchlewski, Dzierżyński, and Hanecki. How then could such a group work with the PPS-Left for whom patriotism was a mere tactical consideration, a matter for opportunistic programme juggling in accordance with the requirements of the moment? As long as Rosa was there, the gap was unbridgeable. Only Zalewski or Warszawski could have overcome it— and in 1918 only the latter was left to do it, with the help of a PPS-Left leadership now approaching Socialist totality.

Having participated in the general Russian post-mortem on the revolution at the London congress—though everyone still strove officiously to keep the patient alive—the SDKPiL set about polishing its own analysis of these great events, and drawing lessons for the future. Once more Rosa wrote one of her major policy summaries for the Polish review, a broad explanatory justification of her party's policy in *combating* the liberals, Russian as well as Polish, in order to *achieve* a liberal monarchy.[2]

More important—and certainly livelier, because not for publication— were the proceedings of the SDKPiL's sixth party congress, which in retrospect were to assume such importance after the split in the party. This congress took place in semi-secret in Prague in December 1908. Rosa Luxemburg did not attend, apparently by her own wish—she was in a highly nervous state and the prospect of lengthy claustrophobic confinement with Jogiches was too much for her. But her influence at the congress was strong. Her article was the Central Committee's brief for its report to the congress. Jogiches' keynote speech had been discussed with her at length and had her full approval; as early as 22 July 1908 Rosa had written to a friend with evident self-satisfaction that 'the *Slaventag* [Polish congress] will be a resounding triumph for my views'.[3]

Jogiches' speech was a curious hotch-potch of Bolshevik and Men-

---

[1] For the PPS programme, see F. Tych (ed.), *PPS Lewica 1906–1918, Materiały i dokumenty*, Vol. I (1906–10), Warsaw 1961, pp. 279–86 (1907) and pp. 389–95 (1908).

[2] 'Nauki trzech Dum' (The lessons of three Dumas), *Przegląd Socjaldemokratyczny*, Vol. V (1908), No. 3, pp. 177–94.

[3] Unpublished letters, ZHP, Warsaw.

shevik ideas, with much self-conscious emphasis on a distinct Polish approach separate from either Russian view. On the peasant question the Poles showed the same neo-classical Marxist incomprehension of tactics as the Mensheviks. 'The government', solemnly intoned Jogiches, '*does the work of the revolution for it* by getting rid of obsolete agrarian forms, creating a landed proletariat and, by causing the accumulation of land ownership in the hands of the village bourgeoisie, will [actually] bring about greater class contradictions and an increase in the [overall] revolutionary potential.'[1]

This prognosis need only be contrasted with Lenin's on the same government's policy as expressed by Stolypin's land reforms: 'If this continues for long . . . it may well force us to renounce any agrarian programme whatsoever . . . agriculture will become capitalistic and any [revolutionary] "solution" of the agrarian problem—radical or otherwise—will become impossible under capitalism.'[2] It is all the more surprising since there was present at the congress the one man who really knew something about the peasant question, and particularly the extent to which Polish agrarian relations differed from those in Russia in generating a far lower revolutionary potential on the land. But Julian Marchlewski delivered his report on the agrarian question in his usual rather involved and learned style without making much impact.[3] The SDKPiL was never specially interested in or practical about peasants, and neglected this question almost disdainfully; already in London Rosa Luxemburg had been challenged by the Russians on this score.[4] Jogiches' formulations now were surprisingly similar in tone and content to Rosa's speeches three years earlier.

None the less, the challenging slogan of the Bolsheviks could not simply be ignored—'Revolutionary democratic dictatorship of the proletariat and the peasantry'; not least because there was too much that was admirable and worth supporting about the Bolsheviks as a group. So the Poles produced their own slogan—this was Jogiches rather than Rosa Luxemburg: 'The dictatorship of the proletariat supported by the peasantry.'

When the proletariat comes to try and exploit the achievements of the revolution, its allies—the peasantry—will certainly turn against it . . . the political make-up of the peasantry disbars it from any active or independent role and prevents it from achieving its own class representation. . . . By nature it is bourgeois and

---

[1] *Sprawozdanie z obrad zjazdu VI zjazd* ZHP, p. 101. My italics.

[2] Quoted by Bertram D. Wolfe, *Three who made a Revolution*, p. 361. Cf. Lenin, *Sochineniya*, Vol. XV, p. 30.

[3] For his writings on the peasant question see Julian Marchlewski, *Pisma Wybrane* (Selected Writings), Warsaw 1956, Vol. I, pp. 559 ff., 567 ff.

[4] *Protokoly Londonskii s"ezd*, p. 321.

shows its reactionary essence clearly in certain fields. ... That is why the proposition before the congress speaks of the dictatorship of the proletariat alone *supported* by the peasantry. ... Peasantry must assist proletariat, not the proletariat the peasantry in the achievement of the latter's wishes.[1]

Whatever concessions to the role of the peasantry had been made in the keynote speech, they were largely obliterated in the discussion. 'In the Bolshevik conception the peasantry plays the role of a third man in bedroom farces whom the author produces whenever he is in trouble and unable to resolve his situation in a natural way. ... The peasantry cannot play the autonomous role alongside the proletariat which the Bolsheviks have ascribed to it.' One speaker did briefly recognize a distinctive feature of the peasant in Poland—only to dismiss him altogether from the revolutionary stage.[2]

All this meant emphasis, even over-emphasis, on the role of the proletariat, not only at the expense of the peasant but at the expense of the middle classes as well. Here the SDKPiL followed the Bolsheviks closely, and Jogiches again borrowed extensively from Rosa Luxemburg. The earlier reservations about armed uprising had largely disappeared. As one speaker put it: 'The proletariat has to impose its own solution . . . by an uprising and fighting at the barricades, by reaching a class dictatorship, by capturing the heights of power in order to lift up and help to extend the power of its own eventual antagonists, the bourgeoisie.'[3] This was the Bolshevik line exactly—except for Lenin's one famous but isolated pledge to continuous revolution in 1905: 'We shall . . . straightaway . . . pass on to the Socialist revolution . . . we shall not stop halfway'; and it differed sharply from the daring projection of permanent revolution on a moving belt worked out by Trotsky 'supported by' Parvus.[4] When it came to the question of organization, however, Jogiches remained faithful to the principles enunciated by Rosa Luxemburg in 1904.

We are a mass party, we try to increase the proletariat's consciousness of its role, we can lead it but we cannot—and in no sense must we try to—be a substitute for it in the class struggle. ... On the other hand we must equally not obliterate the distinction between the party organization and the politically shapeless mass—like the opportunist wing of the RSDRP suggests.[5]

Without any specific pointer, this was clearly a sidesweep at the Bolsheviks, only slightly tempered by the formal warning against the

---

[1] *Sprawozdanie... VI zjazd*, p. 105.
[2] Ibid., p. 117.   [3] Ibid., p. 114.
[4] L. Trotsky, 'W czym sie różnimy (Losy rewolucji rosyjskiej)' (Over what do we differ? (the fate of the Russian revolution)), *Przegląd Socjaldemokratyczny*, 1908, No. 5, pp. 405–18.
[5] *Sprawozdanie...VI zjazd*, pp. 105–6.

dangers of shapelessness. And as a statement of policy it had its share of savage irony, for nothing was further from the way the SDKPiL leadership worked in practice. Jogiches was of course referring to the mass-following the party had acquired during the revolution, which it was desperately anxious to retain, and to the need to associate the entire membership in the class struggle. To his listeners, however, some of whom were on the edge of revolt against his personal arbitrariness and the whole oligarchical leadership abroad, these words must have appeared cynical in the extreme. Not being present at the congress, Rosa Luxemburg was unaware of the overtones of coming trouble, but it is easy to see why she considered the congress to have been a triumph for her views and guiding principles.

On one subject, however, there was almost complete consensus of opinion in the SDKPiL—the national question. There was no need for any long elaboration of views that were well established. Nevertheless this subject too was given a brilliant theoretical polish by Rosa in the review, in the form of an up-to-date and complete statement of the SDKPiL position. Her article 'Autonomy and the National Question' was the most complete and sophisticated statement of her own point of view ever to come from her pen, and the one that Lenin later used when he took up the subject as a weapon against her. The fact that the article provided one of the classic texts on the national question, and the sophisticated and elaborate form of the discussion in the course of later polemics, make it preferable for us to examine the problem separately (see Appendix).[1]

It will have become obvious that the SDKPiL, apart from matters of policy and conscious attitudes, had undergone other more subtle but profound changes. For the first time since its foundation it had achieved its desire—indeed its official *raison d'être*—of gaining mass support. The decline of revolutionary possibilities in Russia made great inroads on SDKPiL support, but though no figures are available, the party was never again reduced to the straits of being a leadership without a following. None the less, the emphasis of policy-making, the entire political centre of gravity, shifted abroad once more, partly to Cracow— the nearest point of contact with Russian-occupied Poland—and partly back to Germany where Jogiches, Rosa Luxemburg, Marchlewski, and other leaders lived. The role of the SDKPiL within the Russian party created a third Polish centre of gravity in Paris, where the Russian headquarters were established from 1908 till 1912 when Lenin moved

[1] 'Kwestia narodowościowa i autonomia', *Przegląd Socjaldemokratyczny*, 1908, Vols. VII–XII, No. 6, pp. 482–515; No. 7, pp. 597–631; Nos. 8–9, pp. 687–710; No. 10, pp. 795–818; 1909, Vols. VI–IX, No. 12, pp. 136–63; Nos. 14–15, pp. 351–76. Reprinted *in toto* in Rosa Luxemburg, *Wybór pism* (Selected Works), Vol. II, pp. 114–67. Lenin's polemics in *Prosveshchenie*, 1913–14, reprinted in *Sochineniya*, Vol. XX, pp. 365–424.

his Bolshevik committee to Cracow and split the RSDRP. This, however, did not lead to any loosening of the SDKPiL organizational structure. Far from submitting itself to more democratic control as a result of the revolutionary accretion, the leadership actually tightened its grip on policy and organization. To some extent this was a normal, if hidden, process which always accompanies the growth of parties—and corresponded, for instance, to developments within the SPD. But apart from any relationship between leaders and members, the tendency also affected the relationship of the leaders with each other. Unlike the Bolsheviks, the SDKPiL had before the revolution been much more of a loose association of brilliant individuals co-operating for certain purposes and going their own way in others—the peer group we have already described. Since his return from Warsaw, however, Jogiches had tightened his grip on the party to an extent which closely resembled Lenin's. The history of the SDKPiL from 1907 to 1914 cannot be understood without understanding its boss, Leo Jogiches.

The flat tone and formal argument of his speeches should not deceive us into confusing appearance with reality. He could be an extremely harsh and intolerant leader who brooked little opposition; his methods of dealing with opponents, if less polemical than Lenin's, were at least as effective. Those who disagreed with him found it simpler to resign, and between 1908 and 1911 several prominent members of the SDKPiL Central Committee—the Polish executive—quietly dropped out. Those who remained were subjected to increasingly rigid discipline and cavalier treatment—the choice was to put up and shut up, or go. At the end of 1912 Rosa Luxemburg reproached him: 'Julek [Marchlewski] in spite of his faults you know how to treat properly, but Adolf [Warszawski] you insist on treating like a servant. He suffers from this and does not deserve it.'[1] Later still, Marchlewski and Rosa Luxemburg, who out of loyalty and conviction both supported Jogiches in the struggle against the breakaway organization, none the less insisted on sharing in the formulation of policy, particularly when it came to dealing with the dissidents. On 4 October 1913 Rosa Luxemburg wrote sharply: 'I insist on a weekly conference à trois with Julek [and me] about party affairs, failing which I simply will do no more work.' And to ensure that the point was well taken Marchlewski wrote a postscript joining in the demand for regular meetings.[2] These two glimpses among many indicate a situation quite different from the outward appearance of uniformity presented by the SDKPiL, which made the split in 1911 seem so utterly incomprehensible to all spectators.

Rosa Luxemburg's position in the Polish movement during these years showed evidence of an unusual, for her almost unique, submission

---

[1] Jogiches letters, IML (M).   [2] Jogiches letters, 4 October 1913, IML (M).

to a discipline which intellectually she respected, but which she personally disliked and despised. The physical presence of Jogiches was painful to her, yet at the same time she never tried to avoid any necessary meetings or refuse any party task. To Luise Kautsky she complained half-humorously on several occasions about the imposition of her duties to 'my Poles', yet she knew that her role in the Polish movement was vital. Until 1911 she was the main spokesman for the SDKPiL in matters of theory. She was not only the most important contributor to the Polish party's theoretical journal, *Przegląd Socjaldemokratyczny*, but Jogiches' main adviser on editorial policy. Every article passed through her hands and the bulk of her letters to Jogiches during this period are concerned with editorial comments. To a large extent the reputation of the SDKPiL in the Russian party and beyond was due to the quality of this review; for a time it was probably the most interesting and stimulating of all Socialist publications in the Second International. The subjects treated ranged as widely as those in *Neue Zeit* but without the latter's pedantry and often excessively academic atmosphere. The Lenin–Trotsky debate on the nature of the revolution took place partly in the pages of *Przegląd Socjaldemokratyczny* in the course of 1908.[1] In fact every major question of the day was covered—if not by outside contributors then Rosa Luxemburg was called upon, often at short notice, to step into the breach. Jogiches and Rosa Luxemburg made every effort to maintain the more popular party paper for clandestine distribution in Poland alongside the theoretical 'heavy'; *Czerwony Sztandar* continued publication—though intermittently—until just before the war. In 1910 a new paper, *Młot* (The Hammer), was followed in 1911 by a further new venture, *Wolny Głos* (Free Voice), and by four others at various times before 1914. The best of Polish talent wrote also for these more popular papers. The SDKPiL was better served with papers, both in quality and in successful distribution at home, than any other Russian or Polish organization.

Rosa Luxemburg was also peculiarly the representative of her Polish party in the SPD. This was a logical consequence of her position in the German movement; she and Marchlewski were the only Poles who were *persona grata* and personally well known to the German leaders. But there was a danger in exploiting this position indiscriminately, so much so that she was obliged to point out to Jogiches after the split in the Polish party that 'I cannot run to the Germans with every major and

---

[1] Lenin, 'Przycynek do oceny rewolucji rosyjskiej' (Comment on the evaluation of the Russian revolution), *Przegląd Socjaldemokratyczny*, 1908, No. 2, pp. 102–11; *Sochineniya*, Vol. XV, pp. 35–47; Trotsky's reply, above, p. 340, note 4. Lenin's translation may have been undertaken by Rosa Luxemburg (though that privilege was later claimed by one Waclaw Konderski).

minor party scandal without endangering our entire position'.[1] Yet on the whole she carried out these orders punctiliously too, and it is a measure of her success that her *entrée* to the German executive was apparently not diminished by her own increasingly oppositional stand in German party affairs.

Yet all these activities were to some extent marginal. Her role in formulating SDKPiL policy, as opposed to elaborating it in writing or negotiating with the Germans, was obviously less than it had been before the revolution—and it was decreasing all the time. The suggestions contained in the letters to Jogiches were ignored more often than not—and Rosa Luxemburg was not the person to accept such a situation for ever.[2] In the end, therefore, her interest in the Polish movement declined. She dutifully served her stint in the dispute with the party opposition—her sharp and clear pen was essential for the public battle in the Polish and German press and to defend the Central Committee's case before the International. But significantly the quantity of her writing on Polish affairs was much reduced after 1911; in 1913 she published only one article in Polish and thereafter nothing more.

Frequent reference has been made to the split in the SDKPiL and we must now launch into one of the most obscure and difficult episodes in the history of Polish Socialism, even though Rosa Luxemburg was herself not directly concerned.[3] It was not entirely a parochial squabble. The split of the SDKPiL into two separate and noisily polemical groups had wider repercussions in the Russian movement, and also obtruded itself into the German consciousness, mainly through the Radek case—although they never really understood what it was all about. It greatly affected the stability and development of Polish Socialism, in which Rosa Luxemburg was an important figure; it also accelerated her own disillusionment with the SDKPiL and indirectly concentrated her attention more firmly on the affairs of the International and of the German party. But as Jogiches' adviser—increasingly self-appointed since he consistently ignored her advice—Rosa Luxemburg could not escape private or public participation in the polemics generated by the

---

[1] Jogiches letters, IML (M).

[2] The evidence is indirect but conclusive. As the Jogiches letters show (and those of Marchlewski to Jogiches, and Rosa Luxemburg to Marchlewski), she gave her views on various matters—sometimes unsolicited, sometimes on request. Similarly she was kept informed on most decisions by the Central Committee, though not on all. But the proceedings of the Central Committee, most of which have survived, do not indicate any reference made, or attention given, to her views. (*Sprawozdanie ZG* . . . in ZHP.)

[3] There is an enormous amount of polemical material following the split, with each side denouncing the other and using not always accurate versions of past events. Much original source material about these events is in the SDKPiL Archives at ZHP in Warsaw, as well as in the SPD Archives in Bonn and IISH in Amsterdam.

affair. Though she was not a member of the Central Committee—the pre-war self-denying ordinance remained in force—her name appears on several of the public broadsides which headquarters fired at the opposition.

Two distinct factors contributed to the split. The first was Jogiches' leadership of the SDKPiL. At the sixth congress in December 1908 a certain amount of dissatisfaction blew up in the face of the leadership. This took the form of policy criticism; as in Germany, the personal and social antagonisms within the party tended to find expression in arguments over policies rather than actions or even roles. Between 1908 and 1911 three important Polish leaders resigned from the executive in turn, Małecki, Hanecki, and Leder.

The actual questions of policy over which there was disagreement centred at first round the problem of trade unions. The revolution had created a largely spontaneous extension of trade-union activity and, in spite of a rapid decline of members after 1907, some organizational cohesion was maintained. Government legislation had established the possibility of legal trade unions, provided that these were not connected with any political movements. The debate in the SDKPiL was focused on the alternative of supporting—at least in part—independently organized and legal trade unions or relying on illegal but closely controlled and necessarily much smaller organizations. Radek, Leder and others supported the idea of legal trade unions—just as there was a body of opinion in the Russian party in their favour. The executive was firmly against this proposal; Jogiches saw little point in mass organizations which he could not control, while Rosa had seen quite enough of the activities of trade unionists free from party control in Germany to insist that any such organization in Poland must be strictly subordinated to political Social Democracy from the start. She wrote to Jogiches that she was firmly against independent trade unions, saw no point in letting such a proposal gain ground in the Polish party, and did not even want it discussed.[1]

Another contentious item was the relationship with the PPS. There was a quiet but growing sentiment among many party members in favour of the PPS-Left; the conviction that since the expulsion of the revolutionary fraction the combat position of the two parties had lost much of its meaning. Instead of continually attacking the PPS, efforts should be made to bring it more firmly into the Social-Democratic orbit. Here again both Leo Jogiches and Rosa Luxemburg thought alike and their views were strictly negative. To them the differences had a content far deeper than was apparent to the newer members, those more closely involved with the daily problems of confrontation in Poland itself.

---

[1] Jogiches letters, 1909 (?), IML (M).

It was noticeable that the opposition was forming round a geographical nucleus in Cracow, which in turn had the closest relations with the
organizations at home. Both the support for legal trade unions and the
desire for a *rapprochement* with the PPS were to some extent the expression of practical workers, who faced the daily conflict with the PPS as
well as the harassment of indiscriminate police activities, while the intransigence of the party leadership dated partly from old and alien
experiences (Switzerland and Germany) and was largely a refusal to
budge from a well-founded theoretical position. But there was more to
it than a mere rivalry between Cracow and Berlin, between practical
activists and intellectual émigrés. Those like Radek and Leder who
reflected the opposition's views among the émigrés necessarily propagated their opinions informally; even a few carefully worded articles in
the party press before 1911 are hardly evidence for the existence of any
real opposition. In the summer of 1910 Jogiches could still succeed in
persuading Radek to withdraw an already accepted article for *Czerwony
Sztandar* on the ground that it 'was opportunistic in spirit' and that its
publication could only do harm.

Jogiches' high-handed refusal to give way to the mounting pressure
for more general discussion of these policy matters brought things to a
head. In the course of 1910 Hanecki travelled round Germany and
Austria and discussed the possibility of a more outspoken opposition
with various well-known party members.[1] This journey by an important
party leader who had been a member of the Central Committee since
1903 and whose connections with the organizations inside Poland and
Russia were second to none, proved decisive. The vague, inchoate, and
largely personal feelings of resentment precipitated into an organized
attempt to oppose the policy of the Central Committee and soon to
challenge the actual authority of that body. Only recently party unity
had been strained in a dispute with Trusiewicz, who had created an
oppositional group ('Solidarność') within the SDKPiL to counter the
intransigent anti-PPS attitude of the Central Committee. It was to prove
a harbinger of more serious events.[2]

On top of these Polish problems came the backwash of the factional
manœuvring in the Russian party in which the SDKPiL had become
heavily involved. On the whole the SDKPiL supported the Bolsheviks,
as we have seen. In a letter to Jogiches Rosa Luxemburg characterized
the Polish party's preference for the Bolsheviks as a matter of principle

[1] Karl Radek, *Meine Abrechnung*, Bremen 1913, p. 57.

[2] Trusiewicz (Zalewski) had long been the stormy petrel of Polish Social Democracy.
He more than anyone had recently stood for *rapprochement* with the PPS-Left. The party
court which considered his case in 1909 was a typical sign of the times—and incidentally a
precedent for the Radek affair. Some of the documents relating to the proceedings against
him are preserved (*Sąd partyjny nad K. Zalewskim*, ZHP). Trusiewicz joined the Bolsheviks in 1918 and died a year later.

as well as tactics—even though there were aspects of 'Tartar-Mongolian savagery' about Lenin and the Bolsheviks which were bound to make the relationship uncomfortable at times.[1] As long as it was a question of assuring Bolshevik ascendancy in a united party and the success of Lenin's policy, the Bolsheviks could count on Polish support. In the course of 1910, however, this supremacy, which required constant negotiation with allies and manœuvring within the RSDRP, no longer satisfied Lenin. He had become determined either to throw the Mensheviks and the so-called Liquidators out of the organizational framework of the RSDRP altogether or to establish an entirely separate organization for the Bolsheviks. But being Lenin he did not intend to be left as an isolated splinter movement; he would not only leave but take his opponents' clothes as well. The Bolsheviks were to be *the* RSDRP and the others the isolated splinter group. But this intention was not clear at the time, and Lenin of course did his best to disguise it. Moreover, the manœuvres and negotiations throughout 1910 and 1911 were not only highly complicated but took place in a profusion of committees and organizations of a purely temporary and tactical nature. Each group tried to proliferate such organizations and claim legitimacy for them within the party.

The Poles had played a particularly important role in the struggle for control of the central organ of the RSDRP, *Sotsial-Demokrat*. Jogiches had been active in the editorial commission and after 1907 handed his function to Warszawski who lived permanently in Paris and was almost wholly involved in Russian affairs. He fell under the spell of Lenin; to a considerable extent he began to stand for the Bolshevik point of view in the SDKPiL Central Committee more than he represented the latter in the councils of the Russian party.[2] As such he was made to feel 'the shortcomings of the Berlin Troika' whenever there was any air of disagreement between the Bolsheviks and the Poles.[3] The Berlin Troika was Jogiches, Leder, and Marchlewski. As Lenin's tactics became more openly centrifugal, the attitude of the Central Committee hardened and Warszawski's letters hardened too—in protest against this 'change of direction'. In the end Warszawski was recalled by the Central Committee in September 1910 and his place taken by the 'harder' Leder. Soon Leder seems to have fallen under the same spell. In the course of 1910 'he had often voiced anti-Bolshevik views in the editorial commission which were against his own conscience'.[4]

---

[1] Extract from Jogiches letters, 10 August 1909. *Protokoly soveshchaniya rasshirennoi redaktsii 'Proletariia' iiul' 1909*, Moscow, 1934, pp. 260–3.

[2] See his letters to the Central Committee during this period in the collection *Pisma A. Warski z Paryża do ZG w Berlinie*, in ZHP, Warsaw. See also Jan Sobczak, 'Z dziejów udzialu . . .'.

[3] Sobczak, loc. cit.   [4] ZHP, Fund 179, No. 623.

But contacts between the two parties were not confined to this. The manœuvres inside the Russian party were largely a confrontation of power, based on votes and funds. In return for their support for Bolshevik policies, the SDKPiL was subsidized by the Bolsheviks out of the accumulated takings from the armed raids in Russia and other sources.[1] Towards the end of 1910 we find Jogiches at various meetings in Paris called by Lenin of his close supporters, together with Kamenev, Zinoviev, and Rykov.[2] When the Mensheviks and *Bund* delegates had been manœuvred into leaving the Central Committee of the Russian party, Jogiches again figured among the remaining Bolshevik supporters. But now there emerged from among Lenin's own Bolshevik supporters a body of opinion that was not willing to go through to the final and official split. These became known as the Bolshevik 'conciliators'—one of Lenin's contemptuous designations of opponents or lukewarm supporters. In accordance with the established SDKPiL policy to preserve at least the appearance of unity, Jogiches was one of the leading figures of this group. Confronted with the clear alternatives of one Russian party or two, the conciliators and Lenin's loyal Bolsheviks faced each other in open disagreement. In the late summer of 1911 the 'Russian manœuvres', as Rosa Luxemburg put it, resolved themselves into a head-on conflict between Lenin and Jogiches.

Jogiches' strength came from two main sources. One was the support for the Polish point of view expressed by a growing group of conciliators. These controlled the organizations which Lenin had himself helped to set up to break the power of the Central Committee, in which the Mensheviks were strong. Now these creations—the Organizing Commission and the Technical Commission—became the organs in which the strength of the conciliators was marshalled against him. The other base from which Jogiches mobilized against Lenin was his German connection. This was currently of great importance in the Russian party. A sum of money—the so-called Schmidt inheritance—which had been willed to the RSDRP by a young Social-Democrat sympathizer had had to be placed under the control of three trustees—Kautsky, Mehring, Clara Zetkin—pending agreement between Bolsheviks and Mensheviks. Easy access to these trustees and the power to persuade them became a vital weapon in the Russian struggle for power. Here Jogiches could rely on Rosa Luxemburg who was personally very friendly with Clara Zetkin and knew Mehring well, though in the

[1] See *Protokoly soveshchaniya . . . 1909*, p. 126. These are the proceedings of the editorial board of *Proletarii*, for a time the Bolshevik paper until Lenin's group obtained virtual control of the official organ, *Sotsial-Demokrat*. The editorial board of *Proletarii* acted more or less as the group's organizational centre. The subsidy for the Poles and other allies was regularly discussed at these meetings.

[2] L. Schapiro, *The CPSU*, p. 120.

summer of 1911 she was still on indifferent terms with him, and of course locked in dispute with Kautsky. None the less, all three trustees —reluctant custodians of what proved to be a hornets' nest—were only too glad of the advice of anyone who could save them from the buzz of self-interest which emanated from every Russian quarter. Jogiches was in a strong position. The type of close in-fighting in prospect was congenial to both of them.[1]

It was Jogiches who lost the fight, a combination of bad luck and inferior generalship. His most important supporters in the Russian party, who had gone to Russia to prepare for an all-party conference, were promptly arrested—Nogin and Lindov in April 1911, Rykov in August of that year.[2] The Russian police at that time had a particular interest in supporting the Bolsheviks who stood for disunity. In order to prevent a united and therefore more dangerous Social Democracy, Okhrana instructions were to concentrate on the arrest of the conciliators.[3] With the number of his supporters thus depleted, the organizations in which Jogiches was entrenched could not survive. In October 1911 Jogiches openly showed his hand. The Technical Commission refused to provide further funds for the publication of *Sotsial-Demokrat* and the Bolsheviks had to borrow. Lenin was determined that both the Organizing and the Technical Commissions should cease to exist. In November he recalled his members and they walked out of both organizations, taking the cash assets with them. All that Jogiches could now do was to denounce Lenin in public, which he did. But in this he was only one of the many whose sole means of revenge for Lenin's objectionable but successful splitting tactics was a recourse to literature.

It is difficult to reconstruct Rosa Luxemburg's position in all this. She confessed to Luise Kautsky that she did not know much about the events in the 'Russian battlefield in Paris, in which Leo is immersed

---

[1] Jogiches' position can best be seen from the following extract from letters to Kautsky: 'Correct as Lenin's accusations against Martov, Dan and their tendency may be . . . he is not at all objective in his judgement of other groups, *Vpered* and *Pravda* [Trotsky]. These groups which he calls anarchists and "liquidators" completely accept the basis of recognizing the illegal party. . . . Co-operation with these elements . . . is not only possible but essential. . . . [Lenin] wants to use the chaos in the party to get the money for his own faction and to deal a death blow to the party as a whole before any plenum can meet.' (30 June 1911.)

'An immediate and negative answer to Lenin's demand for a final decision about the money seems essential to me, since Lenin expressed the intention of removing his representatives from the commission and breaking it up.' (10 July 1911.) Fund G4 (*Russenfond*), IISH. The relationship between money and power in the RSDRP at this time is clear from the last sentence.

[2] The latter was denounced by a police agent disguised as a member of the Bolshevik faction.

[3] See M. A. Tsyavolvskii (ed.), *Bolsheviki: Dokumenty po istorii bolshevizma . . . byvsh moskovskago okhrannogo otdeleniya . . .*, Moscow 1918, pp. 48 ff.

up to his neck, with daily telegrams and letters'.[1] Her suggestions for
dealing with the fractious Russians reflected his own faithfully enough—
without the element of personal involvement; a conference by all means,
but of the party members in Russia, and not merely the incorrigible
'fighting cocks' abroad. But probably this ignorance of detail was partly
feigned. She did deal with Clara Zetkin and Kautsky about the money
on Jogiches' behalf, though she took care not to importune or appear
too obviously partisan. But when Martov published a pamphlet exposing
the Bolsheviks' financial skulduggery she joined the chorus of outraged
protest—for the benefit of German ears—and Kautsky no doubt took
his own cue of condemnation from her.[2] To the Mensheviks Rosa
Luxemburg was quite simply Lenin's most active partisan in Germany,
and for all practical purposes she also drew the naïve Clara Zetkin in
her wake. Akselrod and Trotsky came and slipped in behind the scenes
of the SPD congress at Jena in September 1911 to wheedle a favourable
decision about the money out of Kautsky. Haase too was solicited; the
main thing was not to be spotted by 'any delegates close to Zetkin and
Luxemburg'.[3] As late as February 1912, when relations between Lenin
and Jogiches had already been broken off, Rosa Luxemburg still got
Lenin's emissary Poletaev an introduction to Kautsky.[4] Most important
of all, she begged Jogiches on at least two occasions not to use the money
as blackmail, once with regard to the trustees, and the second time
when the Technical Commission under Jogiches' chairmanship refused
Lenin funds to publish *Sotsial-Demokrat*. But she phrased her warnings
dispassionately and coldly, without much expectation of being listened
to.[5] As we shall see, she was not prepared to follow Jogiches into unbridled condemnation of Lenin after the dust-up in Paris, not even
when Lenin attacked her openly and specifically in 1912.

These events had their effect in the Polish party itself, which since
1910 had been on the brink of division. Though in the main Jogiches
acted within the established policy of the SDKPiL, most of the Polish
leaders felt that his involvement had a more personal aspect in pursuit
of private aims and ambitions. The virtual eviction of the SDKPiL
from the councils of the 'live' section of the Russian party provided
useful ammunition for an already restive leadership against Jogiches.

[1] *Letters to Karl and Luise Kautsky*, p. 160.
[2] I. Martov, *Spasiteli ili uprazdniteli* (Saviours or Wreckers), Paris 1911. *Letters to Karl and Luise Kautsky*, p. 161. See also the special collection of papers (*Russenfond*) appertaining to Kautsky's trustee activity in IISH, Amsterdam—now withdrawn pending publication (perhaps within the next decade!).
[3] *Pisma P. B. Akselroda i I. O. Martova*, Berlin 1924, p. 217.
[4] *Russenfond*, IISH. See also N. Poletaev, *Vospominaniya o V. I. Lenine*, Moscow 1956, Vol. I, p. 272. O. Pyatnitskii, *Zapiski bolshevika*, p. 153.
[5] Jogiches letters, beginning of October 1911, IML(M).

The Berlin section of the SDKPiL wrote a strong letter of protest to the Central Committee in which they spoke of the latter's 'gross neglect' in failing to keep the party informed of these events.[1] But we should not take this document too literally, as evidence of neglect; it was mainly an offensive weapon.

The opposition in the party did not intend to force any Lenin-style breakaway. Since they had particularly close relations with the local organizations in Warsaw and Łódź, Hanecki and his colleagues were able to manipulate their supporters into positions of authority. But when two representatives of the opposition came to Berlin to negotiate with the Central Committee, they were promptly handed over to a party court.[2] After this, in the autumn of 1911, the two local organizations, particularly the Warsaw one, openly challenged the Berlin leadership, and organized an oppositional conference in the capital in December. After some heated public exchanges the Central Committee declared both local organizations dissolved. They refused to accept their own dissolution and announced their intention of remaining in existence, independent of the Central Committee. Thereupon the latter circularized the International Bureau as well as the German and other parties to the effect that a dissident organization now existed which had no standing in the party. The break was now official and public. It split the organizations in the two main towns and elsewhere into two: one continuing to owe allegiance to the Central Committee in Berlin (*zarządowcy*) and the other supporting the 'splitters' (*rosłamowcy*)—or, as they were sometimes known, the SDKPiL Opposition (*opozycja*). Early in 1914 the Opposition organized an executive committee of its own, known as the National Committee (*Zarząd Krajowy*) in Cracow, while the executive in Berlin continued to be known by its old title (*Zarząd Główny*).

The loyal supporters of the Central Committee centred round the nucleus of those who had founded the original SDKP and nursed it through its infancy before 1900. The four musketeers remained together —Jogiches, Rosa Luxemburg, Marchlewski, and Warszawski. Apart from old loyalties, it is hard to say why; Marchlewski and Jogiches did not get on personally though they always treated each other with circumspection. Warszawski had been drawn into the Bolshevik orbit in Paris and was recalled for that reason; Jogiches treated him very offhandedly. And Warszawski in fact could certainly never bring himself to feel as strongly about the opposition as Jogiches. But, like the others,

---

[1] *List sekcji berlińskiej SDKPiL do ZG*, 22 July 1910, ZHP, Warsaw.

[2] See letter of Leder to Henke, 17 January 1913. This was later addressed as an open letter in Polish to the Central Committee of the SDKPiL. Copies are in the Henke papers in the SPD Archives, Bonn (in German) and a printed pamphlet in ZHP, Warsaw (in Polish).

he did have a very real love for the party which he had helped to found, and it was he who was to be primarily instrumental in reunifying it during the war. More than the others, Warszawski stood for the practical realization of working-class unity, not only in the divided Social Democracy but with the PPS-Left as well. Among those who pledged their support to the Central Committee was Feliks Dzierżyński. It was only after the arrest of this fanatic personality and devoted organizer that the National Committee could be established on home ground. His adherence was all the more surprising since Lenin, who had a very sharp eye for potential revolutionaries and supporters, had known Dzierżyński since 1906 and wooed him relentlessly—and was in fact to obtain his whole-hearted allegiance in 1917. For the few months he remained at liberty after the open split, Dzierżyński played an oddly schizophrenic role, supporting the Central Committee on the Polish question, but equally firmly supporting Lenin in Cracow in his own Russian splitting tactics.[1]

[1] Many western historians of Bolshevik history have become so fascinated with Lenin's manœuvres that they see his hand in every factional split within the orbit of the RSDRP before 1914 (e.g. Leonard Schapiro, *The Communist Party of the Soviet Union*, pp. 106, 123-4 and particularly p. 129: '[Lenin] had shortly afterwards engineered a breakaway in the Polish Social-Democratic party. This split was designed to leave the two leaders Tyszka and Rosa Luxemburg isolated in their party.'). A close study of Dzierżyński's role and attitude in this period shows clearly that whatever benefit Lenin may later have derived from the Polish split, he certainly did not engineer it. Dzierżyński was Lenin's closest supporter among the Poles in Russian affairs. 'As regards the policy of the CO [*Sotsial-Demokrat*, the party's central organ], I am in agreement with it as far as my knowledge of these matters goes—only I want to go even further and express my full solidarity with Lenin's policies.' (Dzierżyński to Jogiches, 13–14 February 1911, ZHP, 25/4, No. 593 K1.) Similarly he specifically endorsed nearly every one of Lenin's manœuvres during the spring and summer of 1911, against the *golosowcy* (those aligned with the Menshevik paper *Golos sotsial-demokrata*). Dzierżyński admitted frankly that he could only love and hate completely and never in part. His heart was 'completely Bolshevik' (ZHP, 25/5, No. 685 K1). See also Z. Dzerzhinskaya, *V gody velikikh boev*, Moscow 1964, pp. 160–8 (the memoirs of Dzierżyński's widow). He berated Jogiches for not clarifying his policy in Russian matters to his colleagues; Lenin should long ago have 'spat on the efforts [to create] unity [in the RSDRP] and carried out his policy without any further hindrance' (ZHP, 25/6, No. 754, K1–2). But Dzierżyński, like the other Poles and in spite of his close personal attachment to Lenin and his Bolshevik heart, drew the line at the final split. He disapproved of the action of the Bolshevik 'Russian organizing commission' in calling for the Prague conference in January 1912 at which the Bolsheviks constituted themselves the official Russian party. 'In this way the party would simply split into seven parts and this would mean the end of effective unity. The situation is extremely complex and we [Dzierżyński and Jogiches] have to sit here and somehow find a way out.' (ZHP, 25/5, M679, K1 and 25/6, M789.) After the conference itself Dzierżyński supported the Bolsheviks on principle but also the stand taken by the Central Committee in Polish matters. In his remaining months of freedom he condemned the *roslamowcy* uncompromisingly. By the time Lenin entered the Polish lists officially, Dzierżyński had been captured and was thus saved from open opposition to Lenin at a time when Polish and Russian matters could no longer be treated separately.

Against the old leadership were ranged Hanecki, Unszlicht, Małecki, and Ettinger, together with a host of younger recruits like the Stein brothers—and of course Radek. Hanecki was the undisputed leader of the opposition. Neither their past history nor future careers provide any satisfactory general explanation of their alignment. Hanecki became Lenin's confidential agent, which was much more than being just a Bolshevik; by 1917 he had practically severed his connection with the Polish movement and was in Stockholm conducting Lenin's top-secret negotiations with Germany for funds and support. Some of Lenin's close associates viewed his role with suspicion, and did not take to his debonair appearance, which included an ostentatious, invariable button-hole, but Lenin always defended him stoutly. Unszlicht, too, joined the Bolsheviks after the revolution and was for some time Dzierżyński's assistant in the Cheka (Soviet security police), later serving as a Bolshevik diplomat and official. But both Dzierżyński and Marchlewski also joined the Bolsheviks, in 1917 and 1918 respectively, so it is wrong to read too much into this connection between the Polish opposition and the Bolsheviks.

A few leaders took up neutral or intermediate positions similar to that of Trotsky in the Russian party before 1914. The most important was Leder who worked in Vienna during this period. Condemning the Central Committee for its intolerance and particularly for its handling of the Radek case, Leder none the less refused to countenance the split and gave his allegiance to neither side. It was no wonder that the split in the SDKPiL remained incomprehensible to the rest of the Socialist world. The polemics and accusations (which included accusations of harbouring and shielding Okhrana spies) flew back and forth in the next few years in all languages and only helped to confuse the issues still further.[1]

The events inside Poland itself, interesting and little known though they are, do not concern us here. Rosa Luxemburg had nothing to do with them and her activity in the Polish movement was confined to émigré aspects. She, too, disapproved of Jogiches' tactics but, like Warszawski, felt deeply attached to the SDKPiL, her first political home. From 1911 onwards Rosa Luxemburg was therefore in the unusual position—for her—of enforcing a policy with which she had little sympathy. She drafted many of the Central Committee's public statements on the subject of the split, the announcements to the International

---

[1] The Central Committee had singled Unszlicht out for the role of *agent provocateur*, though without mentioning his name. As far as I can discover, there was no vestige of truth in the accusation. There were some spies, in the second rank of the *rosłamowcy* organization, but this was common to all clandestine groups at the time.

Socialist Bureau and to the German party.[1] The task of liaison with the German executive was not always easy. If Jogiches had had his way, she would have been at the German executive offices every second day with the latest aspect of the scandal—a proceeding which would soon disgust the Germans, as she well knew.[2] Printing polemics costs money, which was especially scarce now that Bolshevik support had been cut off as had a substantial part of the dues-paying membership. Rosa Luxemburg therefore had the unpleasant task of squeezing money out of an SPD leadership to which in German affairs she stood in vocal opposition. Nevertheless she succeeded, though the sums were less than had been hoped. Jogiches wanted to send one donation back to the Germans with a contemptuous note and it was only when Rosa remonstrated at the pointlessness of such a gesture that he desisted.[3]

She was necessarily involved up to the hilt in the Radek case. This was less troublesome for her conscience since she disliked Radek herself—though again she did not fully approve of the severity of Jogiches' action. The latter had decided to make an example of the hapless Radek who was within target range in Germany and whose position in the SPD was tenuous. Radek had a sharp and lively pen and his destruction would silence one of the Central Committee's most persuasive critics. An old scandal—or rather string of scandals—was dug up and in December 1911 the evidence was placed first before a commission to look into the charges of theft—charges against which Jogiches, Rosa Luxemburg, and Marchlewski had indignantly defended Radek in September 1910 when they were raised by Häcker, Rosa's old PPS opponent in Germany, and Niemojewski in the very hostile paper, *Myśl Niepodległa*, as part of an anti-Semitic onslaught against the SDKPiL leadership.[4] The commission dragged on and was repeatedly hustled by Jogiches—and finally dissolved amid its own protests on 30 July 1912. The next step was the hard-working party court. It met in August 1912 and with little ceremony sentenced Radek to expulsion. The German executive was officially informed of the decision on 24 August, in a document signed, not by Rosa Luxemburg, but by Marchlewski, one of the court's conveners.[5] In doing so the Polish

[1] See, for instance, 'Do ogółu partii', *Pismo ulotne ZG SDKPiL*, June 1912, ZHP; also *Czerwony Sztandar*, July 1912, No. 188, pp. 4–6. Unfortunately there are few references in her letters to Jogiches on the subject of the split; no doubt they talked out their exchange of views on this subject. What there is, however, indicates her general line quite clearly: see below, p. 361.

[2] See Jogiches letters, end of 1912 (?), IML (M).

[3] Ibid.

[4] Karl Radek, *Meine Abrechnung*, p. 57. For Rosa Luxemburg's articles, see *Młot*, 1, 8, 15, 29 October 1910.

[5] 'God help him, for he knows not what he does', wrote Radek. The thefts of which he was accused were several:

Central Committee used Radek's real name and thus broke his pseudonym; according to him his departure for Bremen in 1912 was due to the danger from the police in the capital.

Rosa was against the whole formal proceedings. 'I consider Radek's potential as a centre of opposition grossly exaggerated and am against your plan [of a party court].'[1] Jogiches took not the slightest notice. As expected, Radek got the explicit support of all the *rosłamowcy* as well as Leder who now came out strongly against the executive. As the Polish support for Radek increased, Jogiches pressed ever more strongly for parallel action against him from the German party and it was Rosa who had to press the SPD executive to expel him. Circumstances in Germany helped her considerably, though here too the very action which made Radek unpopular in Germany helped to assure him of the support of the radical party organization in Bremen, itself in opposition to the SPD executive. As a result of their support Rosa Luxemburg now fell out with her old friends in the north, Henke and Knief, as well as Pannekoek. At one stage her position was almost schizophrenic— Polish pressure was forcing her into a German attitude of which in the end she could not but disapprove. At the 1913 German congress in Jena, where Radek was formally expelled from the German party, she voted against the measure of automatic expulsion, because it set a dangerous precedent for all nonconformists in the German party. At the same time the Polish decision had to be validated and respected. She and Marchlewski had to fight hard with Jogiches to obtain his approval for offering the German party at least a review of the Polish evidence against Radek at the party court, if it was called for. But it never was.[2]

Part of the campaign conducted by Rosa Luxemburg against Radek in Germany was to show that he was an outsider with no significant support. 'Among the Russians only unimportant and out-of-date personalities like Plekhanov and Akselrod support him, only the ruins of the former Russian party', she wrote in a letter to *Vorwärts* who reluctantly printed it at the second attempt as the statement of 'the

---

1. Books belonging to a party newspaper library—these were the subject of Häcker's attack.

2. A coat (or some clothes) belonging to a comrade. This became the traditional item in German party mythology (see Ruth Fischer, *Stalin and German Communism*, pp. 201–2).

3. Money. This was the most serious charge which Radek insistently denied, then and later, though he admitted the books and the clothes.

The case deserves further study, especially in view of Radek's later eminent position in the Russian party and his influence on German left-wing affairs.

[1] Jogiches letters, 1912 (?), IML (M).

[2] Jogiches letters, November 1913, IML (M). For the Germany story, see above, pp. 315–7.

best-known representative of the SDKPiL'.[1]

But Radek now got strong support from an unexpected quarter. The person who replied to Rosa Luxemburg was not one of those contemptuously referred to as a ruin, but none other than Lenin. He sent a blistering letter to *Vorwärts* entitled 'Rosa Luxemburg and the Polish "Central Committee" in Martov's footsteps', which the paper did not print but which remained to gather dust in the *Vorwärts* archives.[2] Though he made a point of not enthusing too openly about the merits of Radek's case, he compared the Central Committee's action to the underhand revengefulness of Martov's public 'exposures'. The suggestion that the SDKPiL were no better than the Mensheviks was harnessed to repeated assertions that both were empty shells, without revolutionary guts or for that matter any following; the intended audience for these dramatics was, of course, the SPD leadership. From then onwards Lenin became Radek's strongest supporter outside Polish Socialism and the Central Committee's most vituperative opponent.

The extent of Lenin's responsibility for the Polish split is an intriguing question which can only partially be solved from the available evidence. The split in the Polish party was at least partially connected with the break-up of the Russian party. Having out-manœuvred Jogiches and his conciliator supporters, Lenin moved to the offensive in his opponent's territory—he was not the man to let Jogiches polemicize against him without retort. In the summer of 1912 he moved his headquarters to Cracow and, as his wife charmingly puts it, 'Vladimir Ilyich had there the opportunity of coming into closer contact with the Polish Social Democrats and of studying their point of view on the national question.'[3] The move to Cracow had long ago been suggested by Dzierżyński, but now it was the *rosłamowcy* who welcomed him.[4] 'Since the Warsaw Committee [of the opposition] demanded that the Polish party take up a more definite position in the internal party affairs of the RSDRP, Vladimir Ilyich took the side of the Warsaw committee. . . . He could not remain an onlooker . . . to an important part of the general struggle within the party which was so acute at the time.'[5]

Outside the RSDRP the most obvious assistance which Lenin could give the rebels was on the international plane. Like Rosa he was a member of the International Socialist Bureau. It was as one of the

---

[1] *Vorwärts*, 14 September 1912.

[2] For translation and fuller discussion of the circumstances see J. P. Nettl, 'An unpublished Lenin article from September 1912', *International Review of Social History*, Vol. IX (1964), Part 3, pp. 470–82.

[3] Nadezhda Krupskaya, *Memories of Lenin*, p. 175.

[4] Ibid., p. 176.

[5] Ibid., p. 179. Dare one detect here a slight touch of bad conscience about such obvious fishing in other people's troubled waters?

RSDRP representatives—Plekhanov was the other—that he replied to the Central Committee's announcement with one of his own. Rosa Luxemburg had written on 8 July 1912 that

a splinter group has established itself in Warsaw . . . and a small group of organized members have committed a series of severe violations against the statutes, discipline and unity of the [Polish] party and would not submit to the proceedings of party justice against two of their representatives. [This is not the result of any] political differences of opinion but merely the fruit of indiscipline and disorganization by a few individuals and . . . *agents provocateurs*. They have been formally excluded both from the Polish Social Democracy and from the RSDRP of which the former is an autonomous member.[1]

Lenin replied on 31 August. He denied the SDKPiL Central Committee's entire version of the split.

1. The Central Committee has no right to decide or to announce who belongs to the RSDRP or not. The [Polish] Central Committee has no connection with and does not belong to our party, whose Central Committee I represent.
2. The split has already been in existence since Hanecki *was excluded* from the Polish Central Committee in 1910.[2]

The organ of the dissidents printed this statement with gleeful comments.[3]

Lenin now threw the whole weight of his attack against the Central Committee, which he described as 'a committee without a party'.[4] Jogiches and Rosa Luxemburg, faithful supporters of the Bolsheviks for so long, were speedily promoted from conciliators to liquidators—the blockbuster accusation of the immediate pre-war period.[5] Naturally Jogiches replied in kind, with a whole batch of pamphlets denouncing Lenin's splitting tactics in the Russian party and his iniquitous influence on the Poles. Having bombarded Kautsky with letters in favour of his Technical Commission in the summer of 1911—Rosa's activities were not decisive enough—he now berated him for not being financially firm enough with Lenin. The dispute blared its way across 1912 and 1913, deafening those whose ears were attuned to Russian or Polish, with even a number of assiduous translations into German. For the Central Committee Lenin was now the particular enemy.

Yet it should not be wholly surprising to find that in 1912 personal contact between Rosa Luxemburg and Lenin still existed. At the end

---

[1] Central Committee to International Bureau, 8 July 1912, Henke papers, SPD Archives, Bonn.
[2] Lenin, *Sochineniya*, Vol. XVIII, pp. 252–3. My italics. Hanecki actually resigned.
[3] *Gazeta Robotnicza*, No. 19, November 1912.
[4] Lenin, *Sochineniya*, Vol. XVIII, p. 383.
[5] For the history of the term, and its justification, see Schapiro, *The CPSU*, Chapters 6 and 7.

of February of that year Lenin came to Berlin personally to succeed where Poletaev had failed, and carried out an assault on Kautsky for further payments of the trustee moneys. He took the opportunity of calling upon Rosa Luxemburg several times in two days. 'Lenin was here yesterday and has been back four times today. I like talking to him, he is clever and educated—I like seeing his ugly mug. . . . He found Mimi [Rosa's cat, whose approval of visitors was an essential preliminary to her mistress's sympathy] very imposing, a *barskii kot* [a lordly cat].' It was not until the row in the International Bureau at the end of 1913 that personal animosity really grew between them. One should never take Lenin's polemics as an automatic guide to his personal attitudes. Russian habits were the exact opposite of German, *c'était la musique qui faisait le ton.*

The break, and the opportunity for a Polish counter-attack, came when Lenin carried out the final split in the Russian party by insisting on a division, not only of the respective party organizations, but of the Social-Democratic representation in the fourth Duma. The RSDRP Duma representatives, though divided into Mensheviks and Bolsheviks, were loosely controlled by the respective group leaders, and in the course of 1912 developed an institutional pull of their own towards unity. It was the old dichotomy between local activists, legal or illegal, and foreign leaders. Throughout 1913 Lenin planned to split 'his' parliamentary delegates off completely. It was only a matter of waiting for a favourable opportunity. This, with suitable manœuvres for blame-throwing, came in October 1913.[1] The Russian Social-Democratic parliamentary group was now split formally in two—six Bolsheviks and seven Mensheviks.[2] Whatever the mysteries of the internal struggle, which even Rosa Luxemburg confessed 'made her head swim', this was a public act of disunity for all to see. The dismay was universal.

Towards the end of 1913 the reluctant International Bureau had the Russian question on its agenda once more. At the meeting in London in mid-December—the last occasion on which Rosa Luxemburg visited that city—plans for reunification were to be discussed. The formal motion for including the Russian split was Rosa Luxemburg's. She cited the split in the Duma delegation as 'the last act in two years of compromising the growing labour movement in Russia . . . on the part of Lenin's group'. As a special sideswipe at Lenin, the motion empha-

[1] See A. Badaev, *Bolsheviki v gosudarstvennoi dume. Vospominaniya*, Moscow 1954.

[2] Hence the crucial importance of the Jagiello election in Warsaw in 1913. To Rosa's sardonic amusement, both Warszawski and Marchlewski tried to get Kautsky to publish articles in *Neue Zeit*. But the editor had had enough of Poles and Russians, and politely told them so—'at the risk of contemptuous remarks about by opportunism and lack of character'. (Karl Kautsky to Adolf Warszawski, 22 January 1913, C. 756, IISH.)

sized 'the irregularity of Russian representation in the International Bureau, one of whose two representatives merely represents a splinter group created by himself'. Rosa Luxemburg called for 'steps . . . to bring about unity . . . failing which the . . . problem [was] to be submitted to the . . . International congress in Vienna [in 1914], in the same way that French reunification had been dealt with at the 1904 Amsterdam congress'[1]

Lenin replied by getting some of his *rosłamowcy* supporters to write to the Bureau and urge priority for the question of the Polish split, but Rosa was able to prevent this from being adopted for the agenda.[2]

At the meeting of the Bureau even Plekhanov, who had been an unexpected but redoubtable ally of Lenin's for the last two years, now deserted him, and resigned his mandate (the second RSDRP mandate) to the Bureau, who gave it to an orthodox Menshevik. Unfortunately Kautsky, though he was heartily sick of Russian affairs after his experience as trustee, still made it his business to oppose Rosa's formula. Where she proposed that only those parties represented in the Bureau and who were members of the RSDRP should be called upon to get together to prepare for a general conference on reunification, Kautsky called for a broader base of 'all interested parties who consider themselves Social Democrats . . . we must avoid any judgements about the past and concentrate only on the future.'[3]

On the face of it this was a repetition of Lenin's and Martov's tight and loose versions of Socialist membership at the famous second RSDRP congress in 1903. But in reality Rosa's rather obstinate defence of her tighter definition had another purpose. Her formula was meant to exclude the *rosłamowcy*, who were not represented in the International Bureau, while Kautsky's plan would have included them. Though probably Kautsky's motives were in the main a sincere desire for unity and not any great interest in pre-judging contending groups, the sharp exchange between him and Rosa Luxemburg showed clearly that the personal element between them was still smouldering. Kautsky reported with glee to Victor Adler afterwards that he had been able 'to spike her guns'. But in fact a compromise was reached. Without being impeded from eventually dealing with anyone it pleased, the Bureau was to take soundings from those 'parties affiliated to the International before a more general conference is called'. As Rosa Luxemburg

[1] *Vorwärts*, 21 November 1913, 1st Supplement ('Aus der Partei').

[2] *Supplement to Bulletin ISB*, No. 11. Meeting of ISB London, 13–14 December 1913. The text of the letter is not given or the authorship disclosed. For Lenin's correspondence with the secretary of ISB in trying to ward off that body's interference in Russian affairs, see *Correspondance entre Lénine et Camille Huysmans 1905–14*, Paris/The Hague 1963, pp. 100 ff., 119 ff.

[3] Ibid., p. 4. See also *Vorwärts*, 18 December 1913.

specially emphasized in one of her perpetual 'corrections' to the press, the principle was to reunite an existing party, not to found a new one.[1] The main issue, involvement of the International in the affairs of the RSDRP, had been achieved.

But it was circumstances more than any effective action by Rosa which aligned opinions in the International Bureau when the problem of Russian unity next and finally came up for discussion in July 1914. Early in that year Vandervelde, chairman of the Bureau, had visited Russia on its behalf and had discussed the problem of unity with all factions.[2] His report showed that the main obstacle to unity was Bolshevik intransigence. The meeting in July was called to consider it, and the next steps to be taken. It took the form of an enlarged conference of all interested groups in accordance with the Bureau resolution of December 1913. Apart from the two Russian groups—once more including Plekhanov—the *Bund*, the Letts, and both sections of Polish Social Democracy, as well as the PPS-Left, were represented. The SDKPiL opposition was present only because of a Bolshevik ultimatum to the effect that if their Polish allies were not invited, they themselves would not attend. Jogiches himself had been prepared to denounce the whole conference in Brussels if it meant a participation of the *rosłamowcy*, but Rosa dissuaded him: 'I am for this conference even if it does bring difficulties with it and I would be in favour of admitting them [*rosłamowcy*] under clearly defined conditions'. Unfortunately, no official record of the discussions and speeches exist, except for the reports of Russian police informers who attended under their respective Bolshevik and Menshevik disguises, and a part of the Bureau Secretary's handwritten notes.[3] Though a member of the Bureau, Lenin, furious at all this interference in his affairs, did not himself attend; he claimed to have better things to do. He sent his trusted supporter and close personal friend, Inessa Armand, with an enormous and detailed memorandum which instructed her to block every effort at unity and to meet all persuasion with the now familiar '*niet*'.[4]

Inessa Armand found herself almost completely alone. Plekhanov, who never did anything in moderation, now turned against the Bolsheviks as incontinently as he had recently supported them, and indulged his sharp tongue to such an extent that the chairman had to call

---

[1] *Vorwärts*, 23 December 1913 ('Aus der Partei').

[2] E. Vandervelde, *Three Aspects of the Russian Revolution*, London 1918, p. 19.

[3] M. A. Tsyavlovskii, *Bolsheviki. Dokumenty . . . okhrannogo . . .*, pp. 146–8.

[4] Lenin, *Sochineniya*, Vol. XX, pp. 463–94 (official report and instructions of the Central Committee), pp. 495–502 (for Lenin's private instructions and tactical guide lines). It is interesting to compare this latter document with Rosa Luxemburg's instructions to Warszawski at the second Russian congress in 1903 (above, pp. 189–91). Though Lenin's style was harder and more abrupt, both met a somewhat similar diplomatic problem in a

him to order. Rosa Luxemburg also spoke. She represented not only the view of the Polish Central Committee, but carried all the authority of a long-standing protagonist of Russian unity with acknowledged expertise in this difficult question. It was her insistence which prevailed upon the conference to submit the report of the meeting to the forthcoming International Socialist congress due to meet in Vienna in August 1914. This would make continued Bolshevik refusal to agree to the conditions of unity proposed by the conference nothing less than open defiance of the entire International.[1]

Rosa could be well satisfied with the achievements of the conference.[2] The long-standing Polish desire for unity had received the official stamp of International approval—even the *roslamowcy* representatives voted for the resolution and against the Bolsheviks; Russian unity was as much their policy as the Central Committee's, provided that it did not involve their own diminution. Rosa's activities for Russian reunification could not but raise the prestige of the SDKPiL Central Committee in the eyes of the International. Moreover, the question of the Polish split had once more been kept off the official agenda in spite of Lenin's strenuous efforts to focus attention on it (to many outsiders the whole purpose of the meeting had been to discuss 'the present situation of Social Democracy in Russia *and Poland*') And finally, Lenin had been exposed as the single obstacle to unity.[3]

---

very similar way—and both were determined to lay down not only policy but the precise manner of its execution. For some recently published documents on how Bolshevik policy was formulated and carried out on this occasion, see *Istoricheski Arkhiv*, No. 4 (1959), pp. 9–38 (particularly M. Litvinov's letter which incidentally identified Rosa Luxemburg as the prime mover in forcing the meeting on the Russians).

[1] Rosa Luxemburg's remarks have to be deduced from scattered references in her correspondence at the time, particularly in her letters to Jogiches; also from the notes relating to the discussion taken down by hand, still preserved in M. Huysmans's private papers. The conditions for unity were fivefold: acceptance of the party programme, recognition of majority decisions, acceptance of the need for secrecy in party organization (this was against Menshevik wishes), prohibition of all formation of parliamentary blocs with bourgeois parties, and agreement to participate in a general unification congress (O. H. Gankin and H. H. Fisher, *The Bolsheviks and the World War*, pp. 131–2). The official resolution of the meeting was published in *Le Peuple* (Brussels), 20 July 1914, No. 201, p. 1.

[2] To Kautsky's unexpected pleasure, he found himself in full agreement with Rosa for the first time for four years—and the last. Both agreed on the policy for reunification against Bolshevik intransigence. Kautsky acknowledged the pleasant fact gracefully ('Karl Liebknecht und Rosa Luxemburg zum Gedächtnis', *Der Sozialist*, 24 January 1919, Vol. V, No. 4, p. 56)—the Bolsheviks later used this single identity of views as heavy ammunition against her.

[3] For a different (but I think naïve) interpretation of Lenin as committed to some form of Social-Democratic unity right up to the time of the allied intervention in Russia after the war, see Rudolf Schlesinger, 'Lenin as a Member of the International Socialist Bureau', *Soviet Studies*, Vol. XVI, No. 4 (April 1965), pp. 448–58, especially p. 451.

When war broke out the Polish leaders in Germany were automatically cut off from contact with the organizations in Russian Poland. By strenuous efforts Jogiches managed to retain a limited amount of contact during these early years via Scandinavia, the classic secret route by which Russian émigrés kept in touch with their homeland.[1] In any case the labour movement in Poland as well as in Russia had fallen into a parlous state by 1914, which the sudden wave of massive strikes in the summer of 1914 could only partially revive. The declaration of war anyhow pole-axed this rally completely. For a brief moment all Polish and *Bund* Socialist groups decided to collaborate but the attempt did not last long; soon organized Socialism broke once more into its inimical constituent parts. Piłsudski backed the Central Powers to the hilt. Not until the German offensive of 1915 overflowed the greater part of Poland was it possible for the émigré leadership of the SDKPiL and PPS-Left to re-establish contact with local organizations. In this respect the *rozłamowcy*, most of whom were in Switzerland, were better off than the Central Committee in Berlin, limited by the severe restrictions on all Socialist activity in war-time. Rosa Luxemburg anyhow had her hands more than full with the birth-pains of an effective Left opposition in the SPD, while Jogiches increasingly took over the vacant role of organizer for the *Spartakusbund*.

But the bleak issues of the war had irrevocably made nonsense of the largely personal differences between the two Polish groups. It fell to Warszawski in Switzerland to undertake reunification, a task close to his heart. He travelled to Warsaw in the summer of 1916 and by November of that year the local organizations of the SDKPiL were once more merged into one.[2] For Warszawski it was only a preliminary step to the more difficult task of bringing together the SDKPiL and the PPS-Left, though he only achieved this when the Communist Party was formed at the end of the war. Warszawski was known to favour unity strongly—and had to pay the usual Communist penalty for enthusiasm when he failed to be elected to the first central committee of the new Polish party because he was considered to have been too soft in the negotiations with the PPS-Left. But he had Rosa's approval.[3] The programme of the new Communist Party of Poland was sent post-haste and under difficult conditions to Berlin and obtained the approval of

[1] For a graphic analysis of these routes, see Michael Futrell, *Northern Underground*, London 1962.

[2] See the documents in O. B. Szmidt, *Dokumenty*, Vol. III, pp. 169–71; also *Czerwony Sztandar*, June 1917, No. 191.

[3] See below, pp. 444–5. For Warszawski, see his article in *Nasza Trybuna*, No. 5, 13 December 1918, which talked about a merger instead of a capitulation. In general see Józef Kowalski, *Zarys Historii polskiego ruchu robotniczego 1918–38*, Vol. I (1918–1928), Warsaw 1962, p. 110. This is an official party history.

the two great leaders. Fittingly, this last act of Jogiches and Rosa Luxemburg for Polish Socialism was one of unity and approval. Rosa Luxemburg had other things to think about in November 1918, but we may assume that this great achievement, particularly the acceptance by the PPS-Left of all that the SDKPiL had stood for, caused her satisfaction.

By the time the curtains parted at the end of the war, most of the actors had emerged in new and different roles. Many were attracted by the magnet of the Russian revolution. Marchlewski had been bailed out by the Bolsheviks after the peace of Brest-Litovsk and joined the Russian party, though he still continued to speak with authority on Polish affairs. Dzierżyński, too, was released from prison by the revolution of March 1917 and henceforward devoted his fierce talents and loyalties entirely to the Russian Bolshevik party. Hanecki was Lenin's secret confidential agent in Stockholm. But none made such a dramatic reappearance on the scene as Karl Radek, who travelled to Germany illegally in December 1918 as the representative of the Bolshevik party, wearing the mantle of enormous prestige which membership of Lenin's entourage now commanded. It was a moment of mixed feelings for Jogiches and Rosa Luxemburg. The momentary resuscitation of their old political community, and the somewhat nostalgic atmosphere in which the brilliant post-revolutionary careers of so many friends and comrades were discussed, provide their own ironic contribution to the end of Rosa Luxemburg's story.[1]

Rosa's legacy to Polish Socialism was thus very different from, though not less than, that to German Socialism. She was directly associated with the left wing in Germany until her death. As we shall see, the creation of the German Communist Party was in large measure due to her and its policies were shaped for many years by her ideas. In Poland, on the other hand, there was a break. The creation of the Polish Communist Party had nothing to do with her; many of the personalities associated with the party after the war did not even know her personally; even though her influence in the creation of the SDKPiL and the emergence of its mature policy was acknowledged to be great, it was that of an historical figure. Thus in the report of the meeting of the organizing committee of the new Communist Party of Poland in December 1918 no mention is made either of Jogiches or Rosa Luxemburg.[2] But, at Warszawski's instigation, a man called Ciszewski—a member of the PPS-Left—travelled to Berlin before the congress and

---

[1] See below, pp. 467–8.

[2] *Sprawozdanie ze zjazdu organizacyjnego KPRP (Zjednoczonych SDKPiL i Lewicy PPS)*, Warsaw 1919. The minutes of the founding congress have not survived; possibly there were speeches of tribute to the two great leaders.

submitted the unity proposals to Rosa and Jogiches, who approved them with few alterations. Even if it was a mere formality, the new Polish Communist Party therefore had the official blessing of Rosa Luxemburg—while she in turn had the satisfaction of seeting it created even before the German party, a product of fusion with the PPS-Left and not of separation like the KPD.[1]

Polish Socialism divided sharply into the periods before and after the war; to connect the two is the task of historians and political philosophers, not of contemporary politicians. The sense of a clean start in 1918 was far greater in Polish than in German Communism. The Stalinist assault on the pre-war Left did not therefore touch the Polish past—or Rosa Luxemburg—as directly as in Germany, and after the death of Stalin the Poles took out her reputation almost unaltered from the casket in which it had been stored for the duration. All that was needed was interest enough to polish and brighten it with research, and this has now been amply forthcoming.

In Germany, however, she was, and still is, a disputed figure, not only historically but in terms of present policies. The continuity of her influence, the fact that she was indisputably linked with modern German Communism, makes any discussion of Rosa Luxemburg both controversial and dangerous. Hence the flood of Polish publications and the limited and highly selective treatment of Rosa Luxemburg in East Germany.

---

[1] See J. Ciszewski, 'Wspomnienia z roku', *Z Pola Walki*, Moscow 1928, Nos. 7–8; also *Z Pola Walki*, 1958, No. 4, pp. 39–63.

XIII

THE WAR

IN the Marxist calendar 4 August 1914 is a watershed date. For a decade one had only to mention the 4th of August in German Socialist circles and everyone knew what was meant: not the declaration of war so much as the SPD's official support for it. While everyone later agreed that this was not the outcome of a sudden shock but a natural reaction (or in hostile eyes the culmination of a long process of decay), we must not be dazzled by hindsight. At the time the vote of the SPD *Reichstag* delegation for the war credits was a momentous decision, and a shock to all but the immediate participants. As with most profound innovations, inevitability was a plea of immediate psychological defence. 'We couldn't help it', is the classic cry of all conservatives who carry out a revolution.

The first real confrontation of the European Socialist leaders with their own impotence was at a meeting of the Bureau of the Socialist International in Brussels on 29 July 1914. Rosa Luxemburg was present as usual on behalf of the SDKPiL; she had been in Brussels since mid-July in search of the perennial but elusive panacea for unifying the centrifugal Russian party, and only knew what was going on in Berlin at second hand. The newspapers, however, spoke clearly, and the German delegation was able to complete the picture when the members arrived in the course of 28 July. And the other national delegations told their stories, from Vienna and from Paris. The tone of the resolution adopted was familiar enough. 'The International Socialist Bureau charges proletarians of all nations concerned not only to pursue but even to intensify their demonstrations against war. . . .'[1] But the speeches in private session reflected very different opinions. Victor Adler declared his party's complete helplessness. He implied that the only choice was between the destruction of organized Socialism or alignment to the furore of the Vienna crowds; all his hearers were struck by the ghastly realism of his resignation, which none the less

---

[1] Translated from the French from A. Zévaes, *Jaurès*, Paris 1951, p. 245. The full text of the resolutions is reprinted in Carl Grünberg, 'Die Internationale und der Weltkrieg', *Archiv für die Geschichte des Sozialismus und der Arbeiterbewegung*, Vol. I (1916), p. 405.

bore the usual stamp of his authority. But most of the delegates would not accept the full implication of his words; the militants, Rosa among them, dissented strongly. In the words of one participant, she was 'utterly outraged' by such defeatism; 'the meeting cannot proceed in such an atmosphere.' Jaurès too was optimistic; the Germans divided among themselves.[1] The meeting considered a change of locale for the coming International congress, due to take place in Vienna in August; this city, heaving with popular nationalism, was obviously unsuitable. Rosa Luxemburg and Jean Jaurès pressed the alternative claims of Paris; there the congress would be accompanied by monster demonstrations against war.[2] All the hopes of the delegates now focused on this congress. But two days later Jaurès was to be assassinated in Paris.

That evening a representative group of participants spoke to a huge crowd in the Cirque Royal, which 'literally shook at the end of Jaurès's magnificent speech'.[3] The Brussels gathering was the epitome of all that was best and most hopeless in the Second International, the belief that idealism, public opinion, popular goodwill could be summoned at will by the leaders and would engulf or at least divert the course of history. Rosa was exhausted by her Russian negotiations and by the ever clearer impotence of the last meeting of the International Bureau.[4] She took no part in the desultory small talk of the delegates, but sat silent and withdrawn.

The Brussels meeting was distinguished not only by those who participated but by those who did not come. Significantly, some of the 'realists' kept away; the right wing of the PPS could see nothing but good for Poland in a war between Russia and the Central Powers, while the Bolsheviks too had no interest in powerless public squawks about unity and war. The revolutionary forces had recently been growing and fermenting in Russia, and the prospect of war was almost too good to expect. 'Franz Josef and Nikolasha won't do us the favour', Lenin commented, with an optimistic glint in his eye; he had gone climbing in the Slovakian Tatra to mark his contempt for the International Bureau's unity meeting.[5]

---

[1] A brief résumé of the speeches at this meeting is in *Compte Rendu de la Réunion du BSI tenue à Bruxelles le 29–30 juillet 1914*, in M. Huysmans's private papers. For a recent account with documents, see Georges Haupt, *Le Congrès manqué*, Paris 1965 who cites the Spanish Socialist Fabra-Ribas on Rosa Luxemburg's attitude at the meeting.

[2] Carl Grünberg, loc. cit.

[3] Angelica Balabanoff, op. cit., p. 134. According to her, Rosa also spoke; Grünberg does not mention her.

[4] Camille Huysmans to Benedikt Kautsky, 11 March 1949, in *Briefe an Freunde*, p. 116.

[5] In a letter to Maxim Gorky, quoted in Bertram D. Wolfe, *Three who made a Revolution* p. 608.

Haase, Rosa Luxemburg, and the other German delegates returned to Berlin on 31 July. There, too, the speed of events had obliterated realistic perceptions. In a manifesto of 25 July the SPD executive almost pre-empted the call of the International; all the weakness and hesitation of 1911 seemed to have disappeared. 'The class-conscious German proletariat . . . raises a flaming protest against the criminal machinations of the warmongers. . . . Not a drop of any German soldier's blood must be sacrificed to the power hunger of the Austrian ruling clique, to the Imperialist profiteers.'[1] Similar denunciations followed daily, but in less than a week the senior members of the executive had returned from the last holiday of peace and decided jointly and severally that there was precisely nothing that the SPD could do against war. The automatic phrases of defiance pumped out by their juniors under Haase's influence—no holiday for this busy lawyer—had lost all point, for war abroad and military government at home loomed certain and imminent; indeed, they could only do harm to the SPD. The executive issued a new manifesto, apologetic and quietist in tone, whose urgent message was—no risks![2] At the same time, with a furtive backward glance at history, one of its members was sent to Paris to talk to the French; 'it will not have been for want of trying'. The crucial question of voting for the inevitable war credits in the *Reichstag* was already being discussed, as yet inconclusively.[3] Some sections of the party press were still faithfully echoing the anti-militarist sentiments so painfully hammered out during the years of Socialist self-sufficiency, with *Vorwärts* in the van.[4] For a while the press ran on in its well-accustomed grooves —it knew after all no other language—while the leaders hesitated. All depended on the hope that the German government would not back the madmen in Vienna.

But it did. And once Germany was in, the whole perspective changed. On the one hand was fear: fear of isolation from the masses, Bebel's old fear of the all-powerful military dictatorship—the party had had a glimpse in 1910 of what the military commanders were simply longing

---

[1] Reprinted in Carl Grünberg, op. cit., p. 423. The phraseology directly echoes Bismarck's famous remark about the Balkans not being worth the bones of a single Pomeranian grenadier, which had already been quoted *verbatim* in a resolution of the party executive dated 15 October 1912. The SPD was always highly receptive to slogans from any source and went on repeating them faithfully; during the last ten years of its pre-war existence it had become a 'slogan' party.

[2] Grünberg, op. cit., pp. 435–6, dated 31 July.

[3] Karl Liebknecht, *Klassenkampf gegen den Krieg*, Berlin 1919, p. 11.

[4] *Vorwärts*, 30 July 1914. 'The Socialist proletariat refuses all responsibility for the events which are being conjured up by a ruling class blinded to the point of madness. . . .' This was still the moderately radical *Vorwärts* created after November 1905, of which Rosa Luxemburg had been an editor for a few weeks.

to do to Social Democracy,[1] also the knowledge of complete impotence in case of war, which Bebel had also foreseen in private four years earlier.[2] On the other side was the practical legacy of so many years of isolation, firmly established after the victory over the revisionists. In its present need society stretched out its hand and Social Democracy seized it. For some it was a catharsis, the end of a dark period of useless penance; as in France, a small group of left-wing radicals now became the most vociferous supporters of the war.[3] For most of the others it was a welcome by-product of an unhappy situation. The ruling classes, it turned out, were not blood-thirsty monsters, they were merely people with a rather different background and views, but one could work with them. 'No reader of Scheidemann can miss the genuine pleasure which he felt in being invited to discuss matters on an equal footing with the ministers of state.'[4] Noske was even more blatant. The same sentiment, a little better disguised, appears also in the memoirs of Ebert and Keil, the Württemberg leader.[5] But it would be unfair to see all these men as merely Social Democrats *faute de mieux*. There were two crucial new factors in their life: a war which they had opposed but could not prevent; and, more important still, a defensive war against the old bogey-man of progressive Europe, Tsarist Russia. With a queer mixture of arrogance and historical conservatism they suddenly saw themselves as helping a relatively progressive Germany to destroy Tsarism. We now know that this was a more predictable reaction than it seemed at the time; recent documentary evidence suggests that the German chancellor's hesitation in ordering full-scale mobilization was merely a manoeuvre to precipitate the Russians into mobilizing first and thus ensure the patriotic support of the SPD.[6]

The last of the defiance of 30 July, when Ebert and Otto Braun were sent to Zürich with the party chest as a precaution against outlawry,

[1] *Protokoll . . . 1910*, p. 430. An appeal by General von Bissing referring to his confidence in 'our so reliable working class'—a confidence that 'must not be shaken in any way'—appeared in *Vorwärts*, 17 August 1914, with the editorial comment that 'with this latest proclamation Herr von Bissing has placed himself beyond all criticism'.

[2] For a curious glimpse of this side of Bebel from an English point of view, see letter of Sir Henry Angst to William Braithwaite, 22 October 1910, in W. J. Braithwaite, *Lloyd George's Ambulance Wagon*, London 1957, pp. 65–66.

[3] For Konrad Haenisch's conversion see his personal statement in Eugen Prager, *Geschichte der USPD*, Berlin 1922, p. 34; also his more 'political' reasoning in *Hamburger Echo*, 1 December 1914, No. 280.

[4] Schorske, *German Social Democracy*, p. 292. There was also the incident at an Imperial reception when an over-carefully briefed Kaiser leapt to welcome a guest whom he mistakenly believed to be Schiedemann.

[5] Gustav Noske, *Erlebtes aus Aufstieg und Niedergang einer Demokratie*, Offenbach 1947, pp. 39, 43, 55. Friedrich Ebert, *Kämpfe und Ziele*, Dresden, no date [1924?]. Wilhelm Keil, *Erlebnisse eines Sozialdemokraten*, Stuttgart 1947, Vol. I, p. 306.

[6] See Imanuel Geiss (ed.), *Julikrise und Kriegsausbruch 1914*, a collection of documents, Vol. II, Hanover, 1965.

had already dissolved by 3 August. The *Reichstag* debate on the war credits was imminent; how would the 110 members of the SPD vote? Considering what later proved to have been at stake—the whole future of twentieth-century Socialism—the discussion was flat and brief. The perspectives of the majority had narrowed. For them, 'it was now exclusively a matter of deciding whether at a time when the enemy had already entered the country and [that enemy] anyhow was Russia, a party representing a full third of the German people could deny the means of defence and protection to those called upon to defend them and their families. . . . Impossible.' As against that, a small minority, 'between a sixth and a seventh', felt doubts—not an opposing certainty, but doubts. 'Could one envisage the vote for war credits, when the information as to the events was one-sided, and anyhow came from the side of the enemies of Social Democracy . . .? It would be in contradiction with itself, would make the worst impression on the workers of other countries and create confusion in the Socialist International.'[1] Thus the majority were sure of their duty while the minority were not. The twenty strongest supporters of voting for war credits later declared that they would have voted for them, if necessary, against the party, while the fourteen opponents could not bring themselves to break the long tradition of discipline, especially since the party had already resolved to speak and vote unanimously in the *Reichstag* next day, one way or the other.[2] At the caucus meeting of the opposition, some suggested abstention, with the precedent of Bebel and Wilhelm Liebknecht in 1870; others—including the grand old man's son Karl—wanted a loud negative vote. But finally it was decided to support the government. Ironically Hugo Haase, an opponent of the affirmative vote, was chosen to deliver the SPD declaration in the *Reichstag*—in his role of first chairman of the party. He did it in the spirit of the large majority, not his own. And the bourgeois deputies loudly applauded him.

Today we are no longer surprised, for the decision was the inexorable consequence of twenty years of party history. The threads of inevitability have been drawn two ways, by objective historians who could evaluate material knowing how the story ended—and therefore emphasize what was 'real' and show up what was 'false'—and by the Communists searching for ever earlier evidence of a great betrayal. With their different objectives and techniques both came to similar conclusions: the vote for war credits was the end of a long process, not the beginning;

---

[1] Eduard Bernstein, in *Archiv für Sozialwissenshaft und Sozialpolitik*, *II*, Kriegsheft 1915, pp. 19–20. There are other accounts, including an apologia by Kautsky in *Neue Zeit* (1915–16, Vol. I, p. 322), the veracity of which was questioned by Mehring (*Die Internationale*, April 1915, editorial comment, p. 10). Bernstein, a pacifist but not a radical, gives the most sober and least egocentric account.

[2] *Die Internationale* April 1915, p. 49; Karl Liebknecht, *Klassenkampf gegen den Krieg*, Berlin 1919, p. 55.

a logical consequence of past actions, not a brutal aberration. But contemporaries did not see it like that. Those most affected saw a temporary
wavering which would, indeed must, soon be corrected. Lenin in Switzerland, which he reached a few weeks after his release from custody in
Austrian Cracow, could hardly believe it. For the German party was
the jewel of the International; however unreliable the other parties
might be, with their history of splits and wavering, the SPD had so
often declared its solid hatred of the imperial state and imperial military
policy, its determination to prevent or abort any war. Any moment
now the executive, the *Reichstag* caucus, would call for action. But no.
Since twenty years of history in which they had participated could not
just be a lie, the minority of revolutionary Socialists everywhere began
to feel that the German Socialist leaders had betrayed the cause.
Nothing else could explain it. Now they must be garrotted with their
own string of words.

The SPD executive instinctively knew that it was on parole with the
government, for its own good behaviour and for that of the party
membership. The party-truce (*Burgfrieden*) meant in effect suspending
all worth-while opposition for the duration, except for such minor
concessions as could be negotiated amicably. Chief beneficiary of these
concessions was not the party, but the unions. But at least the party and
its organizations were allowed to exist unmolested; members were able
to speak in the *Reichstag*, however minute the chances of influencing
the government. In return the SPD had to prove that its continued
existence kept labour aligned to the war effort. The discipline which
the executive had once exercised for the benefit of Socialist isolation
was now wielded on behalf of the war cabinet, and had a twofold role:
to quell opposition to itself and to the *Burgfrieden* (which became synonymous in all Socialist eyes), and to plead the cause of minor, inadvertent
offenders with the military; a dual responsibility to party and to state.[1]
On 4 August 1914 the SPD became, like the other parties in imperial
Germany, a pressure group which articulated special interests (though
mutely in war-time) but without hope of taking or wielding power in
the state.

Not that everything divided and at once fell neatly into place. Whatever some of the local papers might say—they always tended to be
extreme in either direction—the main leaders of the SPD were neither
joyful revisionists nor chauvinists. They sincerely believed that they
had done what they could, that it had failed, but they had to go on living
in a situation that was not of their own making. The fact that good

---

[1] On 27 September 1914 the SPD executive met and decided on measures to enforce
uniformity in the party (*Protokoll . . . 1917*, p. 29). Already on 5 August the coming party
congress at Wurzburg, fixed only a week earlier, had been postponed *sine die* (*Vorwärts*,
6 August 1914).

might come out of it was incidental.[1] After all, war and the threat of invasion were realities; most of the boys at the front were also working men. The leaders shouldered their responsibility as they saw it. They believed that everyone would soon come round to their point of view. Almost all the papers soon did so, with occasional lapses. The censorship twice suspended publication of *Vorwärts* during September. *Sozialdemokratische Korrespondenz* was one of the censor's favourite clients. Scheidemann reported that 'every single day we had to plead for one newspaper or another'.[2]

For the first few weeks the main feeling among the Centre and the Left was unease and shame, a knowledge that things had not gone as they should, yet without any clear notion of what more could have been done. Kautsky again took to his pen, producing historical apologias for his own position and incidentally a special war-time philosophy for the SPD that was to be truly Socialist and yet conformist as well.[3] Both Rosa Luxemburg and Clara Zetkin suffered nervous prostration, and were at one moment near to suicide.[4] Together they still tried, on 2 and 3 August, to plan an agitation against war; they contacted twenty SPD members of the *Reichstag* with known radical views, but got the support of only Liebknecht and Mehring.[5] Rosa herself naturally did not admit to despair as easily as Clara Zetkin, but she too could only emphasize her isolation and the difficulties of making an impact on a party 'besotted with war. . . . The party life of the masses is completely stifled.'[6]

[1] See Schorske, p. 294, n. 26.

[2] Philipp Scheidemann, *Memoiren eines Sozialdemokraten*, Dresden 1928, Vol. I, p. 271.

[3] Karl Kautsky, *Der politische Massenstreik*, Berlin 1914; 'Die Sozialdemokratie im Weltkrieg', *NZ*, 1915–16, Vol. I, p. 322; 'Der Krieg', *NZ*, 1913–14, Vol. II, p. 843.

[4] Clara Zetkin, letter to Helen Ankersmit dated 3 December 1914, in *Ausgewählte Reden und Schriften*, Vol. I, p. 639. This letter is a dramatic account, perhaps excessively so, of the personal tragedy in the collapse of a hitherto secure Socialist world. For Rosa Luxemburg's feelings, as reported by Luise Kautsky, see Maurice Berger, *La nouvelle Allemagne*, Paris 1919, p. 262: 'Le 4 août, j'ai voulu m'enlever la vie, mes amis m'en ont empechés.'

[5] Clara Zetkin, *Reden und Schriften*, Vol. II, p. 129. Clara Zetkin first told this story in a speech in the provincial constituent assembly for Württemberg on 14 April 1919, in which she represented the KPD. Her opponents laughed: 'If you had joined with Rosa Luxemberg to meet the French [armies] they would certainly have run away once they had seen you two.' Parliamentary gallantry was one of the courtesies that did not survive the war.

[6] See letter to Karl Moor in Switzerland, 12 October 1914, first printed in *Niedersächsische Arbeiterzeitung*, 7 August 1926; reprinted in *Germanskoe rabochee dvizhenie v novoe vremya* (The German Labour Movement in recent times), Moscow 1962, pp. 402–4. This reprint of extracts from various Luxemburg letters is interesting, since the letter to Karl Moor is given as being to 'an unknown addressee in Switzerland'. Moor, a Swiss Socialist whom Rosa had met in Brussels in July 1914 where he represented the Swiss party in the Bureau, became an ardent supporter of Lenin and the Bolsheviks and went to Russia after the revolution. Later, Lenin's reservations proved justified: the German Foreign Office documents revealed him as a German and—on the quiet—an Austrian agent as well. He is now an 'unperson'—hence the unknown addressee. The original of the letter is in IML (M).

Now the first task was to dissociate themselves from the *Reichstag* vote, both in the eyes of the 'masses outside in the country' and of foreign comrades. Rosa at once called a conference of her close friends at her flat on the evening of 4 August, as soon as the news of the vote was out. Present were Mehring, Julian Marchlewski—still under close police surveillance—Ernst Meyer, Hermann Duncker and his wife Käthe, and Wilhelm Pieck. Rosa sent 300 telegrams to local officials who were thought to be oppositional, asking for their attitude to the vote and inviting them to Berlin for an urgent conference. The results were pitiful. 'Clara Zetkin was the only one who immediately and unreservedly cabled her support. The others—those who even bothered to send an answer—did so with stupid or lazy excuses.'[1] The first public disclaimer of official SPD policy appeared in September 1914 in the form of a bald notice to the effect that there *was* an opposition in Germany, no more and no less.

Comrades Dr. Südekum and Richard Fischer have made an attempt in the party press abroad [in Sweden, Italy and Switzerland] to present the attitude of German Social Democracy during the present war in the light of their own conceptions. We therefore find it necessary to assure foreign comrades that we, and certainly many other German Social Democrats, regard the war, its origins, its character, as well as the role of Social Democracy in the present situation from an entirely different standpoint, and one which does not correspond to that of Comrades Südekum and Fischer. Martial law presently makes it impossible for us to enlarge upon our point of view publicly. Signed—Karl Liebknecht Dr. Franz Mehring, Dr. Rosa Luxemburg, Clara Zetkin.[2]

The idea of sending the letter, and its mild tone—in the vain hope of attracting further signatories—were particularly Rosa Luxemburg's; it was she who persuaded Clara Zetkin to sign during a short visit to Stuttgart in September, and also approached Mehring and Liebknecht for permission to use their names. 'Would you authorize us', Rosa wrote to Mehring, 'to append your signature? You are so well known abroad that it would be of great moral value and a well-earned slap in the face

---

[1] Hugo Eberlein, *Die Revolution*, 1924, No. 2. This is the best account of the meeting and subsequent action taken. This issue of *Die Revolution* celebrated the 10-year jubilee of the foundation of the *Spartakusbund*. The article is anonymous but can probably be attributed to Eberlein who was the confidential agent of the radical leadership since he was a relatively obscure figure and therefore not marked within the SPD (see *Briefe an Freunde*, p. 137, to Marta Rosenbaum, dated 5 January 1915). See also Ernst Meyer, *Spartakus im Kriege*, Berlin 1928, p. 6.

[2] *Dokumente und Materialien zur Geschichte der Deutschen Arbeiterbewegung*, Berlin 1958, Series 2, Vol. I, p. 31. The letter appeared in two Swiss papers; I do not know whether it was reprinted in Italy or in Sweden. Its appearance in Switzerland was duly noted by Lenin (*Sochineniya*, Vol. XXI, pp. 16–17). This declaration was later picked out as the first concrete step in the creation of a separate Communist party (*Bericht über den Gründungsparteitag der KPD Spartakusbund*, Welcome Speech by Ernst Meyer, Berlin 1919, p. 1).

[*Ohrfeige*] for the infamous protestations by the party executive. In the near future Karl L[iebknecht] will be coming here and I hope he will sign as well. Please reply by cable immediately on receipt of these lines.'[1]

In private Rosa gave full vent to the frustrations of getting the motley group of oppositionists together for any concerted and effective action. For their cohesion was a negative one, dislike of the attitude of the party, without any compensatory agreement on what to do instead. It was a rocking boat in which the foursome sailed into the official wind, and Rosa had her work cut out at the helm.

I want to undertake the sharpest possible action against the activities of the [*Reichstag*] delegates. Unfortunately I get little co-operation from my [collection of] incoherent personalities ... Karl [Liebknecht] can't ever be got hold of, since he dashes about like a cloud in the sky; Franz [Mehring] has little sympathy for any but literary campaigns, [Clara Zetkin's] reaction is hysteria and the blackest despair. But in spite of all this I intend to try to see what can be achieved.[2]

The extent to which Rosa was the focal point of the opposition had been acknowledged by her opponents all along. Ebert had written of the effect of 'war ... on the "Rosa group" which would inspire the latter to all kinds of "new plans" '.[3] In November 1914 Kautsky, writing to his friend Victor Adler, characterized the situation like this:

... [Karl Liebknecht's intended vote against the budget in the *Reichstag*] certainly does not mean a split [in the party] right now. The only result could be that the unhappy boy Karl will not make himself a terror but a laughing stock. It could however be the beginning of a split.

I am not in any contact with the far left camp. But from various indications I assume that Rosa is feverishly busy trying to split the party. She too prefers to be the first in the village rather than the second in Rome. If she cannot rule the big party, she wants a small one which swears by her. Soon she will have to serve her sentence and apparently wants to carry out the split before then. She is probably afraid that once she is behind bars, the present critical phase of the war will pass without a split and when she comes out she will once more be faced with the solid and united class party of peace-time in which there won't be any room for her.

How far the splitting tactics will be successful it is hard to say. Up to the present Rosa's following is very small. ... The group of David, Südekum, Heine, and the trade unions are working for her, though unintentionally. ... If the 'Marxist centre' appears as the ally of this group then quite a few workers will go over to the Luxemburg group. If, however, we oppose the right wing openly, then they will in turn denounce us to the masses as '*Rosaurier*', as Ledebour puts it; people who only differ from Rosa in our lack of guts.[4]

---

[1] Rosa Luxemburg to Franz Mehring, 13 September 1914, from Stuttgart, IML (M), Fund 201, No. 857.

[2] Letter to Konstantin Zetkin, end of 1914.

[3] Friedrich Ebert, *Schriften Aufzeichnungen Reden*, Dresden 1926, Vol. I, p. 309.

[4] Victor Adler, *Briefwechsel*, pp. 606–7, dated 28 November 1914.

There was at this stage little to choose between the official party view and that of the Centre in their view of the Left, at least as far as ascription of motives was concerned. Among the many ligaments torn by the war was the benefit of doubt which Socialists had always accorded to each other's motivations. In any case neither the German government nor the SPD had any doubts that Rosa Luxemburg was the intellectual centre of gravity behind the radical opposition. It has been the privilege of Stalinist historians to question the primacy of her role at this time.[1]

It was also decided to make personal contact with anti-war groups in other countries; at the suggestion of the British Independent Labour Party, Franz Mehring, Karl Liebknecht, and Rosa Luxemburg in December 1914 each wrote somewhat stiff, formal greetings to the newspaper *Labour Leader* in London.[2]

In addition to the disastrous situation in Germany itself, the havoc caused by the war within the International had to be taken into account. Every party had voted for its belligerant government except two lonely Serbians and the Bolshevik caucus in the Russian Duma. But at least the Independent Labour Party was coming out against the war in England, if only for a time, and the neutrals in Switzerland and Italy were strongly in favour of the old International's opposition to war. It was vital for someone to raise the same flag in Germany.

These protests, subdued and careful as they were, crystallized for the first time a sentiment that was to distinguish the left-wing opposition in Germany from this time onwards—a growing hatred of organized German Social Democracy, of the symbol SPD, which in time became as virulent as the original opposition to capitalism and to the capitalist state. To some extent it was the violence of juxtaposition, which had made the SDKPiL hate the neighbouring PPS most of all; which made the SPD concentrate its electoral fire on the Liberals. But there was also a strong personal element in it: the eternal, ill-suppressed impatience and frustration of émigrés like Rosa Luxemburg with the ponderous and 'official' Germans. Not only émigrés, however: they were all of them strong and sincere haters in their different ways—Rosa, Karl Liebknecht, and Mehring. Only Clara Zetkin turned to Communism from loyalty and love. Yet why should they, who had so often in the last few years thundered against the decay of revolutionary ideals in the SPD, have been astonished now? Did they think that they were

---

[1] Foreword (anonymous) by Central Committee of SED, to Clara Zetkin, *Ausgewählte Reden und Schriften*, Vol. I. This was written in 1951. More recent historical writing has viewed Rosa's role more favourably.

[2] *Dokumente und Materialien*, Vol. I, pp. 78–9; also Drahn und Leonhard, *Unterirdische Literatur . . .*, p. 15. The letters were smuggled out via Holland.

dealing only with a few misguided or wrong-headed leaders, while the masses—those fabulous, sensitive, incorruptible working classes— would still know what to do when the time came? Myths are sometimes harder to explode than realities or even the ideology in which realities are mirrored—and so the myths remain when all else is shattered. The violent reaction of the Russian Bolsheviks is easier to understand, for they were always ignorant about realities in the SPD and merely had to overcome in a short time their many years of admiration and deference. For the German Left, the war released a flood of pent-up resentment. It became a matter of honour to hate one's own traitors the most; in each country the task of those faithful to the old principles of international Socialism was to fight the enemy at home—as a dialectical reply to all those eager to find salvation by fighting the enemy abroad. In an illegal handbill issued by the *Spartakusbund* in the summer of 1916, entitled 'A Policy for Dogs' (*Hundepolitik*), Rosa Luxemburg took up the remarks of Dr. David—an old revisionist—who characterized Liebknecht's attitude as that of a dog who barks but does not bite.

A dog is someone who licks the boots of his master for serving him out kicks for many years.

A dog is someone who gaily wags his tail in the muzzle of martial law and faithfully gazes up to his masters, the military dictators, quietly whining for mercy.

A dog is someone who barks at a person—particularly in his absence—and who fetches and carries for his immediate masters.

A dog is someone who, on the orders of the governments, covers the entire sacred history of a party with slime and kicks it in the dirt.

Dogs are and always were the Davids, Landsbergs and comrades and they will get their well-earned kick from the German working classes when the day of reckoning comes.[1]

Similar comments flowed from the pen of Karl Liebknecht. The Left strove to love internationally and hate on home ground. Eventually this culminated in the Liebknecht formulation: 'The main enemy is at home'.

There was therefore some basis for the accusation that the German radicals were hoping for the defeat of Germany, just as the Bolsheviks specifically counted on the defeat of Tsarist Russia.[2] With the breakdown of the International, each party—or oppositional group within it —had the special responsibility of taking on the enemy at home. From this to revolutionary defeatism was a small step; Lenin sitting in

[1] *Selected Works* Vol. II, p. 561.
[2] One of Rosa's personal enemies, Georg Ledebour, himself a radical, even accused her of Russian patriotism, of wishing a Tsarist victory over Germany. Karl Kautsky to Victor Adler, 28 November 1914, in *Briefwechsel* pp. 606–7.

Switzerland was easily able to take it. The Germans never quite took the final step. What prevented Rosa Luxemburg from openly celebrating the hopes of a German disaster was her immense and often repeated concern with the human loss involved. She was torn between two conflicting desires: the defeat of German imperialism as the most evil manifestation of all; but equally the ending of the war as quickly as possible to save further bloodshed, above all the slaughter of soldiers who were nothing but proletarians temporarily dressed in field grey.[1] What prevented the German radicals from the cheerful adoption of Bolshevik revolutionary defeatism was precisely the legacy of optimism of a mass party in a highly developed capitalist country. The reaction from optimism is not pessimism but despair; the destruction of society by war not progress but barbarism.

The main effort thus lay at home. After initial hesitation—not what to do but how to do it—and a desperate if ineffective search for weapons, Karl Liebknecht determined to use his position as a deputy of both the Prussian diet and the *Reichstag*. This gave him a better means of focusing opposition in his person than Rosa's relative isolation. He was not so much the obvious choice, the clearly destined leader—like Lenin or even Hitler; he was inevitable by being all alone. He had not been a disciple, much less a colleague, of Rosa's; in the last seven years they had clashed almost as often as they had agreed, and Rosa's opinion of him, if tolerant, was never flattering. In January 1915, a month after his lonely protest in the *Reichstag*, she wrote, 'He is an excellent chap, but. . . .'[2] This fiercely opinionated lawyer, with his good heart and his passion for drama, had for years bombarded party personalities with heavily underlined good advice as to the line to be taken.[3] The party leadership had clashed with him over his radical proposals for a youth policy from 1904 to 1907, and had never taken him seriously; they

---

[1] Occasionally in *Die Krise der Sozialdemokratie*, Zürich 1916, she remarked that 'a nation that capitulates before the external enemy has no dignity' (p. 68), and 'the Social Democrats have an obligation to defend their country in a great historical crisis' (p. 80). These statements have been pulled wholly out of context to suggest that Rosa Luxemburg gave qualified support to a war of national defence. Since the whole pamphlet is concerned to show that the First World War was not such a war as far as Germany was concerned, these remarks are meaningless as evidence for such a view.

Rosa Luxemburg's argument against war, as costing mainly proletarian lives, was later contrasted contemptuously by Communist party historians under Stalin with Lenin's revolutionary defeatism (Lenin himself never listed this argument among her faults). Curiously, Khrushchev used exactly the same argument against the Chinese Communists in 1963: '. . . . in time of war the working classes die most of all. [The need for war] has nothing to do with Marxism-Leninism' (speech in Moscow, 23 May 1963, reported in the [*Manchester*] *Guardian*, 24 May, p. 13).

[2] Letter to Konstantin Zetkin, January 1915.

[3] For instance, letters to Karl Kautsky from 1907 onwards in IISH, D XV.

considered him an unbalanced and unworthy successor to his great father.

To this apparently unqualified man now fell the public representation of his group, and he accepted the challenge whole-heartedly. He was apparently not present at the first meeting in Rosa Luxemburg's flat, nor did he stand out in the *Reichstag* caucus debate on 3 August.[1] But a tour to the Western Front as a *Reichstag* deputy in October seems to have decided him finally that a few cautious letters of protest were no longer sufficient.[2]

In November he began his bombardment of the SPD *Reichstag* delegates for a negative vote in the next budget debate. He followed this with a personal campaign the week before the debate itself.[3] But in the end he was the only one who broke party discipline, the *Burgfrieden* —a complete break, just as he had wished; he voted alone against the credits. His name instantly became the symbol of the things and people he stood for, to his enemies and to the watchers abroad for a break in the thick German mists. His written explanation to the Speaker of the *Reichstag*, which the latter refused to have entered in the written record, was distributed illegally and became the forerunner of the *Spartakus* letters. At first these were part of the information circulars distributed to sympathetic party functionaries through the good offices of the local party organization in Niederbarnim, an electoral district of Berlin controlled by the radicals. Here Rosa Luxemburg had often spoken in the past; here she now used all her magnetic charm and persuasion to build up a nucleus of protest. Its influence was at first confined to the capital, but gradually spread to other cities, with better distribution of material and more contacts. There were other radical centres in Germany, in Bremen, Stuttgart, Brunswick, Leipzig.

Rosa Luxemburg was also working feverishly in her own field. In December 1914 she went into hospital for a short while; the long isolation and the disaster of the war were too much for her. She had violent changes of mood; at the beginning of November she had written to Hans Diefenbach that 'my first despair has quite changed. Not that things are rosier, quite the contrary. But one gets used to a hailstorm of blows better than a single one . . . precisely the growing dimensions of the disaster . . . call for objective judgement.'[4] The prison sentence passed on her in Frankfurt at the beginning of the year became due in December, but was postponed to 31 March 1915 on account of her

---

[1] Frölich, p. 232. *Spartakusbriefe*, Introduction, p. x.
[2] Camille Huysmans to Benedikt Kautsky, 11 March 1949, in *Briefe an Freunde*, pp. 69–70.
[3] Drahn und Leonhard, *Unterirdische Literatur*, p. 13.
[4] *Briefe an Freunde*, p. 71, 1 November 1914.

illness.[1] None the less, she knew that time was short. The *Sozialdemokratische Korrespondenz* had almost outlived its purpose; it could no longer whip up support in other papers since these were all censored, even if they had wanted to take material. What was needed was a broader, more theoretical paper, a central organ for the faithful, which could get by the censorship and yet announce as widely as possible the basis on which the party must meet the new challenge of war and the actions of a wrong-headed if not yet treacherous leadership. Under Rosa's particular guidance *Die Internationale* was prepared, with the collaboration of Franz Mehring and Julian Marchlewski. Everything had to be found from scratch, money scraped together, a printer found—this proved very difficult, and with reason: contributors, publisher, and printer were all later indicted.[2] Even after her arrest Rosa was able, through the visits of her secretary Mathilde Jacob, to keep abreast of the last-minute rush to get *Die Internationale* out. Carefully coded verbal communications took place via Mathilde Jacob between Rosa and Leo Jogiches—the latter, as usual, the practical hand behind the scenes, shuttling between authors, publishers, and printers, arranging for the distribution, and all the while keeping Rosa informed on how things were going.[3] It is even possible that Rosa received assistance from one of the staff at the Barnimstrasse prison called Schrick, who was known among the *Spartakus* leaders to be well disposed towards the prisoner.[4] The fact that the conception and form were essentially Rosa's work was acknowledged by Mehring in the introduction when the one and only issue appeared in April 1915; the censor immediately confiscated all copies he could find and prohibited further issues.[5] By that time she had already been in prison for two months.

In early March she had planned to accompany Clara Zetkin to an international women's conference in Holland—even a women's conference was now no longer to be despised. But on 18 February she was suddenly arrested and taken to the women's prison in the Barnimstrasse.

[1] Above, p. 322. The appeal against the verdict had been rejected by the Court of Appeal (*Reichsgericht*) on 20 October.

[2] On 20 July 1915 an indictment was laid against the authors and the publishers of the journal—Rosa Luxemburg, Franz Mehring, and Clara Zetkin as authors, Berten and Pfeiffer as publishers. The indictment was made out against the 'authoress Rosa Luxemburg and comrades', and was based on the High Treason paragraph 9C of the Emergency Regulations. However, the office of the Reich prosecutors advised against proceedings as it was not likely that an indictment for high treason could be made to stick. The hearing, originally planned for 22 March 1916, was adjourned *sine die* and proceedings stopped. The state prosecutor's files in the matter are in IML (M), Fund 209, No. 1356.

[3] Leo Jogiches to Mathilde Jacob, 2 April 1915, in *International Review of Social History*, Vol. VIII, 1963, part 1, p. 100.

[4] Letters from this woman to Mathilde Jacob still exist in the Hoover Institution, Stanford University, California.

[5] *Die Internationale*, 15 April 1915, p. 10.

The arrest was entirely unexpected, and carried out by the criminal police department, not the state prosecutor's office. The *Deutsche Tageszeitung*, with good official connections, reported that the arrest was due to the fact that Rosa Luxemburg—'the red Prima Donna'— had organized meetings in Niederbarnim.[1] Karl Liebknecht spoke in the Prussian *Landtag* in support of his 'close party friend'. 'It shows the nature of our *Burgfrieden*, the peace on the home front. [But] we don't even bother to complain that this highly political—in a party political sense—sentence imposed in peace-time should suddenly be carried out in spite of the *Burgfrieden*. . . . I know that my friend Luxemburg can only feel honoured by this execution of judgement, just as I do. . . .'[2] Liebknect's great one-man propaganda campaign had begun. With Rosa Luxemburg behind bars, his main intellectual stimulus had gone. He was now more alone than ever.

However much she may have told her personal friends that she wanted time to write and think, it was a most unfortunate moment from a political point of view to be immured in prison. 'Half a year ago I was looking forward to it, now the honour falls on me much as an Iron Cross would fall on you.'[3]

At this moment her removal from the political scene was too great a blow to the opposition to be supported with her usual equanimity. Still, *Die Internationale* was ready; now in prison would come 'the study of the war' which she 'naturally' wanted to write, and at last perhaps the outline of the book on economics from her school lecture notes.[4] The study of the war became *The Crisis of Social Democracy*, known more generally as the *Juniusbrochüre* because of the pseudonym Junius. She also wrote an answer to the critics of her *Accumulation of Capital*—another job that had had to be left for an unexpected period of peace and quiet in the midst of war.

Rosa always loosened up in prison, as though her political personality were normally held together only by the pressure of life. It was almost as if everything now had to grow to fill the political vacuum, and the component parts of her personality became separated from each other in the process. Rosa the recluse, the thinker, the botanist, and the literary critic emerged and floated away as extensions of Rosa the woman. There was a sudden upsurge of letters to friends, all carefully tailored to suit the personality of the recipient. To her housekeeper,

---

[1] See *Vorwärts*, 20 February 1915.

[2] *Berichte über die Verhandlungen des Preussischen Haus der Abgeordneten*, XXII Legislative Period, II Session 1914–15, Berlin 1916, Vol. VII, column 8754.

[3] *Briefe an Freunde*, p. 74, letter to Hans Diefenbach, 1 November 1914.

[4] Ibid. She never did the latter; only the outline remained and was published with a few comments and additions by Paul Levi in 1925 (*Einführung in die Nationalökonomie*).

Gertrud Zlottko, Rosa wrote roughly in unsentimental peasant tones:
'Your resigned tone really doesn't go down with me. . . . Pfui, Gertrud,
no point in that! I like my people to be gay. Work is the order of the
day; do your bit and for the rest don't take things to heart. . . . Keep your
spirits up.'[1] To Luise Kautsky she was 'a perpetually serious person
from whom people always expected something clever—worse luck . . .
I have to have *someone* who believes me when I say that I am only in
the maelstrom of world history by accident, in fact I was really born
to look after a chicken farm. You have to believe it, do you hear?'[2]

But there was always another important aspect to her activities: her
practical contact with the struggle outside. Following the effort of the
previous months, this was at its lowest ebb during the first nine months
of 1915. Germany seemed to be winning the war, and a number of
SPD members began to feel the itch of Germany's civilizing mission in
French revolutionary terms, as something to be carried forward on
bayonets. At the same time the SPD executive inevitably mounted a
counter-attack against the party opposition—what remained of the old,
and what had begun to manifest itself of the new. In Württemberg the
Land organization had simply taken over the opposition *Schwäbische
Tagwacht* as early as November 1914 and, in view of the success of the
coup, the Reich executive supported it gladly.[3] Elsewhere, too, the last
embers of independence on the part of local papers were stamped out
as far as possible. *Vorwärts* was harder to tackle. The party's arbitration
tribunal, the Control Commission, was well left of centre; its senior
member was still Clara Zetkin and 'it was no use appealing from the
devil to the devil's own grandmother . . .'.[4] But the executive merely
bided its time before launching a coup against the remaining recalci-
trants on the paper; restraint in publication was no longer enough, the
government wanted genuine and enthusiastic support for official policy.
The French and English examples of Socialist partnership in war-time
government, which the SPD executive quoted with so much envy, were
unfortunately misleading. No real share of power, at local or central
level, was ever offered by the German government, only verbiage and
trappings; but in the absence of spontaneous enthusiasm for the government the need for disciplined labour support was all the greater.

Between Luxemburg and Liebknecht on the one hand and the executive majority on the other, stood the 'Centre'. These men were unhappy

---

[1] *Briefe an Freunde*, p. 185, dated 25 May 1915. To help keep these spirits high, Rosa
drew funny pictures for her on the tops of her letters and encouraged the other women to
do the same.

[2] *Letters to Karl and Luise Kautsky*, p. 172, dated 18 September 1915.

[3] W. Keil, *Erlebnisse* Vol. I, pp. 306–7; also Ossip K. Flechtheim, *Die Kommunistische
Partei Deutschlands in der Weimarer Republik*, Offenbach 1948, p. 13.

[4] Scheidemann, *Memoiren*, Vol. I, p. 268.

about the majority's unanimous certainties but they were also repelled by the violence, the doctrinaire intransigence, of the Left which seemed to them to ignore all war-time reality. They too were by no means a homogeneous group.[1] Some, like Bernstein and Eisner, opposed the executive only because they were convinced, English-type pacifists. Others were more revolutionary but they felt they must wait for conditions to approximate once more to their beliefs. All were deeply attached to party unity. In March 1915 came a still more severe test of loyalty versus orthodoxy than in August or December 1914; for the first time the *Reichstag* was now voting, not the special war credits but the normal annual budget, the obstacle at which the SPD had always baulked as a matter of course. War or no war, this was the occasion for the traditionalists to speak their mind. Liebknecht was joined by Otto Rühle in his negative vote, but thirty others now abstained. A special amendment to the old rule of unanimity had been accepted by a reluctant executive on 3 February 1915, to avoid further defections to Liebknecht. Most of the centrists still saw Liebknecht as a cantankerous crank, of the same lurid hue as Rosa Luxemburg in her fight with Kautsky in 1910. Opposition there might yet have to be, they argued, but not this way; not deliberate provocation to which there could be only one effective reply. In August 1915 once more there was the same grouping over the same vote, except that Rühle now abstained instead of voting with Liebknecht; the latter was alone again.

In April *Die Internationale* came out; a philosophy to clothe the action. In the strongest tone Rosa Luxemburg's leader 'Der Wiederaufbau der Internationalen' (The Rebuilding of the International) posed the alternatives.

The new version of historical imperialism [as amended by the leadership of the SPD] produces an either/or. Either the class struggle is the all-powerful *raison d'être* for the proletariat even during the war, and the proclamation of class harmony by the party authorities is blasphemy against the very life interest of the working classes. Or the class struggle even in peace-time is blasphemy against the 'national interests' and the 'security of the fatherland'. . . . Either Social Democracy will get up before the bourgeoisie of the fatherland and say 'Father, I have sinned' and change its whole tactic and principles in peace-time as well. . . . Or it will stand before the national working-class movement and say 'Father, I have sinned' and will adapt its present war-time attitude to the normal requirements of peace. . . . Either Bethmann-Hollweg [the German Chancellor] or Liebknecht, either imperialism or Socialism as Marx understood it. . . . The International will not be revived by bringing out the old grind [*die alte Leier*] after the war. . . . Only through a cruel and thorough mockery of our own half-heartedness and weaknesses, of our own moral collapse since 4 August,

---

[1] For a contemporary account see Eugen Prager, *Die Geschichte der USPD*, Berlin 1922.

can the recreation of the International begin and the first step in this direction can only be the rapid termination of the war.[1]

August the 4th could no longer be forgotten or forgiven; it must be burnt out from the party, along with those responsible. As a functioning organism of Social Democracy the Second International was dead; its leaders had betrayed it. But the idea was alive as long as there were a few people who maintained its principles untarnished.

It was here that Rosa Luxemburg differed from Lenin. He saw the collapse not only in terms of a few treacherous leaders—though that too[2]—but because the whole loose federal structure of the International had contributed to its undoing. The passion for size, for unity at all costs, had destroyed the real unity of discipline and of thorough adherence to revolutionary principles. There could be no question of reconstituting the old International under new leaders; a *different* International was required, containing only those who accepted its tight organization as well as its new ideals.[3]

Lenin's view was simpler, less sophisticated, than Rosa Luxemburg's complicated cataclysm. In his own mind he had long equated opportunism in matters of principle with opportunism in organizational questions; the failure of the SPD and of the International was simply due to a particularly virulent strain of the old, old disease of opportunism. Although shattered at first by the events of 4 August, he quickly recovered. Unlike Rosa Luxemburg, who groped for new and deeper causes hitherto unknown for a moral and political cataclysm on a unique scale, the mere understanding of which taxed her greater powers to the full, Lenin was merely preoccupied by the *size* of the problem; its nature was familiar enough. He made his diagnosis and through it passed on to the remedy—a split, a new organization; his old precepts for organizational integrity had been triumphantly vindicated. It was satisfying to have been proved right so completely. Thus, while Rosa Luxemburg suffered acutely, Lenin was cheerful and relaxed. Perceptively he commented on the *Juniusbrochüre*—of whose authorship he was not then aware:

One senses the outsider who, like a lone wolf, has no comrades linked to him in an illegal organization, accustomed to thinking through revolutionary solutions right to the end and to educating the masses in that spirit. But these short-

---

[1] *Die Internationale*, April, 1915, pp. 6–7.

[2] '. . . the claim that the masses of proletarians turned away from Socialism is a lie; the masses *were never asked*, the masses were misled, frightened, split, held down by the state of emergency. *Only* the leaders could vote freely and they voted *for* the bourgeoisie and *against* the proletariat.' (Lenin, *Sochineniya*, Vol. XXI, p. 405.)

[3] See Lenin's report on the Zimmerwald Conference, 5–8 September 1915, in *Sochineniya*, Vol. XXI, pp. 350–55; also *Sozialdemokrat*, Geneva, Nos. 45–46, 11 October 1915.

comings—and it would be entirely wrong to forget it—are not personal failures in Junius but the result of the weakness of the *entire* German Left, hemmed in on all sides by the infamous net of Kautskyite hypocrisy, pedantry, and all the 'goodwill' of the opportunists.[1]

Blandly he assumed that Junius's violent rejection of official SPD policy must inevitably lead to his own conception of revolutionary civil war.

Junius nearly gets the right answer to the question and the right solution—civil war *against* the bourgeoisie and *for* Socialism; however, at the same time he turns *back once more* to the fantasy of a 'national' war in the years 1914, 1915 and 1916 as though he were afraid to speak the truth right through to the end. . . . To 'proclaim' the *revolution*—[even though] with an *incorrect* revolutionary programme.

In the same place Junius states quite correctly that you cannot 'make' a revolution. Yet the revolution was on the programme [of history] in the years 1914–1916. It is contained in this womb of the war, it would have *emerged* from the war. This should have been *proclaimed* in the name of revolutionary classes: *their* programme should have been fearlessly developed. . . .[2]

In one respect Lenin was bound to acknowledge Rosa Luxemburg's superior and earlier perception. In a letter to Shlyapnikov in October 1914 he admitted: 'Rosa Luxemburg was right. She realized long ago that Kautsky was a time-serving theorist, serving the majority of the party, serving opportunism in short.'[3] It was a curious admission, for Kautsky had so long been Lenin's weak spot. Both he and Trotsky had admired him greatly. Both had found Rosa's quarrel with him absolutely unjustified at the time.[4] Now they too discovered what Rosa had long known, that Kautsky used Marxism like plasticine, to soften the contours of an imperialist war. Lenin turned violently and very personally against him, and thereby exaggerated his importance all over again.[5] When Clara Zetkin was in Moscow in 1920 they had trouble with the lift in Lenin's apartment which instantly induced him to exclaim angrily: '[It is] just like Kautsky, perfect in theory but lets you down as soon as it comes to the point.'[6]

[1] Lenin, *Sochineniya*, Vol. XXII, p. 305.   [2] Ibid., pp. 302–3.
[3] *Sochineniya*, Vol. XXXV, p. 120; also Frölich, p. 236.
[4] See above, p. 292.
[5] Lenin's later polemics against Kautsky—which are by implication polemics against his own earlier adulation—are many and bitter. Everything Lenin hated in the USPD was turned into a personal indictment of Kautsky. Perhaps the best description (with which Lenin would no doubt have agreed) of Kautsky's Marxism was by Parvus: 'Marx's ideas, Kautsky's style, and the whole thing brought down to the level . . . of popular description, all the wholesome guts knocked out of it. Out of Marx's good raw dough, Kautsky made *matzes*.' (*Die Glocke*, Vol. I (1915), p. 20.)
[6] Clara Zetkin, *Reminiscences of Lenin*, London 1929, p. 13.

Rosa, on the other hand, soon realized the isolation and declining importance of her former friend. With the exception of a few fleeting references in future articles and in her private correspondence with Luise Kautsky, she never bothered with him again. Her political fire was concentrated elsewhere. The real leaders of the centrist opposition were not Kautsky, Eisner, and Bernstein, but Haase, Dittmann, and Ledebour, a fact which Lenin did not realize until the end of 1917.

If Lenin's views, as expressed in his articles at the time and in the policy statements of the Zimmerwald Left, are mentioned here at some length, it is an admitted piece of hindsight. The history of the German Left since the beginning of the First World War has been so firmly in the grip of Bolshevik party history (and still is) that a factual Lenin–Luxemburg confrontation becomes essential. Yet it must be said that until 1917 the opinions of the Bolsheviks on the war had practically no influence on Rosa Luxemburg and her friends; for purely physical reasons they were probably unaware of what was being said in Switzerland. The only personal contact was with Radek's friend Knief in Bremen, which first found some local expression in the pages of the *Bremer Bürgerzeitung* and from June 1916 in the weekly *Arbeiterpolitik*. Then there were the two meetings, at Zimmerwald near Bern in September 1915 and at Kienthal at Easter 1916. At the first conference there were ten German delegates, six from the centre under Ledebour and Hoffmann, three from Rosa's and Liebknecht's group which took the name of the defunct paper, 'Internationale', and Julian Borchardt, representing a minute splinter group and its paper *Lichtstrahlen*. Lenin proposed a new International and the thesis: 'Turn the imperialist war into civil war'. For this he got seven votes against thirty, and among the Germans only Borchardt supported him. He gave way under the pressure of his friends, and a compromise resolution was issued calling in general terms for class war against an annexationist peace and condemning those Social Democrats who supported the war. But Lenin went on trying behind the scenes; the Zimmerwald Left was a potential splinter group. The importance attached to its views in Germany can best be judged by the fact that the *Spartakus* letter of November 1915 which reported the conference, devoted precisely one sentence to Lenin and the Bolsheviks.[1]

At Kienthal the next year Lenin was prepared to break up the conference if the German centrist delegates again insisted that they could

[1] *Spartakusbriefe*, p. 81. See also Arthur Rosenberg, *Geschichte des Bolschewismus von Marx bis zur Gegenwart*, Berlin 1932, p. 81. The Zimmerwald literature is vast; for a recent summary see F. Tych, 'La participation des partis ouvriers polonais au mouvement de Zimmerwald', *Annali dell'Istituto Giangiacomo Feltrinelli*, year IV, 1961, p. 90. See also O. H. Gankin and H. H. Fisher (eds.), *The Bolsheviks and the World War. The Origins of the Third International*, Stanford/London 1940, especially the bibliography.

not be bound in their actions at home by any conference resolutions. Hoffmann proposed that the International Socialist Bureau, which had now moved from Brussels to The Hague, be called upon to meet, but this proposal was lost, with the two *Spartakus* delegates, Bertha Thalheimer and Ernst Meyer, also voting against it.[1] In the end a compromise was found which specifically called upon 'the representatives of Socialist parties' at once to abandon the support of all belligerent governments and specifically to vote against war credits. In the course of the debate the German delegate from Bremen, Paul Frölich, criticized both the centrist group in the *Reichstag* and the 'Internationale' opposition for their continued refusal to make a clean organizational break with the SPD.

The later Communist claim that the radicals had moved significantly towards the Bolsheviks by April 1916 is true only in part.[2] They never joined the Zimmerwald Left, and the idea of a new splinter International, however pure, repelled them. In November 1914 Rosa Luxemburg could still write to Camille Huysmans: 'I congratulate you on the solution which you found for the Ex-[ecutive] Committee [to move to Holland]. I beg you to keep at it and to stay at your post in spite of all attempts which might be made to take away your powers or to persuade you to give them up.'[3] By 1915 she had accepted the collapse of the old International. In her polemics against Kautsky in the *Juniusbrochüre* she specifically mocked the hope of simply forgiving and forgetting. She called for a clean reconstructed International in the *Juniusbrochüre*, one from which the old elements had been purged. The difference was between the expulsion of undesirables from a tarnished but still essential organization and the creation of a totally new one. Even at the end of the war she still could not face the creation of a new International under the auspices of the victorious Bolsheviks. Probably the question belongs to that large undefined area of problems which only the real, the physical revolution could and would solve. Meantime organizational wire-pulling was so much irresponsible self-deception.

In collaboration with Liebknecht, Rosa had worked out some guiding principles to be submitted to the first conference at Zimmerwald. They did not in fact reach the conference, either officially or privately; the last-minute arrangements for the meeting, the need for secrecy, above

---

[1] See Ernst Meyer, Introduction to *Spartakusbriefe* (first edition), Berlin 1926, Vol. I, p. 7. Bertha Thalheimer was the sister of Rosa's old protégé August Thalheimer (see letter to Konrad Haenisch, 24 April 1910, in *Briefe an Freunde*, p. 25).

[2] See Ernst Meyer, loc. cit. The claim became increasingly emphatic in later German and Russian works, till in 1930 Stalin ordered a reversal and the systematic denigration of the role of the non-Bolshevik Left in Europe.

[3] *Briefe an Freunde*, p. 67, dated 10 November 1914 (in French). None the less, she opposed any attempt to call a meeting of the Bureau. Letter to Karl Moor, above, p. 371, note 6.

all the difficulty of communicating from prison, prevented the draft from being completed in time, which annoyed Rosa considerably. They were later printed as an illegal handbill, and first appeared as an appendix to the *Juniusbrochüre* in 1916[1] As might have been expected, the outline was not a programme or even a recommendation for specific policies, but a declaratory statement of principles—an international Socialist's Bill of Rights. As such, they served as a masthead to the *Spartakus* letters, and provided, if not a platform, at least an affirmation of faith round which the Left opposition could rally.

If they seem to be vague statements of principles rather than specific slogans or demands, and to avoid anything which might resemble a Bolshevik platform around which to assemble supporters, Rosa Luxemburg, who did all the drafting, had nevertheless to fight for such specific points as there were. Liebknecht wrote that her draft contained 'altogether too much mention of discipline, not enough spontaneity'; it was 'too mechanical and centralistic'. Rosa accepted many of his minor suggestions for rewording, but on the question of international discipline —her own version was anything but harsh even by contemporary standards—she remained adamant.[2]

The correspondence between Rosa in prison and Karl at the front illustrates the nature of their relationship, and that of the whole *Spartakus* leadership; much more like the old SDKPiL than the SPD. Once more Rosa emerges if not as the leader at least as the main inspirer of the Left opposition and of its ideas. The quality of intellectual self-discipline, of commitment rather than control, unmistakably bears her stamp. It was she who coaxed Liebknecht, not to act, which he could do on his own, but to think and formulate, she who flattered Mehring and soothed Clara Zetkin. After approval by Liebknecht and Mehring, Jogiches got the theses printed and they were adopted by the meeting of *Spartakus* members on 1 January 1916.

Rosa Luxemburg had completed the *Juniusbrochüre* in prison by the end of April 1915 and succeeded in smuggling it out, though owing to the difficulties of finding a printer, it could not be published until early the following year. 'On her release from prison early in 1916 she found the manuscript still untouched on her desk.'[3] It took her three more months to bring it out. At first she insisted on using her own name but was dissuaded; the pseudonym finally chosen was meant to illustrate an historical parallel with the English eighteenth century. The pamphlet reflected the atmosphere of early 1915, when revolutionary Socialists

[1] See below, p. 387, note 1.
[2] Ernst Meyer, 'Zur Entstehungsgeschichte der Juniusthesen', *Unter dem Banner des Marxismus*, Year I, 1925–26, No. 2, p. 423.
[3] Frölich, p. 245.

were in a vacuum of despair and self-abasement, as yet unfilled by any alternative policy. Its title predicted its content, the history of a disaster.[1] Like the later essay on the Russian revolution, it was a private purgative as much as a political tract. We must not forget that both were written in prison.

This pamphlet also contains one of Rosa's clearest and most heartfelt statements of proletarian ethics. Like Marx, she never set out to discuss one subject today, another tomorrow—the ant-heap approach to Marxism. The whole point of Luxemburgism—if there is such a thing— is not this or that variation from Bolshevism or any other neo-Marxist doctrine, but the totality of its approach at all times.[2] Ethics are very much part of this totality, but unconscious ethics, not lectures about how to behave. The *Juniusbrochüre* positively bristles with an indictment of imperialist ethics: brutal, hypocritical, in which lives are the cheapest and most expendable commodity of all, especially proletarian lives.

The railway trains full with reservists are no longer accompanied by the loud acclamations of the young ladies, the soldiers no longer smile at the populace out of their carriage windows; instead they slink silently through the streets, their packs in their hands, while the public follows its daily preoccupation with sour faces. In the sober atmosphere of the morning after, another chorus takes the stage: the hoarse cries of the vultures and hyenas which appear on every battle-field: ten thousand tents guaranteed to specification! A hundred tons of bacon, cocoa, coffee substitute, instant delivery but cash only, hand grenades, tools, ammunition belts, marriage brokers for the widows of the fallen, agencies for government supply—only serious offers considered! The cannon fodder inflated with patriotism and carried off in August and September 1914 now rots in Belgium, in the Vosges, in the Masurian swamps, creating fertile plains of death on which profits can grow. Hurry, for the rich harvest must be gathered into the granaries—a thousand greedy hands stretch across the ocean to help.[3]

The Junius pamphlet welds the general to the particular. In Rosa Luxemburg's persuasive historical style the reader is helped over the small steps of historical fact and hustled at one and the same time over much larger assumptions. Having exposed the lie of the defensive war, Rosa Luxemburg went on to state a general proposition: 'In the era of imperialism there can be no more [justified] national wars' since 'there is complete harmony between the patriotic interests and the class

---

[1] Junius, *Die Krise der Sozialdemokratie*, Zürich 1916, reprinted in 1920 with an introduction by Clara Zetkin. Quotations are taken from the original edition. The work has also been reprinted in Rosa Luxemburg, *Selected Works*, Vol. I, pp. 258–399. When *Die Krise der Sozialdemokratie* came out in 1916 there were appended to it the 11 propositions and 6 policy headings which had all been adopted as a programme by the 'Gruppe Internationale' on New Year's Day 1916; see above, p. 386.

[2] As George Lukács has so perceptively stated in *Geschichte und Klassenbewusstsein*, Berlin 1923.

[3] *Die Krise der Sozialdemokratie*, p. 3.

interests of the proletarian International, in war as well as in peace; both demand the most energetic development of the class struggle and the most emphatic pursuit of the Social-Democratic programme.'[1] In the last resort it was a matter of personal commitment to the world around her. There is no tragedy without commitment; no negation, even, without it. The opposite of love—and hate—is indifference, abstraction. Lenin, disengaged, sat in Switzerland and shrank Rosa's general propositions to their particular context and relevance—and then attacked them in that context. And not for the first time: in their polemics two years earlier Lenin had attacked her views on the national question by treating it, not as a universal proposition, but in the context of the constitution and tactics of his party. It is unprofitable to ask whether Rosa's negation of any wars of national defence did or did not apply to emergent colonial nations in Africa and India, since the pamphlet was not written with these in mind. The denial of all national wars at this stage was intended to prevent any more attempts to prove that Germany was engaged in a war of defence; to kill the argument not with denials, but by destroying the foundations on which it rested. Just as Polish self-determination was wrong, because all self-determination was wrong, so the war was not a German war of patriotic defence because such things no longer existed. An excessive claim? Perhaps, but Rosa Luxemburg always put up the maximum stake. Lenin enlarged tactics into a philosophy, while Rosa used philosophy to justify tactic.

The Junius pamphlet was the last item Rosa was able to smuggle out of prison for some months. She probably had the assistance of an unknown member of the staff, and was later to have help again at the Wronke fortress. 'Perhaps her treatment now became more severe as a result of an encounter that she had with an insolent detective who came to examine her. What actually happened is not quite clear but Rosa Luxemburg put an end to the interview by throwing a book at his head and for this she received further punishment.'[2]

Rosa was becoming personally isolated by political developments. She had now lost many old political friends; Parvus, Kautsky, Lensch, Haenisch, Dittmann, Stadthagen, Wurm—all had become opponents. From her foreign friends she was cut off. This left Jogiches and Marchlewski in Berlin. The latter was arrested in January 1916 before Rosa herself came out of prison.[3] Clara Zetkin had been taken into custody

---

[1] Ibid., pp. 82, 97.

[2] Frölich, p. 242. It is safe to assume that Frölich heard of these incidents from Rosa Luxemburg herself. However, since an almost identical incident took place on 22 September 1916, to which Frölich does not refer, it may be that he mixed up the two.

[3] He was released early in 1918 under the exchange arrangements of the Brest-Litovsk treaty, and went to Russia, where he joined the Bolsheviks.

in June 1915 and was only released early in 1916 on account of severe ill health. She spent some time with Rosa in Berlin during the first months of 1916, the last time the two friends were to see each other. The second echelon of the new Left consisted of a younger generation to whom Rosa was never personally close. Mehring, now 70, was an old, if delicate, friend. Rosa's relations with Liebknecht were politically close and destined to become closer still, but they were never personal friends. She admired his courage and despised his slapdash existence. To Hans Diefenbach, before whom no political pretence was necessary, she described the war-time Liebknecht:

You probably know the manner of his existence for many years: entirely wrapped up in parliament, meetings, commissions, discussions; in haste, in hurry, everlastingly jumping from the underground into the tram and from the tram into a car. Every pocket stuffed with notebooks, his arms full of the latest newspapers which he will never find time to read, body and soul covered with street dust and yet always with a kind and cheerful smile on his face.[1]

But his courage—which was undoubted—contained an element of recklessness which made her and many of his friends apprehensive. At the end of October 1915 she asked a comrade who was acting as intermediary between her and Liebknecht to have a tactful word with him on this subject. As a result of a 'mysterious misunderstanding', some of Liebknecht's comments on the political situation, written from the Russian front, had appeared in her mail. 'I consider it most dangerous for Karl to develop these literary activities at this distance and you would be doing him a good turn if you could find a suitable way of advising him against it.'[2]

Friends there were, but private ones, mostly women; and political admirers and disciples, like Hugo Eberlein, the Dunckers, the Thalheimers, Pieck (her former student at the party school), and Paul Levi, who had defended her in court and was one day to succeed to her double

[1] *Briefe an Freunde*, pp. 93–94, letter to Hans Diefenbach dated 30 March 1917. Rosa wrote an identical characterization to Luise Kautsky at about the same time (*Letters to Karl and Luise Kautsky*, pp. 199–200). In the latter case the description continues: '. . . in his heart of hearts he is of a poetical nature as few people are, and can take an almost childish delight in almost every little flower'. This is the most obvious instance of a phenomenon that strikes the careful reader of Rosa Luxemburg's letters: not only the continued use of certain phrases throughout her correspondence but the thrifty hoarding of descriptions and incidents. Spontaneity? Cf. below, p. 426, note 2.

[2] Rosa Luxemburg to Fanny Jezierska, probably end of October 1915, in IISH Archives, Amsterdam. Radek also advised Liebknecht from Switzerland in 1915 not to take unnecessary risks. Karl Radek, *Rosa Luxemburg, Karl Liebknecht, Leo Jogiches*, Hamburg 1921, p. 33. Karl Liebknecht wrote to Fanny Jezierska on 18 October 1915: 'I don't know what to do, and count on you . . . I know you have plenty to do yourself but I don't know who else to turn to; 5 o'clock in the morning, half an hour's sleep . . . I am dead. I cannot leave my [real] work in spite of all the literary duties, so I never get a rest.'

position as leader of the party and later its most severe critic.[1]
Without appreciating the personal as well as the political vacuum of
those war years it is not possible to understand Rosa in prison, and
especially not the Rosa of the last hectic months after her release in
1918. Soon things were to look up, however, as the *Spartakusbund*
became better organized and extended the range and quality of its
appeal; and Rosa's friends rallied round closely to lighten the mental
and physical burden of her second long imprisonment.

On 29 December 1915 twenty SPD deputies finally voted against
new war credits, while another twenty-two abstained. Articulate opposition to the executive was growing. Loyalty to pre-war principles rotted
the war-time discipline. Why? The war was no quick walkover; and
nothing fails like failure. As long as the German government was imprisoned by the idea of a decisive victory, the war might continue for
ever. All this gave stifled doubts a chance to reassert themselves. The
SPD leadership's commitment to the war now looked like an option,
no longer a necessity. The opposition thought it could feel the disillusion among the rank and file—precisely that same rank and file whose
acceptance of patriotic unanimity had so far kept the opposition quiet.
The main feature of the centrists, the later USPD, was their essentially
democratic base; they were never willing, then or later, to lose contact
with mass reality by moving into heroic isolation. The Left's idea of
creating mass support with a revolutionary gesture was repugnant to
them. They too were a revolutionary party, but only if the masses
shouted their desire for revolution. On the left, the 'Gruppe Internationale' began to exercise a pull. As their influence grew, there was a
real danger that they would run away with the support on which the
Centre relied. As one of their most sensible members, and a former
friend of Rosa's, had written in April 1915:

The editors of *Neue Zeit*, especially you [Kautsky], none the less have a duty to
answer the attacks of the group I[nternationale]; silence will be taken as
abandonment of the position . . . the fact remains that the I[nternationale] is
now being distributed throughout Germany; thanks to the devoted work of
Rosa's friends it was being handed out at all the local meetings [*Zahlabende*]
in Greater Berlin last Tuesday. The masses are restive about the war and
especially over the rising cost of living, they have no one on whom to vent their

[1] Eberlein was mentioned by Rosa as 'completely devoted to us' in a letter to Marta
Rosenbaum, 5 January 1915, *Briefe an Freunde*, p. 137. Before the war Rosa had recommended Pieck for a job with the following comment, especially interesting in view of his
political career and eminent capacity for survival. 'He is energetic, possesses initiative,
idealism, and great enthusiasm, and he is a diligent reader' (*Letters to Karl and Luise
Kautsky*, p. 166, dated 9 January 1913).

rage and since they can't get at the government the party becomes the scapegoat. That is the 'action' which Rosa is screaming for. . . .[1]

Some centrists went into opposition willingly, others with a heavy sigh. There was no unanimity about motives. The first abstention in the credit vote, in March 1915, had been justified by one of the leaders, not as opposition to the war effort, but as a means of avoiding a direct vote of confidence in the government.[2]

Thus the break between Centre and majority led first to the eviction of the recusants from the party caucus on 24 March 1916, and finally in January 1917 to the formation of a new, oppositional Socialist party, the USPD.[3] The organizational break was a long and difficult process. Those who voted against the credits from March 1915 onwards believed that they were exercising the undeniable demands of their conscience; they had no wish to break with the SPD. It was the majority who gradually drove them out; from informal consultations as early as the summer of 1915, from official membership of the *Reichstag* delegation in March the following year. Had there been any party congress, a move might well have been made to expel them from the party altogether. The creation of an opposition bloc in the *Reichstag*, and later of a new party, was not what the dissenters wanted but the consequence of majority intolerance—as the Left gleefully pointed out. And incidentally it is significant that the emergence of articulate opposition in the SPD was from the top downwards—not the expression of local dissent against the Centre, masses against authority; nor was it even a party phenomenon—everything sprang from the bosom of the *Reichstag* caucus, which officially had no constitutional significance whatever in the SPD.

None of this narrowed the gap between the Left—the 'thorough' (*entschieden*) opposition as Meyer called it—and the Centre, the *Arbeitsgemeinschaft*, as the loose association of expellees in the *Reichstag* came to be known.[4] On the contrary, it became wider. The Left had the same fear of the Centre as the latter had of the Left—the stealing of each other's mass support, or, to use the combat phrase, the confusion of the masses. Liebknecht sharply attacked the 'December men of 1915' with historical echoes of the Russian Decembrists. Never had historical analogy been harder worked than by the German Left, a sure sign of intellectual doubt and stress.[5]

[1] Emmanuel Wurm to Karl Kautsky, 21 April 1915. IISH Archives, D XXIII, 259.

[2] Hugo Haase to Freidrich Ebert, 5 March 1915, in Ernst Haase, *Hugo Haase sein Leben und Wirken*, Berlin n.d. [1929?], p. 105.

[3] For the Centre's declaration on their vote against the budget, and the withdrawal of the whip, see Prager, *USPD*, pp. 94–96.

[4] 'Ad hoc working group' would be the most accurate translation. For Meyer, see *Spartakus im Kriege*, Berlin 1928.

[5] 'Die Dezembermänner von 1915', *Spartakusbriefe*, p. 86.

Hitherto the Centre's doings and sayings had merely been quoted in the letters without much comment. But since Liebknecht had been evicted from the caucus on 12 January 1916, the Left had become more confident and better organized. In spite of decimation—Mehring, Marchlewski, Clara Zetkin arrested by the beginning of 1916; Meyer, Eberlein, Westmeyer, and Pieck arrested or drafted—they now had their own network of agents, established at a secret conference in March 1915, largely to arrange distribution of *Die Internationale*.[1] On 1 January 1916 an important meeting took place at Liebknecht's law office. Delegates arrived in great secrecy, in twos and threes.[2] This was the real moment of decision for the Left, and they agreed to maintain a nucleus of opposition to the party executive as well as to the newly-created *Arbeitsgemeinschaft*, but also to work within the party for as long as possible. As a programme this conference adopted the 12 declarations and 6 propositions which Rosa Luxemburg had evolved for Zimmerwald and smuggled out of prison in December 1915. They read as follows:

1. The World War has destroyed the result of 40 years of work of European Socialism. . . . It has destroyed the revolutionary working class as a political instrument of power. . . . It has destroyed the proletarian international and has . . . chained the hopes and wishes of the broad masses to the chariot of imperialism.
2. By voting for war credits and by proclaiming the *Burgfrieden* the official leaders of the Socialist parties in Germany, France, and England (with the exception of the Independent Labour Party) have strengthened imperialism and have . . . taken over the responsibility for the war and its consequences.
3. This tactic is treason against the most elementary lessons of international Socialism. . . . As a result, Socialist policy has been condemned to impotence even in those countries where the party leaders have remained faithful to their duty; in Russia, Serbia, Italy and—with one exception—Bulgaria.
4. By giving up the class struggle during the war official Social Democracy has given the ruling class in each country the chance to strengthen its position enormously at the expense of the proletariat in the economic, political, and military spheres.
5. The World War serves neither national defence nor the economic or political interests of the masses anywhere; it is merely an outcrop of imperialist rivalry between capitalist classes of different countries for the attainment of world domination and for a monopoly to exploit countries not yet developed by capital.[3]

---

[1] Introduction, *Spartakusbriefe*, p. xiii.
[2] *Dokumente und Materialien*, Vol. 1, p. 283. Report from memory by Rudolf Lindau, one of the participants, in *Neues Deutschland*, No. 1, 1 January 1956.
[3] It is curious to note that with this sentence Rosa Luxemburg in fact got the approval of the entire German Left for the particular thesis of her *Accumulation of Capital*, although at the time no prominent Marxists were willing to subscribe to her analysis of capitalism and its collapse.

In the present era of unabashed imperialism national wars are not longer possible. National interests serve only as deception, to make the working classes the tool of their deadly enemy, imperialism.

6. From the policy of imperialist states and from this imperialist war no subject nation can possibly obtain independence and freedom.

7. The present World War, whether it brings victory or defeat for anyone, can only mean the defeat of Socialism and democracy. Whatever its end—excepting revolutionary intervention of the international proletariat—it can only lead to the strengthening of militarism, to the sharpening of international contradictions, and to world economic rivalries. Today's World War thus develops simultaneously with the pre-conditions for new wars.[1]

8. World peace cannot be assured through apparently utopian but basically reactionary plans, such as international arbitration by capitalist diplomats, diplomatic arrangements about 'disarmament', 'freedom of the seas' . . . 'European communities' [Staatenbünde], 'Central European customs unions', 'national buffer states' and the like. The only means . . . of ensuring world peace is the political capacity for action and the revolutionary will of the international proletariat to throw its weight into the scales.

9. Imperialism as the last phase of the political world power of capitalism is the common enemy of the working classes of all countries, but it shares the same fate as previous phases of capitalism in that its own development increases the strength of its enemy pro rata. . . . Against imperialism the worker's class struggle must be intensified in peace as in war. This struggle is . . . both the proletariat's struggle for political power as well as the final confrontation between Socialism and capitalism.

10. In this connection the main task of Socialism today is to bring together the proletariat of all countries into a living revolutionary force. . . .

11. The Second International has been destroyed by the war. Its decrepitude has been proved by its inability to act as an effective barrier against the splintering nationalism during the war, and by its inability to carry out jointly a general tactic and action with the working classes of all countries.

12. In view of the betrayal of aims and interests of the working classes by their official representatives . . . it has become a vital necessity for Socialism to create a new workers' International which will take over the leadership and co-ordination of the revolutionary classes' war against imperialism everywhere.[2]

Propositions:

1. The class war within bourgeois states against the ruling classes and the international solidarity of proletarians of all countries are two indivisible and vital rules for the working classes in their struggle for liberation. There is no Socialism outside the international solidarity of the proletariat and there is no Socialism without class war. Neither in time of war nor peace can the Socialist proletariat renounce class war or international solidarity without at the same time committing suicide.

---

[1] This is as complete a contradiction of Lenin's thesis regarding the revolutionary potential of the First World War as can be found in German left-wing literature of the time.

[2] Cf. above, p. 385.

2. The class action of the proletariat of all countries must have as its main object the struggle against imperialism and the prevention of wars. Parliamentary action, trade-union action, indeed the entire activity of working-class movements must be made subject to the sharpest confrontation in every country against its national bourgeoisie.

3. The centre of gravity of class organization is in the International. In peacetime the International decide the tactic of the national sections in questions of militarism, colonial policy, economic policy, the May Day celebrations—as well as the tactic to be followed in case of war.

4. The duty to carry out the resolutions of the International precedes all other organizational duties. National sections which go against these resolutions automatically place themselves outside the International.

5. In the struggle against imperialism and war, the decisive effort can only be made by the compact masses of the proletariat. The main task of the tactic of the national sections, therefore, must tend to educate the broad masses to take a determined initiative in political action. It must also ensure the cohesion of mass action, must develop political and trade-union organization in such a way that rapid co-operation of all sections will be ensured, and that the will of the International be transformed into the action of the working masses in all countries.

6. The next task of Socialism is the spiritual liberation of the proletariat from the tutelage of the bourgeoisie which makes its influence felt through its nationalist ideology. The national sections must develop their agitation in parliament and in the press towards the denunciation of the out-of-date phraseology of nationalism which is merely a means of bourgeois domination. The only real defence of genuine national freedom today is the revolutionary class struggle against imperialism. The fatherland of all proletarians is the Socialist International, and defence of this must take priority over everything else.[1]

All the stress was on internationalism, against national sentiment. Rosa placed her faith in this against the fallible vagaries of national parties; a shift of emphasis rather than a new tactic. It was perhaps the high-water mark of the international ideal among the *Spartakus* group. Probably no one but Rosa Luxemburg would have envisaged an organizational structure in which national parties were made truly subservient to the International. 'National' parties in this context was a pejorative term, and also a piece of loose thinking—the result of being dominated by the recent German experience. The RSDRP for instance, as Rosa well knew, did not consider itself a 'national' party, neither did the Austrian Social-Democratic Party. In any case the intellectual and extreme international emphasis proved transient; from then on the Liebknecht tactic that 'the main enemy is at home' increasingly dominated, with its positive revolutionary tinge.[2] The difference between Rosa Luxemburg and Liebknecht was admittedly one of emphasis

---

[1] *Dokumente und Materialien*, Vol. I, pp. 279–82. Henceforward each of the *Spartakusbriefe* was headed by extracts from one or several of these propositions.

[2] 'Der Hauptfeind steht im eigenen Land', illegal handbill of May 1915, printed in Drahn und Leonhard, op. cit., pp. 24–27.

rather than of policy, but it is noticeable all the same. The fact that her conception was adopted shows again how powerful was her influence on *Spartakus* thinking in the first two years of the war.

But there was complete agreement between her and Liebknecht on sharpening the issues between *Spartakus* and *Arbeitsgemeinschaft*. The conference of 1 January 1916 decided to drive forward relentlessly with the 'clarification process' of attacking the centrist leaders in order to steal their mass support. Rosa wrote her own comment on the 'men of December', more personal and also more profound than Liebknecht's; these men had all at one time been her collaborators and friends. 'I know thy works, that thou art neither cold nor hot: I would that thou wert cold or hot. So then because thou art lukewarm, and neither cold nor hot, I will spew thee out of my mouth.'[1]

Rosa was released from prison on 22 January 1916, though the public prosecutor was still mulling over the leading article of *Die Internationale* with a view to an indictment. On the day of her release she had to shake hundreds of well-wishers' hands. 'I have returned to "freedom" with a tremendous appetite for work.'[2] Karl Liebknecht was on extended leave from his regiment to attend the *Reichstag* session; much as the High Command and police authorities would have liked to lock him up, they could not touch him—yet.[3] He was making use of parliamentary question time, the only chance for private members to make a nuisance of themselves; each question was designed to needle the government and to reiterate his thesis of imperialist and aggressive war. The right-wing and liberal deputies even tried physical assault on him; they thought that he had gone literally out of his mind.[4] There were insistent

[1] Revelation, iii. 15–16. From 'Entweder-Oder' (Either-Or), in *Selected Works*, II, p. 533. The piece was circulated as an illegal handbill in typewritten form. It was cited in the testimony to the *Reichstag* commission which sat from 1925–9 to examine the causes of Germany's defeat. *Untersuchungskommission des Reichstages, Vierte Reihe ; Die Ursachen des deutschen Zusammenbruches im Jahre 1918, Der innere Zusammenbruch* (The Internal Collapse), Vol. IV, pp. 102–3.

[2] Rosa Luxemburg to Regina Ruben, dated 25 February 1916, IML (B). See also *Letters to Karl and Luise Kautsky*, p. 196: 'You have no idea of the torture it was having to receive 80 (literally 80) people [in my flat] on the very first day and say a few words to each one of them after a year in the Barnimstrasse.' (Undated—probably early 1917.)

[3] *Dokumente und Materialien*, Vol. I, p. 336. (Confidential report from the Berlin police president to the Prussian Minister of the Interior, dated 31 March 1916.) See also p. 355 (Chancellor's telegram to the Emperor's Privy Council, dated 9 April 1916).

[4] See report of *Reichstag* debate, during which Karl Liebknecht was constantly interrupted by shouts of 'nonsense!' 'madness!' 'lunatic asylum!' (*Reichstagsverhandlungen*, 13th legislative period, 2nd session, Berlin 1916, Vol. CCCVII, Column 952–3). History does have a habit of repeating itself, at least in its minutiae. Karl Liebknecht's solitary stand, the tone of his speech and the attitude of his opponents, were almost an exact repetition of the occasion when Janko Sakasoff made an anti-war speech on behalf of the Bulgarian Social Democrats in the *Sobranje*, 8 October 1912 (see *Bulletin Périodique*, International Socialist Bureau, Brussels, 1913, 2nd Supplement to Vol. 3, No. 9, p. 7).

demands in the *Reichstag* and press that an end be put to his treacherous performance and to the machinations of his friends. The police reports of the time bristle with material about *Spartakus*, predicting the perpetual imminence of a revolutionary outbreak; though based on real information, it is clear that the conclusions the agents wrote up were those which their superiors wanted to hear. To the authorities *Spartakus* looked much more menacing than it really was, and it was good politics to keep it so.[1]

It was a period of intense activity for Rosa Luxemburg and Karl Liebknecht. In moments snatched from meetings and editorial work they walked throughout the spring on the outskirts of Berlin, lighthearted with the pleasure of action. Karl was emotionally less stable; it was he who did handsprings and unpredictably burst into song, while Rosa watched tolerantly, though herself unable to join in such transports.[2] The friendship between Rosa and Karl's young Russian wife Sonia grew into an intense protective relationship. Later, when Karl was in the penitentiary and Rosa herself immured in a fortress, she bombarded Sonia with letters intended to cauterize the young woman's pain at the separation. As with others, Rosa undertook not only the moral protection but also the education of her friend, though these efforts did not always succeed as she hoped; the effect this correspondence had on Rosa herself was often that of a 'cracked glass'.[3] She saw all her friends, including Hans Diefenbach, now serving as a doctor on the eastern front. These six months were the last time in her life that Rosa was able to lead anything like a normal existence.

[1] See the extracts of the secret police reports and instructions published in *Dokumente und Materialien*, Vol. I. For 1917 onwards see Leo Stern, *Der Einfluss der grossen sozialistischen Oktoberrevolution auf Deutschland und die deutsche Arbeiterbewegung*, Berlin (East) 1958). A detailed discussion of this subject hardly belongs here. The East German historians have found this material useful for proving the significance of 'mass' opposition to the war as well as to the official party organizations; but the wish is father to the proof.

[2] *Briefe an Freunde*, p. 94, letter to Hans Diefenbach dated 30 March 1917. See also *Letters from Prison*, Berlin 1923. This is a translation of Rosa Luxemburg's collected letters to Sonia Liebknecht, published as *Briefe aus dem Gefängnis*, Berlin 1920. References to quotations are from the English edition, though frequently I have retranslated the original German.

[3] *Letters to Karl and Luise Kautsky*, p. 188. 'Sonia sent a whole packet of literature for me to read—all hopeless.' (*Briefe an Freunde*, p. 128, letter to Hans Diefenbach dated 13 August 1917.) Sonia Liebknecht is still living in East Berlin, and recently emerged from a long silence to threaten the West German government with legal proceedings for whitewashing one of her husband's murderers. See below, p. 487, note 2. Sonia Liebknecht may have appeared more naïve than she was. She herself was a university graduate; a recent writer has described her as 'attractive, apparently ingenuous, but perfectly capable of delivering important messages for her husband in prison and fully involved in his political activity'. See Okhrana Archives of Russian Secret Police dossiers from 1870 to 1917 in the Hoover Institution at Stanford University, California, quoted in Ralph H. Lutz, 'Rosa Luxemburg's Unpublished Prison Letters 1916–18', *Journal of Central European Affairs*, October 1963, Vol. XXIII, No. 3, p. 305.

But it would not have been normal if it had not also been crammed with political activity. Between the government and *Spartakus* stood two shock-absorbers, which cushioned the necessary and ardently desired class struggle; these were the first obstacles to be removed. First, there was the majority SPD and its executive. The latter had taken the offensive; now that the opposition was prepared to come out into the open there could no longer, in Ebert's and Scheidemann's minds, be any reason for half measures. Besides, the increasing pressure of the government and the military on the majority Socialists—press censorship, restriction of 'discussable' subjects on public platforms, in some cases prohibition of SPD meetings altogether—in turn made the executive press harder on the opposition whom it blamed for its troubles.[1] Doubtful district organizations were simply taken over by suitable nominees from the centre, and the silencing of oppositional party papers culminated in the executive's physical seizure of *Vorwärts* in October 1916, after various attempts to regulate its policy. This was a theft which the Berlin party organization, which regarded *Vorwärts* traditionally as its own, never forgave.

But the real struggle, the close in-fighting, was with the centrists, themselves by now in opposition to the majority in the party. The *Spartakusbriefe* contained one warning after another against mistaking centrist opposition for 'real' opposition, and against confusing tactical manœuvres with struggle. 'What the 24th of March [the second centrist vote against the budget] offers in the nature of progress is precisely due to the ruthless criticism by the radicals of all half measures'—halfness, wholeness: Liebknecht's favourite words—'it confirms the fruitfulness of this criticism for the *general strengthening of the spirit of opposition.*'[2] And he concluded: 'Whoever strays about between armies locked in battle will get shot down in the crossfire, if he doesn't seek refuge on one side or the other. But then he arrives, not as a hero, but as a refugee.'[3]

The solution, however, was still not Lenin's: democracy, not splits; looser and not tighter discipline.

Upwards from below. The broadest masses of comrades in party and trade unions must be reached, in doing battle for the party, *in* the party . . . the handcuffs of the bureaucracy must be cracked open . . . no financial support, no contributions, not a farthing for the executive . . . not splitting or unity, not new party or old party, but *recapture* of the party upwards from below through mass rebellion . . . not words but deeds of rebellion. . . .[4]

Though Rosa Luxemburg attended innumerable committee meetings of the party as well, in which a running battle for control was being

---

[1] *Reichstagsverhandlungen*, 1916, Vol. CCCVI, Col. 716; CCCVII, Cols. 943, 1244.
[2] *Spartakusbriefe*, p. 130. My italics. Unsigned, but clearly by Liebknecht.
[3] Ibid.
[4] Ibid., pp. 132–3. This was one of the earliest suggestions of a financial embargo.

fought with the centrists, she did so from loyalty rather than conviction. This was not the struggle she wanted; it was narrow rather than broad—much better to forget about the formal bureaucratic structure and broaden the battle outwards and down to the masses. After a year in prison her patience had anyhow worn thin. 'I cannot attach any importance to this pygmy battle [*Froschmäusekrieg*] within the official bodies . . . our "proletarians" grossly overrate this bureaucratic dogfight', she complained to Clara Zetkin.[1]

The activities of the radical opposition were strongest in Berlin. Only here, under the critical eye of the leadership, was it possible to achieve that precise theoretical separation of *Spartakus* from the *Arbeitsgemeinschaft* which was supposed to prevent working-class confusion. But any history based on the pronouncements of the leaders is misleading, for at regional and still more at local level *Spartakus* and *Arbeitsgemeinschaft* were largely indistinguishable, and to most local functionaries Rosa Luxemburg's 'either-or' would have been meaningless, as it still was for a time after the war.[2]

The situation was very confused. It was hard enough to decide between official and opposition members of the SPD outside the *Reichstag*. Even in the Berlin organization there was confusion. On 31 March a general meeting of the Greater Berlin organization reviewed the *Reichstag* events of 24 March, the latest vote against the budget. A resolution was adopted favouring the *Arbeitsgemeinschaft*, which appeared in *Vorwärts* next day, fitfully blacked out by the censorship. Rosa Luxemburg, who was present, failed to obtain permission even to bring an amendment to the resolution. Her request to *Vorwärts* to print her criticisms of the resolution was refused—for did it not represent the unanimous view of the opposition? At about the same time the executive made the first attempt to regulate the policy of *Vorwärts*. This time Rosa Luxemburg was able to bring a resolution in the local Press Commission more pointed than the one submitted by the centrist opposition. Her resolution was lost by a small majority—only because it had been submitted by Rosa. Eight days later, however, the executive of the Berlin provincial organization adopted Rosa's same rejected resolution *verbatim*, over the heads of its own Press Commission.[3] Each side drew the wrong conclusion about the disarray in the opposing ranks—the disarray was universal.

[1] Rosa Luxemburg to Clara Zetkin, 30 April 1916, IML (M), Fund 209, photocopy IML (B), NL2–20, p. 130.

[2] East German history emphasizes the contrary and claims a clear distinction between Centre and Left at all levels. The point must be made, otherwise *Spartakus* is wrongly seen as a compact, well-defined group behind equally well-defined, articulate leaders—which is nonsense.

[3] *Spartakusbriefe*, pp. 149–52. See also *Vorwärts* of relevant dates, 1 April, 7 April, 15 April 1916.

On 22 April 1916 Rosa Luxemburg moved to the offensive. Deeds, not words, was the mounting refrain. It was decided to make a real, visible, tangible gesture: to call a demonstration for 1 May in the centre of Berlin. Even the mildest May Day celebrations had been put away for the duration. All the more reason to make a memorable show now. There were negotiations with the 'Ledebour group'—it was either the Ledebour group, the Haase group, the Kautsky group, according to choice; these personal attributions were always derogatory. In the end no joint action could be agreed. Madness, said the centrists—there was insufficient evidence of revolutionary feeling among the masses, no evidence at all of a desire for patent suicide; failure could only make the opposition ridiculous.[1] So Rosa Luxemburg and Karl Liebknecht, with a few supporters, decided to go it alone, after much agitation and advertisement of their intentions.[2] This naturally brought the police out in force. 'At eight o'clock sharp . . . in the middle of the Potsdamer-platz, the sonorous voice of Karl Liebknecht rang out: "Down with the government, down with the war".' He was instantly arrested, but apparently the other leaders were not molested. The arrest itself was followed by a larger if quieter demonstration for several hours, though it is never easy on such occasions to distinguish participants from spectators; the very presence of large police reinforcements increased the number of curious onlookers.

Liebknecht was first sentenced to two and a half years' hard labour on 28 June; unexpectedly—for all concerned—this caused the first large political strike of the war. In due course the higher military court (*Oberkriegsgericht*) increased the sentence to four years one month.[3]

[1] *Spartakusbriefe*, p. 166.

[2] She spoke of 'an imposing demonstration', 'a dense crowd', without giving figures (ibid.). According to contemporary eye-witnesses, hostile and friendly, the numbers in the original demonstration seem to have been a few hundred, though some days later news of Liebknecht's arrest produced rather larger demonstrations. See *Dokumente und Materialien*, Vol. I, p. 379; also the report mentioned but not printed here in *Archiv der Reichskanzlei*, Nr. 8/7, 'Social Democrats', Vol. XI, Sheet 189, in IML (B). A facsimile of the illegal proclamation calling for the demonstration is printed in *Dokumente und Materialien*, Vol. I, p. 373.

[3] In Germany sentence to hard labour or penitentiary—as opposed to prison—involved the loss of civil rights, in Karl Liebknecht's case for six years. This meant disbarment from legal practice—he was a lawyer—from voting and of course he could not stand as a candidate for Reich or provincial legislatures.

Germany military sentences during the war fell into three categories: penitentiary or hard labour for treasonable activity, imprisonment for lesser offences, and administrative custody, often in a fortress—the easiest and most convenient way of dealing with Social Democrats without the expense and trouble of a trial. Fortress was more 'political' and less rigorous than prison. By the standard of today's methods of dealing with war-time sedition, both the sentences imposed on *Spartakus* leaders and the treatment in prison were mild. The vociferous protests of the *Spartakus* group against the arrest and imprisonment of their leaders should not mislead us into believing the contrary.

An appeal to the Reich High Court was disallowed and he began his sentence on 6 December 1916 at Luckau in Saxony. The *Reichstag* had hastened, within a few days of Liebknecht's arrest, to lift his immunity, and a majority of Socialists had voted with the 'class enemy' for this measure. Most of them had not the slightest sympathy with or understanding of his action.[1]

At least Liebknecht's arrest if not his demonstration brought him the personal support and sympathy of Hugo Haase, the leader of the *Arbeitsgemeinschaft* and former party chairman. A new effort was made to collaborate with *Spartakus*. In July Haase reported to his wife that there was 'full understanding with the Rosa group'. The arrest of Liebknecht had 'pushed all problems of personality into the background'.[2]

This did not mean that he would encourage or countenance what he considered further foolishness.

At the general meeting [of the Berlin constituency organizations] Rosa made a very skilful speech . . . with strong effect, the more so as she did not in the end insist on an embargo of membership dues, but her proposal was dangerous [all the same]; it reeked of separatist organizational measures. The party executive would have risen to this at once, and therefore I fought against it with such success that only a handful [of people] remained with Rosa in the end. How right I was in practice became clear at once. The executive proved unable to attack the adopted resolution . . . I agree with you, the unity of the opposition in the country must be strengthened.[3]

But Rosa Luxemburg and her friends were not prepared to seize the proffered hand with conditions of 'sensible' behaviour. On the contrary, the original refusal to collaborate on 1 May made the present offers of unity and reconciliation 'the height of creepy shamelessness' as far as Rosa herself was concerned. She administered 'a well deserved kick in the pants', and *Spartakus* continued to draw the sharpest lines of distinction between the *Arbeitsgemeinschaft* and itself.

---

[1] 'Gentlemen . . . in Liebknecht we are dealing with a man who wanted, through an appeal to the masses, to force the government to make peace, a government moreover which has repeatedly expressed its sincere desire for peace before the whole world. . . . This war is a war for our very homes . . . how grotesque was this enterprise . . . how can anyone imagine that [Liebknecht] could influence the fate of the world, play at high policy [*hohe Politik machen*] by shoving handbills at people, by creating a demonstration in the Potsdamerplatz. . . . Contrast this pathological instability with our [party's official] clear-headed and sensible calm. . . .'
(*Reichstagverhandlungen*, loc. cit., Cols. 1027–28, speech by Landsberg. The remarks about 'high policy' are an interesting example of the official SPD's 'deference' attitude to government.

[2] Ernst Haase, *Haase*, pp. 120, 125.

[3] Ibid. The full report of Rosa's speech and Haase's reply at the meeting on 25 June 1916, in which the Left opposition and the *Arbeitsgemeinschaft* met head on, is in *Vorwärts*, 27 June 1916.

In the two months of liberty that were left to Rosa she continued to battle against the party authorities, particularly in the oppositional districts of Berlin. She appeared at all possible meetings and bombarded them with lively resolutions—everything to turn the centrists' common sense into something more positive. Politically Rosa was almost alone. Only a few Left leaders were at liberty and this meant all the more work for her. Jogiches was there, unobtrusive and efficient; the technical processes of duplicating, distribution, and control of the *Spartakus* literature were almost entirely in his hands. After the arrest of Ernst Meyer in August 1916 he took over the formal leadership of *Spartakus* under the pseudonym of W. Kraft. From August 1916 onwards he was able at last to make printing arrangements for the group; henceforth the letters were no longer hectographed. A few of his circulars exist— laconic, matter-of-fact, unemotional, without any of the charisma of Luxemburg or Liebknecht; flatter even in German than in Polish.[1] But effective. He had never in the past taken any interest in German affairs except in so far as they impinged on the SDKPiL; other than as Rosa's friend and *éminence grise* he was completely unknown in the SPD. None the less it was he who did all the work of clandestine organization, and emerged in 1916 as the effective manager of the Left opposition—a remarkable achievement which has not yet been documented. Without him there would have been no *Spartakusbund*; the scintillating figures associated with the intellectual leadership of the Left were none of them capable of performing the dour conspiratorial work of building a vehicle for their policies.

On 10 July Rosa was suddenly rearrested.[2] She spent the first weeks at the women's prison in the Barnimstrasse where she had been before, but was then transferred to the interrogation cells at police headquarters in the Alexanderplatz—the famous 'Alex' of Berlin satire and of grimmer memory under the Third Reich.

At the time the police had still not decided whether to put her on trial or merely to keep her in custody; a decision for the latter course was made some time in the early autumn. The six weeks at the Alexanderplatz were the worst prison experience of Rosa's life. 'The hell-hole at the Alexanderplatz where my cell was exactly 11 cubic metres, no light

---

[1] *Spartakusbriefe*, p. 206.

[2] Some sources say 10 June, but wrongly. (Meyer, Introduction, *Spartakusbriefe*, Vol. I, p. viii.) Meyer's wrong dating is all the more surprising since he was present when she was arrested. 'Dr. Ernst Meyer . . . and Eduard Fuchs accompanied her home that Sunday. Mathilde Jacob awaited them with the bad news that two very suspicious men wished to speak to Rosa about some leaflets. The next morning at the crack of dawn the same men reappeared, identified themselves as secret police, placed Rosa under arrest and took her eventually to the women's prison. . . .' Ralph H. Lutz, *Journal of Central European Affairs*, October 1963, Vol. XXIII, No. 3, p. 309. This story is clearly put together from details in some of Mathilde Jacob's correspondence. See below, p. 418.

mornings and nights, squashed in between cold [water tap] (but no hot) and an iron plank.'[1] For a time she was held almost completely incommunicado.[2]

In October she was at last transferred to the old fortress at Wronke (Wronki) in Posen (Poznań); slothful, comfortable, grass-infested. She had privacy, and the privilege of walking up and down the same battlements as the sentries. Above all, she must have worked out an arrangement with at least one member of the staff; her correspondence, both legal and illicit, reached flood level. She knew that it would be a long while before she would be released; a whole new way of life became necessary. She continued her output of illegal material but, shut off as she was from the struggle outside, there was little development in her thought; for a year her writing was static, even repetitious. Only her temperament and her lively style prevented it from sounding stale.

Within the new circumstances she still found means of giving full rein to her personality. In the many letters written to friends during the next two years her personality reached out of prison like an octopus, wooing, embracing, and scolding her friends, dragging them into the orbit of her intellect and emotions. It did not matter whether she was writing on politics, literature, or life. Prison life, instead of stifling her, in fact enabled her to reach a spiritual and emotional maturity which is remarkable—as are the means which she developed to convey the flow of feelings and ideas. For the next two years the political aspect of her life was bound to cede primacy to the demands of a bursting personality confined in a relatively small space.

---

[1] *Briefe an Freunde*, p. 45, letter to Mathilde Wurm dated 28 December 1916.

[2] The *Spartakus* letter of 20 September 1916 contains two—naturally unsigned contributions by Rosa Luxemburg. The first, 'Der Rhodus' (*Hic Rhodus, hic salta*—the quotation is from Marx, *The 18th Brumaire of Louis Bonaparte*), was probably written before her arrest in July (*Sparkatusbriefe*, pp. 211–17). The second, 'Liebknecht', deals with the upward revision of the latter's sentence on 23 August and must therefore have been smuggled out of the Barnimstrasse prison through either Mathilde Jacob or Fanny Jezierska (ibid., pp. 217–20).

XIV

PRISON IN GERMANY,

REVOLUTION IN RUSSIA

O N the surface of war-time Germany the Liebknecht incident caused hardly a ripple. Neither our own preoccupation with this small group of revolutionaries nor the solemn prolixity of police reports can alter the fact that the great majority of Germans hardly knew that *Spartakus* existed. Though the euphoria of early victories had gone, the need to 'see it through' (*durchhalten*)—the phrase which *Spartakus* echoed with such contempt—was still official SPD policy. The war was now bound to be a long and costly one. It was this realization which brought the first stirring, not yet of opposition, but at least of self-consciousness among the SPD leaders. They bethought themselves of the government's frequent protestations of peaceful and purely defensive intentions, and of their own commitment against a war of conquest. As a stiffener, a Reich conference was held—no properly constituted party congress could be envisaged for the duration—from 21 to 23 September 1916. For the last time representatives of all shades of opinion met together within the old and ample bosom of the SPD, the last occasion that executive, centrists, and *Spartakus* confronted each other in one party.

The *Gruppe Internationale* (as *Spartakus* was to be officially known until the end of 1918) sent Käthe Duncker and Paul Frassek as its representatives. In the restrained language required on public occasions in war-time—the hall was spattered with police—these two tried to put the views of *Spartakus* on the question of war. They marked themselves off so firmly from the centrist *Arbeitsgemeinschaft* that their strictures against the latter often drew laughter and approval from the majority.[1]

Frassek submitted what was to be the opposition's last official declaration within the SPD.

The Reich conference has come together under the throttling conditions of the state of siege. . . . The state of siege and the censorship make every free discussion of policy impossible from the start; the stage of siege, in giving every

---

[1] *Protokoll der Reichskonferenz der Sozialdemokratie Deutschlands von 21, 22 und 23 September 1916*, Berlin, no date, p. 85.

advantage to the supporters of the so-called majority within the party, puts those belonging to the genuine opposition at a particularly heavy disadvantage, decimated as we are by prosecutions, arrests and military service. In any case the election of delegates has not been carried out by the members or delegates of individual constituencies, but through the local committees or executives of the party organization. Under these circumstances it is clear that any resolutions adopted by this conference cannot have the least political or moral value.[1]

A further declaration by *Spartakus* at this conference, couched in stronger language, was not accepted by the conference chairman, and consequently did not even appear in the *Protokoll*.[2]

Spartakus could not expect that its speeches and resolutions at the conference would sway the majority of delegates. The real purpose was propaganda. Like all Socialist representatives elected into hostile assemblies, the two *Spartakists* were merely 'speaking through the window' to the—it was assumed—attentive masses outside. For their purposes the SPD leadership was impugned as a mere stooge of the Reich government.

On 17 October 1916 the successful coup against *Vorwärts* was finally carried out; at last that same 'Kosher' editorial board of which Rosa Luxemburg had been a member for a few weeks in 1905 was removed. On 5 December the *Bremer Bürgerzeitung* and on 30 March 1917 the Brunswick *Volksfreund* went the same way. Among the major papers, only the *Leipziger Volkszeitung* remained under centrist control while the Left was confined solely to *Der Kampf*, which they had started in Duisberg on 1 July 1916 as their legal paper.

With the executive counter-attacking strongly on all fronts, there was no point in the *Arbeitsgemeinschaft* continuing within the SPD, deprived of all influence. An attempt was afoot to elbow its members out of the party altogether. To forestall this, on 7 January 1917 a Reich conference of the Social-Democratic opposition took place in Berlin. This public defiance led to an open breach; the SPD executive formally decided to cut off all party connection with the conference participants and there was nothing for the latter now but to start their own party. The founding congress of the Independent Social-Democratic Party of Germany (USPD) took place in Gotha in the first week of April amid nostalgic thoughts of the founding congress of the old SPD held nearly fifty years earlier in the same town.

Communist historians have strongly reproached *Spartakus* for failing to make an organizational break with the SPD before the war, but especially after 4 August 1914. Here was another obvious opportunity. With historical sleight-of-hand they point to Lenin's coherent yet democratic organization—leaders and members in harmony—which

---

[1] Ibid., p. 14.   [2] See *Die Internationale*, 1927, Vol. 12, pp. 379–80.

was soon to make possible the capture of an entire state, unilaterally and without official allies. It is true that *Spartakus* gave little or no importance to purely organizational problems. There were strong historical reasons for this—the proud exclusiveness of a powerful mass party before the war, and the oppositional thesis so long advocated by Rosa Luxemburg of the need to maintain contact with the masses at any cost. Disputes within the party—from 1910, opposition to all party authority—were one thing, but contracting out of the organized working class of Germany was another. In Rosa Luxemburg's eyes contact with the masses was emphatically more important even than any mistaken policy. She had strenuously advised her friend Henriette Roland-Holst against such a move in 1908.

A splintering of Marxists (not to be confused with differences of opinion) is fatal. Now that you want to leave the party, I want to hinder you from this with all my might. . . . Your resignation from the SDAP [the Dutch *Sociaal-Democratische Arbeiderspartij*] simply means your resignation from the Social Democratic movement. This you must not do, none of us must! We cannot stand outside the organization, outside contact with the masses. *The worst working-class party is better than none.*[1]

Now, on 6 January 1917, the day before the planned conference of the party opposition, she wrote:

Understandable and praiseworthy as the impatience and bitter anger of our best elements may be . . . flight is flight. For us it is a betrayal of the masses, who will merely be handed over helpless into the stranglehold of a Schiedemann or a Legien . . . into the hands of the bourgeoisie, to struggle but to be strangled in the end. One can 'leave' sects or conventicles when these no longer suit and one can always found new sects and conventicles. But it is nothing but childish fantasy to talk of liberating the whole mass of proletarians from their bitter and terrible fate by simply 'leaving' and in this way setting them a brave example. Throwing away one's party card as a gesture of liberation is nothing but a mad caricature of the illusion that the party card is in itself an instrument of power. Both are nothing but the opposite poles of organizational cretinism, this constitutional disease of the old German Social Democracy. . . .[2]

None the less, this heartfelt appeal for remaining in the party and continuing the struggle against the treacherous authorities from within, did not mean that Rosa Luxemburg modified by one jot her criticism of the insincerity of the men who had called the opposition conference.

The sharpest criticism of the centrist leaders and their policy, but no organized split from the existing party: the policy of *Spartakus* towards the new Independent Socialist party was the same as it had always been

[1] Roland-Holst, p. 221, letter dated 11 August [1908].
[2] *Der Kampf*, No. 31, 6 January 1917. This article, smuggled out from the fortress at Wronke with the assistance of Mathilde Jacob, appeared under the pseudonym Gracchus.

in the old SPD. In a circular to sympathizers on 25 December 1916 Jogiches made some proposals for the attitude to be adopted by *Spartakus* delegates at the impending opposition conference to which *Spartakus* had been invited. These stressed the need and means of exposing the SPD's policy to the masses by every available means—elections, meetings, handbills, etc.; the emphasis was on mass propaganda not on problems of separate organization.[1] And *Spartakus* went to the conference to wait and see; insistent on maintaining its own political line but without distinct organizational conditions. It accepted the decision of the conference to separate from the SPD and form a new party. All that was required was the maintenance of its own identity. 'If those representing our direction decide on participation in a joint conference [with the *Arbeitsgemeinschaft*] then we will of course do so as a separate, independent, and self-sufficient group.'[2] This from the pen of the most professional organizer on the Left outside the ranks of the Bolsheviks. If the *Arbeitsgemeinschaft* had not constituted itself an Independent Socialist party—against Rosa's advice—*Spartakus* would have preferred to remain within the SPD—that 'stinking corpse of 4 August 1914'— rather than set up on its own in what might well prove to be a political vacuum.

The USPD leaders, and Haase in particular, concentrated the attention of the conference on practical matters instead of first principles. They too wanted a new unity—and public debate of presently unrealizable principles was the best means of dividing the new party right from the start. Everything depended on how events would shape; it was precisely the absurd lip-service to empty principles which in their view had bedevilled the pre-war SPD. The USPD was determined not to tie its hands in advance, and above all not to *Spartakus*. In the end the latter joined the USPD without the clear definition which Jogiches had demanded. But *Spartakus* went on urging its own policy within the USPD, and Rosa Luxemburg continued to ridicule its leaders in public as hitherto.

The relationship between them was uneasy, but less so than the tone of the *Spartakus* polemics might suggest. The fierce denunciations at the top did not penetrate far down into the amorphous Socialist membership. Kautsky still saw the main function of the USPD as an honest David struggling against two Goliaths—the predatory SPD executive on one side and *Spartakus* on the other. Yet the centrist view of *Spartakus* had subtly changed. Instead of talking of the 'Rosa group'

---

[1] *Spartakusbriefe*, pp. 206–10. His draft proposals formed the basis of the resolutions brought by *Spartakus* at the opposition conference. (*Protokoll . . . Gründungsparteitag der USPD 6–8 April 1917 in Gotha*, Berlin 1921, pp. 98–99.)
[2] *Spartakusbriefe*, p. 207.

—a few arrogant, clever, intransigent Marxists whose ambition drove them to prefer a minute but devoted splinter group to a democratic mass party—the USPD leaders were now faced by a powerful myth—the hero-worship of Karl Liebknecht. His demonstrations in April and May 1916 had not only closed the opposition ranks, but had provided the simplest rallying cry—a name. 'The boy Karl has become a real menace [*fürchterlich*]. If we in the *Arbeitsgemeinschaft* had not appeared and proved that we too exist, the irresistibly growing opposition would simply have gone over to *Spartakus* altogether. If a break has been avoided and *Spartakus* held at bay, that is entirely to our credit. The right-wing has not helped us but has only helped *Spartakus*.'[1]

Kautsky was right, at least in one respect: Liebknecht had become a byword in the farthest corners of Europe, which *Spartakus* did its utmost to keep alive. Some French soldiers talk in the trenches about the futility of their own part in the war.

'And yet,' said one 'look! There is one person who has risen above the whole beastly war; who stands illuminated with all the beauty and importance of great courage . . . Liebknecht. . . .' Once more Bertrand emerged from his frozen silence. 'The future, the future. The work of the future will be to wipe out all this . . . as something abominable and shameful.'[2]

Lenin, too, increasingly identified opposition to the war and the revolutionary movement in Germany with the name of Karl Liebknecht. It became a convenient shorthand which everyone would understand. 'The future belongs to those who brought forth a Karl Liebknecht, who created the *Spartakus* group, whose point of view is in the *Bremer Arbeiterpolitik*.'[3] As the embodiment of *Spartakus*, Liebknecht became one of those political bogie-wheels on which Lenin's ideas could move along smoothly and comprehensibly. 'The revolutionary propaganda of the *Spartakus* group becomes more and more intense, the name Liebknecht becomes more popular in Germany every day.'[4] This identification of *Spartakus* with the person of Liebknecht was to have important consequences. A dead martyr can be manipulated by his heirs, a living one is apt to drag his colleagues with him to the extremes dictated by the contingent pressures of his martyrdom.

The search of *Spartakus* for its distinct identity, of which Karl Liebknecht became the symbol, was most clearly articulated by Rosa

---

[1] Victor Adler, *Briefwechsel*, pp. 634–5: letter from Karl Kautsky dated 28 February 1917.

[2] Henri Barbusse, *Le Feu (Journal d'une escouade)*, Paris 1916 (Prix Goncourt), p. 280. Together with Erich Maria Remarque, *Im Westen nichts Neues*, this became one of the most famous anti-war novels of the time.

[3] Lenin, 'Farewell letter to the workers of Switzerland', *Sochineniya*, Vol. XXIII, p. 363.

[4] Lenin's speech on 4 November 1917, *Sochineniya*, Vol. XXVI, p. 258.

Luxemburg. It went well beyond 'mere' politics. Between *Spartakus* and the Independents were two concepts of life which differed in their most fundamental aspects. It is impossible to understand Rosa Luxemburg as a political person without accepting her capacity for judging everything in the form of an extreme dichotomy—words or action, hope or desire, living or dying. Mere political differences were mealy-mouthed understatements; what was happening was a miniature private dialectic of her own, the birth of a new world amid the dust and ashes of the *Arbeitsgemeinschaft*. Rosa's contributions to the *Spartakus* letters were distinguished by this 'either/or' frenzy, infused with all the temperament of which she was capable—but it was only in her private correspondence that this essentially personal parting of the ways could be presented in all its stark relief. The following letter, to the wife of Emmanuel Wurm, speaks more for Rosa Luxemburg than any official document ever could.

Wronke, 28 December 1916.
My dear Tilde,
  I want to answer your Christmas letter immediately while I am still in the grip of the rage which it inspired. Yes, your letter made me absolutely wild [*fuchsteu-felswild*] because short as it was every line showed clearly the extent to which you are imprisoned within your surroundings [*im Bann deines Milieus stehst*]; this weepy-weepy tone, this lament for the 'disappointments' which you have suffered —allegedly due to others; instead of for once looking in the mirror to see the per-fect image of humanity's whole mystery! 'We' in your language now means the other toads of your particular sewer; once upon a time when you were with me it meant my company and me. All right, then I shall deal with you in your desired plural [*dann wart, ich werde Dich per 'Ihr' behandeln*].
  You are 'not radical enough' you suggest sadly. 'Not enough' is hardly the word! You aren't radical at all, just spineless. *It is not a matter of degree but of kind.* 'You' are a totally different zoological species from me and never have I hated your miserable, acidulated, cowardly and half-hearted existence as much as I do now. You wouldn't mind being radical, you say, only the trouble is that one gets put inside and can't be of use any longer. You miserable, pettifogging souls, you would be perfectly prepared to offer a modicum of heroism but only against cash, as long as you can see an immediate return on it; a straight 'yes'—the simple words of that honest and straightforward man: 'Here I stand, I can do no other, God help me'—none of it was spoken for you.[1] Lucky that world history to date has not been made by people like you, otherwise there wouldn't have been any reformation and we would still be stuck with feudalism.
  As far as I am concerned I was never soft, but in recent months I have become as hard as polished steel and I will not make the slightest concession in future,

---

[1] This is, of course, Martin Luther's famous saying. Rosa closed the article in *Der Kampf*, cited above (p. 405, note 2), with the same sentence. Not only the phrase but the whole concept expressed her own view exactly. The present letter is interesting because it was written at the same time and in the same mood as the article in question, yet the one sums up for political restraint, and the other for personal intransigence.

either politically or in my personal friendships. I have only to conjure up the portrait gallery of your heroes to feel like caterwauling: that sweet Haase, Dittmann with his cultivated beard and those cultivated speeches in the Reichstag, that limping shepherd Kautsky, whom your husband naturally follows through thick and thin, the magnificent Arthur [Stadthagen]—*ah je n'en finirai!* I swear to you—I would rather sit here for years—I do not even say here, which is approaching paradise, but rather in the hell-hole in the Alexanderplatz where in a minute cell, without light, I recited my favourite poets—than 'fight' your heroes or for that matter have anything to do with them! I would rather have Graf Westarp [the leader of the Conservative party in the *Reichstag*] —not because he once spoke in the Reichstag of my almond-shaped velvet eyes— but because he is a *man.* I swear to you, let me once get out of prison and I shall hunt and disperse your company of singing toads with trumpets, whips and bloodhounds—I wanted to say like Penthesilea, but then by God you are no Achilles.[1] Had enough of my New Year's greeting? Then see to it that you remain a *human being.* To be human is the main thing, and that means to be strong and clear and *of good cheer* in spite and because of everything, for tears are the preoccupation of weakness. To be human means throwing one's life 'on to the scales of destiny' if need be, to be joyful for every fine day and every beautiful cloud—oh, I can't write you any recipes how to be human, I only know how to *be* human and you too used to know it when we walked for a few hours in the fields outside Berlin and watched the red sunset over the corn. The world is so beautiful in spite of all the misery and would be even more beautiful if there were no half-wits and cowards in it.

Come, you get a kiss after all, because you are basically a good soul. Happy New Year![2]

The recipient must have defended herself as stoutly as she knew how, for on 16 February Rosa wrote again:

Never mind, even though you answered me so bravely and even offered trial by combat, I shall always be well disposed towards you. That you want to take me on makes me smile. My dear girl, I sit firmly in the saddle, no one has yet unseated me. I would like to see the one who does it. But I had to smile for another reason; you do not even want to take me on and are much closer to me politically than you are prepared to admit. I shall remain your compass because your honest nature tells you that *I* am the one with the unmistaken judgement— since I do not suffer from the destroying minor symptoms: fearfulness, being in a rut, the parliamentary cretinism which affects the judgement of others. . . . My dear girl, 'disappointment with the masses' is always the most lamentable excuse for a political leader. A real leader doesn't adjust his tactic in accordance with the attitude of the masses, but in accordance with the development of history. He sticks to his tactic in spite of disappointments and waits for history to complete its work. Let us close the debate on this note. I shall be happy to remain your friend. Whether I can remain your teacher too, depends on *you.*[3]

[1] Penthesilea was a Queen of the Amazons who fought against the Greeks at Troy and was slain by Achilles.

[2] *Briefe an Freunde*, pp. 44–6, to Mathilde Wurm. Rosa Luxemburg's italics.

[3] Ibid., pp. 46–7.

In her prison Rosa Luxemburg felt more firmly attached to the realities of political life, however disagreeable and hard, than ever before.[1] Political life, not politics; an enlargement, not a contraction—that was the consequence of her situation. Every act and interest became life writ large, and took its place in the composite but vital business of living. This was the message of optimism which poured out of prison at her friends. Cut off from the collective life of the community, the individual, instead of shrinking, had to grow large enough to speak not only for itself, but for everything. Things had to substitute for people—plants, flowers, animals, large and small. The old fortress of Wronke became a universe with its own laws and purposes, strong enough to reach out into the consciousness of all Rosa's friends. They must have rubbed their eyes over the morning mail and wondered whether they were not the ones cut off from reality.

Rosa Luxemburg remained at Wronke from October 1916 until July 1917. It was an easy-going routine; conditions were spacious, even moderately comfortable. She had the run of the fortress, could walk along its grass-grown walls and give herself completely to the sight and smell of the surrounding countryside.

Today it rained in torrents, none the less I spent two hours wandering round the little garden—as usual without an umbrella, just my old hat and in Grandmother Kautsky's cape [probably the one she had been given when she went to Warsaw at the end of 1905]. It was lovely to think and dream while walking, even though the rain penetrated hat and hair and ran down my neck in rivulets. Even the birds were awake. One of them, with whom I have become chummy, often walks with me, like this: I always walk on two sides of the garden along the wall, and the bird keeps step with me by hopping from bush to bush. Isn't this nice? We both brave every weather and have already walked our daily round in a snowstorm. Today the bird looked so blown about, wet and miserable, I probably too; and yet we both felt very well. All the same in the afternoon it got so stormy that we just daren't go out at all. The bird sits on the bars of my window and tilts its head right and left in order to look in through the glass. I sit at my desk and enjoy the ticking of the clock which makes a comfortable noise in the room and so I work.[2]

With vigour she took up again some of the interests which had fascinated her some years earlier.

How happy I am that three years ago I threw myself into botany with my usual intense absorption, with my whole self; so much so that the whole world, the

---

[1] The different effects of prison on revolutionaries would make an interesting study. Parvus felt utterly handicapped in isolation and did nothing but complain. A few cells along, in the Peter-Paul Fortress in 1906, Trotsky immersed himself in fruitful political analysis of a wholly abstract nature; prison provided the peace and quiet he needed for this type of work. Rosa, admittedly 'in' for longer, re-created her normal life; like those of a blind man, her remaining faculties for communication—letters—grew larger than life to compensate for the absence of personal contact.

[2] *Briefe an Freunde*, pp. 97–98, to Hans Diefenbach, 16 April 1917.

party, and my work disappeared and one sole longing possessed me—to wander about in the spring fields, to stuff my arms full of plants and then, after sorting them out at home, enter them in my books. I spent the whole spring as in the throes of a fever. How much I suffered when I sat in front of a new plant and for a long time could not recognize it or classify it correctly. I almost fainted with the effort so that Gertrud [Zlottko] used to threaten to take away my plants altogether. But at least I am now at home in this green world. I captured it—by storm and with devotion; for whatever you give yourself to with such intensity takes strong root in you.[1]

But the war was never far away. It loomed over wasp and watering-can indiscriminately; as soon as one was lulled by the ferocious microcosms of nature the scene was brutally changed to the clangour of men at war.

I had such a pang recently. In the courtyard where I walk army lorries often arrive, laden with haversacks or old tunics and shirts from the front; sometimes they are stained with blood. They are sent to the women's cells to be mended, and then go back to the army for use. The other day one of these lorries was drawn by a team of buffaloes instead of horses. I had never seen the creatures close at hand before. They are much more powerfully built than our oxen, with flattened heads, and horns strongly curved back so that their skulls are shaped something like a sheep's skull. They are black and have huge, soft eyes. The buffaloes are war booty from Rumania. The soldier-drivers said that it was very difficult to catch these animals who had always run wild, and still more difficult to break them in to harness. They had been unmercifully flogged—on the principle of 'vae victis'. There are about a hundred head in Breslau alone. They have been accustomed to the luxuriant Rumanian pastures and have here to put up with lean and scanty fodder. Unsparingly exploited, yoked to heavy loads, they are soon worked to death. The other day a lorry came laden with sacks, so overladen indeed that the buffaloes were unable to drag it across the threshold of the gate. The soldier-driver, a brute of a fellow, belaboured the poor beasts so savagely with the butt end of his whip that the wardress at the gate, indignant at the sight, asked him if he had no compassion for animals. 'No more than anyone has compassion for us men', he answered with an evil smile, and redoubled his blows. At length the buffaloes succeeded in drawing the load over the obstacle, but one of them was bleeding. You know their hide is proverbial for its thickness and toughness, but it had been torn. While the lorry was being unloaded the beasts, utterly exhausted, stood perfectly still. The one that was bleeding had an expression on its black face and in its soft black eyes like that of a weeping child— one that has been severely thrashed and does not know why, nor how to escape from the torment of ill-treatment. I stood in front of the team; the beast looked at me; the tears welled from my own eyes. The suffering of a dearly loved brother could hardly have moved me more profoundly than I was moved by my impotence in face of this mute agony. Far distant, lost for ever, were the green lush meadows of Rumania. How different there the light of the sun, the breath of the wind; how different there the song of the birds and the melodious call of the herdsman. Instead the hideous street, the foetid stable, the rank hay mingled with

[1] *Briefe an Freunde*, p. 93, to Hans Diefenbach, 30 March 1917.

mouldy straw, the strange and terrible men—blow upon blow, and blood running from gaping wounds. Poor wretch, I am as powerless, as dumb, as yourself; I am at one with you in my pain, my weakness, and my longing.

Meanwhile, the women prisoners were jostling one another as they busily unloaded the dray and carried the heavy sacks into the building. The driver, hands in pockets, was striding up and down the courtyard, smiling to himself as he whistled a popular air. I had a vision of all the splendour of war! . . .[1]

With flowers and plants Rosa still had the professional touch acquired from the studies in Zürich long ago. The equally intense comments on art—literature, music, painting—were those of a gifted amateur. But once again the reverberations of a solitary routine brought to the surface a more intense and systematic involvement with art. Rosa no longer saw or read, she re-absorbed and criticized and analysed, and fed off art like a plant off compost—herself and her friends, who were regaled by her feast. This, too, was part of the foundation of her new self-sufficiency.

As ever, Rosa had distinct preferences. Fulsomeness, excessive decoration, mere skill—indeed any excess—was repugnant to her. She was always attracted by simplicity precisely because social questions were essentially simple:

I have just finished Ricarda Huch's *Wallenstein* . . . in the end the portrayal comes to nought. No complete picture emerges from so much detail and decoration . . . I cannot help it, German thoroughness makes it impossible to create a delicate, living portrait of an age or a person. . . . She lacks, although she is a woman, the mental *finesse* which should have told her that the pursuit of every detail must ultimately tire and repel any sensitive person. . .

Rosa's interest in the Russian language—'the language of the future' —continued unashamed and undiminished. The choice for a translation fell on Vladimir Korolenko's autobiography *History of my Contemporary* (*Istoriya moego sovremennika*). Her correspondence with publishers and with Luise Kautsky clearly shows the desire to help fill a gap in the study of modern Russian writing. But the value of this work was social as well as literary. Her preface to the translation emphasized the link. It placed Korolenko in the majestic tradition of Russian literature— and although Rosa Luxemburg never set up as a literary critic by allocating marks of merit and demerit, she emphatically claimed a high place for him among living writers. In addition she analysed Korolenko's

---

[1] *Letters from Prison*, pp. 56–58. Whatever Sonia Liebknecht may have replied, she could not help feeling that Rosa's vicarious sufferings were much less than the more direct ones of her husband, and she unburdened herself feelingly to Mathilde Jacob about the difference in the circumstances of Rosa Luxemburg and her husband, Karl. See Ralph H. Lutz, 'Rosa Luxemburg's . . . letters', *Journal of Central European Affairs*, October 1963, Vol. XXIII, No. 3, p. 310.

[2] *Briefe an Freunde*, pp. 102–3.

writings in the context of social history. Here her judgements were un-inhibited. Writers like Tolstoy and Korolenko himself, who were aware of what *was* and in what way it was changing, earned her approval over those who ran away from social realities into introspective and spiritual absorptions. Within the chosen group of socially conscious writers, Rosa particularly contrasted Gorky and Korolenko. The latter was still interested in the countryside, in peasants, while Gorky,

the devoted follower of German scientific socialism, was already preoccupied with the town labourer, and his shadow, the Lumpenproletariat ... Korolenko, like Turgenev—whom he so highly esteemed—had a thoroughly lyrical and receptive nature, he was a man of mood; Gorky, on the other hand, followed the tradition of Dostoievsky—a man with a thoroughly dramatic conception, bulging with energy, bursting for action— ... if drama is the poetry of action, then [Korolenko's writings were] only half poetry but wholly truth, like everything that is part of life.[1]

Korolenko combined an unassuming literary style—reportage but deeply felt—with an irrevocable attachment to society around him. These virtues are mirrored in her introduction. There were no blaring assertions, none of the catchwords of Marxism, only joy at the continu-ous social protest yet individually expressed. Rosa gave a brief biography of Korolenko and the reader feels with her the unbearable necessity of protest and action rather than any rationalized thesis of opposition. Korolenko—and she herself—were no longer dealing with Russians, Poles, or Jews, but with people.

It is one of the necessities of modern society that human society, whenever it gets a bit uncomfortable for one reason or another, should immediately find a scapegoat in members of another nation, or race, or religion, or colour; having stilled its bad temper on them it returns refreshed to its own routine. And it is natural that the only suitable scapegoats are always economically, historically, and socially backward nationalities.[2]

Enlarged by Rosa's growing emphasis on wholeness, protest no longer consisted in *doing* but demanded *being*; individual gestures of protest lost their significance and perhaps did more harm than good. 'Was not the obstinate *eppur si muove*—Galileo's pointless and empty gesture—without any practical result other than the revenge of the Holy Office ... if indeed it ever took place at all.'[3] But what then of Liebknecht? He too

---

[1] *Die Geschichte meines Zeitenossen*, Berlin 1919–20, p. 50 (Introduction).
[2] Ibid., p. 44 (Introduction).
[3] Ibid., p. 31. This contemptuous dismissal of Galileo, for hundreds of years a symbol of the intellectual revolt against darkness and obscurantism—scientific truth against religious dogma—had no echo at the time, but was both prophetic and fascinating. Modern research (in the West, not in the East) has exposed Galileo as the intransigent dogmatist against a flexible, political, above all responsible church forced to take action, not against the inroads of modern science but the irresponsible disturber of the peace. (See George de Santillana,

was undergoing his enlargement in prison, though through a process of violent oscillation rather than Rosa's direct and well-proportioned growth. How could anyone imagine that either of these two could ever again fit into the personal and political limits of a pre-war SPD?

The translation of Korolenko and her economic writings in prison were a self-imposed discipline. She still pressed hard against the limits of her existence. Occasional visits and letters were the only form of communication with the living world outside. But she was determined to live—perhaps more fully than she had ever lived before; and her friends were turned into delegates, pressed and moulded to live her life for her. Whether encouraging others to be brave and strong; whether insisting on a new closeness with Luise Kautsky or Marta Rosenbaum through an arrangement of symbols on paper which she had probably never sought in the intimacy of speech; whether binding a disciple like Hans Diefenbach close to her by perpetually displaying her scintillating personality for his benefit—it was her life and not theirs that was at stake. The choice of vehicles was so limited—literature, politics, the instant, timeless speck of life minutely observed and captured; broad-based judgements alternating with the ruthlessly critical penetrations of a needle—they follow on each other's heels in a bewildering and complex procession. The present and the past became welded into one flexible whole—where most other prisoners would choose to moan about the contrast. Some minute and fleeting vision in the prison yard was captured, made to conjure up a shared experience of the past. Yet such was Rosa's skill that she breathed life into her correspondents—so that they took on new and sharper dimensions. Luise Kautsky, much the same age as Rosa, needed only a hint, a snap of the finger, to drop everything and join Rosa in spirit at Wronke. In return Rosa could be cold, even brutal; the reader knows or feels that Luise left more of herself in pawn to her friend than she received in return, for friendship is never equal, or for that matter just. In a passage which Luise Kautsky omitted from her edition of Rosa's letters, the latter ironically chided Luise for her sentimental refusal to look the situation in the face and honestly accept her emotional attachment to another man.[1]

'Phases of the Conflict between Totalitarianism and Science' in Carl J. Friedrich (ed.), *Totalitarianism*, Cambridge (Mass.) 1954, pp. 244–62, and his book *The Crime of Galileo*.) It is surprising that the analogy between Galileo and, say, Pasternak from the Soviet point of view as a conflict between spontaneity and discipline has never struck any Soviet theorists. And what price Rosa Luxemburg's spontaneity in view of her dismissal of Galileo's 'pointless and empty gesture'?

[1] This passage occurs in letter No. 93 dated 19 December 1917. All the originals of Rosa's letters to the Kautskys are at IISH. Since it was Luise Kautsky's special wish that this particular aspect of her life should not be made public, I have confined myself to this comment.

This passage is revealing because it indicates a facet of Rosa's character which none of her biographers has mentioned—and of which perhaps only Luise Kautsky was aware. Rosa Luxemburg was not interested in any high-principled campaign for women's rights—unlike her friend Clara Zetkin.[1] Like anti-Semitism, the inferior status of women was a social feature which would be eliminated only by the advent of Socialism; in the meantime there was no point in making any special issue of it. But disinterest in public did not mean private indifference. Since the break-up of her own 'marriage' to Leo Jogiches in 1907, Rosa had undertaken a campaign for the possession of the souls of her women friends, especially against those husbands who were also her political opponents. This subtle enticement had been carried out with Rosa's usual blend of intellect and emotion; a war on two fronts. From prison the campaign moved into high gear.

The same increase of pace is clear from the letters to Hans Diefenbach. This became a very special friendship, and in her letters to the young army doctor during the war Rosa unleashed a many-splendoured offensive, with an emotional skill which she never surpassed. Even today one can still feel her tentacles reaching out from prison like those of a passionate and demanding octopus. Nowhere is the mixture of emotion, ethics, politics, and aesthetics more skilfully and tidily woven; past, present, and future more dialectically fused, than in these outpourings coming apparently straight from the heart. From the descriptions of contemporaries and from the few letters of his that remain, we know Diefenbach to have been a reserved, somewhat stiff young man who had difficulty in keeping his end up among all his highly verbal and incisive friends.[2] The slightly cannibalistic streak in Rosa's friendships caused her to hammer unmercifully at Diefenbach's dilettantism: 'Hänschen regrettably has more talent than knowledge . . .', she told him, ' . . . and if your temperament is a little too much like over-refined white flour [*semmelblond*] and your perpetually cool hands irritate me at times, I still say: "Blessed are those without temperament as long as this lack of temperament means that they will never trade on the happiness or peace of other people." ' And to his sister she wrote after his death:

His weaknesses—naturally he also had these—were those of a child not equipped for life's realities, for the struggle and for the inevitable brutalities; he was always slightly afraid of life. I always feared that he might remain an everlasting dilettante, buffeted by all the storms of life; I tried as far as I could to apply gentle pressure on him so that he might eventually take root in life after all.[3]

---

[1] One of Clara Zetkin's favourite themes was a quotation from Engels (*Ursprung der Familie* . . .): '*He* is the bourgeois in the family, the woman represents the proletariat.' See for instance Clara Zektin, *Ausgewählte Reden und Schriften*, Berlin 1957, Vol. I, p. 95.

[2] See the brief sketch by Benedikt Kautsky, the son of Karl and Luise, in *Briefe an Freunde*, pp. 16–17.

[3] *Briefe an Freunde*, pp. 77, 78, 134.

What effect did these marvellous letters have on their recipients? In Diefenbach's case we do not know. She always addressed him as 'Sie'—the polite form—but this was the only restraint. For the rest, the letters have an intensely provocative, erotic quality, almost daring this restrained young man to be shocked and to protest. Yet she could not have gone on in this vein if there had not been some response. 'Good God, if I sense in the slightest that somebody doesn't like me, my very thoughts flee from his presence like those of a scared bird; for me even to look him in the face again seems too much.'[1] Diefenbach's devotion to his volatile and fascinating friend was of long standing, though perhaps tinged with hopelessness, after all the years of Rosa wilfully blowing hot and cold. Then, in 1914, the friendship was suddenly and mysteriously promoted. With Konstantin Zetkin gone and the circle of friends narrowed by political defection, who but the faithful, unromantic, but transparently decent and fastidious Hans Diefenbach, so often the object of amused pity and derision, should now advance to the grail of her close affection, surrounded by a glow of virtue? The need for a single, supreme confidant was greater than ever in the impersonal routine of Wronke fortress. Rosa's friends were all delighted; the marriage of scarlet and alabaster, so suitable for both, became their fond hope for the conclusion of the war.[2] But there was also nothing naïve about Diefenbach's affection for Rosa Luxemburg. He may not have realized the circumstances of his own promotion, but he did know Rosa's weaknesses as well as her great strengths. With slightly mocking affection he provided for Rosa in his will—a sum of money to be held in strict trust, lest among other things she should spend it 'politically'. 'The money must be managed by some responsible person—e.g. my sister—and the beneficiary shall get the interest annually until the date of her death. I make this disposition because my excellent friend may not prove as great a genius in her personal economy as in her understanding of the economics of a whole society.'[3] Despite her great grief, Rosa was annoyed rather than flattered when this came out after his death in action in 1917.[4]

Many of Rosa's letters from prison were published as an act of piety. They were meant to show that the red revolutionary, the enthusiastic propagandist of violence and destruction, was in fact a highly sensitive, easily hurt, kindly woman who suffered with every frozen wasp and had a deep love of life and of living creatures. What Luise Kautsky

[1] *Briefe an Freunde*, p. 77.
[2] Reported by Blumenburg. But Luise Kautsky's statement that the marriage was an 'understood thing' is, I am sure, an exaggeration—at least as far as Rosa was concerned. Cf. above, p. 251, note 1.
[3] *Gedenkbuch*, p. 53.
[4] Letter to Luise Kautsky, dated 29 May 1918, in *International Review of Social History*, 1963, Vol. VIII, Part 1, pp. 106–7.

and her son Benedikt have done is to say to us: choose—between the public and the private Rosa; at least observe the contrast between the two. Rosa herself would probably have laughed at this attempt and poured scorn on such sentimentality. For what is implied is that we must take these letters as evidence of another Rosa, a spontaneous and much more human Rosa, to set against the intensely political being of her public writings. The error is to see her political writings as artefacts, the letters as natural, bursting through in a torrent of temperament. In fact, there was nothing spontaneous about these letters at all. They were written quickly, but writing them was as disciplined and deliberate an activity as any of her political work. Phrases, thoughts, run through them like sudden inspirations—but they are raw material, bait, not ends in themselves. Every syllable serves a purpose. The real, the only, spontaneity of which Rosa was ever capable was—silence. When she was really moved she could not communicate at all. But silence cannot be quoted or recorded and so we must rely on her own occasional references to it. Thus after the death of her father Rosa wrote to Minna Kautsky: 'This blow shook me so deeply that I could not communicate for many months either by letter or word of mouth.'[1] And after one of the worst blows of her life, the death of her devoted Hans Diefenbach: 'I have just received word that Hans has fallen. For the moment I am unable to write more. Brevity and frankness are the most merciful things, just as with a difficult operation. I am unable to find words.'[2] This was still the same woman who years before had shyly written of her own compulsive need for self-communion, and wondered if there was something peculiar about her on account of it—as though it were some terrible evidence of failure.[3]

Last but not least, there was the imperceptible re-creation of *Spartakus* —quite apart from its political purposes—as an ideal peer group, very much like that comfortable if highly sprung sociological mattress—the original SDKPiL.

She swore that after the war, whatever happened, she would not go back to the boredom and bureaucratic mincing-machine of the pre-war party—'no more meetings, no more conventicles. Where great things are in the making, where the wind roars about the ears, that's where I'll be in the thick of it, but not the daily treadmill.'[4] In the meantime Rosa would deal only with real political 'friends'—friends almost in the English sense of being like-minded; a selection made by circumstances and by herself: no more need for reservations, for tact, for all those political concessions which had disfigured the sociology of the old

---

[1] 30 December 1900. IISH Archives, now printed ibid., p. 97.
[2] *Letters to Karl and Luise Kautsky*, p. 204, 10 and 15 November 1917.
[3] Seidel letters, p. 70.
[4] Rosa Luxemburg to Clara Zetkin, 1 July 1917, photocopy IML (B), NL5iii-A/14.

SPD. The new peer group mustered for Franz Mehring's 70th birthday. 'We honoured the old man with speeches, all serious and suitable to the occasion. Quite different from that Jamboree with Bebel, do you remember?'[1] A peer group imposes personal responsibilities. Even from prison Rosa encouraged the old man with all the means at her disposal, for every member of that small band was immensely valuable.

How wrong you are to think that your bad mood has anything to do with age. What better evidence of youthfulness than your indestructible pleasure in your work, in fighting and laughing, the way you still set about it every day [*Sie noch jeden Tag in die Pfanne hauen*]. You cannot imagine to what extent the example of your wonderful capacity for work, the thought of your mental flexibility and even the hope of earning your approval, egg me on. How I look forward to sitting again in your comfortable study at the small table to talk with you and laugh with you.[2]

Both Mehring and Clara Zetkin spent some time in custody during the war and both were in very poor health. Rosa organized a complete almoner's service for Clara Zetkin's benefit, nagging her friends to call on her or at least to keep writing; Rosa was not above berating Hans Diefenbach for visiting Stuttgart without making a point of calling on Clara Zetkin.[3] The almoner-in-chief was none other than Mathilde Jacob, Rosa's secretary. Her war-time letters to Clara Zetkin are preserved, and while they contain little of political interest—Mathilde Jacob was not a very political person but *was* devoted to Rosa—they do reflect the stream of instructions, queries, and suggestions which emanated from Wronke and Breslau for the better preservation of Clara Zetkin. The latter was a hypersensitive, often obstinate woman who had to be coaxed—and this, under precise instruction from Rosa, larded with concrete tokens of regard like books and flowers, was Mathilde's job.[4]

It is noticeable that Rosa's concern was largely with the older generation, with the small group of intellectuals who had broken loose with such agony after 4 August 1914. There are only a few references to younger sympathizers, the new shock troops of radicalism, later to dominate the KPD until many of them, too, were flung off the dizzy turntable of Bolshevization. To this extent Rosa was anchored in the

---

[1] Rosa Luxemburg to Clara Zetkin, 9 March 1916; File 209, No. 494, IML (M).

[2] Ibid., File 201, No. 858, IML (M).

[3] *Briefe an Freunde*, p. 102.

[4] The letters are in IML (M). Many of Mathilde Jacob's other letters are preserved in the Hoover Institution, Stanford University, as are some 125 letters from Rosa Luxemburg to Mathilde Jacob from 10 July 1916 to 8 November 1918. This collection is discussed, unfortunately in a very haphazard and unsystematic way, by Ralph H. Lutz in *Journal of Central European Affairs*, Vol. XXIII, No. 3, October 1963, pp. 303–12. Although this article contains many errors of fact, one must presume that its quotations and direct references from Mathilde Jacob's letters are reliable.

Second International; in her personal relations she looked backwards to the past rather than to the future. Only when a different social organization was found to be required in order to make effective an old philosophy did the new men begin to come into their own.

Not that the work of care and protection all went one way. A determined effort was made to cushion Rosa Luxemburg from the exigencies of prison—and the only reason this remained unsung was that its inspirer and director was Leo Jogiches, furtive as ever. Rosa had always suffered from a delicate stomach, and now more than ever; the collection of rice to supply her with the right diet was no easy task in blockaded, war-time Germany. Rosi Wolffstein, Rosa's ex-student, had helped significantly in this effort, and was summoned to a secret meeting with the redoubtable Dr. Krystałowicz (Leo Jogiches) at a station café to receive his formal thanks on Rosa's behalf.[1] Indeed, Jogiches now devoted himself to Rosa in the most touching way, thus opening up the third and last period of peace in their long and often stormy relationship.

The February revolution in Russia was the first crack in the dishearteningly monolithic pursuit of imperialist war. But no one dreamt that the events in Petrograd would eventually end Russia's participation in the alliance against Germany. On the contrary, a more popular government was expected to release national energy into more effective prosecution of the war. No one quite knew what to make of the events— whether they were a good or bad omen for Germany, or for the Socialists for that matter. Rosa Luxemburg's first reaction was personal. 'So many old friends, locked up for years in Moscow, Petersburg, Orel or Riga, now walking about free! How much easier that makes my own incarceration. It is a strange change of roles, isn't it? But I am satisfied and don't begrudge them their freedom, even though it means *my* chances have got so much the worse.'[2] In July 1917, and again the next year, the question arose as to whether Rosa might claim Russian citizenship and benefit from deportation, like Marchlewski. Another alternative was a special exchange of distinguished revolutionaries; such a move was at one time envisaged for Karl Liebknecht. Rosa was undecided; 'perhaps, maybe—a difficult question'. In the end she declined. What mattered was the inevitable German revolution, and she wanted to be on hand for it—even if it meant longer imprisonment meanwhile.[3]

For her information about events in Russia she necessarily depended on the newspapers, and the newspapers were cautious. Right from the start the German government had worked out precise directions to the

---

[1] This story was told to the author by Frau Frölich herself.

[2] *Briefe an Freunde*, pp. 87–88, 27 May 1917.

[3] Rosa Luxemburg to Mathilde Jacob, 29 July 1917, photocopy IML (B), NL2 III-A/16, p. 20.

press about its reporting of the events in Russia. No discussion of the new constitutional forms which had emerged from the Russian revolution was permitted, since 'they only indicate how one should proceed here in case of an upheaval'. Even after the October revolution, which was clearly to Germany's advantage, the German authorities would only permit such comments on the Soviet state as served as a frightening example; 'all that explains or praises the proceedings of the revolutionaries in Russia must be suppressed'.[1]

Rosa's first official reaction in the *Spartakus* letter of April 1917 was also cautious.[2] The analysis was historical, backward-looking—a sure sign of uncertainty. All that could be done was to hark back to the events of 1905–1906. Almost syllabically the next objectives are spelled out: democratic republic, eight-hour day, confiscation of large landed properties; above all, an end to the imperialist war. Peace was just the first of several demands that must be put forward, less in the hope of achieving them than as a means of galvanizing working-class action. This was the old idea of a programme, not as a political expression of wants but as a process of political stimulation. It is important to understand this if the reaction of *Spartakus* to the unexpected conclusion of peace by the Bolsheviks less than a year later is to make sense. The demand for peace was a weapon, not something which one could actually hope to achieve.

The second part of the article was a reckoning with the claim of the German government and its SPD supporters that the war against Russia was a war of liberation from Tsarist absolutism.

Events in Russia have also faced the German proletariat with a vital question of honour. . . . Once the Russian proletariat has burst the solidarity of the home front through open revolution, the German proletariat unashamedly stabs it in the back by continuing to support the war. From now on the German troops in the East do not fight against Tsarism any longer, but against the revolution; as soon as the Russian proletariat comes out openly for peace the German proletariat by remaining silent will become the accomplice to an open betrayal of its Russian brethren—if it remains silent. Russia has liberated herself, but who will liberate Germany from military dictatorship, from *Junker* reaction, from the imperialist slaughter?[3]

In the next *Spartakus* letter of May 1917 there were two lengthy articles by Rosa Luxemburg.[4] There had been time to read and think.

[1] *Revolutionäre Ereignisse und Probleme in Deutschland während der Periode der grossen sozialistischen Oktoberrevolution 1917–18*, Berlin (East) 1957, p. 282, quoting a minute from the Ministry of the Interior.

[2] 'Die Revolution in Russland', *Spartakusbriefe*, pp. 302–5. The attribution to Rosa Luxemburg is mine.

[3] Ibid., p. 305.

[4] 'Der alte Maulwurf' (The Old Mole), *Spartakusbriefe*, pp. 322–9; 'Zwei Osterbotschaften' (Two Easter Messages), ibid., pp. 347–51.

Preoccupation with the past was pushed aside in favour of a more rigorous examination of the present.

In the stuffy atmosphere of Europe, in which everything has been effectively stifled for three years, a window has at last been torn open, and a fresh and lively current of air is blowing in. . . . But even with the greatest heroism the proletariat of a single country cannot break the stranglehold [of the world war] by itself. Thus the Russian revolution inevitably grows into an international problem. The Russian workers' striving for peace comes into the strongest conflict not only with their own middle class but with that of England, France, and Italy. . . . As for the German bourgeoisie . . . it only wants to use the Russian proletariat to get itself out of a war on two fronts, seeing how unfavourable the strategic situtation is abroad and how poor the supply position at home. This is the same machination by German imperialism to make use of the Russian revolution for its own self-interested purposes as that attempted by the allied powers, only in the opposite way. The western powers want to harness the bourgeois liberal tendency of the revolution in order to . . . defeat their German competitors. The German imperialists want to use the proletarian tendencies of the revolution to avoid a military defeat—and why not, gentlemen? German Social Democracy has served so faithfully and long in dressing up mass slaughter as 'liberation' from Russian Tsarism; now the Russian Social Democrats are called upon to assist by helping the 'liberator' out of his unhappy involvement in an unsuccessful war.[1]

Scheidemann's role as a go-between for Russia and Germany had been engineered by Parvus's string-pulling behind the scenes, with the blessing of the German Foreign Office. Some of this was known to *Spartakus* though they did not yet realize the full purpose of the originators of the plan. Rosa sensed that Ebert's and Scheidemann's initiative in Copenhagen was part of an official flirtation with Russian revolutionaries *against* the Russian liberals who had declared their support for the war. She was certain that such a mission 'could only get a kick in the pants from Russian Socialists of all shades', but she was wrong. Parvus short-circuited the SPD at this stage and got the German authorities to deal with Lenin direct, instead of with the Workers' and Soldiers' Soviet in Petrograd.[2]

Having all too correctly analysed the interests of the belligerent governments and their supporters, Rosa turned once more to the interests of the Russian and German working classes. In her view it was now possible at last to talk of a real war of liberation, the kind of defensive struggle she had indicated in the *Juniusbrochüre*.

The outbreak of the revolution and the powerful position of the proletariat as a result have changed the [character of] imperialist war in Russia to something akin to that claimed in the propaganda of the ruling classes in all countries: a war

---

[1] Ibid., pp. 323–5.
[2] Philipp Scheidemann, *Memoiren eines Sozialdemokraten*, Vol. I, pp. 420–7.

of defence. The liberals, with their dreams of a Russian Constantinople, have had their plans stuffed down their throats; the solution of a patriotic war of defence has suddenly become reality. The Russian proletariat, however, can only end the war and make peace in good conscience when their work—the achievements of the revolution and its unhampered progress—is assured. The Russian workers are today the only ones who *really* defend freedom, progress and democracy.[1]

Already the analysis diverged sharply from that of Lenin. Looking outwards from Russia, it was the same old imperialist war, now carried on by Kerensky and Chkheidze instead of Nicholas and his ministers—to be combated by exactly the same means; any means, including German help. Looking out from Germany, however, the Russian revolution had achieved something worth defending against the strong and unrepentant German reaction, which might want peace with Russia for tactical reasons, but in the long run would want even more to destroy the revolution. This in essence was to be the *Spartakus* position for the next eighteen months. They recognized the need for peace as the only way to open up further revolutionary horizons, but not a peace which left imperial Germany triumphant. The *x* in the equation was the German revolution.

Even before the pact between Lenin and Trotsky, in which the one accepted Bolshevik organization and the other armed insurrection as the motor of the 'permanent' revolution, Rosa Luxemburg in her German jail had announced the complete dependence of the Russian revolution on revolutions elsewhere. To succeed, the revolution in Russia had to spark off revolutionary outbreaks—above all in Germany. This was the key. Scheidemann's negotiations for a possible peace between the Russian revolution and German imperialism were only mentioned in order to show them as grotesque absurdities. Rosa knew nothing of the assiduous negotiations between Parvus, Karl Moor, and the German Foreign Office, of the impending journey of Lenin and his entourage through Germany in a sealed train provided by the German government. She believed such eventualities to be not only undesirable but impossible. Her task and that of her friends now lay in bringing about a revolutionary outbreak in Germany. Every effort of *Spartakus* from now on was directed to achieving this aim. If only the masses could be awakened, and made to see their own interest! To that end she now directed her efforts, with an increasingly bitter and sarcastic tone as her words scattered like useless autumn leaves among passers-by preoccupied with other worries than saving the Russian revolution.

Spartakus openly greeted the events of February and propagated them as widely as possible in Germany. Certainly *Spartakus* articles

[1] *Spartakusbriefe*, pp. 326–7.

written by other comrades followed Rosa Luxemburg's analysis very closely. In August 1917 the unknown author of an article entitled 'Burning questions of the time' foresaw in Russia the emergence of a dictatorship of the proletariat, but added: 'Here begins the fatal destiny of the Russian revolution. The dictatorship of the proletariat in Russia is destined to suffer a desperate defeat compared to which the fate of the Paris Commune was child's play—unless the international proletarian revolution gives it support in good time.'[1]

Here also are to be found the first traces of that profound pessimism for the short term which characterized Rosa's thinking about the Russian, and later the German, revolutions. It was not an easy point to make in public, especially while the war was on. As early as April 1917 Rosa wrote to Marta Rosenbaum:

Of course the marvels in Russia are like a new lease of life for me. They are a saving grace [heilsbotschaft] for all of us. I only fear that you all do not appreciate them enough, do not recognize sufficiently that it is our own cause which is winning there. It *must* and *will* have a salutary effect on the whole world, it must radiate outwards into the whole of Europe; I am absolutely certain that it will bring a new epoch and that the war cannot last long.[2]

But this enthusiasm was for a distant future. An epoch was a long-term concept; as soon as her friends began to cast favourable horoscopes for the immediate political scene Rosa blew cold at once: 'We must not count on permanent success [in Russia], though in any case even the attempt to seize power is already a slap in the face for our Social Democrats and the whole miserable International.'[3] And to Luise Kautsky she predicted even more baldly that 'of course, the Bolsheviks will never be able to maintain themselves'.[4] Once more she reflected and also created *Spartakus* opinion—though both Franz Mehring and Clara Zetkin were to prove more optimistic after the events of October.[5]

Neither the circumstances of the October revolution nor the implications of Lenin's policy of peace and land distribution to the peasants were clear to anyone in Germany—except perhaps to the German government. The Left, particularly the leaders in prison, were unable to distinguish the inevitable from the peculiar, the historical from the 'man-made', in the events in Russia. That was why they could not see

---

[1] *Spartakusbriefe*, p. 356. According to the style of this article, it could well be by Leo Jogiches.

[2] *Briefe an Freunde*, p. 157.

[3] *Briefe an Freunde*, pp. 160–1. The East German historian, Leo Stern, summarizing the reaction of the German Left to the outbreak of the revolution in Russia, gives the cheerful quotation, but not the pessimistic one (*Der Einfluss der grossen Oktoberrevolution* p. 79).

[4] *Letters to Karl and Luise Kautsky*, p. 207.

[5] See below, pp. 425, 428.

the factors making for Bolshevik survival. Their disapproval of these factors once they knew them, and their ability to pass judgement on them—which the Bolsheviks later questioned precisely as being ill-informed—was, as we shall see, quite a different matter.

In July 1917 the wheels of the German security administration ground out Rosa's transfer from the fortress in Wronke to the town prison of Breslau. This was much closer confinement, in terms of physical space as well as visits and facilities. There is no evidence that the transfer was a punishment for any breach of discipline or that the smuggling of illegal material through Mathilde Jacob and Marta Rosenbaum was suspected.

Here I am leading the existence of a proper convict, i.e. day and night they lock me into my cell and all I can see outside is the men's prison ... I limit my presence [in the yard where I can see all the other prisoners running about] to the minimum prescribed by the doctor for health reasons and during my walks I look around as little as possible. The difference from Wronke is in every respect a sharp one, though this is not a complaint but merely an explanation if for the time being I do not write letters woven out of the scent of roses, the azure colour of the sky and the wisps of cloud to which you have hitherto been accustomed. . . .[1]

In addition, Rosa's health had worsened again. 'My stomach has been rebelling strongly for several weeks and I actually had to spend part of the time in bed; even now I exist mainly on warm bandages and very thin soup. The cause is uncertain, probably nervous reaction to the sudden worsening of my general circumstances.'[2]

From the end of 1917 onwards Rosa Luxemburg's influence on the tactics and policy of *Spartakus* undoubtedly suffered a decline. Various factors contributed to this, partly on Rosa's side, partly arising out of the situation. With her transfer to Breslau she was more cut off, her state of mind necessarily became more self-absorbed. The *Spartakus* letters had largely been her inspiration and effort; without her frequent contributions they lost much of their lustre. Moreover, her immediate circle of political friends, for whom she had acted as the fountain-head of strategy as well as tactics, began to lose its grip on events. Leo Jogiches was arrested on 24 March 1918; the authorities knew that with his arrest they had captured the main organizer of *Spartakus* activities as well as the willing vehicle of Rosa Luxemburg's ideas.[3] This left Franz Mehring, now seventy years old, Ernst Meyer and Paul Levi in charge. More important still, the development of the opposition in Germany

---

[1] *Briefe an Freunde*, pp. 126–7.   [2] Ibid., p. 127.
[3] *Archivalische Forschungen*, 4/III, p. 1282. See also *Dokumente und Materialien*, Vol. II, p. 131.

was temporarily moving against *Spartakist* influence. There were two waves of strikes, one in April 1917, another far bigger in January 1918—the first to have distinctly political overtones. But although these events had full *Spartakus* support with handbills and appeals, they were not under its direction nor had *Spartakus* exercised any significant influence on them.[1] Out of these strikes, and leading them, there emerged an elusive organization of workers based on the larger factories of Berlin, and with it the first traces of workers' councils. In spite of arrests and the military draft of thousands of restive workers, the organization remained more or less intact throughout the war and found its political expression in the Revolutionary Shop Stewards (*Revolutionäre Obleute*) who were to play such a significant role in the period from November 1918 to March 1919.

Spartakus was following rather than making events in Germany from the end of 1917 onwards. The intellectuals, who provided *Spartakus* with its sophisticated programme and the necessary Marxist analysis of the situation, now had no significant function to fulfil, especially not from prison. Karl Liebknecht and Rosa Luxemburg were too honest to claim for themselves a leading role which at the time they did not play; Liebknecht, whose correspondence was very restricted by prison regulations, merely noted down a continual commentary on events, while Rosa's letters gave no more than fleeting, desperate references. There was remoteness, self-absorption; her remaining efforts were concentrated on the one event on which she could speak with unchallenged authority —the Russian revolution.

Among the first public commentators on the Bolshevik victory at the beginning of November 1917 Rosa Luxemburg was noticeably absent. This may have been due to physical difficulties. The most enthusiastic support came from Radek's old friends in Bremen, and from Clara Zetkin.[2] Both these articles, while stressing the dangers and difficulties, pledged immediate and complete support for the Bolsheviks. But in private Rosa Luxemburg asked Luise Kautsky on 24 November:

Are you happy about the Russians? Of course, they will not be able to maintain themselves in this witches' Sabbath, not because statistics show economic development in Russia to be too backward as your clever husband has figured out, but because Social Democracy in the highly developed West consists of miserable and wretched cowards who will look quietly on and let the Russians bleed to death. But such an end is better than 'living on for the fatherland'; it is an act of historical significance whose traces will not have disappeared even after

[1] For summary and sources of this evidence, see E. Kolb, *Die Arbeiterräte in der deutschen Innenpolitik, 1918–19*, Düsseldorf 1962, p. 49.

[2] *Arbeiterpolitik*, No. 46, 14 November 1917. See also Clara Zetkin in the women's supplement of *LV*, 30 November 1917.

many ages have passed. I expect great things to come in the next few years, but how I wish that I did not have to admire world history only through the bars of my cage.[1]

To Mathilde Wurm she had written a week earlier: 'My heart is heavy for the Russians, I don't expect the continued victory of the Leninists, but still—such an end is better than "living on for the fatherland".'[2]

By the middle of November the impending peace negotiations with the Bolsheviks had been written up in the German press and Rosa's private comments became much more incisive.

Yes, the Bolsheviks; of course they don't please me either with their fanatical determination to make peace at any price [*Friedensfanatizismus*] but after all *they* are not to blame. They are in a cleft stick and have only the choice between two sets of troubles, and are choosing the lesser. *Others* are responsible for the fact that the devil is the beneficiary of the Russian revolution. . . . Consequently, let us first sweep before our own doors. On the whole the events there are glorious and will have immeasurable results.[3]

Doubts about the wisdom of a Russian revolutionary peace with German imperialism were expressed in the first public *Spartakus* comment on the events of October. A curious reversal in the roles of USPD and *Spartakus* had taken place. The former now hailed the prospect of negotiations and attempted to use the events in Russia for bringing pressure on the German government in the direction of Kautsky's old scheme for a 'just' peace without annexations.[4] They had thus inherited *Spartakus*'s slogan of peace at any price, first and foremost, if there was to be anything left of the proletariat. *Spartakus*, on the other hand, now saw in the conclusion of peace with Russia nothing but benefit for German imperialism and its wish to destroy the Russian revolution. The article 'Historical Responsibility' in the *Spartakus* letter of January 1918 was sour and unhappy in tone; the anonymous author could see no good from any of the probable alternatives in the near future. Now that an armistice had been concluded, a separate peace treaty between Germany and Russia was only a matter of time.

[1] *Letters to Karl and Luise Kautsky*, p. 207. This letter was written almost immediately after the death of Hans Diefenbach, during a period when Rosa was emotionally handicapped in her ability to write.

[2] *Briefe an Freunde*, p. 55, 15 November 1917. Once more the partially identical phraseology of these two letters is an interesting example of Rosa's careful 'rationing' of words and feelings, and incidental evidence that her letters were deliberate, not spontaneous, creations. The contemptuous reference to 'living on for the fatherland' [instead of dying] is based on Heinrich Heine's sarcastic portrait of the heroically posturing but perpetually surviving Polish revolutionary émigrés of his day.

[3] *Letters to Karl and Luise Kautsky*, pp. 214–15, 19 December 1917.

[4] *LV*, 12 November 1917.

It is psychologically understandable that the Bolsheviks should see a prestige success in that most important question of peace and should present themselves as successful to the Russian people. But a second look shows the Bolsheviks in another light. The immediate effect of the armistice in the East will merely be that German troops will be moved from there to the West. . . . Already the last bloody German advances in Flanders and in the South, the new 'marvellous' successes in Italy, are the direct results of Bolshevik victory in Petersburg . . . the mask of virtue and restraint which was forced on German imperialism by its precarious military situation up till now will be thrown into the lap of the Scheidemanns. With the help of God—who is undoubtedly on the side of the big battalions—a 'German peace' will be dictated. . . . This is how the situation really is and the Bolsheviks are only deceiving themselves and others if they hear the melody of peace on earth. . . . The last laugh about the Russian revolution has hitherto been exclusively enjoyed by Hindenburg and the German nationalists.[1]

January 1918—the lowest ebb of confidence and hope. The unknown Jeremiah could not even offer any good advice, for every avenue of progress was blocked. In fact the article has all the makings of an epitaph.

The German workers continue to watch the spectacle good-naturedly, continue to be mere spectators, and so Soviet rule in Russia cannot find a fate different from the Paris Commune. This connection [between Germany and Russia] is already visible in the deterioration of Bolshevik policy. Only the desperate search for some sign of proletarian action in Germany can for instance explain— even if it does not excuse—the fact that the Bolsheviks even for one moment allowed themselves to carry on negotiations with the German official Socialists. Their negotiations with Hindenburg and Hertling [the new German Chancellor] may in their eyes be nothing but sad necessity which merely illuminates the evil German circumstances, but at least they do not cast any reflection on those in power in St. Petersburg. The fact that they find it necessary to spread revolution into the German masses through such dirty channels as Parvus-Scheidemann proves that they too suffer from a lack of principle [*zerfahrene Zweideutigkeit*], which is completely at variance with their usual severe morality and intolerance of compromise.[2]

---

[1] *Spartakusbriefe*, pp. 406–9.

[2] *Spartakusbriefe*, pp. 415–16. I do not feel able to identify the author of this depressing article with any confidence. The flat and uncompromising despair does not conjure up Rosa Luxemburg at all. On the other hand the long discussion of Polish and Lithuanian self-determination makes the authorship of Leo Jogiches at least possible.

The reference to Parvus and Scheidemann concerns the Social Democrat leaders' visit to Stockholm in December 1917 at Parvus's request, to negotiate a possible peace with the Russians. This visit took place with the knowledge and approval of the German authorities, who wanted to put out an unofficial feeler to the Soviet government to find out its terms. Parvus had been in financial and political contact with the Bolshevik Bureau in Stockholm since the summer. The attempt failed; the Russians in the end would not deal with the SPD, while the SPD executive were not prepared to carry out the Russian wishes for real peace agitation at home. See Philipp Scheidemann, *Memoiren eines Sozialdemokraten*, Vol. II, pp. 123 ff.

It was the severest public criticism of the Bolsheviks ever to be uttered by the German Left—typical of the profound pessimism and the deep self-hatred of this black period.

After the conclusion of the peace of Brest-Litovsk in March 1918, public comment by *Spartakus* surprisingly became more favourable again. Lenin had gone to great trouble to explain and excuse the separate peace; he felt, quite correctly, that it would certainly be misunderstood and resented in Germany. It was, he declared, to the accompaniment of stormy applause, 'the only way out for the survival of the efforts of the proletariat and the poor peasants . . . however hard the conditions it has imposed'. In return he excused the inaction of the German working class: was it perhaps a veiled form of moral bargain? 'It is unjust to accuse the German workers of not making a revolution . . . things don't go like that. Revolutions cannot be made to order . . . they ripen as part of the historical development. . . .'[1] And, in any case, 'the [German] working masses will understand, will say: "the Bolsheviks have acted correctly".'[2]

Apart from the emotional enthusiasm of Clara Zetkin and the concurrence of the small Bremen group, historical justification of the Bolsheviks was chiefly provided by Franz Mehring. Already at the end of 1917 he had adopted in public the long view which Rosa Luxemburg was content to express in her private letters.

Revolutions have a long wind—if they are real; the English revolution of the seventeenth century, the French revolution of the eighteenth, took forty years to impose themselves [on history] and yet how the tasks of these revolutions shrink—one might almost say into *minutiae*—compared to the enormous problems with which the Russian revolution has to struggle.[3]

At the beginning of 1918 and throughout the year Franz Mehring continued his propagation of 'the long wind of history'. It was not only the need to justify the Russian events in public at any price, which *Spartakus* and—though reluctantly—Rosa Luxemburg accepted. Even Karl Liebknecht, almost completely isolated in Luckau jail—'unable once again to get a proper grip on Russian problems', he complained bitterly—had marked an early outburst against the Bolshevik peace policy in his private notes: 'Not to be printed! With all reserve, owing danger of misdirection. Only intended as basis for discussion. . . . We must avoid any basic tendency to anti-Leninism. Greatest care and tact in all German criticism of Russian proletariat!'[4] Mehring was more

[1] Speech at the conference of factory committees of Moscow region, 23 July 1918, *Pravda*, No. 153, 24 July; Lenin, *Sochineniya*, Vol. XXVII, pp. 506–7.

[2] Speech at session of All-Russian Central Executive, 23 February 1918, *Sochineniya*, Vol. XXVII, p. 26.

[3] *LV*, 31 December 1917.

[4] Karl Liebknecht, *Politische Aufzeichnungen*, pp. 32, 102.

positive. He had never been interested in tactics. In contrast to all his hatreds and self-hatreds, he had a real love for the impersonal processes of history. Where Rosa had primarily abhorred the physical annihilation and suffering of the working classes during the war, where Lenin had seen the value of death and destruction for revolutionary purposes, Franz Mehring merely saw abstract history in the making. His increasing support for the Bolsheviks—though he too had criticized the separate peace—and his faith in their survival had a highly personal colouring and certainly does not provide any evidence for the later Bolshevik thesis that their action actually served the best interests of the German proletariat.

Mehring apart, *Spartakus's* increasing commitment to the Bolsheviks was inevitable if the German working classes were not to be boxed in by the sort of negatives implied in the *Spartakus* letter of January 1918. Following the treaty of Brest-Litovsk German troops occupied the Ukraine in spring and summer 1918, together with large parts of the Baltic States and Finland. Violent opposition to what were practically annexations of large parts of Russia was intended to help the Bolsheviks in spite of themselves; to all intents and purposes Germany was once more at war with Russia and the problems of conscience posed by a separate peace were things of the past. Moreover the USPD, which had welcomed the February and October events in Russia, was now becoming sharply critical of the Bolsheviks. On 15 November 1917 Kautsky had analysed Russian conditions and found them wanting; according to the best Marxist standards, conditions in Russia were not ripe for Socialist rule. This thesis produced an immediate reaction from Franz Mehring in *Der Sozialdemokrat* on 5 January 1918; it also induced Rosa Luxemburg to mock Kautsky in public as well as in private. If it was a matter of fighting the USPD leadership or arguing with Kautsky, Rosa at once took up arms on behalf of the Bolsheviks.[1]

But the long wind of revolution in Russia crippled the chance of any German version in the foreseeable future. Rosa was not willing to say this in public, but Franz Mehring was. In an open letter to the Bolsheviks he wrote: 'If only I could send you better news from the internal life of the German working-class world. But official Socialism grows like an oil stain, even though it may be close to moral and political bankruptcy and daily continues to come closer to it.'[2] By declaring bankrupt all German revolutionary potential, Mehring necessarily admitted the failure of the whole *Spartakus* policy; with him it was intellectually in for a penny, in for a pound. 'We have made one big mistake, namely that from an organizational point of view we joined the independents in the

[1] *Letters to Karl and Luise Kautsky*, p. 207. For Lenin's opinion of this support, see below, pp. 438–9.
[2] *Dokumente und Materialien*, Vol. II, p. 158.

hope of driving them forward. This hope we have had to give up. . . .'[1]
And as late as 5 September 1918 Ernst Meyer wrote to Lenin in much
the same vein.[2]

Rosa Luxemburg had announced her intention of publishing her
criticisms of the Russian revolution in the form of a pamphlet and was
trying to get Franz Mehring to do the same. All efforts to dissuade her
seemed doomed to failure.[3] In the *Spartakus* letter of September 1918
Rosa broke a considerable period of silence and published a sharp
critique of the Bolsheviks, which the editors only published with a
cautionary note of their own.[4] She wrote a further article containing a
still sharper attack on the supplementary protocols to the Treaty of
Brest-Litovsk—and this time Levi, Meyer, and Leviné decided not to
print it.[5]

After the second article was delivered in Berlin through the usual
good offices of Mathilde Jacob, Paul Levi travelled to Breslau to have
it out once and for all with the impenitent critic. The only record
of this meeting is his own, and then only a brief reference.[6]

They had an obstinate and lengthy argument, but in the end he
succeeded—perhaps the only occasion in the last decade that Rosa had
been talked out of an intention to publish. Even then, it was only the
argument that her remarks would be misused by enemies which convinced her. But after Levi's departure she nevertheless sat down at once
and wrote out a draft which she sent him in September 1918 through an
intermediary: 'I am writing this pamphlet only for you and if I can
convince *you* then the effort isn't wasted', she assured him.[7]

Rosa Luxemburg could afford to be more forthright and detailed in
what was practically a private discussion, just as Karl Liebknecht in
prison had poured himself without reserve into his private notebooks.
She now went back to first principles. Her pamphlet was not only a
comment on the Russian revolution but a critique of the very notion

---

[1] Ibid., p. 161.

[2] Ibid., p. 195. Cf. his own rather different version in *Rote Fahne*, 15 January 1922: 'In
vain did I make every effort to impress on Comrade Luxemburg that we were able to look
forward to great revolutionary events in Germany in the very near future.' The article was
written as part of the KPD's defence against Paul Levi's publication and Meyer, a most
punctilious person, may be forgiven his retrospective optimism.

[3] Clara Zetkin, *Um Rosa Luxemburgs Stellung zur russischen Revolution*, Hamburg 1922,
reprinted in Clara Zetkin, *Ausgewählte Reden und Schriften*, Vol. II, p. 385.

[4] *Spartakusbriefe*, p. 453.

[5] See Ernst Meyer, 'Rosa Luxemburgs Kritik der Bolschewiki', *Rote Fahne*, 15 January
1922.

[6] Paul Levi's introduction to Rosa Luxemburg, *Die Russische Revolution*, Berlin 1922.

[7] Ibid., p. 1. Quotations are taken from the English edition by Bertram D. Wolfe, *The
Russian Revolution*, Ann Arbor (Michigan) 1961.

of Socialist revolution. The pamphlet was rigorously divided into heads and sections like a legal brief. Bouquets first.

The party of Lenin was the only one which grasped the mandate and duty of a truly revolutionary party; with the slogan—'all power in the hands of the proletariat and peasantry'—they insured the continued move forward of the revolution. Thereby the Bolsheviks solved the famous problem of 'winning a majority of the people' which has always weighed on the German Social Democracy like a nightmare. . . . Only a party which knows how to lead, that is to advance things, wins support in stormy times. The determination with which, at the decisive moment, Lenin and his comrades offered the only solution . . . transformed them almost overnight from a persecuted, slandered, outlawed minority whose leader had to hide like Marat in cellars, into the absolute masters of the situation.[1]

This passage has always presented a problem. The Bolsheviks see it as a rather involved way of presenting a blank cheque of approval, slightly marred by the ill-informed criticism immediately following; but for Social Democrats it is the example-extraordinary of a deep-down democrat who insists on seeing democracy even in the arbitrary tyranny of Bolshevism—though not without doing violence to every demand of logic and evidence. And in formal democratic terms the idea of a Bolshevik majority is nonsense. But that was not what Rosa Luxemburg meant. There was no question of elections or mandates. 'Winning a majority' was the same doctrine of revolutionary action as a solvent for static opposition—movement against rigidity—as she had preached in the SPD from 1910 to 1914. By moving and not talking, the Bolsheviks had utilized their revolutionary period to the full and swept the masses along. For the moment. But there followed a bill of particulars which cut sharply into the general plethora of praise.

1. *Land Policy.* The fact that the Soviet government had not carried out full-scale nationalization of large and middle-sized estates could not be made the subject of reproach.

It would be a sorry jest indeed to demand or expect of Lenin and his comrades that in the brief period of their rule they should already have solved or even tackled one of the most difficult tasks, indeed we can safely say *the* most difficult task in a Socialist transformation of society . . . but a Socialist government must at least do one thing when it comes to power, it must take measures which lead in the direction of a later Socialist reform of agriculture; it must at least avoid everything which may bar the way to those measures in future. Now the slogan launched by the Bolsheviks—immediate seizure and distribution of the land to the peasants—necessarily tended in the opposite direction. Not only is it not a Socialist measure; it even cuts off the way to such measures; it piles up insurmountable obstacles to the Socialist transformation of agrarian relations. . . .

[1] *The Russian Revolution*, pp. 38–39.

[In short,] the Leninist agrarian reform has created a new and powerful layer of enemies of Socialism in the countryside, enemies whose resistance will be much more dangerous and stubborn than that of the large aristocratic landowners.[1]

2. *The Nationality Question.* This chapter was a classic restatement of Rosa's lifelong view of the essential economic and political unity of the Russian empire, and the error of hawking the concept of national self-determination to all and every constituent member of the Russian empire, large or small.

It is exactly as if the people living on the north coast of Germany should want to found a new nation and government. And this ridiculous pose of a few university professors and students was inflated into a political force by Lenin and his comrades . . . to what was at first a mere farce they lent such importance that the farce became a matter of the most deadly earnest—not a serious national movement for which . . . there are no roots at all, but a single and rallying flag for counter-revolution. At Brest[-Litovsk], out of this addled egg crept the German bayonets.[2]

This much could have been written against the PPS. But then the argument became more fundamental.

The 'right of national self-determination' constitutes the battle-cry of the coming reckoning of international Socialism with the bourgeoisie. It is obvious that the . . . entire nationalist movement which at present constitutes the greatest danger for international Socialism has experienced an extraordinary strengthening from the . . . Russian revolution and the Brest[-Litovsk] negotiations . . . from all this the terror and the strangling of democracy followed directly.[3]

Neither the particular nor the general statement was new. But what was brilliant was the sudden intuition at the end, which linked this problem specifically to that of terror. Because of the weak edges of the revolution, because of the mistaken tactic which permitted the creation of strongly inimical movements and régimes in the Ukraine, the Baltic states, and elsewhere, the government at home was obliged to resort to the fiercest measures in order to maintain itself on that territory to which, by its arbitrary acceptance of national self-determination, it had been confined. In this she was right. The centrifugal pressures of nationality were in the end to bring out the repressive policy of Stalin, Ordzhonikidze, and Dzierżyński, three non-Russians, whose practical views on national self-determination differed totally from those of Lenin and against whose rigid terror his last important efforts were directed.[4]

[1] Ibid., pp. 43, 46.
[2] Ibid., pp. 54–55.   [3] Ibid., pp. 55–56.
[4] For this and further discussion of the differences in the national question between Rosa Luxemburg and Lenin, see below, pp. 510–6.

3. *Constituent Assembly and Suffrage.* The next two items in *The Russian Revolution* dealt with Bolshevik policy with regard to the Constituent Assembly and suffrage. Rosa Luxemburg criticized the Bolsheviks' action in dispersing the Constituent Assembly, which they themselves had called, and in restricting the suffrage. The details were not important, and these—but only these—she later retracted.[1]

But again she was concerned with tactics only as examples of principle. She took issue with Trotsky's theory—he too was quick to elaborate theories—that institutions tend to lead a life of their own and, if they did not reflect the particular reality assigned to them, must be destroyed: a fear of reification which strongly survived in Soviet constitutional practice. To this she opposed her own long-held view about mass influence *on* institutions. 'The living fluid of popular mood, continually forced round representative bodies, penetrates them, guides them ... even in bourgeois parliaments.'[2]

Similarly, on suffrage:

... freedom of the press, the rights of association and assembly all have been outlawed for all opponents of the Soviet régime ... on the other hand it is a well-known and indisputable fact that without a free and untrammelled press, without the unlimited right of association and assembly, the role of the broad mass of the people is entirely unthinkable.[3]

On the face of it, this could only mean that the existing institutions should have been preserved, full freedom of the press and of assembly guaranteed, and so on. No doubt Bolshevik rule was to be an example for the future, for the eventual and final Socialist revolution (in Germany?), and not simply a means of clinging to power at the price of deformation and compromise. Therefore, purity of Socialist principles needed emphasizing continually, at the expense of tactical success. But more important still, Rosa Luxemburg was not putting forward concrete alternatives to Bolshevik mistakes. She was not writing for the Bolsheviks at all, but for the future, for German revolutionaries. In the last analysis the present was unimportant; present, past, and future had equal weight. She was wrong in supposing that a kind of mass pressure on a Constituent Assembly in Russia, moving it forward and keeping it Socialist, was available; quite the contrary. She did not realize the extent to which the Bolsheviks were a minority in the country; she caught only a glimpse of the fact that Bolshevik rule was possible only by toleration of the peasants, who were more interested in peace and land than in Socialism. But this was secondary to the more general proposition that arbitrary curtailment of inconvenient institutions and popular processes after a revolution was bound to be self-generating

[1] See below, pp. 444–6.
[2] *The Russian Revolution*, p. 60.   [3] Ibid., pp. 66–67.

and repetitive, bad habits which would lead the government farther and farther away from contact with the masses.

4. *Dictatorship*. The same feeling of malaise was expressed in the last sections dealing with the problem of dictatorship.

Freedom only for the supporters of the government, only for the members of one party—however numerous they may be—is no freedom at all. Freedom is always and exclusively freedom for the one who thinks differently. Not because of any fanatical conception of 'justice' but because all that is instructive, wholesome and purifying in political freedom depends on this essential characteristic; and its effectiveness vanishes when 'freedom' becomes a special privilege.[1]

Of course this was not a plea for bourgeois democracy but for the democracy which Socialists had always believed to be possible only after the success of a revolution. No doubt it assumed mass enthusiasm for the Bolsheviks which did not exist, but more important was the feeling that the Bolsheviks were imposing democracy from above rather than building on it from below.

Lenin is completely mistaken in the means he employs. Decree, dictatorial force of the factory overseer, draconic penalties, rule by terror, all these things are but palliatives. The only way to rebirth is the school of public life itself, the most unlimited, the broadest democracy and public opinion. It is rule by terror which demoralizes.[2]

Rosa Luxemburg, who did not mind in the last resort whether the Bolsheviks maintained themselves or not—and this perhaps was the major difference between her and them—was far more afraid of a deformed revolution than an unsuccessful one. She took Lenin's organizational abilities and objects seriously enough and extended them through time to their inevitable consequences.

With the repression of political life in the land as a whole, life in the Soviets must also become more crippled . . . life dies out in every public institution, becomes a mere semblance of life, in which only the bureaucracy remains as the active element. Public life gradually falls asleep. The few dozen party leaders of inexhaustible energy and boundless experience direct and rule. Among them only a dozen outstanding heads do the leading and an élite of the working class is invited from time to time to meetings where they are to applaud the speeches of the leaders, and to approve proposed resolutions unanimously—at bottom then a clique affair. A dictatorship to be sure; not the dictatorship of the proletariat, however, but only a dictatorship of a handful of politicians in the bourgeois sense . . . yes, we can go even further: such conditions must inevitably cause a brutalization of public life. . . .[3]

----

[1] Ibid., p. 69.   [2] Ibid., p. 71.
[1] Ibid., pp. 76–77.

Khrushchev could have used these words in his speech denouncing Stalin's régime at the Twentieth Congress if he had thought of them! They contain all that he said—if one substitutes 'one man' for 'a few leaders', admittedly an important difference—only much more concisely than his own long speech.

Finally, Rosa Luxemburg turned once again to the remedy for these tendencies. 'Lenin and Trotsky and their friends were the *first* who went ahead as an example to the proletariat of the world. . . . But in Russia the problem could only be posed. It could not be solved there. In *this* sense, the future everywhere belongs to Bolshevism.[1]

How far then was Rosa Luxemburg right? The fact that she accepted the notion of Soviets (workers' and soldiers' councils) in Germany and fought bitterly against the calling of the German Constituent Assembly, her willingness to draw a line under the old Russian polemics during the German revolution and not to haggle with Radek over this part of the past when he arrived on 19 December 1918, her admission to Warszawski that she had changed her mind about a lot of things (unspecified)—all these later caused Communist historians to talk of a general withdrawal of her criticisms.[2] But this seems to me to be a one-sided judgement. No doubt she changed her mind about details, though even here she herself pointed out in her speech to the KPD's founding congress in December 1918 that her opposition to the Constituent Assembly was based on the fact that Germany still had an anti-Communist government, and that a comparison with the Russia of November 1917 was therefore incorrect. More significant than changing her mind was her unwillingness, in the middle of the German revolution, to grub around in the Russian past. But most important of all, the pamphlet on the Russian revolution was not primarily a discussion of detailed policies. It was an examination of the basic propositions of revolution and in fact the only glimpse from Rosa's pen of how she envisaged the future. Her general conclusions had little or nothing to do with the details she was criticizing; rather she was applying well-established, systematic conclusions to a new set of facts. 'The Russian Revolution' happened to be the title of the particular frame passing through Rosa Luxemburg's mental epidiascope at the time. In this sense her argument was highly deductive; she was arguing from an attitude—her particular attitude—to the facts and not, as appears at first sight, using the facts available about Russia to construct a theory of revolution.

Unlike Lenin, Rosa Luxemburg did not accept a difference between party life and eventual public life, between party and post-revolutionary society; for her the Socialist revolution was nothing more than the

---

[1] See below, p. 495.   [2] See below, pp. 445–6.

expansion of Socialism from the party to the whole society. The idea of *Socialists* in control of *capitalist* society was hardly thinkable, the idea of accepting and temporarily even strengthening such a *status quo* and calling it stability could only be lunacy. If this last is a necessary condition of Bolshevism then Rosa was truly anchored in the Second International. Lenin on the other hand did make the sharp distinction. He evolved a theory of party discipline and organization which he put into effect with every means at his disposal. His approach to public life after the revolution was, however, highly empirical; provided the party was properly organized, it could afford every change of tactic, survive every manœuvre, could fortify or discard at will, if necessary, every single institution in society. Only the constitution of the party mattered. The Bolshevik view of society did not change much before and after the revolution, except in terms of their power within it; there was still 'we' and 'it'. Party discipline could not relax, but rather became tighter. Only in this way could rapid tactical changes in government policy be undertaken without lack of cohesion. It was Stalin who later completed the picture, first by making society conform to the graveyard discipline of the party, from the centre towards the periphery; then, finding alteration of policy a course too brusque for party cohesion, he reversed the thrust of power, and made the party as empty as society, from the periphery towards the centre. In 'balancing' society and party, Stalin was closer to Rosa Luxemburg than to Lenin, though their methods were somewhat different.

Rosa Luxemburg's pamphlet on the Russian revolution has become famous as an almost clairvoyant indictment of the Bolsheviks. In part this is justified. But its purpose will be better served if we see it as an analysis of ideal revolution based, like so much of Rosa Luxemburg's work, on a form of critical dialogue, in this case with the Bolshevik October revolution. Those who are made joyful by criticism of the fundamentals of the Bolshevik revolution would do better to turn elsewhere.

XV

1918—THE GERMAN REVOLUTION

BEGINS

POLITICALLY, *Spartakus* was at a very low ebb in the summer of 1918. Most of the leaders were immured in indefinite confinement while the war dragged on, incapable of decision. Judging from the bulk of the press and from official German reactions, the outlook for the revolution in Russia was gloomy—the Bolsheviks unlikely to maintain their position in spite of the very policies which had helped to prolong the radical agony in Germany. 'Oh God, my nerves, my nerves. I cannot sleep at all', Rosa wrote to Luise Kautsky in July 1918. 'Clara too has been silent for too long, has not even thanked me for my birthday letter, a thing quite unheard of in her case. I cannot contain the fear within me. . . . For myself I am full of courage. To bear the sorrow of *others*, for that I lack courage and strength. All these are merely thoughts, ghosts. . . .'[1]

Then, unexpectedly and spectacularly, the Western Front collapsed in September. The worst fears of the German High Command soon communicated themselves to the capital; as so often, people were overtaken by events, those committed to the *status quo* as well as those who aspired to overthrow it. In September 1918 a new wave of strikes broke out. On 28 September the German General Staff informed the imperial government that armistice negotiations were essential if a catastrophe was to be avoided. On 1 October Lenin notified his colleagues that the situation in Germany was sufficiently ripe for action by the Russian government.[2] The executives of the SPD and the USPD had to consider their position now that the German government belatedly tried to associate wider political groups in the liquidation of the unsuccessful war policy. On 23 September 1918 the SPD executive and the *Reichstag* group of SPD deputies jointly stated their minimum demands for participation in any government.[3]

Quicker off the mark, the USPD leaders and the Revolutionary Shop

---

[1] *Letters to Karl and Luise Kautsky*, pp. 220–2, dated 25 July 1918.
[2] Lenin, *Sochineniya*, Vol. XXXV, pp. 302–2.
[3] *Vorwärts*, 24 September 1918.

Stewards had begun to meet regularly and discuss how the impending situation could be turned to good account. They too issued an appeal to the population, which contained their immediate demands from the government—more extreme in tone and content than that of the SPD.[1] *Spartakus* issued two final letters, in September and October 1918. In neither of these was there any optimistic prognosis for the coming months, any signs that the long-predicted collapse of the imperial government was imminent. The September letter contained Rosa Luxemburg's gloomy analysis of events in Russia which we have already discussed. Though *Spartakus* had already indicated some of the methods and techniques of the future revolution in outline, taken over from the Russian experience, there was little evidence that the group foresaw any imminent application of these ideas. The later investigations of the German *Reichstag* into the causes of the German collapse as well as modern historical research both show how little *Spartakus* was able to contribute in the summer and early autumn of 1918 to the development of events in Germany.[2] Interesting evidence from a source most unlikely to denigrate *Spartakus* comes from Lenin, who had an extremely sharp eye not only for revolutionary potential but equally for weakness and ineffectiveness. On 20 September 1918 he wrote to Vorovskii, one of his representatives in Stockholm:

. . . Is it to be tolerated that even people like Mehring and Zetkin are more concerned to take issue with Kautsky from a *moral* (if one may use this term) point of view, rather than a *theoretical* one? Kautsky, they say, really ought to have better things to do than to write [polemics] against the Bolsheviks.

Is this any kind of argument? Can one weaken one's own position to such an extent? This means nothing else but to arm Kautsky gratuitously.[3]

---

[1] *Dokumente und Materialien*, Vol. II, pp. 207–10.

[2] These researches must be set against German nationalist claims for the effectiveness of internal left-wing sabotage in order to save the 'honour' of the German army. The police reports on *Spartakus* activity, on which these claims were based, are misleading; clearly police informers, in Germany as elsewhere, provided precisely the kind of evidence their employers hoped to get from them.

In this connection it is an interesting irony of history that pre-war Communist historians, with every natural incentive to write up the significance of their own *Spartakus* ancestry, sometimes resolutely refused to do so. Thus P. Langner, *Der Massenstreik im Kampf des Proletåriats*, Leipzig 1931, p. 49: 'The collapse of Wilhelminian Germany [in] . . . 1918 did not take place as a result of the struggles of the working classes against imperialist war and the bourgeoisie. It came from inside, as a result of the physical incapacity to continue the war.' Nothing shows up the nationalist *Dolchstoss* (stab in the back) myth more clearly than this. However, post-war East Germany history on the whole tends to exaggerate the importance of *Spartakus*. All the recent evidence, including the substantial East German literature, is summarized in an appendix to E. Kolb, *Die Arbeiterräte in der deutschen Innenpolitik 1918–19*, Düsseldorf 1962, pp. 410–14.

[3] First published in *Pravda*, No. 17, 21 January 1925, quoted from *Sochineniya*, Vol. XXXV, p. 299.

This criticism of too much *Spartakus* 'morality' instead of aggressive theoretical combat clearly showed that Lenin had somehow sniffed out the exhaustion of *Spartakus* and its unpreparedness for coming events. By early October the German government was visibly beginning to disintegrate. *Spartakus* and the Left radicals from Bremen had finally decided to collaborate closely. Both recognized at last the impending revolutionary possibilities. The first thing was to break the existing government and in particular the state of martial law. An appeal by the *Spartakus* group in October 1918 therefore called on the people to rise, to create 'conditions of freedom for the class struggle of the workers, for a real democracy, for a real and lasting peace and for Socialism'.[1] Shortly afterwards a more positive appeal was launched calling upon the workers as well as the soldiers to organize. But the form of organization was not yet specified: 'the spontaneous mutinies among the soldiers must be supported by all means and be led towards an armed uprising, the armed uprising for the struggle to gain the entire power [of the state] for the workers and soldiers . . . '.[2]

On 7 October *Spartakus* held a national conference, the first for nearly two years. Nothing is known of the discussions at the conference; but a report, together with the resolutions and an appeal to the workers, was circulated illegally, and part of it appeared in the last *Spartakus* letter in October.[3] The joint conference itself produced a lengthier analysis of the world situation and more strenuous and precise demands, but again they were confined to an attempt to obtain particular concessions from existing authority rather than the destruction of that authority itself. The whole process was intended as a continual raising of revolutionary sights so that the ponderous and reluctant dragon of the German working classes could finally be induced to snort and move. But there was still nothing about the organizational forms of the coming struggle, much less about the way to implement any future working-class victory.

On 12 October the Prussian government and some of the other provincial governments declared an amnesty for political prisoners. Three days later the *Bundesrat*—the upper house of the Reich legislature—officially announced the participation of both *Bundesrat* and *Reichstag* in the coming bid for peace. The German government was still hopeful of saving its authority by broadening its base, even though the allies had already declared that the Emperor at least must be sacrified before any armistice negotiations would be entertained. Karl Liebknecht was among the first to be released under the amnesty. He returned to Berlin on 23 October and was escorted by a crowd of workers from the station

---

[1] *D. & M.* Vol. II, p. 225.   [2] Ibid., p. 227.
[3] For the full text, see *D. & M.*, Vol. II, pp. 228–34.

straight to the Soviet Embassy. Nothing is known in detail of the discussions he had there; a short and somewhat ominous sentence of Karl Radek's merely confirms complete agreement: 'The night after [Karl Liebknecht's] release Bukharin told us that Karl was in complete agreement with us . . . if he had at that time been able to come to us, no king would have been welcomed as Liebknecht would have been welcomed by the Russian workers.'[1]

From the moment of his release Liebknecht automatically took over the leadership of the *Spartakus* group. His reputation and moral authority had never been higher. On 25 October the executive of the USPD offered to co-opt him, but Liebknecht stipulated that he would only accept if the USPD altered its programme and tactics and fell into line with *Spartakus*. Though not refused outright, this stipulation cooled USPD enthusiasm, as it was meant to do.

While the discussions were going on, the revolution itself broke out at the naval base in Kiel, the same place where in August 1917 the only significant mutiny of the war had taken place. The inability of the government to do more than send a negotiating commission brought the ferment out into the open everywhere. From the beginning of November onwards Soldiers' Councils appeared at the front and Workers' Councils sprang up in most of the major cities of Germany. As yet these were demonstrations of revolt rather than instruments of revolution, and in most places they had no clear programme except to attempt to impose their authority—or at least their right to exist—on local authorities and army commanders. The Sailors' Council at Kiel sent a radio message to Moscow from which the Russian leaders deduced that revolution in Germany was now under way.

For a short time the situation in the provinces was more revolutionary than in Berlin. Representatives of the USPD, the Revolutionary Shop Stewards, and *Spartakus* represented by Liebknecht and Piek—fatal partnership—began to plan an organized rising and fixed the day for 4 November. However, in full meeting the Revolutionary Shop Stewards, though they accepted the principle, refused to accept the early date agreed by their negotiators. A few days later, on 6 November, in view of the evident success of the mutiny in Kiel and the ferment in the provinces, the Revolutionary Shop Stewards finally settled the 11th as 'the day'. Liebknecht's immediate proposal to bring this date forward to the 8th was lost by a considerable majority in the meeting. Was it the hope that events would overtake them after all?

Meantime the SPD too had been drawn into the impending negotia-

---

[1] Karl Liebknecht, *Klassenkampf*, p. 108 (Appendix: 'In memory of Karl Liebknecht', first published in February 1919 in *Izvestiya*). The same comment is made by Radek in his biographical sketch in memory of the three German leaders, *Karl Liebknecht, Rosa Luxemburg, Leo Jogiches*, Hamburg 1921. See also below, p. 443.

tions for a change of government. However, the executive was treating with two sides, with those who planned an uprising, and also with the government itself about a peaceful hand-over of power. Notes passed backwards and forwards; the negotiations with the government appeared to reach deadlock when the SPD insisted that the Emperor must abdicate. In order to reinforce its position during these negotiations, the government brought in troops on 7 November to occupy the main factories, and forbade a proposed mass demonstration to celebrate the anniversary of the Russian revolution. Finally, on the same day, the SPD leaders sent an ultimatum to the Chancellor; if he refused it they were determined to join the rising.

In the end all these elaborate plans came to nothing. On 9 November, two days before the deadline, a general strike took place in Berlin and large groups of armed workers and soldiers thronged the streets. It was the effective end of the Empire. The Chancellor, Prince Max of Baden, formally handed over his power to SPD chairman Ebert. But even then the SPD's advent to power was not the result of its own efforts. Liebknecht had gauged the potential of the demonstrations correctly; in a speech from the balcony of the Imperial Palace shortly after midday, he proclaimed the Socialist Republic. When the news of these events reached the *Reichstag*, where the SPD caucus was in permanent session, Scheidemann was persuaded to declare the Democratic Republic then and there to prevent a complete *Spartakus* takeover.

Now I saw clearly what was afoot. I knew [Liebknecht's] slogan—supreme authority for the workers' and soldiers' councils—and Germany would therefore be a Russian province, a branch of the Soviet. No, no, a thousand times no! . . . A few working men and soldiers accompanied me into the hall. 'Scheidemann has proclaimed the Republic.' Ebert's face turned livid with wrath when he heard what I had done. . . . 'You have not the right to proclaim the Republic, what becomes of Germany . . . whether she becomes a republic or something else—a constituent assembly must decide.'[1]

Immediate negotiations took place between the two Socialist parties with a view to forming a joint government based on equal representation. The concession of parity by the SPD was generous; but in return almost all those radical conditions posed by the executive of the Independents to which the SPD took exception were withdrawn, 'to cement the revolutionary Socialist achievements'. Now that the day had come, pressure for unity among the leaders was strong. The new Reich executive, known as the Council of People's Commissioners (*Rat der*

[1] Philipp Scheidemann, *The Making of a New Germany*, New York, 1929, Vol. II, pp. 261–2.

Volksbeauftragten), consisted of three SPD and three USPD delegates.[1] The *Spartakus* group—which of course was an organized pressure group within the USPD—had called for the 'Russian example' on 7 November, the anniversary of the Bolshevik revolution—at least for the Russian spirit if not yet for the Russian facts. This meant no compromises. But all mention of Russia frightened the leaders of the two Socialist parties to death. On 9 November *Spartakus* issued a special supplement to the new *Rote Fahne* in which it called for a more advanced and detailed programme of revolutionary steps. By now *Spartakus* demands were far exceeding the realities that were in process of achievement. The intention was quite clear. With the first release of revolutionary activity, the goals had at once to be set higher, and so on in continuous progression.

This then was the situation when Rosa Luxemburg was released from the city jail in Breslau. Apparently the amnesty of 12 October had been deemed to apply only to those serving a specified sentence; the large number interned under administrative order were either forgotten or had been deliberately ignored at some stage in the administrative chain. Only when the revolutionary wave reached Breslau on 9 November were the gates of the prison opened. The last few weeks had tried her nerves and patience to the utmost. She had refused all visits, since

my mood is such that the presence of my friends under supervision has become impossible. I have suffered everything patiently, and under other circumstances would have remained patient for a long time. But the general situation . . . has wrecked my psychological detachment. These conversations under supervision, the impossibility of talking about things that really interest me, have become such a burden that I prefer to renounce every visit until we can meet as free people. It cannot take long. . . .[2]

Her first task on release was naturally to address the expectant crowds in the central square of Breslau, from the balcony of the old *Rathaus* where the judgements of the city elders had long ago been given to the citizens. She was no stranger to the city, or to them. Now she was able to judge the new temper from which she had been cut off for so long.[3] And late that afternoon she hastened to Berlin where she was greeted with joy by all her old friends, but also with concealed sadness, for they suddenly realized what the years is prison had done to her. She had aged terribly and her black hair had gone quite white. She was a sick woman.'[4]

---

[1] Part of the correspondence is reprinted in *D. & M.*, Vol. II, p. 331 (SPD) and p. 346 (USPD).

[2] *Letters from Prison*, p. 78, dated 18 October 1918, to Sonia Liebknecht.

[3] Frölich, p. 288; *LV*, 10 November 1918. Frölich wrongly gives the date of her release as the 8th instead of the 9th. Publication of the Breslau *Volkswacht* had been suspended by the government for a few days.

[4] Frölich, loc. cit.

The outbreak of revolution in Berlin, whose extension was only prevented by the speed with which the joys of government were accepted by SPD and USPD alike, had established a pattern which was already set when Rosa Luxemburg arrived on the scene. There was no question of altering the arrangements that were being made on the 9th between the leaders of the official Social Democrats and the Independents. Indeed, *Spartakus* accepted this solution as fulfilling the immediate needs of the present. In the words of Rosa Luxemburg: 'The image of the German government corresponds to the inner ripeness of German conditions. Scheidemann-Ebert are the proper [*berufene*] government of the German revolution in its present stage.'[1] The task of *Spartakus*—which ceased to be the *Gruppe Internationale* and finally adopted '*Spartakus*' as an official title on 11 November 1918—now was to prepare and hasten the conditions in which the next stage of the revolution could take place. There had been no question on 9 November of hustling aside the SPD, much less the USPD, and taking over power itself. Even Liebknecht's proclamation of the 'Socialist Republic' from the Palace had been a declaration of intent rather than a practical proposal for action; a means of pushing the Independents. *Spartakus* was barely equipped to provide an organized and coherent ginger group within the USPD; its immediate preoccupation was the growth of its influence and support, and the formation of a tactic to act upon the masses. To take over the government was out of the question; they had far less chance of success than the Bolsheviks in October 1917.

Thus the situation set objective limits to the possibilities of the group. However, there were also severe subjective limitations to its policy. Liebknecht, whose personality and attitudes dominated the activities of *Spartakus* for the next two months, was quite adamant in his refusal to make any compromise with either SPD or the Independents. He refused participation both in the government of 9 November which had been suggested by the negotiators on both sides and, as we have seen, would not even serve on the executive of the USPD. This policy of abstention from any commitment to parties which did not accept the total *Spartakus* programme was no doubt shared by all his colleagues. But the programme itself had also been set: no Constituent Assembly, all power to the Workers' and Soldiers' Councils. This was the policy borrowed from the Russian experience. It was concerning the wholehearted acceptance of this tactic that Radek reported that 'Liebknecht and we are in complete agreement'.

There is no reason to suppose that Rosa Luxemburg disagreed either in her evaluation of the situation or about the tactics to be adopted. Just as she had taken over the leading role in interpreting the Polish

[1] *Die Rote Fahne*, 18 November 1918.

Revolution in 1905–6, she now took on the same task in Germany. Her special skill consisted as always in analysing events in revolutionary Marxist terms and in emphasizing the role of *Spartakus* within the necessities of the situation. She was a superb propagandist. All her writings were directed towards persuading a proletariat assumed to be more aware than ever of its needs and possibilities; waiting only to be guided in the required direction. Her emphasis was above all on clarity. As it had been necessary for so long to dig a demarcation ditch between the PPS and the Polish Social Democracy and to refute the false appeal of the seducer, so it was now essential to demarcate even more clearly a correct working-class policy when the false siren-calls were legion. The militant crowds were being harangued from all sides, SPD, USPD, *Spartakus*, Revolutionary Shop Stewards; last, but not least, by middle-class interest groups. Soon, moreover, there developed a further complication in the shape of a younger group of ultra-radicals, who wanted complete dissociation from the mêlée, a disdainful withdrawal till history placed its chance before them on a silver platter. In practice this merely amounted to forgoing all the possible opportunities of revolution, like the brief refusal of the Bolsheviks to participate in the 1906 Duma elections. As confusion increased, so necessarily did the temper of the voice of clarity. Rosa's inflammatory tone was in the first instance due to a desire not so much to create positive revolutionary action as to provide a firm and unmistakable channel for the streams of advice and proposals unleashed by all the various socialist parties. Clarity came to mean volume and pitch as much as correct analysis.

Any search in Rosa's writing for specific approval or disapproval of the Russian example during these months is based on a misunderstanding of her attitude and her situation. The sharp criticism of Lenin and the Bolsheviks contained in her writings in prison has been contrasted by Communist historians with her tacit acceptance of the Russian programme after November 1918—the result of a conversion. Rosa Luxemburg's few specific statements have been carefully culled as valuable evidence of a definite change of mind. Thus a few years later Warszawski reported the receipt of a letter at the end of November, brought to Warsaw by a German soldier. This was Rosa's answer to Warszawski's questions about the attitude to be adopted towards the Russian revolution. 'If our party [SDKPiL] is full of enthusiasm for Bolshevism and at the same time opposed the Bolshevik peace of Brest-Litovsk, and also opposes their propagation of national self-determination as a solution, then it is no more than enthusiasm coupled with the spirit of criticism—what more can people want from us?' With most of the old SDKPiL leaders now in Russia and working closely with the Bolsheviks (Dzierżyński, Hanecki, Unszlicht, Leder, Radek, as well as

Marchlewski—the split had long been healed), there was naturally great pressure on the local Polish party headed by Warszawski with its still official links with Rosa Luxemburg and Jogiches in Germany. 'What shall I do?' Warszawski had asked, and Rosa continued:

I shared all your reservations and doubts, but have dropped them in the most important questions, and in others I never went as far as you. Terrorism is evidence of grave internal weakness, but it is directed against internal enemies, who . . . get support and encouragement from foreign capitalists outside Russia. Once the European revolution comes, the Russian counter-revolutionaries lose not only this support, but—what is more important—they must lose all courage. Bolshevik terror is above all the expression of the weakness of the European proletariat. Naturally the agrarian circumstances there have created the sorest, most dangerous problem of the Russian revolution. But here too the saying is valid—even the greatest revolution can only achieve that which has become ripe [through the development of] social circumstances. This sore too can only be healed through the European revolution. And this is coming![1]

Similarly Clara Zetkin reported that Rosa's two urgent requests to her in the summer of 1918 to get Mehring to arrange a scientific and critical analysis of the Russian revolution, on the basis of her own work, were not pursued, and that she made no further reference to these requests or to any need for them.[2]

Both conclude that Rosa Luxemburg was wrong about certain aspects of the Russian revolution in the first place, and that in any case she changed her mind after her release from prison. The criticism of Bolshevik suppression of other parties Clara Zetkin ascribed to Rosa's 'somewhat schematic, abstract notion of democracy'. She claims that Rosa misunderstood the discriminatory electoral laws in Russia, the dismissal of the Constituent Assembly and the refusal to elect another; that she failed to grasp the essence of 'proletarian dictatorship', the need and nature of terror, and the Bolshevik relationship between party and masses.[3] Warszawski's conclusions were identical. None the less, he qualified the 'errors' of his old and brilliant comrade.

We have seen that the opinions which Rosa Luxemburg stated in her pamphlet were no longer her opinions from November 1918 and until her death. All the same, in spite of all the errors and incompletions of her work, it is revolutionary work. Rosa Luxemburg's criticism differs from opportunistic criticism because it can never harm the cause or the party of revolution, it can only enliven it and help it—because it is revolutionary criticism.[4]

[1] Adolf Warski, *Rosa Luxemburgs Stellung zu den taktischen Problemen der Revolution*, Hamburg 1922, pp. 6–7.
[2] Clara Zetkin, *Um Rosa Luxemburgs Stellung zur russischen Revolution*, Hamburg 1922, reprinted in Clara Zetkin, *Ausgewälte Reden und Schriften*, Berlin 1957, Vol. II, p. 385.
[3] Ibid., pp. 392, 396–8, 393, 400, 404, 408.   [4] Warski, op. cit., p. 37.

Thus both Adolf Warszawski and Clara Zetkin deduced—admittedly on instructions from the executive of the KPD and the Comintern in its dispute with Paul Levi—a fundamental revision of Rosa's attitude to the Russian revolution. Whatever she did not revise were alleged to be errors. However, like so many discussions which involve the projection of someone's views from one period to a totally different one, especially after their death, the problem is largely irrelevant. Rosa was never quick to change her mind. She was obstinate and had considerable confidence in her own powers of analysis, and in this case there was anyway no real need to recant. New circumstances could always invalidate the practical relevance of ideas, though not necessarily their validity in the past. There is no reason to suppose that she now approved of those aspects of the Russian revolution which three months earlier she had criticized; in fact she took pains to reiterate some of her criticisms.[1] In any case, she had always postulated most strenuously that most of the bad features of the Russian revolution would dissolve in the melting-pot of a European revolution; the advent of that revolution automatically altered the context of most of her remarks. With this, the problems that had bothered her in the summer of 1918 ceased to matter so urgently.

In any case, all the evidence shows that she was willing and anxious to collaborate with the Russians, to learn from their experience, and to agitate as strongly as possible for a link between revolutionary Russia and revolutionary Germany. Right from the start *Spartakus* demanded that the Soviet Legation, which had been closed on 5 November after allegations that it was abusing its diplomatic immunity by smuggling propaganda material should be re-opened as soon as possible. But this did not imply any admission of Russian precedence, or the subordination of German tactics to the dictates of Moscow. As we shall see, she resisted this possibility to the end of her days. In November 1918 this problem simply did not exist. Lenin and the Bolsheviks were still willing to admit, if not the primacy of the German revolution over the Russian —though there is some evidence of this—at least the critical importance to the Soviet Union of Communist success in Germany. The Bolsheviks were prepared to make real sacrifices for this. In short, by 9 November 1918 the rights and wrongs of the Russian revolution had for the moment become irrelevant.

As in the spring of 1916, the leadership of *Spartakus* was once again in the hands of Karl Liebknecht, Rosa Luxemburg, and Leo Jogiches (released from his Berlin prison on 9 November). With them in the executive were Meyer and Levi, who had between them run *Spartakus* after the arrest of its other leaders, Lange, H. Duncker and his wife Käthe, A. Thalheimer, Pieck, Eberlein, and Paul Frölich, back in the

---

[1] See above, pp. 433, 435.

fold after his Zimmerwald-Left period during the war. Clara Zetkin was in Stuttgart and Mehring was too old and ill for active participation. On 10 November *Spartakus* issued its new programme based on the events of the previous day. More strongly than ever it emphasized the need to get rid of all parliaments and to substitute Workers' and Soldiers' Councils everywhere in Germany, with all administrative and legislative power. The need was for centralization, the slogan 'the unified Socialist Republic of Germany'. Unlike the Russians, with their fetish about nationality rights, federalism had no place in a *Spartakist* Germany; semi-autonomous provinces were merely a guarantee of reaction. No one apparently considered that the decentralization accompanying hundreds of councils, each supreme, would be far more chaotic than provincial governments.

At the same time the appeal underlined the poverty of what had been achieved to date.

Nothing is gained by the fact that a few additional government Socialists have achieved power. . . . See to it that power, which you have captured, does not slip out of your hands and that you use it for your own goal. . . . No 'Schiedemann' must sit in the government, no Socialist must enter government as long as a governmental Socialist is still in it. No co-operation with those who betrayed you for four years.[1]

Already the fatal weakness of *Spartakus* had made its appearance, the incitement to remove the present government without the stipulation of a clear alternative. While this was based on a definite tactic—and not merely unclear thinking—it was a tactic that led, as we shall see, to confusion and not to clarity.

On 10 November a joint meeting of all the Berlin Workers' and Soldiers' Councils took place at the Circus Busch—the traditional place of assembly for large popular gatherings. This meeting elected an executive which, pending the calling of a national congress of Workers' and Soldiers' Councils, was to act as its trustee and representative. Its functions were not clearly defined, but given the spontaneous nature of the Councils it was a miracle that anything as concrete as an executive emerged at all. The meeting confirmed the six People's Commissioners as the provisional national executive but its own functions and role vis-à-vis this latter body were left unclear. The Commissioners considered themselves legitimately if provisionally invested with supreme authority, responsible only to the Constituent Assembly to be elected in January, or as soon as practicable. *Spartakus*, on the other hand, which considered the executive of the Workers' and Soldiers' Councils as the supreme authority, responsible only to the coming national congress of councils,

[1] *D. & M.* Vol. I, pp. 341–2.

immediately agitated against any resignation of power into the hands of the Commissioners. Thus the differing conceptions of revolutionary power immediately led to a tactical divergence between the two extreme Socialist camps. Both fastened their slogans on to institutions, *Spartakus* on the Councils, the SPD on the coming Constituent Assembly. The Independents swung in between, accepting the Constituent Assembly as inevitable—they always had a clear sense of the limits of revolutionary possibilities; pending the election, however, which they wished to put off as long as they could, the revolutionary power of the Councils was to be built up as much as possible. They accepted the duality, which the groups on either side would not; *Spartakus* opposed any parliament, while the SPD expected the Councils to wither away once a legitimate government came into being.

These articulate opinions existed, we must repeat, only at the top. They were by no means reflected in the membership of the Workers' and Soldiers' Councils in Berlin, still less in the rest of Germany. In Berlin and in most of the Reich, SPD members, or soldiers and civilians unattached to any party but conservative on the whole, formed the majority on the Councils. The USPD provided a consistent and sometimes substantial minority, though in a few places it dominated the Councils; and its left wing, *Spartakus*, for a period controlled a few Councils, in Brunswick and Stuttgart. The *Spartakus* call for all power to be given to the Councils was therefore not primarily intended to promote institutions which they did not in fact control, or in which they did not have even a substantial minority. No doubt they hoped that more power for the Councils would make the membership more radical, that the slogan itself would sharpen the situation generally without too much immediate institutional emphasis just as it had done in Russia. But for the moment, while agitating strongly on their behalf, *Spartakus* was not even able to get its main leaders co-opted on to the provisional executive of the Councils in Berlin. The demand of *Rote Fahne* on 10 November 1918, that Rosa Luxemburg be asked to join this executive, was ignored. Later attempts of *Spartakus* leaders to join or influence the meetings of the executive, or of the national congress of Councils in December, all failed, on the fine legal point that Liebknecht and Rosa Luxemburg were neither workers nor soldiers! German precision and orderliness lent its particular flavour even to the revolution. Had Rosa Luxemburg forgotten all her expletives about the psychology of German Social Democracy?

Another immediate preoccupation of *Spartakus* and of the USPD was to get their papers published. *Spartakus* in Berlin adopted, at Jogiches' suggestion, the technique of the SDKPiL in Warsaw during the 1905 revolution. A small group, with Liebknecht at its head, occupied the offices of the *Berliner Lokalanzeiger* on 9 November, while raids were also made on other papers in Berlin. The occupiers insisted on the production of the newspaper under the title *Die Rote Fahne* (The Red Flag) and the second evening issue of Friday 9 November carried this title for the first time. But the loyalty of the printers to their management, and their threat to down tools, jeopardized the chances of any further such issues. Rosa Luxemburg had just arrived from Breslau by train and had gone straight to the newspaper offices; her first physical contribution to the German revolution was an eloquent appeal to the printers' proletarian conscience—never in the past famous for its militancy.[1] Even this was no use; next morning the printers, under instructions from the old management, firmly refused to print any more. Karl Liebknecht and Rosa Luxemburg, now in charge of all *Spartakus* publications, were turned out on 11 November.[2] Reference to the local Workers' and Soldiers' Council produced a directive that the occupation was illegal. On 12 November, however, the executive of the Berlin Councils authorized the use of printing and distribution facilities for the production of *Rote Fahne*. Rosa Luxemburg and Karl Liebknecht, accompanied by an escort of workers, personally carried the authorization back to the firms offices. But the management was now adamant in its refusal—the fear of *Spartakus* was not so great when commercial interests were at stake—and turned to Ebert personally: 'Our firm has been suffering twinges of conscience in case this authorization is really to be followed. . . . We are determined to trust the government programme for peace and quiet and the assurances for the safety of private property. This authorization, however, would place the vast resources of the firm at the disposal of quite the contrary tendency.' The People's Commissioners thereupon consulted with the Council of Workers and Soldiers; a brief laconic comment across the firm's protest states: 'The order against the publishers will not be carried out, further orders of this sort will not be given.'[3] Rosa Luxemburg thereupon tried to make a more commercial arrangement with the firm for bringing out *Rote Fahne* but, assured of government support, the management refused this as well.[4]

After this *Rote Fahne* did not appear again until 18 November. An unfavourable contract had finally to be made with a new publisher, which was expensive for *Spartakus*. This, and the small ration of paper allocated to the radicals, greatly hampered the range of their distribution.

---

[1] Hermann Duncker, 'Wie die erste Nummer der *Roten Fahne* erschien' in *Einführungen in den Marxismus*, Berlin (East) 1958, Vol. I, p. 395. Also *Rote Fahne*, 9 November 1928.

[2] Wilhelm Pieck, *Die Gründung der KPD*, Berlin 1928, reprinted in *Reden und Aufsätze*, Berlin (East) 1951, Vol. I, pp. 97–98.

[3] *D. & M.* Vol. II, pp. 289–392.

[4] *Der Ledebour-Prozess*, Berlin 1919, p. 513, Meyer's testimony.

The USPD also had difficulties, and their main organ, *Freiheit*, first appeared only on 16 November.[1]

Thus *Spartakus* could not hope to influence the main organs of government directly. All it could hope to do was to direct and influence the genuine revolutionary potential of the masses with the limited means at its disposal, and on this objective all its efforts were henceforward concentrated. It was freely admitted that the *Spartakus* organization was embryonic. But, contrary to the assumption of some later anti-Communist historians, *Spartakus* was well aware of these limitations, even if it conveniently did not admit them in public; the agitational policy was adopted partly because it suited the political philosophy of Liebknecht and Rosa Luxemburg, but particularly because they and their colleagues knew well that their situation permitted no other form of action. On 9, 10, and 11 November the leadership of *Spartakus* was in almost continuous session to formulate policy and to review negotiations with both Revolutionary Shop Stewards and USPD. The agitational demands of *Spartakus* on both these groups were still being consistently refused, just as the Revolutionary Shop Stewards had overruled Liebknecht with regard to the date of the proposed uprising. If anything the USPD, who had allowed Liebknecht to formulate their demands in the correspondence with the SPD after 9 November and had wanted him on their executive, were more susceptible to *Spartakus* influence than the Revolutionary Shop Stewards.[2] From the USPD side, at any rate, there was still a fund of old comradely loyalty. If only *Spartakus* were prepared to negotiate seriously instead of resorting constantly to demagogy! *Spartakus*, however, negotiated by means of abuse; its terms were nothing less than the complete adherence of Goliath to David.

The Revolutionary Shop Stewards, on the other hand, were possibly the only group of the three who had anything like an effective organization—though even this varied greatly from factory to factory. They were determined to preserve it. They stressed the necessity for keeping the revolutionary demands in line with the organizational possibilities—as opposed to the USPD's more political preoccupations: Liebknecht's conception of continuous mass action was mere 'revolutionary gymnastics'. *Spartakus* in turn accused them of suffering from a 'mechanical conception which places far too much emphasis on technical prepara-

---

[1] *Ledebour-Prozess*, p. 514.

[2] Richard Müller, *Vom Kaiserreich zur Republik*, Berlin 1924–5, Vol. II, p. 29; Pieck, *Reden*, Vol. I, p. 99.

One *Spartakist*, Schreiner, who had joined the left-wing Socialist cabinet in Württemberg (Stuttgart), was forced to resign on 15 November because *Spartakus* would not sit in any commission or government with the SPD (Wilheim Keil, *Erlebnisse*, Vol. II, p. 107).

tions'. Monotonously *Spartakus* dinned its only lesson, mass action, into unreceptive ears—at least as far as its potential allies were concerned.[1] The *Spartakus* leaders knew they had no effective mass organization. The main historical burden of the German Communists to this day has been their failure to build up an organization during and particularly at the end of the First World War. But it certainly was not due to any oversight. The *Spartakus* leaders deliberately decided to forgo any sustained attempt to create an organization in November 1918. They held that the revolutionary possibilities made this an unnecessary dispersal of effort; by concentrating on organizational work and neglecting the inspiration and leadership of an existing if uncertain mass movement, they might miss the bus of revolution altogether. The fact that the rising of 9 November had taken place spontaneously, that the organized parties had followed and not led, seemed to justify this decision. At the meeting of 11 November Rosa Luxemburg particularly stressed the need for *Spartakus* to remain within the organizational network of the USPD as long as possible, so that the masses might be captured for the *Spartakus* programme or possibly the Independent leaders be removed by democratic processes. After all, here was an organization ready-made —the USPD. To achieve all this, a full USPD party congress was considered necessary, and this Rosa immediately demanded. Jogiches, who knew the organizational possibilities better than anyone, supported her whole-heartedly, and the meeting once more adopted a programme whose main emphasis was on propaganda. Rosa laid down as immediate tasks the reissue of their daily paper, the production of a more theoretical weekly, special papers for youth and for women, a soldiers' paper, syndication of leading articles to be offered to other newspapers— shades of *Sozialdemokratische Korrespondenz*; finally, the creation of a special department for propaganda in the army.[2] Never had a revolution had such a paper base.

Organizationally, therefore, *Spartakus* was slow to develop; in most of the important provincial cities it evolved an organized centre only in the course of December and in many cases not until February or March 1919. The remarkable exception was Stuttgart where there had been an important *Spartakus* centre since the summer of 1918, which

---

[1] For the Revolutionary Shop Stewards, see Richard Müller, *Vom Kaiserreich zur Republik*, Vol. I, pp. 129 ff., and Emil Barth, *Aus der Werkstatt der deutschen Revolution*, Berlin, no date, pp. 30 ff.; for *Spartakus*, *Illustrierte Geschichte der deutschen Revolution*, Berlin 1929.

Liebknecht, who had the habit of sketching his views for his own benefit in revolutionary shorthand, characterized his own policy as: 'slogan [*Parole*]—mass action—further raising [of all demands]' (*Illustrierte Geschichte*, pp. 203 ff.).

[2] Pieck, *Reden*, Vol. I, p. 100. H. Duncker, *Erinnerungen von Veteranen der deutschen Gewerkschaftsbewegung an die Novemberrevolution*, Berlin (East) 1958, p. 21.

had, among other things, acted as a collection point for deserters from the German army.[1]

By the same token *Spartakus* had no means of bringing direct and personal pressure to bear in the Workers' and Soldiers' Councils. Attempts to arrange caucus meetings of *Spartakus* sympathizers within the Berlin Workers' and Soldiers' Councils did not produce satisfactory results, and an independent Communist caucus within the Berlin Council was formed only on 20 February 1919.[2] Attempts to have well-known *Spartakus* leaders co-opted to the Workers' and Soldiers' Councils in Berlin failed with monotonous regularity.

By mid-November 1918 *Spartakus* had exhausted its capacity for direct influence on the USPD leadership and was openly quarrelling on tactics with the Revolutionary Shop Stewards. It now adopted a wholly oppositional attitude and had to rely exlusively on mass action to bring its programme to fruition. Rosa Luxemburg did not participate in the early decisions which had produced this configuration but there is no reason whatever to suppose that she disagreed with it. When reading her articles in *Rote Fahne* it is essential to bear in mind the circumstances we have described, all resulting from the positive tactical decisions forced on *Spartakus* on the one hand, and from its isolation, partly deliberate, partly circumstantial, from both majority Socialists and Independents on the other. 'The revolution has begun; not joy over what has been achieved, not triumph over the beaten enemy are the orders of the day, but the strongest self-criticism and iron conservation of energy to continue the work that has only been initiated. Our achievements are slight, and the enemy is *not* beaten', she wrote, as early as 18 November in the first issue of *Rote Fahne* after the printing hiatus had been overcome.[3]

The proposal of the provisional executive of People's Commissioners to call a Constituent Assembly as soon as possible was the first point of attack.

Constituent Assembly as the bourgeois solution, Councils of Workers and Soldiers as the Socialist one. Among the open or disguised agents of the ruling classes the slogan [of a Constituent Assembly] is natural. With the guardians of capitalist money hoards we never argue *in* the legislature or *about* the legislature. But now even the Independents take their place among the guardians of capital on this vital question.[4]

As yet Rosa still made some concession to the good intentions of the Independent leaders; it was their mistaken and feeble application of

[1] Keil, *Erlebnisse*, Vol. II, p. 12.
[2] *Rote Fahne*, 21 February 1919.
[3] *Rote Fahne*, 18 November 1918.
[4] 'Die Nationalversammlung', *Rote Fahne*, 20 November 1918.

Marxism which led them to misunderstand the real nature of a Constituent Assembly.

They have forgotten that the bourgeoisie is not a political party but a ruling class . . . but once profits are really in question, private property really in danger, then all easy-going talk of democracy immediately comes to an end. . . . As soon as the famous Constituent Assembly really decides to put Socialism fully and completely into practice . . . the battle begins. . . . All this is inevitable. This battle must be fought out, the enemy destroyed—with or without a Constituent Assembly. 'Civil war', which they are so anxious to cut out of the revolution, cannot be cut out. For civil war is simply another name for class war, and the thought that Socialism could be achieved without class war, that it follows from a mere majority resolution in parliament, is a ridiculous petit-bourgeois conception.[1]

Thus the very *conception* of a Constituent Assembly was a negation of the class war and therefore unacceptable to Socialists.

The clearest statement of the alternative was made a month later—it was Liebknecht's ascending revolutionary progression in literary terms—when the Reich Conference of Workers' and Soldiers' Councils in turn adopted the proposal of the People's Commissioners for elections to a Constituent Assembly. History was pressed into service, the history of the English revolution:

Not in the debates [of the Long Parliament] in Westminster Abbey, though it may have contained the intellectual centre of the revolution, but on the battlefields of Marston Moor and Naseby, not in glowing speeches, but through the peasant cavalry which formed Cromwell's Ironsides, was the fate of the English revolution decided.[2]

Parliaments were thus useless as means of ensuring revolution, even bourgeois revolution; they were merely the end product of revolutions achieved by other means, in physical and social battle.

But just as the masses had to be clear about their situation, so it was from time to time regrettably necessary to defend *Spartakus* in the eyes of the masses. This was where Rosa Luxemburg made her own particular contribution to the writings of the time. Here especially she left statements which rose above the immediate necessities of revolutionary action and have remained as a valid commentary on what is best in proletarian revolution for all time. More perhaps than any other member of *Spartakus*, she was at all times concerned with the ethics of revolution, both as an essential part of revolution itself and as a tactical

---

[1] Ibid.
[2] 'Nationalversammlung oder Räteregierung?', *Rote Fahne*, 17 December 1918.

reminder to all its detractors of the moral purposes of revolution. She poured scorn on the rumour-mongers:

Liebknecht has killed 200 officers, has been killed himself, has looted the shops, has distributed money among the soldiers to incite them to destroy the revolution. . . . Whenever a window pane crashes on to the pavement, or a tyre bursts in the street, the Philistines at once look over their shoulders; their hair standing on end and pimply with gooseflesh, they whisper: 'Aha, here comes *Sparktakus*'.

A number of people have been writing to Liebknecht with touching personal requests to save wife, nephew or aunt from the coming mass slaughter, which *Spartakus* has planned. We have come to this in the first year and month of the glorious German revolution! . . . Behind these rumours, ridiculous fantasies, and shameless lies there is a serious purpose. The whole thing is planned . . . to create an atmosphere of pogrom and to shoot *Spartakus* politically in the back. They [the official Social Democrats] consciously and deliberately misrepresent our Socialist aims as banditry. They yell against putsches, murder and similar rubbish, but they mean Socialism . . . but the game will not succeed . . . though yet vacillating sections of workers and soldiers may be inveigled into opposing us. Even if a momentary return of the counter-revolutionary wave should throw us back into those prisons which we have only just left—the iron course of revolution cannot be held up. Our voice will sound loud and clear, the masses will understand us, and then they will turn all the more fiercely against the propagandists of hate and pogroms.[1]

Against the constant accusation of being a party of terror Rosa had this to say.

[Those] who sent 1½ million German men and youths to the slaughter without blinking an eyelid, [those] who supported with all the means at their disposal for four years the greatest blood-letting which humanity has ever experienced— they now scream hoarsely about 'terror', about the alleged 'monstrosities' threatened by the dictatorship of the proletariat. But these gentlemen should look at their own history.

The revolution that had brought them into power long ago had used its fair share of force.

Terror and fear were the weapons of bourgeois revolution with which to destroy illusions and hopeless resistance to the mainstream of history. The Socialist proletariat, however, thanks to the theory of scientific Socialism, enters into its revolution without illusions, with a clear comprehension of the ultimate consequences of its historical mission, of the unbridgeable contradictions of society, of the bitter enmity to bourgeois society as a whole. It enters the revolution not in order to follow utopian illusions *against* the course of history, but to complete the iron necessities of development, to make Socialism *real*. . . . It therefore does not require to destroy its own illusions with bloody acts of

---

[1] 'Das alte Spiel', *Rote Fahne*, 18 November 1918.

violence in order to create a contradiction between itself and bourgeois society. What it needs is the entire political power of private capital, of wage-slavery, of middle-class domination, in order to build up a new Socialist society. But there are others who need terror, anarchy, and the rule of violence today: the middle classes who are shaking in their shoes for their property, their privileges, and their profits. It is they who fabricate the myths about anarchy and putsches, and pile all these on to the shoulders of the proletariat, in order to unleash their real putsches, their own real anarchy, in order to stifle the proletarian revolution, to drown Socialist dictatorship in chaos, and to create on the ruins of the revolution a class dictatorship of capital for ever and ever.[1]

Rosa Luxemburg's conception of terror, which she developed in the coming weeks, was later to be attacked both by the Communists—for not being radical or clear enough—and by 'neutral' historians, who claimed that this was mere phraseology to disguise planned and necessary terror in all its consequences. Certainly Rosa Luxemburg's formulations differ substantially from those of the Russians, particularly Radek, who for some years to come was to be the spokesman of the official Russian view in German Communist affairs. 'When the Independents, like Hilferding and Ledebour, said that they accept dictatorship but without terror, without force, they show that they do not accept dictatorship of the working classes at all. . . . Dictatorship without the willingness to apply terror is a knife without a blade.'[2] Other members of *Spartakus* did not find it necessary to write on this question at the time; those who survived only denounced Rosa Luxemburg's conception much later, on Stalin's orders. When Radek arrived in Berlin illegally on 20 December, this was one of the first subjects he discussed with Liebknecht and Rosa Luxemburg—had the comments in the *Spartakus* letters struck home to them more than the Bolsheviks were openly prepared to admit?

Our argument was mostly concerned with terror. Rosa was hurt that Dzierżyński had accepted the post of heading the Cheka [the Russian security police]. 'After all terror had never beaten us; why should we have to depend on it?' 'But with the help of terror,' I answered her, 'by persecuting us, they throw us back a full five years. We plan for world revolution, we need a few year's grace. How can you deny the need for terror under those circumstances? Anyhow terror is valueless when applied against a young class, representing the future of social change and therefore full of enthusiasm and self-sacrifice. The case is quite different with classes whom history has sentenced to death, and who in addition bear the responsibility for the crime of the world war.' Liebknecht supported me warmly. Rosa said, 'Perhaps you are right, but how can Josef [Dzierżyński] be

[1] 'Ein gewagtes Spiel', *Rote Fahne*, 24 November 1918.
[2] Struthahn (Karl Radek), *Die Entwicklung der deutschen Revolution und die Aufgaben der Kommunistischen Partei*, Stuttgart 1919, p. 5.

so cruel?' Tyshka [Jogiches] laughed and said: 'If the need arises, you can do it too.'[1]

Once again there is no need to isolate Rosa's conceptions from their context. She had strong personal reservations about terror, but had necessarily accepted Russian events as being the result of particular circumstances. The revolution in Germany was improving those circumstances and making the use of terror unnecessary in both countries. Out of earshot of the daily propaganda bulletin, the founding members of the German Communist Party heard her declare that, in the long view, 'the working-class revolution needs no terrors for its ends, it hates and despises cold-blooded murder'.[2]

At the same time she was fully conscious that terror would be applied as a weapon of defence by the opponents of the revolution; that many Socialists, including possibly herself, would yet fall victim to it. She was not squeamish; mass action in all its forms must result in frequent destruction of life as well as property. Revolution was not a drawing-room game, or an abstraction; it was simply inevitable. This view differed, however, from the organized and deliberate terror on the part of the revolutionaries which she had condemned in Russia. While it is therefore correct that Rosa Luxemburg never occupied herself with the technique of terror, her attitude cannot be described as 'clever sophistry', or as an attempt 'to avoid a clear confrontation with this issue through self-deception, and with the help of subtle dialectic'.[3]

Finally Rosa supported every available means of keeping the masses awake and on their toes. *Spartakus* organized repeated demonstrations, not only in reply to what it considered major provocations by the government but as a constant check on its own ability to call up mass support. Thus on 21 November there were big meetings in Berlin at which, among others, Liebknecht and Rosa Luxemburg addressed the crowd. On 1 December there were a further six public meetings.[4] From then on *Spartakus* was continuously mobilizing support in the streets. Rosa Luxemburg analysed these mass movements as 'Acheron on the move':

They console the masses with the promise of golden rewards from a future democratic parliament ... but the healthy class instinct of the proletariat rises up against this conception of parliamentary cretinism. ... The strike movement now unleashed is proof that the political revolution has crashed into the basic

---

[1] Karl Radek, 'November—A small page out of my memoirs', originally in *Krasnaya Nov*', 1926, No. 10, pp. 139–75, reprinted in Otto-Ernst Schüddekopf, 'Karl Radek in Berlin, Ein Kapitel deutsch-russischer Beziehungen im Jahre 1919', *Archiv für Sozialgeschichte*, 1962, Vol. II, p. 133. This will in future be cited as Radek, *Dairy*.

[2] *Bericht über den Gründungstag der KPD*, p. 53.

[3] Kolb, *Arbeiterräte*, p. 140.

[4] *Rote Fahne*, 2 December 1918.

structure of society. The revolution returns to its basic roots, it pushes aside the paper props of ministerial changes and resolutions . . . and enters the stage on its own behalf . . . in the present revolution. The recent strikes are not trade-union agreements about trivial details . . . they are the natural answer of the masses to the enormous tremors which capital has suffered as a result of the collapse of German imperialism . . . they are the early beginnings of a general confrontation between capital and labour in Germany. . . . Acheron is on the move, and the dwarfs who carry on their little games at the head of the revolution will either be thrown off the stage or they will finally learn to understand the colossal scale of the historical drama in which they are participating.[1]

This joyful indulgence in mass movement, this persistent call for action and clarity, helped to create the conditions for the hopeless January rising in which both Karl Liebknecht and Rosa Luxemburg were killed. Her writings, with their heightened tone and sharp revolutionary formulation, are often considered to have whipped up the unjustified and premature action. But this judgement assumes first of all that the *Spartakus* appeals in general and Rosa's writings in particular—certainly the best writing and the most provocative challenges of the day—received wide publicity, and were acted upon. No direct evidence of the effects of *Spartakus* propaganda on the masses is available; we do not know whether the mass demonstrations took place because of appeals by *Spartakus* or USPD sympathizers in the factories, or as a result of public announcements in the press, or spontaneously, or all three. The confusion of political allegiance in factories, councils, and other organizations make a clear identification of *Spartakus* influence almost impossible. Moreover, there is no substantial evidence that the mass actions which had overtaken the leading organizations before and on 9 November had ever been brought under any effective control. The case for connecting *Spartakus* propaganda directly and causally to the popular manifestations in November, December, and January has still to be proven.

Direct incitement to action was anyhow not the prime purpose of Rosa Luxemburg's writing. Her essays, full of historical parallels and scientific analyses, may have been intended as rather emphatic commentary on events, but not to an excited mass of half-demobilized soldiers and unemployed workers. It was the situation which made *Rote Fahne* inflammatory, not its content. The only alternative was out of the question—adjusting the tenor of one's appeals to the tactical demands of the moment, hot and cold, stop and go, like the Bebel leadership of the SPD before the war.

The answer to this apparent dilemma is simply that Karl Liebknecht

---

[1] 'Der Acheron in Bewegung', *Rote Fahne*, 27 November 1918. Acheron is the mythological river of woe that seals off Hades.

and Rosa Luxemburg, both of whom had already paid for their revolutionary determination during the war, accepted the full consequences of what they were doing as a part of historical necessity. If indeed the masses rose and were defeated then this would clarify the situation still further; it was part of the inevitable process of education in a revolutionary situation. In the last resort, leaders who are themselves willing to accept the sacrifice of their liberty and life are probably the only ones who can justifiably call upon their supporters to do the same, particularly when these sacrifices are a necessary part of distant though inevitable victory. That the whole conception of revolution may have been mistaken, that there was really no prospect of long- or short-term victory in Germany, is another question; given the circumstances and traditions of the *Spartakus* leaders, it is not meaningful to ask why they did not act 'Russian' during this period. The Independents' policy of compromise, accepting the inevitable Constituent Assembly and hoping to develop a revolutionary tactic within it, was anathema to *Spartakus*. When Kurt Eisner came from Munich to Berlin at the end of November for the conference of provincial Prime Ministers (he had by this time been elected Prime Minister of Bavaria), he had a long dialogue with Liebknecht. He attempted to persuade the latter to make common cause with the more moderate revolutionaries, even to form joint governments with them, in order to ensure that present revolutionary achievements might at least be maintained and a decent peace obtained from the allies; but he was answered with a stern 'no'. 'The achievement of Socialism is only possible if everything is pulled down completely; only after the destruction of the entire capitalist system can reconstruction begin.'[1]

If anything, the membership of *Spartakus* was even more revolutionary than the leaders. The pressure for action came from below—just as Rosa Luxemburg had always predicted. In December several mass demonstrations led to attacks on public buildings by groups of young *Spartakus* members. On 21 November an attempt, with resultant casualties, had been made to storm police headquarters, in spite of the fact that the Berlin Police President was a left-wing Independent—later a Communist—and probably the only senior official in the capital who sympathized with *Spartakus*.[2] On 8 December detachments went once more from a public meeting to the military headquarters and stormed

---

[1] H. Roland-Holst, *Rosa Luxemburg*, pp. 189–90. The official note of the conversation, with a depressing hand-written comment on its failure, is in *Geheimes Staatsarchiv München*, Political Archives, VII, Series 115, handwritten note of conversation Eisner-Liebknecht, 24 November 1918.

[2] Eduard Bernstein, *Die deutsche Revolution ihr Ursprung ihr Verlauf und ihr Werk*, Berlin 1921, Vol. I, p. 71; *Geheimes Staatsarchiv München*, Political Archives, VII, No. 79, folio 7.

it.[1] And at many *Spartakus* meetings official speakers were often followed on to the rostrum by unexpected members of the crowd, who sometimes made hair-raising but seriously-meant demands, including the liberation of prisoners in all the jails and the instant capture of various prominent personalities. Almost each day there were rival meetings called by the different groups which sometimes clashed.[2]

Rosa Luxemburg knew that in revolutionary times irresponsible elements attached themselves to the revolutionary parties: 'The proletarian revolution will always have to reckon and fight with this particular enemy and tool of the counter-revolution.'[3] In the crowds there were no doubt some footloose criminals, but the bulk were young uncompromising radicals, who wanted the constant warnings against any truck with the enemy translated into a complete personal break with all the coat-tails of society—and into action, above all action. We should know all about this primary urge for the experience of action from the American and German students of our otherwise far less revolutionary present. During these stormy weeks at the end of 1918, and particularly at the founding congress of the German Communist Party, the leadership collided with some of these elements, and was sometimes overruled by them. But they were part of the stuff of proletarian revolution; there were more important things to do than to condemn them for their impetuousness. That task can be left to German middle-class historians anxious to pick over the dungheap of the 1918 national disgrace—just as condemnation of the left-wing students of 1967–8 can safely be left to the comfortable gentlemen of the Kiesinger coalition, which of course includes a good share of Socialists!

[1] Pieck, *Reden*, Vol. I, p. 104.
[2] Ibid.
[3] Rosa Luxemburg, *The Russian Revolution* (ed. Bertram D. Wolfe), p. 74.

XVI

IRRESISTIBLE FORCE AND

IMMOVABLE OBJECT

HAVING obtained confirmation of their authority from the Berlin Workers' and Soldiers' Council, the provisional government of People's Commissioners quickly set about making it real. Legitimacy was no limitation on power. Ebert—though the phrase. 'I hate social revolution like the plague' cannot be attributed to him with certainty— decided that order and a return to normal were the immediate priorities of the situation. He was willing and able to accept all the responsibility. More than his two Social-Democrat colleagues in the government, Scheidemann and Landsberg, he had a strong sense of legitimacy, with regard both to the institutions he had inherited from his predecessors and the new forms of power which had tentatively emerged on 9 November. Ebert was a literal man. Most of the demands put forward by the pre-war SPD under Bebel's leadership and his own, as an unrealizable slogan, had unexpectedly become reality. The notion of revolutionary progression, in which the present stage was but a small step, seemed nonsense to him. What was needed was a period of revolutionary digestion. Accordingly, the government asked for and obtained from the executive of the Workers' and Soldiers' Councils increased powers to cope with the situation. And on 21 December 1918 the national Congress of German Workers' and Soldiers' Councils set the seal of its confirmation and approval on Ebert's government.

This same preoccupation with legitimacy, from which followed the urge for 'peace and quiet', made him resort without hesitation to any available means of achieving his mandate. The most obvious and convenient tool was the army. The High Command had sworn allegiance to the Republic, and this commitment was sufficient guarantee for Ebert, a man for whom an oath was an oath. He considered the delicate negotiations with the army as his personal function, and did not deem it necessary to submit them to the approval of his USPD colleagues— for, after all, they were only intended to achieve an object that had already been agreed on by all the People's Commissioners. As far as he was concerned, any over-eagerness on the part of the army to intervene was only a reaction to *Spartakus*'s encouragement of revolutionary excesses—the inevitable results of a disturbed situation.

The course of events in December and January hinged largely on a number of incidents which appeared to disturb the slow process of consolidation by the government. On 6 December troops occupied the editorial offices of *Rote Fahne* and attempted to arrest the executive of the Berlin Workers' and Soldiers' Council, and were only with difficulty persuaded to leave; at the same time there were calls to make Ebert President. There is no conclusive evidence that Ebert inspired this or wished it to happen, but he did nothing to issue any denial or to denounce and punish the instigators.[1] None the less, these events were followed by mass demonstrations and strikes. Then, on 21 December, the government attempted to deal with the People's Naval Division (*Volksmarinedivision*), a unit of revolutionaries and mutineers, who had installed themselves in the Marstall, the stables of the Imperial Palace, and were pressing their somewhat mercenary services on the revolutionary government. Their idealism for the government of the revolution was heavily tinged with concrete demands for pay and privileges. The negotiations with the government, partly over these and partly over the continued presence and even existence of the unit, came to an abrupt end when troops under the command of Otto Wels, the Social-Democrat Commandant of Berlin, made an unsuccessful assault on the stables. This incident, and particularly the sharp manner in which the negotiations had been broken off and an attack mounted without warning, caused the three Independent members of the provisional government to resign. Henceforth the USPD was wholly in opposition once again. Finally, the government's attempt to remove the left-wing police president of Berlin, Emil Eichhorn, on 3 and 4 January, led directly to the events of the January rising, as a result of which Rosa Luxemburg and Karl Liebknecht were murdered.

Each of these incidents provoked a reaction which was in no proportion to its actual importance. The situation was largely beyond the control of both the government and its opponents. Having decided for itself that the government and its Independent supporters were mere agents of the counter-revolution, *Spartakus* saw all these events as signposts along a predicted road, and called out its troops on each occasion. Though it continued, at any rate until the end of the year, to call for the *advance* of the revolution, it was soon obliged to call its supporters not so much to advance as to defend existing achievements against the attacks of the government. These rallying cries for defence were actually a more effective tactic than any call for further advances. *Spartakus* was on its own in demanding rapid and total advance on all

---

[1] Arthur Rosenberg, *Geschichte der deutschen Republik*, Karlsbad 1935, p. 84. For a view of Ebert's complicity, see Walter Oehme, *Damals in der Reichskanzlei, Erinnerungen aus den Jahren 1918–19*, Berlin (East) 1958, pp. 62 ff. All the main sources carry slightly different versions of this controversial event.

fronts, but it could and did find ready allies for the defence against counter-revolution, real or imagined. The workers of Berlin, the Revolutionary Shop Stewards, as well as the USPD leadership—particularly after their members left the government—were much more disposed to support action of this kind, for it was precise and not vague or irresponsible. At times the People's Naval Division signified its support, especially when its own interests were threatened. But although events more or less forced co-operation on these groups, it was not too effective. *Spartakus* always mistrusted the intentions and good faith of its allies. While co-operating with them in practice, it went on demarcating its own position from theirs, and continued to show them up in public as cowards and weaklings. The rapid tactical realignments of Lenin had never taken hold in Germany, not even among the radicals. *Spartakus* was imprisoned in the limitations of its commitment to purity and principles as public weapons instead of a private hoard of strength. This made tactical adjustments impossible.

Now that the Independents were in opposition to the government once more, they began to split on the issue of co-operation with *Spartakus*. On 8 December one of their right-wing members, Ströbel, had stated openly that *Spartakus* and the USPD were irreconcilably separated by the difference between German and Russian methods. He saw *Spartakus* as the slavish imitators of Russian methods and the Bolshevik programme; the preoccupation with giving exclusive power to the Councils seemed alien and remote to Germany.[1] He and others advocated for the USPD a clear separation both from Left and Right. Too many compromises on both sides were responsible for the fact that the Independents were being pulled apart. The alternative was to make a decision between the two extremes. 'We have no policy. We have appeals and leading articles, we have speeches and resolutions, but we have no policy. . . . There are only two possibilities for the USPD: exit from the cabinet and adherence to *Spartakus*—or continuation in the government and sharp demarcation from the Left.'[2]

The internal struggle between *Spartakus* and the Independent leadership for the control of USPD policy and the direction of its substantial membership came to a head in December. *Spartakus* had been pressing for a party congress and it was this issue which dominated the general meeting of the USPD of Greater Berlin on 15 December. An influential group of USPD had altogether lost interest in discussing the problem of Councils or Constituent Assembly as alternatives; they considered it a 'waste of time'.[3] At the meeting Hilferding brought

[1] *Die Freiheit*, No. 43, 8 December 1918.
[2] Rudolf Breitscheid in *Der Sozialist*, IV (50), 12 December 1918.
[3] Rudolf Hilferding in *Die Freiheit*, No. 57, 16 December 1918.

a resolution to the effect that the next task was to accept the elections as inevitable and to ensure the greatest possible success for the Independents. At the same time he stipulated the tasks as 'to ensure the safety and increase of our revolutionary achievements with complete decisiveness and without feeble compromise'.

Rosa Luxemburg made an impassioned speech against this whole conception. She and Haase appeared as main speakers on the question of policy and presented their different views. She sketched the history of the last few weeks.

Five weeks have passed since 9 November. The picture is totally changed. Reaction is much stronger today that on the first day of the revolution. And Haase tells us 'Look how wonderfully far we have come'. His duty should have been to show us the advance of the counter-revolution, supported by the government of which Haase is a member. . . . We are still prepared to enter the government today if it carries out Socialist policy based on proper principles.

Precisely the adherence to the policy of the existing government had cost the Independents votes in the elections for the first all-German congress of councils.

Haase has also accused us of bowing to the views of the masses. [According to him] we are not prepared to take over the government without the agreement of the masses. We do not bow, but we also do not simply wait around. . . . Yes, conditions within the USPD are intolerable, since there are elements in it who do not belong together. Either you agree to go the same way as the social patriots, or you joint *Sparkatus*. Only a party congress can decide this question, but in demanding a party congress, we find Haase's ears just as closed as we found those of Scheidemann when we made similar demands during the war.[1]

Rosa Luxemburg submitted her own resolution against Hilferding's. She demanded the immediate exit of the USPD members from the government (it was six days before the Marstall incident), resolute opposition to the Constituent Assembly, the immediate seizure of power by the Workers' and Soldiers' Councils, the dissolution of the Council of People's Commissioners, and finally the immediate convocation of a USPD congress. Her resolution was lost by a large majority, 195 votes against 485 for Hilferding. The Berlin members did not want to accept the choice which Rosa Luxemburg and Breitscheid wished to impose on them. They felt that the middle position of the USPD could be maintained against both alternatives, and that it was the correct policy.

This vote also showed *Spartakus* how illusory for the moment were

[1] *Die Freiheit*, No. 57, 16 December 1918.

its hopes of discrediting the USPD leaders in the eyes of the membership, or of forcing them at least to submit to a vote of confidence by a party congress. The fact that Rosa really believed in the possibility of sweeping aside the USPD leadership is born out by her private assessment of the situation for Clara Zetkin's benefit. Rosa explained that people were really behind *Spartakus*. They admired and followed *Rote Fahne* far more than *Freiheit* and actually felt that *Spartakus* did not take the Independent leadership to task sharply enough. Only Haase and Hilferding defended their paper—weakly. 'That is why we insist on the party congress.'[1] Not that a party congress would in the event have produced an alignment different from that at the Berlin members' meeting. The delusion that negative votes of this sort were the result of the leaders' narrow manipulations, and that a broader discussion would also produce a more radical attitude, died hard. For the moment *Spartakus* was balked; and there was no point in continuing as an ineffective ginger group within the USPD. At once the leaders made preparations for the founding of a separate party of their own. It was the organizational break at last—but even now not without grave doubts on the part of Rosa and Leo Jogiches.

If they could not have a USPD congress, at least there was the national congress of Workers' and Soldiers' Councils four days later, on 20 December. Here was another opportunity of 'testing' the masses. *Spartakus* placed great hopes on the congress, called for welcoming mass demonstrations—which would show the delegates how radical the masses were. The majority Socialists' analysis of the situation used many of the same words as *Spartakus*, but with strangely different meaning.

When William the deserter himself deserted, and the Junkers and middle classes took refuge in their rat holes, the entire working population of Germany looked hopefully towards the only political power which was left, the power of the labour movement. . . . The congress which begins today has the proud task of justifying this confidence, and of reinforcing it where it has already begun to weaken. Certain quarters have been pressing the slogan 'All power to the Workers' and Soldiers' Councils'. The congress has supreme power today, for it is the parliament of the revolution, which can break the revolution's government or give it the strong support which the government needs to master the incalculable difficulties before it. The majority of the congress . . . will be sensible enough to recognize the weakness of its composition. The elections which brought it into being were regrettably neither general nor equal nor direct, in many cases not even secret. Such as they were, they were only an expedient . . .;

---

[1] 29 November 1918, photocopy IML (B), NL5III-A/15, p. 85. A month later, still optimistic, she wrote that the USPD 'is in the process of complete dissolution . . . in the provinces the reunion of USP and the *Scheidemen* is in full cry' (ibid., p. 92). Did Rosa mean leaders or masses? One wonders!

for all these weaknesses the only remedy can be found in the spirit of the new orderly system of liberty, and in that strong sense of right which is part of the basis of the German working-class movement. . . .

The discussion 'Constituent Assembly or Councils' may have led to qualification even before its final discussions here. Social Democracy does not recognize these alternatives, since its sacred duty lies in giving the entire population as quickly as possible a full and democratic possibility of self-determination, thus bringing forward the elections for the Constituent [Assembly] to the earliest possible date. Until then the government of the Reich, supported by the confidence of the people, must have liberty of action. Additional governments . . . must not be tolerated . . . it depends on [the Left Independent–*Spartakist* movement] whether the sittings [of the congress] are carried out in a spirit of dignity and in full cognizance of the importance of the matters in hand. As far as can be seen, the Social Democrats, with which we equally count the right wing of the Independents, have a vast majority . . . the far Left . . . can be no menace at any elections. But was it not they who announced 'All power to the Councils'? All right then! They have recognized the Workers' and Soldiers' Councils as the highest power and will have to submit to the decision [of the Congress], even if they do not like it.

How easy it must have seemed to the leadership to hoist *Spartakus* with its own petard!

The recommendations to the delegates concluded with the following sentence:

The men who have the enormous task of leading the people in these troubled times must be restrained, clear, quiet and decisive. We need men of action, not men of words.[1]

This declaration is quoted at length because it highlights the different conceptions of revolution held by SPD and *Spartakus*—part of the confusion arose from the absence of a distinct revolutionary vocabulary, and both sides had to use the same old words. As regards programme, the SPD was for consolidation. They recognized the revolutionary achievements as real, and believed that the Socialist society of their conception was at hand. They would go on clinging to this idea until in the 1920s they were pushed out of power by the same democratic system they had created; even when a Nazi government, as indifferent to classifying its opponents as the old imperial governments of Russia and Germany had been, persecuted Socialists indiscriminately with Communists, they still believed that the appearances of 1918 had been realities and that only the *Spartakus* excesses had revived forces which history had already pronounced dead.

But the differences between left- and right-wing socialists were not only programmatic. The Social Democrats saw themselves as men of

[1] *Vorwärts*, 16 December 1918.

action, 'restrained, quiet, decisive'; *Spartakus* were cheap manufacturers of revolutionary phrases, without any sense of responsibility. Ascriptive phrases like 'calm deliberation' and 'worthy' abound in party speeches of the time. There was a strong sense of inheritance—not only of power, but of a tradition of rule which retrospectively made all the pre-war denunciations sound like envy. It was no longer the system which was blamed, but individuals: the Kaiser, Ludendorff, Bethmann-Hollweg. The class lessons were thrown to the winds. And yet, to the fury of the Left, the old words still served—there were no others—causing confusion and an almost hysterial fury at such theft.

More than any differences in programme, this quarrel over an inheritance made any co-operation impossible, even in the future. In France and Italy, in spite of the same ideological splits, there was never the same sharp social differentiation; under certain future circumstances a 'Popular Front' co-operation between Communists and Socialists proved possible. In Germany this was not the case, and the two groups were unable to co-operate even against the rise of National Socialism, which menaced them equally. For this reason, too, the intermediate position of the USPD became impossible, so that inevitably its own Right and Left configurations soon split and joined the more natural habitats of SPD and KPD respectively. The choice was not only ideological but social, and therefore harsher.[1]

The congress did as *Vorwärts* had predicted, in spite of every effort by *Spartakus* to impose its programme from within and without. *Rote Fahne* reprinted resolution after resolution at public meetings against Ebert and against the SPD majority of the congress, but all to no avail.[2] A resolution submitted by the delegation of the Stuttgart Council, which was largely *Spartakus*-orientated, for the admission of Liebknecht and Rosa Luxemburg as 'guests with a consultative voice' was defeated by a considerable majority.

An orthodox SPD speaker from Berlin stated that there was no point in admitting Karl Liebknecht and Rosa Luxemburg since 'we in Berlin at least, but I think all over the Reich, know very well exactly what we have to expect from these comrades'.[3] After the vote was taken, one of the delegates called upon the congress 'to rise for a man who has sat in jail for four years', but he was shouted down with the traditional German '*pfui*'; had they not all suffered, if not like lions, then at least like lambs?

[1] In spite of twelve years' common persecution, this social differentiation was carried through to 1946, and has been a feature of the SED in East Germany ever since—embodied in the isolation of the old SPD element within the united party.

[2] E.g. *Rote Fahne*, 17 December 1918.

[3] *Allgemeiner Kongress der Arbeiter- und Soldatenräte Deutschlands vom 16 bis 21 Dezember 1918, Stenographische Berichte*, Berlin, no date, pp. 26–27.

The Soviet government had attempted to send a delegation to the congress. Although the executive of the Berlin Workers' and Soldiers' Councils had recommended the government to admit this delegation, the local commanders in the East had refused to let it pass, and indeed the SPD/USPD government had decided after lengthy discussions not to allow the Russian Legation to return to Berlin for the time being.[1] There was complete agreement between majority and Independent Socialists on the dangers of Russian intervention in the German revolution, if on nothing else. When the delegation was turned back by the German military authorities in Kovno, Radek, a member of the delegation, obtained the agreement of the Soviet Council of People's Commissars to try and cross the frontier illegally. He arrived in Berlin on 19 or 20 December.[2] Though he could have attended the last two sessions of the congress, the *Spartakus* leaders told him that his presence there would be useless—everything was going against them. He arrived just at the time when they had definitely decided to found their party without further delay, and he assisted in the preparations.

As a good if recently-converted Leninist, his first questions concerned the *Spartakus* organization.

How many people had we at the congress? There was not even a *Spartakus* caucus. . . . And in the Berlin Workers' and Soldiers' Council? There too we had no organized group. In the provinces things were better here and there. In Bremen we had managed to capture a substantial portion of the council under the command of Knief. In Chemnitz, Brandler was working. 'And how large is our organization in Berlin?' I asked. 'We are only collecting our forces. When the revolution began we did not have more than 50 people organized in Berlin.'

I drove with Paul Levi to the offices of the central committee to meet Jogiches. It was like an apiary. The old secretary Mathilde Jacob met me . . . she led me to Jogiches. He had aged a lot, my old teacher. . . . There was still a certain amount of tension between us, since the split in the Polish Social Democracy in 1912 . . . we did not talk about these old matters. He asked after Lenin, Trotsky, Zinoviev, Dzierżyński. After a few minutes we were back to our old relationship, open and simple.[3]

---

[1] Philipp Scheidemann, *Der Zusammenbruch*, Berlin 1921, p. 224. For the negotiations regarding the Soviet delegation to the congress, see *D. & M.* Vol. II, p. 501 and Scheidemann, p. 227.

[2] See Radek, *Diary*, p. 132. Although Radek in his later writings on the German revolution became less and less reliable about facts as well as interpretation, he wrote this diary shortly after the events described, and some of the earlier details are borne out exactly by a recent biography: Willy Brandt and Richard Löwenthal, *Ernst Reuter. Ein Leben für die Freiheit*, Munich 1957. Reuter, the Mayor of West Berlin until his death, was a Communist in the years immediately after the First World War, known as Reuter-Friesland. He had been a prisoner of war in Russia and, together with a man called Felix Wolf or Rackow, accompanied Radek in his illegal journey from Russia to Berlin.

[3] Radek, *Diary*, pp. 132–4.

A curious moment, Radek's arrival in Berlin, the official delegate of the victorious Bolsheviks—a moment of mixed feelings and memories even in the midst of a hailstorm of present events. Radek, the outcast of Polish and German Social Democracy, the snide journalist with the poison pen who had clutched Lenin's coat-tails in 1914 for protection against Jogiches and Rosa Luxemburg, Radek the '*genus* whore' who had poisoned Rosa's relations with her Bremen friends, had deepened the split in the SDKPiL, had written that the 'Tyshka and Luxemburg clique is finished'—Lenin's plenipotentiary! Radek himself glided elegantly over the personal undertone of the first meeting. And we may well believe that Jogiches, who had really mellowed during the war, soon let the past remain buried—as with Lenin, actual revolution simply buried old personal feuds under its majestic rubble. But Rosa? Radek said nothing. But she stayed with him that first day not one moment longer than was necessary, and would not join them for dinner. The coldness of their encounter became proverbial in the Communist Party.[1]

The programme for the new party was entirely written by Rosa Luxemburg and had been published on 14 December [2]

Rosa wrote a draft of a party programme. It was discussed among the leaders and caused no argument at all. The only argument arose over the relationship to the Constituent Assembly. Liebknecht said that he woke up in the morning opposed to participation in the elections, and by the evening supported it. It was a very tempting suggestion to oppose the conception of a Constituent [Assembly] with the slogan of the Councils, but the congress of Councils had itself opted for the Constituent [Assembly]. This fact could not be overcome. Rosa and Liebknecht admitted it, and Jogiches emphasized it continually. But the youths in the party [—like the 'youths' in the SPD of 1891—] were bitterly opposed to it. 'We shall chase them away with machine guns' [they said].[3]

Throughout these weeks Rosa was the most consistent exponent of the notion that success was really a long way off, and that the processes of revolution would, though inevitable, be slow. Now she could elaborate this idea, untrammelled by any tactical slogans. Liebknecht, too, admitted this, at least in private.[4] But while he was much more influenced

---

[1] Ruth Fischer took an extreme view. 'Luxemburg refused even to see him and had to be persuaded by Levi that this was an impossible procedure.' *Stalin and German Communism*, London 1948, p. 76. Ruth Fischer was not then in Berlin and is generally unreliable; in places deliberately so. Consequently I am very reluctant to accept any interpretation of hers without corroboration. For example, 'Liebknecht and his friends opposed Luxemburg's concept as a dangerously unrealistic interpretation of the ... situation in Germany.' (Ibid.) This story is, in fact, an inversion of the truth.

[2] 'Was will der Spartakusbund?', *Rote Fahne*, 14 December 1918.

[3] Radek, *Dairy*, pp. 134–5.

[4] A. Rosenberg, *Geschichte*, pp. 28, 61, 73. This author is most emphatic; also Radek, *Dairy*, p. 133.

by the apparent revolutionary reification of his surroundings—he spoke at meetings almost daily and was in closer contact with the leaders of the USPD and Revolutionary Shop Stewards—Rosa Luxemburg maintained her stable, almost philosophical, vision intact. Her draft programme reflected this. She talked continually of a 'tough, inexhaustible struggle' over a long period of time.

For the benefit of her immediate party audience she also contrasted sharply the alternatives of chaos and victory, challenging the easy notion that victory was inevitable, irrespective of Socialist mistakes. She had frequently hinted at this in *Rote Fahne*; now she spelt it out for the young radical optimists in the movement who were piling on pressure. She warned them solemnly that the counter-revolution would prefer chaos to admitting a Socialist victory.[1] The core of Rosa's ideas was contained in the summary at the end.

This is what *Spartakus* stands for.

And because it stands for these things, because it is the moving spirit, the Socialist conscience of the revolution, it is hated, persecuted and slandered by all the open and secret enemies of the revolution itself. 'Crucify it', cry the capitalists, trembling for their hoards. 'Crucify it', cry the lower middle classes, the officers, the anti-Semites, the newspaper satraps of the bourgeoisie, trembling for the fleshpots of class domination.

'Crucify it', the misled and deluded sections of the working classes and soldiers echo, those who do not yet realize that they are raging against their own flesh and blood when they rage against *Spartakus*.

In hate and slander against *Spartakus* all the counter-revolutionary, anti-social, dubious, dark and dangerous elements combine. This alone shows clearly that the real heart of the revolution beats with *Spartakus*, that the future is with it. *Spartakus* is not a party which wishes to obtain power over the working classes or by 'using' the working classes. *Spartakus* is no more than the self-conscious part of the proletariat, which points out to the broad masses their historic tasks at every step, which represents at every stage of the revolution the final goal and acts in the interest of proletarian world revolution in all national questions. *Spartakus* refuses to share the government with the servants of the middle classes, with Scheidemann-Ebert, because it considers such co-operation treason to the very foundations of Socialism, a source of strength to the counter-revolution, and the crippling of the revolution itself.

Spartakus will also refuse to accept power merely because Scheidemann-Ebert have gone bankrupt and because the Independents find themselves in a blind alley as a result of their co-operation with them.

Spartakus will never undertake to govern other than through the clear and unmistakable wish of the great majority of the proletarian masses of Germany, and never without their conscious agreement with the ideas, aims, and methods

[1] *Bericht über den Gründungsparteitag der kommunistischen Partei Deutschlands (Spartakusbund) vom 30 Dezember 1918 bis 1 Januar 1919*, Berlin, no date, pp. 53–55 (cited hereafter as *Bericht KPD*).

of *Spartakus*. Government by the proletariat can only battle its way to complete clarity and readiness, step by step, through a long valley of sorrows, of bitter experience, of defeats and victories. The victory of *Spartakus* is not at the beginning but at the end of the revolution: it is the same thing as the victory of the great masses of the Socialist proletariat. . . .[1]

To the well-ordered tranquillity of the historian, this appeal must seem naïve and highly romantic. And so, perhaps, it was. She had waited so long for the revolution, had defended its coming against so many powerful and learned detractors—and here it was, the apparent result, not of party manœuvres, but of conscious proletarian action in its own interest and on its own behalf, just as she had always claimed. But it would be absurd to dismiss this declaration of faith as an attempt to cover ice-cold calculations with a little attractive warmth. It was not just a mantle thrown over hard organizational realities. This was what *Spartakus* had to offer *instead of* organization.

It was optimistic, in the sense that there opened up enormous vistas of a better life, but at the same time the distance of the projection and the warnings of defeats and sorrows convey an aura of profound pessimism in practical, immediate terms. Contrary to appearances, the historical belief in objective situations tends to be pessimistic; those who rely on their own action, who draw the circle of their world tight enough to encompass only the range of their own personal possibilities—these are the real optimists. This declaration of faith, tacked on to a party political programme, reads like a testament. Lenin, too, pinned such a testament to the wall before dying; when the years of tactical polemics, of firm proposals for action, suddenly opened out on an objective situation almost beyond remedy, at this late moment he challenged his too-powerful lientenants: 'I shall fight Great Russian chauvinism to the end of my life.' The *Spartakus* programme was Rosa's testament, just as it is also the concise summary of her life's work. Here was the famous statement that *Spartakus* would take power only with the support of the majority of the masses, which has led to such bitter squabbling between Social Democrats and Communists over Rosa's intellectual corpse. It was this idealism, this apparent commitment to orthodox liberal democracy, which later brought a powerful section of the German Communist Party under the leadership of Ruth Fischer to diagnose Rosa Luxemburg's influence in the German working-class movement as 'syphilitic'.

We already know that to look for vestigial traces of orthodox or mere majority democracy in Rosa's thought is misleading.[2] Emphatically

---

| [1] *Bericht KPD*, pp. 55–56.

[2] Arguing against national self-determination in Poland and those who claimed support for it from 'a majority in the nation', Rosa Luxemburg had written as far back as 1908:

she did not believe—and continually fought against—the idea that the genius of a central committee and a lot of power sufficed to establish a correct policy. But equally there was no question of waiting for, or soliciting the masses. The masses meant action—in the right situation; through action to a majority and not, as in orthodox democracy, consensus first and maybe action later. Rosa Luxemburg had no doubt that the support of the masses must come with action and could come in no other way, but that it was a sporadic and not a continuous process; finally, that it coincided with the seizure of power and the advent of Socialism. The creation of only two alternatives, Bolshevism or Social Democracy as they developed, retrospectively narrowed the area of choice; at the time Rosa's ideas were a lively third alternative.[1]

The decision to found an independent party was not taken lightly, as we have seen. In spite of the failures at the USPD meeting and the Council congress, Rosa Luxemburg in particular was still preoccupied with the need to remain inside an existing organization and so keep contact with the masses. Isolation meant not merely an organizational vacuum, it meant leaving the real world of Socialism for a void. In the end, however, Rosa Luxemburg accepted the majority's decision to organize a separate party; of the leadership, only Jogiches actually voted against it—and he the organizing expert. Only the delegates from Brunswick voted with him.[2] Nevertheless, Clara Zetkin was persuaded by urgent letters from Rosa and Jogiches to remain in the USPD for the time being. There were still right-minded members to be stolen, and it was her job to steal them.[3] Jogiches' doubts about the wisdom of the organizational break merely confirmed the doubts of no less a Leninist than Radek; even at the party congress itself, 'I still did not

---

'Woe to the Social-Democratic party that should ever consider this principle [of legitimate majority rule] authoritative. It would be equivalent to a death sentence on Social Democracy as a revolutionary party. . . . "The will of the nation", or of its majority, is not a sort of God for Social Democracy, before which it humbly prostrates itself; on the contrary, Social Democracy's whole historic mission depends above all on revolutionizing, on forming the will of the "nation"—that is, its working majority.' (*Przegląd Socjaldemokratyczny*, No. 6, August 1908; *Wybór Pism*, Vol. II, pp. 155 ff.) The sentiment is genuine enough, though the pregnant phraseology was more suitable for 1908 Poland than 1918 Germany. Later Bolshevik critics of Luxemburgism's excessive preoccupation with majorities and democracy were clearly unfamiliar with this excerpt—as with almost all her Polish writing.

[1] This narrowing corridor between a Stalinist 'Left' and a *petit-bourgeois* 'Right'—or otherwise minute sectarianism—is despairingly illustrated for a later (still narrower) period in Simone de Beauvoir's novel of post-1945 French politics, *Les Mandarins*.

[2] Hans Wenzel, *Das Revolutionsjahr 1918–19 in Braunschweig*. Unpublished thesis (Brunswick), p. 119; *Die Oktoberrevolution und Deutschland, Protokoll der wissenschaftlichen Tagung in Leipzig 25–30 November 1957*, Berlin (East) 1958, p. 137.

[3] Clara Zetkin, *Ausgewählte Reden*, Vol. II, Introduction, p. xiii; also pp. 100 ff. She left the USPD only after the party congress in May 1919.

feel that I was in the presence of a party'.[1]

But by an overwhelming majority a preliminary all-German conference of the *Spartakusbund* decided on 29 December 1918 to go ahead with the creation of a new party. The founding congress of the KPD followed on immediately in the reception hall of the Berlin City Council, from 30 December 1918 to 1 January 1919. The political situation was very tense. After the incidents with the People's Naval Division on 24 December, groups of *Spartakus* members had again occupied *Vorwärts* and forced the production of issues sympathetic to their own cause. The Independents had left the government a few days earlier and were now officially in opposition. The first groups of *Freikorps*— volunteer associations of soldiers and officers to combat the revolution— had been formed, and leaflets calling for the murder of the *Spartakus* leaders were already in circulation. There were persistent rumours that Karl Liebknecht had been killed and on 7 December an attempt had in fact been made to kill him.[2] It was in this atmosphere that the KPD was constituted.

Reports were made by various members of the executive on the major questions of the day. The congress laid down the conditions for further co-operation with both USPD and the Revolutionary Shop Stewards; in theory this still depended on their unqualified adhesion to *Spartakus* policy. A telegram of greetings and solidarity was sent to the Soviet government. When Radek spoke in the name of the Russian party and officially welcomed the founding of the KPD on its behalf, there was a minor sensation; all the journalists reporting the congress, which was held in public, rushed off to telephone the news that an illegal Russian representative had arrived—and what a representative! But sly and cautious Pieck had temporarily had the doors locked.[3]

Then came the climax of the proceedings. Shortly after half-past two on the last day of 1918, Rosa Luxemburg made a long speech on the subject of 'our programme and the political situation'.[4] The bellyful of compromises, of submissions to the organizational exigencies of large parties, of loyalty to an old though ruinously betrayed idea—all this had finally come to an end. For the first time Rosa Luxemburg was

---

[1] Radek, *Dairy*, p. 136. When Radek remonstrated with Rosa Luxemburg about the extreme tone of her articles she replied that 'when a healthy child is born, it struggles and yells and doesn't bleat'. The same argument, in practically the same words, was used in the discussions of the Central Committee of the RSDRP about the German terms for peace in January 1918. Lenin said that 'the Western revolutions were still foetal while the Russian revolution was a healthy and loudly yelling infant demanding the right to be heard' (*Protokoly Tsentralnogo Komiteta RSDRP, Avgust 1917–Fevral' 1918*, Moscow 1929, p. 198). This is another incidental example of the strikingly common pool of left-wing similes.

[2] *Ich war, Ich bin, Ich werde sein*, Berlin (East) 1958, Introduction, p. 20.

[3] Radek, *Dairy*, p. 136.   [4] *Bericht KPD*, pp. 18–42.

able to weave a Germany party directly into the very tissue of Marx and Engels, unadulterated by the glosses and dilutions of their patrician disciples. Her speech was full of references to the Communist Manifesto. One of the aspects of the new party was that greater respect would be paid to the texts of the Old Masters. In this sense the founding of the KPD was the Marxist Reformation, against the indulgences of Pope Kautsky.

We are at a moment when the Social-Democratic, or Socialist, programme of the proletariat must be put on a totally new basis. Party comrades, we shall now take up the thread which Marx and Engels first spun 70 years ago with the Communist Manifesto. . . . Consciously, and in contradiction to the results of the last 70 years, together with the entire conception on which the Erfurt programme was based, we liquidate all of this and with it the consequences that led directly to the world war. There is no longer a minimum and a maximum programme. Socialism is both of these at the same time, and is itself the minimum that we have to achieve.[1]

Finally, Rosa Luxemburg again elevated the masses into the mainstream of the revolution.

The battle for Socialism can only be carried on by the masses, directly against capitalism, in every factory, by every proletarian against his particular employer. . . . Socialism cannot be made and will not be made by order, not even by the best and most capable Socialist government. It must be made by the masses, through every proletarian individual. Precisely there where the proletarians are chained to capital, the chain must be broken. That is Socialism, only in this way can Socialism be created. And what is the form of the struggle for Socialism? It is the strike. And that is why we have seen that the economic phase has now moved into the foreground in the second period of the revolution.[2]

Nothing shows more clearly that Rosa Luxemburg had retained her basic concept of revolution since 1906, and was far from adopting Bolshevik methods in Germany. But the less one forgets the less one learns, and this doctrine of mass confrontation was central to her thought.

The congress murmured approval of the Marx formulations, of the commitment to the masses, of the rather arid and formal remarks about agriculture: 'The most important conception of the Socialist economy is to remove the contradiction and the division between town and country. Industry cannot even be reorganized in a Socialist direction without a

---

[1] *Bericht KPD*, pp. 19, 26.

[2] Ibid., p. 33. These sentences had all been marked for deletion in the copy of the KPD *Bericht* used by the present author. This belonged at one time to a Communist journalist of the thirties, who had been editing a new version of the speech for publication—without the emphasis on economic 'spontaneity'.

live connection with an equally reorganized agriculture.' The storms of applause came when Rosa attacked the SPD and USPD leaders personally. She pointed to the build-up of troops in the East, to the government's horse-trading with the military leaders in Germany. The congress had applauded Karl Liebknecht too when he said: 'We only remained in the USPD to drive it forward, to keep it within reach of our whip, to steal its best elements. . . . We may not have captured the leaders, but a good part of the masses.'[1] But in other matters Rosa Luxemburg and her immediate friends did not find things so easy. The congress turned down the executive's proposal to participate in the elections for the Constituent Assembly. On the first day Rosa's appearance had been met with the enthusiasm befitting a distinguished revolutionary leader. But her speech in favour of participating in the election was met by 'weak applause'.[2] Paul Levi, who had presented the executive's resolution on the subject and supported it at length, had to face repeated dissent, while the floor speakers who fulminated against participation were greeted with great enthusiasm. Participation was finally lost in a vote of 62 against 23. Rosa mildly rebuked the delegates, with the memory of the Duma boycott in her mind.

We understand and value the motives from which stems the opposition to the executive's point of view. Our pleasure is, however, not wholehearted. Comrades, you take your radicalism rather too easily. With all our stormy impatience we must not lose the necessary seriousness and the need for reflection. The Russian example against the Constituent [Assembly] does not apply. When the Constituent [Assembly] was driven out, our Russian comrades already had a Trotsky–Lenin government. We still have Ebert–Scheidemann.[3]

Leo Jogiches, on the other hand, who alone had opposed the creation of a separate party on such very weak organizational foundations, now proposed to his colleagues that in view of the leadership's defeat on such a vital question of tactics the whole KPD project and congress should be abandoned—though he was soon persuaded to withdraw this suggestion.[4]

An SPD historian later underlined the essential contradiction of the Communist Party Congress. 'If the Communists considered that the immediate removal of the government was out of the question as a political aim, they should have avoided raising the hope among their followers with all the means at their disposal that the government could be overthrown. Under those circumstances it was frivolous to drive the workers into the streets. . . .'[5] Neither then nor later did her opponents

[1] Ibid., p. 4.   [2] Ibid., pp. 10–11.   [3] Ibid.
[4] Paul Levi, 'The Congress of the Communist Party', Die Internationale, 1920, Vol. II, No. 26, p. 43.
[5] Hermann Müller, Die Novemberrevolution. Erinnerungen, Berlin 1931, p. 252.

understand the difference between a speech to party members and an appeal to the masses which in Rosa Luxemburg's eyes were two fundamentally different things, and yet were both halves of the truth. When Radek challenged her about the extreme tone of her articles, far in excess of the real potential of *Spartakus*, she said: 'When a healthy child is born, it struggles and yells and doesn't bleat.'[1] Strong language was a fatal habit in Polish and Russian politics.

In spite of the pressure of events, and the admitted infancy of the new party, it was a great occasion. If the new party was not the result of Rosa's ardent wish, here it was none the less—at least the like-minded now shared a communal yet exclusive organization. Now that the decision had been made to 'go it alone', Rosa had no regrets or doubts. She was more optimistic than at any time since 1914. 'The separation from the USPD had become absolutely inevitable for *political* reasons,' she wrote to Clara Zetkin, 'even if the *people* [in it] are still the same as they were at Gotha [the USPD's founding congress] the situation has entirely changed.' And she berated her absent and easily despairing friend for taking the negative vote against the executive over participation in the Constituent Assembly elections far too seriously.

Our 'defeat' was merely the triumph of a somewhat childish, half-baked, narrow-minded radicalism. In any case that happened at the beginning of the conference. Later contact between us [the executive] and the delegates was established . . . an entirely different atmosphere [*Resomanz*] than at the start. . . . *Spartakisten* are a fresh generation, free from the cretinous traditions of the 'good old party'. . . . We all decided unanimously not to make the matter into a cardinal question [*Kabinettsfrage*] and not to take it too seriously.[2]

We have already speculated on the valedictory note in the programme and its accompanying speech, and it would add drama if we could show some awareness in Rosa that these were the last weeks of her life. But, hindsight apart, the evidence suggests the contrary. Rosa was always conscious of the possibility of death in action, and repeatedly mentioned it to her friends—though not always without a touch of rhetoric.[3] But this was a general, almost abstract preoccupation, not even heightened by the events at the end of 1918—except perhaps in the very last days. On 25 December Rosa wrote to Clara Zetkin that she had received 'urgent warning "from official sources" that the assassins are looking for Karl and myself, and we shouldn't sleep at home . . . it finally got on my nerves and I simply went back to Südende'. And on 11 January,

[1] Radek, *Dairy*, p. 133.
[2] Photocopy IML (B), NL5, III-A/15, p. 118.
[3] 'My dear young friend, I assure you that I would never flee even if the gallows threatened . . . because . . . I believe sacrifices to be part of a Socialist's stock-in-trade.' (Letter to Walter Stöcker, 11 March 1914, IML (B); see *Selected Works*, Vol. II, p. 304.)

perhaps the last actual letter from Rosa's pen: 'Right now the battle is raging through Berlin, a lot of our brave boys have fallen. . . . Now I must close.'[1] There was of course plenty of very real danger, only Rosa was not fully conscious of it or simply ignored it.

Little is known of how Rosa Luxemburg lived during these two months. The work of writing and editing *Rote Fahne*, of drafting the programme and appeal of *Spartakus*, would have been a full-time job under any circumstances. *Rote Fahne* was her main worry—'will it come out, will it not come out. At last, here it is . . . technically not yet up to much', she wrote to Clara Zetkin on 18 November.[2] She insisted on seeing every word that appeared.[3] All the *Spartakus* leaders, but particularly Karl Liebknecht and Rosa Luxemburg, were living two or three full-time lives at the same time. While Rosa was writing and editing, Karl Liebknecht was negotiating continually within and on behalf of *Spartakus*. There were long and regular meetings of the *Spartakus* executive. Both made continual appearances at public meetings. Apart from the large open gatherings, which took place several times a week, there were meetings in factories in various suburbs of Berlin. By the end of December it was no longer possible for Rosa and Liebknecht to remain safely in their own apartments. At first Rosa lived for a few nights at a time in various hotels, calling at the flat only for mail and clothes; during and after the January risings they were billeted with different sympathizers and changed lodgings every night. It was only during Christmas that Rosa was able even to visit her own home, much less live in it. Mathilde Jacob was her post office once more.

Occasionally Rosa was able to walk anonymously among the crowds of Berlin, to obtain the 'feel' of the revolution as an outsider as well as a participant. Radek describes a dinner with Liebknecht, Jogiches, and Paul Levi on the day after his arrival in Berlin. 'The owner of the tavern regarded Liebknecht with special affection, and gave him far more to eat than us. . . Afterwards we went for a walk. Great masses of people in the streets. Not pedestrians and strollers as usual, but swarms of people talking about politics, their faces full of interest and

---

[1] Rosa Luxemburg to Clara Zetkin, 11 January 1919, IML (M), photocopy IML (B), NL5, III-A/15, partly quoted in Luise Dornemann, *Clara Zetkin*, Berlin (East) 1957, p. 288. Clara Zetkin had asked for advice a week earlier on whether she should come to Berlin. The letter only reached Rosa in Berlin on 10 January and she answered it the next day. Clara Zetkin's final reply, her last letter to her closest friend, had an almost prophetic echo of impending doom. 'Will this letter, will my love still be able to reach you? . . . Oh Rosa, what days! I see before me so clearly the historic greatness and meanings of all your actions, but my knowledge of these things cannot still the urgent demands of my heart, I cannot overcome my terrible worry and fear for you personally.' (Clara Zetkin to Rosa Luxemburg, 13 January 1919, ibid., p. 290.)

[2] Photocopy IML (B), NL III-A/15, p. 75.

[3] Clara Zetkin, *Reden*, Vol. III, p. 423.

joy. We talked politics with one of the drivers in another café.' Later that night Radek spoke at a meeting, and was challenged as a reactionary when he spoke of the hardships in Russia. 'Some worker . . . had misunderstood my remarks about conditions of the battle. They could not imagine what a revolution was really like . . . I spent New Year's Eve with Liebknecht. In spite of his exhaustion he was as happy as a child.'[1]

During these hectic weeks Rosa made a sporadic effort to maintain her connections with at least a few of her closer friends, but she did not see any of them again. There was no time, and the world was too divided. But Rosa hoped that all would be well again later, during the inevitable ebb. Meantime her universe was public meetings, the editorial staff of *Rote Fahne*—including faithful Mathilde Jacob and Fanny Jezierska—and the colleagues of the *Spartakus* executive. A narrow universe but warm, kept warm by the events outside.

No doubt this was the way that Rosa had always wished to live, all her natural impatience and energy absorbed in the manifold activities of real, not theoretical, revolution, with a few intimates only. Rock-like though reserved as ever was Leo Jogiches, still her oldest, closest friend. The glimpses of him during these weeks are of the briefest, but there he was, his main preoccupation the support and protection of Rosa, to whose pre-eminence he at last almost subordinated his own strong personality. And perhaps his presence helped her to develop that extraordinary reserve of nervous energy. It was as though the forcible contraction of effort during the years in prison now catapulted her forward more fiercely than ever. Those who knew her in these weeks all spoke of her inexhaustible energy, of her disregard for tiredness and the constant headaches and nausea. What price would she have paid with her health if she had survived?

The event that sparked off the January fighting began in a small way, like all the others since 9 November. The continuous large crowds on the move in Berlin, the demonstrations and uncontrolled mass meetings, the many minor and more serious incidents, finally caused the government to take action against the police president, Emil Eichhorn. Under his command, the police seemed to be turning into a revolutionary institution. The SPD was determined that this sensitive post should no longer be occupied by one of its Independent opponents. The government put in Ernst, a right-wing Social Democrat; someone reliable. The last straw was Eichhorn's refusal to submit himself to the authority of the Prussian Ministry of the Interior; he claimed that he was responsible in the last resort only to the executive of the Workers' and Soldiers' Council. *Vorwärts* had been running a campaign against

[1] Radek, *Diary*, pp. 133-4, 136.

him since 1 January, hinting that he was a Russian agent since he had once worked for a Russian news agency; it was a handy and effective denunciation, even though it was entirely unfounded.[1]

There was no reason to suppose that this legitimate if inadvisable dismissal would lead to more than the usual protests and demonstrations. On 4 January he was officially sacked, but refused to leave his office. On the evening of the same day a routine meeting of the executive of the USPD organization of Greater Berlin reacted to the news with a unanimous resolution that 'the attack on Eichhorn must be repelled', but what to do or how far to go was not settled or even discussed at any length.[2] For once the USPD decided to put the potential of the masses to the test, before deciding on any course of action. But while the Independents merely called for a protest demonstration on 5 January, *Rote Fahne*, in line with its usual practice, called for the strongest popular reaction.[3] *Spartakus* could not afford to admit the need of a popular thermometer. A meeting of the KPD executive specifically rejected any attempt to take over the government—'we can hold out for two weeks at the most'—but a call was made for the usual arming of the workers and disarming of the troops.[4]

The demonstrations of the 5th turned out to be larger than anyone had expected. The revolutionary leaders, particularly the KPD, now saw complete justification for their policy; if such a turn-out did not call for action, nothing ever would. It was reported—wrongly, as it turned out—that the troops too were ready to join in.[5]

The great moment seemed unexpectedly to have struck, and the revolutionary groups bowed to it. A fatally loose organizational co-operation was worked out. On 5 January the Berlin USPD leadership, the Revolutionary Shop Stewards, and the executive of the KPD issued a joint proclamation, calling on the masses 'not to accept the attempt of the government to stifle the revolution with bayonets. With the attack on the Berlin police authorities, the entire German proletariat, the entire German revolution is at stake.'[6] A similar call for further demonstrations was made on the 6th. By this time the *Vorwärts* offices had been occupied once more by demonstrators, and a revolutionary issue appeared on the 6th under the anonymous sponsorship of 'The Revo-

---

[1] Paul Hirsch, *Der Weg der Sozialdemokratie zur Macht in Preussen*, Berlin 1929, pp. 133 ff. *Vorwärts*, 1 January 1919 onwards; also *Preussischer Untersuchungsausschuss, Bericht über die Januar Unruhen in Berlin*, No. 4121A, Col. 28 ff. Eichhorn's own story is in Emil Eichhorn, *Uber die Januarereignisse*, Berlin 1919, pp. 60 ff.

[2] Richard Müller, *Der Bürgerkrieg in Deutschland*, Berlin 1925, p. 30. All the sources agree that no decision on any course of action was taken at this meeting.

[3] *Ledebour-Prozess*, p. 44, testimony of Ledebour; *Rote Fahne*, 5 January 1919.

[4] Richard Müller, *Bürgerkrieg*, loc. cit.

[5] *Ledebour-Prozess*, p. 51.   [6] *D. & M.* Vol. III, p. 10.

lutionary Workers of Greater Berlin', specifically calling for the removal of the traitors Ebert and Scheidemann, seizure of power by the Council, and arming of the masses.[1] Almost simultaneously, that same Workers' and Soldiers' Council—the object of the revolutionaries' affection—announced to the population its own confirmation of Eichhorn's dismissal and thus removed the last ground of legitimate complaint.[2]

The first-fruits of the co-operation of the three revolutionary groups was the formation of a Revolutionary Executive of thirty-three members. This in turn created a directorate of three: Liebknecht, Ledebour, and Scholze, representing the KPD, the Independents, and the Revolutionary Shop Stewards respectively. Much doubt exists as to the exact purpose of this executive— whether it was merely to direct the movement, as its participants later claimed, or whether it was to take over the government once the existing incumbents had been removed.[3] This was the classic 'unmade' revolution as propounded by the German Left: let the events dictate the institutions; mass pressure on institutions could make them infinitely flexible. The concept may have been peculiarly Rosa Luxemburg's, but for the moment it was accepted even by her personal opponents in the USPD.

The exact motives of each group and the precise connection of events have never been entirely clarified. At the meeting of 5 January, consisting of delegates from all three groups, the decision to overturn the government had been approved against the opposition of a strong minority from among the Revolutionary Shop Stewards; precisely the group that had been the most active in bringing their organized workers out on the streets. Nor had the executive of the KPD by any means committed itself to the removal of the government; indeed, most of the evidence shows that the representatives of the KPD in the joint meetings, Liebknecht and Pieck, agreed to the sharp resolutions and maximum demands *against* the specific instructions of their party.[4] Apparently, the news of the occupation of *Vorwärts* and other newspaper offices reached the revolutionary executive after it had made its non-decisions about the future, and caused considerable surprise.[5] This in turn gave rise to a general wave of euphoria.

The *Volksmarinedivision*, the People's Naval Division, whose continued existence had been assured by popular support during its conflict with the government at the end of December, now refused to come in on the side of the insurgents. They remained neutral, their leaders making themselves conspicuous by their absence when attempts were

[1] Ibid., p. 14.   [2] Ibid., p. 15.   [3] *Ledebour-Prozess*, p. 53.
[4] R. Müller, *Bürgerkrieg*, pp. 32 ff. Pieck, *Reden*, Vol. I, pp. 115–16. See also Karl Heinz Luther, 'Die nachrevolutionären Machtkämpfe in Berlin', *Jahrbücher für die Geschichte Mittel- und Ostdeutschlands*, Vol. VIII (1959), p. 212.
[5] *Ledebour-Prozess*, pp. 62, 82.

made by revolutionary emissaries to enlist their aid.[1] Thus the insurgents lost the services of the only body of armed revolutionary troops.

Already by the afternoon of the 6th the Revolutionary Executive was in some doubt as to its ability to control events, and began to support the initiative of the official USPD leadership for negotiation with the government. It was clear probably by the evening of the 6th, certainly by the morning of the 7th, that there was no chance of overturning the government, and troops were known to be moving steadily into Berlin. But having been carried along like everyone else on the wave of events, the Communists saw negotiations at this stage as a complete betrayal, the old SPD executive tactic of 1910. Rosa Luxemburg wrote of 'the complete neglect of the most elementary rules of revolutionary action'. Instead of occupying the real positions of power, only a few newspapers and news agencies had been captured. For this, however, she blamed the leadership, not the masses. In any case,

when one is in the middle of the sharpest struggle against the government of Ebert–Schiedemann, one does not at the same time start 'negotiations' with the government. . . . Such negotiations can only lead to one of two results: either to a compromise or—far more probably—to a dragging out of the situation, which will be used by Ebert's men for the most brutal measures of repression. . . .

The masses are ready to support any revolutionary action, to go through fire and water for Socialism. But they need clear guidance, and ruthless determined leadership. . . . Germany has always been the classic country of organization, and still more of the fanatic organization mentality, but . . . the organization of revolutionary actions can and must be learnt in revolution itself, as one can only learn swimming in the water. . . . The lesson of the last three days calls loudly to the leaders of the workers: do not talk, do not discuss endlessly, do not negotiate, act.[2]

Almost quixotically, Rosa Luxemburg and the KPD were springing to the defence of a revolutionary effort which they had not initiated, whose aim they could not support, but which equally must not be allowed to fail. The lesson was clear—and it was the old lesson of 1907–10: you cannot manipulate the crowds into revolutionary action and then manipulate them out again. For that reason she and her colleagues had initially opposed the insurrection designed to remove the government. But once the masses were out on the streets, you could not negotiate over their heads, even though the result might be a bloody defeat. The same lesson was repeated more emphatically in her other articles; all turned on this question of commitment to the masses,

[1] Ibid., pp. 189–94, testimony of sailor Milowski; also Eric Waldman, *The Spartakist Uprising of 1919 and the Crisis of the German Socialist Movement*, Milwaukee (U.S.A.) 1958, p. 176.
[2] 'Versäumte Pflichten', *Rote Fahne*, 8 January 1919.

irrespective of tactical results.[1] The emphasis is continually on the leaders and their failures. Nor was this unjustified: the revolutionary leadership was able neither to drive the movement forward nor to negotiate whole-heartedly to bring it to a rapid end. Thus the government was able to mount its counter-action undisturbed, to turn stalemate or disengagement into victory. Radek had all along been firmly against the whole thing, and especially against Communist participation. He now advised complete about-turn and withdrawal; the KPD must propose formally to the Revolutionary Shop Stewards that fighting must cease; if necessary the armed workers must give up their arms. At the same time, a manifesto was to be issued justifying the retreat and calling for new elections to the Workers' and Soldiers' Councils.[2] This was the Leninist tactic of liquidating mistakes brutally and quickly. The proposal was supported in principle by the KPD executive. How to make it effective?

Next day, the 10th, the KPD Central Committee claimed that it wrote to the Revolutionary Executive withdrawing its two representatives, 'even in their consultative capacity ... [since] the clarity and strength of the revolutionary movement demands an immediate revision of our relationship with the Revolutionary Shop Stewards.. We are always available for an exchange of views ... and will fight shoulder to shoulder ... if a really thorough revolutionary action is envisaged.' The letter, signed by Pieck himself—to give the appearance of solidarity; did Liebknecht refuse to sign?—could not be delivered by hand as intended owing to the practical disintegration of the Revolutionary Executive; it was printed instead in *Rote Fahne* on 13 January 1919. Thus it had no practical value, and perhaps was never intended to have; the editorial comment accompanying it in *Rote Fahne* suggested that it was part of the 'clarity' process by which the KPD executive dissociated itself from the vacillating leadership of the revolt. Was the letter ever sent, or meant to be? We do not really know.

Little is known of the details of the internal discussions. In any case, a tradition later grew up in leading Communist circles according to which the KPD delegates to the Revolutionary Executive, Liebknecht and Pieck, acted against the instructions of their party executive, and the KPD leaders tried unsuccessfully to end the participation of their representatives in the disastrous venture. Pieck in his memoirs glided over his own part by painting a picture full of objective difficulties.

---

[1] Was machen die Führer?', *Rote Fahne*, 7 January 1919. 'Das Versagen der Führer', *Rote Fahne*, 11 January 1919.

[2] *Illustrierte Geschichte*, p. 282. Radek's letter to the KPD executive dated 9 January and expressing these negative views was reprinted only here. A discussion of KPD attitudes is in Eric Waldman, *The Spartakist Uprising*.

The executive of the KPD could not be kept informed about these decisions, nor was it possible to inform them of what was decided [by the Revolutionary Executive]. Only at a later meeting of the KPD executive it appeared that they were in agreement with the struggle against the government's measures, but not with the aims of the enterprise: the fight for government power. Out of this arose considerable differences of opinion, with regard to the activities of Liebknecht and myself among the Revolutionary Shop Stewards during the enterprise. The cause of this was the lack of decision and lack of clarity on the part of the USPD and the Revolutionary Shop Stewards, as a result of which the USPD leadership began negotiations with the Social Democrats and naturally had not the least interest thereafter in intensifying the common effort. The KPD executive none the less supported the action with all its strength, and enormous masses followed its appeal for demonstrations.[1]

A later historian put it more bluntly: 'On January 10 the *Spartakusbund* tried again to end its connection with the Shop Stewards. Again it forbade the participation of Liebknecht, but without effect.'[2] The KPD leadership disapproved both of the 'putsch' mentality of the Revolutionary Executive, and of the tentative negotiations attempted both by the USPD and a section of the Revolutionary Shop Stewards. What it advocated instead, however, is not clear. According to Rosi Wolffstein, the *rapporteuse* of the KPD founding congress, who was not in Berlin during the January events, Rosa taxed Liebknecht with the following reproach when he returned to the party offices after one meeting of the Revolutionary Executive: 'But Karl, how could you, and what about our programme?'[3]

Rote Fahne certainly did not reflect Radek's advice to write off the action as ill advised and premature, and to withdraw from it in as good order as possible. Instead, the mass action was reported as a victory; only the negotiations were clearly labelled as a betrayal and capitulation of the revolutionary workers. 'The Communist Party naturally does not participate in this shameful policy, and refuses any responsibility for it. We continue to regard it as our duty to drive the revolution forward . . . and to warn the masses with the sharpest criticism of the dangers of the Shop Stewards' policy of hesitation and the bog[ged down] policy of the Independents.'[4]

The constant hammering on clarity, at a time when the mass action

---

[1] Quoted in Pieck, *Reden*, Vol. I, pp. 115–16.

[2] Ruth Fischer, *Stalin and German Communism*, London 1948, p. 97. Ruth Fischer had every interest in showing up the January action as a good example of the disorganized conditions which her later policy of 'Bolshevization' was designed to remedy. She was not present in Berlin during January, but reported—perhaps exaggerated—a tradition that became well established a few years later.

[3] In an interview with the author. Rosi Wolffstein is the widow of Paul Frölich. The story had already become a KPD legend within a few weeks of Rosa's and Karl's deaths.

[4] *Rote Fahne*, 11 January 1919.

had failed and the city was being occupied by troops bent on revenge and repression, contained more pathos and courage than good sense. To analyse the situation on 13 January as though profound historical insights were being opened up by current events, as though history itself was now writing the indictment of the Independent leaders as the working class's false friends, can hardly have contributed much to keeping up the spirits of defeated workers.[1] Emphasis on the perspective of history at a moment of defeat is typically the consolation of an intellectual élite.

But leaders who sincerely believed that the long-term prospect could carry any amount of present failure could naturally resort to this kind of analysis on the grounds that it could actually contribute to greater success next time. The implication was clear: it was the co-operation with the Shop Stewards and the Independents—both indecisive elements—which had brought about the failure of the present action. Next time the masses must follow the lead of the only organization able to recognize reality beneath all the fictions and pretences—the KPD.

What of the glaring contradiction between the desire of the Communists to disengage, and the public castigation of the revolutionary leadership for negotiating? Negotiations of this sort were a betrayal of the masses, and deliberately both Rosa Luxemburg and Karl Liebknecht in their last articles preferred once again to commit *Spartakus* in public to the action of the masses, however disastrous. In future it would be possible to show that *Spartakus*, which had not wanted or called for the overthrow of the government, had still supported the people while the other leaders, who had first set themselves and the masses impossible goals, soon betrayed their followers once it was politic or necessary to do so. There was no time to develop this idea; by the evening of 15 January both Karl Liebknecht and Rosa Luxemburg were dead. But already the outline of the future apologia was clear. As for the differences within the Communist leadership, these could await serious self-criticism as soon as the situation was calmer.

The attempt to negotiate had anyhow not succeeded. On 11 January the government insisted on acceptance of all its conditions, otherwise their counter-attack would begin with an assault on the captured *Vorwärts* building. Although by this time mass support for the whole action had ebbed considerably, the government troops under Noske formally paraded into central Berlin from the suburbs on 13 January and took the *Vorwärts* building by storm. On 12 January the senior military leaders had informed the government that they did not wish to have further negotiations with *Spartakus* under any circumstances; this might make their own troops unreliable. This was pure military

[1] 'Kartenhäuser', *Rote Fahne*, 13 January 1919.

propaganda, since *Spartakus* itself deliberately refused to participate in any of the negotiations; in fact it was the only group to do so. It is to be noted that the name *Spartakus* had now become the invariable synonym for all insurgents—used by the government, SPD, and military alike. Delegates sent to negotiate with the government, who consisted largely of Revolutionary Shop Stewards and Independents, were invariably referred to as *Spartakists*.[1] At the same time the government's determination to impose its will in exemplary fashion on the Left was not matched by similar toughness towards the army. Whatever the truth of the story of Ebert's sell-out to the military as early as November, by the beginning of January the government had placed itself formally in the hands of the armed services. Kautsky wrote: 'From a purely military point of view the government could permit itself to refuse more or less outright any further negotiations. . . . It may truly emerge victorious from this battle and indeed have gained in strength, but only by ceding larger powers to the middle class and military factors, with whose help it was able to triumph.'[2] And indeed victory in the January fighting made the government undertake a wholesale offensive against even the relatively harmless Workers' and Soldiers' Councils as undesirable revolutionary institutions—still under the guise of dealing with *Spartakus*, of securing law and order.

In the eyes of the public the blame for the revolt appeared to lie largely with *Spartakus*. The Revolutionary Shop Stewards, who had never had either the talent or the means for propaganda, remained largely anonymous and now went underground in their factories. Ledebour had already been arrested on the night of 10–11 January, and the USPD leadership fell into the hands of less committed right-wing leaders. *Spartakus* as a group was easily the most exposed. Middle-class organizations and *Freikorps* leaders encouraged the belief that if the Communist leaders could be dealt with personally, the end of all these troubles would be in sight. This notion, which led to the production of handbills calling for the killing of Liebknecht, was never discouraged by the SPD. Such personal attainders had been appearing since November, but now reached a crescendo. On 13 January a poem appeared in *Vorwärts* under the name of Arthur Zickler, a regular contributor, which roundly accused the *Spartakus* leaders of cowardice by skulking in their hiding places while honest workers were being killed.

> Many hundred corpses in a row,
> Proletarians,
> Karl, Rosa, Radek and Co.,
> Not one of them is there,
> Proletarians.

---

[1] Noske, *Von Kiel bis Kapp*, p. 73. [2] *Die Freiheit*, 13 January 1919.

The atmosphere in Berlin at this time can therefore be imagined. Both Rosa Luxemburg and Karl Liebknecht, the best-known figures of *Spartakus*, were particularly exposed. At least unofficially there was a substantial price on their heads, offered by right-wing private enterprise, and Scheidemann may well have known of this and encouraged it.[1] Both were now on the run, moving from flat to flat every night. Whatever their differences over the tactics of the revolt, their situations were identical, for in the eyes of the world they *were Spartakus*, two halves of a hermaphrodite whole.[2] The offices of the KPD were occupied and ransacked by the military. Even then, it took persuasion and the arrest of three leading colleagues to convince Rosa and Karl to take better measures for their own safety.[3] They still insisted on continuing the editing of *Rote Fahne*. On the 12th and 13th they stayed in the working-class district of Neukölin. Apparently the comings and goings in connection with *Rote Fahne* made this hiding place too conspicuous and on the 14th they moved to a middle-class district in Wilmersdorf. It was from there that Rosa Luxemburg wrote her last article, 'Order reigns in Berlin', and Karl Liebknecht 'In spite of all'.[4]

'Order reigns in Berlin' was a bitter attack on the rule of bourgeois 'order', with all its brutalities and repression.

But even in the middle of the battle, amid the triumphant screams of the counter-revolution, the revolutionary proletariat must make its reckoning with recent events and measure these and their results on the scale of history. Revolution has no time to lose, it marches on—over the graves, not yet filled in, over 'victories and defeats'—towards its great tasks. To follow its direction in full consciousness is the first task of the soldiers for international Socialism.[5]

Could a final victory of the revolutionary proletariat and the removal of Ebert-Scheidemann have been expected, Rosa asked. Could a revolutionary dictatorship have been established? No, if the degree of ripeness of the German proletariat is taken into account. The *permanent* victory in this context was not yet possible. Not that the revolt was pointless or unnecessary, for it was the provocation of the government that had brought it about.

---

[1] Frölich, p. 330.

[2] The idea of a party being headed equally by a man and a woman was an unattractive by-product of revolutionaty socialism in the eyes of the *gente per bene*. There were repeated hints of orgies and at the very least Rosa and Karl were believed to be lovers—an idea that has proved remarkably durable.

[3] Pieck, *Reden*, Vol. I, p. 118.

[4] 'Die Ordnung herrscht in Berlin', *Rote Fahne*, 14 January 1919; 'Trotz alledem', *Rote Fahne*, 15 January 1919. This was the last date of publication before the paper had to go underground. It did not appear again legally until February.

[5] *Rote Fahne*, 14 January 1919.

It was a *matter of honour* for the revolution to ward off this attack with all its energy, if the counter-revolution was not to be encouraged to further efforts. . . . It is an inner law of revolution not to stand still on its achievements. Attack is the best form of defence. . . . The revolutions so far have brought us nothing but defeat, but these inevitable defeats are themselves one stepping-stone on top of another to the final victory. . . .

But the leadership has failed. None the less, the leadership can and must be rebuilt by the masses out of the masses. The masses are crucial, they are the rock on which the final victory of revolution will be built. The masses were up to the mark, they have forged this defeat into the chain of those historical battles which are themselves the strength and pride of international Socialism. And that is why a future victory will blossom from this 'defeat'.

'Order rules in Berlin.' You stupid lackeys! Your 'order' is built on sand. Tomorrow the revolution will rear ahead once more and announce to your horror amid the brass of trumpets: 'I was, I am, I always will be!'

The next day Karl Liebknecht added his own valediction:

Hold hard. We have not fled. We are not beaten . . . for *Spartakus*—that means fire and spirit, heart and soul, will and deed of the proletarian revolution. For *Spartakus*—that stands for all the longing for achievement, all the embattled resolution of the class-conscious proletariat . . . whether or not we shall survive when all is achieved, our programme will live; it will dominate the world of liberated peoples. In spite of all.[1]

The farewell was intended to be temporary, actors whose play had come to the end of the run, whose backers had withdrawn. But in fact the two leaders were saying goodbye to life itself.

On 15 January a section of troops arrested Karl Liebknecht and Rosa Luxemburg towards nine o'clock in the evening. No one knows how their hiding place was discovered, but it may well be that the presence of these two strange guests in this respectable middle-class block of flats caused some other tenants to notify the military, or one of the anti-revolutionary defence organizations.[2] Pieck was present by accident; on the instruction of the Communist executive he had brought them false papers and the latest information from party headquarters.[3] The owner of the flat, Frau Markussohn, later described Rosa's appearance to Luise Kautsky. 'Her sunken cheeks and the dark rings under her eyes from so many sleepless nights were evidence of her physical exhaustion, but her strength of will remained unimpaired.'[4] When the soldiers came she was resting; she now suffered constantly from headaches. She packed a small case, and took some books—a further spell

---

[1] 'Trotz alledem.'   [2] H. Roland-Holst, op. cit., p. 207.
[3] Wilhelm Pieck, 'Der 15 Januar 1919', first published in *Internationale Pressekorrespondenz*, Moscow, 10 January 1928. Reprinted in Pieck, *Reden*, Vol. I, p. 432. The account of the arrest given below follows Pieck's narrative.
[4] H. Roland-Holst, loc. cit.

in jail was inevitable. An attempt to give false names was of no avail: the soldiers knew well with whom they were dealing.[1] Karl Liebknecht was taken away first, then Rosa Luxemburg and Pieck followed in another car which drove to the Eden Hotel, the temporary headquarters of one of the para-military divisions in the centre of Berlin. Their arrival had been notified in advance, for Rosa Luxemburg was greeted with sarcastic taunts and much abuse. She was taken to the first floor of the hotel, where a Captain Pabst went through a formal interrogation.[2] It was already late at night.

It has never been entirely clear how premeditated the subsequent murders were, and how many people knew of them before and immediately afterwards. Pabst himself—who survived all the subsequent events in Germany with profit though without much honour—stated in 1962 that 'in practice the authority of the State was in the hands of the Freikorps, but they had the full support of Noske', then a member of the government and People's Commissioner in charge of military affairs.[3] Possibly Rosa's stinging replies helped to enrage the officers still further.[4] According to investigations carried out shortly afterwards by Jogiches and published in Rote Fahne during February, the whole plot was worked out in advance, as soon as it was known to the leaders of this particular division that Rosa Luxemburg and Karl Liebknecht had been apprehended and would be brought into their headquarters.[5] The obvious participants were later brought to trial before a military court in which the soldier Runge was sentenced to two years and two weeks' imprisonment, while Lieutenant Vogel got four months. The other accused were acquitted. Reference to these events, particularly as far as knowledge and approval of them were concerned, was made in a number of libel actions ten years later.[6]

[1] Frölich, p. 332.

[2] Pabst's role in the affair has had some unexpected recent publicity. Pabst himself, who is still alive, published an account of the events of 15 January 1919 in a German newspaper in January 1962. Following this, the 'Bulletin of the Press and Information Office of the German Federal Republic' commented officially that the account given by Pabst was substantially correct, and that the murder of the two revolutionary leaders was 'an execution in accordance with martial law' (Standrechtliche Erschiessung). Bulletin des Presse und Informationsamtes der Bundesregierung, 8 February 1962, No. 27, p. 223.

Der Spiegel, the editors of which were shortly thereafter indicted for treasonable activities on other counts, published a sarcastic interview with Pabst (Der Spiegel, No. 16, 18 April 1962). Karl Liebknecht's widow, Sophie (or Sonia) Liebknecht, at present living in East Berlin, announced that she would take proceedings against the head of the West German Information Department for 'glorifying murder'.

[3] Der Spiegel, No. 16, pp. 38–39.

[4] Maurice Berger, La nouvelle Allemagne, Paris 1919, p. 275.

[5] Rote Fahne, 13–16 February, 19 February 1919.

[6] These mostly centred round Jörns (or Jorns), the examining magistrate charged with the investigation of Rosa's murder. He was strongly suspected of suppressing evidence, or

There is little point in going through the mountains of conflicting evidence, but within certain limits the course of events is moderately clear. The government certainly did not issue express orders for the murder of any of the *Spartakus* leaders. At the same time Noske did nothing to restrain his bloodthirsty auxiliaries. The *Freikorps* members, at the time and later, felt they could rely on Noske's support in any subsequent proceedings, should these arise. In addition, a number of precedents for unpunished summary action had already been set. The negotiators on behalf of the group that had occupied the *Vorwärts* building were shot down on 11 January while carrying their flag of truce, and some of the other occupants were severely beaten up.[1] No proceedings were ever taken or envisaged against those responsible. The maltreatment of individual revolutionaries had by then become a common occurrence.

None the less, the officers of the *Garde-Kavallerie-Schützen-Division*, of which Pabst was first Staff Captain, knew that the murder of these two well-known *Spartakus* leaders was an event of greater importance than any shooting of hostages in the course of street fighting. Probably when the news was telephoned through that the two leaders had been captured the problem was discussed and it was decided to deal with them summarily. Soldier Runge, who later felt that he had been shabbily treated by his superiors and unloaded his own version in the newspapers, was persuaded or bribed or ordered—or all three—to stand by the side door of the Eden Hotel and to hit the emerging *Spartakus* leaders over the head with his rifle butt.[2] For the sake of appearances the official instructions were to take Liebknecht and Luxemburg to the civil prison at Moabit, where all the other leaders of the revolt so far captured had been taken. Pieck, waiting in the passage outside the interrogation room, heard the officers say to each other that not one of the three would leave the hotel alive.

Karl Liebknecht was led out first before the curious and unsympathetic eyes of the soldiers and a few hotel guests. So this was what the

rather of ensuring the nothing came out that might require suppression. In 1928 this allegation was printed in *Das Tagebuch* (e.g. 24 March), and Jörns accordingly sued the editor, Josef Bornstein, for libel. At that time Jörns was already well-established as a Reich Procurator (*Reichsanwalt*). The fact that he was a thoroughly political lawyer is shown by his later career in the Nazi People's Court. For the evidence of political loading of the administration of justice against the Left, even in the early days of the Weimar Republic, see J. Gumbel, *Vier Jahre Mord*, Berlin 1923, particularly pp. 81, 101–2, where a comparative table of sentences against Left and Right is given. See also F. K. Kaul, *Justiz wird zum Verbrechen*, Berlin (East) 1953, p. 280.

1 *Ledebour-Prozess*, pp. 206 ff. Hermann Müller, *Novemberrevolution*, p. 267.

2 See his own 'confession' made to *Rote Fahne*, 11 January 1921. Though his evidence tallies precisely with Pieck's, he was quite clearly capable of saying whatever suited the occasion. Cf. also below, p. 494, note 1.

legendary *Spartakist* looked like! As he emerged from a side door into a deserted street—nothing indicates premeditation more than this complete absence of passers-by—Runge carried out his instructions, and hit him hard over the head with his rifle butt. Liebknecht was then half dragged, half hustled into a waiting car, which went off in the opposite direction to that of the prison. In the Tiergarten he was made to get out of the car and was shot within a few yards. The fatal shot was actually fired by Captain von Pflugk-Hartung. The body was delivered to a local mortuary as that of an unknown man found by the roadside. On return to the Eden Hotel this section reported to their chief that Liebknecht had been 'shot while trying to escape'.

Shortly afterwards it was Rosa Luxemburg's turn. Already in the lobby of the hotel some of the soldiers had been exercising their muscles on her. Pieck heard one of the maids say, 'I shall never forget how they knocked the poor woman down and dragged her around.'[1]

The transport of Rosa Luxemburg was in charge of a Lieutenant Vogel. Runge punctiliously performed again and, half-dead, she was dragged into another waiting car. There the messy proceedings were quickly brought to an end inside the car by a shot in the head from the officer in charge. The car stopped at a bridge over the Landwehr Canal and the body was thrown over into the murky waters, where it remained until March. Here the story was that an angry mob had stopped the car and carried Rosa Luxemburg off to an unknown destination. The soldiers were unanimously sorry; they had nothing definite to report about her fate.

Although the Communist leaders knew that the report that Liebknecht had been shot while attempting to escape was a lie, they had no facts as yet to set against the story of his death and Rosa Luxemburg's disappearance. Since *Rote Fahne* was out of action for the moment, it fell to the Independents' *Freiheit* on 17 January to challenge the official government announcement regarding the two deaths; this was of course based on the agreed version of the murderers.[2] However, long before her body was found, the real facts began to emerge and were published in *Rote Fahne*. Certainly by April the government knew the facts if not the motives, but still refused publicly to amend the statement of 16

---

[1] Pieck, 'Der 15 Januar 1919'.

[2] This announcement, in part published by *Vorwärts* on 17 January, is reprinted with comments in Ferdinand Runkel, *Die deutsche Revolution*, Leipzig 1919, pp. 217–20. The SPD version is in Hermann Müller, *Novemberrevolution*, pp. 271–9. The *Freikorps* view also got a public airing. All was the fault of the bloodthirsty Socialist government, who ordered the soldiers to do it; the latter were mere instruments of legitimate authority. F. W. von Örtzen, *Die deutschen Freikorps 1918–23*, 2nd ed., Munich 1937, pp. 284–9. The shifting of all responsibility on to a higher authority which the war criminals of the Second World War were to make so notorious, did not begin with Hitler.

January. For a time a Barbarossa-type myth about Rosa Luxemburg was in circulation, that she had gone underground to direct operations and would emerge once more in due course. However, *Rote Fahne* made it its business to scotch this false hope.

There was a widespread feeling of horror, even in SPD circles. When *Rote Fahne* began its disclosures, *Vorwärts* wrote on 13 February that 'the full force of the law must be invoked against the murderers'. Representatives of the Berlin Workers' and Soldiers' Council for a time sat in on the judicial proceedings against the murderers. But no prosecution could be made to stick. Demands for a civil as opposed to a military court to try the murderers were refused by the government on the grounds that this would interfere with the process of justice already in motion. The old Socialist conviction about the class 'justice' handed out by the imperial courts had withered away into a more anaemic respect now that six Socialist ministers *were* the Reich government. Besides, the regiment claimed jurisdiction; the allegations referred to acts committed on duty. The minimal sentences actually handed out were based on the derisory charge against Lieutenant Vogel of failing to report a corpse and illegally disposing of it, and against Runge of *attempted* manslaughter. The latter maintained that he had indeed hit Rosa Luxemburg—unexpectedly, there were witnesses—but not enough to inflict serious injury. Vogel's role did not emerge at all. The military court did make an attempt to penetrate the regimental solidarity of the murderers' 'don't knows', but to little avail. Even then, Vogel was hurried away by his friends, with false papers, after a very short period of arrest, and waited abroad for the inevitable amnesty. By the end of February Jörns, the investigating magistrate, had succeeded in manœuvring the representatives of the Workers' and Soldiers' Council into a state of impotence; by the time the trial itself took place, they renounced their participation, and there was no one except *Rote Fahne* to ask awkward questions.[1] Besides, other trials were waiting: there were fresher murders to tickle the public palate—Eisner assassinated in Munich in February, Haase shot at the end of 1919; hardly a year passed without at least one sensational political murder. The death of Rosa Luxemburg and Karl Liebknecht very soon lost its flavour of tragic immediacy.[2]

[1] For the reports of the Workers' and Soldiers' Council's delegate to the Council itself on their efforts, see *Protokoll, 56, 57. Sitzung des Zentralrates der deutschen Sozialistischen Republik, 15 Feb. 1919.* These protocols are in typewritten form in IISH, shortly to be published.

[2] This brief account of the proceedings is based on the newspaper reports and later testimony of the participants in a string of libel actions connected with Jörns, the examining magistrate. In addition, the official record of the public proceedings is still available (Prussian Ministry of Justice papers, now *Bundesarchiv* Koblenz, P.135/11759), but adds little that was not published in the newspapers. Almost all the witnesses were waiters, male

This attempt to stifle the real story of the murders, with all its political implications, should not merely be seen as an attempt of a small if powerful and obstinate clique operating behind the scenes. The January fighting represented a high-water mark of the revolutionary tide in Germany. Afterwards there was a strong reaction against disorder, which found expression in widespread if tacit support for the government. The waverers came down on the side of law and order—that very 'order' which Rosa had pilloried in her last article. In reporting the death of the *Spartakist* leaders, the bourgeois press did not even attempt to mumble the usual hypocritical phrases. Totally incomprehensible in life and actions to the vast majority of middle-class Germans, the death of the *Spartakist* leaders seemed no more than the inevitable consequence of their madness. *Tägliche Rundschau* wrote that the deaths of Rosa Luxemburg and Karl Liebknecht were the 'proper expiation for the blood bath which they unleashed . . . the results of her own action killed the woman from Galicia [*sic*]. . . . The day of judgement on Luxemburg and Liebknecht is over. Germany has peace, it can breathe again.' And the *Deutsche Tageszeitung* on 16 January took the line that newspapers always did when reporting murder trials. The fate of *Spartakists* was that of 'criminals pure and simple who without any self-restraint had long lost all power to distinguish between good and evil'. With the reassertion of such opinions under the aegis of the Socialist government, no enthusiasm for punishing what were considered to be society's executioners could have been expected. Though the issue was settled in the capital, *Spartakists*, at least in the eyes of their beholders, were still flickering wanly in the north and in Munich; there was little point in public sympathy for those who, though dead, were still kicking fitfully.

The news of the murder naturally did evoke sympathy and immediate outrage against the government from the articulate sections of the working population. Telegrams of protest came in from the Soviet Union and many other countries. The executive of the Communist Party, now underground, issued an appeal on 17 January written by Leo Jogiches, in which they asked their supporters to avoid 'terroristic attempts at revenge against the leaders of the treacherous government . . . the moment for the final battle has not yet come, and we warn you against rash attempts.'[1] The Independent leaders also issued an appeal, calling for a protest strike and warning their supporters that what the government was doing to the *Spartakists* today, it would do to all

---

and female (a profession with a curious propensity for inconclusive testimony at police proceedings, when not actually employed by the police or the secret service). Only one 'inside story' from the side of the participants was ever published, that of Runge.

[1] *D. & M.* Vol. III, pp. 85 ff.

workers tomorrow.[1] A meeting on the same day of the Plenum of the Berlin Workers' and Soldiers' Council expressed their deep disgust for the murders and protested against the government's excessive use of terror following their successful defeat of *Spartakus*.[2] But the workers werc exhausted; the strike was feebly supported.

After the defeat of January, a new chapter in the relationship between *Spartakus* and the rest of society had begun. For with these murders, the abyss which the Communists had pictured in theory had become real and, unmistakably, it was the abyss of the grave; above the arguments about revolutionary theory and tactic towered the inescapable responsibility for the murder of the two great leaders, condoned if not actually encouraged by the SPD leadership.

Among Rosa's few close friends there was an irreparable sense of loss and tragedy. Outwardly tough, as befitted a veteran revolutionary, Leo Jogiches sent Lenin a laconic telegram on 17 January: 'Rosa Luxemburg and Karl Liebknecht have carried out their ultimate revolutionary duty.'[3] Clara Zetkin in Stuttgart wrote a letter on 18 January to Mathilde Jacob. She had read of Rosa's arrest in the papers on the 16th, of Rosa's probable death on the morning of the 17th. This good-hearted, loyal woman could hardly find words to express her sense of personal and political loss when the brightest star on the Socialist horizon was extinguished.[4]

Franz Mehring was in a sanatorium on the outskirts of Berlin, old and very weak; his friends hardly dared to bring him the news. Finally one of his and Rosa's mutual friends was charged with the terrible task.

You can imagine how he reacted to the terrible news. The old man did not want to believe that such a thing was possible . . . he wandered up and down his room for hours . . . until his old body sank exhausted into a chair. But then he immediately got up again and continued his restless pacing. His eyes were dry but his face marked with scorn and hatred. 'No government has ever sunk lower', he kept murmuring.[5]

His wife was ill herself and could not help him; a few days later Mehring contracted pneumonia and had not the strength to survive it. He died on 29 January 1919, in large part the victim of the death of his friends.

Jogiches was less demonstrative. But he more than anyone must have felt the whole point of his existence crumbling. As much as was possible for such a highly political person, he had lived these last weeks mainly to keep Rosa going—there was no longer a trace of discord between them. He himself had been arrested on 14 January but had managed to escape

---

[1] *Die Freiheit*, 17 January 1919.
[2] *D. & M.* Vol. III, p. 104.
[3] Clara Zetkin, *Reden*, Vol. II, p. 444.   [4] Ibid., Vol. III, p. 71.
[5] Quoted by Schleifstein, *Mehring*, p. 76.

without being identified. Karl Radek saw him late in the evening of the 16th when he appeared at the secret flat looking ten years older. 'Feverishly he began to speak of the past, of our old quarrels. "Now that Rosa is no longer with us, we must reassemble all our old friends".' He was waiting more anxiously than ever for the return of Marchlewski from Russia which had been requested in December by Rosa Luxemburg and the KPD executive to help them in their work.[1] The two men met again next day. Radek asked him whether he had not thought of leaving for the south and safety, but Jogiches answered with a smile: 'Somebody has to stay, at least to write all our epitaphs.'[2]

Jogiches and Clara Zetkin went to work on Rosa's papers, or such as were left after the soldiers had finished their searches in Rosa's flat in Südende. Though Jogiches now took over the leadership of *Spartakus*, his heart was in the past; he was above all concerned with the identification and punishment of the murderers and the saving of as much of Rosa's writing as possible. 'Now that she has gone, we must all stick more closely together', he told Clara Zetkin. They discussed the future almost exclusively in the context of the past. 'Much of this stuff could be thrown away, since Rosa changed her mind on all that', he is reported to have added, his mind on her certain immortality.[3]

Jogiches himself had not long to live. His own safety hardly mattered to him any longer. On 10 March he was arrested and this time identified at once. At police headquarters in the Alexanderplatz one of the detectives in charge was an ex-Sergeant-Major Tamschick, a notorious bully who had once been the terror of his recruits. He knew Jogiches as one of the leaders of *Spartakus* and shot him in cold blood at the first opportunity. No attempt to punish him was ever made.[4]

Pieck himself managed to escape after a few days. He was carrying false papers when arrested together with Liebknecht and Rosa, and was apparently not identified—indeed, he was hardly known. There was never any suggestion that he was in any way concerned with the arrest of the two leaders, but Pabst stated later that he was released because he had supplied information about other *Spartakus* personalities, which facilitated their arrest. Pabst's own statements are confusing and contradictory. However, there were sufficient grounds for suspicion to enable Thälmann, later the leader of the KPD, to bring charges against Pieck in retaliation for participating in an unsuccessful attempt to wrest

---

[1] *Julian Marchlewski*, p. 92; Pieck, *Reden*, Vol. I, p. 547.

[2] Radek, *Dairy*, pp. 139–40.

[3] Ibid., also Clara Zetkin, *Reden*, Vol. II, p. 387.

[4] Soon afterwards Tamschick also murdered Dorrenbach, one of the leaders of the People's Naval Division, in the same way—a shot in the back. Tamschick enjoyed a peaceful career with promotion in the Prussian police. For his military past, see the highly coloured memoirs of one of his recruits in *Neues Deutschland*, 13 June 1959.

the KPD leadership from him in 1928. A party Court of Honour was constituted in 1929 under the chairmanship of Kippenberger, who was in charge of the Communist military apparatus and a member of the *Reichstag*. The findings were not disclosed and no further action was taken at the time. Kippenberger later fell out with Ulbricht in exile in Paris and was among the first of many German Communists to be quietly executed in Russia in 1936.[1]

On 25 January 1919 thirty-two comrades killed in the January fighting were buried with Karl Liebknecht. An empty coffin was placed at his side. Only on 31 May was the body of Rosa Luxemburg washed up unexpectedly at one of the locks of the canal, and was taken to its last resting place on 13 June. The government feared large-scale demonstrations, and Noske ordered the body to be kept at a local army camp pending burial. Although the train of mourners was large, the demonstration was silent and orderly. The funeral was at the Friedrichsfelde Cemetery, which in time became a common shrine for all prominent Communist leaders. On 13 June 1926 a memorial was unveiled to commemorate their last resting place: Rosa Luxemburg, Karl Liebknecht, Franz Mehring, Leo Jogiches, and Julian Marchlewski, who had died in 1925 in an Italian sanatorium, a respected senior Bolshevik official.[2] The cemetery was razed to the ground under the Nazis and rebuilt after the war by the East German government; party members make organized annual pilgrimages at which they see much of Ulbricht and less of the shrine.

Both Rosa Luxemburg and Karl Liebknecht had considered death in action to be the highest honour for a Social Democrat. For Rosa it was a fitting end which helped to preserve her from Stalin's special form

[1] This story is set out at length in Erich Wollenberg, 'Der Apparat; Stalins fünfte Kolonne', *Ost Probleme*, Vol. III, No. 19, 12 May 1951, pp. 576–8. This account, in a none too impartial journal, ties Kippenberger's execution to a definite intrigue by Pieck, for which there is no other evidence. The fact that there was an investigation against Pieck proves nothing except the existence of a rumour and the methods of power politics inside the KPD; the campaign against Thälmann's leadership was based on a financial scandal involving not him but his brother-in-law. It was Stalin personally who overruled the KPD Central Committee's decision to remove Thälmann rather than any private intrigue by Pieck. The latter's reputation among his colleagues in the 1920s was that of a tough, resourceful, if devious militant.

None the less, Runge's own story—which Pieck certified as accurate (*Rote Fahne*, 11 January 1921)—contains the following rather odd passage (in italics). Runge had been ordered to shoot the *Rote Fahne* editor (wrongly thought to be Pieck) in the corridor of the hotel. 'I had doubts . . . the man from the *Rote Fahne* came up to me and said *he had a commission to carry out [Auftrag zu erledigen]*. He was led away into a room and when he emerged an officer instructed one of the guards: "Take this man away *and see to it that nothing happens*." '(My italics.)

[2] *Die Rote Fahne*, 15 June 1926. Marchlewski's ashes were returned to Poland at the request of the Polish government in March 1950.

of Bolshevik dishonour. There was something larger than life about her ideas and the rigid prescription she had set herself in a life devoted to revolutionary politics, yet always combined with a deep respect for human values and culture. She died in the firm belief that her cause would win in the end; that she could advance it by dying as much as by living. At the time of her death she recognized a temporary defeat in Germany, but in the context of great advances there and in Russia. A truly Marxist party had been created under her auspices in Germany and, as far as she could, she had set guiding lines for its future development. Her eyes closed on a German revolution at last beginning to come into its own as the centrepiece of the international revolution in which she so fervently believed. Her presence in Germany for so many years, in a milieu basically anti-pathetic to her, seemed fully justified. Although she recognized the success of the Bolsheviks in Russia, she was not willing to accept their direction of the international movement, or to subordinate her party to the Bolsheviks. In the last two months she treated Lenin as a friend and an equal—no more. A hasty letter she wrote him in Russian on 20 December 1918 shows the respect of an equal but no deference.

Dear Vladimir,
I am profiting from uncle's journey to send you all hearty greetings from the family, from Karl, Franz [Mehring] and the others. May God grant that the coming year will fulfil all our wishes. All the best! Uncle will report about our life and doings, meantime I press your hand,
With best regards,
Rosa.[1]

The 'uncle' carrying the letter was Eduard Fuchs, a lawyer and journalist and member of the *Spartakusbund*. No details are known about his visit to Moscow but it was inevitably connected with the Russian plans for the new International. Almost certainly Fuchs's task was to express to Lenin the strong reservations against this intended creation harboured by both Rosa Luxemburg and Leo Jogiches. At the same time they had to discover Lenin's precise intentions. His conversations with the Bolshevik leader were kept strictly unofficial if not secret; none of Lenin's colleagues were officially informed. In the event the German reservations and objections only served to confirm Lenin in his determination to proceed as quickly as possible with the foundation of the Third International. 'We must hasten [before the departure of the "Spartakist"] to prepare for the international socialist conference which will found the Third International.'[2]

[1] *Pravda*, 15 January 1925; reprinted in facsimile in *Selected Works*, Vol. II, opposite p. 624.
[2] Lenin, *Sochineniya* 5th edition, Vol. L, pp. 227–30. See also ibid., p. 460, note 246.

On his return Fuchs reported Lenin's intentions. Rosa Luxemburg's worst fears were confirmed: she was more determined than ever that the German communist party should not participate. She instructed the German delegates to vote against the creation of a new International at this time and in present circumstances. She considered it premature with only one Socialist party, the Bolsheviks, precariously on top in one country, and was afraid that, if formed, the new International would be entirely under Russian domination—as indeed it was.[1] In the event Eberlein, the only German delegate to the founding congress, did not vote against the resolution to found the Third International but acceded to strong Russian pressure and merely abstained. By this time—March 1919—Rosa Luxemburg was dead.

After her death German Communist policy—in fact the whole party —was suspended in a vacuum for a time. The January rising in Berlin was followed by successful local insurrections in Bremen and Munich, while attempts were made in other cities. The government was able to deal with all these in turn; only in Munich had the forces of the Bavarian countryside to be thrown against the revolutionary capital, and here too the Communists took over a hopeless situation which they had originally opposed, and suffered the consequences. Eugen Leviné, who should have gone to Russia with Eberlein, was sent to Munich instead, and executed in June 1919. The leadership in Germany went underground. Only in February was *Rote Fahne* able to appear again. Its first concern was to identify the perpetrators of the murder. For a time, Communist political activity was confined to the periphery; Marchlewski worked in the Ruhr, and Clara Zetkin in Württemberg. After the death of Leo Jogiches the leadership of the party passed to Paul Levi and his main task for the next twelve months was the creation of an organization and the regrouping of Communist forces. Levi at any rate had learnt his lesson in January. When the activists made another attempt in March 1921 to raise the banner of revolt, this time with more careful 'planning' and better 'organization', but less popular

---

[1] Hugo Eberlein was the only German delegate able to make the journey. He found a haphazard gathering. Representatives of various nationalities who happened to be in Moscow constituted themselves as delegates of their countries.

At the start, the Russians offered to meet the objections of the vital German party and treat the proceedings as preliminary rather than constituent. But Eberlein was soon under considerable Russian pressure not to oppose the plans of the Bolsheviks, and in the end abstained from the constituent vote of the International, rather than vote against it as instructed. See *Der 1 Kongress der Kommunistischen Internationale: Protokoll der Verhandlungen in Moskau vom 2 bis zum 19 März 1919*, Hamburg 1921, Vol. I, p. 131. The official Russian version emphasized the Russian party's forbearance with Eberlein's crisis of conscience and his spontaneous conversion rather than any Bolshevik pressure on him to swing the vital German vote into line. See report of G. Zinoviev, *Vosmoi s"ezd RKP(B),mart 1919 goda, Protokoly*, Moscow 1959, p. 135.

support, he opposed them bitterly and eventually threw the weight of Rosa Luxemburg's words against them by publishing her pamphlet on the Russian revolution and hinting at the disputes within the Communist leadership in January. Another in the series of dramatic exits from the KPD took place. Both Levi and the Central Committee claimed the authority of Rosa Luxemburg for their point of view, and fired suitable quotations from her writings at each other. This too was to become a habit of left-wing politics for the next ten years.

Communist leaders in Russia and elsewhere were well aware that German revolutionary Socialism had lost its outstanding leaders. In Leningrad and Moscow meetings were held at which the Bolshevik leadership paid tribute to their German comrades. Inevitably this blow in Germany was bound to set back the hopes of international revolution. But for the Russians the event had its useful side, for with Rosa Luxemburg and Leo Jogiches there disappeared two determined opponents of Bolshevik control of international Socialism. Henceforth the Russians were the more easily able to impose their will on the German party, and after the adhesion of the larger part of the USPD to the KPD in the summer of 1920, a real mass base was at last available to the Communists. In spite of all the sects and personalities which were thrown off the main body of the party like sparks from a catherine wheel for the next twelve years, as the Russians tightened their grip and oscillated the orientation of German Communism to suit their present needs, the KPD never again lost its organizational hold on at least a part of the masses.

What would have happened if Rosa had remained alive? There was no doubt that the January fighting had ended the revolutionary phase of German post-war development which nothing could have revived for the time being. The government used its victory to impose its will and weight on all the revolutionary institutions in Germany, and in its shadow the army stood waiting, swollen with the support of the *Freikorps*, enthusiastic volunteers against the revolution. Now both lunged forward into the power vacuum. Rosa Luxemburg's sarcastic prediction that the *bourgeoisie* would soon rid itself of its Social-Democrat agents and assume power on its own account nearly came true in the Kapp *putsch* of March 1920; only the unexpected general strike called by the right-wing trade-union leaders she had always so heartily despised actually prevented the success of the military mutineers. All this was inevitable after January.

The fascinating question obviously is how a Communist leadership under Rosa Luxemburg and Karl Liebknecht would have utilized the mass strength which came through the adhesion to the USPD. The terms for the merger were in fact dictated from Moscow, and probably would have been similar if Rosa had written them. Rosa Luxemburg always dreamed of this particular eventuality, pushing aside the Independent leaders and taking over their supporters. With such a mass base, she would have been better able to resist Zinoviev's take-over on behalf of the Third International and the Russian party, but whether she could have revitalized the engine of revolution within Germany is another question. No doubt she would have resisted the further Communist attempts to seize power in March 1921 and in 1923, both carefully engineered and prepared—and hopelessly unsuccessful. But this is as far as we can go. Why should she have been able to stand out successfully against Stalinization when no one else could? Or would she have left with Paul Levi, if the March 1921 action had been imposed in the face of her opposition?

What of the long run? SPD or KPD, Nazi concentration camp or emigration—and if so, West or East? In 1933 the world of Stalin would have been grotesquely unfamiliar to a woman of sixty-three—and for this woman, dangerous. Would it have been Harvard, a special professorship, a thick black book of apologia, with all the aseptic admiration of young, neutrally academic professionals in their discreet bow-ties? Or perhaps sociology, that refuge of clever European Marxists? Or suicide, the last resort, with Marta Rosenbaum and so many others whose hearts were broken? We cannot tell, for Rosa had something in common with them all.

It is always convenient for biographers to take the death of their subject as the end of a period. Apart from the seductive convenience, it may sometimes even be justified. The principles for which Rosa Luxemburg stood and the influence she exercised might not have survived even if she had remained alive. Without a successful German revolution, the increase of Russian power and control over Communist parties everywhere was inevitable; there was no reason why Germany should have remained outside this development. The painful dislocation of loyalties which this brought about for so many Communist leaders was spared Rosa Luxemburg, though her ideas—largely the misrepresentation of her ideas—served as a football for the power game within the world Communist movement. Having died orthodox, she exercised a claim to be heard. She could never be written off as someone who had consciously departed from what was to be the correct course, like Trotsky or Bukharin or Karl Kautsky.

The long process of litigation over Rosa Luxemburg's intellectual and political heritage is itself a history of distortion. The truth, and Rosa's position in it, are simple enough. Marx left two great alternatives —one basic, one derived. The basic variable was revolution—formal or real, objective or subjective, an event that happened or one that had to be made. (Extreme positions, these, with an infinity of possibilities in between.) The irreparable break, which transformed possibilities into irreconcilable alternatives, took place in 1910 with Rosa Luxemburg and Karl Kautsky holding the two sawn-off ends. (The revisionist controversy was about 'how', not 'what'; about the small present, not the great future—really a second-rate dispute.) From this first break derived the second variable: Socialists *making* the revolution, or *leading* it. The pull of the Russian October revolution prevented any intermediate positions from developing and produced a new break right away—only Rosa Luxemburg's death prevented her from developing and defending her leadership of an alternative revolutionary Marxist tradition against other claimants. But none the less, the position was rightfully hers—not the reward of those, including Trotsky, who later broke out of the Bolshevik collectivity, but of the forceful, perpetually foreign woman who belonged to many Socialisms and to none. Only Rosa Luxemburg was actively concerned with both the great divisions of modern Marxism, and partly helped to create them. That is her role in history, and the reason for this book.

At the same time, her influence extends far beyond the formal confines of Marxism. No uncommitted student of political thought can afford to ignore a corpus of ideas which combines without equal a complete loyalty to dialectical materialism with absolute insistence on the humanistic and self-liberating aspects of revolutionary democracy. Those who believe that the discipline of change and improvement must be largely self-imposed, that the modern industrial economy of the West is at once the harshest prison for the human spirit and the only key to its liberation; those in short who hold that the revolutionary steps to progress must lead directly from highly developed capitalism to Socialism without the historically retrograde control by a small élite which serves progress in relatively backward societies, will all find no better guide or inspiration than the life and work of Rosa Luxemburg. In the last few years the revolutionary exhaustion, the materialist introspection of the highly developed industrial societies of the West has suddenly given way to new, at the time of writing as yet inchoate, movements of social protest, in part with revolutionary overtones. Intellectuals, students and underprivileged racial minorities have seized the standard of social revolution from the frozen hands of organized labour, and are excitingly carrying it aloft. Once more there is hope that the impetus of change may come from within highly industrialized societies, and not only from without and against them, in Asia and Latin America.

Rosa Luxemburg's actual solutions may have been utopian. But if the validity of the European experience and its acceptance as a means to further progress are to be maintained, then her over-all contribution is highly relevant.

THE NATIONAL QUESTION

R OSA LUXEMBURG did not invent the notion that Socialism and national self-determination might be conflicting ideas. The difficulty of finding the right emphasis and relationship between them in practical politics already bedevilled Polish Socialists in the early 1880s. In the Polish context it is as old as Socialism itself. It even goes all the way back to Marx and Engels. Though Marx hailed the re-establishment of Poland as progressive and worthy of the First International's support, his motives were not simply based on some concept of abstract right or justice. Karl Marx, with his long-range vision of history, worked out a correspondingly long-range revolutionary strategy—aimed largely at defeating Russia, then the geo-political heartland of European reaction. In general Marx's and Engel's conception of the national-geographical rearrangement of Europe was based on four criteria: the development of progress, the creation of large-scale economic units, the weighting of approval and disapproval in accordance with revolutionary possibilities, and their specific enmity to Russia.[1] Their attitude to Poland—with all due allowance for the persistent intrusion of this particular issue—fits into their general framework and in fact illustrates it.

In order to move the German revolution forward it was necessary to separate Germany from Russia. The creation of a democratic Poland was the first pre-condition for the creation of a democratic Germany. That this formulation contradicted the absorptionist policies of the Prussian government with regard to non-German minorities suited Marx all the better.[2] The fact that Marx stressed that Germany's honour was at stake in the need to re-create Poland may be taken as much as a propagandistic weapon as evidence of any genuine attachment to such unmaterialistic motivations. Once in exile in London, the stress on right and honour largely disappeared. The anti-Russian accent grew stronger. The desirable political constellation of East Europe became the celebrated anti-Russian *cordon sanitaire* of containment.[3] Reflecting

---

[1] See Wehler, *Sozialdemokratie*, p. 15.

[2] See *Neue Rheinische Zeitung*, 12 July, 12 August, 20 August 1848.

[3] K. Bittel (ed.), *Neue Rehinische Zeitung*, new edition, Berlin (East) 1955, No. 2, February 1850, pp. 116 ff. See also F. Engels in *Sozialdemokrat*, Zürich, 13 March 1884.

on the new post-revolutionary situation in Europe, Engels wrote to Marx in May 1851: 'The more I reflect about history the clearer it appears to me that the Poles are a *nation foutue*, useful as a means only until Russia herself is drawn into the agrarian revolution. From that moment on Poland has absolutely no more *raison d'être*.'[1]

This subordination of any autonomous interest to the wider strategical necessity of defeating or at least containing Russia was partly eroded by the widespread support for Polish national aspirations among many of Marx's associates, particularly in England. In the course of the rising of 1863 Marx again came out more strongly in favour of an historical reward for so much revolutionary effort.[2] But it is noticeable that even during this resurgence of interest in Polish self-determination there is no attempt to broaden support for a reconstituted Poland into any general doctrine of self-determination. Nor did Marx's various attempts to commit the First International to a specific Polish policy meet with universal enthusiasm in that organization.[3] 'Marx and Engels were interested in the "20 million heroes between Europe and Asia" not as a nation but as a revolutionary and strategical potential.'[4] Engels especially was concerned to emphasize the functional role of Poland as a vehicle for revolution; a role limited in time to the dawn of revolutionary incandescence in Russia itself. When in the late 1870s the Narodniks first gave signs of a revolutionary potential there, the importance of Poland rapidly declined in his conception.[5]

But at the same time the very decline of Poland's functional role caused Engels to examine the specific question of Polish nationality somewhat more generously. As a separate Polish Socialist movement began to emerge in the 1880s Engels was exercised by the tactical problem of giving it as wide an appeal as possible. He developed a more precise thesis about the relationship between revolutionary progress and national states. The national unit was the 'normal political constitution

---

[1] Letter dated 23 May 1851. See also W. Conze's Introduction to W. Conze and D. Hertz-Eichenrode (eds.), *Karl Marx, Manuskripte über die polnische Frage (1863-4)*, s'Gravenhage (Holland) 1961, pp. 25 ff. (hereafter cited as 'Conze').

[2] See letter from Marx to Engels, 2 December 1856, and letters of 13, 17, 19, 21 February 1863. A resolution on the subject is in Leon Wasilewski, 'Karl Marx und der Aufstand von 1863', *Polen*, Vol. I, No. 27, Vienna 1915, reprinted in Conze, pp. 91-96.

[3] See N. Rjasanoff, 'Karl Marx and F. Engels on the Polish question', *Archiv für die Geschichte des Sozialismus und der Arbeiterbewegung*, 1916, No. 6, pp. 192 ff., 210 ff. See particularly Marx's arguments at the first conference of the International, ibid., pp. 194 ff.

[4] Wehler, *Sozialdemokratie*, p. 21. The phrase quoted here comes from Paul W. Blackstock and B. F. Hoselitz (eds.), *The Russian Menace to Europe by Karl Marx and Freidrich Engels*, Glencoe (Illinois) 1952, p. 108.

[5] Helmut Krause, *Marx und Engels und das zeitgenössische Russland*, Giessen 1959, pp. 37, 78 ff.; Conze, pp. 23 ff.

of the European bourgeoisie' in which it could best develop. 'No great people can seriously discuss its internal problems as long as national independence is absent.' In order to avoid any discrepancy between Socialist policy and the obvious desire for national unity and independence, it was necessary for Polish Socialists to 'place the liberation of their country at the head of their programme. An international proletarian movement . . . can only grow out of the existence of independent nations.'[1]

Thus both Marx and Engels established some sort of a tradition of proletarian support for national self-determination—at least of major peoples—in general and for Polish self-determination in particular. This tradition was taken over and developed by the leaders of Social Democracy in Germany, Austria, and elsewhere. Wilhelm Liebknecht especially became the major protagonist of this thesis both in its general and Polish aspects. But in the course of time the motivations changed. The revolutionary strategy, according to which Poland was a cog in the anti-Russian policy of containment and destruction, became emasculated. With the emergence of a Socialist movement in Poland and following Engel's narrower preoccupation with the resurrection of Poland as desirable *per se*, the question of right and justice altered the wider strategy. Wilhelm Liebknecht—and to some extent his colleague Bebel —based the ideological legitimacy of his leadership of the growing German Social-Democratic movement on specific negation of the expansionist policies of the Prussian state and German empire. The occupation of substantial Polish areas was a flagrant example; it was thus natural that support for Polish self-determination became an integral part of the 'mortal enmity' which was ritually (and annually) hurled at existing society and its political superstructure.[2] For German Social Democracy, particularly after the end of the anti-Socialist laws, the problem was not merely part of the permanent confrontation with the government. In the 1890s the Poles in Germany were being organized by their own new Polish Socialist party; the relationship between it and the SPD became a practical problem to which the intellectual commitment to Polish independence had to be accommodated. The relationship between traditional commitment to a concept and its application to sensitive but intractable questions of organization at home provided a fruitful source of trouble in the future.

---

[1] See letter from Engels to Kautsky, 7 February 1882, in Freidrich Engels, *Breifwechsel mit K. Kautsky*, 2nd ed., Vienna 1955, p. 50. This was to be exactly Kautsky's attitude for the rest of his life.

[2] For Liebknecht's position, see his article 'The process of education', *Neue Deutsche Rundschau*, 1898, No. 9, pp. 396–406; see also his speech in the *Reichstag* (Sixth legislative period, first session, Volume I, p. 422, 17 December 1874).

At the end of 1892 the foundation of the PPS completed the emergence of organized Polish Socialism in all three areas of occupation. Each of the three parties in Austrian, German, and Russian Poland was committed to fight for the revival of a Polish state. The fact that three separate parties had to be founded was no more than a temporary concession to the factual division of Poland. The three separate parties did their utmost to collaborate closely and founded an organization in London to co-ordinate their efforts.

When Rosa Luxemburg and a small group of friends broke out of the PPS of Russian Poland in 1893, it was the national question which soon emerged as the main bone of contention between them. No doubt it had played a major part in causing the split but there were other issues as well, more personal and less suitable for public polemic. The national question was as much a means of differentiation as its cause; the reason for digging a moat and also the tool with which it was dug deep and insurmountable. Ends and means snowballed until the national question had become the accepted touchstone of their differences.

It was not until 1895 that the first full theoretical justification for the SDKP position on the Polish question was published.[1] Between 1895 and 1897, in a series of articles, Rosa Luxemburg elaborated the theoretical foundations of her anti-nationalist position, and extended it beyond the context of Poland. It was not yet a full-blown condemnation of national self-determination as an historically dated—and therefore reactionary—concept, but an extension of the Polish experience, and above all of the method of analysis, to other areas. Her case was based on two main assumptions. First, that national and Socialist aspirations were incompatible and that a commitment to national self-determination by Socialist parties must subordinate those parties to bourgeois nationalism instead of opposing one to the other. A programme of national self-determination thus became the first of Rosa Luxemburg's many indices of an opportunism which tied Socialism to the chariot of the class enemy—a concept that was to be elaborated and refined during the revisionist debate. To this extent Rosa Luxemburg invented the concept of modern Socialist opportunism, its characterization and its identification as a bourgeois (i.e. hostile) influence within the Socialist movement. Secondly, Rosa Luxemburg attacked the premises of national self-determination in the particular context of the Russian question. Far from being the bulwark of reaction, to be destroyed or contained by independent states carved out of the Tsar's empire by nationalist revolution, Russia was itself moving into the era of social revolution—not yet the possible epicentre which it was to become after 1905 but

---

[1] M. Rózga, *Niepodległa Polska a sprawa robotnicza*, Paris 1895.

already a link in the chain of growing European capitalism in which bourgeois and finally proletarian revolution could ripen. Russian Poland as well as other non-Russian areas in the Tsarist empire now depended for their release, not on nationalist separation from Russia, but on the proletarian revolution within Russia itself. National separation was in fact a retrograde step. Revolution in Russian Poland would come more quickly if Polish industrial development could flourish in its all-Russian context; by cutting off Polish industry from its Russian markets Poland's industrial development—and hence the development of the class struggle—could only be retarded.[1]

The furore raised by this argumentation was due not so much to the argument itself but to the fact that it was a self-conscious amendment and revision of Marx and Engels—at least of the current conception of their views. According to her critics, Rosa Luxemburg grossly over-emphasized the revolutionary potential of Russia. The revolutionary flicker of the later seventies and early eighties had largely died out; in any case it had hardly been an organized mass effort of the type likely to endear itself to men like Wilhelm Liebknecht or Victor Adler. The PPS tried hard to contradict Rosa Luxemburg's economic argumentation. They asserted most tellingly that her policy played straight into the hands of the hated Russian autocracy; no one but the Russian police could benefit from it. The stigma of alliance between SDKP and Colonel Markgrawski of the Warsaw Gendarmerie—whether coincidental or more than that—was exploited to the utmost in the rumour-prone circles of Polish and Russian emigration. To the Germans Rosa Luxemburg's analysis seemed in addition to everything else a betrayal of their moral obligation towards the underprivileged Poles in the Reich.

On a deeper level the argument turned on the general question of self-determination. Rosa Luxemburg claimed that it was not Social Democracy's duty to found minute new capitalist states that could never be viable. Contemptuously she cited the example of the North German coast; if every group possessing its distinct dialect could now claim the right to its own state, Europe would lapse into truly feudal anarchy.[2] The days when national self-determination was indeed progressive had long since passed. But it had had its historical importance; correct application of Marxist techniques brought up to date must surely lead Socialists to call for national self-determination in hopeless multi-national units like Turkey which had proved incapable of any economic

---

[1] The economic argument was developed in Rosa Luxemburg's doctoral dissertation, *Die industrielle Entwicklung Polens*, Leipzig 1898.

[2] If she had been more receptive to English history and social circumstances, she might have picked on what is in fact the classic illustration of her thesis—the failure of Wales and Scotland to develop nationalist mass movements against the dominant bourgeois tendency for economic integration with England since the industrial revolution.

development and progress, instead of helping to shore up these archaic monsters against Russia.[1] However much Rosa Luxemburg stressed her own orthodoxy in applying Marx's techniques to a changed situation, Liebknecht, Kautsky, and Plekhanov all dismissed her amendments as inadmissible if not downright sacrilegious. Rosa Luxemburg had turned Marxist strategy exactly upside down. Marx had called for an independent Poland and a strong Turkey in order to weaken Russia, while this argumentative hen in Zürich ridiculed the possibility and value of Polish independence and called for the break-up of the Turkish empire instead. The fact that much of Marx's thinking had been strategic, and abstracted from the development of a revolutionary situation in Russia itself, was ignored. The independence of Poland had suddenly become a Marxist object unto itself, like a meteor falling into the deliberations of the astronomers.

In the heat of the argument, Rosa Luxemburg no doubt adopted an extreme and uncompromising position. Though publicly committed to autonomy for Poland, she began by confessing in private that even this was a concession; she would have preferred to do without autonomy as well.[2] Some of her colleagues, like Marchlewski, though they shared her basic position, did not follow her all the way—especially not in her insatiable appetite for public polemics on the subject.[3] But in general Rosa Luxemburg provided both stuffing and framework for the view that Social Democrats must take the geography of Europe much as they find it, that self-determination is a tactical and intellectual concession to the *bourgeoisie*, and that Polish Social Democracy must find the satisfaction of its proletarian aims within the framework of a Russian revolution. To this position she adhered strenuously until her death. It provided the mainstay of twenty years of polemic against the PPS, the most important criticism of the Bolsheviks after the October revolution, and a steady prop for the extreme internationalism with which she confronted the patriotic capitulations during the First World War. 'In the era of rampaging Imperialism there can be no more national wars. [The assertion of] national interests can serve only as a means of deception, of betraying the working masses of the people to their deadly enemy, Imperialism.'[4]

---

[1] For Rosa Luxemburg's articles on the Turkish question and contemporary replies, see above, pp. 65–6.

[2] 'I have even managed to frown a little on autonomy [in the proclamation].' Jogiches letters, 11 April 1894, *Z Pola Walki*, Moscow 1930, Nos. 9–10, p. 127. There are various references to the 'concession to autonomy' in this period.

[3] For a note of Marchlewski's writings on this question, see J. Kaczankowska, *Bibliografia prac Juliana Marchlewskiego*, Łódź 1954. See also above, p. 64.

[4] *Die Krise der Sozialdemokratie*, appendix, fifth thesis; quoted from Rosa Luxemburg's *Selected Works*, Vol. I, p. 395.

In 1908 Rosa Luxemburg's views on the national question in general, refined by many years of political campaigning in the German, Russian, and Polish parties, were treated to a systematic exposition for the first time.[1] It was a self-conscious exercise in deduction, arguing from an established theory to the many scattered instances and facts. She put forward her thesis essentially as the product of the present historical epoch; any other view was wrong because it was out of date. For in this one sector the general advance of social relations and Marxist analysis of them in the course of the past fifty years had left a curious pocket of pre-scientific utopian idealism. 'Social Democracy, which has based its entire policy on the scientific method of historical materialism and the class war, cannot make exceptions in the question of nationality.'[2] Now that the gap had been discovered, it had to be made good at once. The whole basis of Rosa Luxemburg's thesis on the national question was that, far from raising the dialectic to new and possibly insecure levels, she merely brought scientific Socialism up to the level it had attained everywhere else. Words like 'right', 'ethics', 'duties', and 'obligations' were clear evidence of outdated modes of thought. The most telling analogy was with the right to work:

In the 1840s the formulation of a 'right to work' was the dearly beloved postulate of French Socialism, providing an immediate and total solution of all social questions. After the briefest attempt to put it into practice during the 1848 revolution, however, this 'right' ended in a complete fiasco. . . .[3]

The entire notion of abstract rights was contemptuously characterized as being like Chernyshevsky's 'right of every man to eat from golden platters'—a notion to which only anarchists subscribed. The identity of Socialists who propagated the right of nations to self-determination, with anarchists, who specialized in the achievement of so many other abstractions, was constantly asserted.[4] This dashing method of 'pairing' the unlikeliest opponents—in this case bourgeois nationalists and anarchists—puts Rosa Luxemburg right in the mainstream of classical Marxist polemic. She was herself to be a distinguished victim of the method a few years after her death.

One of the most interesting aspects of Rosa Luxemburg's argument was the hint that the very concept of 'nation' was temporary. Instead of being an absolute and permanent standard of measurement she suggested that it might be no more than the particular form in which bourgeois society encapsulated its structural arrangement—and that it would pass away with the end of the capitalist phase of history. This

---

[1] 'The question of nationality and autonomy', *Przegląd Socjaldemokatyczny*, August 1908, No. 6, reprinted in *Wybór Pism*, Vol. II, pp. 114–66. As far as I know it has never been translated into any other language.

[2] *Wybór Pism*, Vol. II, p. 114.   [3] Ibid., p. 135.   [4] Ibid., p. 140.

moment was coming closer, and it behoved Marxists to grasp the future and not cling to the past.

Speaking of the right of nations to self-determination we dispense with the idea of a nation as a whole. It becomes merely a social and political unit [for purposes of measurement]. But it was just this concept of nations as one of the categories of bourgeois ideology that Marxist theory attacked most fiercely, pointing out that under slogans like 'national self-determination'—or 'freedom of the citizen', 'equality before the law'—there lurks all the time a twisted and limited meaning. In a society based on classes, the nation as a uniform social-political whole simply does not exist. Instead there exist within each nation classes with antagonistic interests and 'rights'. There is literally no social arena—from the strongest material relationship to the most subtle moral one—in which the possessing classes and a self-conscious proletariat could take one and the same position and figure as one undifferentiated national whole.[1]

The historical limitation to the concept of nationality and nation was only hinted at. Orthodox Marxism, Kautsky's as well as Lenin's, preferred to *equate* the national interest with that of the proletariat rather than, like Rosa Luxemburg, *subsuming* the one by the other. In any case events proved Rosa Luxemburg's prognosis incorrect—at least in its application to the immediate future; the outbreak of war showed clearly that when the crunch came class antagonisms were swept aside by national solidarity. Perhaps this is why Lenin preferred to equate rather than subsume, and why in 1914 Rosa Luxemburg felt that so much of her view of the world had shattered into a thousand fragments.

The claim that national self-determination was an historically superseded Utopia seemed specious, but Rosa Luxemburg proceeded to clothe it with historical examples. Though unaware of the extent of Marx's and Engels's own strategic approach to the problem of Polish nationality (most of the private correspondence between them had not then been published), she was perceptive enough to recognize that Marx was far too good a practitioner of his own methods to fall into any sentimental commitment to abstract or natural rights. Rosa Luxemburg emphasized that particular predictions of strength and weakness for any of the national movements in the middle of the nineteenth century had proved extremely fallible and that the validity of Marx's own analysis did not in the least depend on his—as it turned out—erroneous support for the hopeless Turkish empire or his derogatory prognosis for Czech nationalism.[2] By now Rosa Luxemburg was careful not to rely too much on the Polish example (no one in the Second International would have

---

[1] Ibid., pp. 147–8.
[2] Ibid., pp. 123–8. It should be noted that this was written almost at the end of the period when Rosa thought that German history was the precursor to the history of her neighbours.

accepted any general analysis based on Poland). But she did illustrate the progress from utopian nationalism to scientific internationalism from her own Polish experience.

The mystic sentimental Socialism which ran wild in Germany in the 1830s, represented by Karl Grün and Moses Hess, emerged in a suitably messy version after forty years in the ideas of Limanowski—the *Lud polski* at the beginning and the *pobudka* at the end of the 80s of the last century; a striving for all that is fine and beautiful. Mr. Limanowski, the later leader of the PPS, united Polish Socialism on the basis that Socialism is undoubtedly a beautiful idea and patriotism a no less beautiful idea; hence 'why should not two such beautiful ideas unite together?'[1]

All along Rosa Luxemburg confronted idealism and beauty with the pessimism of historical necessity. Certainly the revolution would finally liberate the innate potential of human nature; but right now her task was not to stress the moral aspect of Marxist revolution against its bourgeois detractors and their 'law and order', but on the contrary to emphasize the often harsh necessities of historical laws. Cheap propagandistic appeals to potential but temporary allies of the working class could only prove fatal. In any case it was strictly against the tradition of scientific Socialism.

Marx and Engels in reality paid no tribute at all to party or class egoism and certainly did not sacrifice the needs of Western European democracy to [the concept of] nation, as might have appeared at first glance. It is true that it sounds far more big-hearted and attractive for the exuberant imagination of young intellectuals when Socialists announce a general and universal amnesty for all presently subjected nations. But such an attempt to bestow on all nations, countries, groups and on all of human creation the right to freedom, equality and happiness with a single stroke of the pen typically characterizes only the adolescence of the Socialist movement—and even more the boastful phraseology of anarchism.

The Socialism of the modern working class—scientific Socialism—does not go in for merely generous-sounding solutions of social and national conflicts. . . . Social Democracy does not distinguish itself through the magnanimity of its programmes and is in this respect constantly outstripped by Socialist parties which are not tied by any scientific doctrine. These always have their pockets full of attractive gifts for everyone. Thus for example in Russia the Socialist Revolutionaries leave Social Democracy far behind in their solution for agriculture, seeing that they have at their disposal a recipe for the benefit of the peasants—the instant partial introduction of Socialism into the countryside without any [of our] dull attendance on the growth of the right conditions for the elimination of industrial capital through revolution. In comparison with such parties Social Democracy is and always will be a poor party, just as Marx was poor in comparison with the generous and all-promising Bakunin. . .

1 Ibid., pp. 150–1.
2 Ibid., p. 134.

This was perhaps the only occasion when Rosa Luxemburg underpinned the neglect of the peasants by the SDKPiL and the later *Spartakusbund* with full theoretical justification. Yet this position follows logically from her entire analysis of the national question. Just as nationalism was an unsuitable bed-fellow for Socialist aspirations, so peasant discontent could only divert the energy of working-class Socialism into petit-bourgeois channels. In Rosa Luxemburg's view the primary role of the proletariat in the Russian revolution of 1905–6 —a conception shared fully by the Bolsheviks—necessarily led her to refuse alliances with peasants and nationalists just as firmly as with the bourgeois liberals. It was a logical enough conclusion, but for Lenin its very logic made it abstract and dogmatic. He was to oppose Rosa Luxemburg's concept with logic of a different kind: autonomous role of the proletariat, yes—but alliances with all elements who historically had to move forward (in a revolutionary sense) before they moved back; no alliance on the other hand with liberals who had already reached the fullest extent of their revolutionary push and who, whatever they *said* they were doing, were in fact already moving back.

Rosa Luxemburg's argument was at its weakest when she tried specifically to apply it to Russia. The last section of her article is a curiously garbled *reductio ad absurdum* of the deep and personal impact which this question had made on the thinking of all those concerned with the revolutionary future of Russia. Each paragraph begins with 'suppose that . . .'—evidence that abstractions are about to be substituted for realities.[1]

It is perhaps tactically significant (and no more) that Rosa Luxemburg quoted and criticized a Menshevik formulation of the national question rather than a Bolshevik one, even though on this there was for once little difference between them. And it certainly did not save her from a generous discharge of Lenin's wrath; unerringly he picked out the weakest point of her argument—though not until six years later, when it suited him for other reasons to splash a little mud on the Berlin Poles.

In practical terms Rosa Luxemburg's opposition to the PPS and its policy of self-determination made her the most efficient ally of the SPD's policy of organizational integration for minorities in Germany. She was equally committed to integration into the all-Russian party— at least in theory; but here the state of the Russian party itself and a reluctance to dissolve the SDKPiL as a going concern prevented any application of this policy. Such failure to match words with deeds provided suitable ammunition to her PPS opponents, and much of Rosa Luxemburg's writing had to be devoted to an elaborate attempt to

[1] Ibid., pp. 156 ff.

justify the SDKPiL's continued independence as a party. But though her tactics fitted into the general orientation well enough, the precise relationship between party policy and national policy was never explored. As usual, Rosa was silent as soon as it came to the logic of organization. She might oppose the policy of self-determination, and berate those parties advocating it, but she obstinately defended her own party's resistance (and by implication that of all other parties) to being submerged into supra-national wholes. Thus she attacked the Austrian party and its leaders for advocating national self-determination in a socio-political context, while the Bolsheviks attacked them for the opposite reason—giving the national right of self-determination concrete organizational expression in party terms. The Austrians clearly succeeded in pleasing nobody. But more important is the fact that both the SDKPiL's and the Bolsheviks' positions contained serious and self-destructive contradictions.

The Bolshevik dichotomy party/society was to lead them into some very awkward adjustments after 1917, with Stalin almost destroying the old party in order to break the excessive traditional distinction between them. But at least Lenin recognized the need to justify the separation and hammered away at the dialectical unity between national self-determination in its social context and absolute organizational subordination to the centre in a party context. Rosa Luxemburg saw neither problem nor contradiction, and merely combined party independence with its denial for aspiring nations. The notion that party organization could be functionally related to the theoretical or practical solution of social problems, could even set a precedent for post-revolutionary society, was entirely unreal for her. To anyone who believed that the most significant meaning of the revolutionary process was the equation, the fusion, of party and society, the organizational subordination or independence of one Socialist party from another could not be a matter of any importance—and therefore did not need to fit into any theory of revolution.

Rosa Luxemburg made little attempt to distinguish between the positions of those who disagreed with her. As Lenin at one time dumped his various opponents into a few collective dustbins simply marked liquidators and opportunists, so Rosa Luxemburg created the over-simplified category of nationalists or social patriots. Just as the later Communists steadily refused to see any significant difference between Centrism and Reformism after 1914, so Rosa Luxemburg refused to distinguish in the Polish movement between the open nationalism of the right-wing PPS and the policy of the PPS-Left; between those who in the wider context promoted national self-determination to an absolute priority and those, like Lenin and Kautsky, who gave it conditional and limited support.[1] In her argument with Lenin, particularly, a number of entirely different questions became entangled. These can roughly be divided into two categories. First the question of self-determination as an element of revolutionary policy, secondly the question of party relationships in a multi-national situation.

Until 1914 Kautsky acted as the chief interpreter of Marxism in the national question as in almost all others. In most of his substantial writing on the national question Lenin based himself on Kautsky first and foremost—and Rosa Luxemburg, too, considered him the weightiest of her opponents. Her attempts to confuse their views with those of the PPS were often deliberate mystification. In fact Kautsky and Lenin both differentiated sharply between overt nationalism and the Socialist policy of self-determination which, though it admitted the validity of national aspirations, subordinated these formally and at all times to the demands of the class struggle. In 1903 Lenin and Martov, preparing a platform for the second congress, both stated clearly that their acceptance of the right of self-determination implied not one whit less attachment to, and concentration on, the Socialist revolution. For Lenin, particularly, the national question had a twofold importance. It was an untapped source of revolutionary potential to weaken and destroy the Tsarist autocracy. He did not in the least accept Rosa Luxemburg's abstracted caricature of his policy as a utopian guarantee of national self-determination for ethnic groups who, for geographical and other reasons, obviously could never build a separate state and had never had one in the past. But at the same time Lenin certainly went further in his national policy than any mere canalization of revolutionary energy in this direction—as with the peasants. He had a real feeling for the iniquity of great Russian chauvinism which went beyond tactical considerations. The evidence suggests that on this subject Lenin was anchored to a personal view of right and wrong that did not just switch on and off as required.[2] By insisting on the inclusion of the right

---

[1] Rosa Luxemburg's role as a pioneer of polemical methodology is marginally interesting. She did not invent Marxist 'pairing' (Marx himself did that) but she was an expert practitioner years before Lenin. Opportunism in the Second International was partly her discovery—certainly she conceptualized it, and she 'invented' social patriotism.

[2] Even at the very end of his life Lenin was prepared to enter into a conflict with his closest followers on this question. At the end of 1922 he was ready to conduct a one-man campaign against the collective nationality policy of the party, had his second stroke not incapacitated him. See his notes in *Sochineniya*, Vol. XXXVII, pp. 553–9, first published in the Soviet Union in 1956. His final indictment of Stalin's character was partly based on the latter's handling of the Georgian Bolsheviks. See I. Deutscher, *Stalin, A Political Biography*, London 1949, pp. 241 ff. For a short but accurate summary of Lenin's attitude to and policy on the national question, see Alfred G. Meyer, *Leninism*, 2nd ed., New York 1962, pp. 145–55, particularly pp. 152 ff. for his earlier arguments against chauvinistic tendencies in the leadership of his own party.

of self-determination in Paragraph 7 of the Russian party programme—where it remained for fifteen years until it was incorporated into the constitution of the Soviet Union—Lenin was following his deep convictions as well as the obvious tactical requirements of a Russian revolution. It was this point more than any other that had separated him from the Narodniks in the 1890s and was to bring him into continual conflict with the Socialist Revolutionaries in the new century.

But there was a sharp difference between Lenin's views on the national question as a programme for revolution and the relationship of different parties within the RSDRP. On this Lenin made no concession whatever. It was the *Bund*'s insistence on party autonomy more than any claim for Jewish national separateness which inspired *Iskra*'s manœuvres to force the *Bund* to withdraw from the second congress. Though prepared to accommodate the Poles temporarily, Lenin also refused to enter into any federal party commitment with them. In 1906 at Stockholm a compromise was reached, which left Poles and Letts intact as separate member parties of the RSDRP, but Lenin never found this situation comfortable; he was only too pleased to exorcise these sometimes useful but unreliable allies from *de jure* participation after 1912. There was thus a significant difference between self-determination as a propagandistic weapon of revolution and its application as a form of party structure; in party matters Lenin was and continued to be rigidly unitarian and centralistic.

How were the two opposing views to be combined after the revolution, once the revolutionary potential of self-determination had played its required part? Lenin did not throw overboard the promised right of self-determination; indeed he insisted on it in 1917 and 1918 against the murmurings of many of his colleagues.

The right of self-determination [if necessary secession] is an *exception* to our general policy of centralism. This exception is absolutely necessary in view of great Russian arch-reactionary nationalism. The slightest renunciation of this exception is equivalent to opportunism—it is a simple-minded capitulation into the hands of great Russian arch-reactionary chauvinism.[1]

But this did not give the formerly oppressed border nations the right to choose any loose form of association with the Soviet Union. Either they exercised the right of self-determination and seceded, or they stayed in the Soviet Union; no intermediate form of partial association—the best of both worlds—was possible. Where the Communist parties of these countries were concerned, there could be no concession to the federal principle whatever; democratic centralism was the only possible party relationship. If they came to power and chose to integrate with Russia—the logical step which Lenin freely expected them to take—

---

[1] Lenin, letter to S. G. Shaumyan, *Sochineniya*, 3rd ed., Vol. XVII, p. 90.

then the relationship of party to society would solve itself. Bolshevik Russia's 'generosity' could only help the fortunes of its local allies. The difference between Rosa Luxemburg and Lenin in practical matters was thus not nearly as great as the polemics over fundamentals indicated. Lenin insisted much less on the universal validity of his thesis than Rosa Luxemburg on hers. All he wanted was to be left alone to apply his own views in his own party; though he believed in the universal right of national self-determination, he did not campaign for its adoption by every party.

No Russian Marxist ever thought of blaming the Polish Social Democrats for being opposed to the secession of Poland. These Social Democrats err only when, like Rosa Luxemburg, they try to deny the necessity of including the recognition of the right of self-determination in the programme of the *Russian* Marxists.[1]

Three years later, between the first and second Russian revolutions, the permissive freedom for other parties to display whatever views on self-determination might seem most suitable to them was now sharpened into a dialectical alternative.

They [the SDKPiL] have a perfect right to oppose Polish separation, but they fail to understand that in order to propagate internationalism we need not all repeat each others' exact words. In Russia we *must* stress the right of separation for subject peoples while in Poland we *must* stress the right of such nations to unity.[2]

The 'may' had become a 'must'; the pronoun 'we' applied both to Russia and Poland. By this time a powerful group of Poles had joined the Bolsheviks for better or for worse, and it seemed natural to speak of 'we' in both Russian and Polish contexts. Different tactics might still apply to different national areas but one and the same policy clearly emanated from the single Bolshevik centre. Of course the Poles did not approve of Lenin's more sympathetic formulation either—nor would Rosa Luxemburg, imprisoned in Wronke, have done so; loyal Bolsheviks like Dzierżyński, Marchlewski, and Hanecki continued to propagate the old unadulterated SDKPiL thesis within the Russian party.[3] Only

---

[1] Lenin, 'On the right of nations to self determination', *Sochineniya*, Vol. XX, p. 400.

[2] Lenin's speech on the national question at the 7th all-Russian conference of RSDRP (Bolsheviks) on 29 April (12 May) 1917 in reply to Dzierżyński; see *Sochineniya*, Vol. XXIV, p. 265. My italics.

[3] The same problem was chewed over again in much the same form at the eighth party congress in March 1919, when Lenin uttered one of his fiercest denunciations of latent chauvinism in party circles; *Protokoly VIII s"ezda RKP(B)*, Moscow 1933, p. 107. In the particular Polish context Lenin and Marchlewski argued the same toss all over again, with Marchlewski still claiming that the Poles were going to succeed against the policy of self-determination where the Russians had failed. Lenin, *Sochineniya*, Vol. XXIX, pp. 153-4.

the patent failure of the invasion of Poland finally put paid to this view in the Russian as well as the Polish parties. Dzierżyński, perhaps the bitterest opponent of all to self-determination for Poland, did not publicly recant until almost the end of his life.[1]

All this puts Lenin's onslaught on Rosa Luxemburg over the national question in 1914 into a particular perspective. The harshness of his attack on her compared with the tone of his simultaneous polemics with Radek and other *rozłamowcy* had little to do with the national question itself. Lenin was hitting not so much at Rosa Luxemburg but through her at second-rank opponents in his Russian orbit—a fact that he admitted quite deliberately in his article.[2] Besides, Rosa Luxemburg's offending text had been written in 1908 and had certainly been read by Lenin long before 1914; it was the high point of their co-operation. Lenin himself admitted that Rosa Luxemburg's criticism of the Russian party programme on the national question had no tactical significance at all.

When the Poles entered [our] party in 1906 they *never* . . . brought a single motion to alter paragraph 9 [at the time paragraph 7] of the Russian programme!! This is a fact. And this fact proves clearly, contrary to all assertions and assurances, that Rosa Luxemburg's friends considered the debate in the programme commission of the second congress as resolved by the resolution of that congress, that they silently admitted their mistake and made it good when in 1906 they entered the party after having left the party congress in 1903, without making a single attempt to reopen the question of revising paragraph 9 in *the proper party manner*.

Rosa Luxemburg's article . . . appeared in 1908—naturally it does not occur to anyone to deny party writers the right to criticize the programme—but even *after* her article *no single* official body of the Polish Marxists reopened the question of revising paragraph 9.[3]

As Lenin recognized, 'Rosa Luxemburg consistently loses herself in general comments about self-determination . . . without ever posing the clear and precise question that is at issue—mere juridical definitions or the experiences of the national movements of the whole world.'[4]

Thus the Russian national question was organically divided into tactical considerations, which could be adjusted to the varying circumstances of different countries, and questions of strategy which would always be centrally controlled by a united, cohesive party. The dialectical connection between these two aspects was obvious as long as it was a question of preparing the revolution. But as soon as it had succeeded,

---

[1] Feliks Dzierżyński only talked of 'the mistake about self-determination' as late as 3 October 1925, 'Do robotników Dolbysza', in *Pisma Wybrane*, Warsaw 1952, p. 416.

[2] Lenin, 'On the right of nations to self-determination', *Sochineniya*, Vol. XX, p. 365. See also 'Critical remarks on the national question', ibid., pp. 1–34.

[3] *Sochineniya*, Vol. XX, pp. 416–7.   [4] Ibid., p. 366.

the complementarities became paradoxes, and the theoretical paradox soon grew the sharp teeth of political incompatibility. Lenin obstinately retained his formulation and his assumptions in the face of all practical difficulties and opposition from his colleagues. But without these assumptions his thesis, suitably interpreted, now provided a means of dealing with the national question quite differently from the way he had intended. In writing on the national question under Lenin's guidance and direction before the war, Stalin had attacked the federal party of the Austrians:

In this way a united class movement has been broken up into separate national streams. . . . This only helps to aggravate and confuse the problem by creating conditions which actually favour the destruction of the unity of the working-class movement, which foster national division among the workers and intensify friction between them.[1]

This emphasis on party cohesion if necessary at the expense of national separation was to be significant. By 1918 Stalin, now the established party expert on the question of nationalities, had redefined Lenin's thesis even more ominously—and almost like a caricature of Rosa Luxemburg.

All this leads to the necessity of interpreting the principle of self-determination not as a right for the bourgeoisie but [exclusively] for the working masses of the nation concerned. The principle of self-determination must be an instrument in the struggle for Socialism and must be subordinated to the principles of Socialism.[2]

Self-determination had now lost its specific meaning. So many of Stalin's linguistic efforts emptied useful and fairly precise words into a series of flat slogans which all had the same generalized lack of content. Henceforward it would not be difficult to label a demand for secession as bourgeois and contrast it with the progressive demand for unity with Russia coming from the (assumed) working masses—and call both the latter as well as the former self-determination. In this way a minority could be held to speak for the masses and Russia could confidently refuse the desire for secession—or even too much autonomy—by any border nation on the grounds that such a demand could only be bourgeois and therefore not the will of the masses.

[1] Stalin, 'Marxism and the national question', *Sochineniya*, Vol. II, pp. 331–2.
[2] Stalin, 'Report on the national question (1918)', *Sochineniya*, Vol. IV, pp. 31–32. Rosa Luxemburg had frequently stated that if national self-determination were made completely subordinate to Socialism, if only such self-determination were admissible as really furthering Socialism—then self-determination was self-liquidating because it had no meaning at all. The argument seemed sterile precisely because no one held such an abstract view of self-determination.
Whereas Stalin reinterpreted Leninism while claiming devotion to it, others tried more honestly to reformulate Lenin's official thesis, and therefore clashed with him publicly. See *Protokoly VIII s"ezd RKP(B)*, pp. 88 ff., 92 ff.

And this is what happened in practice.[1] But of course it is not what Rosa Luxemburg wanted. The abandonment of the national right of self-determination had to come autonomously from Poles and Letts, not be dictated by Russia. The Bolshevik encouragement of self-determination had produced a serious weakening of the revolutionary heartland in 1918 which Rosa Luxemburg repeatedly lamented at the time. In *The Russian Revolution*, she foresaw that just this self-imposed weakness might eventually lead to Bolshevik harshness and rigidity in order to overcome the problem they had themselves helped to create. Already the terror, the suppression of all other papers and parties, were the derived results of Lenin's fatal policy. She preferred an open campaign of argument against the outdated right of self-determination to Stalin's over-subtle but repressive reinterpretation of this right in the throes of necessity. The ultimate effects of both Stalin's and Rosa Luxemburg's policy might have been similar—cultural and local autonomy for different nationalities but administrative and political inclusion in the Soviet Union with central control—but certainly Rosa Luxemburg would never have accepted the methods by which this was ultimately achieved. It was in her acute, almost visionary, characterization of the methodological consequences of Bolshevik nationality policy that Rosa Luxemburg rose to greater intellectual heights—not in her persistent denials of the strength and revolutionary potential of nationalism. Perhaps it was historically insoluble, like the peasant question; probably Lenin's policy could only lead to Stalin's practical application, and Rosa Luxemburg's campaign for a revolutionary Socialism without nationalism was doomed to the realm of theory.

Rosa Luxemburg's extreme and assertive internationalism has puzzled many commentators. Communist history sees it as an aberration—one of many; an aberration, however, that can only be understood in relation to 'correct' Leninism. The fact that it was not singled out for more precise attack in the early 1920s speaks as much for the importance of so many of her ex-colleagues in the Russian party as for any sympathy with her views as such. Non-Communist (or ex-Communist) writers like Paul Frölich have tried to connect Rosa Luxemburg's anti-nationalism with her social origin as a member of an underprivileged minority. Occasionally attempts have been made to discover a specifically Jewish aspect in her internationalist philosophy.

This is not a simple question. First there is the denial of a specific Polish right to self-determination—not the same as a denial of Polish

---

[1] The best treatment of Soviet nationality policy in practice is in Richard Pipes, *The Formation of the Soviet Union*, Cambridge (Mass.) 1954; E. H. Carr, *A History of Soviet Russia*, London 1951, Vol. I, part 3. For a comprehensive treatment of the problem up to the present, see Walter Kolarz, *Communism and Colonialism*, London 1964.

nationality. She always recognized this distinct national identity. Though Rosa Luxemburg herself probably gave more weight to Polish autonomy for tactical reasons than she initially wanted, the assertion of her own Polish background was a constant means of differentiation from the Germans whom she so disliked. This assertion was always Polish rather than Jewish. Though fond of using pithy Yiddish shorthand, she had no time for self-conscious Jewishness, either as a pattern of behaviour or as a basis for personal identity. In 1917 when many of her friends were looking for a rationalization of their despair she rapped Mathilde Wurm sharply over the emotional knuckles:

Why do you come with your special Jewish sorrows? I feel just as sorry for the wretched Indian victims in Putamayo, the negroes in Africa. ... The 'lofty silence of the eternal' in which so many cries have echoed away unheard resounds so strongly within me that I cannot find a special corner in my heart for the ghetto. I feel at home in the entire world wherever there are clouds and birds and human tears.[1]

So we must distinguish between national consciousness and patriotism. One was permissibly personal, a qualitative selection of characteristics which Rosa liked or disliked in others—and, one presumes, liked and disliked in herself. She was given to unrestrained generalizations in this: person x was typically German, quality y typically Russian. Scandinavians were hell; the English too, on the whole—and such dissimulators into the bargain. Lenin's intransigence was 'Tartar-Mongolian savagery'. And so on. But this never interfered with politics, either overtly or subconsciously; none of her German biographers seems even to have been aware that she disliked the men and *mores* of a society for which she laid down her life. What turns national into patriotic consciousness is conceptualization of personal feelings into policy, connecting discrete personal sensations into a coherent system of beliefs and attitudes. The distinction may seem artificial because it is unfamiliar. For most people a strong and critical sense of attributes turns automatically into a system of patriotic consciousness. But not in the case of Rosa Luxemburg. The notion of a national fatherland, even of a special cultural home, was entirely alien.

Was Rosa Luxemburg then one of the first world citizens able to conceptualize an internationality with the same profound and personal meaning that nationality has for ordinary mortals? This has been the usual answer. I believe it to be false. Such internationalism, where it does exist, is usually a negative not a positive quality, a revolt against national disappointment rather than an embrace of a wider, more diffuse unity. Most rebels of this sort seek a fervent new nationalism, some a millenarian (or other) religion, a few become citizens of the world—

[1] *Briefe an Freunde*, pp. 48–49, dated 16 February 1917.

but always in negation. It is easier for Marxists—new hatreds and new loyalties. Communists objectify their personal relations with a tight collective. The emotions that usually find fulfilment in patriotism become stunted, and in the resultant empty space others proliferate instead. But many of the patriotic characteristics and attitudes remain. Lenin combined a precise and specific hatred of Russian chauvinism with full acceptance and manifestation of Russian culture and attitudes; was he an internationalist? Rosa Luxemburg's 'patriotic' emotions remained precise and concentrated—but they did not happen to be rooted in the *Gestalt* of geographical boundaries or ethnic similarities. She, more than any other Marxist, succeeded in transposing her loyalties from *nation* to *class*—intact.

The public prosecutor went to town in his closing remarks on the subject of the German citizen, the patriot, whose function it is to guard the honour and decency of the German Reich against me, a creature without a home. As regards the question of being an expatriate, I wouldn't swop with the public prosecutor on any account. I have a dearer, greater home than any Prussian prosecutor. . . . What other fatherland is there than the great mass of working men and women? What other fatherland is there than the improvement of life, the improvement of morality, the improvement of the intellectual strength of the great masses which constitute a people?[1]

Rosa Luxemburg transferred all the energy and satisfactions of patriotic consciousness to class consciousness—to the working class. This was neither an effort of the intellect nor a ritual of ideological purification, but a genuine objectification of class as a focus for personal loyalties.[2] Loyalties must necessarily be limited in every person; unless the human personality is totally reconstructed there can be no reserve fund of loyalties to new concepts or structures. All that is possible is transference; taking from one and giving to another—a form of substitution. Either some loyalties wither at the expense of others, or they are transferred intact to a different set of relations. This is what Rosa Luxemburg achieved. Not only she, but the whole group of 'her' Poles —some Jewish, some distinctly not—with whom she was associated for so long. We see it in Marchlewski's periodic immersions in a working-class life so ill-suited to his patrician personality. We see it in Dzierżyński's persistent refusal to accept the Bolshevik policy of national self-determination in spite of his fervent embrace of all other Bolshevik

[1] Rosa Luxemburg's speech at Freiburg in *Volkswacht*, Freiburg, No. 57, 9 March 1914, reprinted in *Rosa Luxemburg . . . gegen . . . Militarismus*, p. 97.
[2] The fact that such a transfer is possible seems to me to invalidate the this-far-but-no-further neo-Marxist sociology of Ralf Dahrendorf and his school. Class—still the basic tool of his social analysis—is there defined as the social unit exercising the function of authority, or having authority exercised over it. This is fine. How does one develop quasi-patriotic loyalty to an objective social function, or lack of one?

doctrines. We see it finally in Radek's impish desire to *épater les bourgeois* in the Germany which he hated and to which he always longed to return—with all its self-conscious stress on national virtue. In their various ways they were all immediately sensitive to manifestations of patriotism, in institutions as much as in individuals. Their campaign against nationalism was as much against the latent, intangible, purely personal patriotism of their contemporaries as against any manifest policies of parties.

Is it possible to be a Marxist without achieving not only a substitution of class consciousness for patriotic consciousness, but an immersion in class *instead* of nation? Have any of the leading Marxists in Russia or China achieved it today? Or is the whole substantial return to the national unit as fact and concept the most retrograde step of all? Rosa Luxemburg stands at the apex of the attempt to make operational the Marxist concept of class as the primary social referent, and to break once and for all the old alternative stranglehold of nation. In this respect her contribution is second to none.

SELECT BIBLIOGRAPHY

I. ROSA LUXEMBURG'S WORKS

A full bibliography of Rosa Luxemburg's writings will be found in my two-volume edition of *Rosa Luxemburg*.

Only *The Accumulation of Capital* (London 1951, paperback ed. 1963), 'Organizational Questions In the Russian Social Democracy' and 'The Russian Revolution' (published together under the title of *Leninism or Marxism? The Russian Revolution*, ed. Bertram D. Wolfe, Ann Arbor paperback 1961) have been published in a readily accessible version in English. The bulk of her major writings are now available in German, a few only in Polish. The main collections are:

1. *Gesammelte Werke* (Collected Works), ed. Paul Frölich, Berlin 1923 onwards. This was planned as a complete edition of Rosa Luxemburg's works in 9 volumes. Only Vol. VI, *The Accumulation of Capital* (1923); III, *Against Revisionism* (1925); and IV, *Trade Union Struggle and Mass Strike* (1928) appeared. Vol. III contains the important 'Social Reform or Revolution' and most of her anti-revisionist writing, Vol. IV the Mass Strike pamphlet and other writings on this subject and on trade union affairs generally.

2. *Ausgewählte Reden und Schriften* (Selected Works), issued by the Marks-Engels-Lenin Institute, Berlin (East) 1951, 2 vols. Contains the 'Introduction to Political Economy', the Mass Strike pamphlet, the war-time Junius pamphlet ('The Crisis of Social Democracy'), and various speeches and articles. Also contains some of Lenin's and Stalin's major anti-Luxemburg polemics.

3. *Politische Schriften* (Political Writings), ed. Ossip K. Flechtheim, Frankfurt 1966, 2 vols. Contains 'Social Reform or Revolution', the Mass Strike Pamphlet, the Junius pamphlet, the speech to the Court in Frankfurt in 1914, the Spartakus Programme, the main speech at the Founding Congress of the KPD, and Rosa's last articles in *Rote Fahne*.

4. *Rosa Luxemburg in Kampf gegen den deutschen Militarismus*, Berlin (East) 1960. Articles and speeches from 1913–15 against German militarism, particularly in connection with the two prosecutions against her in 1914.

5. *Ich war, ich bin, ich werde sein!*, Berlin (East) 1958, selected articles from *Rote Fahne*, November 1918–January 1919.

6. *Wybór pism*, ed. B. Krauze, Warsaw 1959, 2 vols. Mainly Polish writings, including the important 'The National Question and Autonomy'.
7. *Scritti scelti* (Selected Works), ed. Luciano Amodio, Milan 1963. Various selected works, especially on revisionism, useful bibliography and excellent introduction.

Readers interested in pursuing her major themes are recommended to read the major articles mentioned above with reference to these collections.

II. WORKS ON ROSA LUXEMBURG

1. The main biography (written from a Marxist but anti-Stalinist point of view) is Paul Frölich: *Rosa Luxemburg, Her Life and Work*, London 1940. The most recent and comprehensive German edition of this book is *Rosa Luxemburg, Gedanke und Tat*, Frankfurt 1967.
The main Stalinist work on Rosa Luxemburg is:
2. Oelssner, Fred: *Rosa Luxemburg. Eine kritische biographische Skizze*, Berlin (East) 1951. An orthodox communist biography of the Stalin period, with then relevant critical assessments of her work. Now mainly of historical interest as a period piece.
3. Kautsky, Luise: *Rosa Luxemburg: Ein Gedenkbuch*, Berlin 1929, is a personal memoir by one of Rosa Luxemburg's most intimate friends.
The best personal biography is:
4. Roland-Holst-van der Schalk, Henriette: *Rosa Luxemburg. Ihr Leben und Wirken*, Zürich 1937. The author was politically close to Rosa for a period, but the book is a mixture of personal and political reminiscence and somewhat too impressionistic and interpretative. A useful, if brief, English discussion of Rosa Luxemburg's mainly economic ideas with a critique is:
5. Cliff, Tony: *Rosa Luxemburg*, London 1959.

III. GENERAL BIBLIOGRAPHY

1. Adler, Victor: *Briefwechsel mit August Bebel und Karl Kautsky*, Vienna 1954. Contains many letters between Adler, the Austrian socialist leader, and important German socialists like Bebel and Kautsky. Gives a very useful glimpse into the thinking of the Establishment on many questions of the times.
2. Angel, Pierre: *Eduard Bernstein et l'évolution du socialisme allemand*, Paris 1961. The most recent and perhaps best evaluation of Bernstein and revisionism.
3. Angress, W. T.: *Still Born Revolution*, Princeton 1963. A profes-

sional historian's analysis of the attempted communist revolution in Germany in 1921. Covers much of the history immediately following Rosa's death.

4. Badia, Gilbert: *Les Spartakistes*, Paris 1966. The most recent treatment of Spartakus in popular form, by a young French historian who had access to unpublished documents in East Berlin.

5. Balabanoff, Angelica: *My Life as a Rebel*, London 1938. Reminiscences of Lenin's war-time scretary and an acquaintance of Rosa Luxemburg. Good on some of the war-time problems from the Russian point of view.

6. Dziewanowski, M. K.: *The Communist Party of Poland*, Cambridge (Mass.) 1959. The only account of the history of the Polish communist party in English. Useful as an introduction to the very early period, sketchy and less reliable from 1904 onwards.

7. Gankin, O. H., & Fisher, H. H. (eds.): *The Bolsheviks and the World War*, London and Stanford 1940. A major collection of documents relating to the formulation of Bolshevik policy just before and during the First World War.

8. Gay, Peter: *The Dilemma of Democratic Socialism*, New York 1952. The best account in English of the revisionist controversy and particularly Bernstein's views, with a number of documents.

9. Geyer, Dietrich: *Lenin in der russischen Sozialdemokratie*, Cologne 1962. Probably the best account and analysis of Lenin's activity in the Russian Social Democratic Party between 1898 and 1906. Contains detailed material on the relationship with the Poles.

10. Haupt, Georges: *Le Congrès manqué*, Paris 1965. Introduction and documents relating to the meeting of the International Socialist Bureau in 1914 in connection with the impending outbreak of war.

11. Joll, James: *The Second International*, London 1955. Excellent brief survey of the Second International as a whole. The best introductory reading to this subject in English.

12. Lazitch, Branko: *Lénine et la IIIe Internationale*, Paris 1950. Detailed analysis and discussion of the founding of the Third International.

13. Lichtheim, George: *Marxism*, London 1961. Though advanced and complex, this is one of the best existing books on the development of Marxist thought after the death of Karl Marx.

14. Matthias, Erich: 'Kautsky und der Kautskyanismus', *Marxismusstudien* (second series), Tübingen 1957, pp. 151–197. An excellent introduction to Kautsky's thought and attitudes.

15. Meyer, Alfred G.: *Leninism* (2nd ed.), New York 1962. A useful systematic analysis of Lenin's views on various topics.

16. Nettl, J. P.: 'The German Social-Democratic Party 1890–1914 as a Political Model', *Past and Present*, 1965, No. 30, pp. 65–95. A

theoretical analysis of the organization and ideological problems posed by the SPD as a social structure.

17. Roth, Günter: *The Social Democrats in Imperial Germany*, Totowa (N.Y.) 1963. A sociological analysis of ideology and structure of the SPD. Especially useful for sociologists.

18. Schapiro, Leonard: *The Communist Party of the Soviet Union*, London 1960. The standard English work on the history and origins of the Soviet Communist party. Biased strongly against its subject matter.

19. Schorske, Carl E.: *German Social Democracy 1905–17: The Development of the Great Schism*, Cambridge (Mass.) 1955. This is the best available historical treatment of the German Social Democratic Party in the pre-war period by an extremely shrewd historian. Strongly recommended as main introduction to the period and problems.

20. Schüddekopf, Otto-Ernst: 'Karl Radek in Berlin', *Archiv für Sozialgeschichte*, Vol. II (1962), pp. 87–166. Text of Radek's notes, in the shape of a diary, on his visit to Berlin from the end of December 1918 till 1920. One of the few accounts of Rosa in action during her last weeks.

21. Waldmann, Eric: *The Spartakist Uprising of 1919 and the Crisis of the German Socialist Movement*, Milwaukee 1958. An older account in English of the Spartakus uprising. Somewhat academic and not always accurate.

22. Wehler, Hans-Ulrich: *Sozialdemokratie und Nationalstaat*, Würzburg 1962. A detailed, if sometimes incoherent, analysis of the nationality problem and the SPD. Contains substantial bibliography on this subject.

23. Zeman, Z. A., and Scharlau, W.: *Merchant of Revolution*, London 1965. A biography of Parvus, one-time friend and colleague of Rosa Luxemburg. Quite useful for discussion of the radical attitude in the revisionist controversy and a fascinating account of the relationship between the Bolsheviks and the Germans during the war.

IV. COLLECTIONS OF DOCUMENTS

1. *Dokumente und Materialien zur Geschichte der deutschen Arbeitergung*, Series II, 3 vols., Berlin 1957 on. An exhaustive collection of documents relating to the German working-class movement, especially the crystallization of the communist Left.

2. *SDKPiL. Materialy i dokumenty*, 2 vols., Warsaw 1957. Documents and letters relating to the SDKPiL throughout its entire existence (in Polish).

3. *Spartakusbriefe*, Berlin 1958. A new edition of the complete Spartakus letters.

INDEX

Mass strike (cont.).
8, 209, 211, 226, 248–9, 345
Masses, the, 157–8, 159, 168–70, 287, 372, 394, 486; appeal to, 315; and party, 157–8, 280, 286, 371; revolutionary, 249–50, 453, 473, 480; R. L.'s views of, 168–70, 261, 274, 290, 312, 405, 409, 473; *Spartakus* and, 453, 463–4, 470–2
Matschke, Anna, pseudonym of R. L., 216, 235
Matthias, Erich, cited, 76, 99, 275
May Day, 37, 44, 207, 394, 399
Mazowiecki, M., cited, 28
Mecklenburg, 280
Mehring, Franz, 6, 51, 121, 325, 418, 424; arrested (1916), 392; old and ill, 447, death (1919), 492
Academically qualified, 142
Haenisch and, 310
Journalist, as, 311–2, 378, 429
Kautsky, and, 291, 311, 438
Marxism, and, 149
Memorial, 494
Morality, and, 316
Murders, and, 492
New Left, and, 305
Open letter to Bolsheviks, 429
Party school, and, 263, 264, 267
Revolution, and, 169, 428–9
Rosa Luxemburg, her letters to, 118; relations with, 12, 106–7, 109, 121–3, 127, 216, 237, 291, 305, 309–312, 348
Russian revolution, proposed analysis, 430, 445
Schiller, and, 18
Spartakus, and, 386, 423, 428–9
Trustee of Schmidt inheritance, 348
War, and, 372
Writings, cited, 288, 369
Meiner, Felix, cited, 42, 95
Mendelson, Stanislaw, 39
Mensheviks; Menshevism, 193–4, 240–2, 259, 339, 359
Bolsheviks and, 146, 191, 193, 200–1, 223, 240–2, 292, 329–30, 338, 348, 358–61
Duma representation, 358
Lenin and, 60, 131, 193, 347
National question, and, 509
Revolutionary strategy, 240
Rose Luxemburg and, 193, 200–1, 240–2, 292, 350
SDKPiL and, 240, 330, 356

Merker, P., 294
Merton, R. K., cited, 22, 151, 210
Meyer, Alfred G., 511
Meyer, Ernst, 385, 392, 401, 424, 430, 446; cited, 313, 372, 386
Meyer, Konrad Ferdinand, 18
Michels, Robert, 79
Mickiewicz, 18, 53–4
Middle classes (*see also* Bourgeoisie), 58–9, 75, 217, 218, 250, 279, 284, 290, 304, 326, 340; lower, 233, 331–2, 333
Miedzyński, Florian, cited, 115
Militarism, 164, 253, 267–8, 269–72, 300, 322 5, 367, 393
International Congress resolution (1907), 161, 269–70, 334
Pre-military training in schools, 305
Propaganda among troops, 451
Prussian, 322, 324
Rosa Luxemburg and, 162, 322–5
SPD and, 267, 305, 322
Military service, 43, 244
Militia, people's, 231, 269, 332
Mills, John, 54–5, 62; cited, 56, 68, 69, 175
Millerand, A., 145, 146
Milowski (sailor), 480
Mimi (cat), 107, 358
Minorities, 27, 232, 500, 509
Minsk Congress (RSDRP, 1898), 176
Mlot (The Hammer), 343; cited, 354
Moabit prison, 488
Molkenbuhr, Herman (Brutus), 273, 295–6, 298–9
Moor, Karl, 371, 385, 422
Morality, 310, 316
Morawski, F., 89
Morgan, Roger, cited, 76
Morocco crisis (1905), 161; (1911), 162, 270, 293, 294–300, 306
Moscow, risings (1905), 154, 169, 215, 224, 226, 240, 241; Soviet, 241
Moscow Congress (Internat., 1919), 495
Moscow Congress (Russian Communist Party, 1919), 513
Motor cars, 259
Müller, H., 299, 300; cited, 474, 488
Müller, Richard, cited, 450–1, 478, 479
Munchener Post, cited, 318
Munich, Eisner in, 458, 490; Poles in, 102, 179, 181, 184; rising, 496; *Spartakus* in, 491
Munich Congress (SPD, 1902), 116, 124
Mussolini, Benito, 173

ABOUT THE AUTHOR

The late J. P. Nettl was the author of *The Soviet Achievement, The Eastern Zone and Soviet Policy in Germany 1945–1950*, and several other books. The two-volume edition of *Rosa Luxemburg* appeared to widespread acclaim in 1966, and the abridged edition came out in 1969. At the time of his death in 1968, J. P. Nettl was professor of political science and sociology at the University of Pennsylvania.